International Urban
Growth Policies

International Urban Growth Policies

NEW-TOWN CONTRIBUTIONS

GIDEON GOLANY, Editor

A WILEY-INTERSCIENCE PUBLICATION

JOHN WILEY & SONS, New York • Chichester • Brisbane • Toronto

Library of Congress Cataloging in Publication Data:

Main entry under title:

International urban growth policies.

  Bibliography: p.
  1. New towns—Addresses, essays, lectures.
2. Cities and towns—Growth—Addresses, essays, lectures.
I. Golany, Gideon.

HT166.I65   309.2′62   77-28274
ISBN 0-471-03748-6

Printed in the United States of America

10 9 8 7 6 5 4 3 2 1

To my wife Esther with thanks and . . . . apologies.

Preface

Planning of new urban settlements and their construction has occurred throughout the world since the rise of civilization. The "new" urban settlements of Babylonia and Assyria in ancient Mesopotamia; Mehenjo-Daro of the Indus Valley; Kahun of Egypt; Melitus, Olynthus, and Periene of Greece; the many new urban centers in North Africa and Europe built during the Roman occupation; the thousand new towns built during the Medieval period; and the many innovative, imaginatively designed new towns of the Renaissance were all created for reasons of economic, social, religious, political, and defensive significance. All those new towns were evidence of humanity's intellectual and practical ability for innovation in social, economic, political, and physical design. Today, as in the past, for whatever motive, new towns still flame the imaginations of designers and social scientists who strive for perfection in life.

Although the concept of new towns and their construction are nearly as old as urban settlement, only during this century has the realization of the concept become a worldwide phenomenon. Since Ebenezer Howard's pioneering statement of new-town principles in 1898, the philosophy of new-town development has passed through three identifiable stages. Through the end of World War II, ideology flourished but actual construction faltered. The postwar decade brought construction, legislative recognition of urban development priorities, and the beginning of widespread interest in the development of new towns. During the 1960s and 1970s the significance of new towns and the need for urban growth policies have become internationally recognized. Moreover, the rapid growth of new towns has spawned the concept of new cities. Simultaneously, planning and construction to foster social goals

(rather than a narrow concern for the physical environment) have gained emphasis. Accelerating urbanization continues to provide reasons for supporting the new-town idea. I do not think it coincidental that countries that have developed new urban settlements have become seriously involved in formulating national policies for urban growth. The success or failure of national planning and construction of new settlements depends to a great extent upon the degree of coherence of an existing national urban policy. To foster the recognition of the necessity for such coherence and to share the large store of experience gained by many countries with others that lack such experience have been my primary motives in producing this book.

Our modern civilization has learned how to improve health conditions, increase life span, increase or control birth rates, and improve education; we have also witnessed a concomitant increase in population. Yet we have not been able to direct resources properly to provide shelter and ensure socially and physically pleasing environments for everyone. Since 1945 the social cost of the growth of population and of cities has caused many governments to consider various policies and strategies to cope with this growth. New towns have gained popularity as one possible strategy within the context of national and regional planning.

No one has adequately brought together and summarized in one book the various strategies and policies of new-town planning developed by several different countries. Not since the United Nations Conference on Metropolitan Planning and New Towns in Moscow in 1967 has there been any serious review of national urbanization related to new towns. By presenting here various national experiences in the formulation of policy for new towns, their applications and achievements, we hope to fill this gap.

International Urban Growth Policies: New-Town Contributions is for people involved with future urbanization policy and new settlement development who would like to know about current facts, findings, analyses, and conclusions on the subject. The national experiences described in this book provide policies and other information valuable to the countries that are just beginning to formulate strategies in the planning and development of urban growth policies.

I believe that learning about the concept of new towns and searching for its best use within the framework of national policy must continue in different international forms. The United Nations and the Agency for International Development were catalysts in training experts and making financial resources available for regional planning and development in many developing countries. In this sense those agencies and other international groups have become primary supporters of the development of national urban growth policies and consequently of new urban settlements. Seminars, conferences, publications, and the establishment of an international institute for national urban policy should be encouraged. Such an international institute could be supported by countries experienced in building new towns, such as Great Britain, Israel, Australia, Canada, and the Soviet Union, as well as by the various international agencies concerned with urban development throughout the world. As a meeting ground for international scholars, the institute could collect and disseminate knowledge and experience in this field through seminars, conferences, and other professional activities. With proper support from concerned countries and organizations, the institute could also be a training center granting a diploma to international students in the field of urban policy and new-town planning.

I started to plan this book many years ago, but only in early 1974 did I begin to solicit contributing essays from eminent professionals in this field across the globe. The selection of the contributors and the subjects of their essays was critical in compiling a comprehensive, coherent book for readers in many nations. Some of the contributors are internationally recognized figures, and many of them are among the founders of the new-town movement and contributors to the development of national policies for urban growth in their respective countries.

All the essays presented here (except one) were written especially for this volume. The essay written by Professor Pressman generated further research and has been expanded to a book that will be published. Another paper, Dr. Constandse's, was requested by the United Nations for publication. Dr. McLaughlin's essay is the only one previously published, but for the needs of this book he extensively revised and updated his paper, and many of the illustrations are original.

The editing involved soliciting experts from various countries as contributors who would write about subjects compatible with the topic of the book and preparing manuscripts and illustrations to ensure stylistic consistency. I am grateful to the many students who have helped me in different stages of this work. Rita Lucier and Rhonda De Gatengo, graduate students in the Department of English at The Pennsylvania State University, and Joyce B. Buck helped in the editing of manuscripts. John Elicker, Kevin Scott, and David Balas, students in the Department of Architecture, prepared many of the illustrations. Michael W. Anesko, an honors graduate of the Department of English at The Pennsylvania State University, has worked closely with me in the final stages of manuscript preparation. My deep appreciation is extended to my editorial assistant Mrs. Nancy Daniels for the galley proofreading and for the preparation of the index. My special thanks also to my colleague Professor Raniero Corbelletti for his encouragement and support.

GIDEON GOLANY

The Pennsylvania State University
University Park, Pa.
April 1978

Contents

**24   Soviet Policy for New Towns and
Its Implementation, Achievements, and
Problems, 397**

Jack Underhill

Contributors

DIETER ACKERKNECHT (M. Arch. ETH), architect and planner, is an instructor of city and regional planning at the Institute for National, Regional, and Local Planning (Institut für Orts-, Regional- und Landesplanung) of the Swiss Federal Institute of Technology (ORL-ETH), Zurich. He has also been a visiting lecturer at the Hampton Institute, Hampton, Virginia, and associate professor at the California State Polytechnic University, San Luis Obispo. As leader of a research group at the ORL-Institute, Mr. Ackerknecht has conducted research on topics such as design and planning methods and the development of the Swiss Environmental Information Grid (Informationsraster). His publications include "Landesplanerische Prioritätszonen" and "Informationsraster."

DEBAJYOTI AICHBHAUMIK is associate professor of architecture, the Hampton Institute, Hampton, Virginia. He has also taught at Bengal Engineering College, Howrah, West Bengal, and Jadavpur University, Calcutta. Educated at the University of Calcutta (B. Arch.) and the University of Illinois (M.S.), his architectural experience includes the design and construction of projects for Architect's Atelier, Calcutta and consulting for Calcutta's Zoological Garden, Kalyani University, Kalyani; West Bengal; and West Bengal Development Corporation, Calcutta. Among his publications are "Industrialized Buildings: Building Economy and the Architects," "Decentralization of Industries: a Must for West Bengal," and "Basic Considerations for Industrial Locations."

V. N. BELOUSOV was born in 1928 in Moscow. In 1950 he was graduated from the Moscow Architectural Institute. In the workshop of academician L. Rudnev, he participated in the projection and construction of the building of the Moscow State University on the Lenin Hills. Mr. Belousov is the author of about 80 scientific works, papers, and scientific communications. In 1953 his book *Sovremennaya Arkhitektura Yugoslavii* (*Contemporary Architecture of Yugoslavia*) was published; in 1974 "Sovetskoe Gradostroitel'stvo" (Soviet Town Building) was released by the society *Znanie* (Knowledge). At the present time he heads the planning of the general scheme of settlement in the Soviet Union. Following the plans he created in cooperation with specialists of various professions, residential areas and centers of a series of towns of Siberia and Kazakhstan are being built. Beginning in 1959 he taught in the Department of Town Construction in the Moscow Architectural Institute and rose from an instructor to a professor. Since 1971 he has been the director of the *Tsentral'nyi Nauchno-Issledovatel'skii I Proektnyi Institut Po Gradostroitel'stvu* (Central Research and Design Institute on Town Construction), and since 1965 he has been a secretary of the board of the USSR Union of Architects. In 1974 he was elected a member-correspondent of the Academy of Construction of the German Democratic Republic.

OLLE BENGTZON is Housing Editor for Stockholm's daily evening paper, *Expressen*, where he served earlier as a columnist for housing and planning. A journalist since the age of 19, he has also received a diploma from the Nordic Institute for Civic Planning. He culminated his distinguished journalistic career in 1971 by receiving the Swedish equivalent of the Pulitzer Prize, the Stora Journalistpriset.

ALEXANDER BERLER is Professor of Urban Sociology at the University of Haifa and head of the Socioeconomic Research Department, Ministry of Housing, Jerusalem, Israel. His previous academic experience includes teaching at the University of Warsaw and the University of Technology, Warsaw. Professor Berler received his M.A. from the University of Vienna and his Ph.D. from the University of Lwow. His professional activities have included delivering papers at numerous international conferences and scholarly congresses and writing articles and books in Polish, Hebrew, and English. His books in English include *New Towns in Israel* and *Rural and Urban Relations in Israel*.

ADRIAAN KEES CONSTANDSE is head of the Socioeconomic Research Department of the IJsselmeer Development Authority, The Netherlands, and Professor of Sociology and Urban Planning at the Agricultural University of Wageningen. After serving as a research officer of the IJsselmeer Development Authority and completing his Ph.D. at the University of Utrecht, he became a staff member in the Department of Rural Sociology at Wageningen. Concurrently he was managing editor of *Sociologia Ruralis*, the journal of the European Society for Rural Sociology. Professor Constandse has also taught at the University of Tilburg and was twice a visiting professor at the Louisiana State University, Baton Rouge.

GIDEON GOLANY is Professor of Urban and Regional Planning at The Pennsylvania State University. He has taught previously at the Virginia Polytechnic Institute and State University, Cornell University, and the Technion—Israel Institute of Technology. A specialist in new-town planning and development, Professor Golany has consulted on many projects involving planning in both the

United States and Israel. He received his diploma in comprehensive planning from the Institute of Social Studies, The Hague, and his Ph.D. from The Hebrew University, Jerusalem. His numerous publications include *Urban Planning for Arid Zones: American Experiences and Directions, New-Town Planning: Principles and Practice, Innovations for Future Cities, Strategy for New Community Development in the United States,* and *The Contemporary New Communities Movement in the United States* (co-editor).

JESPER HARVEST is chief planning officer of the City of Odense, Denmark, and chairman for the Town Planning Committee of the Federation of Danish Architects. Educated at the Royal Academy of Fine Arts, Copenhagen, the Danish Town Planning Research Station, the Royal Technical University, Stockholm, and Nordplan (Diploma in Planning), Stockholm, he began his career as an architect designing projects for housing and schools. Since 1960 Mr. Harvest has been active in many planning projects in Denmark and Sweden, including the comprehensive development of Hostebro, Denmark, structure planning with employment and center analysis for Gothenburg, Sweden, center planning for several municipalities in the Copenhagen region, a program of development planning for Kolding, Denmark, and town planning for the New University of Odense, Denmark. He has also delivered lectures on Scandanavian planning at American and British universities, including a visit to the United States at the invitation of the World Affairs Council. He has published articles in *Arkitekten, Byplan,* and *Science and Technology.* In 1976 he published a book on urban renewal in Sweden.

MAYER HILLMAN is an architect and planner who is engaged as a research fellow at Political and Economic Planning on studies of the social aspects of transport planning. He has been a member of several advisory groups on transport policy and was a member of the Independent Commission on Transport. Dr. Hillman has contributed memoranda to subcommittees of the House of Commons inquiring into urban transport planning, the motor industry, energy and preventive medicine, and has read papers at many conferences on various aspects of transport and planning policy. In addition to writing numerous articles on his research, he is co-author of *Personal Mobility and Transport Policy* and *Transport Realities and Planning Policy.*

SAKAE IEMURA is manager of the town planning section of the Tokyu Corporation, which is a leading community developer in Japan and is building Tama Denen New Town. He was born in 1929 at Oita, Japan. After graduating in civil engineering from Tokyo University in 1955 he joined the Tokyu Corporation. Since 1957, he has continuously executed planning, designing, and engineering on the development of Tama Denen New Town, which is one of the largest new towns in Japan with a planned population of 400,000 people. It is served by the railroad that was planned simultaneously.

KISHO KUROKAWA is president of Kisho Kurokawa, Architect and Associates, president of Urban Design Consultant, and director of the Institute of Social Engineering. Among other positions he has been a representative member of the Japan Think-Tank Association since 1973, advisor to the Tokyo metropolitan government, and a member of committees concerned with road and environmental problems, long-range planning for social welfare, future society and communication, and housing and land. Dr. Kurokawa received his B.Arch. from Kyoto University and his Master's and Ph.D. from Tokyo University. An active architect with major works in many cities in Japan and in Italy and Tanzania, he is also author of several books, including *Introduction of Urbanology,*

Dialogue for Futurology, and *Creation of Contemporary Architectures.*

NATHANIEL LICHFIELD is professor of the economics of environmental planning at the University of London and senior partner of Nathaniel Lichfield and Partners, planning, development, transportation, and economic consultants in London, and Lichfield Boneh Lichfield, architects, town planners, and economists of Tel Aviv. Professor Lichfield's academic experience includes visiting professorships in the University of California, The Hebrew University, the Technion, and Tel Aviv University in Israel; occasional lecturer at other centers; research in the Center for Urban Economics, University of California, Berkeley; and director of the Planning Methodology Research Unit, University College, London. His activities as a consultant have included all aspects of the field, primarily in Great Britain and more recently in Israel and on each of the continents. He has written or contributed to more than 80 publications as well as hundreds of consultant reports from his practice. Of particular interest are his commissions relating to new towns which extend to several in Britain (Peterborough, Washington, Milton Keynes, and Cramlington), Shannon in Ireland, all of the Israeli new towns, Canberra in Australia, and Tuy Medio and El Tablazo in Venezuela.

FREDERICK A. MCLAUGHLIN, JR. is assistant administrator for program and policy evaluation in the New Communities Administration of the United States Department of Housing and Urban Development (HUD). He previously was director of HUD's Office of Policy Planning, held three positions in the federal Urban Renewal Agency, and served on the city planning staffs of Poughkeepsie, New York; Bangor, Maine; and Yonkers, New York. Dr. McLaughlin earned his B.S. from the University of Massachusetts and his Master's and Ph.D. from Cornell University. His previous articles include "Growth, No-Growth and the Environment" and "National Growth Policy and New Communities in the United States."

JOHN R. MULLIN is an assistant professor of city planning at Michigan State University. He has worked as a planner for the Boston Redevelopment Authority; the United States Corps of Engineers; and Desmond M. Conner Development Services Ltd., Oakville, Ontario. He now has his own consulting practice. While working for the Corps of Engineers, Dr. Mullin served as the U.S Armed Forces representative and liason to various German city planning agencies where conflicts between the military and the cities required solution. Dr. Mullin holds a B.A. degree from the University of Massachusetts, an M.C.P. from the University of Rhode Island, an MSBA from Boston University, and a Ph.D. from the University of Waterloo (Ontario, Canada). His research efforts are now focused upon European planning with particular emphasis upon German planning in the 1920s.

LYNDSAY NEILSON is a member of the Decentralization Policy Branch of the Australian government's Department of Environment, Housing and Community Development. He has also been a member of Clarke Gazzard and Partners, planning consultants, Sydney; a senior research officer of the National Capital Development Commission; and a research fellow with the Urban Research Unit, the Australian National University. As a member of the former Cities Commission, Mr. Neilson has worked on national urban strategy, including studies relating to growth center policy and national settlement policy. His recent work has included reports on population distribution policy, location policies for Australian government employment, and regional planning principles and guidelines for Australian government programs. He has published a number of papers on new cities and growth center policy, as well as on aspects of population distribution, internal migration, business location, and urban development processes.

DAVID PASS is a program officer and project manager for the New Communities Administration of the United States Department of Housing and Urban Development. From 1970 to 1973 he was New York State Urban Development Corporation program director for new communities. The holder of three advanced degrees, including a doctorate from the Royal Institute of Technology, Stockholm, he has received numerous honors and research grants in the course of his planning work in the United States and Sweden. In addition, Dr. Pass is a member of leading professional organizations in the field of urban planning. His doctoral thesis, *Vallingby and Farsta—From Idea to Reality: The New Community Development Process in Stockholm,* was published by the M.I.T. Press in 1973.

STEPHEN POTTER received his B.Sc. from University College, London, and his Ph.D. from the Open University, Milton Keynes New Town, England. While at University College, London, he assisted in research on museum charges and economic base studies of the West Midlands. At the Open University Mr. Potter assisted the Energy Research Group in the review of the Milton Keynes Master Plan, *Flexibility 1975,* and he collaborated with Mayer Hillman to deliver a paper, "Access and Mobility in New Towns," at the Open University and Regional Studies Association conference Perspectives on New Town Development. Mr. Potter's thesis, *Transport and New Towns,* was published by the New Towns Study Unit in October 1976.

NORMAN E. P. PRESSMAN is associate professor of urban and regional planning at the University of Waterloo. He has also taught at Syracuse University and has been a member of architectural and planning firms in Paris, London, Tel Aviv, and Toronto. Professor Pressman received the B.Arch. from McGill University, the M.Arch from Cornell University, and the certificate in urban and social planning from the University of Manchester. Now serving as editor of *Contact,* he is the compiler of five bibliographies about new towns and author of numerous articles in English and French concerning Canadian and French planning and new communities.

JAMES MAURICE RUBENSTEIN is assistant professor of geography at Miami University at Oxford, Ohio. He received his A.B. from the University of Chicago, his M.Sc. from the London School of Economics and Political Science, and his Ph.D. from the Johns Hopkins University, Baltimore. He was a relocation planner for the Baltimore Department of Housing and Community Development and an assistant for the American-Yugoslav project in the Ljubljana, Yugoslavia, urban region.

FRANK SCHAFFER served for some years with the Board of Inland Revenue in London, after earning his Ll.B. from London University. In 1940 he was appointed to the Secretariat of the Expert Committee on Compensation and Betterment, and in 1942 he joined the staff of Lord Reith's Reconstruction Group, which Winston Churchill established to prepare for postwar reconstruction. As a founding member of the Ministry of Town and Country Planning, Mr. Schaffer engaged mainly in the preparation of legislation necessary for the reconstruction while serving as assistant secretary in the department responsible for the Town and Country Planning Act, 1947. After some years spent administering the act, he was appointed in 1956 to take charge of the new towns division of the Ministry of Housing and Local Government, a post that he left in 1965 to become secretary of the Commission for the New

Towns. Since retiring from that post in 1973, Mr. Schaffer has been writing and lecturing on the British new-town movement. He is author of *The New Town Story.*

ZDZISLAW K. (CHARLES) SZCZEPANSKI is an air quality program officer in the Office of Community Planning and Development of the United States Department of Housing and Urban Development (HUD). He was educated at Warsaw Polytechnic and Ecole des Beaux-Arts, Paris (DPLG); and the University of Paris (city planning). Mr. Szczepanski has worked as an architect, planner, and builder in the United States, Canada, France, and Poland and as associate professor of architecture and city planning at the Catholic University of America. After joining HUD, he was a deputy director, Division of Foreign Research, conducting research on urban and regional planning in European countries. In the Office of Environmental Quality he directs environmental research, develops policies, and conducts staff training. His publications include *Trends in Urban and Regional Planning in the U.S., Urban Land Policy: European Experience,* and *Industralized Housing: European Experience.*

RAY THOMAS has been the director of the New Towns Study Unit at the Open University, Milton Keynes New Town, England, since 1970. The experience of the unit has shown, be says, that the main research need is for comparative studies between the new towns and other types of areas so that the large body of information and findings of research on new towns can be properly evaluated. Mr. Thomas is an economist and was previously employed at Political and Economic Planning, a research institute in London and in the Planning Department of the Greater London Council. He is the author of *London's New Towns, Aycliffe to Cumbernauld,* contributor to Peter Hall et al., *The Containment of Urban England,* and co-author of *The New Town Idea,* and he has written widely elsewhere on Britain's new towns, on the British planning system, and on related topics.

WILLIAM R. TSCHOL, licensed economist (M.Ec., Saint Gall Graduate School of Economics, Business and Public Administration) and holder of a Swiss federal certificate of civil service, has been a research fellow and member of a research group on state and regional land-use planning methods at the Institute of National, Regional, and Local Planning of the Swiss Federal Institute of Technology since 1973. He has been city manager of Rheinau, Switzerland, and a consultant in shopping center planning. His publications include "Kantonale Entwicklungsplanung" and "Die neuen Einkaufszentren Uschter 77 und Illuster prägen eine werdende Innenstadt."

ALAN TURNER is the senior partner of Alan Turner and Associates, environmental planning consultants and architects in London. His experience includes the planning of two new towns in Venezuela, an industrial estate and new town in Angola, and six resource-based new communities in Malaysia. He is currently advising the government of Curacao on housing, urban development, and environmental problems. As the managing partner of the New York office of an international consulting firm, he was responsible for a number of new-town projects in the United States. He received the degrees of B.Arch and Master of Civic Design from the University of Liverpool.

JACK A. UNDERHILL is program analysis officer of the Office of Program and Policy Evaluation, New Communities Administration, the United States Department of Housing and Urban Development (HUD). He received his B.A. from the University of California, Berkeley, his M.A. from Columbia University, and his

M.P.A. from Harvard University, Mr. Underhill's early experience includes serving as executive secretary of the Program Advisory Committee to the Director of the Office of Emergency Planning and Office of Civil and Defense Mobilization. Since joining HUD he has worked on programs relating to open space preservation, historic preservation, other environmental ‚protection programs, and plans and programs since the new communities program was enacted in 1968. He has visited the Soviet Union three times on tours of Soviet planning projects. His publications include "New Communities: Planning Process and National Growth Policy" and "Great Britain Revisited: Some Thoughts on New Towns, Urban Planning and Growth Policy."

HANNA ADAMCZEWSKA-WEJCHERT is professor of architecture at the Warsaw Technical University, chief architect of Tychy New Town, and the architectural partner of her husband, Kazimierz Wejchert. Her realized architectural projects include the House of Culture in Garwolin, some buildings in Tychy New Town, and collective atrium houses in Warsaw. Winner of numerous awards and prizes, including several for projects in Tychy New Town, Dr. Wejchert has also lectured at some 25 national and international conferences and published more than 40 articles. Her books include *The Influence of Execution on Changes in Plan, Town Planning Problems of Towns in South Sweden, Problems of Flat Building,* and *Atrium Houses.*

KAZIMIERZ WEJCHERT is professor of architecture at Warsaw Technical University, director of the Spatial Planning Institute, and chief planner of Tychy New Town. As a teacher, he has directed over 120 diplomas; and his students hold many important posts in Poland and abroad. As director of the institute, he supervises publications on town planning. An active architect and planner, he has entered more than 30 competitions and won first prize for projects such as the Technical University in Gliwice, the general plan of Tychy, and the "Eastern Wall," in Warsaw-centrum. Since 1951 his wife Hanna Adamczewska-Wejchert has collaborated with him on all his projects. Professor Wejchert is author of more than 100 articles, and his books include *The Polish Small Town as a Town Planning Problem, Town in the Making,* and *Elements of Town Planning Compositions.* in 1976 at the University of Vienna he received the Gottfried von Herder International Prize for Architectural Creativity.

CHAPTER 1

New Urban Settlements:
Tools for National Policy

GIDEON GOLANY

Two of the world's major problems caused by population growth are the growth of cities and the decline of rural regions. In most countries the percentage increase of urban population has been much higher than that of the total population, especially since World War II.[1]

The populations and physical sizes of urban areas in developed countries have been growing since the industrial revolution. Urban population growth from natural increases and migration of rural populations seeking industrial jobs has been associated with costly municipal services, physical and mental illness, unemployment, cultural conflicts, and social segregation.

The concomitant physical expansion has been manifested both inside and outside the cities of such countries. Within these cities housing is insufficient, density and congestion have increased, and environments have deteriorated. As these conditions worsened people moved from the cities and created sprawling suburbs. This has had three consequences: the tax base of central cities has decreased and caused municipal services to deteriorate; low-income migrants have moved to these areas and worsened the conditions there;[2] and low-density suburbs have expanded road networks, utilities, and other infrastructure and have used vast quantities of land (see Figure 1).

By contrast, developing countries, which still have large rural populations and therefore many rural settlements and mostly agricultural economies, have experienced urban growth without industrial growth and its corresponding employment opportunities.[3] Estimated growth of the cities of Asia, Africa, and Latin America from rural emigration during the 1960s was 200 million people,[4] which corresponds to as much as 14 percent increase per year in some African capitals.[5]

Existing developments in such cities are most often shanty towns or squatter settlements with enclaves of villagers.[6] Such development has burdened urban utilities and municipal services, increased commuting, and consumed vast quantities of land, leaving inadequate open space. The huge areas covered by this kind of settlement have extended networks of utilities and infrastructure to such a degree that they are very costly. Given these conditions, it is doubtful these cities can begin to provide decent shelter and employment for all of their new residents.

Also, this urban growth in developing countries is so great that native agriculture can no longer support the urban populations. Food has had to be imported, a condition that has retarded economic growth through balance of payments deficits.

Simultaneously, in both developed and developing countries rural regions have lost population. The first migrants to leave were young, unmarried men who sought new economic opportunity and social change. Their leaving weakened the extended family. These

I would like to thank Mr. Ray Thomas for reading this chapter and offering helpful comments about its contents.

1

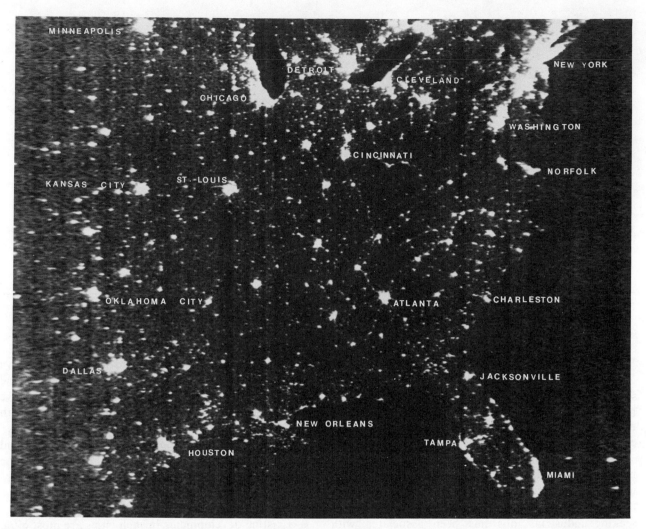

Figure 1. A satellite's night view of the eastern half of the United States, February 13, 1974. God created the earth, and man created the megalopolis. Where should new urban growth go? (This photograph was produced from the Defense Meteorological Satellite Program operated by the U.S. Air Force and distributed through the National Oceanic and Atmospheric Administration [NOAA].)

migrants were followed by married men who sought temporary employment in the big city, where they could save money and then return home to their wives and children. The third group of migrants was comprised of wives and children who joined their husbands and fathers. The result of this migration has been a change in the traditional structure of rural population: this population is now made up of more elderly people.

The impetus of this migration to cities has been population growth beyond what could be supported by agricultural economies. Furthermore, the loss of the most energetic groups of laborers has been associated with rural economic depression, mainly weakening agriculture and the few existing services. In all, the social coherence and economic inde-

pendence of traditional rural society have been disturbed.[7]

Although the conditions of urban growth in developed and developing countries differ, they share the same social cost. The monetary cost cannot be measured, but it is evident in the insecurity, illiteracy, crime, poor sanitation, poor health services, poor social services, overcrowding, and neglect of the environment in cities that once were cultural and economic centers.[8]

I argue that national policies for urban growth and regional planning and new urban settlements as components of such policy can be effective strategies for lessening these threats. In doing so, I emphasize the potential role of new urban settlements for improving the quality of man's life in society.

POLICY

The questions that national governments and their planners face are where the ever-increasing population shall live and how to remove the threat inherent in uncontrolled urbanization. In the past urban managers have had to use expedients to maintain existing standards of life rather than to implement a long-range plan that required many resources. However, I believe that long-range planning is necessary to bring order to the size and function of the settlements of this growing population and that effective planning requires all nations to formulate policies for urban growth.[9] If current trends in urban growth continue, governments will have three choices regarding such policy (see Figure 2).

The first choice is a policy of no policy, which permits growth to occur without planning. This policy may allow special interest groups in one part of a country to gain advantages not available to others. Private developers tend to gain more from a policy of no policy than from an articulated one because without policy they do not have to pay the social and administrative costs of large-scale urban development. The social cost of no policy is the continuation of deplorable conditions in a nation's major cities—a cost that should not have to be paid.

The second choice is an inconsistent, sporadic attempt to influence trends by establishing partial policies for future urban growth with little or no effective coordination among them. Countries with seriously divided political opinion, limited experience and resources, or strong private enterprise may be caught in conditions that lead to such policy.

The third possible choice is to direct and control urban trends with an effective, coordinated, comprehensive national policy for future urban growth.[10] If a government makes the third choice, the policy must incorporate the many determinants and consequences of growth without harming personal freedoms. Because of the relation between urban growth and regional decline, the policy must concern both.[11] It also must concern the management and operation of urban areas; the exploitation of land, water, minerals, and other resources; and the serious threat of depleting physical and social environments (see Figure 3).

Questions Regarding Policy. Having made the third choice, a government must be concerned with the sequential formulation of a policy and the subsequent strategy to implement it, which can provide alterna-

tives for action. One model of this process begins by answering the following questions:

1. End. What are the goals and objectives of such policy? To what degree should the policy achieve them?
2. Type. What kind of policy is needed for the given country? What are the components of such policy?
3. Integration. How is such policy to be integrated with national policy for social, economic, transportation, financial, defensive, or political goals?
4. Execution. How should the national policy for urban growth operate under the given conditions?
5. Strategy and tools. What are the strategies, tools, and phases to implement such a policy? Are the required resources available for implementation?[12]
6. Best urban pattern. What is the best urban pattern for development including population dispersal, centers of economic and social activities, spatial pattern, and the structure of governance?[13]
7. New urban settlements. What are other alternatives of the best urban pattern? What is the position of new urban settlements compared to the expansion of existing ones? What are the land resources required?[14]
8. Cost benefit. What is the cost benefit of the proposed national policy for urban growth and its new urban settlements?[15]

One issue the policy must attempt to resolve is the distribution of population, employment, services, and socioeconomic activities to achieve balance among settlements. For developing countries where most of the population is rural, decentralization of activities, especially employment, may make rural life attractive enough to stem migration.[16] Developed countries can manage centralized activities because they have the necessary resources.

Goals. In formulating policy the definition of goals is difficult because it involves bringing together opinions of diverse national groups, such as residents of cities where great political power exists and residents of the countryside where economic depression may exist. In democratic countries citizens must compromise their views so that the government can formulate a policy. Because publicizing goals is necessary to inform citizens and to give them an opportunity to express their opinions, this phase may be time consuming. Leaders of political parties can help bring about necessary compromise by endorsing the goals and by agreeing on policy.

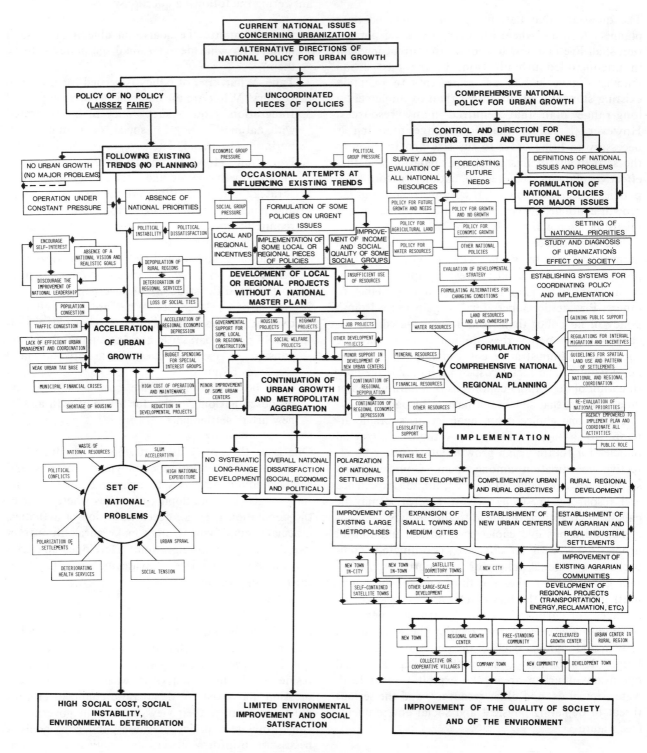

Figure 2. General alternatives of policy for modern urbanization.

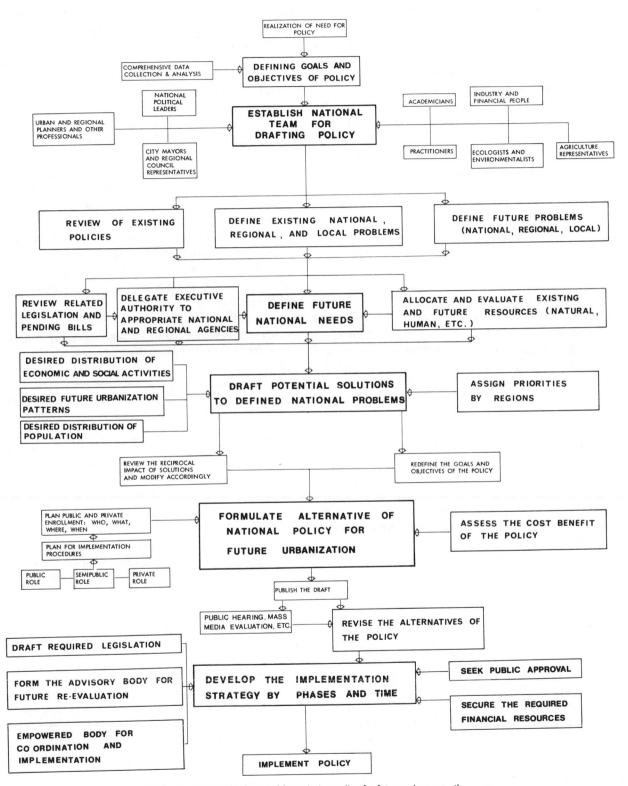

Figure 3. General scheme of formulating policy for future urban growth.

5

The following goals will undoubtedly be among those mentioned in any national discussion:

1. Balanced growth of the population and economy between urban centers and rural regions.
2. Coordination and control of urban, regional, and national development.
3. Development of integrated systems of planning and implementation in which social, economic, transportation, physical, and other developments are all components.
4. Best use of social, economic, natural, and environmental resources.
5. Selection of urban and rural patterns that best suit the unique features of the nation.
6. Social improvement, personal satisfaction, and happiness, to which employment, housing, and services contribute greatly.

Once the government has defined the goals that are acceptable to the country, officials will find themselves in the process of planning. National, regional, and local government bureaucracies become responsible for formulating the methods of reaching those goals. Again, the central government must join all these methods into a coherent unit.

PLANNING AND IMPLEMENTATION

For policy to have meaning, planning and its implementation are necessary.[17] The realization of policy requires a national plan, integrated regional plans, joint private and public contributions, effective coordination (especially among government offices), and best use of national and regional resources.[18]

National Planning. After a nation has approved its policy for future urban growth and has empowered an agency to plan and implement policy, a national plan can be formulated. It should include, at least, an economic plan, a social and population plan, a transportation plan, and a physical plan. Each of these plans should define its goals and objectives, the means to achieve those goals, the cost benefit of the plan, and the mechanism with which it is to be implemented; officials must make each item public.

At least, the economic plan should concern the location and distribution of all national and regional activities, patterns of land ownership and land values, use of economic resources, distribution of public investments, the use of national financial resources,

and systems of taxation.[19] The basic social and population plan should concern population growth and the desired pattern of settlements, migration and population mobility, health and education services, social activities and their best locations, and best forms of settlements. The transportation plan should concern existing and future means of transportation, all arteries and nodes, coordination and development of public and private mass transport, and future technological changes and their effects on the development of patterns of settlements. Finally, the physical plan should include the future pattern of land use, allocation of new settlements and their types,[20] expansion of existing settlements, their relation to transportation networks, natural and mineral resources, major regional networks of infrastructure and utilities, communication systems and their effect on the future pattern of settlements, housing needs, and the impact of any development on the environment.

To implement any plan effectively requires a qualified planning team, strong leadership, an executive agency, an adequate budget, and citizen support of the plan.[21]

Because of its scale, a national plan may be quite general, at least at first. It should, however, function as a master plan for regional ones. Regional plans adopted before the master plan should be changed to conform to it, and any new regional plan should be congruent with the master plan from the beginning.

Regional Planning. Just as national planning realizes national policy, regional planning realizes national planning in a particular administrative, geographic, or cultural area. Regional planning may also apply to a problem common to an area that encompasses more than one administrative unit. Anyone concerned with such planning should conceive it comprehensively rather than singularly; that is, social, economic, transport, and physical problems and their solutions should be conceived in relation to one another.

Regional planning should be viewed as a tool to deal with the causes of the decline of rural communities. Possible goals of regional planning here are the provision of suitable employment, regional services, local and regional transport, training for agricultural improvement, programs of self-help housing, water control, and irrigation and energy supply—all of which in appropriate situations should lead to stable regional populations and improvement of the quality of life. Regions dominated by urban settlements should develop employment opportunities, housing, and various social services. National policy should assure that both types of regions receive balanced treatment.[22]

New Urban Settlements. Accommodation of regional programs will require large-scale development. Such accommodation in rural regions may require either the expansion of existing settlements, and therefore cause one or more rural communities to become urban, or the development of new urban settlements. Because a rural community is usually small, its expansion is equivalent to the development of a new urban settlement. Urban regions may adopt the solution of providing a new town in-town for slum clearance or of decentralizing to new settlements.

Rural-to-urban migration has accelerated the polarization of settlement size at two extremes and has diminished the function of medium-sized cities. The development of new urban centers within rural regions may revive the medium-sized cities. These new cities will meet both goals: those of urban regions by reducing urbanization within the regions and those of rural regions by holding migrants within the regions.

Modern new urban settlements can be categorized according to their economic base and varying levels of economic self-containment. Each type of settlement may be constructed to meet a different goal. The following list gives these settlements, most of which have been realized: (1) new town, (2) new community, (3) company town, (4) development town, (5) regional growth center, (6) freestanding community, (7) accelerated growth center, (8) horizontal city, (9) vertical city, (10) new town in-city, (11) satellite town, (12) metro town, (13) land subdivision, (14) planned unit development, (15) new town in-town, and (16) new city.[23] The advantageous variety of settlements affords examples to fit both urban and regional needs, to offer comprehensive solutions to problems, and to tie urban centers and rural regions together (see Figure 4).

Planning to Improve Society. Social planners agreed long ago that the ultimate goals of planning and its realization are social progress, personal satisfaction, and personal happiness as well as an improved environment for living.[24] In most new-town development these goals have involved alleviating social problems in cities or regions. Having these goals helps to justify the formulation of a national policy for urban growth when we agree that implementing it has the potential to cure other problems such as economic or physical ones.

However, public officials must answer the question, What should be expected in the development of a new town—social cost for economic benefit or economic cost for social benefit? My planning experience has shown me that the best economic investment is the one with the maximum potential social return and that it is a proper long-range investment to pay for social benefits rather than immediate economic ones. The adoption of either of those costs and benefits may influence to a large extent planners' determination and formulation of social goals. The new-town goals of Great Britain, Israel, and other nations have been determined by the social benefits; without such values, it is doubtful whether these new-town movements would have had much success.

Some social goals of a new town and other new urban settlements that planners may set include the following: (1) personal satisfaction and happiness; (2) access to satisfactory social, health, and educational services; (3) a feeling of unity among the community members; (4) safety and security of all residents; (5) availability of various job opportunities; (6) attractive environment; and (7) provision of decent shelter. Within the context of regional planning, new towns need constant coordination with other regional projects unless the new-town goals are very limited or for private economic benefit.

To implement these goals requires social planning, which developers must consider practically. The quality of this planning will influence, to a great extent, the specification of the physical needs in infrastructure, delivery network, housing size and forms, recreational amenities, educational facilities, health services, and safety and security services.[25]

Adopting these goals and building a new town can unify a population and improve citizens' opinions of their government. This improvement may be necessary for emerging national governments in developing countries.[26]

Almost all countries that have planned and initiated new-town policies have included in their goals social integration and the inclusion of low-income families in the new towns. Some planners in the United States have conceived new communities as tools to integrate minority groups.[27] Accordingly, their plans include provisions for jobs and housing. However, most new towns, including publicly implemented ones, have failed to achieve those goals.[28] Instead, the middle class has been enjoying the advantages of these new towns.[29] This failure to attract

CHARACTERISTIC	NEW TOWN	NEW COMMUNITY	NEW CITY	COMPANY TOWN	DEVELOPMENT TOWN	REGIONAL GROWTH CENTER	FREESTANDING COMMUNITY	ACCELERATED GROWTH CENTER	HORIZONTAL CITY	VERTICAL CITY	SATELLITE TOWN	METRO TOWN	LAND SUBDIVISION	PLANNED UNIT DEVELOPMENT	NEW TOWN INTOWN	NEW TOWN IN-CITY
1. PUBLIC OR UNIFIED LAND OWNERSHIP (SEMIPUBLIC)	●	—	◐	—	●	◐	—	—	—	◐	—	◐	—	—	◐	●
2. CONFINED GREEN BELT	●	●	●	●	●	●	●	●	◐	●	—	◐	—	◐	—	●
3. COMBINE TOWN AND COUNTRY	●	●	●	●	●	●	●	◐	●	●	◐	◐	—	◐	—	●
4. INTERSECTING GREEN OPEN SPACE	●	◐	●	●	●	●	●	◐	—	—	—	—	◐	◐	—	●
5. DEFINED AND COMPACT AREA	●	—	●	●	●	●	◐	◐	—	●	—	◐	—	◐	—	●
6. LIMITED POPULATION SIZE	●	—	—	—	●	◐	—	—	—	●	—	◐	—	◐	—	●
7. BALANCED COMMUNITY	●	◐	●	—	●	◐	●	●	●	●	●	●	—	◐	◐	●
8. NEIGHBORHOOD UNITS	●	●	●	●	●	●	◐	◐	●	●	◐	◐	◐	●	●	●
9. SOUND ECONOMIC BASE	●	◐	●	—	●	●	●	●	●	●	—	◐	—	—	—	●
10. PROXIMATE PLACES OF WORK AND RESIDENCES	●	—	●	●	●	●	●	—	●	●	—	◐	—	—	—	●
11. LOCAL PROVISION OF INFRASTRUCTURE	●	◐	●	◐	●	●	●	◐	●	◐	●	●	—	◐	◐	●
12. SUPPORT INDUSTRIAL DECENTRALIZATION	●	◐	●	◐	●	●	●	◐	◐	●	—	●	—	—	◐	●
13. PUBLIC AS MAIN ENTERPRISER	●	—	—	●	●	—	●	—	—	◐	—	—	—	—	◐	●
14. STRONG PLANNING CONTROL	●	◐	●	—	●	●	◐	◐	—	●	◐	●	●	●	●	●

KEY — NOT APPLICABLE
◐ APPLICABLE IN PART
● APPLICABLE

Figure 4. Characteristics of new urban settlements. (Reprinted with permission, from Gideon Golany, *New-Town Planning: Principles and Practice* [John Wiley and Sons, 1976].)

low-income families seems to be due to implementation that does not ensure jobs and housing simultaneously for these families. Social balance in the new-town population must also be reflected in a balance in the employment of residents within the town, and the planning of both should be coherent.[30] Another possible social goal for new towns is cultural integration.[31] Nations such as Canada, Israel, and Australia that encourage immigration as part of their national policy may view new towns as one tool for cultural and social integration. Such a goal, however, requires careful social planning and the necessary investment in the new town.[32] Although social and physical planning supports such integration in the three previously mentioned countries, the cultural differences of the parties to be integrated will determine the degree of integration. Other factors affecting integration are the newness of the settlement and the heterogeneity of the population, both of which make newcomers more receptive to integration than an established city does.

In very congested urban conglomerations with many rural migrants, the development of a new urban settlement in the form of a new town in-city is one way to improve social quality. This new type of settlement should support positive social values that have been retained by the urban villagers. For example, research of African urban villagers has pointed out that in old slum districts of cities there is much social solidarity among slum dwellers and considerable economic exchange among themselves and between poor and rich neighbors.[33] In such circumstances traditional methods of slum clearance will demolish values of social achievement that social planners have been working to establish. However, to retain and strengthen such social achievement, a new town in-city or a new town in-town may be built gradually by sections in the same slum area where clearance took place. As sections are completed, local residents will be able to occupy them and thus not lose their local social ties. Such processes may be combined with schemes for self-help housing for slum dwellers. Such solutions can retain old social solidarity, foster cooperation, maintain existing jobs in the area, and create new ones on the site. Dwellers realize social order, personal satisfaction, and stability. The communal structure of large cities in developing countries may even support the implementation of such a concept and retain both the social and physical unity of their cities.

Anyone who measures the success or failure of new towns in a country should compare national social goals and objectives to their attainment in those new towns.[34] However, circumstances and conditions may change in a country and make reevaluation and adjustments of the new-town policy necessary so that national urban goals may be reached.

STRATEGY

Regardless of the type of new urban settlement planned, a government must have alternative strategies for the implementation of its national and regional plans. Although alternatives will be flexible, such strategy should commit itself to at least the following issues: (1) the use of private and public resources, (2) public incentives for private developers, and (3) the use of industrial development as a tool for generating services and related employment.

Public and Private Roles. New urban settlements are risky enterprises that require immense financial investment. Although some private investors may be able to enter such ventures, it is rarely possible to find enough who are prepared to do so. In circumstances where the public is not responsible for developing new towns and there is no national policy for future urban growth (as in the United States), many government decisions that are not related to new towns may directly affect a private developer and his investment.[35] New towns developed entirely by the public are expected primarily to achieve national goals and objectives and coincide with national policy for future urban growth. Publicly assisted new towns also have primarily social goals.[36] By contrast, privately developed new towns have primarily an economic goal of earning money for the developer.

In general, any of the following enterprises may develop and construct new towns:

1. Public developer only, preceded by comprehensive national policy for future urban growth, as in Great Britain, Israel, and eastern European countries.[37]
2. Private enterprise, with or without public financial support. As in the United States, development may occur without the existence of a national policy for urban growth and will not reach the status of a national new-town movement.
3. A combined effort of public and private enterprises. The public has a defined role of attempting to create and maintain the national interest. National policy may be fully or partially formulated. Canada, France, and Australia each have different degrees and forms of commitments by public enterprise.[38]

In countries that have realized policy and planning of new urban settlements and that execute these cooperatively with private enterprise, the government is committed to aiding private developers. Minimum public commitments are also necessary where private enterprise dominates the development of new urban settlements. Some of the commitments include the following: (1) appropriate legislation, (2) site selection for projected developments, (3) land assemblage and some front-end money, (4) incentives for creating jobs in areas to be developed, and (5) investment for providing minimal services and infrastructure in each new settlement. Such commitments make private development possible by reducing the developer's risks and can offer the opportunity for many small developers to join the construction of new towns. Government also gains by helping private developers because it does not have to provide the entire investment necessary for development. Although this arrangement will make new urban settlements joint ventures, it is still necessary that the public offer incentives so that private investments will be brought to new settlements.

Incentives. Despite the fact that national policy for urban growth concerns systems of cities as a whole and, less frequently, their subsystems, it is the primary responsibility of such policy to indicate clearly where urban growth is desirable and where it is not. In free-market countries the realization of such sections of the policy must be supported by special diverse incentives for citizens, groups, and public, semipublic, and private organizations.

Assignments of priorities of development to regions will lead to commitments to aid agricultural regions, especially those that are losing population because their losses strongly affect other regions. Stabilization of migration from rural areas should be treated by positive means, such as incentives, rather than by compulsory means so that personal freedoms are not harmed. Positive incentives for rural regions to be given by the public to the development of new urban settlements or expanding existing ones[39] may include (1) incentives to private industry and services to move to the region (free land or minimal payments for it, preparation of land grading for industrial use, construction of infrastructure and roads, tax waiver or minimum tax); (2) support for the development of private cooperative employment; (3) subsidies for creating new jobs not necessarily related to agriculture and not requiring skilled people; (4) training people for new jobs other than agriculture for workers no longer accommodated by agricultural employment; (5) introduction of a system of personal tax incentives for local residents and those migrating to the region (income, property, and other taxes); (6) provision of part or all of the moving expenses of population or industries to the region; (7) development of networks of regional roads and transportation to strengthen the region's society, economy, and administration; (8) provision of free or subsidized land for agriculture or for self-constructed housing; (9) low-interest or no-interest loans, grants, and similar financial incentives for self-help housing construction and provision of training and guidance for the construction; (10) allocation of public and semipublic administrative offices to the region; (11) training of local leadership for social, economic, religious, or political activities; (12) provision of a comprehensive educational system that is beneficial to both males and females of all ages; (13) provision of comprehensive social and cultural services and support for development of local and regional cultural events; and (14) provision of minimum health and medical services.

The adoption of all or most of these positive incentives will lead sooner or later to policy development for planning and construction of new (or expanded existing) urban settlements within the rural region to accommodate the new activities. Because national policy for urban growth encompasses the control and direction of growth throughout a nation, the policy must also apply some of these incentives in rapidly growing cities to solve their problems. Any incentives usually lead to new construction. To accommodate this comprehensively to the city may require construction of a new town in-city.[40]

Industry. A new settlement meant to be a new urban center may be a regional growth center to accommodate new industries, new local and regional services and amenities, and new regional transportation and communication. New urban centers should provide jobs for the regional population as well as the local one and provide social services that small communities may not be able to provide adequately. The regional urban growth center and the allied communities of the region as a unit are congruent to the new town unit as economically and socially self-supported and self-sufficient. Israel and some Asian countries have developed such regional growth centers.[41] Mass transportation systems should connect all the units of a region and connect to the national transportation network because the regional network is crucial in helping attract medium-sized or small industries.[42]

Private industries may have difficulties in moving to remote rural regions and may prefer a large urban center. Remote areas may lack conditions necessary to industry such as a supply of skilled labor, energy resources, markets, good services, efficient transportation networks, or proximity to raw materials. However, public provision of infrastructure and incentives may attract industries that suit the needs of a region. The advantages of remote rural areas to some industries include availability of large tracts of land at a low price, nonunion labor, integration with agricultural production, space for possible expansion and for housing, relatively low labor costs, and an attractive environment. Sporadic, uncoordinated development tends to discourage industries from moving to rural regions, but comprehensive regional development encourages private industries to move to such areas.[43]

To avoid economic instability, new towns should not rely on one industry and become company towns.[44] With proper regional planning, new towns will be a tool for implementing further regional planning and development strategy and balancing the economic and social development among the regions.

CONCLUSION

It is becoming more and more obvious that great urban growth in most countries (especially developing ones) and the pace of urbanization and its deficiencies are increasing faster than the improvement offered by national and local governments. For urban improvement to gain momentum, new urban settlements should be considered as large-scale national ventures. The value of developing new urban settlements depends upon the strength of their comprehensive response to short- and long-range national and regional problems. Without this response, their realization may become a national political illusion. For example, if new towns respond only to the housing needs of middle-income groups rather than to the pervasive problems of low-income groups, the towns may only seem to solve national problems.

We have viewed new towns and other new urban settlements as one alternative that may apply within rural regions as well as within metropolitan areas. In either case, new urban settlements depend on a national policy for urban growth. When the planning and development of such settlements is integrated with national policy, we can expect them and their regions to offer the variety of social and economic choices that large cities have always offered.

New towns can be a tool to improve societies, economies, and the environment. Contrary to common opinion and despite its bureaucratic machinery, public enterprise can gain much prestige by sponsoring new-town construction as an instrument for national improvement. For example, new towns can be an instrument for stabilizing the economic fluctuation of regions.

Without a national policy for urban growth and the development of new urban settlements, central governments may be under constant pressure by mayors of large cities and their allies seeking to increase subsidies for their cities. The cost of the urban agglomerate is political as well as economic because one special group may receive aid to the detriment of another. Rather than only subsidizing existing agglomerations, central governments should distribute funds for both existing settlements and new ones because the latter can serve the interest of existing centers. For the long-range national interest, new urban settlements must be viewed as innovative laboratories for social, economic, taxation, governance, physical, and other reforms from which the established city can learn a great deal. Thus it is beneficial for the existing cities to see new urban settlement as part of their process for improvement. The establishment of this relation adds another argument for the necessity of having a national policy for urban growth.

Among the various difficulties impeding the preparation of such a national policy are a lack of qualified administrators and national political machinery (especially in developing countries), the complexity of the issue, unique national conditions that do not allow the transfer of solutions, lack of experts, the comprehensive treatment required, the high cost when limited financial resources are available, and finally, lack of legislation and the hindrance of bureaucratic systems.[46] The major obstacle to implementing policy is the requirement of very skilled professionals and political leaders who must have the knowledge and understanding necessary to treat the issue comprehensively. Regardless of our argument favoring national comprehensive policy and specific policy for urban growth as the most efficient use of national resources, it should also be obvious that such policy is not the magic key that will solve all national problems. Policy is a workable framework that has the potential to unify and channel resources and forces in appropriate directions.

NOTES

1. The world's population grew by 11 percent during the 1920s, 11 percent during the 1930s, 10 percent during the 1940s, and 19 percent during the 1950s. Urban population during those decades increased 30, 30, 25, and 42 percent, respectively. [Department of Economic and Social Affairs, *Urbanization: Development Policies and Planning* (New York: United Nations, 1968), p. 11.]

2. U.S. Advisory Commission on Intergovernmental Relations, *Urban and Rural America: Policies for Future Growth* (Washington, D.C.: U.S. Government Printing Office, 1968), pp. 3–12 and 37–43.

3. Gerald Breese, *Urbanization in Newly Developing Countries* (Englewood Cliffs, N.J.: Prentice-Hall, 1966), pp. 38–72.

4. Department of Economic and Social Affairs, p. 107.

5. Paul R. Ehrlich and Anne H. Ehrlich, *Population Resources Environment: Issues in Human Ecology* (San Francisco: W. H. Freeman, 1970), p. 38.

6. Breese, pp. 102–132.

7. See "Urbanization in Kenya," a working paper prepared for the International Urbanization Survey, the Ford Foundation, New York, 1972.

8. See F. Stuart Chapin, Jr. and Shirley F. Weiss, Eds., *Urban Growth Dynamics* (New York: Wiley, 1962).

9. See Philip H. Friedly, *National Urban Policy Responses to Urban Growth* (Westmead, Farnborough, Hants., England: Saxon House, D. C. Heath, 1974), pp. 3–7; and Department of Economic and Social Affairs, *Planning of Metropolitan Areas and New Towns* (New York: United Nations, 1967).

10. Friedly, pp. 73–117.

11. Lloyd Rodwin, *Nations and Cities* (Boston: Houghton Mifflin, 1970), pp. 8–14.

12. Friedly, pp. 73–117.

13. See Wilbur R. Thompson, "New-On-Old Towns in the System of Cities: A National Perspective," in *New Towns: Why—and For Whom?* Harvey S. Perloff and Neil C. Sandberg, Eds. (New York: Praeger, 1973), pp. 223–236.

14. See Robin Best, "Land Needs of New and Old Towns," in *New Towns: The British Experience,* Hazel Evans, Ed. (New York: Wiley, 1972), pp. 22–28.

15. See Sir Henry Wells, "Agencies and Finance," in *New Towns: The British Experience,* pp. 29–39. Also see Frank Schaffer, *The New Town Story* (London: MacGibbon and Kee, 1970), pp. 182–212.

16. See John Stuart MacDonald, "Migration and the Population of Ciudad Guayana," in *Planning Urban Growth and Regional Development* (Cambridge, Mass., and London: The MIT Press, 1969), pp. 109–125 and Friedly, pp. 39–71.

17. See James Bailey, Ed., *New Towns in America: The Design and Development Process* (New York: Wiley, 1973), pp. 147–153.

18. See Friedly, pp. 121–145; and John Friedman, "The Strategy of Deliberate Urbanization," *Journal of The American Institute of Planners* **34** (November 1968):364–373.

19. See Roberto Alamo Blanco and Alexander Ganz, "The Promotion of Economic Activity," in *Planning Urban Growth and Regional Development,* pp. 60–90.

20. Nathaniel Lichfield, "Economic Opportunity in New Towns," in *New Towns: Why—And For Whom?* p. 50.

21. See Francine F. Rabinowitz and Helene V. Smookler, "Rhetoric Versus Performance: The National Politics of U.S. New Community Legislation," in *New Towns: Why—And For Whom?* pp. 93–112.

22. See Lloyd Rodwin, "Planning Guayana: A General Perspective," in *Planning Urban Growth and Regional Development,* pp. 9–14.

23. See Gideon Golany, *New-Town Planning: Principles and Practice* (New York: Wiley, 1976), pp. 22–59.

24. Department of Economic and Social Affairs, *Urbanization,* p. 1; and Albert J. Robinson, *Economics and New Towns* (New York: Praeger, 1975), pp. 40–42.

25. See Marshall Kaplan, "Social Planning, Perceptions, and New Towns," in *New Towns: Why—And For Whom?* pp. 130–136.

26. See Norma Evenson, *Two Brazilian Capitals* (New Haven, Conn., and London: Yale University Press, 1973), pp. 208–213.

27. See J. Eugene Grisby, "Views on the Feasibility of Integration," in *New Towns: Why—And For Whom?* pp. 189–194.

28. See Neil C. Sandberg, "Can the United States Learn From the Experience of Other Countries? A Commentary," in *New Towns: Why—And For Whom?* pp. 69–80.

29. See Robinson, pp. 128–131.

30. See Peter Cresswell and Ray Thomas, "Employment and Population Balance," in *New Towns: The British Experience,* pp. 71–73.

31. See Neil C. Sandberg, "The Realities of Integration in New and Old Towns," in *New Towns: Why—And For Whom?* pp. 179–188.

32. See Herbert J. Gans, "The Possibilities of Class and Racial Integration in American New Towns: A Policy-Oriented Analysis," in *New Towns: Why—And For Whom?* pp. 137–158.

33. Department of Economic and Social Affairs, *Urbanization,* p. 42.

34. See Robinson, pp. 11–28.

35. See Raymond J. Burby, III and Shirley F. Weiss, *New Communities U.S.A.* (Lexington, Mass.: Lexington Books, 1976), pp. 47–98.

36. See G. Brooke Taylor, "Social Development," in *New Towns: The British Experience,* pp. 124–133.

37. See Peter Self, "Introduction: New Towns in the Modern World," in *New Towns: The British Experience,* pp. 1–10; Alexander Berler, *New Towns in Israel* (Jerusalem: Israel Universities Press, 1970); Department of Economic and Social Affairs, *Urbanization,* pp. 101–104.

38. See Robinson and Chapters 6 and 17 of this book.

39. See Lady Sharp, "The Government's Role," in *New Towns: The British Experience,* pp. 40–45.

40. See Golany, pp. 265–280.

41. See *Regional Cooperation in Israel* (Rehovot, Israel: National and University Institute of Agriculture, Settlement Study Center, n.d.).

42. See Evelyn Denington, "New Towns for Whom?" in *New Towns: The British Experience,* pp. 143–144; *Ekistics* **36,** No. 212 (1973); and *Journal of the American Institute of Planners* **39,** No. 5 (1973).

43. Lichfield, p. 50. Industrial decentralization in some Asian countries has succeeded (Department of Economic and Social Affairs, *Urbanization,* pp. 52–53).

44. See Cresswell and Thomas, pp. 66–79.

45. See Derek Diamond, "New Towns in Their Regional Context," in *New Towns: The British Experience,* pp. 54–65.

46. Department of Economic and Social Affairs, *Urbanization,* p. 4.

CHAPTER 2

The New-Town Movement in Britain

FRANK SCHAFFER

The claim is often made that Britain led the world in the building of new towns. This is not entirely true. Throughout the ages there have been towns and cities built to a predetermined plan: Washington, Canberra, and Philadelphia are some of the better known examples, and there are a score of others, large and small, that made their mark on architectural history. However, the British new towns were different. Started in 1946 in quite a small way, they quickly aroused enormous international interest, with literally thousands of visitors from almost every country in the world coming to see them to find out how they had been created.

In part this interest was due to their success, to the fact that despite all the odds these towns were actually being built and were opening up new and exciting vistas in the field of professional planning. But it was more than that. The British new towns were not isolated projects. They were part of a new, comprehensive system for planning the use of the nation's land resources, guiding the process of physical and economic growth, and improving the living and working conditions of the British people. It is important to see and study them in this context.

ORIGINS

Every generation builds on the ideas—the successes, the failures, the dreams—of those who have gone before. As long ago as 1898 Ebenezer Howard put forward the idea of new towns in his book *Tomor-*

row: A Peaceful Path to Real Reform. He saw garden cities, spaciously planned and set among the green fields, as a way of escape from the smoke and squalor of nineteenth-century Britain. To demonstrate his faith he started Letchworth in 1902 and Welwyn Garden City in 1920. For nearly 40 years he and his small band of followers also carried on an intensive propaganda campaign on behalf of new towns. Yet, in spite of several official reports in the 1920s and 1930s commending new towns to successive governments, nothing happened. In those days the proposal was far too controversial. The breakthrough came after World War II with Lewis Silkin's New Towns Act of 1946.

In the study of history it is usually more important to know why something happened than to know what happened. Whether a new-town program can be instituted, the method of doing it and financing it, the extent to which it can be developed, and the degree of success that can be expected—all depend on the balance of political forces, the economic climate, and the measure of support in the country for new ideas or new experiments to achieve economic and social advance. Each country must fashion its own history.

In Britain the key lay in the political circumstances and emotional upheaval caused by the war. In fact, the British new-town movement was, in a very real sense, born of the war—a war fought by a people who had only just emerged from the chaotic 1930s, with economic slumps, unemployment, hunger marches, slums, and housing shortages. Almost from the start the coalition government under Winston

Churchill recognized the need to keep up morale by assurances that there would be a better deal for all when peace was restored.

So it was that, even at the height of the Battle of Britain, machinery was set up to study the problems that would arise when the country had to face the task of rebuilding the war-torn towns and cities and reestablishing a shattered economy. The need for national planning of land resources was quickly accepted, and as early as 1943 a new ministry—the Ministry of Town and Country Planning—was created. Within a few months legislation was passed to establish planning control over the whole country, and in the following year the Town and Country Planning Act of 1944 enabled local authorities to buy up areas of war-damaged and obsolete properties to secure their replanning as a whole and to aid redevelopment to new and improved standards. These were important achievements; but on other matters, in particular the reform of the land system, the coalition government was sharply divided, and decisions had to be postponed until the normal party system was reestablished.

In the first general election after the war a Labor government, led by Clement Attlee, came to power with an overall majority pledged, for the first time in British history, to major social and economic reforms. In this political context Lewis Silkin, newly appointed Minister of Town and Country Planning, was able to bring to Parliament his New Towns Bill in 1946, to be followed by his even more famous and far-reaching Town and Country Planning Bill of 1947.

New towns, as such, had not been a specific election issue. Indeed they had not been mentioned in any election manifesto. As part of the wartime studies, however, Professor Patrick Abercrombie had been asked to prepare a plan for Greater London. He recommended the building of new towns as an important strategic instrument by which the further growth of London could be limited, a greenbelt established, the best agricultural land protected, and areas of special scenic beauty preserved. In rebuilding the war-damaged and obsolete areas more open space and other social and recreational facilities would have to be provided. This situation, together with the expected natural population increase, would create a surplus of up to 1 million people who could not be housed within the existing London boundaries. Therefore, new settlements beyond the greenbelt, with their own industry and social buildings, would

be the most satisfactory and most economic way of dealing with this overspill of population.

The Attlee government readily accepted the analysis in principle. More difficult and more controversial were the questions: How to do it? Who is to build the new towns? What powers are needed? and above all, Who is to pay for them? There were many who argued that it should be the job of the local authorities—indeed this would have been in keeping with the British tradition—but even the local authorities themselves doubted whether they had the organization, staff, experience, or financial resources for the job.

At this point Lewis Silkin, who had great experience in local government, decided that this crucial question needed expert and unbiased examination. Accordingly he appointed a high-powered committee to advise him and secured as chairman, Lord Reith, creator of the BBC and the first minister appointed by Winston Churchill some years earlier to consider the postwar planning needs. This committee reported unanimously in favor of government-sponsored new towns, financed largely by the Exchequer and directed by semi-independent development corporations operating under the general guidance and control of the minister. The recommendation was adopted and became the basis of the new-town legislation.

In the light of subsequent history, two assertions can safely be made. First, if the legislation on new towns had been postponed for five years, as was at one time seriously considered, it would never have appeared in the statute book. The political opportunity would have been lost. Second, if Silkin had agreed to leave the job to local authorities, there would be no new towns in Britain today.

Many years later, Lord Silkin said that he often thought that his bill had an easy passage through Parliament because the opposition never really believed any new towns would be built, but Silkin himself had no such reservations. Even before the bill became law, he had made a start at Stevenage. Despite the intense, noisy opposition he encountered, within five years no less than 15 new towns had been started. There was pressure to abandon the program, however, when the first postwar economic crisis hit. Fortunately, wiser counsels prevailed, although for a time money was drastically curtailed. Oddly enough, this had a long-term advantage: it enabled the newly formed development corporations to give more thought to the important problems of organization, and it gave them more time to tackle the new, formidable task of planning a complete town.

Features of the 1946 Act. The success of the British new-town movement (nobody now seriously disputes that it has been an outstanding success) stems largely from the statutory powers and machinery of the 1946 act—more specifically four of its features.

First, the act enables the minister, on behalf of the government, to make the initial decision to establish a new town and to propose an area of land that he considers suitable for the purpose. The fact that the initiative lies with the government makes this a valuable instrument for promoting national or regional policies. The minister's decision—tentative at first—is preceded by extensive consultations with other governmental departments and with the local authorities concerned. A public inquiry is held at which the minister's representative explains the proposal and answers questions. Comments and objections are heard and carefully considered. Only then does the minister finally decide whether to go ahead with the proposal; if he does so decide, he makes a final order, designating the land to be used for building a new town.

Second, the act requires the minister to appoint a development corporation to plan and build the town. The corporation is not a political body. It is more like the part-time board of directors of a company. Members are chosen for their ability to work as a team and to direct the general policy and program of building. The corporation appoints its own staff and specialist consultants; because of the attractive and challenging nature of the work, it has been possible from the beginning to attract high-quality professionals in the spheres of planning, architecture, civil engineering, finance, estate management, law, sociology, administration, and public relations. These officers work as a team under the direction and coordination of a general manager, who is directly responsible to the board for the efficient operation of the whole of the corporation's activities.

Moreover, the staff can give their full attention to the job and do not have to fit it in with a score of other statutory responsibilities, as a local authority would have to do; nor are they subject to the departmentalism and committee control that are features of the British system of local government.

Third, the effect of the minister's designation order is to bring into operation all the powers of the New Towns Act. These include in particular the power for the development corporation to buy land in the area, compulsorily if need be, as and when it is required to carry out the building program. Owners are paid the current market value of their land plus compensation for disturbance, but there is one important qualification: any additional value created by the establishment of the new town is excluded.

The fourth feature of the act is that it places on the government the responsibility for providing all the funds needed by the development corporations. This includes the money needed for salaries, fees, equipment, land purchases, provision of services such as roads, sewerage, water supply, and so on and for erecting houses, shops, factories, or other buildings. Interest is payable at the rate current at the time of borrowing, and the whole of the capital and interest is repayable by equal semiannual installments over 60 years. This makes possible a long-term view. Any annual deficiencies—inevitable in the early years—are capitalized on the same terms. When the corporation makes a profit, it can be claimed by the government.

Government Control System. Each corporation has to submit an annual report and audited accounts to the minister, and these are laid before Parliament. The minister is answerable to Parliament for all the activities of the corporations and in addition has to promote a bill every three of four years asking Parliament to vote further money to carry on the program. This process started with the 1946 bill, which included a modest £50 million; by 1975, some 10 bills later, it had reached £2,250 million. When each bill comes forward for discussion, the government presents a detailed report on progress, and both houses of Parliament can debate the matter at length.

There is thus a complete answer to the suggestion sometimes made that because the towns are not under the control of the local authorities, they are undemocratic bodies. The British new towns are national government enterprises, financed by the taxpayer's money, and it is right and proper that ultimate control should rest with Parliament.

This is not to suggest that local authorities and people in the towns have no say in the matter. The process of public participation in planning is becoming increasingly important in Britain. New methods are being developed to test public opinion, analyze reactions and, where practicable, adjust or modify proposals in order to secure the maximum possible degree of public support.

All the new-town areas of course already have the usual elected local authorities responsible for the normal local government functions. The development corporations keep in close touch with these authorities and are required by law to consult them on each building project, though the final decision rests with the minister. The local authorities also participate in the program—building, for example, the schools, civic buildings, fire stations, welfare centers, housing for their own pre-new-town people, and sometimes building new roads and providing water and sewerage services. The development corporations can help toward the capital cost and have paid several million pounds in contributions to the local authorities. Because of the high cost, however, water and sewerage are often taken over by the development corporations, under specific ministerial authority. This will probably not be necessary for any future new towns because regional water and sewerage boards were set up in 1974, and they will probably have adequate resources for any new services needed.

Many other agencies, public and private, also are drawn into the development process, for although a great deal of the development is carried out by the development corporation, the task is essentially one of land assembly. Once the plan for the town has been prepared and the main services have been installed, the program becomes completely flexible. Much land is sold or leased to private builders for construction of houses for sale. Industrialists and commercial organizations can, if they wish, have land on which to build their own factories or shops. Private commercial entertainment companies build the cinemas, dance halls, bowling alleys, and other entertainment facilities. Statutory bodies provide the services for which they are responsible, such as gas and electricity supplies, telephones, and railways. In theory almost all the main building operations could be carried out by private enterprise and the existing local authorities and statutory bodies on land made available to them by the development corporation. In practice it is a shared operation, with the development corporation playing the major role; but one of the great merits of the system is that it can be readily adapted to the political and economic needs of the time, without frustrating the whole enterprise.

With so many separate development corporations, the need for coordinating activities and pooling ideas, information, and experience was soon recognized. For a short time the minister himself held regular meetings with the chairmen; but once the main lines of policy and procedure were established, this arrangement was replaced by periodic meetings of chairmen, general managers, and the various professional officers. Later, a New Towns Association was formed to organize the meetings systematically and to serve as an information center for new-town affairs.

DEVELOPMENT POLICY IN CHANGE

There have been many changes in the social and economic conditions in Britain since the 1946 act was framed. These changes are reflected in the program of new-town building (see Figure 1).

Goals of the Early New Towns. Of the first 15 new towns, 10 were overspill towns serving London and Glasgow. Others had more limited or specific objects such as providing improved living conditions for the steelworkers at Corby or for the coal miners at Peterlee and Glenrothes. At Aycliffe the object was to enable a wartime factory area to be converted to peacetime production by building an adjoining town for the work force. In Wales, people had to travel long distances to work in the Monmouth Valley, so Cwmbran was built to enable them to live nearer their work and to attract more industry and thus create new jobs in the region.

There were a number of other new-town projects under consideration when the Conservatives came to power in 1952, but no further action was taken on them at that time. For a while it was thought the new government might abandon the whole program, but by then the towns were beginning to make a useful contribution to the housing shortage—always a sensitive issue in Britain—and they were allowed to continue. It was nearly 10 years, however, before the success of the new towns was sufficiently established to enable the Conservatives to overcome their traditional dislike of state enterprises. Once they were convinced of the success of these enterprises, however, and when it became clear that they were actually going to be a financial success, the Conservatives went ahead with a second program. New towns had become all-party policy.

Skelmersdale, designated in 1961 to serve the overspill needs of Liverpool, was the first of the new towns in the second program. This was followed in 1963 by Dawley, near Birmingham, later expanded and renamed Telford. In 1964 came Redditch, also serving Birmingham, and Runcorn to give further help to the Liverpool and Merseyside area. In the

Figure 1. The British new towns.

northeast help was given to Tyneside by the designation in 1964 of Washington in County Durham, site of the ancestral home of the family of George Washington. In Scotland, Cumbernauld had been designated in 1955 to help solve the housing problem of Glasgow (the one exception to the decision to suspend the new-town program), and this was followed by Livingston in 1962 and Irvine in 1966. In several cases the process of designation was started by a Conservative government and completed by the Labour government that came back to power in 1964.

Altogether, this was a massive and welcome increase in the new-town program, but there was still an acute housing shortage in London and the southeast. As a first step to remedy this situation, the early new towns near London were asked to review their plans with the object of taking more of London's overspill. Almost all of these towns could accommodate more people without distorting or destroying their carefully planned structures, and new population limits were fixed with, in some cases, the designation of additional land.

Initial Innovations. All the early new towns were of modest size—generally less than 100,000 people—but from this point policy branched out into new fields. Intensive regional planning studies had by then analyzed more fully the national economic needs and prospects, and better statistics were available to forecast population and industrial trends. The new-town method, which had proved so successful in the relatively small projects of earlier years, was now adopted for much larger and more ambitious schemes. An area of 21,000 acres in North Buckinghamshire was designated for the first new city of 250,000 people. Part of the function of the city, to be called Milton Keynes (the name of a small village in the area), was to take further overspill from London, but the area was also chosen for its potential for economic growth. Situated midway between London and Birmingham and served well by the new motorway system, Milton Keynes is particularly attractive to new industry and will make a substantial contribution to the nation's economic expansion.

The second innovation came with the decision to use the new-town powers to expand the ancient cathedral city of Peterborough and the nearby industrial town of Northampton to take more people from London, and, similarly, to expand the town of Warrington to help relieve overcrowding in the Manchester area. These towns are expected to grow to populations well over 200,000. It was thought at one time that the local authorities of Britain's larger towns would strongly resent the intrusion of a government-appointed development corporation, but in fact arrangements were amicably negotiated for development in partnership with the local authorities.

Finally came the designation of nearly 19,000 acres in Lancashire, with the object of reviving the flagging economy of this traditional cotton-spinning area in which the population is expected to increase by over 1 million by the end of the century. Here, the task is not the building of a new town in the traditional sense—indeed the corporation is not named after a town but is merely called the Central Lancashire Development Corporation. The program of development envisages expanding and improving the infrastructure of several existing towns in the area, thus creating growth points for new employment.

In this way, the use of the New Towns Act to meet the needs of a whole subregion is a significant advance in policy and may herald even wider use of the new-town powers and experience. A small step in this direction was taken in Scotland by placing the responsibility for building a new town at Stonehouse, some 30 miles away, on the East Kilbride Development Corporation, but in the economic crisis of 1976 this project was abandoned. In Wales, the Mid-Wales Development Corporation, set up primarily to double the size of Newtown (a 700-year-old town in the area), was assisted by the professional staff at Cwmbran and has now been merged in a new body— the Development Board for Rural Wales—which is responsible for completing the development of Newtown and will also undertake similar developments elsewhere, if any more new towns are designated in Wales. More and more it is being recognized that in some way or other the experience and organizational efficiency of the new-town corporations ought to be called on to play a greater part in the planned development of Britain.

There are now 28 new towns built or being built in Britain, designed to serve various purposes and to meet greatly varying population targets. Yet the basic powers and procedures of Silkin's 1946 act have proved adequate for them all. They have stood the test of time, and the fact that they now have the support of all the main political parties—in itself a considerable achievement—is a credit to the efficiency and objectivity of the development corporations.

Factors Affecting Policy Change. The changes in policy that have influenced the program of new towns over the past 30 years have been matched by advances in planning philosophy and techniques. At the outset there was little experience, except from Ebenezer Howard's slowly growing towns of Letchworth and Welwyn Garden City, and the plans for the first few new towns were relatively simple, following closely the garden city concept. The town was divided into a number of neighborhoods of nicely spaced houses, each with its own small shopping center for day-to-day needs, primary school, church, pub, and other social buildings, and each separated from the next by open land to preserve the identity of the neighborhood and give ready access to open country. Special areas were set aside for industry to keep noise and pollution away from the rest of the town. In time, when the population had increased sufficiently, a town center would be built with the major shops for furniture, clothing, and so on, and with the proper ration of public buildings, meeting halls, and commercial entertainment centers. The whole would be contained within a road system that took local traffic into the town center and routed through traffic onto a ring road to avoid congestion. In all, it was a nice cozy concept of the sort of life people wanted, with a town growing over a period of some 15 years into a self-contained community.

The first major change came with the rapid growth of car ownership in the years after the war. It had been assumed that the prewar pattern—with about one family in 12 owning a car—would return, and garage and parking arrangements were calculated on that basis. The realization a few years later that before long most families would own a car, and many of them more than one, meant radical changes in the road and transport systems. Predictions on population growth also became unreliable, particularly in later years with the increase in family planning. Economic prosperity meant that more people wanted to buy houses rather than pay rent for them. Low-density houses with gardens came under fire from some architects and sociologists, who claimed that for a community to be successful a close-knit urban huddle was essential. Low density meant lack of contact and loneliness, although in fact many new-town dwellers had chosen to move to a new town to escape the congestion of the older urban areas.

With the adoption in Britain of a clean air policy that reduced the problems of smoke and pollution, the planning of industry also became outdated. Industry could now be dispersed throughout the town, even brought into the housing areas themselves, thus reducing rush-hour congestion and giving housewives who wanted it the chance of a job near home.

Many other changing factors have affected the planning of new towns, even within half a generation. Up to a point the new towns being built have been able to adapt their plans and programs, although in the neighborhoods built in the 1950s parking and garage provision remain a problem to this day. But the future is unpredictable. The fuel crisis of 1974 has cast doubts once again on the extent of car ownership and car use, and the economic crisis of 1975 has brought to a halt, for the time being, the steady industrial growth the towns were designed to foster. Somehow or other a new-town plan has to provide for all eventualities.

IMPLEMENTATION

The critical analysis of the early new-town plans led to important changes when the plans for the later towns were drafted. The plan for Cumbernauld, for example, envisaged a much more compact, centralized town, not divided into neighborhoods, but with a large multistory center, readily accessible through pedestrian ways from any part of the town. A center provided for all shopping, commercial, cultural, and social needs. A highly sophisticated road pattern ensured a free flow of traffic with the minimum danger to pedestrians, and this has proved highly successful with an accident rate that is the lowest in Britain.

The plan for Skelmersdale followed much the same principles, but in a modified form. In more recent plans, however, there has been a tendency to go back to the neighborhood concept but with greatly improved public transport systems and a recognition that increased mobility gives people a wider choice of shops, schools, employment, and social activity.

Open space has always been an important aspect of new-town planning, whether in the form of parks, playing fields, children's play spaces, lakes, or merely green wedges of open country left in their natural state around areas of housing, providing pleasant footpaths into the town center or out to the open country. Much attention has also been paid to landscaping. Mature trees have been preserved wherever possible, literally millions of new shrubs and trees have been planted, and areas of scrub and overgrown woodland have been cleared and restored for public use. In all, the new towns, with their attention to landscaping, their attractively laid out industrial areas, and their housing areas with green verges, trees, and small woodlands, are a marked contrast to most of Britain's older industrial towns and cities.

From the earliest days, the layout and design of a town center came under close scrutiny, and prewar ideas were soon discarded. Stevenage was the first town in Europe to build an all-pedestrian main shopping center, in spite of strong opposition from the retail trade organizations. Pedestrian centers are now accepted not only as normal but as essential if the center is to be successful and if it is to attract shoppers from a wide area beyond the town itself.

Housing: The Primary Issue.

In human terms housing is the most important aspect of the new towns and accounts for about 70 percent of the cost. In the early days the emphasis was on rented housing, but now most people who can afford to buy a house prefer to do so. Present policy aims at 50 percent owner occupation, which is about the national average in Britain. The main demand is for a three-bedroom house with a small garden, which suits the average family with two or three children; but dwellings are built to suit all needs, from single-room apartments and bungalows for the elderly, up to the five-bedroom family houses. There are a few tall blocks of apartments, but not many. Most corporations took the view that apartments are not suitable for family living and built them mainly to meet the needs of the young, the elderly, and couples without children who do not want the trouble of maintaining a garden.

There is a great variety of housing architecture and design, ranging from the traditional to the ultramodern, and plots can be bought by those able to afford the luxury of an architect-designed house built to their own personal taste. Variety and freedom of choice, to suit all types, all needs, and all classes, are the keynotes of housing policy.

Private building firms have a large part to play in this wide-ranging housing program, particularly in building houses for owner occupation. Many in the building industry welcome the opportunity to buy from the development corporation land that already has main roads, sewers, water supply, and other services. They can build to their own design but within the framework of an overall plan that carries the promise of all other facilities, such as schools and shops, and in effect gives them a guaranteed market for their houses. Certainly it is more efficient in planning and social terms than the traditional method by which the private builder has to build on whatever piece of land he happens to be able to buy, after negotiating with perhaps a dozen owners to assemble a site large enough for an economic operation, and then building with little or no regard for social needs.

Social Balance.

As a result of this flexible housing policy, most of the new towns have largely achieved the important social objective of creating reasonably balanced communities, in contrast to the one-class housing estates usually built by local authorities and the middle-class suburban sprawl of the private builders. It takes time and is more difficult to achieve in the towns built primarily to meet the needs of a single industry such as coal mining or steel production, but in the overspill towns the population analysis conforms pretty well to the national pattern. Only the unskilled workers are underrepresented. This has caused some concern, particularly to the London authorities, lest the inner city areas become inhabited more and more by the unskilled and underprivileged. There is no easy solution to this. The older city seems to need a much higher proportion of unskilled labor than does a new town, with its modern industry in modern factories. People will not—and should not—move to a new town without a job to go to or at least training opportunities to equip them with new skills.

The answer, if there is one, can lie only at the city end of the operation, through the rebuilding of obsolete areas in a way that will re-create a balanced social pattern by attracting back some of the more affluent people who have fled from the decaying inner ring of obsolete and unsatisfactory housing. The new towns, by taking overspill, were intended to aid this process, and that urban renewal has lagged far behind is a valid criticism of the British achievement.

Financial Problems.

Up to a point, one can generalize about certain basic policies and discern certain trends in planning attitudes. Yet generalizations can be misleading because every new town is different. Each has been individually designed and reflects the individuality of the development corporation and of its planners, architects, and consultants, as well as the opportunities provided by the location, size, shape, and contours of the site. There is no standard plan imposed from above; there is merely an insistence by ministers on the highest standards possible within the limits of the money available, for the supply of money has not been unlimited. On occasion, it has been necessary to scale down programs, and every building project has to be approved by the minister and has to satisfy the test of "showing a return that is reasonable having regard to all the circumstances." It is a delightfully vague formula—even a loss can be reasonable in some circumstances—and its great merit is that it combines firmness in accounting with flexibility in administration. Corporations were not expected, for example, to make a profit from their rented housing. They were expected to do no more than pay their way by fixing rents at a level sufficient to cover all costs after allowing for any government subsidy, although even on this point policy has varied with successive governments, and the rapid inflation of recent years has brought with it some modifications of this simple formula. The general effect, however, has been that the towns depend for financial success on their commercial and industrial prosperity. This creates the level of land values and commercial and industrial rents on which the development corporation must rely to recoup the heavy overheads on roads and services and thus be in a position to repay the government the capital advanced.

In the early 1950s reasonably accurate predictions of cost and income could be made as a basis for a judgment on whether a proposed new town would be a financial success. However, within a few years the rising price of land, increased building costs, inflation, and high interest rates bedevilled all estimates. The same factors of course are reflected in today's higher levels of rent and sale prices, and given expert and enlightened estate management—an essential feature of any new-town organization—there is no reason why a new town on a carefully chosen site should not have a healthy financial outcome. Modern techniques of management accounting and cash-flow analysis were introduced some years ago in the British corporations, and they should provide an effective instrument for maintaining a continuous, critical financial review of development programs.

Financial success is important, but not all-important. Some of the British new towns may not show a monetary profit for many years; however, this can be outweighed by the social benefits achieved, although they cannot be readily given a monetary value. Because the new towns are a national government venture, an overall view can be taken and losses in one place can be offset against profits elsewhere. In practice, almost all the towns started 15 or 20 years ago are now showing a surplus on revenue account, and by the end of the 60-year loan period they can all be expected to produce a highly satisfactory return on the investment. Indeed, the Commission for the New Towns, into whose custody the assets pass when the building of a town is substantially complete, in 1976 was showing an operating surplus of over £58 million from the four towns under its control, and Harlow and Stevenage are also showing substantial surpluses. Some of this money is being ploughed back to finance new development, but the Treasury can claim the balance, and in 1976 a total of £45 million was paid into the Exchequer by these six towns.

CONCLUSION

In a society nothing is static. Ideas advance; laws and procedures are modified or extended to serve changing needs. Even now a new government bill—the New Towns (Amendment) Act of 1976—has passed through Parliament to enable ownership of the rented houses and certain other property to be transferred to the elected local authority for the area. This will ensure that when the job of the development corporation is finished, a new town will take its place as a normal town within the ordinary framework of civic administration. However, ownership of the commercial and industrial property, which is not normally a function of local authority in Britain, will remain with the central government by transfer to the Commission for New Towns.

The need for action to deal with the growing social and economic problems of the inner urban areas has also been recognized, and in 1976 the government decided to emphasize urban renewal and rehabilitation. As a result, the development of Stonehouse as a new town has been abandoned and the released resources are to be used for the improvement of the city of Glasgow. In other parts of Britain the program of new-town building may have to be slowed to enable more money to be spent on urban renewal. Some of the professional staff of the new towns are being made available to help in this work.

In the general field of development and redevelopment, the Community Land Act of 1975 has extended the power and duty of all local planning authorities to buy land for the purpose of giving positive effect to planning proposals. As the minister has said, the new-town development corporations have been doing this successfully for a quarter of a century, and their experience of large-scale comprehensive development is bound to be of great value to the local authorities in carrying out these new duties throughout Britain. In Wales, however, these new duties have been vested in a new Land Authority for Wales. There is pressure from some quarters to set up similar regional boards in England, but for the present the government is relying on the local authorities to organize the programs of development needed in their areas.

In the international field, the reputation and impact of the British new towns has been recognized by setting up of a British Urban Development Services Unit to which other countries can look for help and advice when contemplating large-scale development. This unit, which is a government agency operating on a commercial basis, has already been involved in several projects in the Middle East.

The worldwide interest in new towns was demonstrated at an International New Towns Conference held in Paris in 1975. It was attended by 200 delegates from 22 countries. As a direct result of that conference, an International New Towns Association has been set up, with headquarters in London, to monitor international new-town development and experience and to provide a focus for the dissemination of information.

The new towns represent only a small part of the building going on in Britain today. The carefully planned and coordinated program of comprehensive development, which is their essential characteristic, has not been matched elsewhere in the country. There is a vast amount of work still to be done in the field of new development and economic growth and in the much more difficult, expensive, urgent, and sadly neglected field of urban renewal. Despite extensive programs of slum clearance, there are still many slums in Britain. About one-third of the houses are around 100 years old, and nearly 2 million of them are officially classified as substandard. The inner rings of many of the larger towns and cities are as congested as when Ebenezer Howard wrote about them nearly 80 years ago, and there are scores of industrial towns in the Midlands and the North, grown up in the wake of the industrial revolution, that need almost complete rebuilding if they are to meet the standards of today. It is a formidable task that demands bold leadership, bold action, and a program of intense capital investment for years ahead.

Many countries throughout the world have drawn heavily on the British new-town experience, but even in Britain, there is much to be learned from the example the new towns have set. They are pointing the way ahead for the building of a better Britain.

BIBLIOGRAPHY

This list includes books and reports mentioned in the text together with others that may be of interest to those wishing to study further the history and method of British new towns. A more extensive reading list can be obtained from the New Towns Association, Glen House, Stag Place, London, SWIE 5AJ; and a very full bibliography is available, price £5, from the Librarian, DOE/DTp sub-library, Bldg. No. 6, Victoria Road, S. Ruislip, Middx. AA4 ONZ.

Abercrombie, Patrick. *Greater London Plan.* London: His Majesty's Stationery Office, 1945.

Cullingworth, J. B. *Environmental Planning in Britain: The Official Peacetime History*, Vol. 3, *The New Towns.* To be published by her Majesty's Stationery Office.

Evans, Hazel, Ed. *New Towns: The British Experience.* New York: The Halstead Press, Wiley, 1972.

Howard, Sir Ebenezer. *Garden Cities of Tomorrow.* Edited and with a preface by F. J. Osborn. Introductory essay by Lewis Mumford. London: Faber and Faber. 1965. Reprinted 1970 (paperback). First published in 1898 as *Tomorrow: a Peaceful Path to Real Reform* and reissued with slight revisions in 1902 under the title *Garden Cities of Tomorrow.* A third edition was issued in 1922, with a foreword by Sir Theodore Chambers.

Lord Reith (Chairman). *Reports of the New Towns Committee.* Cmd 6759: *Interim Report.* Cmd 6794: *Second Interim Report.* Cmd. 6876: *Final Report.* London: His Majesty's Stationery Office, 1946.

Osborn, Frederic, and Arnold Whittick. *The New Towns: The Answer to Megalopolis.* 3rd ed. London: Leonard Hill, 1977.

Schaffer, Frank. *The New Town Story.* Foreword by Lord Silkin, London: MacGibbon and Kee, 1970. Rev. ed., Paladin Books, 1972.

Her Majesty's Stationery Office publishes annual reports and accounts in three volumes: (1) the English and Welsh new towns, (2) the Scottish new towns, and (3) the Commission for the New Towns. Master plans for many of the early new towns are out of print, but plans for the more recently designed towns can be purchased from the development corporations.

The New Towns Act 1946, with subsequent amendments up to 1965, is now consolidated as the *New Towns Act 1965.*

An annual review of the progress of the British new towns, including full statistics, is published each year in the February issue of *Town & Country Planning,* the monthly journal of the Town & Country Planning Asociation, 17 Carlton House Terrace, London, SW1Y 5AH.

CHAPTER 3

Britain's New-Town Demonstration Project

RAY THOMAS

By the end of 1975 nearly 2 million people lived in Britain's 29 new towns. The population of the areas covered by these new towns was just under 1 million at the time of designation, so the growth of population by migration and natural increases has been nearly 1 million. By any standards the size of this program of planned development is remarkable (see Table 1).

However, the new towns have accounted for only a small proportion of the total urban growth in postwar Britain. They account, for example, for only about one-tenth of the national population increase in this period. Because the population of all Britain's major cities and conurbations has declined steadily in recent decades, the contribution of the new towns as a proportion of all areas of growth is even smaller—probably only 3 or 4 percent. Britain now appears to face a period of slow population growth or perhaps even a decline; further major new-town designations do not seem likely.

One theme of this chapter is to ask the reasons for the limitation in the size of the contribution made by the new towns. Why does the new-town program seem to amount to nothing more than an experiment, or more generously, a large-scale demonstration project? In summarizing the achievements of the new towns, comment is therefore made on the difference between the new-town situation and other areas of urban growth or potential growth.

A second theme develops from the first. What are the implications of this demonstration project for the art or science of planning in other areas of urban growth or potential growth? Are there lessons for planning at the regional and metropolitan scale? Can other towns benefit from the experience of the new towns? Can the positive character of new-town planning be transferred to other areas?

EMPLOYMENT GROWTH

The major feature that distinguished development in the new towns from other parts of Britain is the growth of employment. A number of qualifications could be made about the detail of the statistics on employment in the new towns given in Table 2, but the broad pattern would not be affected by such qualification. Table 2 shows that the number of jobs in the 14 new towns designated before 1951 had increased by more than 250,000 by 1975 and that employment growth in the new towns designated in the first half of the 1960s is at a comparable rate.

Nationally the growth of employment in Britain in recent decades has been slow. The numbers employed in many traditional centers, such as the central business districts of major cities, has declined. During the postwar period the new towns have been virtually the only major growth centers for employment in Britain.

This success in attracting employment is attributable to a number of factors. One is the location of new towns. Nearly all of them are situated in the hinterlands of London or another major conurbation. Throughout the period since the war, employment (and population) has been decentralizing from these historic centers. The new-town designated areas, which fall mostly within a 30-mile radius of the conurbations, were chosen partly because of the existence of good rail connections with the parent city. As a result, the new towns became natural focal points in accommodating the outward movement of employment.

The growth of employment in the new towns has also been aided by government regional policies. New

Table 1   Original, 1975, and Proposed Population of Britain's New Towns

New Town	Year of Designation	Population (in thousands)		
		Original	1975	Proposed
London's new towns designated between 1946 and 1950				
Basildon	1949	25	88	134
Bracknell	1949	5	43	60
Crawley	1947	9	73	78
Harlow	1947	5	84	Undecided
Hatfield	1948	9	26	29
Hemel Hempstead	1947	21	76	84
Stevenage	1946	7	76	105
Welwyn Garden City	1948	19	40	50
Total (8 new towns)		98	505	(650)
Other new towns designated between 1946 and 1950				
Aycliffe (North East England)	1947	0	26	45
Corby (Midlands)	1950	16	54	83
Cwmbran (Wales)	1949	12	45	55
East Kilbride (Scotland)	1947	2	74	90
Glenrothes (Scotland)	1948	1	32	70
Peterlee (North East England)	1948	0	27	30
Total (7 new towns)		31	257	373
Towns designated since 1950				
Cumbernauld (Scotland)	1955	3	43	100
Skelmersdale (North West England)	1961	10	41	80
Livingston (Scotland)	1962	2	25	100
Redditch (Midlands)	1964	32	52	90
Runcorn (North West England)	1964	29	52	100
Washington (North East England)	1964	20	41	80
Irvine (Scotland)	1966	35	53	120
Milton Keynes (Midlands)	1967	40	70	250
Peterborough (Midlands)	1967	81	103	180
Newtown (Wales)	1967	5	7	13
Northampton (Midlands)	1968	131	151	240
Warrington (North West England)	1968	122	133	202
Telford (Midlands)	1968	70	97	250
Central Lancashire (North West England)	1970	235	244	420
Total (14 new towns)		815	1110	2225
Grand total for Great Britain		944	1872	3250

Note: The original population is that of the designated area at the time of designation. The figures given for the proposed population are for the target planned population including natural increase where this figure is available. Totals for proposed population are estimated on the assumption that the proposed population of Harlow is 110,000.

Source: *Town and Country Planning,* New Towns Special Issue, **44,** No. 2 (February 1976).

Table 2 Employment Growth in Britain's New Towns, 1951-1975

New Town	Employment (in thousands)				
	1951	1961	1966	1971	1975
London's new towns designated between 1946 and 1950					
Basildon	4	19	32	34	39
Brachnell	2	10	15	19	24
Crawley	5	24	34	41	42
Harlow	3	19	30	37	36
Hatfield	13	20	20	21	27
Hemel Hempstead	11	24	30	34	37
Stevenage	4	21	29	31	36
Welwyn Garden City	11	20	23	25	28
Total (8 new towns)	54	158	213	242	268
Other new towns designated between 1946 and 1950					
Aycliffe	4	6	12	13	11
Corby	10	18	23	21	26
Cwmbran	8	12	16	16	16
East Kilbride	n.a.	12	19	26	31
Glenrothes	n.a.	2	6	9	14
Peterlee	1	3	4	7	7
Total (6 new towns)	—	53	80	92	105
New towns designated between 1951 and 1964					
Cumbernauld	—	3	6	8	13
Skelmersdale	—	—	5	10	15
Livingston	—	—	1	4	8
Redditch	—	—	21	21	25
Runcorn	—	—	14	12	20
Washington	—	—	8	11	17
Total (6 new towns)	—	—	55	66	98
Grand total	—	—	348	400	471

Note: The original source of the figures for 1971 and earlier years is from the Census of Population, which includes a question on place of work, and these statistics are not consistent with the figures given for 1975 that have been obtained from the development corporations. The statistics for Hatfield, Hemel Hempstead, and Aycliffe have been adjusted to allow for associated employment centers that do not fall within the designated area of the new town.
Source: Figures for 1951, 1961, and 1966 for the towns designated between 1946 and 1950 are from Ray Thomas, *London's New Towns*, (London: Political and Economic Planning, 1969), and Ray Thomas, *Aycliffe to Cumbernauld* (London: Political and Economic Planning, 1969). Figures for 1971 and for 1966 for the towns designated between 1951 and 1964 are from Census of Population. Figures for 1975 are from *Town and Country Planning*, New Towns Special Issue, **44**, No. 2 (March 1976).

factory building in Britain since the war has required an industrial development certificate (IDC), and since 1963 new office building has required an office development permit (ODP). These instruments of regional policy have been used effectively to encourage the decentralization of industry from historic centers and relocation in the new towns rather than in other locations in the hinterlands of the major conurbations. The new towns in the development areas—the peripheral areas of Britain that suffer from high unemployment—have benefited from various financial incentives from industrialists to locate in these areas as well as from the IDC and ODP systems of control.

The crucial factor in the success of new towns in getting employment has been their ability to offer a complete package of facilities to attract new employers and foster the growth of existing employers. The package includes new housing for rent by employees as well as land or factory space. Many local authorities, particularly those in development areas, have established trading estates with advance factories and land for industrial development, but these local authorities have not usually been able to offer a range of new houses for rent as an additional attraction.

Roughly half of the houses built in Britain in recent decades have been constructed by local authorities for rent, and in recent years the central government encouraged local housing authorities to make their dwellings available to those whose claim to accommodation in the area was based on employment there rather than on existing residence. However, the practice of making dwellings available for rent by migrant employees does not appear to occur on any significant scale. Most local housing authorities have long waiting lists for rented accommodation. These lists are comprised of residents of the area who are also the electors of the councillors who constitute the government of the local authority. For other towns to use the offer of rented accommodation on any substantial scale as a means of attracting new employers seems to be politically unfeasible.

SOCIAL BALANCE

The keynote phrase in the term of reference of the New Towns Committee of 1946 was a reference to the creation of "self-contained and balanced communities for work and living."[1] The Committee's reports gave this phrase a variety of meanings that incorporated a number of different, but related, goals for new-town development. The creation of socially balanced communities was the most pervasive of these.

A number of different motives contributed to the formulation of this goal. The major function of the new towns was to help solve the housing problems of the major cities. The prime purpose was to accommodate members of relatively low-income groups who were inadequately housed in the slum areas of the city, but another aim was to avoid the one-class nature of the earlier public housing estates, such as the London County Council out-of-country estate at Becontree. The aim was to get a fair share of members of high or at least above-average income groups. For some, the motive for social balance was ideological; they believed that a mixing of members of different social classes was an end in itself. For others, the motive may have been the desire for the new towns to be successful; they believed that a fair share of members of high-income groups would be attractive to employers and promote the development of social, cultural, and educational activities of all kinds. Whatever the motive, it was generally accepted, according to the report of the New Towns Committee, that the new towns should "attract a representative cross section of the population."[2]

The new towns have more or less achieved this goal set by the New Towns Committee. Table 3 shows the social composition of Harlow New Town and compares it with that for Greater London and Great Britain as a whole. Harlow is given as an example because it had the smallest initial population of London's new towns and because it is in other

Table 3   Social Composition of Harlow New Town, Greater London, and Great Britain, 1971

	Economically Active Males (%)		
Socioeconomic Group (SEG)	Harlow New Town	Greater London	Great Britain
Professional workers (3 and 4)	6.6	6.1	5.0
Employers and managers (1, 2, and 13)	10.0	13.9	12.3
Other nonmanual (5 and 6)	20.1	23.5	17.5
Skilled manual, etc. (8, 9, 12, and 14)	42.1	32.9	38.9
Semiskilled manual, etc. (7, 10, and 13)	15.0	13.4	15.3
Unskilled (11)	4.5	7.2	7.7
Other (16 and 17)	1.7	3.1	3.2

Note: The numbers of the socioeconomic group headings refer to the sections of the General Register Office classification of socioeconomic groups.
Source: Census of Population, new towns and economic activity volumes.

Table 4   Commuting Patterns in East Kilbride and Cumbernauld, 1966, by Socioeconomic Group[a]

New Towns and Socioeconomic Group (SEG)	Numbers in 10% Sample		
	Reside and Work in the Area	Work in the Area and Reside Outside	Reside in the Area and Work Outside
East Kilbride New Town			
White-collar workers SEGs 1–6	467	242	392
Blue-collar workers SEGs 7–17	687	506	423
Total	1154	748	815
Cumbernauld New Town			
White-collar workers SEGs 1–6	118	71	182
Blue-collar workers SEGs 7–17	224	264	224
Total	342	335	406

[a] See Table 3 for the classification of socioeconomic groups.
Source: Sample Census 1966. Data supplied by the General Register Office, Edinburgh. More detail is shown in Ray Thomas, *Aycliffe to Cumbernauld* (London: Political and Economic Planning, 1969).

ways typical of them. In 1971 Harlow had a substantially lower proportion of unskilled manual workers among its residents than either Greater London or Great Britain. With the exception of this particular group, however, the distribution of socioeconomic groups in Harlow is close to that of both Greater London and Great Britain. It is probably true to say that the social composition of the new town is typically closer to the national average than that of the other towns of similar size.

The achievement of social balance in the new towns can be attributed to development corporation policies in attracting employment. To avoid the problems of economic fluctuations associated with towns dependent upon a single firm or a single industry, the development corporations have sought to obtain a variety of different industries and employers. This variety in employment composition within the town has generated a corresponding variety in the town's social composition.

The importance of this point can be illustrated by the experience of Glasgow's new towns—East Kilbride and Cumbernauld. Like the other new towns, they have attracted a fair variety of employers.

However, because of the proximity of these new towns to Glasgow and the complexities of the Scottish housing market (which are impossible to summarize), they have not attracted a representative cross section of the population. The housing of East Kilbride and Cumbernauld has attracted higher-income, white-collar, and skilled manual workers but to a much lesser degree semi- or unskilled manual workers. The difference between the day and night-time population is manifested in the commuting patterns shown in Table 4. There was, for example, a net commuting flow of blue-collar workers of about 800 daily into East Kilbride, but there was a net commuting flow of about 1500 white-collar workers from East Kilbride. East Kilbride and Cumbernauld are centers of employment for manual workers, receiving a daily inflow of commuters from Glasgow; they are dormitories for white-collar workers, dispatching a daily flow to Glasgow.

The failure of East Kilbride and Cumbernauld to accommodate an appropriate share of low-income workers underlines the most persistent criticism made of the British new-town program. The low proportion of unskilled workers in London's new towns has already been noted, but the criticism has a broader base than could be substantiated by statistics relating to the social composition of the economically active population. It is often suggested, with a certain amount of supporting evidence, that other disadvantaged groups, such as racial minorities, pensioners, and single-parent families, are also underrepresented in the new-town populations. To the extent that this criticism is justified, it can be argued that the new towns have failed to make an adequate contribution to solving the problems of the inner-city areas.

The degree of underrepresentation of disadvantaged groups in the new towns should be viewed in perspective with the overall pattern of urban growth. Outside the new towns the dominant feature of the growth pattern is the construction of houses for sale on suburban sites. The representation of disadvantaged groups among the population who can afford to buy these new houses is probably much less than in new towns, but the fact that the population able to afford to migrate to the suburbs is mostly above-average income intensifies the problems faced by housing authorities of areas in the inner parts of major cities. While the new suburbs take a disproportionate share of the population with above-average incomes, these authorities attempt to deal with the housing and welfare of a population with below-average incomes and perhaps a variety of other problems.

It is easier to identify factors militating against the accommodation of members of disadvantaged minorities in new towns than it is to measure the extent to which disadvantaged minorities have in fact not been accommodated. One factor is the housing allocation procedures. The house-with-job rule has favored the skilled against the unskilled and of course those who are employed as against those without the prospect of a job. Another factor is the cost of living in the new towns, which is generally higher than in the inner areas of the parent city. This is not compensated for by higher wages. People have moved to new towns for better housing and a better physical environment, not for financial reasons. Those without any slack in their household budgets may have been unable to make the move. A third factor of importance is that access to all kinds of urban facilities—including friends and relatives—is more difficult in the new towns than in the inner areas of cities. This must be an important deterrent to those unable to run their own cars (see Chapter 4 by Mayer Hillman and Stephen Potter).

SELF-CONTAINMENT

The problems associated with providing shopping, social, educational, and entertainment facilities for the incoming population are an inescapable part of new-town development. The difficulty with commercial undertakings like shops is that provision cannot be ensured in advance of demand. Retail organizations depend upon current receipts, not future demand, for their profits. When shops do come, they often enjoy fairly monopolistic positions. New-town residents complain of both lack of choice and high prices. The difficulty with all kinds of facilities is that even a generous scale of provision relative to population size will seem inadequate in the early years compared to what migrants from the major cities take for granted. As the new town approaches maturity, the scale of provision of facilities approaches that available in comparably sized historic towns. Many traditional facilities, such as owner-occupied shops, public houses, restaurants, secondhand shops, cinemas, and theaters, are usually underrepresented. The provision in new towns of modern facilities, such as chain stores of all kinds, supermarkets, health centers, and sport facilities, may be equal or superior to that in similarly sized historic towns.

Employment is different in two respects. First, in perhaps the majority of the new towns for most of their history, the number of jobs available has led rather than lagged behind housing. Second, self-containment in the provision of jobs has led to a degree of self-containment with regard to travel patterns. The extent of this effect can be investigated through analysis of the journey-to-work patterns.

In the case of the eight original London new towns the operation of the homes-with-job policy has resulted in an exceptionally high degree of self-containment. For journeys to work, self containment can be measured by comparing the number of local journeys—by people who live and work in the town—with the number of journeys by people who live in the town but work outside or work in the town but live outside. The proportion of such local journeys in the new towns is substantially higher than in other towns in the outer metropolitan area. This distinct feature of the new towns was mostly achieved in the early years of rapid growth of population and employment. From the census data shown in Figure 1, it can be attributed to the pattern of change that occurred over the 1951–1961 decade, but the distinctive pattern has persisted over the 1961–1971 decade.[3]

Most of the difference in the pattern of journeys to

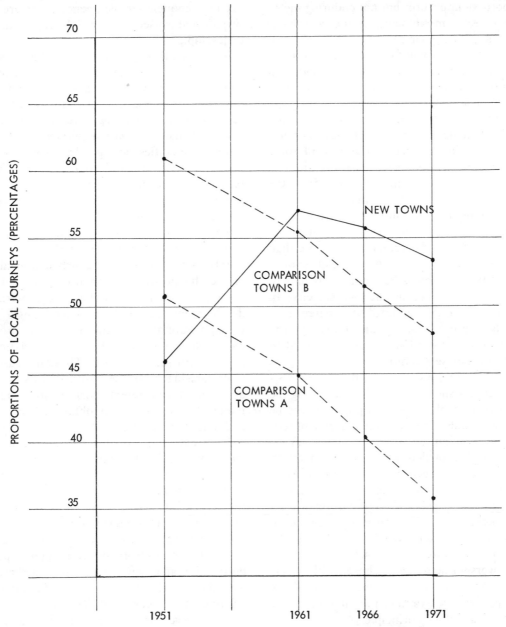

Figure 1. Self-containment in London's new towns and comparison towns 1961–1971. The ratios show local journeys (i.e., journeys by persons living and working in the towns) as a proportion of all journeys by persons living or working in the town (i.e., journeys by persons living and working in the town, plus residents working outside the town, plus workers residing outside the town). The Comparison A towns comprise the 13 other towns in the outer metropolitan area that are situated at a similar distance from London to the new towns and were of comparable size in terms of residential population in 1966. The Comparison B towns comprise Watford, Slough, Luton, Gillingham, Maidstone, and Southend, which constitute the six towns in the outer metropolitan area that are larger than the new towns. Source: Ray Thomas, *Journey to Work Pattern and Londons New Towns 1951–1971* (forthcoming) gives further details.

work between London's new towns and other towns in the outer metropolitan area is attributable to the fact that there is a closer balance between the levels of employment and population in the new towns than in other towns. The net daily commuting flows to towns that are employment centers or net daily flows from the dormitory towns are less in the case of the new towns than they are for towns that are comparable in size and distance from London. The homes-with-job policy, which could be expected to influence the pattern of travel independently of the aggregate balance between the levels of employment and population, has been an important but not enduring factor contributing to self-containment. As the new towns have grown, a growing proportion of people employed in them have either not moved to the towns or have moved from the towns while keeping their job there. The proportion of commuters from the new towns has also increased.

This growth in the volume of commuting independently of aggregate matching of the levels of employment and population poses a question of some significance. Urban theorists such as Hans Blumenfeld have postulated that the major function of "the modern metropolis" is as a labor market, and Blumenfeld actually defines the "modern metropolis" in terms of an urban agglomeration in which the journey-to-work time to the center is not more than 40 minutes.[4] If this theory is accepted, the question is raised, Should the new towns be regarded as part of the same metropolitan area as their parent city? In terms of travel time to the center of their parent city, nearly all of British new towns would so qualify. The idea that they should be self-contained in regard to journeys to work then seems futile.

This does not mean, however, that the British new-town experience has shown the goal of balancing the aggregate levels of employment and population to be in any way undesirable. The distinctive degree of self-containment of London's new towns in journey-to-work patterns is clear evidence that achieving such a balance can effectively reduce the volume of long-distance commuting. This aspect of the goal of balance is wholly consistent with Blumenfeld's maxim that the goal of city planning would be to "minimise the need for commuting and maximise the opportunity for commuting."[5] The selected locations for Britain's overspill new towns, chosen with regard to good rail communications to the center of the parent city, provide an example that illustrates the application of Blumenfeld's principle.

LAND ACQUISITION AND FINANCIAL VIABILITY

The economic theory underlying new-town development is summarized in Figure 2, The Vanishing Point of Landlords Rent, from the original edition of Howard's book *Tomorrow: A Peaceful Path to Real Reform* published in 1898. The new town is built on land acquired at its value for agricultural use. The development agency is thereby able to charge rents that are less than those prevailing in the major cities,

but high enough for the agency to secure a financial surplus that is used to pay off the capital debt incurred in development.

This basic theory is too simple. Large plots of land situated at some distance from the periphery of the city can be bought at values that do not reflect potential urban use. However, low value of such sites reflects the fact that they are costly to develop because of lack of urban services such as roads, sewerage facilities, and good accessibility to schools and shops. New-town development may be cheap in terms of land acquisition but exceptionally expensive in comparison with peripheral development in terms of construction costs.

The financial viability of Britain's new towns has depended upon the ability of the development corporations to provide basic urban amenities and to create the positive externalities that constitute the principal benefit of urban agglomeration. The development corporations have gained financially through capital appreciation of the property they own and have realized this appreciation through increases in rents charged. These increases for new-town housing have been mitigated by public policy, and the development corporations have gained mainly through the rents obtained from commercial and industrial policy.

Land acquisition in Britain's new towns has been aided by special legislation. The development corporations have the power of compulsory purchase of land at its existing value, without any allowance for the potential use associated with the new-town development. This power is rarely exercised, but it dominates the process of negotiation on land acquisition. The compulsory purchase power prevents the designation as a new town from immediately pushing up values to the prevailing level for land zoned for urban use in the region of the new town.

This power is effective in the early stages of development. In the early years the development corporations have been able to acquire all the land needed at its original agricultural value or a little above as a sweetener to soften the clout of compulsory purchase. It is not clear, however, that this power of acquiring land at its existing-use value continues to be effective as the new town grows. Twenty years later, for example, the provisions relating to compulsory purchase are hardly meaningful. There is no realistic basis for estimating the value of an undeveloped site on the assumption that the new town did not exist. The new town is there in reality, and the development corporations cannot insist that

Figure 2. A representation of the economic theory underlying new-town development. Source: Ebenezer Howard, *Tomorrow: A Peaceful Path to Real Reform*, original edition, 1898.

they should pay a different price for property than any other organization or person interested in acquiring property.

IMPLICATIONS FOR OTHER AREAS OF URBAN GROWTH

The experience of the new towns provides a sharp contrast to the pattern of urban growth in other parts of Britain in recent decades. Growth in the new towns has been centered upon employment growth. Elsewhere residential areas have been increasingly separating from the main centers of employment and other facilities because of suburbanization. The new towns have achieved a degree of social balance. The peripheral suburbs of owner-occupied or local authority housing, which have characterized the pattern of growth elsewhere, have increased the physical segregation of social groups. The new towns have proved to be financially viable. Elsewhere the provision of planning services and public housing has become an increasing burden on the public purse.

There is one point of similarity. Urban growth outside as well as in the new towns has been contained in the sense that it has taken the form of infilling and peripheral development at relatively high densities rather than scattered or low development. This feature of the urban growth pattern has preserved greenbelts around towns and cities and limited consumption of agricultural land, but this restrictive policy has greatly inflated prices of land and property. House prices, for example, have moved parallel with incomes at least since the early 1950s (which is as far back as reliable statistics on the topic exist).

One set of factors contributing to the differences between the pattern of development in the new towns and other areas lies in the contrast between the status and powers of the development corporations and those of the local planning authorities who govern the processes of urban growth elsewhere (see Table 5). The development corporations are large organizations devoted solely to development within a small area. They have boards appointed by the central government and are financed by it. They enjoy compulsory purchase powers and effectively monopolize the land and property market within their designated area.

Table 5   Status and Powers of New-Town Development Corporation and Local Planning Authorities

Function	Development Corporation	Local Planning Authority
Policymaking body	Board of development corporation appointed by minister	Planning committee elected by council of local authority
Organization	Development corporation 300–800 employees	Planning section or department usually one of the smallest in the local authority
Special powers	Power of compulsory purchase of property at value disregarding proposed new-town development	Power to zone land for development and to grant or refuse planning permission
Sources of finance	Loans from central government for purposes conducive to new-town development	Primarily rates on property; also grants and loans from central government; but expenditures on planning compete with other local authority expenditures
De facto powers over land and property market	Development corporation dominates property market within the designated area because it is the only major purchaser and developer	Zoning agricultural land for urban use can increase market value of single sites ten or one-hundred fold, but otherwise little influence on the land and property market
De facto powers over development	Development corporation dominates through its own building program and control over other building	Planning authority can restrict or slow down growth through delay or refusal of planning permission; can encourage growth by generous zonings; because of the effect of zoning on value of land, zoning can be counterproductive

By contrast, the planning section or department is one of the smallest in a local authority. The jurisdiction of the local planning authority extends over hundreds rather than tens of square miles. The policymaking body is a planning committee elected by the council. The principal sources of finance are rates on local property, and expenditures on planning compete with other local authority expenditures such as education. The local planning authority has the power to zone land for development and to grant or refuse planning permission in response to planning applications for development. These powers give the local planning authority some influence over the value of single sites or properties through changes in zoning or the granting of planning permission, but the local authority does not otherwise have any major influence in the market for land and property within its area.

The complementary and contrasting nature of the power and status of the development corporations and local planning authorities is illustrated by the fact that in new-town designated areas the two bodies coexist *de jure* without conflict. Formally the designation of a new town and the appointment of a development corporation do not affect the democratic rights of the population already living in the area.

It would be wrong, however, to conclude that the exceptional experience of the new towns is necessarily attributable to the lack of local democratic control over the activities of the development corporations. In the initial years of development, central government control was considered necessary to ensure achievement of the objectives of the New Towns Act: the new towns were intended to meet the needs of the incoming population, not the existing one.[6] Strict control by the central government might in any case be considered essential because the central government is the source of finance; he who pays the piper calls the tune. However, the experience of the expanded towns under the 1952 Town Development Act illustrated that the local democratic control is not inimical to new-town types of development.[7]

Under the 1952 Town Development Act expansion takes place as a result of agreement between the local receiving authority and the exporting authority—that is, London or Glasgow. Under this scheme for expanding towns there are a large number of receiving authorities and expansions, which vary greatly in size. Most receiving authorities and expansions are small, but in a number of cases, such as Swindon,

Basingstoke, and the envisaged expansion of Wellingborough, the scale of the development is comparable to designations under the New Towns Act.

Under the Town Development Act the receiving authority has the powers of compulsory purchase of land at value for existing use, and these powers have been as effective in aiding the purchase of land for urban use at agricultural values as they have been for the new towns. Although Britain's expanded towns have received much less attention and research than the new towns, the expanded towns appear to share most of the characteristics of the new towns, and local democratic control has not seriously inhibited the course of development.

The experience of the expanded towns poses a crucial question: why cannot the benefits of the new-town experience be extended to other areas of growth through granting of compulsory purchase powers to the local planning authorities? One answer to this question is that the granting of such powers is something like what is being envisaged under in the 1975 Community Land Act. The *Land* White Paper, which preceded this act, stated that it is "the Government's intention to lay a duty on local authorities to acquire all land required for private development."[8] This duty would place the local authority on a par with a new-town development corporation but with one important difference. Land in most areas that could be said to be "required for private development" is, or should be, zoned in accordance with the intended use. In acquiring this land the local authority would have to pay the value for potential development rather than the value for existing use. The White Paper does however envisage that "the ultimate basis on which the community will buy all land will be current use value."[9] If this aim were actually achieved, local authorities would possess the crucial power that at present is restricted to development corporations and receiving authorities under the Town Development Act.

The Community Land Act is a controversial proposal, and the difficulties in transferring the benefits of the new-town experience to other areas of urban growth can be illustrated by pointing out some of the objections to the act. One objection is recognized in the *Land* White Paper: for some years the local authorities would be paying an open market price for land already zoned for development. This would mean a cost measured in thousands of pounds per acre instead of a cost measured in hundreds of pounds per acre, which is the prevailing value of agricultural land without zoning for development. The cost of acquisition of such land would require massive finance by the central government.

A second objection is fundamental. There is much room for doubt about whether the power of compulsory purchase at value for existing use could ever be widely effective. In the situation of new and expanded towns two unusual circumstances exist. First, the development agency enjoys a monopolistic position, or more precisely, a monopsonistic position, in a very limited area. Second, a large-scale development was envisaged. This combination of circumstances may be necessary conditions for land acquisition at existing value to be effective. Even in the new towns it is doubtful whether the compulsory purchase powers are effective beyond the early years of development.

The aim of the Community Land Act is in effect to move decision making on new urban development from the private to the public sphere. Such a centralization of decision making has been effective in the new and expanded towns through the creation of large planning organizations able to cope with all the detailed problems that arise in a very limited geographic area. On a wider scale, however, it seems likely to involve many conflicts between the interests of property owners and the planning authority. Such conflicts could be expected to manifest themselves in disputes over the valuation of land.

A third objection is speculative. The process of conversion of land from rural to urban use appears to be unavoidably associated with the possibility of windfall gains by property owners and decisions by planning officials that often have to be based upon criteria that may be difficult to justify clearly and explicitly. The possibilities of corruption are always present. Such possibilities of this kind are reduced in the new towns through supervision by the central government and in the expanded towns through supervision by the exporting authority. It is perhaps the difficulties of such supervision that have limited the number of schemes for new and expanded towns.

A substantial increase in the powers of the local planning authorities envisaged in the *Land* White Paper would greatly increase the risk of corrupt practice. Any supervision of local authorities throughout Britain by the central government could only be nominal. Yet many members of local authorities are major property owners and have or could have direct or indirect financial interests in the property market that would fall under their jurisdiction.

Proposals of the type contained in the *Land* White Paper seem too bold an attempt to transfer the benefits of the new-town experience to other areas. The proposals do not acknowledge the degree of organization and control necessary for planning to play a positive role. However, the proposals assume that what is probably an unrealistic degree of centralization of decision making is necessary so that planning can play a positive role.

The widespread but incremental pressure for urban growth in other areas does not require the centralized decision-making structure associated with the new expanded towns, but the existing system of development control is at the other extreme in its permissive character. As the *Land* White Paper points out, with the existing negative system of planning control, powers to implement plans are restricted "by the price that the market puts on some land, and by the fact that the planners resource is in the hands of private owners rather than at the disposal of the community."[10]

Some positive influence on the land and property market by the local planning authority is desirable. Some means of securing finance from its own resources is necessary if the planning authority is to be able to intervene successfully in the land market in its area. Some organizational integration between the plan-making function and the other activities of local government would give local planning authorities some of the coherence evident in the development agencies in the new and expanded towns.

All of these factors point in the direction of the local planning authority having some kind of fiscal control over the process of land development. The power to influence the course of urban development through taxation would give the local planning authorities the degree of control that is realistic in areas of widespread, incremental growth.

NOTES

1. Ministry of Town and Country Planning, *Final Report of the New Towns Committee,* Cmd 6876 (London: His Majesty's Stationery Office, July 1946), p. 2, gives the following as the terms of reference: "To consider the general questions of the establishment, development, organisation and administration that will arise in the promotion of New Towns in furtherance of a policy of planned decentralisation from congested urban areas; and in accordance therewith to suggest guiding principles on which such Towns should be established and developed as self-contained and balanced communities for work and living."

2. *Ibid.*, p. 10.

3. For an analysis of the aggregate trends in the social balance and self-containment in Britain's major cities and conurbations over the period 1951–1971 see Ray Thomas, "New Towns, New Suburbs, and Urban Renewal," in Ray Thomas, Ed., *"Perspectives on New Towns Development,"* a paper from a conference, New Towns Study Unit, The Open University, 1976.

4. Hans Blumenfeld, "The Modern Metropolis," in *The Modern Metropolis: Selected Essays by Hans Blumenfeld,* Spreiringen Paul D. I., Ed., (Cambridge, Mass.: M.I.T. Press, 1971), pp. 61–62.

5. Blumenfeld, "Transportation in the Modern Metropolis," *The Modern Metropolis,* p. 123.

6. Great Britain, *New Towns Act, 1946.*

7. Great Britain, *Town Development Act, 1952.*

8. Great Britain, Department of the Environment, *Land*, Cmnd 5370 (London: Her Majesty's Stationery Office, September 1974), p. 5.

9. *Ibid.,* p. 6.

10. *Ibid.,* p. 4.

CHAPTER 4

Movement Systems for New Towns

MAYER HILLMAN AND STEPHEN POTTER

Movement systems are primary determinants of urban structure, patterns of land use, and levels of accessibility. The design of an appropriate system is therefore one of the principal ways whereby the advantages of living in towns—access to a wide variety of people and places—can be maximized. Indeed, a good measure of urbanity is the variety of the interaction.

Compared with personal behavioral characteristics, the physical environment may play a relatively small role in this interaction. However, the environmental factor is worth considerable study because it can significantly influence motivation by reducing the costs, inconvenience, and effort of travel, thereby widening available options for activity.

The methods used to aid this interaction in new-town plans vary considerably. The variation is more than can adequately be accounted for in terms of site, size, or population. Indeed, most of this variation can be fully explained only by considering the different planning philosophies and basic assumptions on which urban design is structured.

Since movement systems are the dominant organizational factor of urban design, the importance of the rationale and justification of these assumptions and their related philosophies cannot be overestimated. This chapter explores the rationale of a number of these assumptions and the urban forms that have resulted from them, together with how the problems associated with them have led to a modification of both urban form and philosophy. Three specific case studies—Cumbernauld, Runcorn, and Milton Keynes—serve to illustrate the development of this process in Britain's new towns.

The situation is complicated by the inherent conflicts between the optimal urban forms for the three major modes of transport. In terms of urban design, these forms are hardly comparable and, as a result, require principles according to which priority must be given.

The optimal form for the private car has received most attention, where increasing car ownership and congestion in historic communities has led to the avoidance of this becoming a major planning goal. Given that the use of the car is to be fostered for all possible transport purposes, it is now generally agreed that a loosely knit, low-density, dispersed urban structure, with peak-hour journeys distributed evenly over a high capacity grid or motorway-box network, is the closest to an optimum yet achieved.

The requirements for public transport, however, are quite different. A compact town with high residential densities is preferable, together with well-defined corridors of movement and with the main transport generating land uses conveniently located along them.

With low densities and dispersed destinations, traffic along any single route is likely to be light, except in the peak hour. This does not matter for cars because only one person is needed to make using a car worthwhile. The threshold level for the provision of public transport is much higher, of course, and such a situation is likely to result in a poor provision of public transport, and probably none at all in many marginal situations. The requirement for a compact urban form and corridors of movement generally suggest a linear-type development or an adapted version of the traditional radial-concentric towns that have grown up over the centuries.

A further source of conflict is between motorized and nonmotorized modes (i.e., walking and cycling). This conflict is generally acknowledged in estate layout by pedestrian/vehicle segregation, although this is still not fully satisfactory. However, to bring facilities within walking and cycling distance in urban design, a far more compact layout is needed than for either the car or public transport. A careful arrangement of land uses to minimize journey length is also needed.

In addition to the conflicts between the optimal requirements for the three major transport modes, there are a variety of external costs and benefits associated with each system. Dispersed urban forms use a considerable amount of land. Taking the two extreme densities of new-town development in Britain—Cumbernauld and Milton Keynes—if the latter were built at the original density of Cumbernauld, it would occupy only 30 percent of the area now designated for this purpose. Car-oriented urban forms also generate high flows of traffic, with implications for levels of safety, pollution, health, and noise. In addition, the implications for the conservation of energy and resources of such designs are factors that have become increasingly important in recent years.

The more compact forms, compared to low-density developments, minimize these problems and generally offer a greater freedom of choice between modes, while having the disadvantages associated with high densities: cost, lack of privacy and open space, and greater restriction on the free use of cars.

Thus, there are many public and private conflicts involved in the provision for the three major modes of transport. The planner's purpose of attempting to bring private and public interests into coincidence is more easily met in a new town than in other settlements. Account can be taken of the fact that, whereas the car is the most desirable form of travel from a personal viewpoint owing to its speed, convenience, flexibility, and comfort, the option of using one is limited primarily by age, income, and ability to a minority of the population. Moreover, from the public viewpoint, the car is the least desirable of the major modes because of the space and expenditure required for parking and running it, as well as the environmental externalities previously mentioned.

THE LESSON OF CUMBERNAULD

At present most movement systems proposed for postwar British new towns and other similarly planned communities give preference to either private or public transport. The new town of Cumbernauld probably provides one of the most useful examples of how an initial design philosophy was arrived at, tried in practice, and subsequently modified. The original concept, developed at the time when the American influence of planning for unrestricted motorization was at its height (1958–1961),[1] was to provide an urban structure that could cope with peak car demands at the predicted saturation level of car ownership.[2] Consideration of private transport was the primary organizing factor of the town because the assumption was that the realities of accomodating the car had to be faced and, therefore, that such consideration should be given priority.

The plan, however, was severely restricted by the physical limitations of the site. It was small and lent itself to a compact urban form, which it was hoped, with an extensive system of pedestrian/vehicle segregation, could allow free use of facilities for both the pedestrian and the car user. The target was thus set to locate all dwellings within three-quarters of a mile (1.2 kilometers) of the town center, with two-thirds of the dwellings within one-third of a mile (0.5 kilometers) (see Figure 1).

Public transport had very little influence on the urban form, although it had some detailed influence in relation to the location of underpasses near bus stops, and so on. With walking viewed as the major back-up system to the car, the assumption was that public transport would be little used in the peak hours.

As Cumbernauld developed, a somewhat different picture emerged. The actual roles of the three modes changed very much from those envisaged by the planners in the late 1950s and early 1960s. The town could not be built at the densities proposed in the master plan. Thus today Cumbernauld is intended to occupy about twice the originally designated area. As a result, the pedestrian scale of access in the town has for the most part been lost, and practice has shown that even the high degree of pedestrian/vehicle segregation that exists in Cumbernauld has not fully removed the conflict with vehicles. The provision of a

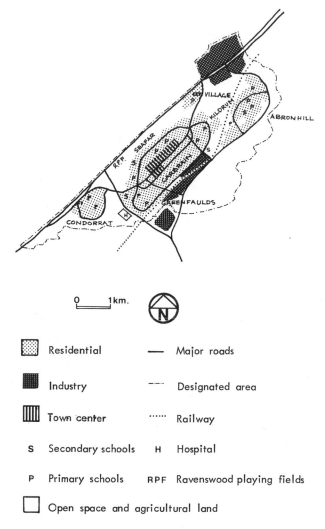

Figure 1. The 1962 plan of Cumbernauld. Source: Osborn and Whittick, *The New Towns: The Answer to Megalopolis.*

road system that will be used in a full motorization situation for only the peak hour has now come to be looked upon more as an expensive extravagance than a necessity when alternative urban designs exist to minimize private transport usage.

By the time the plans for the extension area of Cumbernauld were being prepared (1972–1973), the basic assumptions behind the original plan were obviously in need of considerable revision. The assumption that the family car can provide for the vast majority of transport needs had been proved false, and reliance on the pedestrian system to provide a back-up was no longer possible with a town twice the size. Moreover, the pedestrian system had proved disappointing even in the compact hilltop town; the 1967 household survey showed that 44 percent of journeys to the town center were by car or bus, and a mere 8

percent of the people walked to work. Indeed, a British town the same size as Cumbernauld with a lower proportion of journeys to work by foot is difficult to find (see Figure 2).

The Footpath Network. The problems associated with the development of the Cumbernauld pedestrian network offer some important lessons for planning in other urban areas. Despite the high degree of segregation, a significant proportion of pedestrians use the roads in preference to the footpaths. The 1974 report on road accidents in Cumbernauld stressed this problem and noted an increase in the number of children using the roads as footpaths.[3] Although the town has a low accident rate compared with the rest of Britain, the development corporation still regards it as too high and even suggests that "the most effective deterrent to 'main road pedestrians' would be legislation to permit prosecution of these offenders."

Cumbernauld's footpaths are reasonably direct, although in a number of cases the distance along the roads is shorter; but this is not the problem. The main reason for people choosing to use the road rather than the path is simply that the road appears to be the obvious logical way of getting from A to B. Clarity of the network is the major problem—where roads go is obvious, whereas the footpath network is extremely complex and the standard of layout varies greatly over the town. The problem of people crossing or walking along a road from a bus stop rather than using an underpass is considered insolvable.

Public Transport. The expansion of the new town necessitated a greater emphasis on public transport than was anticipated in the early 1960s. In addition, development elsewhere, especially at Runcorn and Redditch, had indicated the direction in which planning philosophy was going. The detrimental effects of planning a new town's transportation system primarily around the car were becoming obvious. Cumbernauld had suffered from these problems as much as the other new towns; its structure was not conducive to the provision of an attractive bus service because the primary road system was too circuitous. A balanced solution was indeed demanded.

The 1974 Extension Plan. The Outline Plan for the Cumbernauld Extension Area (see Figure 3) is disappointingly devoid of any planning objectives, goals, or any policy statement of this kind.[4] Yet the physical proposals in this document reflect a set of goals and

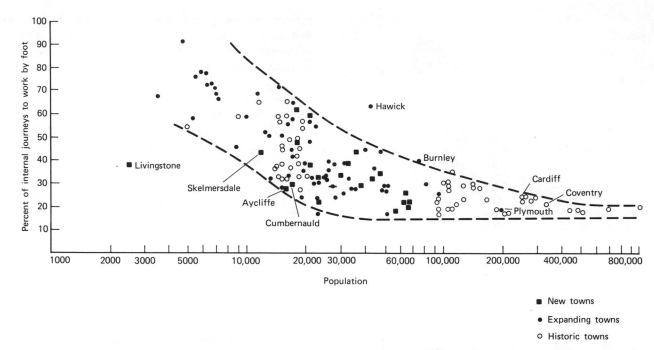

Figure 2. The proportion of journeys to work by foot and town size, United Kingdom, 1966. Small towns obviously have a larger proportion of journeys to work by foot than do large towns, but within this general trend there exists a wide range of figures, representing the influence of the urban form. Where a town of a given size falls within this range depends on how conducive its design is to pedestrian movement for the work journey. Source of data: 1966 United Kingdom Census, Journey to Work and Transportation Tables.

assumptions that represent a very different philosophy from that of the original plan. The attitude of catering for the car at all cost is now gone. The greater emphasis on public transport and the pedestrian and the need for economy in building development have led to a different approach.

Similar physical constraints apply to the extension area as applied to the originally designated hilltop site, and these have largely predetermined both residential and industrial locations. Extending or duplicating the original compact form has not been possible.

In the residential areas the needs of pedestrians and public transport predominate. The loop-road method is used, with the line of the road being determined so as to have every household within a five-minute walk of a bus stop. Strict pedestrian/vehicle segregation is not planned because the lesson of the original hilltop town was that this method gives too much priority to the car—making it more the master than the servant of people. The road is designed to make the car adapt to the needs of pedestrians, not *vice versa*. Pedestrians on and crossing such roads are to be expected, and the needs of the car have to be adapted to conform to this. The bus service is intended to be of the high frequency Superbus type,

as pioneered in Stevenage New Town in the early 1970s.

THE RUNCORN EXPERIMENT

The change in philosophy from auto-dominated planning to more balanced solutions, as reflected in the development of Cumbernauld, owes much to the Runcorn New-Town experiment. Runcorn was designated in 1964; its master plan was developed in 1967.[5] It concentrated more on the function than the needs of transport. The concept that transport was a desirable commodity in itself was at last swept away, to be replaced by the obvious notion that transport is a means and not an end. Thus the goals for transportation in Runcorn were related to the overall objective of achieving "a unity and balance between all elements of the town."[6] Transport, of course, played a vital role in achieving this, but its role and form was constrained by general planning aims. Hence the transport subgoal was "to provide economically for the socially satisfactory movement of people and goods without the environment being dominated by vehicles and communication ways."[7]

However, the plan tended to look at the problem

very much in terms of motorized transport. The concept of bringing facilities close to the people, as tried in Cumbernauld, was not attempted here (largely because the site was considered unsuitable), although this approach also would have been a logical step from such a philosophy. Given the dismissal of this possibility, the rationale behind the town being structured upon a segregated busway system can be readily understood.

The plan emphasized the social need that exists for public transport for shopping, social, school, and work journeys, although strangely, this demand was somewhat underestimated, the master plan referring to "at least 15 percent of the population who will be without the use of a car at a particular time." Even if saturation levels of car ownership are reached, about half of the total population (including one-third of

the adult population) will be without the optional use of a car. Within residential communities, however, pedestrian needs are given priority and movement is on segregated paths. The aim is to provide all the facilities that these areas can support within a five-minute walking distance. The population within such areas amounts to about 8000, which is capable of maintaining a reasonably wide range of shopping, social, and cultural facilities. Certain paths are wide enough to take cyclists also, although no full cycleway system is planned. The master plan did not anticipate much use of this mode.

The form of the town is linear because public transport operates most efficiently along a corridor, but it is modified to form a figure of eight (see Figure 4). Bus stops are provided at the focal points along the corridor in each neighborhood.

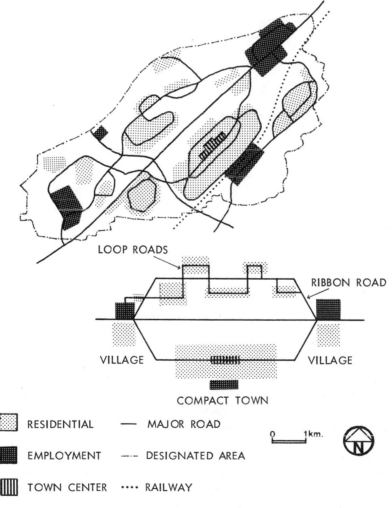

Figure 3. Cumbernauld extension plan: (upper) 1974 land-use and transport plan; (lower) the theoretical structure of the extension. Source of upper diagram: "Cumbernauld Extension Area Outline Plan."

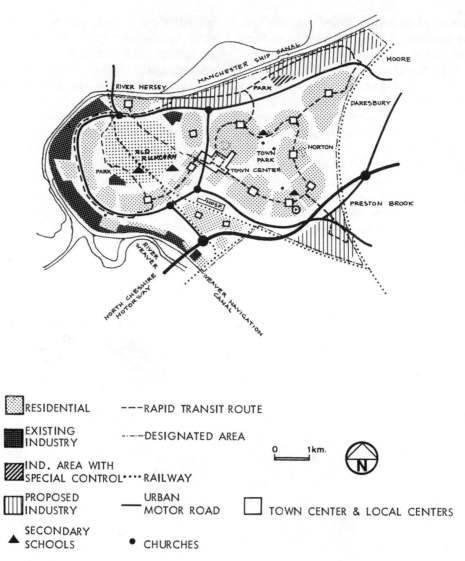

Figure 4. The basic plan of Runcorn (including 1975 amendments).

RESIDENTIAL   ---RAPID TRANSIT ROUTE

EXISTING
INDUSTRY   ---DESIGNATED AREA

IND. AREA WITH
SPECIAL CONTROL ····RAILWAY

PROPOSED   URBAN
INDUSTRY   MOTOR ROAD   TOWN CENTER & LOCAL CENTERS

SECONDARY
SCHOOLS   • CHURCHES

0   1km.

This form encourages a far higher passenger load per route mile than operates on a grid or similar car-oriented layout.[8] With the buses running on a segregated track and with priority ensured by the use of phased traffic lights where it crosses distributor roads, high vehicular speeds are possible. The goal is an average speed of 21 miles per hour (34 kilometers per hour). In 1975, with about half the busway open, buses were averaging 19.5 miles per hour. A modal split of 50/50 between the use of the car and the bus for the work journey was the objective stated in the master plan when car ownership would reach its maximum, but in fact, this ratio has already been achieved.[9] Private vehicular traffic is accommodated on dual two-lane carriageways, with grade-separated junctions and a design speed of 50 miles per hour (80 kilometers per hour).

Despite the priority given to public transport in the structuring of the new town, the planners' own theoretical comparison of work and shopping journeys by car and bus still shows that the car is considerably faster, even when car speed (on a door-to-door basis) is taken at half the design speed of the dual carriageways. Although during the peak periods journey times were expected to be similar for both motorized modes, a typical trip for shopping and other journeys by public transport would take double the time it would by car. For certain purposes (e.g., leisure) it was anticipated that the car would be used for 85 percent of journeys due to the inconvenience and inflexibility of even this high standard bus service when compared to the car. The inherent advantage of the car is considerable.

Even though car-dominated urban forms can undermine the economic operations of public transport, and in the extreme can require the scattering of facilities well beyond convenient pedestrian access, designs that give priority to public transport seem to exhibit comparatively little effect upon the competitiveness of the car. Runcorn is a prime example of this, for although the busway system is expected to alter some car use, especially on the work journey, trends in car ownership are expected to remain unaltered. Those who choose to use the car find that the busway only marginally reduces the convenience of the road system, which is as good as in any new town. In a recent survey, replies to the question, "Comparing walking, driving a car and traveling by bus, which of these do you think Runcorn New Town is best designed for?" residents answered as follows: walking, 26 percent; car, 29 percent; buses, 34 percent; none of these, 2 percent, and don't know, 9 percent.[10] Considering that the figures for car and bus are so close, the resident's perception seems to be that the busway does little to affect the convenience of car use.

Walking, which comes at the bottom of this list, represents the remaining conflict. The main consideration at Runcorn is to balance the car with public transport—hence the use of linear development with a segregated busway. Although the needs of pedestrians predominate within each residential area, their influence upon the design of the new town overall was minimal. Journeys by foot outside and between the residential areas are small because of this. Only 7 percent of journeys to the central shopping area are anticipated to be by nonmotorized transport, and even 45 percent of journeys to secondary schools are expected to be by the motorized means of car and bus.

Within the residential areas, great care has been taken to plan fully for the pedestrian, with walking times to the local centers and bus stops not exceeding five minutes. As noted earlier, the size of these areas is also intended to support "everyday social and shopping needs" within this five-minute walking distance.

The busway, however, has proved to be too successful in this respect, with fewer people using the local shopping facilities than was expected. With such good communications to the town center, even a large proportion of daily shopping requirements are being purchased there. One result is that the development corporation has had to reduce the rent to tenants at one local center.

There are two main lessons to be learned from the Runcorn plan. First, it shows that by giving priority to public transport, facilities for car users can be little affected. One may wonder whether sufficient priority has been given because the development corporation's own calculations show that the car still maintains a substantial advantage over the bus for most trips, particularly those outside the rush hour.

Second, a balance between the car and bus does nothing to reduce the pedestrian/vehicle conflicts previously outlined. Although priority within residential areas has undoubtably been given to the pedestrian, no attempt seems to have been made to amend the form of the town to increase pedestrian access to any other areas. Although far more compact and less wasteful of land than car-oriented urban forms, linear development, even when formed into a figure eight as at Runcorn, still expands the distance that pedestrians have to travel.

A NEW METHODOLOGY: THE LESSON OF MILTON KEYNES

The plan for Runcorn marked an important stage in the development of a fresh methodology for new-town planning. The techniques used and the solutions offered were constantly evaluated according to basic goals of planning.

The plan for Milton Keynes (1970) completed this transition, with a new structure for evaluating planning methods and objectives.[11] The six basic goals, to which each element of the plan had to relate, were established by public seminars. The goals were (1) opportunity and freedom of choice, (2) easy movement and access and good communications, (3) balance and variety, (4) an attractive city, (5) public awareness and participation, and (6) efficient and imaginative use of resources.

The goals bear a close relation to those of Runcorn but are more explicit, with the intention that their influence should show in all aspects of the plan. Transport is now assigned its true role: not an objective in itself, but a means to an end, and in itself a singularly useless commodity. Designing a transport system merely to move people around is to divorce it from its true purpose of contributing to the creation of a community.

In the case of Milton Keynes, these broad objectives led to seven transportation goals:

1. A high degree of accessibility between all activities and places making up the city.
2. Freedom of choice between public and private methods of transport.
3. A high quality public transport system from the beginning of development, not only for those who need it but those who might choose to use it instead of private transport.
4. Provision for the use of the car unrestrained by congestion.
5. Flexibility in the transport system to allow for expansion and change.
6. A safe and environmentally attractive transport system: one which minimizes nuisance from noise and pollution.
7. Provision for free and safe movement as a pedestrian.[12]

Basically, goal 1 is the primary objective, subject to the constraint of goals 5 and 6. Goal 2 is obviously necessary to achieve this, and the goals for the use of the three modes (3, 4 and 7) are needed to maintain freedom of choice (see Figure 5).

The general attitude toward public transport was the same as at Runcorn—that is, a service of good quality would be needed to meet the social goals, but the urban form chosen did not reflect the growing awareness of the practical impossibility of achieving this within a car-determined structure.

The design of the town was oriented toward the maximum convenience of the car user, while at the same time, it was hoped, providing a reliable public transport system and safe pedestrian routes. Because cars afford vastly increased mobility that can be catered for without restriction, the planners of Milton Keynes considered that this should be fully exploited by the provision of a road network capable of accomodating the highest likely levels of use during peak hours. The optimal system established for the movement of cars was that of a grid road system, coupled with very low residential densities (the lowest of any British new town) and dispersed employment centers (see Figure 6). This system would give maximum convenience to car users and provide a competitive public transport system and safe pedestrian (and later bicycle) routes.

Soon after the plan was published, however, it became obvious that the urban form chosen could not fulfill the goals set for it. Its very dispersed, low-density structure was shown to be incapable of supporting the good public transport service demanded by the goals of design. It was hoped that small minibuses might help resolve this problem, but given the structure of Milton Keynes, the cost of running such a system was prohibitive. The technical supplement on transportation concluded: "Thus, in the context of the remainder of the goals established in Milton Keynes and in the light of the selected land use plan, the provision of a competitive form of public transport does not make practical sense. This consideration of maximization of freedom of choice has therefore been discounted."[13]

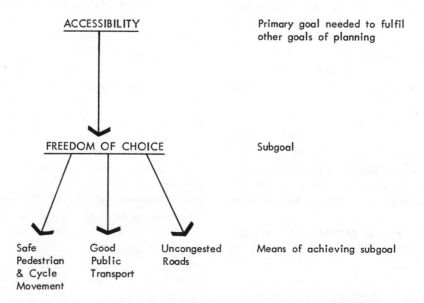

Figure 5.   Relation of goals of planning.

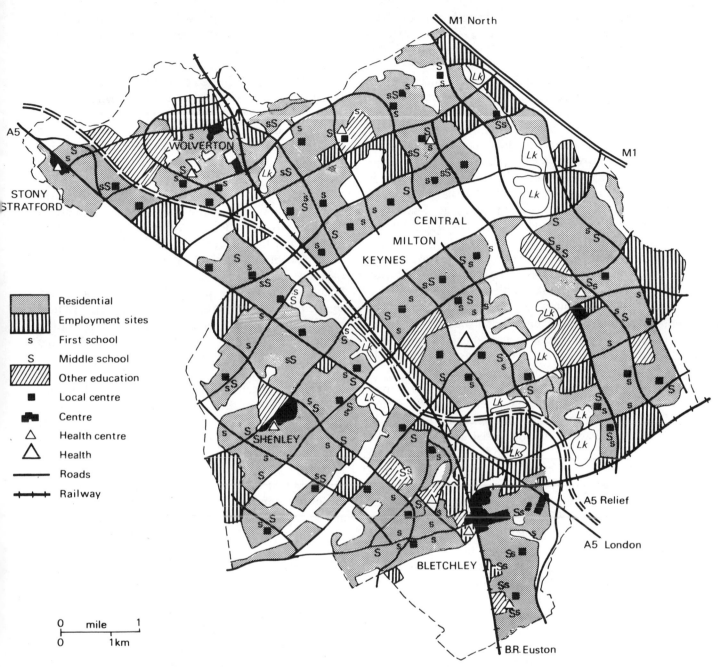

Figure 6. The strategic plan of Milton Keynes. Source: Stephen Potter, "Transport and New Towns. Milton Keynes, England: New Towns Study Unit, The Open University, 1976.

Freedom of choice, of course, depends on the attainment of the goal of accessibility. In suggesting its removal, therefore, the consultants were advocating the abandonment of the whole transport philosophy as established by public consultation before the plan was drafted.

The development corporation has refused to accept this view. However, the provision of a competitive public transport service within a structure deemed unsuitable by its designers, is proving to be quite a problem. The situation regarding this goal is best summed up by the corporation itself in a recent newspaper article aimed at prospective residents: "If you have not got a car, getting about can be a bit difficult and expensive . . . if you haven't got a car, you might have to think about buying one."[14]

One solution being tried experimentally is dial-a-bus, which was introduced in the Woughton area in the spring of 1975 and is proving extremely popular. The number of riders per week has risen from 2300 when the service first started to 4700 in July 1975. The main virtue of dial-a-bus is that it provides passengers with a door-to-door service along no fixed routes and so effectively creates its own corridors of movement where none actually exist, making it very suitable for a low-density situation. However, the system can operate only over a small geographic area; it is extremely slow (because of an average door-to-door speed of less than 5 miles per hour, it is often quicker to walk), due to the bus having to make multiple deviations to pick up passengers; and it is one of the most expensive bus systems to operate due to complicated control equipment and the labor-intensive methods of operation.[15] Fares are higher than for conventional buses, especially when the cost of a telephone call is taken into account.

Owing to the limited field of operation and costs of operating dial-a-bus, conventional buses have to be operated to complement it, providing for longer distance traffic, peak-hour loads, and for people unable or unwilling to pay the high fares of dial-a-bus.

In other words, dial-a-bus is only a partial system of public transport providing a service to one section of the population, while conventional buses, still adversely affected by the dispersed urban form, take other public transport users. In fact, the two systems often compete because many of the dial-a-bus passengers are erstwhile patrons of the conventional service.[16] Moreover, dial-a-bus presents a poor competitor to the car. With the long journey time of the dial-a-bus and the infrequent nature of the conventional services, anyone with the option of using a car does so. No town has been designed exclusively for dial-a-bus; it has always been introduced into areas where proper planning provision for the conventional services has not been made. Lying between the convenience of the taxi and the economy of operation of the bus, this scheme can work well in a dispersed situation, but the full potential of the system can be realized only if it is fully planned, and buses do not have to travel over a wide area, with consequent frustration and delay to passengers. In an historic situation this may be unavoidable. In a new town it is not.

"Provision for free and safe movement as a pedestrian" is one of the transport goals cited in the master plan. In March 1975 a similar policy was also adopted for cyclists. Although an extensive segregated system for both modes is now planned and is partially under construction, obviously this goal has been interpreted in a totally different way than those

relating to motorized transport—that is, free and safe movement within a structure determined by other considerations. Walking and cycling can never be a viable alternative because distances are considerably extended by the dispersed layouts necessary to allow the unrestricted, relatively safe movement of cars. Although housing estates in the city center will be at a higher density,[17] only a very small proportion of the population will be able to walk there, and probably little more than 20 percent will be able to walk to work.

The potential for pedestrian and bicycle movement is considerably reduced by this layout. Pedestrian distances are considerably extended in layouts that permit unrestricted use of vehicles—wide carriageways and infrequent segregated crossings as well as the low density of development and scattered facilities. The small population within each grid square (2000 to 5000) that is within walking distance of a local activity center can support only rather limited facilities, a point fully acknowledged by the development corporation.[18]

By giving priority to the convenience of car travelers, the efficiency of conventional public transport is diminished, and the opportunity to run a dial-a-bus service to a standard probably unequal anywhere in the world has been bypassed. Pedestrian and cycle movement, although safe, is deterred physically and psychologically, and facilities are so dispersed that there is no option but to use motorized means of transport, with their consequent expense and social costs.

THE THREE ALTERNATIVES

The fresh approach to transport planning with which the plan for Milton Keynes began its life must be viewed, to some degree, separately from the subsequent urban form that failed to achieve the goals set for it. The philosophical process was not at fault, only the means by which this was interpreted in a physical form. The impossibility of providing a competitive public transport service in a car-dominated form that was recognized in Runcorn and followed in the Cumbernauld extension plan is further underlined by the failure to provide such a service in Milton Keynes.

As a means by which freedom of choice, and hence accessibility, can be maximized, the system of giving the car priority, followed by the bus and pedestrian, represents the least satisfactory method. For the car user, the system is first-rate, but for the bus user and operator, dispersal of facilities and low density of residential population are unsatisfactory because they lead to multiple, underused routes. Dial-a-bus represents a hope because it can operate under such conditions even though it is not most convenient under them. Conventional buses are still needed to complement dial-a-bus, and their conditions of operation are compounded by the loss of passengers to this better service. Facilities for pedestrians are minimal because distances are often too great, and low residential densities result in only minimal facilities being within walking range.

The linear form, giving priority to the bus, with secondary consideration to the car and pedestrian is close to a satisfactory solution. Facilities for the car are excellent, and the creation of a bus corridor on a segregated, figure-eight track (so that people farthest from the center have the option of picking up a bus going in either direction), has resulted in a relatively high quality service.

THE FOURTH ALTERNATIVE

Satisfactory accessibility can be achieved only by resolving the conflicts between the major transport modes. The old philosophy that universal car ownership would remove the need for such a resolution is dead. The British new-town experience shows that car-dominated urban forms severely prejudice facilities for the public transport user and the pedestrian, whereas public transport and pedestrian forms do little to prejudice facilities for the car.

When alternative designs exist, the provision of road facilities that are likely to be fully used for only two hours a day, and are planned for a level of car ownership that may never be attained, is now increasingly looked on as an unnecessary extravagance.

Finally, arguments indirectly related to transport, such as resource conservation, pollution, and safety, further emphasize the argument that full motorization is not an optimal solution to transportation planning.

The main disadvantage of buses, compared with other methods of travel, is the time involved in using them, when measured as door-to-door travel time. Therefore, a movement system designed to offer a real freedom of choice must make door-to-door journeys beyond walking distance more convenient by bus than by car. To achieve this, pedestrian movement would have to be channeled toward a highly efficient public transport system. Such a solution could

only be viable in circumstances in which its use was optimized and in which it operated a frequent, inexpensive, totally reliable service.

In view of the inherent advantages of the private car to people but its disadvantages to the community, the aim of the movement system for a pedestrian-oriented town would be to promote journeys by other means, but not to restrict travel by car. The road network would be available for those unable or unwilling to walk, such as disabled people, housewives carrying heavy shopping or traveling with children, or businessmen, as well as for all essential motorized traffic.

The availability of an efficient, cheap car hire service could even remove much of the need for car ownership and extend car usage to a significant proportion of the population not owning cars. The car would thereby fulfill the role for which it is best suited because it would be used mainly for diverse and out-of-town activities, especially for leisure purposes.

The application of these principles to urban design would vary according to site conditions and other necessary socioeconomic constraints. Promoting pedestrian and public transport could mean that many facilities would have to be located at the convergence of their routes, while facilities using major space, such as playing fields, parks, and certain types of industry, would have to be on the town's periphery, thereby reducing walking distances while allowing for growth along a linear corridor. The plan of a new town featuring these characteristics (see Figure 7) has been developed from an original proposal by Mayer Hillman and Jonas Lehrman in 1956.[19]

In the zest to provide a real freedom of choice between private and public transport, the humble pedestrian has been forgotten. Merely providing a pleasant environment to walk in without complementary measures to ensure that a wide range of facilities are within walking distance can be considered little more than lip service to pedestrian needs. The importance of pedestrian and cyclist movement has been continually underestimated and discounted in favor of the car and public transport users. Transport experts have argued that, if a real choice can be provided between public and private transport, it does not matter if walking is restricted. However, the rise in the cost of fuel since 1973 has made it increasingly difficult for planners to justify forcing people to use motorized transport when, for a new town at least, alternative designs exist that can minimize dependence upon the car and bus.

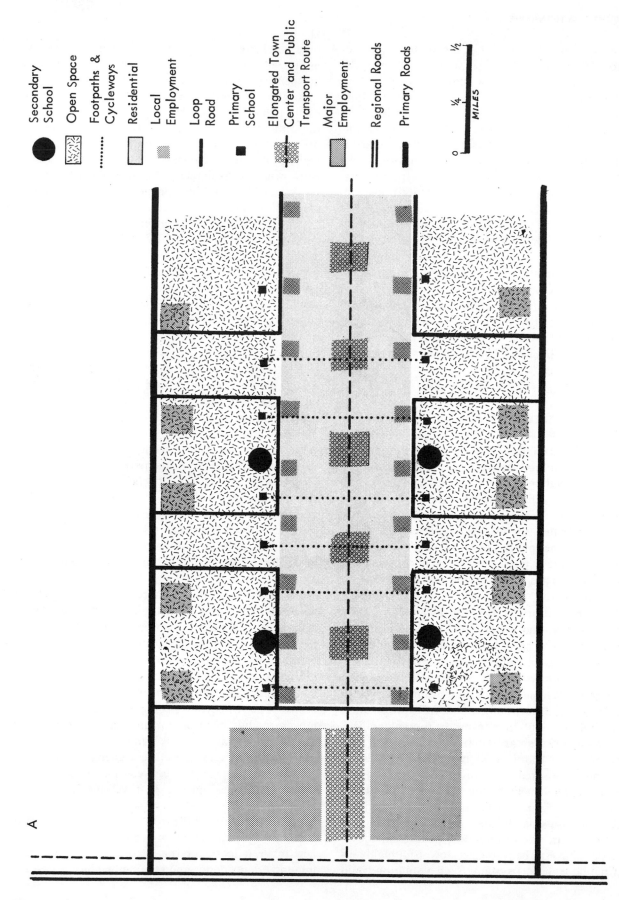

Secondary School

Open Space

Footpaths & Cycleways

Residential

Local Employment

Loop Road

Primary School

Elongated Town Center and Public Transport Route

Major Employment

Regional Roads

Primary Roads

0 ¼ ½

MILES

A

Figure 7. (A) The fourth alternative: a possible design for a pedestrian/public transport-oriented structure; (B) Alternatives for growth of pedestrian/public transport urban structure.

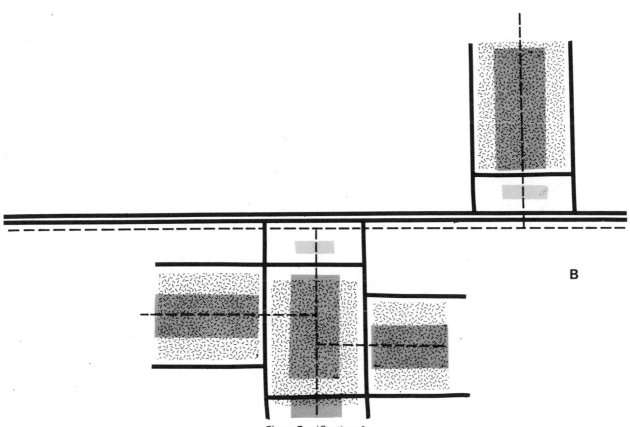

B

Figure 7. *(Continued)*

The percentage of the population who are unable to walk reasonable distances or to travel by public transport is extremely small; thus a primary dependence upon these two modes would ensure that a reasonable level of mobility is not dependent upon adequate age, ability, and income—the three prerequisites of optional car use.

The main advantages of walking and cycling include speed for short distances (up to about one-third of a mile compared to car travel and three-quarters of a mile compared to bus travel), cost (negligible), and risk of accidents (almost nil in segregated layouts). Moreover, the spatial requirements and public costs of accommodating people on foot or cycle are extremely small compared to accommodating them when they travel by motorized means. However, pedestrians have a limited range of movement, are exposed to the weather, and are involved in physical effort when walking long distances, negotiating changes of level, and on occasions having to carry heavy, bulky goods. The opportunity to be able to walk to most destinations would reduce the isolation felt by certain sections of the population, particularly children and elderly people, and social

intercourse would be less restricted by physical factors.

Extremely high residential densities are now unfashionable and unpopular in most Western countries, making it unlikely that attempts will be made again to build towns of 80,000 to 100,000 population or more to an overall pedestrian scale of access, as was attempted in Britain at Cumbernauld and Skelmersdale. However, in countries where high densities are more socially acceptable, this could remain a valid approach—as indeed it would be with smaller new towns or given the choice of a particularly advantageous site.[20] Such social and physical constraints would require a different interpretation of the principles previously outlined.

One urban form that also appears to fulfill these requirements is the cluster, or social city—the original new-town concept formulated by Ebenezer Howard in 1898. A modern interpretation of this is the British new town of Peterborough—an existing settlement, which is being expanded under the New Towns Act by the addition of four satellite townships of some 30,000 population each, around the old city (see Figure 8). With a large population, each of these

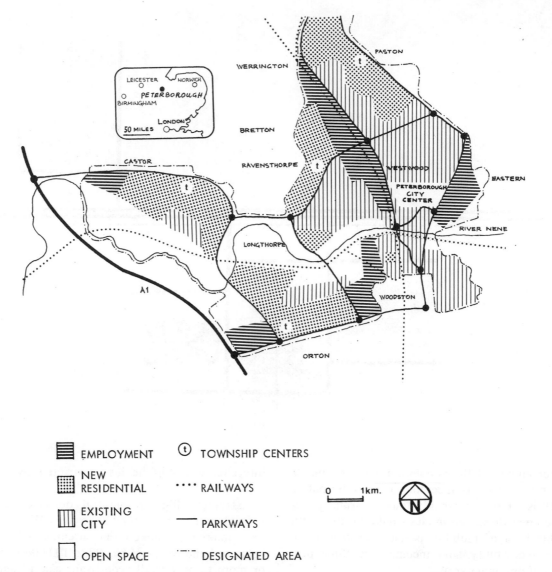

Figure 8.   The basic plan of Peterborough. Source: *The (London) Times*, November 17, 1972, p. II of special supplement on Peterborough.

townships will provide a wide range of facilities within a pedestrian scale of access, while public transport has determined their relative location to provide corridors of movement to maintain an attractive bus service. At the same time, this loose, yet coherent structure can easily provide congestion-free conditions for the private car.

The two examples previously outlined serve to illustrate the different interpretations of the principle of pedestrian and public transport priority in the design of a new town. Such a movement system exploits the virtues of the main transport modes so that each can function optimally without prejudice to the efficiency of the others. A reduction in the need for motorized travel results in a smaller scale of road and parking facilities. At the same time the maximum degree of independence is enjoyed by all.

SUMMARY

Although some of the movement systems approach the provision of a real freedom of choice, none really succeeds in freeing each mode from the adverse conditions imposed upon it by another. Giving priority to public transport frees it from the hostile conditions of car-dominated forms, while the car's flexibility easily adapts it to such an environment.

This form still restricts pedestrian movement to within local areas. However, giving first priority to the pedestrian is just as logical an interpretation of the philosophy discussed as giving it to public transport. A movement system could be structured such that walking and cycling, together with public transport are the predominant modes. Public transport would extend the pedestrian's and cyclist's range, and the car, of course, would still be unrestricted and fulfill its most useful role for long distances or for essential journeys in town transferring people for whom public transport is unsuitable. In this way each element of the movement system could function optimally without severely prejudicing any other.

If the limitations to walking could be reduced by the integration of the pedestrian network with a truly efficient, competitive public transport service, this system would go a long way toward reconciling the conflict between personal and community interests. Such a system, of course, must not be considered in isolation, but must be related to its contribution to the development of the community. Transport is a means, not an end. Conflicts with other elements must be fully allowed for, and the system must be modified to fit in best with the overall needs of the town. Thus several different interpretations of this basic principle are possible.

The car must serve the transport system and not dominate the environment by its presence or considerations of its presence, and a balanced transport system must not be given overriding consideration against what may be considered higher objectives. Transport aids the interaction of land uses. Because planning philosophy structures most of urban design around the transport framework, developing a sound philosophy and a means of interpreting it physically are particularly important.

NOTES

1. *Cumbernauld New Town: Preliminary Planning Proposals* (April 1958), *First Addendum Report* (May 1959), and *Second Addendum Report* (January 1962).

2. 0.45 cars per person.

3. A. Scott, *Report on Road Accidents* (Cumbernauld: Cumbernauld Development Corporation, May 1974).

4. *Cumbernauld Extension Area Outline Plan* (Cumbernauld: Cumbernauld Development Corporation, February 1974).

5. Outline plan, January 1966; A. Ling, *Runcorn New Town Master Plan*, 1967.

6. A. Ling, 1967, p. 66.

7. *Ibid.*

8. For example, there are 2.2 miles (3.5 kilometers) of bus route per 10,000 population in Runcorn compared to 4 miles (6.4 kilometers) per 10,000 in Milton Keynes.

9. A 1975 calculation indicates that an 80/20 modal split between the bus and car may eventually be possible.

10. R. Berthoud, *Runcorn Travel Survey* (London: Social and Community Planning Research, Centre for Sample Surveys, October 1973), p. 12.

11. Llewelyn-Davies, Weeks, Forestier-Walker, and Bor, *The Plan for Milton Keynes*, Vol. 2 (Milton Keynes, England: Milton Keynes Development Corporation, 1970). See also Llewelyn-Davies, Weeks, Forestier-Walker and Bor, *Milton Keynes Plan: Interim Report to the Milton Keynes Development Corporation* (London: Llewelyn-Davies, Weeks, Forestier-Walker and Bor, 1968) and Richard Llewelyn-Davies, "Changing Goals in Design: The Milton Keynes Example," in *New Towns: The British Experience,* Hazel Evans, Ed. (New York: Halsted Press, Wiley, 1972), pp. 102–116.

12. Llewelyn-Davies, Weeks, Forestier-Walker and Bor, *The Plan for Milton Keynes,* Vol. 2, p. 279.

13. *Transportation,* Vol. 2, Technical Supplement No. 7 to *The Plan for Milton Keynes* (Bletchley, England: Milton Keynes Development Corporation, 1970), pp. 33–34.

14. Milton Keynes *Gazette,* July 11, 1975, pp. 16 and 41. Reprinted in *Architectural Design* **40,** (December 1975):729.

15. For example, the Teltram dial-a-bus system in Ann Arbor, Michigan (pop. 100,000) consisting of 45 dial-a-buses and 15 fixed route express buses, cost $1.5 million to subsidize in 1973.

16. For example, in the Maidstone Dial-a-Ride Survey, 70 percent of the trips made were transfers from the conventional services.

17. An increase of 60 percent over elsewhere.

18. See L. A. Shostak and S. F. Fuller, "The Use of Survey Research in Policy Analysis," a paper delivered at New Towns Seminar, Centre of Environmental Studies, London, October 8, 1975.

19. "Project for a Linear New Town," *Architects Journal* **125,** No. 3240 (1957):136–140.

20. For example, the new town of Arcosanti, near Phoenix, Arizona, is planned at an overall average density of 1112 persons per hectare (450 persons per acre). The 1964 plan for the new town of Tsuen Wan (Hong Kong) allowed for an overall density of 946 persons per hectare (383 persons per acre)—a population of 1,200,000 in a town of 1267 hectares (3131 acres).

BIBLIOGRAPHY

Bor, Walter. *The Making of Cities.* London: Leonard Hill, 1972. Esp. pp. 209–210 and "Making a Fresh Start," pp. 218–241.

Berthoud, R. *Runcorn Travel Survey.* London: Social and Community Planning Research, Centre for Sample Surveys, October 1973.

Cumbernauld Development Corporation. *Cumbernauld New Town. Preliminary Planning Proposals, First Addendum Report and Second Addendum Report.* Cumbernauld, Scotland: April 1958, May 1959, and January 1962.

———. *Cumbernauld Extension Outline Plan.* Ref. no. CDC/1/74/p. Cumbernauld: Cumbernauld Development Corporation, 1974.

Hillman, Mayer. "Mobility in New Towns." Ph.D. Dissertation, University of Edinburgh, 1970.

————, Irwin Henderson, and Anne Whalley. *Personal Mobility and Transport Policy.* P.E.P. Broadsheet No. 543. London: Political and Economic Planning, 1973.

———— and Stephen Potter. "Access and Mobility in New Towns." Session 4 of Perspectives on New Town Development, The New Towns Study Unit, The Open University, Milton-Keynes, 1976.

Llewelyn-Davies, Richard. "Changing Goals in Design: The Milton Keynes Example." In *New Towns: The British Experience.* Hazel Evans, Ed. London: Charles Knight; and New York: Halsted Press, Wiley, 1972.

Llewelyn-Davies, Weeks, Forestier-Walker and Bor. *The plan for Milton Keynes.* Vols. 1 and 2. *Transportation,* Technical Supplement No. 7. Vols. 1 and 2. Milton Keynes: Milton Keynes Development Corporation, 1970.

Mercer, J. "People and Transportation: Runcorn New Town." *The Journal of the Institution of Highway Engineers* (January 1974).

Milton Keynes Transport Users Group. "Proceedings of the Conference 'Transport and the Master Plan' (April 1975)." Milton Keynes Community Services Association. *Concern Magazine,* No. 2.

Peterborough Master Plan. Peterborough, England: Peterborough Development Corporation. 1970.

Potter, Stephen. "Transport and New Towns." Milton Keynes, England: New Towns Study Unit, The Open University, 1976.

Slevin, R., and A. D. Ochojna. *Dial-a-Ride in Maidstone.* Cranfield CTS., Report No. 6, Cranfield, Bedford, England: Cranfield Institute of Technology, August 1973.

Thomas, Ray. *Evidence to the Environmental and Home Office Sub-Committee Inquiry into New Towns.* Second Report from the Expenditure Committee. Vol. 3. London: Her Majesty's Stationery Office, 1974, pp. 408–443.

CHAPTER 5

New Towns on the Bottom of the Sea

A. K. CONSTANDSE

The new towns that are discussed in the following pages are indeed built on the bottom of what was some decades ago a vast area of water open to the North Sea, and consequently to the Atlantic (see Figures 1 and 2). This fact is more than a colorful piece of additional information. New towns are not only constructions; they are also products of historic developments and environmental conditions. The new towns discussed in this chapter form a part of a land reclamation project with a history of its own, and therefore, this project and its background will have to be described briefly first.

BACKGROUND

The name of the present Kingdom of The Netherlands, the "low countries," is significant: a large part of it has been formed as a delta by the Rhine River. In an endless interplay between the river bringing clay deposits, thus building land in the sea, and the sea eroding the land, there has been a delicate balance where man found both an extraordinarily rich and fertile environment and an extremely dangerous and unstable habitat. The first inhabitants of these tidal lands could do no more than build large mounds of earth to which they could retreat in times of danger. When the society became better organized, dikes could be built by concerted efforts to hold back the water so that the land could be occupied permanently. Ways were devised for conducting surplus water, which accumulated through rainfall

and seepage in the protected areas, through a network of ditches and canals, to sluices for discharge, which could be used during low tide. In the Middle Ages *polders*, tracts of lowland reclaimed from the sea, came into being. The water management system was maintained by district drainage boards with great authority. These operations started on a small scale as communal affairs by farmers or monks. Once the organization was established, technical inventions were fostered and applied. After the year 1500, power generated by windmills made the use of pumps possible. No longer dependent on the force of gravity alone for the discharge of water, land permanently below sea level could also be drained. An enlargement of scale took place with the rise of capitalistic enterprise; merchants from Amsterdam, seeking a use for their fortunes amassed in overseas trade, became interested in land reclamation and financed large projects. An example is the Beemster Polder in the province of North Holland, a lake of 7000 hectares (17,000 acres), which was drained in the year 1612.

The steam engine, more powerful and more reliable than the windmill, opened up new possibilities, but it was not used immediately because large operations with great investment and uncertainty about immediate returns did not attract private capital. A new stage in the development was reached in the middle of the nineteenth century, when the lake Haarlemmermeer, near Amsterdam, with an area of 18,000 hectares (44,000 acres), was drained by the government. The main reason for doing this was the

53

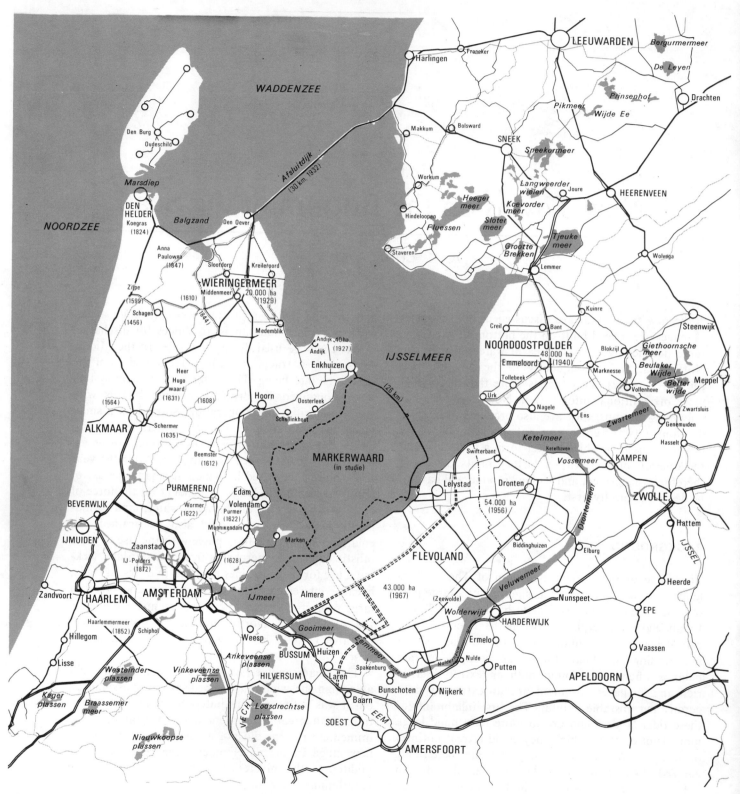

Figure 1. Old and new polders with year of drainage.

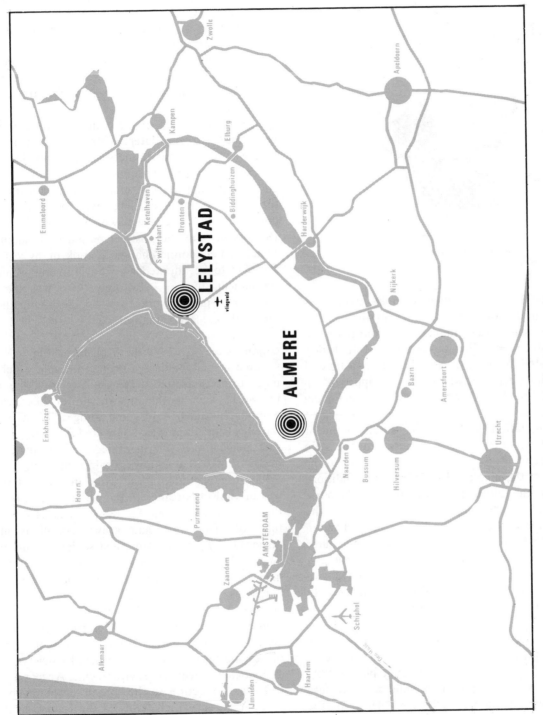

Figure 2. Location of the Holland new towns.

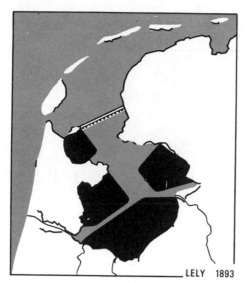

Figure 3. The plan of Lely.

dam into the open sea. Within a few years all the salt water would be washed away, and a valuable basin of fresh water would be obtained. Keeping the central, deepest part of the lake for water storage, the shallower parts could be drained and converted into rich farmland. Five polders, covering a total area of 225,000 hectares (560,000 acres) would be made, adding 10 percent to the total area of cultivated land of the country.

The major quality of the plan, as can be observed more than 80 years later, is its flexibility: once the lake was formed the polders could be made one by one, at times to be chosen at will, in forms to be decided at the appropriate moment and with functions that could be changed. This explains why the plan could survive over two world wars, the Great Depression, and the postwar period of fundamental social and economic change. It took many years for the plan to be adopted as a government project by Parliament, but in 1918, Lely, who was then the minister of public works, saw his ideas embodied in the Zuiderzee (Reclamation) Act.

Organization.   In 1919 the Ministry of Public Works set up a special Zuiderzee Project Branch, which was made responsible for carrying out the civil engineering works, such as the construction of dikes, canals, pumping stations, roads, and bridges. By its efforts the enclosure dam was completed in 1932, and the first polder, the Wieringermeer, measuring 20,000 hectares (50,000 acres), was drained in 1930.

The organization of the work in the first polder was of vital importance to the whole project because there the basis was laid for the procedures still being followed. The state had grown conscious of its responsibility for economic and social welfare of the citizen. The first settlers in polders constructed during the nineteenth century had suffered unusual hardships, and only the second or third generations acquired wealth. The task of the state was no longer seen as merely a matter of acquiring new land, but also of creating good conditions for the growth of a prosperous and well-ordered society in an aesthetically pleasing environment. Accepting this task was a reaction to the chaotic development, the proletarization, which followed the Industrial Revolution, and it was in line with the beginnings of the welfare state.

In 1930 the Ministry of Public Works created the IJsselmeerpolders Development Authority. Its main task at first was to bring the land under cultivation, but soon it made land-use plans, built farms,

threat of the Haarlemmermeer's banks giving way in storms and flooding the surrounding lands. Considerations of actual financial gain did not enter into this decision. The government reluctantly allocated public funds to develop land in that time of liberalism, long before it was politically approved, in the interest of public safety because water was the big enemy.

The accumulation of experience, the development of modern technology, and the entering of the state into the field of project development created, in the second half of the nineteenth century, the conditions necessary for the fulfillment of the dream of Hendric Stevin, about which he had written in 1667—the drainage of the Zuiderzee. The Zuiderzee (in Roman times the lake Flevo) had been enlarged in the course of time by ravaging stormfloods. Though generally not more than 5 meters (17 feet) deep, it acted as a barrier to communication and as a constant threat to the safety of the heart of the country.

The Plan.   After a period in which many plans were made, some taken seriously and others not, the civil engineer Dr. C. Lely published a feasible plan in 1892 (see Figure 3). He proposed to build an enclosure dam of about 30 kilometers in the "neck" of the Zuiderzee, which would shorten the coastline of the open sea by 300 kilometers. South of the dam a lake would be formed, to be called IJsselmeer (Lake IJssel) after the river IJssel, a branch of the Rhine. This river would supply fresh water to the lake, and the surplus water would flow through sluices in the constructed villages, set up public services, and allocated land to farmers. Finally the management and administration of all the state's property (all the land, nearly all the buildings) was entrusted temporarily to its care. It received a budget of its own and was directly responsible to the central government. It was a development corporation *avant la lettre*.

Once the new land had received its first inhabitants, local government had to be established. The adjoining municipalities on the old land were not willing or in a position to manage the new land. A temporary solution was found by creating a civic body with a council and a chairman, who was also the director of the authority. This provisional arrangement for the period between drainage and completion of a reclaimed area formed the model for the local government of the polders that followed and is still being applied. At first the authority appoints a council, which is to be replaced some years later by an elected one. Still later a college of aldermen is formed, all the time chaired by the director. The civic body has the same rights and duties as those of a municipality, with the exception that the planning and development remain in the hands of the authority. As soon as the community is well-equipped and the infrastructure is completed, the normal municipality is instituted, and the authority withdraws from the region.

Execution: A Process of Learning. In 1941 the first polder, the Wieringermeer, received the status of independent municipality. The authority left a prospering area behind and could start its work in the second polder, the Noordoostpolder, an area of 48,000 hectares (120,000 acres), which was drained in 1942. In the first polder the location of villages (service centers) has not been successful. The settlement pattern had not been studied thoroughly, and the planners expected that a spontaneous process of settling would lead to certain clusters at road crossings.

In the much larger second polder a settlement pattern was carefully designed. Because it was one of the rare places in the world where no historic or physical obstacles frustrated the realization of a theoretical geographical model, the hierarchical system of Walter Christaller[1] was applied with some modifications. In the geographic middle of the area a regional center, Emmeloord, was founded, with 10 surrounding villages as local service centers. This polder was handed over to the inhabitants in 1962. It was again mainly an agricultural region and, as such, a success. The settlement pattern, however, quickly demonstrated some shortcomings. The modern agricultural enterprises employed less and less labor. In an area based on an agricultural economy, this directly affects services and, consequently, the total number of the population. In most cases the number of inhabitants of the villages did not reach the target figure, which made it difficult to keep the services feasible and the community viable. In the design of the Noordoostpolder the distances from the periphery of the village region to the center had played an important role. The distance between farm and village should not exceed 5 kilometers because above that, the daily ride for cyclists would be too time-consuming. In the 1960s, however, the private automobile became a common means of transport among rural people, and distance was much less a limiting factor than before. The regional center Emmeloord, which could offer varied services, became a point of attraction at the expense of the villages.

Because no one knew where and when this process of change would end, the planners of the authority decided to stay on the safe side in the third polder, Eastern Flevoland. In this polder, 54,000 hectares (135,000 acres) were drained in 1957. Although larger than the second polder, only four villages, next to a regional center named Dronten, were planned, and only two of these were realized. The region of Dronten, mainly agricultural once more, became a municipality in 1972; at this point the project was halfway in terms of area (over 100,000 hectares), and in the meantime, a new existence had been created for about 60,000 people.

According to the original plans, the next step would have been the establishment of a center of higher order, a capital for the new province, the twelfth, which the four polders in the southern part of lake IJssel would possibly form in the future. This place, called Lelystad in honor of Lely, would be built in the western corner of Eastern Flevoland. There in the center, at the top of the hierarchy, surrounded by the regional centers Emmeloord, Dronten, and two more to be built in the polders to come, it would grow to about 30,000 inhabitants. The construction of Lelystad started in 1965, but with much more ambitious purposes than had been foreseen.[2]

Randstad Development and Policy. Before we can continue the history of the project, we have to look at what happened in another part of the country during the time that the authority was rather self-contained and was working quietly, unobserved by the majority of the population. The territory of the Netherlands is small, but the total population of more than 13 million, which is expected to grow to 15 or 16 million around the year 2000, means that a national density of 475 persons per square kilometer (1200 per square mile) may be reached at that time. The population is unevenly distributed over the country: the three western provinces (North and South Holland and Utrecht) have a population density of 900 per square kilometer (2250 per square mile). The remarkable fact is that, not withstanding these impressive figures, The Netherlands has not a single gigantic urban concentration. There are no cities of over 1 million inhabitants. Due to complex historic circumstances, the western part of the country had a fairly large number of relatively small cities at an early stage. Because industrialization started here later than in other countries, the original structure remained for a long time largely unaffected. Two artificial waterways, the Nieuwe Waterweg, connecting Rotter-

dam with the sea, and the Noordzeekanaal, doing the same for Amsterdam, generated the growth of industry and trade in those areas. A third concentration point came into existence when the center of government, The Hague, began to grow as the tasks of the government were extended considerably. New agglomerations and suburbs came into being, and neighboring towns grew together; but a central area in the ring of cities, now called "the Randstad," remained rural—the Green Heart of Holland (see Figures 4 and 5).

This green heart was considered very valuable, and since the 1950s the preservation of it has been a major issue in the physical planning policy of the government. A consequence of this policy was the plan to guide the spatial growth of the Randstad radially outward (see Figure 6). For the northern wing of the Randstad it meant that two fingers would point into the province of North Holland and one into the new polders. This principle was for the first

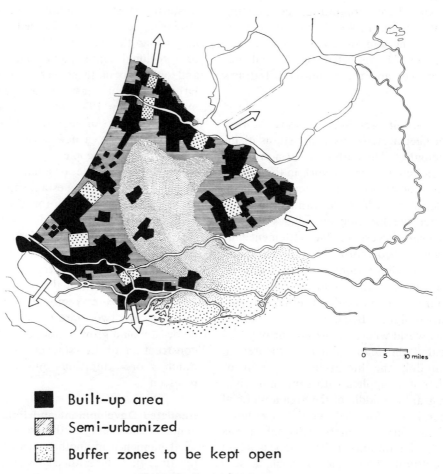

0   5   10 miles

■ Built-up area

▨ Semi-urbanized

▦ Buffer zones to be kept open

Figure 4. Randstad Holland.

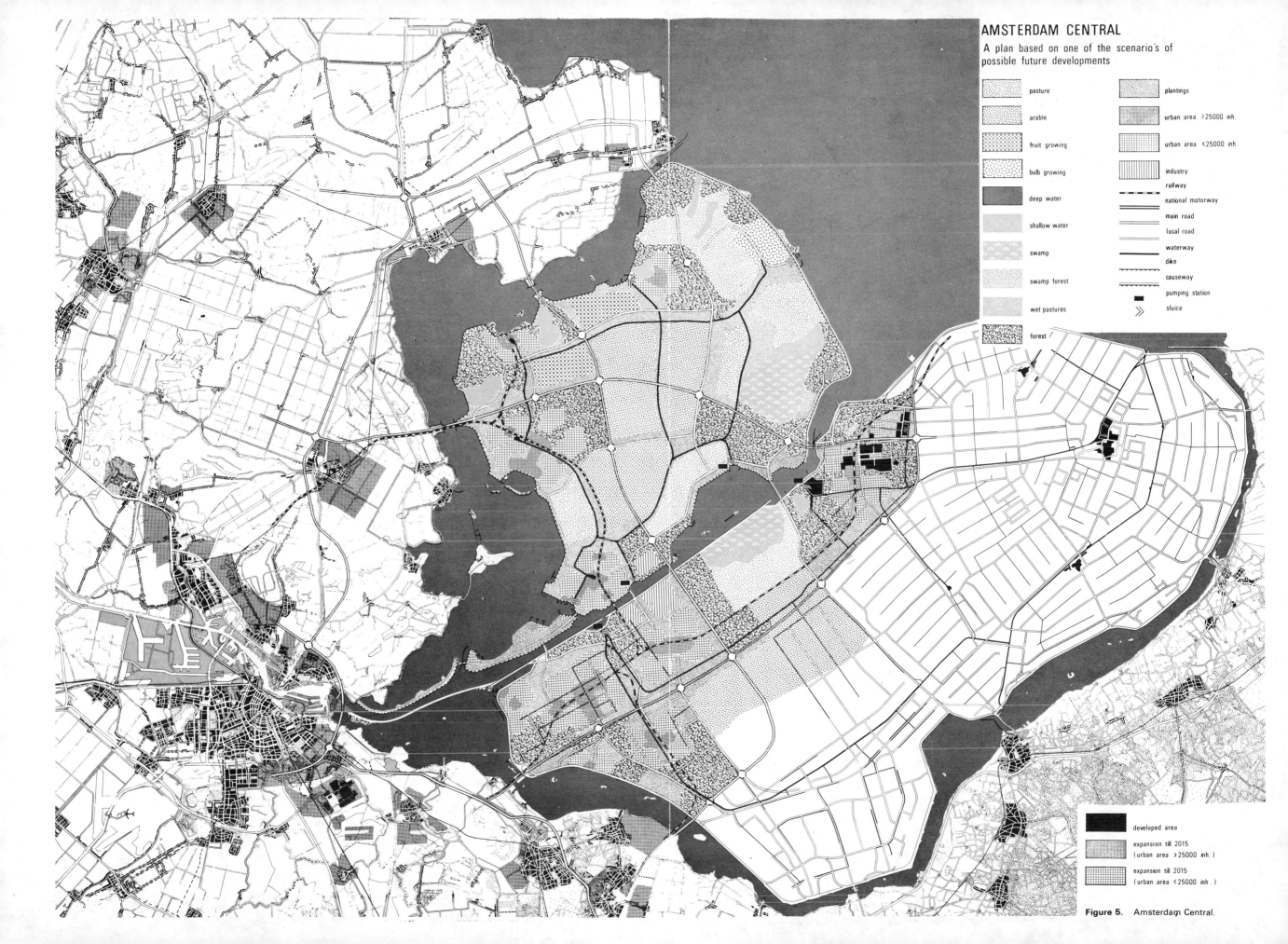

AMSTERDAM CENTRAL
A plan based on one of the scenario's of
possible future developments

pasture

arable

fruit growing

bulb growing

deep water

shallow water

swamp

swamp forest

wet pastures

forest

plantings

urban area >25000 inh.

urban area <25000 inh.

industry

railway

national motorway

main road

local road

waterway

dike

causeway

pumping station

sluice

developed area

expansion till 2015
(urban area >25000 inh.)

expansion till 2015
(urban area <25000 inh.)

Figure 5. Amsterdam Central.

Figure 6. The radial expansion of the Randstad. With Alkmaar, Purmarend, Hoorn, and Almere. Lelystad has been designated to house people and jobs migrating from the northern Randstad (Amsterdam).

national motorway

area within urban sphere

time clearly visualized in "A Structure Plan for the Southern IJsselmeerpolders," published in 1961,[3] and later more concretely in the *Second Report on Physical Planning in the Netherlands* in 1966.[4]

It was stated that the IJsselmeerpolders should create living and working space for half a million people. Lelystad became in this concept the top of a finger pointing northeast from Amsterdam, instead of a provincial capital in the center of an agricultural region. Lelystad should develop into a city of 100,000 inhabitants or more before the year 2000—a new town.

In the fourth polder, Southern Flevoland, 43,000 hectares (108,000 acres), drained in 1968, a second new town, Almere, would be constructed as soon as possible. Later it was decided that this city should be developed for at least 125,000 and at the most 250,000 people, also before the year 2000. The government reports, prepared by the National Physical Planning Agency, contain long-term policy guidelines, which indirectly have a significant influence on the planning process; but the direct powers of the central government are rather limited. The municipalities (there are more than 800) produce the allocation plans, which are legally binding. In theory the central government has many instruments of controlling and manipulating the policies of the municipalities, but in practice the municipality cannot be coerced to participate in national or regional development programs if it is not willing. In the *Third Report on Physical Planning*—the first part published in 1974 and the second part on urbanization in 1976—plans were announced for a better coordination between local, regional, and national planning.[5] But in the last 10 years the actual lag of the growth of the designated growth centers and the fast growth of small centers through suburbanization, in particular in the Randstad, is obvious. The growth centers often have to cope with long procedures for the acquisition of building areas, delays in the realization of necessary infrastructural works and social provisions, financial problems, and shortage of planning staff. The small municipalities can act easily on a small scale, with little investment and without worry about the consequences suburbanization has for regional infrastructure, the damage to the landscape, and so on. Obviously each citizen prefers a house with a garden in a small community to an apartment in a town, and certainly too much high-rise housing has been realized so far. Notwithstanding these countercurrents, the government remains firmly convinced that new housing should be concentrated in a limited number of centers, al-

though in more attractive forms than have been made in the postwar years.

A political complication for the planning is the fact that in 1966 the Dutch population was expected to grow to 20 million by the year 2000, but due to a dramatic change in the birthrate, the predictions went down to 15 or 16 million. This makes many people wonder if it is still necessary to build new towns. Three other facts are important, however: the effects of the decreased birthrate on the housing market will be felt only after 1985, and the number of households continues to grow more than has been expected; the number of marriages remains high, and more single people want to have dwellings of their own. Furthermore, the spatial use per capita has grown faster than was estimated: houses are bigger; the occupancy rate is lower; more parking space, more roads, more sports facilities, and so on are needed. The word "*need*" is used here in the sense of a "felt need," certainly not a vital need. There are good reasons to limit the use of space—for instance, by using it more efficiently, by building in higher density, and by using more public transport facilities and fewer private cars. Although the planners are well aware of this (and their judgments can be found in several policy guidelines such as the *Third Report on Physical Planning*), the fact remains that in the existing towns a great many people are badly housed, particularly in sections built in the nineteenth century. The densities are much higher there than can be tolerated. So the urban reconstruction that has now been started will inevitably lead to a reduced housing capacity of the existing towns. The towns have lost population through suburbanization, and the loss of population will certainly continue, with or without renewal.

Why the new towns on the bottom of the sea are being built may be understood by now. The land in the IJsselmeerpolders is owned by the state; the development is directly financed by the state; there exists a development authority of the state that has been operational during nearly half a century. It is therefore not surprising that the government gave the Development Authority the assignment to develop both new towns, Lelystad and Almere, at a high rate of speed, in order to be able to absorb part of the expected overspill from Amsterdam, in particular, and other parts of the northern wing of the Randstad.

THE NEW TASK

The new towns in one respect constitute the introduction of a new element into the planning process of the

IJsselmeerpolders, but in other respects they fit in a larger complex of the process of continuity and change that has demonstrated itself in other sectors.

We can speak of continuity from the point of view of town planning because since 1930, 18 new settlements, varying in size from a few hundred to over 10,000 inhabitants, have been realized; the only difference is that the new towns now under construction are larger and have to grow faster. We can also speak of discontinuity or fundamental change; because the new towns are created from outside, they are not the result of a regional (agricultural) economy as are the existing settlements, which are part of a hierarchy from the single farmstead through the local regional centers to the provincial capital. The relation of land to people within a closed system has broken down because the polders are now part of a larger system. The size of the planned cities is no longer the result of regional development; it is a national target, and the task of the authority is to create appropriate conditions for that desired growth.

This, however, may not be a reason to consider the new towns as a kind of *Fremdkörper* in the regional system. On the contrary, just because the region as a whole is still under construction, a part of the infrastructure still has to be made and one polder is even not yet drained, there is the unique opportunity not only to build new towns, but also to create an environment in which the new constructions are integrated.

While the new towns are constructed, the work on the project as a whole is continued, and in other sections of the activities, continuity and change can be observed, not as separate developments, but as part of the whole process. There is not a sudden shift from rural to urban planning. Although the polders are not, as was the case, drained solely for the purpose of acquiring more farmland, the cultivation of land for agricultural use proceeds. A part of Southern Flevoland already yields harvests, but there is change too.

An important phenomenon during the past decades is the growth of demand for space for outdoor recreation. The general increase in income and leisure time on weekends and holidays and the increased mobility that results from the automobile coming within reach of the majority of the population put an enormous claim for space on the regions surrounding the cities. Waterfronts were favored. For purely technical, hydrological reasons, stretches of water had to be kept between the old land and the polders. These areas, known as *randmeren* (borderlakes), added a considerable length of new shoreline to the country and could be used for making artificial beaches and marinas. Because their important potential as recreational areas has been recognized, the border lakes have been designed for that purpose, while fulfilling their original function as buffer zones between the low and higher land to maintain the groundwater level of the surrounding areas. The dikes are not only protective; they also form a relation between water and land. In the process of designing the last polder, the Markerwaard, the function of the lakes is of such importance that size and shape of the polder still to be drained partly depend on it. In a recent plan the polder area was reduced from 60,000 to 40,000 hectares.

People favor ancient world landscapes with hills and forests, and newly built landscapes, provided they are in the vicinity of the cities, are also highly appreciated. The observation of this led to a gradual change in landscaping and land allocation. At the outset, parks were made near the settlements with roadside greenery used only for breaking the open space and for sheltering against the prevailing winds, and forests were planted only where the type of soil would make farming unprofitable. Now the forestation covers large areas, serving recreational purposes in the national effort to improve the environmental conditions of the country. To this end, parts of the polders are preserved in their physical condition after field drainage has been finished, or in a following stage, which enables the installation of natural reserves—for instance, migratory bird refuges of great biological importance.

The apparent flexibility of the basic plan, the large variety in potentials, and the abundance of space are like a gift from heaven for the planner. However, for the same reasons, such an area becomes a hunting ground for all people and institutions who are looking for space for uses that are not allowed or are impossible elsewhere. Serving the nation, the Development Authority has to develop a region, and this may lead to serious problems. The new land is regarded as a unique opportunity to create a people's paradise; but it is also a welcome storage bin for everything that hinders, smells, creates noise or danger, or requires an excessive amount of space— from airports and military training grounds to parks for wild animals or counterculture communities. To keep the right balance in granting the claims in the interest of the region itself, to meet as far as possible the demands of interested groups, to promote experiments and innovation, but to do this under the same legal regulations and the same financial limitations and in the same economic system as the existing provinces and municipalities—these are the tasks.

Only after this excursion into history and description of the context can we come to the discussion of the new towns themselves.

LELYSTAD: THE PLAN

In the role of one of the growth centers around the Randstad, Lelystad raises the eyebrows of some people who study the maps of today. Why start here, nearly 60 kilometers from Amsterdam, on empty land without railways or motorways? The answer is simply that at the time when the site for the city as a provincial capital was designated, the land of Southern Flevoland was still the domain of the fishes. Almere was hidden in the womb of the future. The National Physical Planning Agency considered the site as favorable in the future when the polder project had been completed, because it would be at the crossroads of planned lines of communication. The Structure Plan of 1961 showed clearly what was meant—a motorway, a railway, and an important waterway leading from Amsterdam to the north of the country, crossing a connection between the northwest and the south of the country.

The next question was, Why 100,000 inhabitants? Again the answer is simple: in the national planning policy the overspill from the Randstad had to be concentrated in a limited number of growth centers; and according to views about urbanity, city life, with a capacity to maintain a reasonably high level of self-containment, would need a minimum population of about 100,000. No one has been able to indicate the optimum size of a town, so there is no reason to criticize the proposition of that time; it was a working basis.

Although a description of the different stages of plan development would be interesting, lack of space forbids it. Therefore, the Draft Structure Plan of 1975,[6] published at a time when the town already had 17,000 inhabitants, is used as a guideline (see Figure 7). The designated area lies between the waterfront and the motorway that is under construction, which leads from Amsterdam to the north of the country. The structure plan shows a town of five sections, separated from each other by green zones that are connected to forests and open country at the outside. The sections are built up of neighborhoods of 5000 to 6000 inhabitants and a small service center. The sections, which are first residential areas, lie along a so-called central zone in which much of the urban activity—shopping centers, offices, some industry, a hospital, secondary schools, other services, and some housing—is concentrated. For industries that cannot be integrated into the body of the city, three sites have been allotted at the outskirts with the basic idea that Lelystad is to offer an alternative to suburbanization elsewhere: the people should be able to find some of the advantages of suburban life, such as the terrace house with garden, quiet, and safety for children; and the disadvantages of life in remote villages, such as the long travel distance to the job and the absence of urban facilities in the vicinity, can be avoided.

This approach leads to a plan in which the ideas of Christopher Alexander and Jane Jacobs about integration of functions are not pursued, and the principles of the Charter of Athens are not worshipped. Lelystad will not be a big city, but it is not a village or an agglomeration of villages. It is an attempt to reduce the tensions in industrial society that torment people who are not poor enough to be happy with what they have and not rich enough to fulfill all their wishes. One of those wishes is to benefit from both rural and urban qualities. This may sound rather pompous, and in the planning reports, which use more words than can be used here, the wish is not stated that bluntly; but essentially the attempt boils down to that principle.

If Lelystad is built according to the principles laid down in the structure plan, all the people, wherever they live, will have houses with privacy and quiet and simple facilities, such as elementary schools and some shops, within walking distance, but not much more than that. Yet, they will never be more than one or two kilometers from the central zone where they can spend, earn, and communicate in a world of concrete and steel; they will also be only a short distance from the forest, the open fields, or the waterfront, where they can play, rest, or commune with nature (see Figures 8 and 9).

Lelystad is not the answer to megalopolis and not the revival of Ebenezer Howard or the application of a new theory about the quality of urban life. It is the outcome of a process of thought that has taken into account the site of the city, the potential of the environment, its function in the process of development of the Randstad, and the problems of today and tomorrow.

No new town will ever be the answer to everything. Not everybody likes things new: for some people all new towns are loathsome. In addition, a new town is not a universe; it is a part of a larger system, and that

Figure 7. Draft structure plan of Lelystad (1975).

developed area	
residential	
central zone	
town centre	
neighbourhood centre	
light industries	
recreative amenities and residential	
terrain for future use	
green belts	
railway and station	
national motorway and junction	
town motorway	
cyclists' and pedestrians main route	
fly over	
future national motorway	
high voltage	
water	

0   2000m

Figure 8. A section of Lelystad viewed from the air.

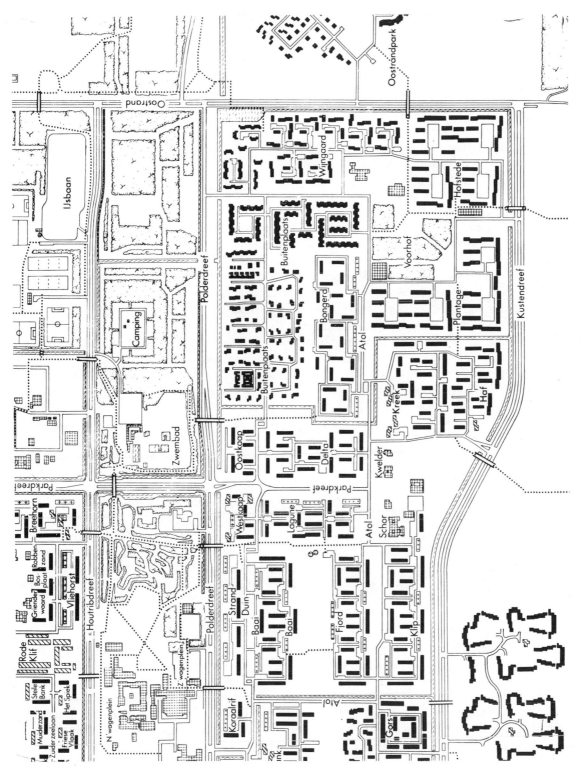

Figure 9. The plan of the area shown in Figure 8.

system should be differentiated internally. The task is not to build a town that is good for all people, but to build a town that fits harmoniously in a larger system and is good for 100,000 people who are part of that system, but who prefer or are obligated to live in that particular place.

Some other characteristics of the structure plan, which are the logical consequence of the planning concept, should be stated. The requirement that the quality of the habitat should offer an alternative to suburbanization forbids the high densities characteristic of the old urban areas, but this does not mean that the lavish land use in suburban developments can be copied. Besides, under the existing regulations for social housing, such densities would not be possible. The final outcome of studies led to an average net density in the residential areas of 30 dwellings per hectare (12 per acre). The requirement that the habitat should have good connections with the central zone and the residential environment should be safe and quiet necessitates the design of a network for pedestrian and cyclist traffic that is separate from motorized traffic. The two networks interfere or overlap only where the intensity of motor traffic does not exceed 300 passages per hour. For all other intersections between the two types of traffic, overpasses have to be constructed. Because distance is important for slow traffic, a system has been developed that makes stretched connections possible for that kind of traffic. Motor traffic, however, is immediately brought from the residential area to a freeway and from there progresses along a widely knit system of roads. The system, guarantees optimal accessibility of the central zone for all kinds of traffic, which is an essential quality of a city center. Lelystad can be called a "pedestrian town" or a "car town" because both characterizations are true in a sense.

The design of the residential areas and traffic system, together with the allocation of green area, lead to a land use of 350 square meters per inhabitant designated as follows: 40 percent for housing, 5 percent for freeways, 18 percent for green areas, 14 percent for industry and the rest for "others," which include shopping centers, cultural facilities, sportfields, and cemeteries. Although no special freeways for public transportation are made, the plan includes an internal transportation system by bus, and space is reserved for a railway from Amsterdam to the north, running along the central zone with locations for two stations.

The structure plan permits development in phases, each of which forms an entity in itself, allowing change and avoiding failure in the case of stagnation or even if the final stage is never reached. The principle is relatively simple: the central zone should be considered as a root stock that grows from north to south and from which nodes or joints sprout at certain places at the appropriate moment. In the meantime, at both sides the neighborhoods are built; as they move southward, they will find new points where activities are concentrated and then generate their potential, thus stimulating their development.

The Development of Lelystad. A plan is a plan; its realization is something else. How is a town built from scratch somewhere in the mud in a remote and unknown area? That was the question raised by several people in 1966 when the first pile for Lelystad was driven into the ground.

The minister in charge did not perceive it as a problem: he gave the assignment to the authority to develop Lelystad to a city of 10,000 to 15,000 inhabitants in the year 1975 as a start for further rapid growth. For this initial period of development, a special fund was raised to encourage the settlement of industry; some money was available for subsidizing the building costs, which were unusually high in the distant place, and the first inhabitants paid reduced rents for their houses, but rents gradually increased.

The project started calmly, at a rate of 300 dwellings per year, with a strong emphasis on amenities, services, and infrastructure for the future. During the first years this showed an odd picture to the visitor: a shopping center, a swimming pool, sportsfields for a few people, pedestrian overpasses over four-lane roads where no traffic was to be seen, and in particular immense acreages of forest planted, without any users around (see Figure 10).

Taking into account the shortage of houses, it would not have been too difficult to populate the town by just building houses; but the explicit aim was to develop employment opportunities in balance with housing facilities. The establishment of a dormitory town at this place was to be avoided. The beginning would have been difficult, if not impossible, if two important employers had not settled in Lelystad. The first was the authority itself: it concentrated in one office building some 1000 employees working before in different offices spread over the area and the border region. The second one was an electrical power plant employing a few hundred people. Some

Figure 10. Social housing in Lelystad.

agricultural and veterinarian institutes, finding space for experimental fields around the city, followed. With another 700 jobs, this completed the basis for further development. A number of private firms, mostly small, some of medium size, decided to move to Lelystad, and of course the building activity itself attracted building firms. Six years after the arrival of the first inhabitants, about 80 percent of the employed persons living in Lelystad also had their jobs in Lelystad, and a few hundred others were coming in daily from elsewhere.

Until this time, the authority had worked along the traditional line of doing all the work of development itself, financed by the government. Knowing that such development could not be accelerated, the authority made successful attempts to interest non-governmental investors for the construction of houses and shops. Furthermore, a housing corporation was established that could borrow money on the free capital market. With the emphasis on the development of infrastructural works and the absence of delaying factors such as land acquisition and time-consuming legal procedures, the building capacity was growing fast. At the same time, the housing problems in the Randstad, particularly in Amsterdam, remained pressing. This led logically to the decision to start with the absorption of not only the indirect, but also the direct, overspill—meaning people who need a house but already have a job.

This policy has advantages. The new town grows faster; arrives in an earlier stage at a level where it can offer its inhabitants a complete environment with all the desired facilities and services, such as schools, a hospital, and a department store; and the "pioneer period" is over sooner. The more people there are, the more varied and large the labor market is. Job opportunities are better for people who want to work in the place where they live, and it is more attractive for new industries and services because there is a better supply of labor than if that policy were not followed. The policy also has disadvantages. During a period of unknown length the number of commuters to Amsterdam is large. It is a socially and economically expensive way of life for the commuters themselves, it drains activity from city life, and it is a burden to the communication system. The advantages weigh heavier than the disadvantages, and as we will see, the coming of the new town, Almere, may relieve the burden as an intervening opportunity.

At the end of 1975, an adequate year to make up the balance because it is the year mentioned in the assignment, the figures were as follows. The government and the housing corporation had built 4300 dwellings and investors and individuals had built more than 1200—5500 in all. More than 1300 were under construction by government (housing corporation), investors, and individuals, leading to a total of 7000. With an average occupation per dwelling of 3.4, the present population of around 19,000 reached 24,000 before the end of 1976. The plans in the course of development and the infrastructural works that are in execution now are all geared to a building capacity of 1500 dwellings per year and lead to a population prediction of 40,000 in the year 1980.

With such fast growth, a major problem concerns the composition of the housing plans according to type and size. For purposes of the city's harmonious development there should be a variety of rents and sizes in adequate numbers for the different income classes, for young and old single people, and for small and large families. The direct demand, however, comes, as in all new towns, from young families with low and medium incomes. While, for example, over 10 percent of the Dutch population is over 65 years of age, only 1.2 percent of the people of Lelystad are aged. While in the Netherlands less than 18 percent of the population is younger than 10 years, in Lelystad nearly 30 percent are in that phase of life. To find the optimal balance each year between the strategic, future-oriented requirements and the necessity to meet direct demand as much as possible, a demographic computer model which allows alertness and flexibility by using feedback and new inputs, has been constructed. The method enables, for example, one to calculate the effects on the age structure if immigration of elderly people is encouraged by the construction of an "overdose" of dwellings designed for the aged groups.

With the incredible rise of building costs recently, it is very difficult to supply low-cost quality houses. Although this is a universal problem that cannot be solved within the context of Lelystad, the new-town problem is specific; there are no prewar or nineteenth-century sections as a refuge for the lowest paid. If the middle-class environment so typical for new developments is to be avoided, emphasis should be laid on the attempt to build for the lower-income groups. The rule that no one should pay more than one-sixth of his income for rent is attempted. About 60 percent of the rented houses have a monthly rent of less than Dfl. 250 per month, and the official minimum income in the same year in the Netherlands is Dfl. 1350 per month. Obviously Lelystad is

not built for the well-to-do in particular, although private building lots are available.

As difficult as a housing policy may seem to be, it is an easily handled steering instrument compared to the policy of developing jobs. Apart from some possibilities to subsidize entrepreneurs who settle in Lelystad and a limited possibility for the government to move its own offices from one place to another, there are virtually no instruments for development. Nevertheless, despite the absence of a railway, a motor road, and the normal urban facilities such as department stores, a hospital, or a soccer stadium, there are no reasons for complaint so far.

At the beginning of 1976 there were 6600 jobs in Lelystad and its agricultural surroundings, some 6300 of the population belonged to the occupied population; over 4100, about 65 percent, found a job in Lelystad itself; the other 35 percent went out, and 2500 came in to fill the remaining jobs. The number of unemployed is about 50 percent lower than the national average. The situation may be enhanced by the fact that some government services settled in an early stage. Of all those living and working in Lelystad, nearly half worked for the government. However, the other half does not, and the two groups together constitute a population of noncommuters who are building up the community for others to come. Gradually and regularly, the others do come in search of space to build up their business and a place that is accessible. Already 83 hectares of the industrial parks have been allotted to 86 small- and medium-sized firms for food processing, printing, metallurgical half products, plastics, and so on. Some offices and businesses in the tertiary sector, separate from the government offices and laboratories, have also come. On the basis of knowledge about what is under construction and who have definitely decided to move to Lelystad, it can be stated that another 1200 jobs will be created soon (see Figures 11 and 12).

Although there is no reason to worry about the present development, the final goals are not yet within easy reach. If, as is stated in the plans, the number of outgoing commuters should not be more than 15 percent of the employed population, about 7000 new jobs will have to be created before the end of this decade. Nearly half of these jobs will be in local services, which grow with the increase of the population. Because of all kinds of thresholds, it is not always easy to keep supply and demand in balance; there may be underdevelopment in one part,

Figure 11. Bus station and pedestrian overpass.

Figure 12. Private housing.

overdevelopment in another at times; and certainly the town suffers from lack of balance at present.

After a stage in which there was a relatively large shopping center (10,000 m²), there is a short period of underservicing now; but a second shopping center is on its way. Due to the application of national norms, the building of schools runs more or less parallel to demand. This is somewhat more difficult with the establishment of a hospital. Because of financial problems, the community center, the so-called *agora* (a multipurpose building with a theater, a churchroom, a swimming pool, a youth center, and a restaurant, all around a market place and under one roof, opening in 1977), will come later than was wished from the viewpoint of harmonious development.[7]

Sociocultural Development of Lelystad. After all the explanations about the physical and economic aspect of a new town, the common question is, What about the people? How does the town come to life? As always, the answer is a little disappointing for the visitor because what can be said after directly questioning the inhabitants sounds too good to be true: everybody is happy with their home and the environment, and criticism is of minor things, such as some facility that is lacking (and which will come next year or tomorrow) or about the fact that a children's playground is designed in the wrong way or at the wrong place.

Of course, this is not the real truth. The researchers are quite aware of it, but they are also well aware of the fact that it is very difficult to find out which of the shortcomings in the environment are deficiencies of the new town and which are of the society itself.

People are relatively happy in Lelystad because they have found a place of their own with the qualities for making a home. The hypothesis is that the happiness is not so much because of the quality of the environment itself, but because of the fact that compared to past experience, residents see improvement; and they cannot see better alternatives. Furthermore, it is a particular kind of happiness, typical for young families with small children; they are home oriented; they spend a lot of money on the house, garden, and car; they look at color TV, they participate in sports; they work during leisure hours in allotment gardens where they grow vegetables.

This picture of a bourgeois society should not give the planner and the social worker the reassuring idea that all is well. There is a huge crowd of teenagers in

the making, and a shift from private to public domain activities can be expected. The environment should be prepared for that. Furthermore, the pretty houses and the flowering gardens conceal the fact of a minority of uprooted people who, in a society growing at such speed, integrate less easily and are more easily forgotten than in an established society. Socially, it would be preferable to have a slower rate of growth; there would be more time for the churches, the schools, and the expressive associations to build up an associative life. Although there is a vigorous associative life now, in which the degree of participation can be measured, not much is known about the condition of life of the nonparticipants.

Again, it is rather difficult to sort out the real social problems. The articulated problems are easy to define, but they are rather trivial and often impossible to solve: trees are too small; there is no corner shop with an old widow; there are no monuments; the center is not very lively, and so on. The fascinating life seen by the planner who knows how it looked when there was nothing and who can imagine how it will be within 25 years is not the life of the citizen who is living between strangers and seeing nothing from the window but twigs that may eventually be trees. Nevertheless, in its few years of existence, Lelystad has developed a thriving society, relatively speaking, perhaps because of its isolated position, not in spite of it.

ALMERE

With Lelystad just off the ground and Southern Flevoland hardly drained, the pressure from the mainland obliged the authority to make a plan for the second new town, Almere, much closer to Amsterdam, bigger than Lelystad and more quickly built (see Figure 13). Almere is close to Amsterdam and is a part of the labor and housing market of that city region and (more than Lelystad) directly built to relieve the problems of that region. But Almere is not intended as just a satellite of Amsterdam. An alternative to suburbanization with its own identity is pursued here as it is in Lelystad. The polynuclear concept is already developed in an early stage of study. It means that the town should be composed of a number of nuclei of different sizes, each large enough to have a satisfactory degree of independence, together forming a town, with one stronger nucleus binding the centers together as a whole (see Figure 14). Between the nuclei open spaces will be

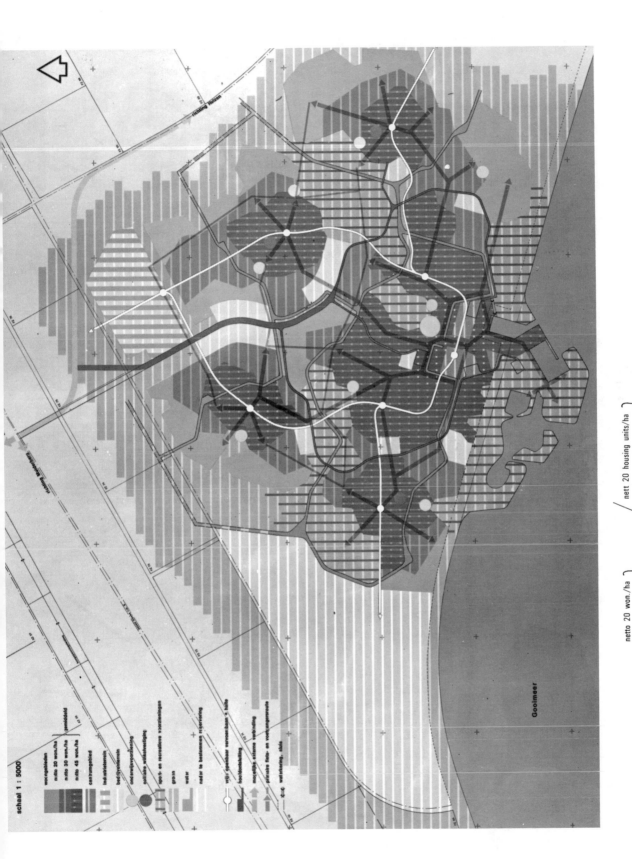

Figure 13. The structural plan of Almere.

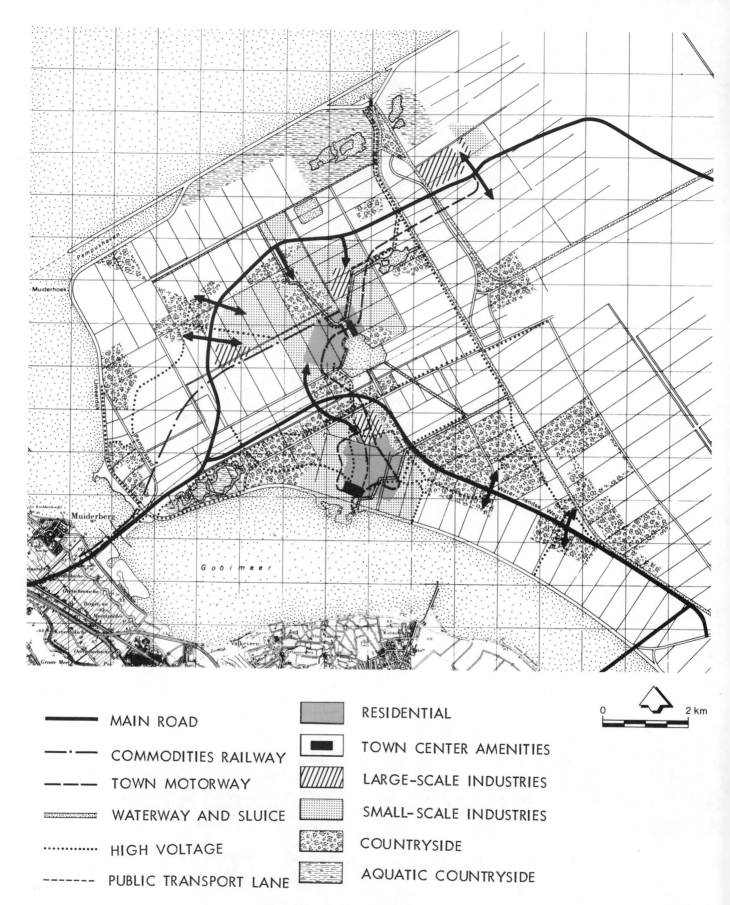

——————— MAIN ROAD	RESIDENTIAL
—·—·—·— COMMODITIES RAILWAY	TOWN CENTER AMENITIES
— — — TOWN MOTORWAY	LARGE-SCALE INDUSTRIES
WATERWAY AND SLUICE	SMALL-SCALE INDUSTRIES
············· HIGH VOLTAGE	COUNTRYSIDE
------- PUBLIC TRANSPORT LANE	AQUATIC COUNTRYSIDE

Figure 14. Structural plan of Almere: Model 3.

preserved to be used for different purposes, varying from intensive recreational use to virtually natural or agricultural areas. In this way the majority of the people will be within walking distance of open green spaces, while living in fairly high density with an urban environment next door. The polynuclear concept provides several advantages: it gives flexibility because it is not necessary to decide definitely about the final size of the town or the exact number and the body of the nuclei. The concept opens the possibility of building at several places simultaneously; so if the total growth of the town has to be large, the growth per locality can be kept at a reasonable level. Of course, some decisions concerning the main structure have to be made at an early stage—for instance, reservations for railway lines and national highways.

This basic concept makes developing a rather sophisticated working method for the planning process possible. In this context it is impossible to describe how it is used and to which alternatives it may lead; only the main outcome for the near future is given here. The locations are given for three nuclei; the construction of the first, on the waterfront, has already started, and the building of the other two should start soon. All three nuclei should have 5000 inhabitants in 1980 (minimum number for the support of elementary services) and 15,000 in 1985 (minimum number for supporting a railway station). The target population is 25,000 in 1980 and 55,000 in 1985. The further growth of the town as a whole to 125,000 or 250,000 can thus be left open for discussion.

Almere-Haven (Harbor), built on the border lake partially across the dike into the lake, received its first inhabitants in 1976. The detailed design is for a center of 25,000 inhabitants with 7000 jobs. The intention is to designate 80 percent of the dwellings for people coming from Amsterdam and the surrounding region, and for those with a lower income to get priority rights, to help solve the problems of Amsterdam. For the same reason the immigration of the elderly is promoted in an attempt to arrive as soon as possible at a normal age structure. One of the goals is to keep the difference between the number of jobs and employed persons below 10 percent to keep commuting at the lowest possible level. Because a high number of jobs does not exclude a high number of commuters, and *vice versa*, and a further growth of the pressure on the infrastructure of the region by private transportation should be avoided, much attention is given in the plan to the development of a good public transportation system:

a freeway is designed and under construction already. At the beginning transportation will be done by a normal bus.

Although many pages could be filled with a further description of the plan and of the development strategy, this discussion is concluded now with the final remark that Almere has a good chance to make a splendid start, much more than Lelystad in its beginning. A great many people, potential inhabitants and entrepreneurs, are showing interest. However, for that same reason the task to be fulfilled is difficult: to meet the demands of people with high expectations, with limited resources at hand, under the pressure of time, while guarding the quality of environment and life, which is the ultimate aim.[8]

FINAL REMARKS

This condensed story of the new towns on the bottom of the sea, seen as a part of the larger project of the IJsselmeer development, is by necessity general and certainly incomplete. It is written by one who is closely involved, which does not guarantee objectivity. Perhaps the chapter does not give enough credit to those who are against parts or all of the project, either because they think the intentions are wrong or because they do not believe it can succeed.[9]

In this densely populated, industrialized country, with serious problems of congestion and pollution, the quantitative aspects of growth raise negative judgments, and the protection of the natural environment ranks high on the list of priorities in planning. The polders do reduce the area of water; the new towns do enlarge the urban area, roads and bridges are built. Therefore, that the project meets resistance is not surprising. In our view, the project should be considered as part of the continuing process of transformation of the environment, which in the Low Countries has always been essential for survival. For a long time, it showed the character of man struggling against nature, with gains and losses alternating on both sides. Although people seem to be more powerful than ever, their knowledge has increased considerably; and in the case of the IJsselmeerpolder project this knowledge is used for guiding a balanced process of transformation to the benefit of both people and environment.

Opposition is also raised by people who do not believe in the national planning concept, and the greenbelt policy; by those who fear that new towns will only contribute to a fast decay of the old existing urban centers; and by those who consider new towns to be unnatural, artificial, and consequently, lifeless constructions, unfit for human existence. In all opposition there is always a possible element of truth; it would be foolish to deny this. Further discussion and continuous reappraisal of the goals is necessary.

Too often the discussion concentrates on the separate elements of the project, obscuring the general view—for example, on Lelystad or Almere separately. Much more emphasis is then laid on competitive aspects than on symbiotic ones. A new regional plan for the Southern IJsselmeerpolders, which is in preparation now, will show that the whole is more than the sum of the parts, that Almere and Lelystad form an integrating part of a new environment, the evolution which continues parallel to the growth of the cities themselves. Almere, within direct view of the Randstad, and Lelystad, now psychologically in some remote empty land, with their outer borders no more than 15 kilometers (10 miles) from each other, will be part of one communication system. They will form one labor and one housing market. If the plans are realized in the proposed way, there will be in 1980, 65,000 people living in the two towns, and possibly 140,000 in 1985.

Although the experience acquired in the past for the Development Authority is of invaluable significance and inspires some confidence, the enlargement of scale produces a number of completely new problems. The gradual absorption of immigrants in the past never made people's participation in the establishment of new communities and the building of institutions a great problem. The people soon identified with their new environment and found their own way. Now it will be different. More social guidance will be necessary, and the development of participation should be institutionalized. The system of temporary local government, which has worked well so far despite its "undemocratic" traits, needs revision. It cannot be maintained until the town is ready, because a town is never ready and because long before the target population is there the number of inhabitants is already so large and local political activity of such importance that the paternalistic system of the pioneer period will no longer work. Studies are now being made for developing a system in which the citizen can fully exercise his legal rights, but at the same time the Development Authority is given power sufficient to execute its task.

A third new circumstance is that at this rate of development, the government cannot endow the authority with such a budget that it can carry out all the work as it used to do. With the foundation of housing corporations, a first step has been made; but for other work an appeal should also be made to the private capital market, which means that institutional investors, banks, and project developers enter into it. Although this change should be considered quite normal and in line with practice elsewhere, it obliges the authority to acquire new skills to protect the ways that lead to the achievement of the goals defined in the plans. Each point raised in these remarks contains in itself enough material for discussion for a new essay, but in this context no more can be said about it.

This chapter tries to explain how attempts of people in the Middle Ages to keep their feet dry can lead to the building of new towns on the bottom of the sea for the people of today and tomorrow.

NOTES

1. Walter Christaller, *Central Places in Southern Germany*, Translated by Carlisle W. Baskin (Englewood Cliffs, N.J.: Prentice-Hall, 1966).

2. Detailed information about this period can be found in English in A. K. Constandse, L. Wijers, and N. C. deRuiter, *Planning and Creation of an Environment: Experiences in the IJsselmeerpolders* (The Hague: Ministerie van Volkshulsvesting en Bouwnijverheid, 1966). Also see *Planning and Development in the Netherlands*, Issue on the IJsselmeerpolders, No. 1 (1970).

3. "A Structure Plan for the Southern IJsselmeerpolders," Rijkswaterstaat Communications, No. 6 (The Hague: Government Printing Office, 1964).

4. *Second Report on Physical Planning in the Netherlands*, cond. ed. (The Hague: Government Printing Office, 1966).

5. *Orienteringsnota Ruimtelijke Ordening, eerste deel van de Derde Nota over de Ruimtelijke Ordening* (The Hague: Government Printing Office, 1974).

6. *Structuurplan Lelystad 1975–2000, Concept* (Lelystad: Rijksdienst voor de IJsselmeerpolders, 1975).

7. Detailed quantitative information is published in the Statistical Yearbooks issued by the Rijksdienst voor de IJsselmeerpolders, Lelystad.

8. *Almere 1985, aanzet tot een ontwikkelingsstrategie 1970–1985–2000* (English summary: Almere 1985: First Steps Towards a Development Strategy 1970–1985–2000) (Lelystad: Rijksdienst voor de IJsselmeerpolders, 1974).

Ontwerp Almere-Haven (Lelystad: Rijksdienst voor de IJsselmeerpolders, 1974).

9. For such an account see David White, "Holland's Growing Pains?" *New Society* (August 15, 1974), 407–410.

CHAPTER 6

French New-Town Policy

JAMES RUBENSTEIN

French planning is best known for the development of national economic growth policies after World War II. The national plans and growth poles are justly celebrated by the international community. In contrast, the French new-town program has received relatively little publicity. This neglect is in part a function of the newness of the policy: large-scale construction did not begin until around 1970. Furthermore, the French have put together a rather complex administrative and financial structure, liberally spiced with acronyms and seemingly irrational relations.

Despite the difficulties involved in making the French new-town policy intelligible to the international planning community, an understanding of the appropriateness of new towns in the development of national urban growth policies should include the French experience. Although the French did not adopt the new-town idea until recently, they are now engaged, with typical French grandeur, in a large-scale effort. By the mid-1970s, nine new towns were under construction—five outside Paris and one each outside Lille, Lyon, Marseille, and Rouen (see Figure 1).[1] The nine new towns are now attracting nearly 20,000 homes and 15,000 new jobs per year, a pace of development comparable to that of the British new towns.

French new-town policy is also important because of the complex administrative and financial arrangements involved. In a basically liberal society with a strong private sector and numerous recalcitrant local authorities, French planners have successfully overcome significant opposition to the new-town concept. The message from French planners to other countries where a public new-town program is considered technically impractical is this: if we could overcome these obstacles in France, any country with the will to see new towns built could.

Nineteenth-Century Heritage. Until World War II planning was virtually nonexistent in France. This situation was due in large part to the peculiar demographic patterns in France. At the start of the industrial era France was arguably the most powerful country in the world. In 1800 it had the largest population in Europe, except for Russia; it also had territorial boundaries that had been virtually unchanged for a century. However, starting about 1814 France suffered through a long period of stagnation, which has completely dissipated only since 1946.

The most significant reflection of the 150-year era of stagnation was the lack of population growth. The large-scale increase in population that swept through Europe in the nineteenth century during the era of industrialization bypassed France. The population of France increased during the first half of that century from 27 million in 1801 to 38 million in 1866, but this was a much slower rate than that of other European countries. After 1866 the population increase was virtually nil. In 1946 France had 40.5 million people, an increase of only 2.5 million in 80 years, an average annual increase of less than 0.1 percent.

This material receives fuller treatment in James Rubenstein, *The French New Towns* (Baltimore: The Johns Hopkins University Press, forthcoming), © The Johns Hopkins University Press.

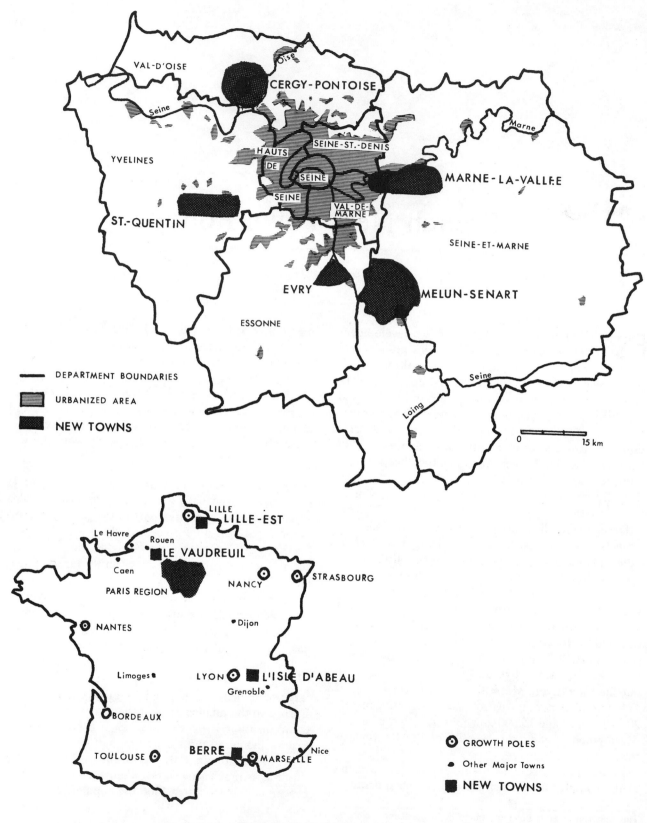

Figure 1. The French new towns.

The lack of population increase is attributable in part to the effects of the Franco-Prussian war in 1870–1871 and the two world wars. However, the other European belligerents in these wars did not show long-term demographic stagnation. The French situation was primarily due to significantly lower birth rates than elsewhere in Europe. The cause of the lower birth rate has been inconclusively debated, with explanations including the lack of economic growth, the inheritance laws, and the sophistication of French civilization.[2]

The overall economic and demographic stagnation in France during the nineteenth and first half of the twentieth centuries masks the dramatic redistribution that was going on inside France. As in other countries, the French cities were growing faster than the rural areas, but in France the effects of these trends were more serious.

During the long period of national stagnation the Paris region grew rapidly. From a city of 0.5 million in 1801, Paris grew to 1.8 million in 1866, 2.5 million in 1891, and 6.6 million in 1946. Between 1866 and 1946 the Paris region increased by 4.8 million people, while France as a whole increased by only 2.3 million people. In fact, four-fifths of the departments of France lost population between 1831 and 1946. Paris increased from 2 percent of the national population in 1801 to 16 percent in 1946.

The dominance of Paris was mainly due to public policy. The government was increasingly centralized in Paris, and the minister of education could boast that in every classroom in France children were reciting the same line of Virgil at the same moment. Public works projects, social services, and higher education were concentrated in Paris. Businesses naturally located in Paris, the hub of the national road and rail systems. Applications for bank loans in the provinces were routed through the Paris offices. The massive improvement projects carried out by Baron Haussman in Paris were financed by the state.[3] The result of these investment patterns and demographic trends was the division of France into two nations: a healthy, growing Paris region and the depopulated, underdeveloped rest of the country.

Since World War II the French situation has changed dramatically. The Paris region has continued to grow, but the decline in the rest of the country has been reversed. From 40.5 million people in 1946, France increased to 42.5 million in 1954, 46.5 million in 1962, 48.5 in 1964, and an estimated 53.8 million in 1975, an average annual increase of

over 1 percent since the war. From the slowest growing country in Europe, France has become one of the fastest. About 20 percent of the increase is due to the migration of people from the former African and Asian colonies, while the remainder is due to both increased birth rates and decreased mortality rates.

The sudden demographic shift put a major burden on the French administration to accommodate the additional population. New investments were needed in the newly expanding regions such as the Riviera and the Rhône Valley. These trends added a sense of urgency to the need for the planning policies that emerged after the war.

Postwar Planning Policies. The national planning policies developed after World War II were based on two principles: the stimulation of economic recovery from the war and long-term growth, and the deflection of development away from the Paris region.

A planning commission (Commissariat Général du Plan) was created in 1946 to oversee the development of a national plan for the reconstruction and managed growth of the French economy. Inspired by Jean Monnet, the plan concentrated investment in six critical industrial sectors: mining, iron and steel, agricultural machinery, electricity, transport, and cement. These sectors were selected because of their importance in stimulating the recovery of other industries and because many of the firms were either nationalized or oligopolistic. The plan, which covered the years 1947–1953, was financed in large measure by the Marshall Plan.[4]

The success of the first plan has led to the creation of a series of multiyear plans. Although the economic objectives of each plan have differed, all have involved the establishment of economic targets and the allocation of funds for capital investments to achieve the goals. In 1975 France completed the sixth plan.

At the same time that the economic planning machinery was initiated, other national planners became concerned with reversing the historic trends toward concentration in Paris.[5] The Ministry of Construction attempted to encourage growth outside of Paris through controls and subsidies and to prevent new developments in Paris by refusing to issue the needed permits. Regional action was also promoted through the creation of regional administrative units. France was divided into 21 regions in 1955 for statistical purposes. Eventually, advisory councils, comprised of local and national officials, were organized for each region. Today each region is headed by a prefect with considerable administrative power. Figure 2 shows the 21 planning regions in France, with average, annual personal income for the residents of each region in 1970. Although the difference between the Paris region and the rest of the country has lessened since World War II, the income per capita in Paris is still nearly 50 percent above the next most prosperous region.[6]

The first generation of French planning was marred by a lack of unity among economic and regional planners, who were separated in different national agencies. The planning programs were not sophisticated enough to achieve the desired objectives,

and regional planners failed to discriminate among different industries. By urging all industries to locate in less-developed areas, regional planners did not take into account the different effects that different industries have on particular regions. The approach was called *soupoudrage* (or powdering), which implied that industries were placed without consideration for the specific regional effect. However, by ignoring the locational implications of new investments, economic planners increased pressure on the Paris region (for most new firms still the optimal site).[7]

Since about 1960 French planning policies have

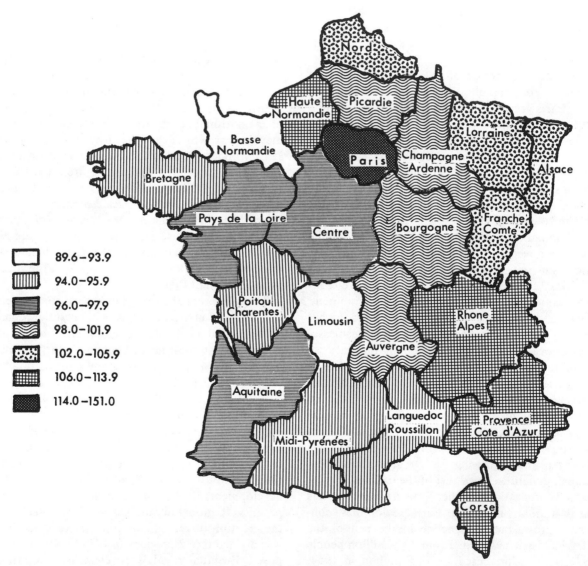

Figure 2. French planning regions in 1970 and relative income per capita for each region. (France as a whole = 100.) For similar map from 1959 see Philippe Pinchemal, *France: A Geographical Survey*, p. 165. In recent years the difference between the Paris region and the poorest areas has lessened, although the Paris region is still nearly 50 percent above the second wealthiest region. Source: *Annuaire Statistique de la France*, 1974, Vol. 79.

continued to be divided into two often conflicting positions, although the basis of the division has changed. Regional and economic planners have achieved a relatively high degree of unity, but planners from the Paris region have reasserted the importance of national investment in the capital.

Beginning with the fourth plan (1962–1965), the national economic planning process was regionalized. This involved breaking down the national plan goals and targets for the different sectors of the economy into separate goals and targets for each region. The national plan therefore became a matrix of targets for particular sectors and regions. For example, the plan would produce a goal for overall housing starts in France but would also divide that total among the various regions. The establishment of both national goals and regional shares was entrusted to the planning commission.

At the same time the Délégation à l'Aménagement du Territoire et à l'Action Regional (DATAR) was created, reporting directly to the prime minister. The functions of DATAR were to formulate regional policies and to work with the different ministries to assure that the patterns of expenditures in each ministry were consistent with national objectives for each region.[8]

The best known policy developed by DATAR was the *métropoles d'equilibres*. Key industries that were most likely to stimulate further growth in a particular region were identified. These propulsive industries were encouraged to locate in one of eight growth poles: Marseille, Lyon, Lille, Bordeaux, Toulouse, Nantes-St. Nazaire, Strasbourg, and Nancy-Metz. The large urban areas were chosen because the strong pull of Paris could be counteracted only by other large cities.[9]

Planning for the Paris Region. While national planners were concerned with organizing the economic development of the provinces, the Paris region continued to grow from 6.6 million to 8.4 million people between 1946 and 1962. The nineteenth-century boulevards, sewers, and structures that had served Paris well for many years were no longer adequate. Effective planning was stymied by the hostility of national planners to the continued growth of Paris. The Paris region therefore expanded in a sprawling, undisciplined fashion, aggravating social problems.

The Paris region was increasingly spatially divided into socially segregated units. The historic center had been claimed for offices and upper-income housing, with factories and low-income housing forced out to the suburbs. Competition for space in the center has led to large price increases and demolition of old structures in favor of modern high rises. Low-income families live in anonymous apartment projects in the suburbs, with inadequate shopping facilities, inconvenient public transport, and long-distance commuting to jobs. Table 1 illustrates this lack of balance.[10]

Planning policies in the Paris region prior to the formulation of the new-town idea have aggravated the existing lack of balance. Housing programs for the Paris region were designed to alleviate the severe shortages after World War II. Large-scale housing estates, called *grands ensembles*, were planned in the suburbs during the 1950s and 1960s. Today some 1 million people, about one-third of the population of the outer suburbs, live in these *grands ensembles*. Nearly one-half of the population increase of the Paris region since 1954 has been concentrated in such housing.

Most French planners today consider the *grands ensembles* to be unsatisfactory living environments. A relatively high degree of crime and other social pathologies have been observed in them. Planners blame the high incidence of social problems on the lack of social and physical diversity in the projects. Because their purpose was to provide a large quantity of housing, the projects generally consist of several high-density apartment towers. Shopping and recreational facilities near the projects are usually inadequate, and employment opportunities are rare. Residents are required to commute long distances to work in central Paris or other suburbs, a task made difficult by the relatively poor public transportation system in the suburbs. One study has shown that 20 percent of the workers in one large project spend more than one hour to reach work.[11]

Table 1 Distribution of Residents and Jobs in the Paris Region (%)

	Population	Jobs	Offices
Central Paris	25.8	47.1	68.2
Inner suburbs[a]	41.5	30.0	26.7
Outer suburbs[b]	32.9	22.9	5.1

[a] The inner suburbs are defined as the departments of Seine-Saint-Denis, Val-de-Marne, and Hauts de Seine.
[b] The outer suburbs are defined as the departments of Essonne, Seine-et-Marne, Val-d'Oise, and Yvelines.
Source: Préfecture de la Région Parisienne, *La Région Parisienne: 4 Anneés d'aménagement et d'equipement 1969–1972.*

The most important planning program affecting the distribution of jobs in the Paris region has been the construction of *La Défense,* a large-scale office complex located in the western suburbs. Like the *grands ensembles, La Défense* has exacerbated the social problems of the Paris region. In response to the pressures for additional office space in the Paris region, the government approved a plan in 1958 to redevelop a large area to the west of the central area. The most important axis in Paris, which extends west from the Louvre, through the Tuileries, Concorde, Champs-Elysées, Arc de Triomphe, and Neuilly, now terminates at the modern high rises of La Défense. The first stage of the operation, on 130 hectares, will be completed in the late 1970s; the project contains around 1.5 million square meters of offices, 300,000 square meters of commercial space, and 100,000 jobs. Future extensions are now being planned. Around 30 percent of the new offices being built in the entire Paris region are now concentrated in La Défense. The result of this concentration is a strengthening of the patterns of spatial segregation in the Paris region, because the project represents an extension of the regional office center along a western axis, rather than a fundamental reorientation of the direction of growth in order to spread offices evenly in the region.[12]

THE NEW TOWNS

Responding to the need for coherent planning policies in the Paris region, President de Gaulle asked his old friend Paul Delouvrier to see what he could do about the situation.[13] A strong, dominant person, Delouvrier is considered the father of French new towns. He is universally cited as the first French planning official to advocate the development of new towns and actively work for their realization. He was able to use his strength and influence, especially with the president and the minister of finance, to realize the vision.

When Delouvrier was placed in charge of the newly created Paris region in 1961, his first task was to create a master plan for development that accurately reflected the demographic realities in the region.[14] Despite national policies designed to discourage location in Paris, the region was still growing. The previous master plan, the Plan d'Aménagement et d'Organisation Générale de la Région Parisienne (PADOG), was published in 1960 and was outdated by 1961.[15] The PADOG had called for a firm boundary around the existing built-up area, with further growth restricted to isolated redevelopment projects and infilling within the urbanized area. In the absence of a plan accepting that growth was occurring, the expansion of Paris would continue in a haphazard manner.

In the early 1960s Delouvrier sent his planners around the world to examine the planning policies in other cities. These investigations strongly supported construction of new towns. New towns were first officially proposed in the 1965 master plan for the Paris region, the Schéma Directeur d'Aménagement et d'Urbanisme de la Région Parisienne (SDAURP).[16] The master plan noted that the Paris region would grow from 8.4 million in 1962 to around 14 million in 2000, due to the excess of births over deaths among existing residents, not due to migration. The problems of the Paris region could be divided into four categories:

1. The disappearance of open space due to the growth of the region in a sprawling fashion, which the French call *tache d'huile,* or oil slick.
2. The development of the suburban housing projects with inadequate provision of services and facilities.
3. The congestion of central Paris due to the lack of suburban facilities.
4. The need for modernization of older areas in central Paris and the inner suburbs, where housing is overcrowded and does not have modern plumbing.[17]

Attacking these problems would, according to the master plan, reduce unhappiness stemming from fatigue and a lack of choice. Fatigue resulted from the need to travel long distances for work, shops, and recreation due to the lack of accessibility or high cost. The region's population increase would aggravate these problems in the absence of policies to counteract the trends.

The master plan proposed to concentrate regional growth in new towns on the periphery of the Paris region. New jobs, shops, and public services would be concentrated in the new towns to serve both existing and new residents. The downtowns would be dynamic centers, with a combination of high-density apartments and nonresidential functions. Single-family homes could be located farther from the downtowns. Eight new towns were proposed to accommodate most of the Paris region's growth until 2000.

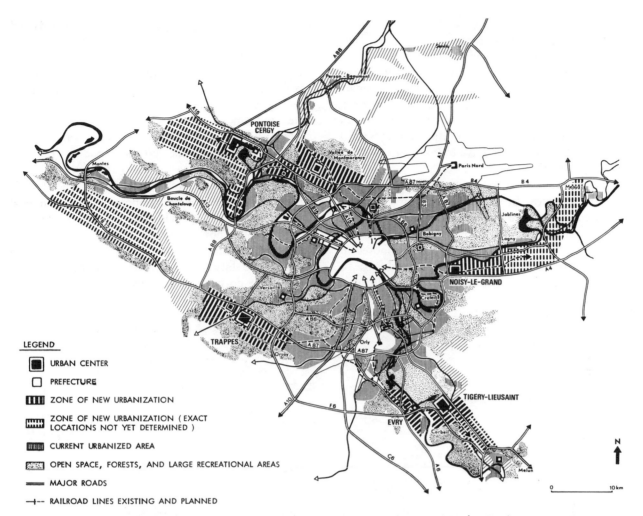

Figure 3. Master plan of the Paris region (SDAURP), 1965. Source: *La Region Parisienne: 4 Années d'aménagement et d'equipement.*

The eight new towns were to be arranged along two development corridors or preferential axes (see Figure 3). These two axes were designed to run parallel to each other, from the southeast to the northwest, tangent to the north and south sides of the existing built-up area. This unorthodox pattern was proposed to break the traditional radioconcentric urban structure that was responsible for the existing problems. The axes would become transportation corridors to promote accessibility to a number of facilities without having to go into the center.

Although new development was to be concentrated in the new towns and preferential axes, the existing built-up areas could not be ignored and would be treated as a unified whole. New transportation investments were required throughout the region. Expressways and rapid transit lines were needed to reduce congestion on existing systems in central

Paris, as well as to provide accessibility to the new towns and poorly served existing suburbs.[18]

One intriguing alternative that was rejected in the master plan called for the construction of one gigantic new town, called Paris B, to house several million people. The Paris B concept was rejected because it was impractical; even if it had been successfully built, it would have replicated many of the congestion problems found in the original Paris.

Of the eight new towns proposed in the master plan, five are now under construction: Cergy-Pontoise and Marne-la-Vallée (formerly Noisy-le-Grand) along the northern axis, and Saint-Quentin-en-Yvelines (formerly Trappes), Evry, and Melun-Sénart (formerly Tigery-Lieusaint) along the southern axis. Two of the proposed new towns were eliminated because of strong opposition from local officials, while Saint-Quentin combined two new town sites into one. Figure 4 shows the revised master plan published in 1969 to reflect the new towns that were actually to be undertaken.

While the Paris regional planners were advocating the construction of new towns, the national planners in DATAR were also attracted to the new-town idea. Studies carried out in the three *metropoles d'equilibres* of Lille, Lyon, and Marseille indicated that regional growth would have to take place outside the existing urbanized areas.

For various reasons new towns were recommended at these metropoles. In the Lille region a new town was needed to provide services and facilities for a large new university complex being built to the east of the city. At Lyon two new towns were proposed to counteract the tendency of the Lyon suburbs to sprawl in all directions. The new towns were located

on the east side of Lyon to preserve the vineyards and other natural amenities elsewhere in the region and to strengthen the development of axes between Lyon and Grenoble, Chambery, and Annecy. One of the two new towns, L'Isle d'Abeau, has been started adjacent to a new airport, which will be the second largest in France.

The new town at Marseille was necessitated by the decision to increase the port's capacity. Because large-scale expansion was blocked at the existing port area, an entirely new port is being built on the Gulf of Fos to the west of Marseille. The adjacent new town of Berre will provide the needed supporting services for the port facilities. A fourth new town is Le Vaudreuil, near Rouen. This new town will help organize the large-scale growth anticipated in the Basse-Seine corridor, which extends from Paris to

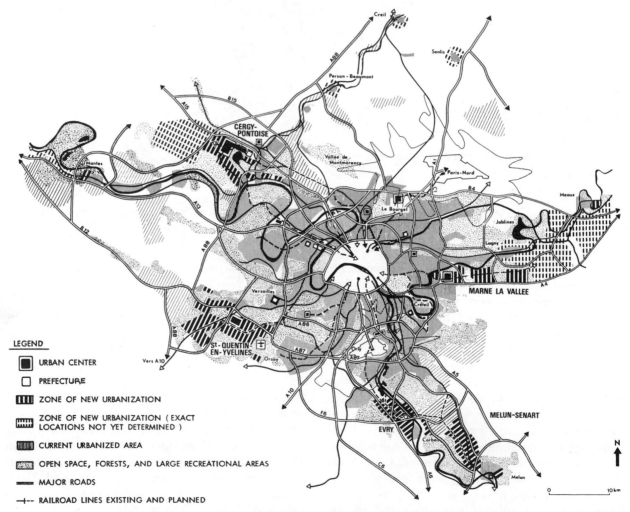

Figure 4. Modifications to the master plan of the Paris region (1969). (Note the removal of new urban centers and zones of new urbanization in the Vallée de Montmorency, Mantes, and the second one near Trappes now Saint-Quentin-en-Yvelines.) Source: *La Region Parisienne: 4 Années d'aménagement et d'equipement.*

the English Channel at Le Havre. The new town is designed to prevent this growth from occurring as a sprawling extension from Paris by channeling development into the new town located well beyond the current limits of the Paris region.

The extent to which DATAR's support for new towns was a result of Delouvrier's pressure is unclear. Aware that national support could not be expected for Paris new towns alone, Delouvrier urged the national planners to consider new towns in the provinces. Whether DATAR would have proposed the provincial new towns without Delouvrier's strong urging is unknown, but support for the Paris new towns certainly represents an exception to the national planners' opposition to new large-scale investments in the Paris region. The reduction in the scope of the Paris new-town program was certainly due in part to the need for balance between the size of the Paris and provincial new-town efforts.

National Integration of New-Town Strategies. The national government has sought to integrate the significant differences in the origins and purposes of the provincial and Paris new towns into a unified policy. This effort was made in the Sixth National Plan, which set down investment priorities for the 1971–1975 period and affirmed in the Seventh National Plan for 1976–1980. The section of new towns included a statement of goals, indicators to measure progress toward the goals, and financial support for the projects.

The Sixth National Plan cited four goals for the new towns:

1. To restructure the suburbs by organizing new concentrations of employment, housing, and services.
2. To reduce the amount of commuting and ease the transport problems in the particular urban regions.
3. To create truly self-contained cities, as measured by a balance between jobs and housing, variety of different jobs and housing, provision of housing and supporting services at the same time and place, the rapid creation of urban centers, and concern for recreational facilities and environmental protection.
4. To serve as laboratories for experiments in urban planning and design.

For the first three goals, the Sixth National Plan provided a set of indicators and targets to measure progress at each of the new towns, including the following:

Goals 1 and 2. Division between secondary- and tertiary-sector jobs.

- Number of permanent jobs created each year.
- Percentage of region's new jobs created in the new town.
- Number of jobs created in the tertiary sector.
- Square meters of offices started.
- Square meters of commercial centers started.
- Number of new jobs in the next two years.

Goals 1 and 2. Housing.

- Number of housing units started and completed, divided among low, middle, and upper income.
- Percentage of region's housing starts located in the new town.
- Percentage of jobs in the new town taken by residents of it—percentage of people living and working in the new town divided by the total number of people working in it.
- Percentage of residents in the new town working in it—percentage of people living and working in the new town divided by the total number of people living in it and working either inside or outside it.
- Average journey-to-work time for new-town residents compared to all residents of the region.

Goal 3. Self-containment and balance.

- Number of new jobs created each year compared to the number of new residents.
- Percentage of new jobs staffed by women.
- Percentage of upper-income housing created.
- Actual housing starts compared to goals.
- Amount of open space per household.

The fourth goal is essentially qualitative. The Sixth National Plan aided the achievement of this goal in three ways: architecture and design of housing; quality of public facilities; and innovative techniques, especially public transportation, environmental protection, and telecommunications systems.[19]

Despite the diverse reasons for planning new towns in France, the nine new towns have many similar characteristics. These new towns are all rather large. The nine new towns range in size from 140,000 at Le Vaudreuil to 375,000 at Berre. The new towns, consequently, are concerned with a large amount of territory, averaging over 10,000 hectares. These sites are not green fields; they are located adjacent to poorly designed and inadequately served suburbs. The new towns are designed to provide needed services to these nearby areas as well as to the incoming residents of the new towns. Table 2 shows the current and projected figures for population and employment.

In many ways the new towns are new downtowns. Each new town will be characterized by a large downtown area in which a high order of commercial activities will be concentrated, including department stores, office buildings, public services, and apartments. These downtowns will be built at high densities, with multilevel transport systems and

pedestrian decks. The high-density downtowns will make the new towns animated regional centers, where residents and nonresidents alike will congregate in the evening as well as during working hours. Neighborhoods will be grouped around the downtown area, with a mixture of styles and cost in the housing. The towns will include a balanced representation among types of people and functions. New road and rail links will be built to aid connections with the main city. Figures 5 and 6 show the plans for the centers of Cergy-Pontoise and Evry, respectively.

Implementation of New-Town Policy. The French new-town administrative structure is quite complex, reflecting the almost Byzantine qualities of the

Table 2   Current and Projected Population and Employment in the Nine French New Towns

		1968	1975	At Completion (1985 or 2000)
Paris region	Population	263,627	417,987	1,380,000
	Employment	112,500	157,700	731,000
Cergy-Pontoise	Population	53,445	84,487	330,000
	Employment	15,000	26,100	150,000
Evry[a]	Population	33,180	53,673	150,000
	Employment	40,000	51,600	155,000
Marne-la-Vallée	Population	61,878	81,624	300,000
	Employment	20,000	22,800	220,000
Melun-Sénart	Population	65,709	94,548	300,000
	Employment	29,000	35,300	101,000
Saint-Quentin	Population	41,405	103,655	300,000
	Employment	8,500	21,900	100,000
Provinces	Population	104,149	150,811	975,000
	Employment	70,000	95,900	318,400
Berre[b]	Population	33,328	57,476	375,000
	Employment	25,900	45,300	125,000
L'Isle d'Abeau	Population	38,213	47,573	250,000
	Employment	13,200	15,900	70,000
Lille-Est	Population	26,288	38,600	210,000
	Employment	28,300	30,900	68,400
Le Vaudruil	Population	6,320	7,162	140,000
	Employment	2,600	3,800	55,000
Total	Population	367,776	568,798	2,355,000
	Employment	182,500	253,600	1,049,400

[a] Within the larger Evry study area there were 160,000 residents in 1968, 200,000 in 1975, and 500,000 planned for 2000.
[b] Within the larger Berre study area there were 76,766 residents in 1968, 120,602 in 1975, and 466,000 planned for 2000.

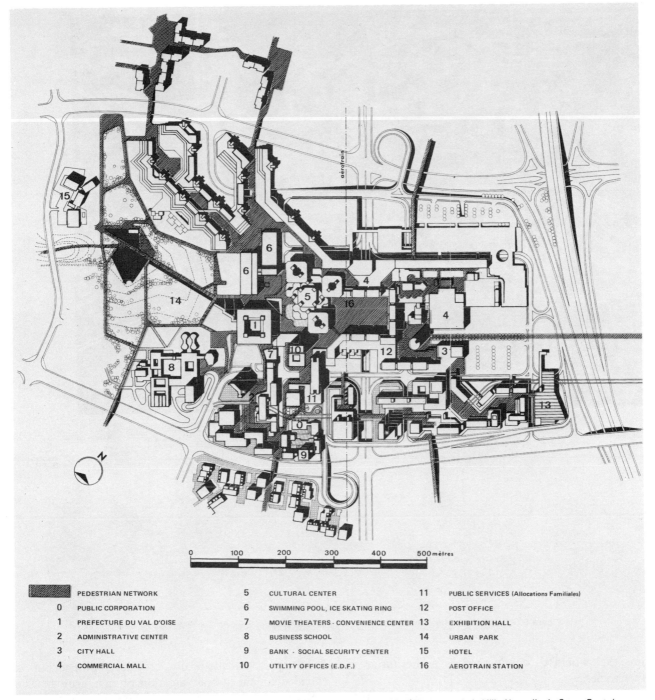

Figure 5. Cergy-Pontoise center, March 1972. Source: *Etablissement Public d'Aménagement de la Ville Nouvelle de Cergy-Pontoise.*

French government system as a whole. Nonetheless, the mere fact that a workable administrative structure has been developed for the new towns indicates the profound changes that have occurred in the French government since World War II. The new-town administrative system, worked out only after much difficulty, would have been completely infea-sible until recent years because by all accounts the French spirit is not conducive to effective government. The typical Frenchman is a staunch individualist who regards the government's intervention as a nuisance. Yet despite this hostility by the public, the French government is permitted to exercise considerable discretion and engage in arbitrary ac-

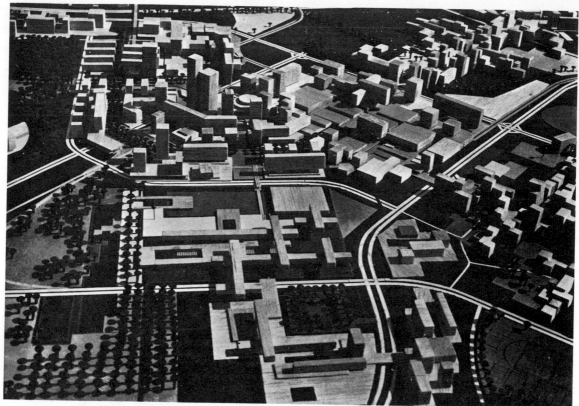

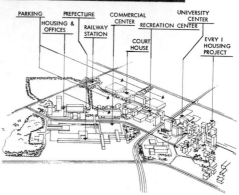

Figure 6. Evry town center. Source: *Etablissement Public d'Aménagement de la Ville Nouvelle d'Evry.*

tions that would be condemned as authoritarian in other societies.

Three national ministries are concerned primarily with the development of new towns. The Ministère de l'Aménagement du Territoire, d'Equipement, du Logement, et du Tourisme (MATELT), brought together a number of smaller ministries concerned with various aspects of urban development, as the long name indicates. The Equipment Ministry, as it is commonly called, is oriented toward encouraging public works projects, such as roads and sewers. The

ministry is unequivocally pro development but is divided on the proper location of that growth. The ministry is now sprinkled liberally with supporters of the new-town program.

The Ministry of Economic Affairs and Finance has traditionally been the most powerful. It serves two roles: preparation of the budget and regulation of the nation's monetary policies. Prior to World War II this ministry practiced extreme financial orthodoxy. In recent years the ministry has adopted a more pragmatic, open policy with regard to investments for urban development. The successful launching of the new-town program is due in large measure to the willingness of the Ministry of Finance to authorize the required financial assistance.

The Ministry of Interior is the voice of local authorities to the national government. The minister appoints many local government officials and has ultimate authority over all local actions. The ministry is considered a very traditional organization, opposed to dramatic administrative changes and concerned primarily with preserving the established political power of local authorities. Many local officials are also members of the national assembly. Although some of these officials have been involved in formulating the administrative reforms needed for the development of new towns, most have avoided active support of them.

The Problem of Local Government. The system of local government in France is rather chaotic. France has three tiers of local government, including the 21 regional governments recently established. The two traditional levels are the departments and communes. There are 95 departments in France, eight of which are in the Paris region. Each is led by a prefect appointed by the minister of interior and by an elected general council. Below the departments are the communes, the government closest to each citizen. France is divided into some 38,000 communes, with a mean area of 1428 hectares and a mean population of 1400. There are 1305 communes in the Paris region alone. The citizens of each commune elect a mayor and municipal council.[20]

In theory the localities have no legal authority. All power is vested in the national government, including the right to abolish or modify the local governments. Local officials are technically agents of the national government and report to the minister of interior.

Over the centuries, however, the government has delegated a good deal of authority to the departments and communes. Although legally the government could take back those powers, political support could never be mustered for a major readjustment. The relatively modest reforms associated with the new-town program represent the extreme to which change can be pushed in the French system.

Localities thus play a major role in the process of urban development. Local governments have the responsibility for providing schools, roads, swimming pools, sewage plants, police, and other social services. The most important power held by the com-

munes and departments is the right to issue building permits for all projects. No one can build anything without receipt of a building permit from the two local governments.

Although local governments have acquired considerable legal responsibility for urban development, they lack the financial means and technical expertise to do very much without national government support. Communes have the right to collect local taxes, but because they are so small the revenues produced are inadequate to pay for new projects. New public works are therefore financed with loans taken out by the communes, usually from the Caisse des Dépôts et Consignations (CDC), which makes long-term, below-market-rate loans to the communes.[21] If the commune's borrowing power is still insufficient to pay for a project, as is the case for most large efforts, the additional funds can come only from direct national grants.

Because of the pattern of financing, it is fair to say that the national government makes most urban growth policy. The national government establishes priorities for investment in new projects and awards grants to the local authorities accordingly. The establishment of local priorities is made primarily by a cadre of civil servants from the various national ministries permanently located in each department. These department agents provide the technical expertise that local authorities cannot afford to hire.

Despite the financial and technical power wielded by the national government, a local authority can still successfully oppose undesired development simply by refusing to apply for grants or to give building permits. These negative actions are likely to receive the support of the Ministry of Interior, which resists attempts by other government agencies to influence local authorities. The development of urban growth policies has thus been for the most part stymied because both the national and local governments exercise primarily negative powers. The national government can block a project by refusing to subsidize it, and the local authorities can block a project by refusing to apply for funding or to grant a building permit.

The local governments are wary of the new-town policy for three reasons. First, the construction of new towns, directed by national planners, represents a threat to the local authorities' power. For the local authorities located on the site of a new town, the threat is immediate. The threat perceived by local officials where new towns are not located is that new towns could prevent them from exercising a choice concerning the nature and amount of growth within their own boundaries. The power to decide its own growth rate by each commune is jealously guarded by local officials through the exercise of the authority to issue building permits. If a new town is proposed in a region, the success of that project is based not only on the creation of positive inducements to attract people and enterprises and a rapid pace of construction, but also on the exercise of negative constraints to discourage construction elsewhere, thereby channeling development into the new-town areas. Local authorities located in areas where building is to be discouraged dislike losing the ability to decide whether development would take place. The irony of this opposition to the new-town policy is that although local officials do not like the idea of being forced to accept a policy that restricts growth in their communes, this is exactly the policy that the majority adopts anyway, given the choice.

Second, communes lack the financial resources to undertake large-scale urban development such as new towns. Because the communes are severely limited in the amount of finances they can raise through local sources, any large-scale project must be financed with both grants and loans from the central government. The need for bank loans and responsible fiscal management to repay the loans and interest limits the amount of activity that a local authority can undertake. Communes welcome new business because they contribute more in taxes than they demand in services, but they do not want new housing because of the drain on public services by new residents. Consequently, many communes will respond negatively to the requests for permits from most housing builders.

Third, because most communes in France are very small, new-town boundaries would have to encompass several. Although communes have agreed in the past to undertake some specific joint projects, such as sewer lines, there was no precedent for the cooperation needed to manage the many aspects of large urban growth. The problem of intercommunal cooperation is exacerbated by the political differences of local officials. It is not uncommon for one commune to have Gaullist officials and the next one to have Communists. Urban development policies are frequently decided by narrow political considerations. For example, the amount of high-rise apartments as opposed to single-family houses is debated along strict party lines, with the left favoring apartments and the right favoring detached houses.

Despite these objections, local authority opposition has been blunted by a political paradox. Right-wing local officials are fearful of new towns because they are likely to lose their offices when large numbers of new low-income, left-voting families settle. However, they do not oppose the new towns because the policy was developed and supported by right-wing national governments. The left is wary of new towns because the government proposed them but does not oppose them because they see long-term political benefits.

Development of a Workable Administrative Structure. The French admired the British new-town administrative structure, in which a single development corporation performed virtually all roles in the development process. However, that approach was politically impossible in France.[22] Instead, responsibility for the development of new towns has been divided among several organizations. In particular, three new agencies have been created to deal with the new towns: Etablissement Public d'Aménagement (development corporation), Syndicat Communautaire d'Aménagement (union of communes for new-town development), and Groupe Central des Villes Nouvelles (national group for new-town development).

Etablissement Public d'Aménagement. Instead of a unitary, all-powerful, British-style development corporation, the French established development corporations with powers limited to certain areas of the development process. One development corporation, called an *Etablissement Public d'Aménagement* (EPA), is appointed for each new town. The EPA has two functions, one related to planning and one to land development. The EPA carries out planning, development, and infrastructure studies; organizes and coordinates land transactions and initial development work; estimates costs and proposes the timetable for building the new town. With regard to land development, the EPA can acquire land by power of eminent domain or through negotiations; develop roads, utilities, and other infrastructure; and resell or lease land to private builders.[23]

The EPA staff includes engineers, architects, planners, and economists. The technical head of the EPA—the director general—is usually either an engineer or economist. Although each EPA is structured somewhat differently, the organization for Saint-Quentin-en-Yvelines, illustrated in Figure 7, is typical. The agency is divided into four units: administration, operations, research and studies, and

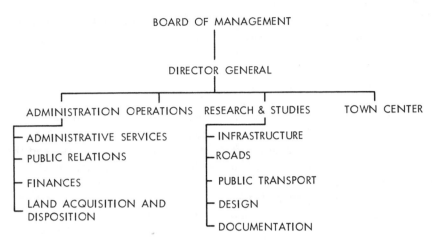

Figure 7. Organization of the Etablissement Public d'Aménagement (EPA), Saint-Quentin-en-Yvelines. Source: Etablissement Public d'Aménagement de la Ville Nouvelle de Saint-Quentin-en-Yvelines.

the town center. About 60 people work for the EPA, some of whom are on loan from regional or national agencies to provide additional technical expertise.

Policy making by the EPA is entrusted to a board of management, which contains 14 members selected as follows: seven representatives of local authorities, including the communes, department, and the Paris regional district, and seven representatives of the state, including the Ministries of Equipment, Interior, Economic Affairs and Finance, and Cultural Affairs.[24] This board is headed by a president, who is also a local official.

The EPA is in a politically sensitive position because it contains many of the tensions and ambiguities involved in French intergovernment relations. Unable to raise taxes in its own right, the EPA is dependent on both local and national officials for loans and loan guarantees. Administrative and planning costs are paid directly by the national government, while the funds for land acquisition and site preparation are received from both the local authorities and the national government.

Syndicat Communautaire d'Aménagement. Many of the administrative problems associated with new-town development were due to the small size of the communes. The EPAs for the nine new towns encompass 115 communes, ranging from four at Berre and Evry to 21 for Marne-la-Vallée and 23 at L'Isle d'Abeau. The obvious first step in the search for a long-term solution to the local government problem was to combine the small communes into one large local authority for each new town. This solution was advocated by national planners as far back as the Fifth National Plan in 1966. However, existing local

authorities and the minister of interior not surprisingly opposed the idea of combining the existing communes into one new one. Such an arrangement would have resulted in the elimination of current local government officials, an action the Ministry of Interior would not support.[25]

In 1968 the Association of French Mayors issued counterproposals, calling for the creation of an association among the communes inside the new towns. This association would be called a community syndicate for development (SCA). The communal boundaries for elections would remain unchanged, but the *syndicat communautaire,* composed of representatives from each municipal council, would directly manage the tax system and budget of the new town. This would be like administering a joint estate consisting only of property acquired after marriage. Construction of the new town is managed jointly and all relevant income and expenditures equally apportioned. The SCA would uniformly set the tax rate for the entire district.[26]

The national assembly settled the issue in 1970 with the passage of the *Loi Boscher.* The communes were given the choice of adopting the SCA method or immediately creating a single new commune, called an *ensemble urbain.*

The first step in the development process is the designation by the government of the relevant zone for development, roughly coinciding with the territory of the *Etablissement Public.*[27] The communes have four months from the date of designation to establish the SCA or *ensemble urbain.* If no agreement can be reached at the end of four months, or if after four more months the local authorities fail to reach an agreement with the EPA concerning the broad program and goals for the new town, the government can then impose its own solution on the communes.

If the *ensemble urbain* is chosen, the local authority is like any other commune. The old communes cease to operate in the new-town area, and the residents vote for representatives of the new commune. The only exception is that for the first years of development a nine-man municipal council is appointed. The residents vote for three more councillors after 2000 dwellings are occupied and three more two and four years after the first three. At this time the council has 18 members, one-half elected and one-half appointed. Within three years of this time the entire council must be elected in the normal way.

Le Vaudreuil has an *ensemble urbain,* but the other eight new towns have SCAs because the local authorities did not wish to vote themselves out of existence. There is one SCA in five new towns: Cergy-Pontoise, Evry, Saint-Quentin-en-Yvelines, Lille-Est, and L'Isle d'Abeau. Berre has two SCAs and Marne-la-Vallée and Melun-Sénart have three each. The rationale for permitting more than one SCA was both technical and political. In the three new towns with more than one SCA, development will take place around more than one center, with large areas of open space separating the urbanized areas. Each district has its own master plan and a SCA to manage the problems unique to the particular area. The method has also been used to separate conservative communes from radical ones.

The SCA is concerned only with managing the development of the new-town area. Inside the new town, the old communes continue to perform routine functions such as policing the streets and recording vital statistics. After 25 years the SCA will become a single commune. This postpones the changeover beyond the political careers of current office holders, although many of these officials will be voted out when there are enough new voters.

Relations between the EPA and SCA are not ideal. The local officials naturally harbor a good deal of mistrust about the outside planners. Planners tend to be impatient with the local authorities who do not have the technical expertise to manage the complexities of a large-scale rapid development process properly. Local officials frequently delay EPA projects by insisting on lengthy hearings. The issues that interest the local officials are usually matters such as which developer will be awarded a particular contract. Local officials who are close to a particular developer may question the choice made by the EPA and try to secure a change to someone who has had

dealings with the local officials in the past. Other local officials may try to stop projects because they are not seen as in the best interest of the existing residents. An example of this would be the building of single-family houses in a working-class commune. The job of smoothing the relations between local officials and planners frequently must be done at the top, among the technical head of the EPA, the political head of the EPA, and the head of the SCA. The latter two jobs are sometimes held by one person to simplify the problems.

Groupe Central des Villes Nouvelles. In 1970 a new national organization, the *Groupe Central des Villes Nouvelles* (GCVN), was created to promote the interests of the new towns inside the government. Its functions are (1) to propose any administrative and financial measures to the ministers concerned to promote smoothness of operations, (2) advise, within the framework of pluriannual programs, on prospects of medium- and long-term financial stability of projects, and (3) propose actions concerning capital endowments and the consistency of annual programs for financing operations out of official appropriations.[28]

The GCVN, like the rest of the French administrative structure, is a rather complex organization, as Figure 8 indicates. The secretary-general for the GCVN plays three roles. First, he is the technical head of a number of research-oriented functions, shown on the right side of Figure 8. These functions relate primarily to the gathering of statistics and the coordination of the financial situation at each of the nine new towns. About 20 people perform these tasks. The policymaking duties are entrusted to a management board, comprised of a president and vice president, and representatives of 12 ministries and the departments where new towns are located.

The secretary-general of the GCVN is at the same time a representative of the Ministry of Equipment. He is in charge of the technical and financial assistance that the Ministry of Equipment has available for the new towns. This arrangement, of course, ensures that the Ministry of Equipment is strongly committed to new towns. The GCVN also provides a special service to the Paris regional government by monitoring the progress of the five Paris new towns more closely than the four provincial ones. Data are therefore much more readily available for the Paris new towns. The GCVN has about 15 people assigned to tasks for the Ministry of Equipment and 10 for monitoring the Paris region.

Figure 9 shows the division of administrative

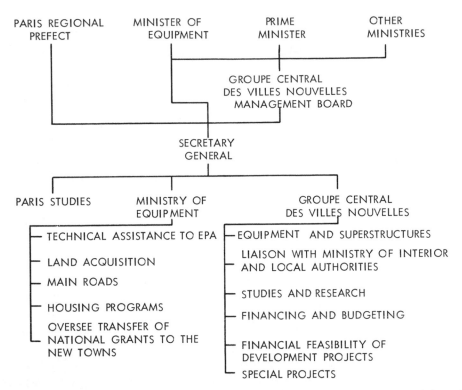

Figure 8. Organization of *Groupe Central des Villes Nouvelles*. Source: Author's translation of an organizational chart of *Groupe Central des Villes Nouvelles*.

responsibilities and financing for the French new towns. The arrangements shown here represent a simplification of the actual development process. Although the national government ultimately pays most of the development costs, the actual procedures for diverting money to the new towns is extremely complicated.

In theory new-town projects are financed as any other urban development program is in France. In other words, new towns are supposed to be financed by local authorities. Despite the fact that local authorities are hopelessly incapable of financing urban development projects, financial arrangements for new towns are based on the myth that the local authorities will soon be ready to assume fiscal control.

No long-term financial solution has been created because everyone is participating in the myth. The result is that, despite the fact that officials in the Ministries of Equipment and Finance support the program, the new towns go from one financial crisis to another.

Because the new towns are considered local government projects in theory, the total amount of local financial support that can be raised is exhausted before the national government intervenes. Since the local tax base is much too small to support large urban development projects, the local authorities are required to borrow as much money as the CDC will lend them. The SCAs qualify for the same 30-year, 8 percent loans as do regular local authorities. This money is used for the construction of schools, sports equipment, hospitals, other social services, and public facilities.

Although the EPA has no borrowing authority, it can in fact borrow money as an agent of the local authority. The CDC makes available six-year loans for land acquisition and site preparation at between 3.75 and 6.5 percent interest. However, if the EPA cannot repay these loans, the SCA is liable. These loans are repaid with receipts from the sale or leasing of land to private developers.

The problem with the system of borrowing money is that the SCAs do not yet have the resources to make repayments. Someday the population of the new towns will be large enough to generate sufficient income, but that time is still far away. Consequently, as a matter of course, local authorities are placed in a position of defaulting on loans unless additional help is given by the national government. Thus the national government perpetuates the myth of local

FUNCTION	WHO DOES IT ?	WHO PAYS ?
PLANNING	AT FIRST: MEA LATER: EPA	GRANTS FROM THE MINISTRY OF EQUIPMENT
LAND ACQUISITION	EPA	ABOUT 50% GRANTS FROM THE MINISTRY OF EQUIPMENT AND 50% LOANS FROM THE CDC REPAID FROM SALE OR LEASING OF THE LAND
SITE PREPARATION (UTILITIES, ROADS, OPEN SPACE, ETC.)	EPA	GRANTS FROM MINISTRIES, LOCAL TAXES, AND LOANS TO THE SCA FROM THE CDC; THE EXACT DIVISION DEPENDS ON THE PARTICULAR PROJECT
HOUSING	PRIVATE OR PUBLIC NONPROFIT DEVELOPERS	LOW INCOME: 1% LOANS FROM THE CDC; MIDDLE INCOME: LOANS AND GUARANTEES FROM A VARIETY OF GOVERNMENT SOURCES; HIGH INCOME: PRIVATE SOURCES OF FINANCING
EMPLOYMENT	PRIVATE DEVELOPERS; EPA NEGOTIATIONS WITH POTENTIAL NEW EMPLOYERS	PRIVATE SOURCES, ALTHOUGH GOVERNMENT SUBSIDIES ARE AVAILABLE IN SOME CASES
SHOPPING	PRIVATE DEVELOPERS, AFTER NEGOTIATIONS WITH EPA	PRIVATE SOURCES
SOCIAL SERVICES (SCHOOLS, HOSPITALS, POLICE, RECREATION, SWIMMING POOLS, DAY-CARE CENTERS, ETC.)	SCA	LOCAL TAXES; LOANS FROM THE CDC TO THE SCA; AND GRANTS FROM THE MINISTRIES OF NATIONAL EDUCATION, HEALTH, SPORTS, ETC.; THE EXACT AMOUNT DEPENDS ON THE INDIVIDUAL PROJECT

Figure 9. Division of administrative responsibilities in French new towns.

authority control by giving them grants to repay loans. Initially, the Ministry of Finance permitted the SCAs to defer the starting of loan repayments to the CDC for four years, but that period has had to be extended. Such deferments are likely to continue on an *ad hoc* basis amidst an air of emergency for some years, with the level of national support depending on the particular financial conditions of each new town.

The national government also makes direct grants that are not related to loan repayments. These grants cover the normal national contribution given for local projects, such as 55 percent for primary roads and 80 percent for elementary schools. These direct grants come from the particular ministries normally concerned with the provision of the function, such as the Ministry of National Education or Equipment. The amount of grants allocated for the new towns each year by the various ministries is isolated from the rest of the budget. This special line is immune to last-minute budget cutting in parliament by order of the prime minister.

This complex financing system makes it almost impossible to determine the strength of the government's commitment to the new towns. Direct grants to the new towns, including loan repayment assistance and administrative costs, are now about 400 million francs a year (about $85 million at current exchange rates). This figure, though, does not include local contributions, loans still outstanding, and subsidies to private developers operating in the new town.

NEW-TOWN DEVELOPMENT STRATEGY AND ITS REALIZATION

France has a fundamentally liberal economy. The relatively limited powers exercised by the EPA, in contrast to the British-style development corporation, illustrate the orientation of the French planning system. The new-town development process is designed to divide responsibility between the public authority and the private sector so as to assure both public control over the location of new development and private profits. Neither national nor local government officials—at least those in power—view the private sector with hostility. There is a considerable amount of personal movement between the private and public sectors.

The distinction between private and public sectors is in fact not very clear in France. Since World War II several industries have been nationalized, but their management policies are indistinguishable from those of private firms.[29] Other firms have not been fully nationalized, but the government has the right to appoint a percentage of the board of directors. Still other firms are privately managed but survive only with government subsidies. Throughout the economy, monopolies and interlocking directorates have been encouraged much more than in other western countries. Therefore, when reference is made to private-sector activities in France, the observer must always be aware that some public involvement is still likely.

The close relation between private and public sectors means that attitudes on economic issues are frequently similar. The urban development process has been created as a partnership. The successful realization of a new project requires great cooperation. Rather sophisticated land controls have been devised to secure new development in the desired location by a large, efficient private developer. Profits come not so much from land speculation as from the ability of private developers to operate on a large scale to meet market demands quickly.

As was the case with the relations between local authorities and the government, the theoretical division of powers on paper does not reflect the true relation. In theory both the national government and local officials have a good deal of power over private developers. Local governments issue building permits, operate planning and zoning controls, and provide infrastructure. The national government provides subsidies to both local officials and private developers and approves local planning proposals. However, in reality large private developers have considerable power, especially with the local authorities who frequently can be persuaded by slick businessmen to issue the needed permits. The most important club available though is the power of the market. If government officials choose not to heed demands from consumers and developers, a good deal of opposition to the government would be generated, and the urban projects would grind to a halt. As in the United States, the planning controls cannot be totally unrelated to the market. The controls can bend the market, but they cannot successfully break it.

From the private developers' viewpoint, France is a booming country today. Part of the demand for new housing is due to factors common to other western countries, such as the trend to smaller households, higher average incomes, and replacement of old substandard units. The boom is particularly strong in France because of the relatively rapid population increase and the failure to recover fully from wartime shortages.

The biggest problem for the private developer is the scarcity of low-cost accessible sites for new construction. The planning system was designed to minimize urban sprawl and the inefficiencies in the site improvement process that stem from disjointed development. The new-town policy was a logical extension of this orientation, especially in the Paris region, where most of the development pressures are still concentrated. However, private developers see the system of planning controls as mostly counterproductive. By restricting the location of new projects, private developers argue, the price of land with planning permission has skyrocketed, inevitably resulting in higher housing costs for the consumer. A rational land policy would be to grant planning permission for more land than is actually needed for urban development. The abundant supply would then bring down land prices.

The basic flaw in this argument is the fact that the problem was not the lack of land with planning permission but a lack of land equipped with utilities and infrastructure. The mere release of a large supply of land would not lower prices unless all of that land had been prepared. Large-scale preparation of sites that may not be used for new projects is not a rational investment policy for the government. As long as the government retained responsibility for financing and installing infrastructure, the rational investment policy was to concentrate new construction rather than encourage further sprawl. Thus the need for carefully managed investment in new infrastructure has led to the general acceptance that government leadership is needed in selecting sites for new development.

The need for government intervention does not of course destroy the influence of the market. Sites with infrastructure located in desirable areas will have a much greater demand than those where consumer demand is lower. The basic problem for the national planners is that the new towns are generally not sited where market pressures are strong. Therefore, the new towns can be developed only through the use of strong legal controls and subsidies to the private sector to stimulate private-sector decisions to locate in new towns and away from undesired areas.

Developmental Tools. Three sets of tools are used to control the location of urban development in France. First is the system of master plans and zoning ordinances. Each new-town EPA submits a master plan for government approval. Under a 1967 act, master plans are also required for areas outside the new-town boundaries.[30] These master plans—or SDAUs as they are called in French—usually cover the territory of several communes. Under the SDAU process the regional prefect decides which communes in the region are subject to growth pressures. He orders these communes singly or jointly to prepare master plans, with the technical assistance of local representatives of the Ministry of Equipment. The master plans must be approved by the commune's municipal council, the prefect of the department, the regional prefect, and the interested national ministries.[31]

The master plans do not tell the public precisely what changes can be expected; they are designed to give the general guidelines of development and the new infrastructure to be located somewhere in the area.[32] The quantity of such new investments are known, but the exact location is not. The function of precisely stating what uses and densities are permitted at particular locations, as well as the exact location of public works projects, is found in the Plan d'Occupation des Sols (POS), documents equivalent to American zoning laws.[33] The POS must conform

with the SDAU and explain in detail the future appearance of the commune. For rapidly growing areas, such as new towns, this precise snapshot is of course impossible. A device that effectively limits large-scale growth, the POS is designed as a comprehensive inventory of the locality.[34]

This system at first glance appears to be a relatively simple method by which national concerns are filtered down to regions and localities; the placement of regional and national expert personnel in local offices would appear to assure that national and regional directives are incorporated into local plans. As one would expect of a planning system that is trying to modify the direction of existing growth trends, developers who prefer to continue construction in the areas of natural growth—that is, through continuous extension of the built-up area in a sprawling fashion—will exert pressure.

Pressures are applied locally where the plans are prepared. Local officials are vulnerable to the pleas of private developers to make a small exception just for them. Many local officials have close relations with private developers and find that the best way to secure a high-paying job in the private sector is to demonstrate how they were able to get planning permission for a project. National planners, more removed from these pressures, look at the total effects of all master plans. These local master plans and zoning ordinances are designed to conform to regional plans, such as the one already described for the Paris region, but the net effect of many small exceptions made for single developers may be to violate the intentions of a regional plan.

The second set of tools is the method of land price freezing and acquisition. If land is acquired at agricultural prices, the development authority can secure the increases associated with urbanization. The problem is how to secure the land at low prices because the mere announcement of a new project induces land speculation.

Since 1962 the French have tried to solve the problem with a technique called Zones d'Aménagement Differée, deferred development zones (ZAD). When a piece of land has been "zaded," its value is frozen at the level of one year before the designation. Any local authority, EPA, or national agency may declare a ZAD. If an owner wishes to sell his land to another private person, the public authority that has declared the ZAD has the right of first refusal to buy the land at the asking price. If the asking price is roughly the same as the frozen value, the public authority is not likely to intervene. When the price is

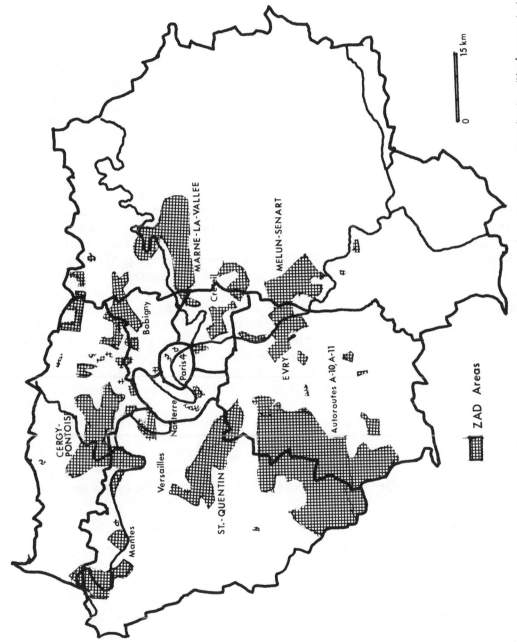

Figure 10. *Zones d'Aménagement Différée* (ZAD) in the Paris region. Source: *La Région Parisienne en Bref.* (Institut d'Aménagement et d'Urbanisme de la Région Parisienne.)

considerably higher—roughly 25 percent above the frozen price—there is likely to be public intervention. The public authority has the choice of negotiating the agreed price or initiating expropriation proceedings. The ZAD declaration lasts for 14 years. Once a piece of land has been under the ZAD system for three years, the owner can demand that the public authority acquire the land through negotiations or expropriation. If the public authority refuses, the land is then revalued and refrozen for 14 more years. Figure 10 shows the land that has been "zaded" in the Paris region, where land speculation pressures are the most intense.

The ZAD system has two purposes: It is a method to ensure that land needed for public action can be acquired at relatively low prices, and the ZAD designation will dampen speculation in areas where future public action is contemplated.[35]

The ZAD has been fairly successful in the new towns. Land has been acquired at considerably lower prices than similarly located "unzaded" sites. Table 3 shows the land situation in the five Paris new towns. More than one-half of the land in the five study areas has been placed under ZAD. ZADs have been created for virtually all of the land that is to be acquired and urbanized, as well as to dampen price rises on territory that should remain undeveloped according to the master plan. As of 1976 nearly 15,000 hectares had actually been acquired in these five new towns.

Two particular problems have developed in the use of ZADs. First, landowners have found that by submitting to expropriation proceedings they are likely to receive a much higher rate than the frozen value. Most judges in France apparently are sympathetic to the notion that the seller is entitled to a portion of the surplus value, even though the buyer is a public agency. Because expropriation takes a long time, the land has a chance to increase in value a bit more before settlement. Thus the price actually paid by the public agency will be a compromise between acquisition at agricultural prices and fully speculative levels.[36]

The second problem is that the ZAD procedure is toothless unless the government's threat of preemption can be backed with actual acquisition if necessary. If the public agency does not have the money to buy the land if demanded by the owner after three years, the owner is free to sell at a speculative price while the public agency is powerless.

Because of the local government fiscal crisis, land acquisition must in some way be financed nationally. Funds are derived from loans taken out by the local authorities from the CDC or direct grants from the Ministry of Equipment. Approximately 1477 million francs had been expended on land acquisition in the nine new towns by the end of 1975. About two-thirds of the money came from state grants and one-third from loans. Land acquisition costs have averaged about 80,000 francs per hectare in the Paris new towns and 59,000 for the provinces (about $6400 and $4720 per acre, respectively, at current exchange rates). The land costs have varied from a low of around 41,000 francs per hectare ($3280 per acre) at L'Isle d'Abeau and 53,000 francs per hectare ($4240 per acre) at Melun-Sénart to a high of 94,000 francs per hectare ($7520 per acre) at Lille-Est and 99,000 francs per hectare ($7920 per acre) at Cergy-Pointoise. While these figures seem high compared to

Table 3   Land Situation in the Paris New Towns (ha)

New Towns	Study Area	Development Area	ZAD Area	Already Acquired
Cergy-Pontoise	10,000	3,700	7,476	2,627
Evry	9,000	1,500	3,486	1,726
Marne-la-Vallée	17,000	5,000	10,057	3,824
Melun-Sénart	17,000	3,500	8,976	3,245
Saint-Quentin	16,000	3,500	11,016	2,863
Total	69,000	18,200	41,011	14,285

Note: Figures are accurate as of 1976. Study area is the original planning territory. Development area is the territory now being intensively developed by the EPA, or likely to be. The development area corresponds to the total area placed under ZAD.
Source: "Situation Foncière dans les Villes Nouvelles de la Région Parisienne," "Rapport d'Execution du VIe Plan," and "Bilan des Villes Nouvelles Au 31 Decembre 1975."

other countries, they are low compared to the rest of the urban areas, particularly the Paris region. Land in the new towns is being bought at prices that are five to 10 times less than for comparable sites outside the new towns.[37]

Most of the land in the new towns will ultimately be sold to private developers and single homeowners. The exception is the town center, which will be leased to private developers rather than sold. As the commercial and employment cores of the new towns, the town centers will yield most of the anticipated profits associated with urban development.

The third basic land development tool is a mechanism for the establishment of public-private cooperation in the provision of needed services and facilities. The creation of a workable system for financing the installation of roads and utilities has been the biggest obstacle for French new-town administrators.

The basic problem, as already shown, is that local authorities are responsible for land development but do not have a sufficient financial base to pay for it. Infrastructure of national interest, such as primary roads, are paid for by the national government, but the cost of local utilities must be generated from local taxes. In practice this system does not work when large-scale development is required because the commune does not have a sufficiently large tax base to make the required local contributions.

One solution for financing infrastructure that has been tried in the new towns, as well as elsewhere in France, is the Zone d'Aménagement Concertée, concerted development zones (ZAC). The ZAC procedure, which has largely replaced earlier programs, is basically a contract between a public authority and a private developer concerning the distribution of costs and responsibilities for creating a new project.[38] The project, by the way, can be for residential or nonresidential use and has been used for rehabilitation projects as well as new construction. The definition of ZAC is as follows: "The 'Zones d'Aménagement Concertée' are the zones within which a public authority has decided to intervene in order to realize or have realized the development of infrastructure for land which the public authority has acquired or will acquire for the ultimate purpose of turning it over to public or private builders."[39] A request for a ZAC can be initiated by local authorities, EPAs, or national officials. Depending on the size of the proposed ZAC, the request must be approved by the prefect of the

department, the regional prefect, the minister of equipment, or the cabinet.

The ZAC procedure is basically a formal mechanism for negotiation between public authorities and private developers. The exact division of responsibilities is subject to the individual negotiations. The usual procedure is for the local authority to grant some sort of tax concessions in exchange for the private developer assuming the local share of the infrastructure costs. This arrangement increases the likelihood that utilities will be ready in time, but it can give the developers a substantial long-term bonus in the form of lower taxes. The division of benefits enjoyed by the private developers and public authorities depends on the relative negotiating competence of the two and the level of market pressure on the site. In the new towns the EPAs do most of the negotiations. Although they are technically competent, EPAs are limited in the bargaining process by the fact that most of the new towns are located in areas with relatively low market pressures. The EPA therefore must frequently make concessions to attract developers.

Virtually all new construction in the new towns is being done through the ZAC procedure.[40] ZACs have not solved the financial problems of the new towns, but they have made some contributions. The ZACs do not address the problem of financing large infrastructure projects, but they are alleviating some of the pressure for the installation of secondary systems.

ZACs are useful in another way. Because the national government must approve any large ZAC, the choice of approved projects is an important element in national policy for urban growth. A project must be designated as a ZAC to receive government priority for infrastructure grants. It is almost impossible to develop a large-scale project outside a ZAC. Therefore, the designation of much of the new towns as ZACs ensures that the new towns are entitled to financial priority. At the same time, the ZAC method institutionalizes procedures for planning the provision of utilities in coordination with other participation in the development process. The EPA, which normally manages the ZAC, can bring together the project plans, private developers who will do the actual construction, and the sources of financing the infrastructure. Although critics have charged that the amount of collusion between local officials and private developers in the ZAC system is unhealthy, the program is a pragmatic attempt to coordinate the development process, given the realities of market pressures.

By contrast to the situation with infrastructure, the government does not usually engage in actual construction of buildings. Instead, construction is left to the private sector, although government often supports it financially.

Housing. Housing in France is built by either private builders or nonprofit organizations. The government, however, provides financial assistance in one form or another for three-fourths of the housing starts. There are three basic types of housing constructed in France.

Très Aidé (Heavily Assisted). About one-third of the housing in France is *très aidé.* It is low-income housing built by nonprofit public or private corporations.[41] Over 90 percent of this category of housing is called HLM (*habitation loyer moderée*), moderate-income, rental housing. The government makes loans to builders at 1 percent interest and decides each year how much to allocate to the HLM program in general from the CDC, and then which building companies will actually receive the loans. Some variations of the HLM program offer higher or lower interest rates to other builders of nonprofit housing; the lower the interest rates, the lower the rents in this housing.

Aidé (Other Assisted). About 40 percent of the annual housing starts are under *aidé* programs. *Aidé* is middle-income housing financed by a variety of government loans and loan guarantees. Guarantees are most frequently handled through the *crédit foncier* (mortgage land bank).[42] Under these programs, developers' profits are limited to around 6 or 7 percent in exchange for the lower rates at which they can borrow with the government guarantee. Another source of funds for *aidé* housing is a 1 percent payroll tax on companies with more than 10 employees.

Nonaidé (Unassisted). One-fourth of new housing is *nonaidé,* upper-income housing built without government assistance. This category includes luxury apartments in the center and single-family homes in the suburbs.

The French system for housing development again reflects the delicate balance that exists among the government, local authorities, and the private sector. As the source of funding for three-fourths of the na-

tion's housing, the government controls the amount of new housing and who will build it. The government, however, does not directly control the location of new housing by type of financing. Once a builder has received the government's financial support, he can build on any piece of land he owns or leases as long as the project conforms to the local master plan. The exact site selected will, to a large extent, depend on the ZAC agreement reached with the local authority concerning the distribution of the costs of site preparation.

In the new towns the EPA planners negotiate with individual builders to secure the desired types of housing. The Sixth National Plan established targets for the amount of *très-aidé, aidé,* and *nonaidé* housing in the nine new towns. For the 1971–1975 period, the plan called for the construction of 40.2 percent *très-aidé,* 51.7 percent *aidé,* and 8.2 percent *nonaidé.* For the 1976–1980 period, the Seventh Plan established targets of 29.5 percent *très-aidé,* 64.4 percent *aidé,* and 6.1 percent *nonaidé.* New-town planners have sought to match those targets by negotiating with an appropriate combination of developers.

The biggest problem has been the attraction of unassisted housing for upper-income families. Table 4 shows the actual distribution of housing starts among the three basic types in the five Paris new towns, compared to the goals and the Paris region as a whole.

Although housing starts have lagged behind the objectives in the new towns, the effort has been impressive, as Table 5 shows. About 183,000 dwelling units were started in the nine new towns between 1971 and 1975, 51,000 of which were in the five Paris new towns. Low-income, nonprofit housing developers have been particularly eager to locate in new towns because the lower land costs will result in a lower rent being passed on to the occupants.[43]

Table 4   Distribution of Housing Starts by Type of Financing in the Paris New Towns, 1971–1975 (%)

Type of Financing	Goal	Reality	Paris Region[a]
Très-aidé (low-income)	40.2	30.6	31.2
Aidé (Middle-income)	51.7	65.1	43.0
Nonaidé (upper-income)	8.2	4.3	25.8

[a] For the years 1969–1972.

Sources: France, Préfecture de la Région Parisienne, *La Région Parisienne: 4 Anneés d'aménagement et d'equipement 1969–1972,* p. 60; France, Premier Ministre, *Programme finalisé des villes nouvelles VIe plan,* p. 13; Groupe Central des Villes Nouvelles.

Table 5   Number of Housing Starts in the French New Towns, 1971–1975

New Towns	Goal	Reality
Paris region	114,790	50,816
Cergy-Pontoise	23,800	10,100
Evry	17,740	10,505
Marne-la-Vallée	23,300	8,584
Melun-Sénart	23,000	4,727
Saint-Quentin	26,950	16,900
Provinces	46,900	32,416
Etang-de-Berre	27,500	20,100
Lille-Est	6,150	6,539
L'Isle d'Abeau	6,750	2,967
Le Vaudreuil	6,500	2,810
Total	161,690	83,232

Source: Groupe Central des Villes Nouvelles.

Most new-town housing is found in high-rise apartment buildings. This is due to a number of factors:

1. Virtually all of the housing is low-cost and government-subsidized.
2. French builders work efficiently at a large scale and can deliver high-rise units at a lower cost than single-family homes.
3. High density is being promoted by planners to foster a lively urban setting.

Nonetheless, the new towns are providing a higher percentage of single-family houses than is normally found in French suburbs today.[44] This effort is designed to attract middle-income families who still usually prefer to live in the center of large cities.

Employment.   Decisions about employment location are influenced primarily by national policies, which are not always beneficial to the new towns. The fear of further economic domination by the Paris region has led to the creation of taxes and quotas for firms locating there. Industries have been moving out of central Paris, as other large cities, because of the difficulties in expansion and the high cost of land. The greatest pressures for location in Paris come from new offices. In addition to the requirement that new businesses secure a permit to locate anywhere in the country, government policy has sought to restrict

new offices in the Paris region through two special programs.

The Restriction of New Office Construction in the Paris Region to One Million Square Meters Per Year.   About half of this total is reserved for single companies seeking to build their own headquarters. The other half goes to the large demand for construction of speculative office buildings, in which no large tenants have been secured prior to development.

The Imposition of Special Taxes for New Firms in the Paris Region.   The Paris region has been divided into several zones. All new firms locating there must pay a special fee, depending on the exact location within the region. Two systems of zones have been developed, one for offices and one for factories. Offices that have received permission to locate in central Paris and the near west suburbs must pay a fee of 400 francs per square meter of space occupied. The rest of the inner area of the region is subject to decreasing rates of surcharges. The outer suburbs, including the new towns, do not have any fees, reflecting the relative difficulty of the outer suburbs to attract offices. In central Paris new factories must pay a fee of 150 francs per square meter; in most of the suburbs the fee is 75 francs per square meter. The new towns charge 25 francs per square meter.

The nine new towns have attracted 71,100 jobs through 1975. As Table 6 shows, this figure is well below the goal established in the Sixth National Plan. For the Paris region in particular, the new

Table 6   Number of Jobs Attracted to the French New Towns, 1971–1975

New Towns	Goal	Reality
Paris region	131,900	45,200
Cergy-Pontoise	35,000	11,100
Evry	30,500	11,600
Marne-la-Vallée	22,400	2,800
Melun-Sénart	20,000	6,300
Saint-Quentin	24,000	13,400
Provinces	51,560	25,900
Etang-de-Berre	34,000	19,400
Lille-Est	7,160	2,600
L'Isle d'Abeau	6,400	2,700
Le Vaudreuil	4,000	1,200
Total	183,460	71,100

Source: Groupe Central des Villes Nouvelles.

towns have had great difficulty competing with the rest of the region, particularly for offices. Nonetheless, the performance is quite substantial at this time. The new towns have sought a long-term balance between the number of jobs and the residents active in the work force. At this time the new towns have achieved a ratio of about six jobs for 10 active residents. This is an achievement of some note for new projects, although additional efforts must be made in the future to bring the employment fully in line with other functions.

Shopping Facilities. The French new towns have been most successful in attracting shopping facilities because the construction of suburban stores has not kept pace with the trends in residential location. Shopping facilities are still concentrated in Paris. Suburban expansion of large department stores and supermarkets started during the 1960s, but strong opposition by small shopkeepers has led to the imposition of restriction on the further expansion of shopping centers in the suburbs. All new ones with more than 1500 square meters must be approved by a department commission comprised of local officials, businessmen in the department, and consumer organizations. These committees have effectively clamped down on small- and medium-sized shopping centers.

A few large subregional centers have been approved, on the theory that the provision of services at this level does not conflict with the small neighborhood business interests. In Paris, for example, the regional officials have implemented a plan that permits the development of 15 regional shopping centers, including one for each of the five new towns under construction. Eight will open by 1976, with three more scheduled to be finished in 1977. Centers have been opened at Cergy-Pontoise and Evry, although neither has reached the planned size.

These large shopping centers are an extremely important design element in the new towns as major components of the downtown areas. The shopping centers are large by United States standards—between 50,000 and 100,000 square meters. Stores are located on different levels, although there is a central covered mall. The centers are designed to simulate the effect of Paris' busy shopping streets. Window-shoppers are encouraged to promenade or sit in sidewalk cafes located along the malls. Recreational facilities such as movies and indoor sports are also located in the complexes. They are connected to offices and other downtown buildings, including parking garages, and they play the most important role in the creation of lively town centers.

The shopping centers are significant generators of income for the new towns. Developers are eager to build the centers in the new towns because of the restrictions on alternative sites. The new-town shopping centers attract customers from a wide area. The first new-town shopping center at Cergy-Pontoise, for example, contains the only department stores northwest of central Paris. When the center opened in 1973 there were 350,000 people living within 20 minutes by car, although fewer than 20,000 were new residents of Cergy-Pontoise. The center is located at an expressway exit and is much closer than central Paris for residents in the northwest quadrant of the region. The Cergy-Pontoise shopping center was built by a private developer on land sold by the EPA. The center makes an annual contribution to the new town based on a percentage of income generated to pay for the management of the parking lots.

With the demonstrated success of the Cergy-Pontoise center, the other new towns have been made more favorable financial arrangements. At Marne-la-Vallée, for example, the EPA negotiated directly with the large Paris department stores. Having obtained commitments from two, the EPA arranged a competition for the rights to attract the smaller stores, construct the facility, and manage it for 70 years, after which it would revert to the EPA or its successor. The first phase of construction included 40,000 square meters of shops and 15,000 square meters of office space. The EPA asked for a cash payment in advance of at least 24 million francs; the high bid was about 80 million francs.[45] In addition, the developer will pay 1 percent of the income generated by the small stores and 0.5 percent of the large ones. These figures will increase to 1.25 and 0.62 percent after 30 years.

CONCLUSION

The French new-town program is still too new for us to reach firm conclusions about its successes and problems. Although the program is now quite large, the effort has been plagued with delays that have arisen primarily because of the conflicting needs and demands of planners, local authorities, and private developers. From a purely quantitative view, the new towns have not yet achieved their objectives, especially in the Paris region, where developers have preferred to build outside the new towns.

Nonetheless, the new towns represent a dramatic improvement over the previous form of peripheral development in France. Compared to the *grands en-*

sembles, ZUPs, and other French projects of the postwar era, the new towns provide a superior living environment. They have more diverse social groups, more shops and job opportunities, better schools and recreational facilities, and more convenient transportation connections than other new projects. Above all, given the immense difficulties in France of achieving any sort of large-scale urban development policies, the fact that the new-town program exists is a success in its own right.

NOTES

1. Several other projects in France could qualify as new towns in the broad sense of the term, including Mourenx, Toulouse-le Mirail, and Hérouville-Saint-Cair. However, these projects are not included in the structure of administration and financing that has been established by the government for the nine new towns referred to here.

2. See, for example, Joseph Spengler, *France Faces Depopulation* (Durham, N.C.: Duke University Press, 1938).

3. See Howard Saalman, *Haussman: Paris Transformed* (New York: George Braziller, 1971).

4. Stephen Cohen, *Modern Capitalist Planning: The French Model* (London: Weidenfeld and Nicolson, 1969), p. 90.

5. The most influential writer on the subject was Jean-François Gravier, whose 1947 book *Paris and the French Desert* aroused public support for decentralization. Gravier documented the long-term trends and showed how public policy had encouraged the domination of Paris. Gravier warned that unless existing policies were changed, France outside Paris would be a cultural and economic wasteland.

6. In 1970 the per capita income in France was about 16,000 francs (about $3200). In the Paris region, the figure was 21,000 francs ($4200). For information about French regional planning policies, see George Ross and Stephen Cohen, *The Politics of French Regional Planning* (Baltimore: The Johns Hopkins University Center for Metropolitan Planning and Research, 1973).

7. See Ross and Cohen.

8. "The DATAR, modeled after the Planning Commission, was deliberately designed not to pose a direct threat to existing ministries. The fact that it was too small in staff and resources and too weak in legal powers to act on its own constituted a fundamental guarantee to the ministries: like the Plan, it cannot replace them; it cannot command them. DATAR cannot become a super-ministry. It must work within the existing structure of bureaucratic competence and power, trying to initiate and coordinate action by other ministries. But unlike the Plan, which developed during a period of weak, unstable governments and strong, independent bureaucracies, and consequently stressed political non-commitment and independence, DATAR was created in a period of strong Gaullist governments. It has been much closer to purely political undertakings than was the Plan in its early days. Though headed by a 'Minister,' DATAR is not an independent ministry. It was attached directly to the Prime Minister's office. The Plan—at various times in its life—had also been attached to the Prime Minister's office. But DATAR's attachment has been more intimate in political terms. Among its other consequences, this close political attachment has been an important source of its influence in dealing with other administrations." Ibid., pp. 19–20. See also Jerome Monod and Philippe de Castelbajac, *L'Aménagement du territoire* (Paris: Presses Universitaires de France, 1973).

9. See Jacques Boudeville, *Problems of Regional Planning* (Edinburgh: Edinburgh University Press, 1966) and Niles Hansen, *French Regional Planning* (Bloomington: Indiana University Press, 1968).

10. The Paris region has also been spatially segregated between the east and west. Population is divided about evenly between east and west, while two-thirds of the jobs are in the west. During the 1960s one-third of the new population, three-fourths of the employment, and four-fifths of the offices were located in the west. See France, Préfecture de la Région Parisienne, *4 Anneés d'Aménagement et d'Equipement* (Paris: Préfecture de la Région Parisienne, 1973).

11. See Jean Duquesne, *Vivre à Sarcelles?* (Paris: Editions Cujas, 1966) and Pierre Merlin, *Les Villes Nouvelles* (Paris: Presses Universitaires de France, 1969), pp. 250–255.

12. The head of La Défense development corporation, Jean Millier, was formerly working with the new-town studies. He has claimed that La Défense is not really in competition with the new towns. However, given the proximity to central Paris and the price advantages, office firms are flocking to La Défense, while the new towns must scramble for them.

13. Delouvrier was with de Gaulle during World War II, helped Monnet create the First National Plan, and served in the Ministry of Finance. Appointed prefect of Algeria by de Gaulle, Delouvrier is credited with playing a crucial role in successfully extricating the French. De Gaulle then asked him to turn his talents to cleaning up the "mess" in Paris.

14. Delouvrier was appointed *délégué général* for the Paris region in 1961. This job was mainly concerned with planning and advising the government. In 1964 a second revision of the Paris regional administration was made. Delouvrier was named regional prefect. The three departments that had comprised the Paris region were divided into eight new ones to serve as a middle tier of local government, with about 1 million inhabitants per department. The communes were not changed at this time. The Paris region is comprised of 1305 communes.

15. France, Ministère de la Construction, *Plan d'Aménagement et d'Organisation Générale de la Région Parisienne* (Paris: Ministère de la Construction, 1961).

16. France, Délégué General au District de la Région de Paris, *Schéma Directeur d'Aménagement et d'Urbanisme de la Région de Paris,* 3 vols. (Paris: Délégation Général au District de la Région, 1966).

17. Ibid., pp. 43–51.

18. Ibid., pp. 64–93.

19. France, Prime Minister, *Programme Finalisé des Villes Nouvelles, VIe Plan* (Paris: Ministére de l'Aménagement du Territoire, l'Equipement, du Logement, et du Tourisme, 1971).

20. Philippe Pinchemel, *France: A Geographical Survey* (New York and Washington: Praeger, 1969), p. 190.

21. *Caisse des Dépôts et Consignations* (CDC) is a national bank established in 1816. The deposits come from savers who bank at their local post office. The funds are used to establish monetary policy (the amount of money circulating in the French economy) and to support a number of national agencies that have the function of loaning money for particular types of projects. *Glossary of French Planning Terms* (Baltimore: The Johns Hopkins University Center for Metropolitan Planning and Research, 1974).

22. J. E. Roullier, *Administrative and Financial Problems of Creating New Towns in the Paris Area* (Paris: Ministère de l'Aménagement du Territoire, d'Equipement, du Logement, et du Tourisme, 1970), p. 18.

23. Ibid., p. 9. The EPA replaced an earlier organization called the *Mission d'Etudes et d'Aménagement* (MEA). The MEA was a task force appointed in 1966 or 1967 by the prime minister for each of the new towns. The MEAs were limited to the research and study functions. MEAs did most of the work on the master plans for the new towns. However, the MEAs could not buy or sell land.

24. Ibid., pp. 20–21.

25. Interview with Paul Delouvrier.

26. Roullier, p. 23.

27. The exact boundaries of the new towns can be rather confusing. There are a number of definitions in use: (1) Study area—the area considered by the MEA during the initial planning efforts, (2) The area of concern for the EPA, (3) The area of concern for the SCA, (4) The territory that will be urbanized—that is, where intensive development efforts will be concentrated. When the planning documents are studied, the MEA or EPA boundaries are used; when the administrative boundaries of the new towns are referred to it is the SCA area.

28. Roullier, p. 29.

29. An example is the automobile industry, which includes the nationalized Renault and the private Chrysler, Peugeot, and Citroën.

30. The *Loi d'Orientation Foncière* (Law concerning the orientation of land development).

31. Préfecture de la Région Parisienne, Etablissement Public d'Aménagement de la Ville Nouvelle de Melun-Sénart, *Schéma Directeur d'Aménagement et d'Urbanisme Rapport* (Paris: Etablissement Public d'Aménagement de la Ville Nouvelle de Melun-Sénart, 1973), pp. 4–5.

32. In 1974 there were 73 master plans being prepared or approved in the Paris region alone, nine of which are for the new towns. This covers about one-half of the territory and two-thirds of the population of the Paris region.

33. "The Urban Development Scheme or SDAU defines the main lines of action and the Ground Occupation Plan or POS gives them legal form; the SDAU guides, while the POS specifies; the SDAU announces, but the POS schedules." (*Urbanisme* **42**, No. 138 (1973): IV.

34. There are about 360 communes currently developing a POS in the Paris region, with another 100 where work is set to start.

35. Yves Brissy, *Les Villes Nouvelles* (Paris: Editions Berger-Levrault, 1974), pp. 68–76.

36. Brissy, pp. 81–84.

37. France, Ministère de l'Aménagement du Territoire, de l'Equipement, du Logement et du Tourisme, "Tableau de Bord 'Villes Nouvelles'" (Paris: November 1973).

38. The ZAC system replaces the ZUPs (*Zones d'Urbanisme en Priorité*). In the ZUP procedure the local authorities received financing from the appropriate ministries to develop the services required in designated zones of concentrated new urbanization. The procedure failed for two reasons. First, the ZUP did not provide for mechanisms of coordination with private developers. Second, the ZUP could only be initiated if the commune met financial guarantees. Virtually all communes were unable to meet the financial requirements before a ZUP could be approved. (Brissy, p. 79.)

39 Ministère de l'Equipement et du Logement, Circular 69–67, June 4, 1969, p. 3 (my translation).

40. Public-private cooperation has also taken other forms, although the ZAC system is the one used in almost every case. Among the other possibilities are the following:

1. The sale of land equipped with a covenant to respect. This is the simplest method and does not differ from the transfer of land in any other situation where some sort of planning control is retained. This method is only possible where the market is sufficiently strong.
2. Association from the time of studies. In certain cases where very large-scale projects are envisioned private developers are brought in to assist with the advance planning. At Marne-la-Vallée several developers contributed to the creation of the master plan, specifically the financial feasibility studies. At Saint-Quentin-en-Yvelines the future urban center, including residential and commercial space, was the subject of a study by a group of private financial experts.
3. Competitions. Competitions have been held at Evry, Marne-la-Vallée and L'Isle d'Abeau for the creation of housing projects.

41. Private profit-making builders will also build nonprofit low-income housing in France. The reason is that by agreeing to construct a certain number of nonprofit units the private developer could receive permission to build a large profit-making project.

42. See Ann Louise Strong, *Planned Urban Environments* (Baltimore: The Johns Hopkins University Press, 1971), p. 359.

43. In the Paris region as a whole, about 100,000 housing units have been started per year. The Paris new towns attempted to secure over 20 percent of the total. Instead, they have achieved less than 15 percent.

44. The percentage of single-family houses being built in the Paris new towns is as follows: Cergy-Pontoise 29; Evry 33; Marne-la-Vallée 32; Melun-Sénart 46; Saint-Quentin 25. Total: 31. In the Paris Region: 19.

45. The specific method of computation of the asking and received prices may be of interest. The following table shows the way the figures were derived:

Marne-la-Vallée Shopping Center

Function	Area (m²)	Price Asked	
		Francs/m²	Total (francs)
Shops	40,000	400	16,000,000
Offices	15,000	200	3,000,000
Piazza	2,000	2500	5,000,000
Total			24,000,000

Function	Area (m²)	Price Received	
		Francs/m²	Total (francs)
Shops	40,000	1660	66,400,000
Offices	15,000	550	8,250,000
Piazza	2,000	2700	5,400,000
Total			80,050,000

BIBLIOGRAPHY

Boudeville, Jacques. *Problems of Regional Economic Planning.* Edinburgh: Edinburgh University Press, 1966.

Brissy, Yves. *Les Villes nouvelles.* Paris: Editions Berger-Levrault, 1974.

Clera, Paul. *Les Grands ensembles banlieues nouvelles.* Paris: Presses Universitaires de France, 1967.

Cohen, Stephen B. *Modern Capitalist Planning: The French Model.* London: Weidenfeld and Nicolson, 1969.

Crozier, Michel. *The Bureaucratic Phenomenon.* Chicago: The University of Chicago Press, 1964.

Duquesne, Jean. *Vivre à sarcelles? Le Grand ensemble et ses problemes.* Paris: Editions Cujas, 1966.

Fondation Nationale Des Sciences Politiques. *L'Experience Française des villes nouvelles.* Paris: Armand Colin, 1970.

France, Délégué Général au District de la Région de Paris. *Schéma directeur d'aménagement et d'urbanisme de la région de Paris.* 3 vols. Paris: Délégation Général au District de la Région, 1966.

France, Préfecture de la Région Parisienne. *La Région Parisienne: 4 années d'aménagement et d'equipement 1969–1972.* Paris: Préfecture de la Région Parisienne, 1973.

France, Premier Ministre. *Programme finalisé des villes nouvelles, VIe plan,* 1971. Paris: Ministère l'Aménagement, du Territoire, de l'Equipement, du Logement et du Tourisme.

France, Préfecture de la Région Parisienne. *Schéma directeur d'aménagement et d'urbanisme de la région Parisienne, April 1975.* Paris: Préfecture de la Région Parisienne, 1975.

Glossary of French Planning Terms. Baltimore: The Johns Hopkins University Center for Metropolitan Planning and Research, 1974.

Gravier, J. F. *L'Aménagement du territoire et l'avenir des régions Francaises.* Paris: Flammarion, 1964.

Hansen, Niles. *French Regional Planning.* Bloomington: Indiana University Press, 1968.

Lacaze, J. P. *The Role of the French New Towns in Regional Development and Regional Life.* Paris: Ministère de l'Aménagement de Territoire, d'Equipement, du Logement, et du Tourisme, 1972.

Merlin, Pierre. *Les Villes nouvelles.* Paris: Presses Universitaires de France, 1969.

Monod, Jerome and Philipe Castelbajac. *L'Aménagement du territoire.* Paris: Presses Universitaires de France, 1973.

Pinchemel, Philippe. *France: A Geographical Survey.* New York and Washington: Praeger, 1969.

Ross, George and Stephen Cohen. *The Politics of French Regional Planning.* Baltimore: The Johns Hopkins University Center for Metropolitan Planning and Research, 1973.

Roullier, J. E. *Administrative and Financial Problems of Creating New Towns in the Paris Area.* Paris: Ministère de l'Aménagement du Territoire, d'Equipement, du Logement, et du Tourisme, 1970.

———. *French New Towns and Innovation.* Paris: Ministère de l'Aménagement du Territoire, d'Equipement, du Logement, et du Tourisme, 1973.

Saalman, Howard. *Haussman: Paris Transformed.* New York: George Braziller, 1971.

Spengler, Joseph. *France Faces Depopulation.* Durham, N.C.: Duke University Press, 1938.

Strong, Ann Louise. *Planned Urban Environments.* Baltimore: The Johns Hopkins University Press, 1971.

Zublena, A. *Urban Centers in French New Towns.* Paris: Ministère de l'Aménagement du Territoire, d'Equipement, du Logement, et du Tourisme, 1972.

CHAPTER 7
Danish National Planning Policy

JESPER HARVEST

Denmark has about 5 million inhabitants and an annual population increase of 0.5 percent. With this modest increase, a population of 6 million inhabitants will not be reached until after the year 2000.

Internationally, Denmark is considered to be primarily an agricultural country. Agriculture does still play an important economic role, but most of the working population is now employed in industry and services. Of the 5 million inhabitants, only 1 million live in rural areas, whereas 4 million people are urban inhabitants. The tendency is toward an increase of employment in services and a decrease of employment in manufacturing.

The country is rather small: the area of Denmark proper is 43,000 square kilometers. Of this, built-up areas occupy about 7 percent, while 75 percent is cultivated, and the remaining 18 percent is woods and uncultivated land (see Figure 1). For the size of the country, the coastline is very long, and the sea is less than 100 kilometers from any place in the country. It has many islands. Greenland, also part of Denmark, has an area of 2 million square kilometers. From the point of view of planning, it is interesting that there is no private land ownership in Greenland, but the inhabitants have long-term rights of use.

Denmark is a representative democracy. Parliament has one chamber with 179 members. Local government consists of 14 county councils and 277 municipal ones. As a general rule, physical planning is decided by both municipal and county councils.

Evolution of Settlements. Denmark is an old country that has been inhabited and cultivated continuously for more than 1000 years. The old subdivisions and roads are still traceable and form an important basis for the present pattern. In medieval times most of the population lived in villages for cooperation in farming and protection against intruders.

Land was the source of wealth. Much of the land was owned by the Church, but with the Reformation in 1536, the king confiscated most of its property. The great farmers became the nobility who gathered more land and were the ruling class for centuries. The nobility resided on their lands, first in fortified houses and gradually in more luxurious castles, many of which are now tourist attractions.

Towns developed slowly. Some of them were based on serving a royal castle. To forward their growth, the king granted the towns rights of trade and forbade this right to other parts of the nation. A far-reaching reform of land ownership and farming methods was initiated by noblemen with foresight who formed the royal government in the latter half of the eighteenth century. Hitherto farmers had all been in villages and their land scattered in the outlying areas so that each had a part of the good soil, a part of moorland, and so on. At this time land was gathered in units suitable for one farm, and the farmers moved to the land. As a result, the old village pattern was broken. Along with the agricultural reforms, a public school system was introduced in the beginning of the nineteenth century.

New farming methods and a beginning specialization and industrialization gave a basis for the beginning growth of towns that became very marked in the last quarter of the nineteenth century. As a result of

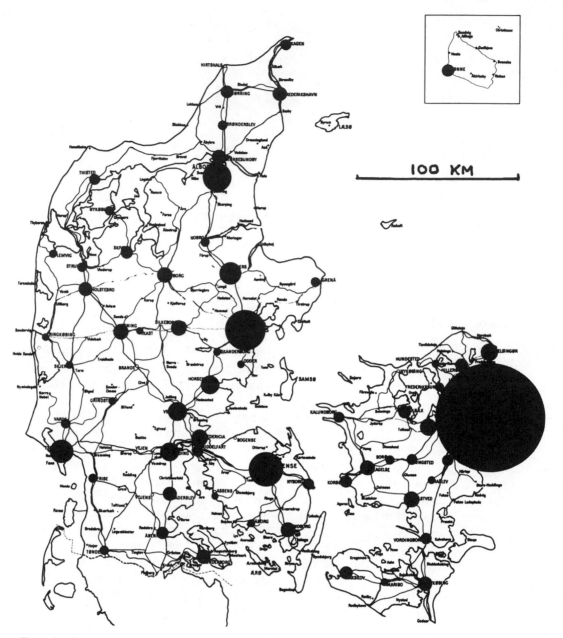

Figure 1. Comparative sizes of Danish towns. The largest circle is Copenhagen with approximately 2 million inhabitants.

inexpensive grain obtainable from America, traditional farming was not profitable anymore. Farming was then changed from grain cultivation to animal feed production, which for a long time proved to be more profitable than grain cultivation and gave the basis for an important export of bacon and butter, primarily to the English market. The famous cooperative movement was a necessary part of this development. The farmers united and formed still existing cooperative dairies and societies for the purchasing of feed.

With the expansion in farming, the towns grew as service centers for their surrounding farming areas. Most towns developed around existing smaller towns. There were many towns because distances were difficult to overcome when it was necessary to be able to travel between town and the farm by horse and carriage in one day.

The railways of the nineteenth century were established primarily to connect existing towns. This new method of inexpensive, fast transportation, along with industrialization, not only resulted in further growth, but also in massive rebuilding of the existing towns that continued until World War I. A few new towns were built in connection with the establishment of the railway system in a period of growth and optimism. Many buildings that later would have been considered important to preserve were replaced by new ones. Buildings of this period still constitute the bulk of old parts of towns.

The rural districts were also changed. As a result of a war with Germany in 1864, Denmark was reduced in size. This was compensated for by the cultivation of moors and difficult soils that had not been used for production. Because of an even distribution of farming and population and the limited possibilities for overcoming distances, a large number of moderate-sized towns were developed. With so many towns, it was not realistic later to think of establishing new towns to any large extent.

The Growth of Copenhagen. Copenhagen has always enjoyed a special position in the country. The town was established and grew as a natural trading place at the entrance to the Baltic Sea. Centrally placed in the old Danish monarchy, Copenhagen was easily accessible by sea. It was chosen by the king for his residence, and as a result of a war in 1658 when the citizens successfully defended the town, it enjoyed special privileges. For the glorification of himself and the country, the king built palaces and initiated and regulated the erection of large districts.

The town grew with the expansion of central government. In 1850 Copenhagen, with 100,000 people, was much larger than any other town in the monarchy. With subsequent industrialization and economic development, the town experienced a rapid growth in population. Large working-class districts were built over a short period, especially after the 1880s, and by World War I the town had about 700,000 inhabitants. Growth has continued, and the Copenhagen region now has more than 2 million inhabitants.

In the past decade, however, growth has been moderate. There has been a marked decrease in the number of inhabitants in the older parts of the region, primarily in the Copenhagen municipality. This is a result of a higher standard of living: middle class families have acquired a taste for more spacious quarters available in suburban settings.

With a more moderate national increase in population, higher costs of buildings, and more difficult transportation, there has been a tendency toward stagnation in the number of inhabitants for the region as a whole. The increase has instead taken place in middle-sized towns, those with 30,000 to 50,000 inhabitants.

DEVELOPMENTAL POLICY

At the time of rapid urban growth in the nineteenth century, there was very little planning. Industry and housing became integrated, which often caused nuisances near the dwellings. The acceptance of the need for planning was caused by the existence of unhealthy living conditions. The first law dealing with town planning was passed in 1924. It was, however, too early to provide public authority over privately owned land, so the law proved to be ineffective. A new, more effective law that is still the basis for the planning system was passed in 1938. The implementation of this law was interrupted, however, by World War II. With more experience, planners found it necessary to use a more flexible planning system than was originally intended. The law and the Danish administrative system were sufficiently flexible to allow such an evolution.

Because of its larger population and more rapid growth, urban problems occurred especially in Copenhagen. Thus most Danish planning laws have been initiated because of the capital's problems.

By the time of World War II Copenhagen had grown so much that transportation by the existing tramway system was too difficult; it took too long to reach the center of the city. As the town spread out, it became impossible to provide all districts with this public transportation.

During and immediately after the war, a small group of planners worked out the famous Fingerplan agreed upon by local authorities in 1947 (see Figure 2). Development according to the Fingerplan should take place in corridors along systems for both private and public transport. There should be no urban development between the fingers because the areas here should be used for recreation for the adjoining urban corridors.

To implement the Fingerplan it was necessary to establish planning powers and distinguish between rural and urban use. Such powers were obtained with the Urban Development Act in 1949. According to this act, special committees were authorized to set limits for urban development. Originally this limit had a duration of 15 years. In 1970, however, the system was changed in principle to prescribe permanent limits. The system was created especially

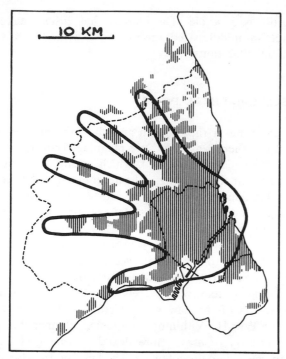

Figure 2. A simplified version of the 1947 Fingerplan. It shows existing development and future urban growth in corridors along with roads and public transport.

for the Copenhagen situation; gradually it was enforced in other parts of the country. With the 1970 reform, the system was made national. At present, then, the whole country is divided into separate urban and rural zones; the change of an area from rural to urban zone can take place only according to a plan. Such a change in zoning is followed by certain tax increases for the area. The background for the adoption of a system covering the whole country was a beginning of national planning. One of the first results of this national planning was a zone plan in 1962, which showed both acceptable locations of future urban development and areas where freedom from urban development was desirable because of scientific or aesthetic values (see Figure 3).

With the purpose of forwarding natural conservation, more detailed planning was adopted, and today there exists for the entire country a record of landscape values that are considered important to protect.

Otherwise national planning mostly has been realized in the form of development plans for single sectors. There is on-going planning for the national and regional road network. The state railways have carried out a perspective plan for the improvement in

services up to the year 1990. The state railways are responsible not only for the national rail services but also for the regional passenger services in Copenhagen and for a number of important ferry routes to many islands.

With the introduction of national planning, a regional development policy also emerged. Certain differences between the living conditions in the various parts of the country existed. Average wages were higher in Copenhagen and the larger towns than in the rest of the country. Unemployment was more common in the west and south; in these districts there were fewer possibilities for high school education, and the hospitals and public facilities were not well equipped. A law on regional development was passed in 1958. According to it, the government can grant certain financial aid to promote the location of private industry in the development areas (see Figure 4). Establishing more areas of employment will give a basis for growth in existing towns and a gradual realization of equal living conditions throughout the country. An active national localization policy has not yet been practiced, but it is possible by moving certain government functions from Copenhagen and establishing new public facilities in the development areas.

In connection with a reform of local government in 1970, adequate public services everywhere in the country were also considered. The number of counties and municipalities was reduced to create administrative units with a sufficiently large population to support management, schools, hospitals, and other public amenities. The number of counties was reduced from 23 to 14 and the number of municipalities from over 1200 to 277.

Beginning in 1974 national and regional physical planning has been realized according to a separate law. The planning system is different from that known in other countries because it is realized in a continuous process of cooperation between the municipalities and counties. Furthermore, regional planning begins with proposals from each municipality. Each county is responsible for deciding a number of alternatives for a regional plan. This plan has to be negotiated with the municipalities, and as a new action, the regional and municipal councils have to hold discussions with the general public about the goals and contents of the regional plan before a final proposal can be formulated.

Regional plans must be approved by the central government, which can also issue certain guidelines for regional planning, but cannot work out a national

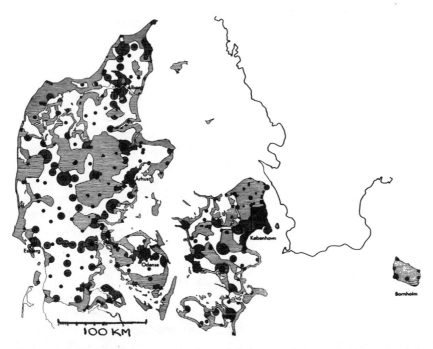

Figure 3. Zoneplan 1962. Existing and future urban development is shown as dark area. Shading indicates landscape values.

plan as such. This system leaves the development to the decision of the local authority. For the Copenhagen region, which covers three counties as well as central Copenhagen, there is a special regional planning agency.

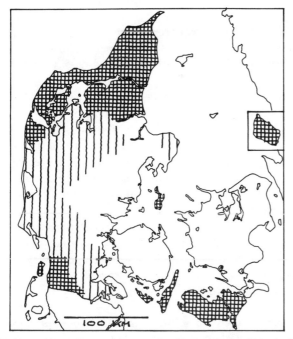

Figure 4. Regional development areas. Financial state aid is obtainable for new industries within the indicated districts.

PLANNING IMPLEMENTATION

For a long time, planning was considered primarily an architectural skill. After the isolation of Denmark during World War II, new influences came, above all, from Great Britain. When the British new towns began to emerge, Danish architects and planners admired and studied them. The idea of beginning a new society on virgin soil was attractive to many planners. A town could be created without unhealthy dwellings and the traffic congestion that began to appear as the private car came within economic reach of much of the population.

New towns are considered to be independent, self-contained communities with minimum commuting and attractive neighborhoods with school and shops within walking distance. The ideal, however, was more difficult to reach in a small country with many existing towns, a limited population growth, and strong local self-government.

The most ambitious idea for a Danish new town was for a large town to be built in the west of the country as a center to counterbalance Copenhagen in the east. With a location between the three existing towns of Kolding, Vejle, and Fredericia, planners thought of a new regional and national center. However, none of the existing towns in the region wanted to stop their individual growth in favor of the new idea. There was no political or organizational basis for a new town. The practical application of the idea became some housing districts with inadequate local services and long distances to work.

In general it is the policy of the municipalities to expand their existing towns. The delineation in 1970 of the new municipalities was in fact carried out so that each town was completely within one municipality and so that each municipality should preferably have one main town. Lately some municipalities have considered more moderate growth in their main town in favor of controlled growth in the villages, with the aim of securing a better basis for the local school and services, which are in danger of being closed.

A Danish municipality can, if necessary, expropriate land for the purpose of building roads, preserving open green space, constructing schools, and initiating other public works. A plan can designate the location, density, and use of buildings on privately owned land. If necessary private development can be legally deferred until adequate infrastructure can be provided. A municipality, however, cannot decide if and when development is to take place unless it also owns the land. Many municipalities purchase land with the purpose of securing a supply of adequate sites, especially for housing and industry. If an owner wishes to sell vacant land within the urban zone, he must offer it first to the municipality, which then has the option of buying it.

Decisions about establishing and running industries, shops, and many local services are made almost entirely within the private sector. The main method of influence available to the municipality is to work out plans and carry out development with regard to infrastructure, which is sufficiently attractive to the private sector.

Køge Bay Regional Development. In Copenhagen the Fingerplan indicated that most development was to take place towards the western "thumb." This development on virgin soil most closely resembles new towns elsewhere. The area suitable for development was within eight municipalities and two counties. The existing local authorities and the limited number of inhabitants did not give a sufficient basis for a new, large development.

These circumstances led to the adoption of the Køge Bay Area Planning Act in 1961. According to it, the government appointed a special committee to assist the municipalities in providing a basis for development and to coordinate urban planning, both physically and functionally. Physically, the Køge Bay

development is a new town. Functionally, it is a part of the Copenhagen region.

The task turned out to be more difficult than expected; coordination was especially difficult to obtain, and the necessary state investments for roads and public transport were delayed again and again. In the long run, however, the plan was successful. The development is certainly much better than what could have been expected without the plan. There are 10 urban units along a 30-kilometer span, each with a station along a new railway line. Single units accommodate from 5000 to 24,000 inhabitants. From 12,000 inhabitants in 1960, the population is expected to grow to a total of about 150,000 at the end of the 1980s. Køge Bay consists primarily of housing districts, and the population growth is provided by the growth of the region, especially the thinning out of inner Copenhagen.

The plan provides for adequate open green space, a differentiated road system, and a separate system of foot and bicycle paths. The railway stations with their shopping centers are at the natural junctions of the system of paths.

Houses are placed suitable distances away from the noise and fumes of major roads (see Figure 5). Earth walls are built along the west motorway to screen traffic noise. The walls are designed to give motorists a pleasing view, and the inner slope is harmonized with the buildings behind. The landscaping is coordinated with the traditional vegetation of the region.

Because the urban area is long and narrow, there is only a short distance to the open countryside and coast. Waterfront land is reclaimed over a stretch of seven kilometers to provide a basis for watersport activities. Among other facilities there will be moorings for a total of about 5400 boats.

The most notable deviation from the original plan involved the local centers, which were to be sprinkled throughout each urban unit. Because of larger shopping units and general economic development, all the desired local shopping facilities could not be provided.

Because development was considered to be sufficiently well advanced and a new regional planning authority had been provided with the necessary planning powers, the period of the special planning committee was terminated in 1974.

A New Town as a Regional Development Experiment. Another successful Danish new town from modern times must be mentioned; it is successful in

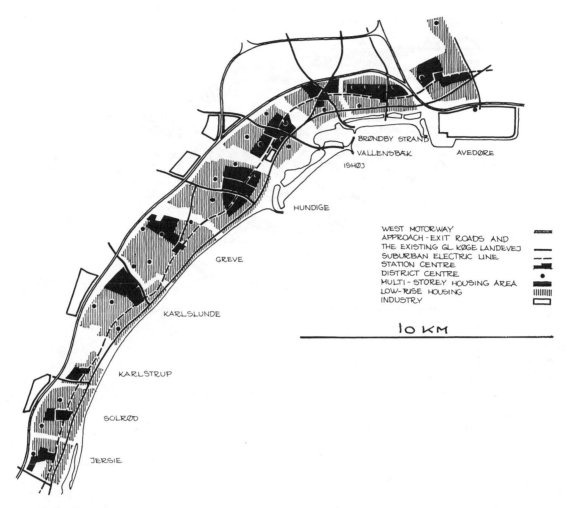

Figure 5. Køge Bay area development plan, final version of 1966. Housing is grouped within walking distance from the stations along the railway.

the same sense that the town is under construction. The town is on the west coast of Jutland where economic difficulties and population decreases have become all too familiar (see Figure 6).

Fishing is the principal natural resource in this district. To promote fishing and settlement, the state, after long discussions, decided to build a new harbor in Hanstholm in the northwest where it would never be bound by ice. The decision was made before World War II; but the erection was delayed, and afterwards the plans were modified. During the war the Germans built a large underground fortress to guard the entrance to the Baltic. Construction on the harbor was started seriously some years after the war, and the harbor was opened after a construction period of about 25 years.

A new town was also planned and is now growing slowly in the hills above the harbor. Planning and erection of the town was carried out with special aid from the state. Land was bought in advance by the public authorities and is leased to the users on long terms. Without land speculation and with favorable interest for the public loans, the inhabitants have received considerable aid.

The town is approaching 3000 inhabitants, and the plan is sufficiently open to allow a much larger town. Further growth is, however, entirely dependent on the possibilities for new industries. The town can be expanded in stages up to a population of 20,000 or more, but it can also function with fewer inhabitants.

Heavy storms occur regularly on the west coast, and the harbor needs constant repairs and improvements. The town itself is sheltered by a forest that is planted around it to the west and north. To make

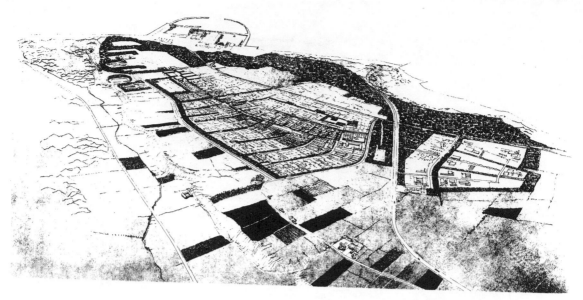

Figure 6. Perspective of the new town and harbor of Hanstholm on the northwest coast of Jutland.

trees grow in this district requires special methods and naturally takes more time than in other parts of the country.

Urban-Rural Dilemma. Apart from the two examples described previously there are no new towns under construction in Denmark. The national policy is aimed at expanding and improving the existing towns; the most recent planning acts show this rather clearly, and the Urban and Rural Zones Act was implemented to protect the open countryside. With the increased mobility afforded by the private car, there is a tendency toward settlement over wide distances from the large towns.

In a small country, if there were no restrictions on where people are allowed to build, the tendencies toward sprawl could easily result in the disappearance of open countryside suitable for farming and recreation. The Urban and Rural Zones Act limits, to a large degree, future urban development to an expansion of the existing towns. It is the municipalities that have the initiative and the necessary possibilities for investing in new urban districts. Zoning of new land for urban purposes is undertaken only when shortages of land occur in the existing towns.

Since the industrial expansion in the nineteenth century, the larger towns, especially Copenhagen, have possessed a fairly large number of old, substandard working-class flats. Such housing has been cause for much social indignation since the 1930s.

In the beginning, there was no doubt that the right solution was to move the inhabitants to new districts with the intention of tearing down the old houses and replacing them with better flats, offices, and shops. However, people living in the older developments did not want to move to outlying, more expensive flats. Construction costs and rents in new flats escalated. As time passed more and more voices were heard in favor of keeping the old, densely built districts. Their original construction was not inadequate, and the houses could be improved with bathrooms and central heating. The former slum clearance policy is now changing to one of conservation and improvement. The old districts are becoming attractive to many people, and the new districts are frequently criticized for lack of friendliness and local services. There seems to be a departure from the belief that a new town can be made much better than the old.

Current Tendencies in Regional and Environmental Planning. The plans for the Copenhagen region are influenced by the previously described experiences. The emphasis is on an open structure for the location of urban development along transport corridors. There is unanimous agreement on keeping the northeastern part of the region free of any further development. The remaining areas will be kept permanently open for farming and recreation. The bulk of the development is directed toward the west where there is land suitable for building. Development will, however, be based on the existing administrative structure with 52 municipalities in the region. Earlier ideas about amalgamating the municipalities have been abandoned. One of the tendencies of the day is toward concern for the local community and the right of local decision making.

The regional plan also indicates some projects that are very serious economically, the most important being the relocation of Copenhagen Airport. The plan also proposes two bridge-and-tunnel connections to Sweden. However, none of these projects is final. More and more politicians are beginning to doubt their necessity and to question the possibility of raising the money for such huge investments at the same time that heavy demands on the social security and educational systems are being made.

The environment and its protection now play an important role. New legislation has been passed with the aim of limiting the pollution of water and air and bringing the noises of traffic and industry under control. The Danish are gradually realizing that such measures will require large investments in the immediate future if decay is to be halted.

FUTURE DEVELOPMENT

The future looks far less optimistic than the postwar period with its steady growth. The present economic difficulties appear to be of a more lasting nature. Denmark has a high income level and standard of living, but it has no raw materials. Higher prices for oil and other sources of energy have been met with programs for conservation. The high-income level brings high costs for establishing new work places and for the upkeep and operation of schools, hospitals, and other institutions. This will leave a narrow margin for large new public investments that will be needed for the protection of the environment.

Population increases are moderate. New develop-

ment is primarily caused by a redistribution of people, expansion of industries and services, and an increased housing standard. There is a tendency toward spreading the population growth to a fairly large number of existing towns, resulting in a moderate increase in each town. Many people prefer living in smaller communities and, by doing so, seek a connection with the past in a world of otherwise rapid change. A return to a former economic balance with small production units is, however, unlikely, and the work places in both industry and services will be concentrated in large units. The rather moderate distances between the various towns, however, does not mean that there will also be a concentration of the population. How far the dispersal of people will go will depend partly on the price for personal mobility. If the price for using the private automobile continues to go up, more commuters will return to the central urban regions.

There are also a number of people who prefer to live in the central parts of the large towns, provided that houses are modernized, open space provided, and traffic noise reduced. The interest in preserving old buildings is also increasing.

At present new-town development does not seem to be an important part of the Danish future. There will be new development but mostly in connection with existing towns. The idea of solving urban problems by building new towns on a large scale is probably an idea that is valid under special conditions and for a limited period only. An important part of the reform of the Danish planning system is that the inhabitants are to be provided with information about the plans and entitled to have their opinions heard before the final decisions are made. This will, I think, result in a greater concern for the existing towns and landscape values. There will probably be resistance to large changes and reduced interest for projects built upon imaginary pictures of a future distant and difficult to reach.

CHAPTER 8

Swedish Urbanization Policy: Contributions of New City Districts

DAVID PASS

The City of Stockholm has demonstrated a responsiveness to the pressures of urbanization and to national policies of the Swedish government. Initial national housing policies, combined with practical, enlightened municipal concerns for physical development to meet the perceived needs of people, were reflected by municipal elected officials and professional staff. During the 1940s and 1950s the city developed new city districts on vacant, municipally owned land, constructed a rail rapid transit system linking the new city districts to the city core, worked within the constraints of national labor market policy, and succeeded in achieving school investment policy recognition of the special needs of new city districts while balancing local public and private sector needs and interests. These accomplishments are best illustrated at the Vällingby development area northwest of the city core and the Farsta development area south of the city core (see Figure 1).[1]

PLANNING AND DEVELOPMENT FOR NEW CITY DISTRICTS

Population studies at the beginning of the 1940s showed that earlier figures for Stockholm were too conservative. The supply of housing in Stockholm had been plentiful during the 1930s. With the coming of World War II, production diminished—ceasing altogether about 1940—and the city began to experience a housing shortage. The national government had stepped up its policy in the housing field through rent control and long-term, low interest loans for new housing construction, in addition to nationally established housing quality norms and national assignment of responsibility to localities to solve housing shortages.

By the 1940s it had become necessary for Stockholm to undertake residential development on a new scale. Previously, small neighborhoods of detached single family homes on their own parcels of land or three-story apartment dwellings had been constructed amid a framework of narrow streets and suburban trolley-car lines with a few neighborhood shops.

Planning for rail rapid transit construction and central business district redevelopment was underway. A June 1945 work plan, *Stockholm in the Future: Principles of the Outline Plan of Stockholm*, for the preparation of a proposed Stockholm master plan distinguished between the requirements for a satellite town and a new city district. A satellite town was to be geographically separated from and external to a large mother city; there must be good transportation between the satellite and the city; and the satellite must have a suitable proportion of employment opportunities and housing.

A city district in social composition would form a Stockholm in miniature. Each district would have a limited number of inhabitants determined with regard to a suitable population size for different

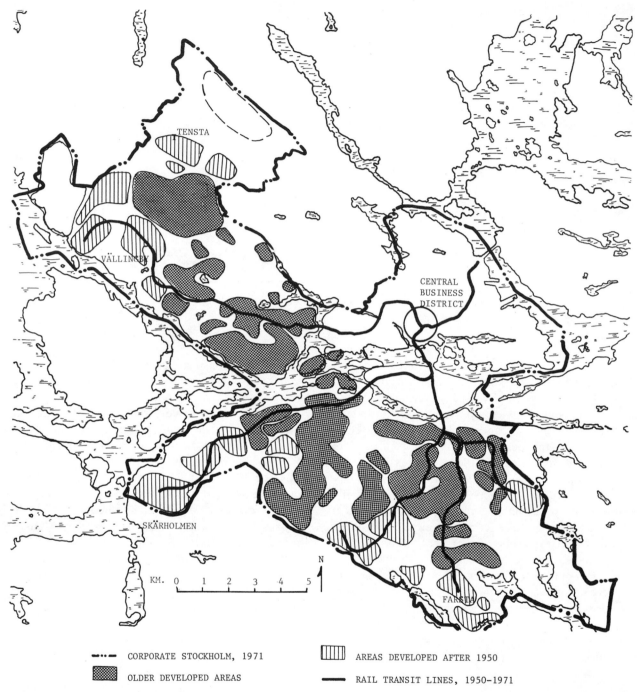

Figure 1. Stockholm's new city districts. Courtesy of Stockholms Stadsbyggnadskontor.

Legend:
- - - CORPORATE STOCKHOLM, 1971
▨ OLDER DEVELOPED AREAS
▥ AREAS DEVELOPED AFTER 1950
— RAIL TRANSIT LINES, 1950–1971

social and common services. Between 10,000 and 15,000 persons was a maximum in relation to a larger Stockholm secondary school. Each district would be provided with its own commercial facilities necessary for the comfort of the inhabitants. There would be a school, day nurseries, laundries, a post of-

fice, library, movie theater, restaurant or coffee shop, community hall, and other shops, all centrally located, in contrast to their scattered location in many existing residential areas (see Figure 2).

The new city district would (1) be a part of the city and a miniature of the entire city, neither a dormi-

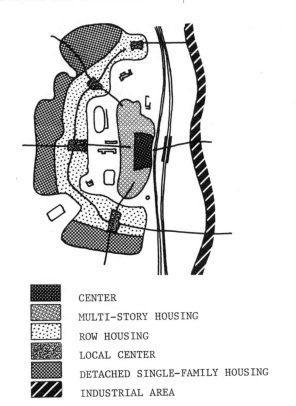

CENTER

MULTI-STORY HOUSING

ROW HOUSING

LOCAL CENTER

DETACHED SINGLE-FAMILY HOUSING

INDUSTRIAL AREA

Figure 2. Conceptual sketch of suburban development area in a new city district of Stockholm. David Pass, *Vällingby and Farsta—From Idea to Reality: The New Community Development Process in Stockholm* (Cambridge: The MIT Press, 1973), p. 118. © The MIT Press. Reprinted with permission.

tory suburb nor an independent satellite, and (2) contain a community center providing social, cultural, educational, retail, and recreational facilities. These principles are reflected in the planning and development of the new city districts of the 1940s and 1950s.

Beginning in 1948 new city districts were developed along rail rapid transit lines extending northwest and south of the Stockholm core; by 1965, 17 had been completed or were nearing completion.

By 1950 it had been determined that 25,000 persons, rather than 10,000 persons, were needed to support a complete range of shopping facilities. One district within each group of three or four new city districts would be singled out to contain an areawide shopping center larger and better equipped than the others. This center would serve both the inhabitants in the immediate vicinity and for the wider area where centers did not provide such a broad range of shops (see Figure 3).

Centers of this size built by 1960 served three different groups of city districts. Vällingby was the center for five other city districts, Farsta for six, Högdalen for three.

Swedish planners developed a hierarchy of different sizes of shopping centers in the new city districts. Here and there within a city district, Neighborhood centers (D centers) provided a small group of three to five neighborhood shops adequate for the needs of 3000 to 6000 people. District centers (C centers) were centrally located in a city district of 12,000 to 15,000 people and adjacent to a rapid transit station and included day-to-day and some specialized shops and short-term parking facilities. Area centers (B centers) provided facilities for a primary clientele of 12,000 to 15,000 and a secondary clientele of 70,000.

By the end of World War II, Stockholm was faced with the government-assigned responsibility of housing large numbers of people. The development of a rail rapid transit system was underway to link what were then considered outlying corporate areas with the city core. Large-scale development for new facilities to meet new needs required large amounts of vacant land, preferably municipally owned and municipally governed.

Southern Spånga, a large area to the northwest, was vacant and municipally owned; by 1949 it was municipally governed. The land was available, and plans that recognized the need for higher-density residential use around the centers located at the transit stations were being prepared. Earlier plans for primarily low-density single family detached dwellings were discarded as too costly to service with public transportation.

Land, governance, land-use plans, transit—now for development. The municipal role over land development had traditionally been a regulatory function of prescribing permitted land use. The city had little control over the timetable for private-sector assumption of new development. Indeed, because of the relative remoteness of the Vällingby development area, the private sector initially was uninterested in undertaking development there. However, the city, which had been acquiring or establishing development companies to aid in meeting residential construction goals, had the development vehicle, particularly in AB Svenska Bostäder, which developed the Vällingby Center.

The general goals advanced by the city council for the new city districts included the possibility of a job near home. In addition to offering a pleasant and convenient way of life, a practical consequence of walking to work was that the city would not have to enlarge municipal facilities further for commuter transport. An early slogan hailed the new city districts as self-contained employment, residential, and recreational units.

In an attempt to implement this goal, a municipal interagency agreement was established in 1952 to give residential priority to persons with jobs in the new development area. Between 1952 and 1958 more than 2000 priority requests were filled, primarily in Vällingby and Farsta. However, in response to increasing demand and an apparent worsening of the housing situation—waiting time almost doubled between 1952 and 1958—further implementation of the agreement was suspended.

To implement a national labor market policy and a location policy the National Labor Market Board was responsible for regulating the use of capital, materials, and labor. Techniques at its disposal included the work permit and consultation between the board and localities concerning plans for urban expansion. All new construction activities were covered—hous-

ing, shops, department stores, roads and streets, schools, hospitals, industries. The major effect of the work-permit requirement was primarily the delay of construction, although board-administered industrial location policy opposed the location of small industries and workshops at Vällingby. The board also generally refused permission for businesses or industries in the Stockholm region to move to Vällingby to expand.

Conditions that contributed to obstruct the realization of the walk-to-work goal included the inability to secure housing in the new city district, national employment location policy, the relative immobility of residents within the Stockholm region due to the housing shortage, and eventually, the rapid expansion in Sweden of car ownership and highways.

Some observers have said that the meaning of the walk-to-work idea was only to create jobs in the area equal in number to about 50 percent of the gainfully employed local residents. In 1965 the Vällingby Development Area contained employment opportu-

Figure 3. New city district center in Skärholmen. Courtesy of Stockholms Stadsbyggnadskontor.

Figure 4. Six-story multi-family housing in the new city district of Tensta. Courtesy of Stockholms Stadsbyggnadskontor.

nities for 54 percent of the gainfully employed local residents. However, only 24 percent of the employed local residents were to be found in these working places; the rest (76 percent) were commuters who worked elsewhere. Of the total number of persons working within the development area, 44 percent also lived there. Results at Farsta were similar; in both cases less than half of the workers walked to their jobs.

As we have seen with labor-market policy, national investment policies and formulas do not always recognize new development situations; however, accommodations are sometimes possible. National capital grants for new school construction, for example, were based upon a standard population formula that reflected the age heterogeneity of Swedish localities. The new Stockholm city districts, however, attracted relatively greater numbers of young families with school-aged children.

Fortunately, Stockholm had a large professional

staff of experts; for to receive the national funds needed, the city had to make and document its case. And while the inevitable delays occurred, an agreement was eventually reached whereby the national school construction funds were made available.

The development of Vällingby Center was accomplished by the public sector, the private sector having been uninterested in committing large resources to an untried and untested idea. With the reports of financial success at Vällingby Center not only meeting but outstripping projections and the information that the city was planning a similar center at Farsta, the private sector marshalled its resources in building, banking, and commerce. At least three nonmunicipal organizations expressed a strong desire to develop Farsta Center. Now that the private sector wanted to participate in the needed investments and commercial development activities, the municipal government, at this time business oriented, was able to recognize the importance of concentrating the reserves of the municipal development companies exclusively in the field of housing (see Figure 4).

CONCLUSION

The development of new city districts during the 1940s and 1950s, and later during the 1960s and 1970s, reflected an enlightened response of a relatively wealthy city to the demands of growth while at the same time renewing its core. Particularly in the first decades, development was believed to be needed and was accepted as a nonpolitical issue. The official process utilized a fairly extensive system of plan and proposal review for advice and comment which included local and national government agencies and established private-sector interest groups. Of importance, however, is that the city has been able to initiate and continue to develop responsible solutions at an appropriate scale to what it has perceived as major growth and urbanization pressures.

NOTES

1. The examples are drawn from research published by the author in Sweden. For further detail, see David Pass, *Vällingby and Farsta—From Idea to Reality: The New Community Development Process in Stockholm* (Cambridge: The MIT Press, 1973).

BIBLIOGRAPHY

Anton, Thomas, "Politics and Planning in a Swedish Suburb." *Journal of the American Institute of Planners* **35** (July 1969), 253–263.

Åström, Kell. *City Planning in Sweden.* Stockholm: The Swedish Institute, 1967.

Holm, Per. *Swedish Housing.* Stockholm: The Swedish Institute, 1957.

Housing, Building, and Planning in Sweden. Stockholm: Ministry of Housing and Physical Planning, 1974.

Larsson, Yngve, et al. *Stockholm Regional and City Planning.* Stockholm: Planning Commission of the City of Stockholm, 1964.

Markelius, Sven. "The Structure of the Town of Stockholm." *Byggmasteren (A.),* Architectural Edition (1956), 71–76.

Ödmann, Ella and Dahlberg, Gun-Britt. *Urbanization in Sweden.* Stockholm: Allmänna Förlaget, 1970.

Physical Planning in Sweden. Stockholm: National Board of Urban Planning, 1972.

Planning Sweden: Regional Development Planning and Management of Land and Water Resources. Stockholm: Ministries of Labor and Housing and Physical Planning and Local Government, 1973.

Popenoe, David. *The Suburban Environment: Sweden and the United States.* Chicago: University of Chicago Press, 1977.

Sidenbladh, Göran. "Stockholm: A Planned City." *Scientific American* **213** (September 1965), 107–118.

Stein, Clarence S. "Stockholm Builds a New Town." *Planning.* Chicago: American Society of Planning Officials, 1952, 56–64.

Strong, Ann Louise. *Planned Urban Environments: Sweden, Finland, Israel, The Netherlands, and France.* Baltimore: Johns Hopkins Press, 1971.

Svensson, Ronny. *Swedish Land Policy in Practical Application: Experience of the Effects of Swedish Land Policy at the Local Government Level—Successes and Failures.* Stockholm: Swedish Council for Building Research, 1976.

CHAPTER 9

Swedish Urbanization Policy: A Critical Appraisal

OLLE BENGTZON

Sweden has been the world leader in housing construction. During the 10-year period 1965–1975, 1 million dwellings were mass produced in accordance with Parliament decisions.

In a small country with only slightly over 8 million inhabitants, this means an annual average of more than 12 new dwellings per 1000 inhabitants. In certain years the number of rooms for housing purposes increased 10 times faster than the population.

PROBLEMS OF PROSPERITY

This unparalleled housing construction, however, has not been without its problems. The society has come to suffer from severe growing pains. Swedish city planning, regarded in many countries as exemplary, nowadays is able to provide some warning examples also. The building fever resulted in a bad hangover.

Urban construction proliferated in Sweden after World War II, and social development has not been able to keep pace with the building cranes.

The Industrial Transformation of Sweden. In half a century Sweden has been transformed from a poor agricultural society into an affluent industrial nation. Until World War I three-quarters of the population still lived by farming and forestry. During the 1970s less than 10 percent are occupied in farming.

The insignificant city population lived in narrow and poor dwellings. Far into the 1930s one room and a kitchen or only a kitchen was by far the most common apartment size in Stockholm and several other cities.

Far-sighted administrators had made it clear early that purposeful city planning is the prerequisite for improving the housing standard. During the 1920s the tenants' organization began constructing well-planned apartments for workers' families and thereby functioned as a prompting force.

Depressions in the period between the wars, however, hit Sweden severely and left little room for improvements. During the war years 1939–1945, housing construction came almost to a standstill in spite of the fact that Sweden stayed out of the war.

The Social Democratic government that had taken over in 1932 had created a committee to study long-term housing policy. In its final report, presented at the end of the war, the committee suggested that a good dwelling ought to be considered a social right and that housing construction should be shielded from all speculative interests. State subsidies were given to both private and public housing projects, but cooperative and local-government-owned enterprises gradually came to dominate the construction of new housing.

As a neutral island in devastated postwar Europe, Sweden started from a favorable position. The manufacturing industries flourished, which resulted in a rapid migration into the cities. Rising income levels increased still the demand for housing.

The construction of new housing could not keep pace with this demand. Thus a housing shortage developed and continued for many years. There were long waiting lists and a black market where even poor and narrow prewar apartments came to be in great demand.

The housing shortage prevented a much-needed restoration of old housing and also triggered a panicky building boom in many fast-growing communities. Municipal housing enterprises were tempted into badly planned construction of oversized buildings on small pieces of land on the outskirts which local governments were able to put their hands on in a hurry. A mechanized construction industry was developed too late, but the sudden appearance of building cranes encouraged high-rise building and severe exploitation even in small communities. The scattered high-rise buildings were never popular; but because of the housing shortage, people were forced to move into them.

Stockholm and a few other cities were better prepared from the start. In contrast to conservative policy in later years, farsighted conservative politicians in power in Stockholm at the turn of the century had arranged for the city to buy a number of large landed estates around the capital.

Thus the city of Stockholm was in control of large areas of land in neighboring communities. During the first part of the twentieth century, Stockholm also arranged a number of city planning contests especially centered on the problems of outer city planning. These contests attracted attention internationally.

Demographic Implications. All this led to the development of neighborhoods comprised of between 10,000 and 15,000 inhabitants and consisting of various types of buildings. Stockholm's authorities were very exacting about layout design and services. The new parts of the city were well provided with schools, leisure facilities, and neighborhood stores. But when it came to finding work opportunities and cultural and social services, they were dependent on the downtown of Stockholm.

THE PROMISING FUTURE: A MODEL OF SUCCESS

During the first postwar years the development continued on the same lines with new development in

an ever-widening circle around the old city core. Not until the creation of Vällingby was the satellite town introduced—the specifically Swedish model that gained world renown.

Vällingby. The Vällingby idea was developed in a clearly purposeful cooperation between socially committed politicians like Dr. Yngve Larsson and Stockholm's well-known city planning director Sven Markelius. Also responsible for the groundwork of the Stockholm 1952 general plan were the two closest collaborators of Markelius, Göran Sidenbladh, who later succeeded Markelius, and C-F. Ahlberg, who became the first regional planning director for Greater Stockholm.

Unlike England's new towns, for instance, Vällingby was not placed far out in the countryside. It was located at a convenient commuting distance from Stockholm—20 minutes by the new subway which was a prerequisite for this kind of new thinking in city building in Stockholm. In spite of the short distance to the city, Vällingby was to be given a large degree of independence and it was publicized as the ABC-city, an acronym of the Swedish words for work, housing, and center.

Vällingby was completed at a relatively slow pace during the 1950s on one of the estates that Stockholm had acquired at an early stage some six miles west of the old city core. Moderately dimensioned and carefully differentiated buildings were fit into the topography of small, undulating hills (see Figure 1).

Minutely planned neighborhoods were grouped around a well-equipped local city which was also intended to serve other parts of the town with all kinds of social, cultural, and commercial facilities. Altogether the plan included some 50,000 people. Vällingby was also furnished with job opportunities both in industries and in administrative offices.

Vällingby came to be regarded—and rightly so—as a model of social city planning and has influenced the construction of new housing in many countries. According to the Stockholm general plan, the ABC-idea was to be developed further in future projects along other subway branch satellite lines.

THE RETROGRESSIVE REALITIES: SOCIAL AND ECONOMIC REVERSES

Vällingby has not been surpassed. More recent city building in Stockholm might rather be considered retrogressive. The reasons are several and concurring. Pressure from the waiting line increased still

Figure 1. Aerial view of a district center in Vällingby reveals a concern for a successfully integrated urban environment: housing, schools, shopping facilities, and places of employment are grouped in a pleasing and effective manner. Photo courtesy of EXPRESSEN Jan Delden.

more in connection with the economic boom during the 1960s. No longer did Stockholm discourage young people—by means of advertising campaigns—from moving into the crowded capital.

Quite to the contrary, local politicians of all parties seemed to be caught with elephantiasis. They were inflated by the optimistic progress of the 1960s and inspired with a religious faith in unlimited growth. Stockholm politicians and economists in their following spoke seriously of a Greater Stockholm encompassing 25 percent of Sweden's popula-

tion and competing with metropolitan areas like Hamburg and the Ruhr.

The big city visions made building extensively and quickly paramount. The appetite grew stronger—not least in the public housing enterprises. Buildings increased in number and in size.

In spite of the fact that planning legislation in Sweden provides society with better instruments for controlling city building than in most countries, to a large extent the construction industry got the upper hand. Both public and private construction enterprises insisted on constructing uniform buildings in large series in order to be able to fulfill the 1-million-dwelling program enacted by Parliament.

The buildings and parts of the town dictated by the contractors lacked social purpose. The lately accomplished mechanization of the construction industry had been dedicated solely to the construction process, not to improving the end product. The great opportunities provided by modern technology and new materials like glass, steel, concrete, and plastics for freely designing buildings in accordance with human needs were not utilized. To the contrary, the old mistakes were repeated and aggravated with the assistance of cranes and other construction machinery. In uniform mass production all the variations and detailed planning still typical of Vällingby disappeared.

The basic discussion of goals, of how to shape the city society, was neglected while construction went on at an increasing pace. City planning and building were left to a large extent to the free play of forces. Sweden became another victim of what Harvard economist Galbraith has referred to as large-scale production's control of the technoeconomic system.

Maximization of profit and profitability became a guiding factor even in state and local administration, and both planners and decision makers were influenced, consciously or unconsciously, by such considerations.

The distance from ordinary people grew both figuratively speaking and literally because of large-scale handling of matters inside and outside public administration. Buildings and parts of the town were shaped no longer in accordance with the needs of future residents but to fit into a given production and administration system.

The people who were to live in the buildings came to be looked upon as a substrate for reciprocally conflicting private and public interests. Housing contractors, traffic companies, retail business, schools, hospitals and other institutions all wanted maximum efficiency heedless of motives other than their own. In this continuous tug-of-war, the combatants lost sight of the whole and of the people.

Early warnings that large-scale production and handling might lead to ruthless exploitation went unheeded by the politicians. They were enthralled by growth; and whenever quality-conscious city planners in Stockholm protested against obvious abuses, the public housing enterprises had only to turn to one of Stockholm's neighboring communities where they were allowed to build as densely, as high and as much as they liked.

Budding discontent among dwellers could be ignored by the housing enterprises as long as the waiting line was endless. They exploited the shortage and had residents move in long before buildings and surroundings were completed. This meant that even ambitiously planned housing developments in Stockholm proper came as horrifying experiences to their first inhabitants.

Tensta. Most notorious of all new housing developments was Tensta, constructed at a hasty pace beginning in the fall of 1966. During the following three years, 20,000 people moved in and found themselves living on a dangerous building site. Often the buildings lacked staircase handrails and lighting, balconies, and plaster on the external walls. There were no sidewalks along the streets. Children were left to play among blast stone and ravenous construction machines (see Figure 2).

All the things which, according to the city plan, were to contribute to protection and well-being had been delayed. For years both children and adults were relegated to an unhospitable stony landscape with no vegetation and no security. Day nurseries, schools, leisure facilities, and other social services were also delayed. The first dwellers would have to wait 10 years for the subway and meanwhile make shift with slow buses reaching their destinations only after several transfers.

Settling in such an unhospitable and insecure environment naturally caused many problems for the many, often young and recently married, homeless couples who had to move to Tensta and other unfinished housing developments. As was to be expected, social workers and authorities began to observe a nascent slum in not yet completed buildings resulting in mentally injured children and stress-ridden adults.

Social workers reported many cases of an epidemic social disease which has been termed "broken child's sickness" by English social-medical experts. It is rife among young, professionally trained mothers who have involuntarily experienced a radical change in their everyday life.

The housing shortages prevented them from choosing their residence; they were forced to accept what they got. Many years' waiting for admittance to day nurseries compelled them to stay home with their children and thus to desist from stimulating companionship at a place of work. Their husbands often took on extra jobs to be able to pay rents and keep cars that were necessary as a means of transportation

Figure 2. Rapid but uncoordinated development at Tensta has made life there uncomfortable—and even dangerous. Planners neglected the importance of exterior space as they raced to complete large numbers of living units. Photo courtesy of EXPRESSEN Jan Delden.

to distant places of work and as an entry in the status race provoked by hard-sell advertising.

The young mothers were left in solitude and became isolated in a strange and dismal environment. Discontent in an apparently hopeless situation released unconscious aggression against the children as being the immediate cause of the change in their everyday conditions. This sometimes led to both physical and mental ill-treatment. Some mothers returned in sheer desperation to their places of work, abandoning even small children without care.

A number of responsible psychiatrists and doctors wrote an official letter warning regional authorities in Greater Stockholm of these developments. They stated that "mental conflicts and disorders among the inhabitants of areas like Tensta are causing serious alarm. Among children such symptoms as insecurity, fear, restlessness, bed-wetting, sleeplessness, violence and shoplifting is common. Sniffing of paint thinner is prevalent among children in their early teens and even at lower ages. . . ."

It is, they claimed, large-scale planning and construction methods that have thrown society out of balance. They urged that alleged but never proved economic advantages of large-scale production be weighed against "human suffering," "human discontent," and "an alarming increase in social aid expenditure."

The concentration of young families—and other families not given any choice—to unfinished colonists' camps lacking in service facilities creates serious conflicts and problems. Children, two or three years old, wander about in bands. The laws of the jungle rule even in the playground, and children at an early age learn how to assert themselves fighting with their fists.

Those who are finally accepted by day-care centers prove to have difficulties in cooperating in group activities. Many of them are unable to stand 12 hours of waiting in the day-care center for parents coming to pick them up after tiring journeys from distant places of work.

Adults feel tormented by their own situation and that of their children. An incessant struggle for work, for a place to live, for space in the day-care center, for a seat in the rush-hour subway train, certainly does not help them create the kind of secure home environment that children need to grow up as free, generous, and positive individuals. With parents who are losers in the competitive race, failure causes indifference, alienation, and anxiety, which of course affects their children in a vicious circle (see Figure 3).

Doctors and psychologists doing field-studies in fast-growing outer parts of the city also observed, with increasing concern, an entirely new type of people emerge: insecure, distrustful, aggressive egoists. The first symptoms manifested themselves in day-care centers and kindergartens. Many preschool children suffered from grave psychic disorders.

Self-assertion and inability to cooperate persists through the school years. People living under an incessant urge for self-assertion have difficulties in appreciating values such as equality, solidarity, and

companionship. The strongest develop into ruthless egoists feathering their nests at the expense of others. The weaker give up or become openly hostile toward society. This may result in a rapid increase both of the number of social dropouts and of crime involving gross violence.

Stockholm, for its part, took a lesson from the mistakes committed in Tensta. Housing development within the city limits is now better coordinated so that the exterior environment—yards, playgrounds, protected pedestrian paths, day-care centers, schools and other public services—is completed at the same time as the buildings.

Neighboring communities as well as several other Swedish cities, however, went on building just as haphazardly and jerkily as before—until suddenly they could no longer find tenants for apartments in unfinished developments. This came as an unpleasant surprise to builders and local politicians who had been convinced by 25 years of uninterrupted housing shortage that almost anything could be let at almost any price.

In the mid 1970s uninhabited apartments in certain areas increased to more than 25 percent. In part this was due to the market being saturated by record-breaking rush building, but the main explanation was that the growth of large city regions did not at all fulfill the expectations of progress optimists in the 1960s. The ever-rising economic boom turned into recession.

Botkyrka.   Hardest hit were those communities outside Stockholm which had counted on unchecked growth and surrendered control of housing to the housing enterprises. In one of Stockholm's neighboring municipalities, Botkyrka, where only 15,000 people lived in the mid 1960s, the public housing enterprises of Stockholm had plans drawn up for a wholly new and decidedly production-controlled high-rise town for close to 50,000 inhabitants. It was constructed in a period of five years. Botkyrka borrowed 75 million kronor for its public investments, expecting to regain 100 million after five years. But instead the debts have grown to 100 million, and social problems are getting worse day by day (see Figure 4).

When the housing shortage eased, consumers on the housing market were able to make their own choices. Everyone who found an opportunity and could afford it moved away from the uncomfortable and monotonous high-rise parts of town which had been constructed at the dictate of building cranes and

Figure 3. A victim of poor planning at Tensta. Photo courtesy of EXPRESSEN Jan Delden.

Figure 4. Monotony of construction at Botkyrka has given a barren quality to the urban environment. The development has experienced serious social and financial reverses. Photo courtesy of EXPRESSEN Jan Delden.

concrete block factories. Left behind are the economically and socially weakest. It will take a long time to rehabilitate many of the areas in communities all over Sweden which were built too hastily during the record years.

The rented apartments involved great losses which brought on a panic among responsible local politicians. Construction of apartment blocks in the whole country dwindled from some 75,000 a year to less than 20,000.

Many communities practically ceased to build multi-family buildings. What came instead was often ill-planned and spread-out construction of one family homes, in many cases far away from city stores and places of work.

THE USES OF THE PAST

Smart manufacturers of family houses deliberately profited by popular aversion to right-angled concrete apartment blocks and began to offer red cottages with white corners, trellis-windows, and front porches. This deliberate emphasis on nostalgia no doubt has been advantageous to the building enterprises but hardly to the buyers.

Areas with thinly spread-out single houses can never provide the public service transport, child care, and shared facilities necessary where overwhelming numbers of parents both go to work. Many new family house areas have been just as haphazardly planned as the high-rise areas of the 1960s and may very soon cause just as serious social problems in the form of alienated stay-at-home mothers or abandoned children.

Upplands Väsby. We can, however, in this picture of capsized city building in Sweden, find some communities where those responsible have listened to consumers and then carefully planned housing in accordance with the needs of the dwellers. Upplands

Figure 5.   More successful planning efforts are seen in Upplands Väsby, north of Stockholm. Development of both internal and external environments has been coordinated to provide residents with harmonious living conditions. Photo courtesy of EXPRESSEN Jan Delden.

Väsby is one of the few municipalities in the vicinity of Stockholm where both ills have been avoided—mighty, large-scale production interests and heavy speculation in single houses.

The publicly owned housing enterprise in the municipality, Väsbyhem, in close cooperation with socially conscious city planners and well-informed tenants, has succeeded in creating comfort and human warmth in newly developed housing areas. Low buildings placed close to each other and with apartments close to the ground provide both freedom of movement and natural community between dwellers (see Figure 5).

The best of traditional construction methods in older Swedish towns have been reinstated in a new form. Streets running between the houses converge on an inviting center. Interior and exterior facilities for education and leisure are shared, which means that more plentiful social service can be offered here than in the large-scale constructed high-rise areas—and at lower rent levels.

Upplands Väsby now can boast the fact that quality social planning is profitable. In contrast with other communities, Upplands Väsby has escaped million kronor losses on account of unhired apartments. On the contrary, there is a line of more than 1000 applicants waiting for their popular close-to-the-ground apartments. Upplands Väsby now attracts more study groups from abroad than Vällingby.

CHAPTER 10

German New Towns: Perspective and Overview

JOHN ROBERT MULLIN

German new towns through the twentieth century have been steeped in controversy. Government, ideology, the iconographic beliefs of the citizenry, physical designs, locations, and purposes have all contributed to this state. Yet the German approach to new towns has also produced several outstanding innovations in the government's role, financing, site selection, planning processes, tenant-selection, and methods of tying new towns into the existing community fabric. Although all of these innovations are worthy of review, very little has been written about them in English. This is due, at least in part, to problems of language, culture, lingering wartime feelings, and a lack of research opportunities. With these points in mind, this chapter is intended to serve as an introduction to the evolution and modern practice of German new-town planning.

Before the evolution of German new towns can be understood, however, it is necessary to define the term *new town* as it is understood in Germany. Several years ago Purdom, in a study of satellite cities in England, noted that the term *Garden City* inevitably lost its precise meaning when translated into other languages.[1] A similar statement can be made concerning the term *new town*. In fact, the word in Germany is used indiscriminately in reference to any large-scale development built under the auspices of a unified authority. There are at least eight settlement forms that can be considered as being new towns. These include the growth point (*schwerpunkt*), the satellite town inside the city-centered region (*satellitenstadt*), the neighboring town (*nebenstadt*), the independent neighboring town (*selbständige nachbarstadt*), the suburban town (*randstadt*), the satellite town outside the urban region (*trabentenstadt*), the ribbon city that ties two cities together (*bandstadt*), and the dormitory town (*wohnstadt*).[2] None of these eight forms can be compared directly with the self-contained new towns of the British experience. In fact, with the exception of Wolfsburg, initially planned over 35 years ago, there have been no provisions made for planning entirely separate, self-sufficient new towns. Instead, each proposed town, regardless of form, is built under regional auspices in a defined relation to a large core city. This approach has been found to be both administratively and sociopsychologically quite successful in Germany (see Figure 1).

HISTORIC EVOLUTION

Long before the formation of the Bonn Republic, Germany had a strong tradition of new-town planning and development. Factors such as the evolution of anti-urbanist ideology, the rapid rise of the industrial city with all its dehumanizing effects, and government support of rural interests intertwined to create an atmosphere that continually sought the development of new towns as a means toward the

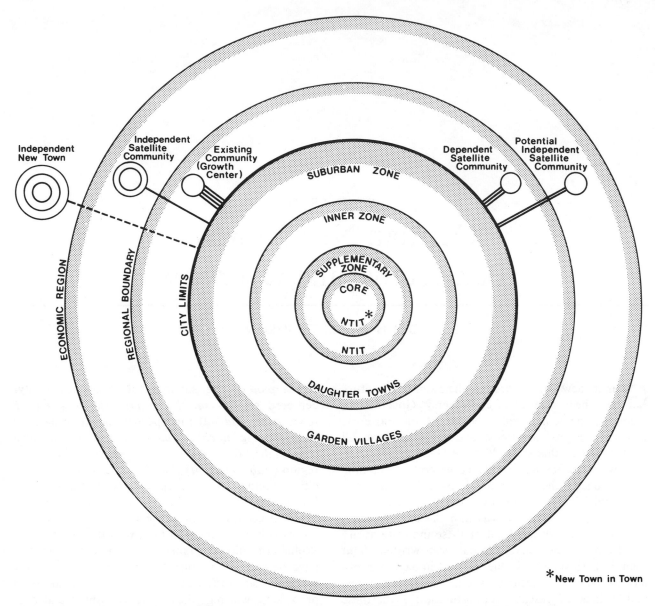

Figure 1.   German new communities: schematic of regional location and association.

creation of a new society.[3] This phenomenon was present in all national German governments from the Bismarckian Era through the Third Reich.

The Bismarckian-Wilhelmian Era.   With the formation of the Bismarckian Reich in 1871 came the economic stimulus that led to a massive shift from an *agrarstadt* to an *industriestadt*. This shift touched virtually every social and economic class in the nation and, in turn, gave rise to an ideological split between the industrially minded urban liberals and the tradition-bound, rural-oriented landowners.[4] This split has had ramifications lasting well into the

present, for ideology has affected virtually all new-town proposals.

Between 1871 and the turn of the century, very few new towns were undertaken. Yet the romantic ideas of Riehl, Langbehn, Lagarde, and Moeller van den Brucke provided a great stimulus for the rejection of the city as an acceptable place to live.[5] They saw the highly stratified society of the fixed-sized *mitte-lalterlichstadt* as being the ideal. In terms of spatial living arrangements, it was essential to these men that each man have his own plot of ground to raise his food and that he live in a small village. The love of the medieval life was also prevalent in the ideas of one of the greatest planning theorists of the period—Camillo Sitte.[6] From the ideas of the ideologists and Sitte came a major impetus for the German Garden City Movement.

Most planners credit Ebenezer Howard as being the main creator of the concept of the garden city, but Theodor Fritsch, a disciple of the aforementioned ideologists, developed a German version in *Stadt der Zukunft* several years before Howard.[7] Fritsch's intention was to save the middle classes from being crushed by the new industrialism and urbanism. Within this focus he developed a scheme for new communities in which the land was to be held in common ownership. The concept was designed to control land speculation, eliminate overcrowding, and return incremental increases in property values to the community as a whole[8] As Mumford noted, in terms of conceptualizing space, there were only minimal differences between the ideas of Fitsch and Howard.[9] Unlike Howard, however, Fritsch did not create any new communities, but several of the ideas he proposed were implemented in new communities developed after the turn of the century. In particular, his ideas could be found in the developments built at Eden, Donnershag, and Sigfried.[10] These new communities were built under a set of utopian guidelines, which included free land, an internal barter system, cooperative buying, and communal living. Perhaps more importantly, from the ideologists came several of the guiding principles under which the *Deutsche Werkbund* was founded in 1907. This organization, far more than any other in Germany, provided the stimulus for the international new style communities of the 1920s and included several of the world's most respected planners and architects.[11]

There were several other new German communities developed prior to World War I that received praise throughout the western world. These included the Krupp "company" communities of Margarethenhöhe and Alfredshof in Essen; the garden village at Gmindersdorf, which was designed by Theodor Fischer, one of the most renowned planners of the period and one of the earliest practitioners of the Garden City approach; Perlach, near Munich, and the Slaughter House Area in Dresden.[12]

None of these was of the scale proposed for Letchworth or Welwyn, and none was part of any realistic policy to relieve the overcrowded conditions of the city. They were simply single attempts to create new settlements that reflected the ideological preferences of the developers and architects. These preferences included a village atmosphere, provisions for farming, and a place where the resident could have his own home, sunlight, green space, and privacy.

While the garden city concepts had little effect in terms of the total population, they represented the housing ideal for the residents of the high-density, vermin-ridden, dank *mietbaracken* structures of the German city.[13] The ideal represented not only an alternative to the evils of urban life, but also the strong desire of the population to find a sense of community in which a feeling of belonging could be attained.[14] This idea, noted by the *Werkbund* before World War I, was an important element of the new settlement policies of the 1920s, was used in the National Socialist resettlement program and has continued to a degree into the present in the creation of satellite communities. Regardless of the type of government in power or the ideological basis of its policies, there has been a continuous movement to build settlements that reflect nonurban values. Dahrendorf has noted this phenomenon in his study of German society: "The large city has never really been accepted in Germany as an environment worth living in. Where writers dealt favorably with city life their works were soon denounced as asphalt literature. . . . This is common in first grade primers and government policy."[15]

To write that Ebenezer Howard's concepts were not accepted would be false. His ideas were eagerly adopted and were a major stimulus to the formal creation of the German Garden City Association in 1904.[16] His influence could also be noted in the ideas and theories of Hermann Muthesius, one of the founders of the *Deutsche Werkbund*. Muthesius had become familiar with the British experience when he was serving as a cultural attaché in the German Embassy. After returning to Germany, he became one of the most active advocates for the use of garden-city principles. In fact, he endeavored to develop the idea of the low-density English cottage settlement in Berlin. However, due to the scarcity of suitable low-cost land for building and the extensive government control held by real estate interests, his concept proved unfeasible. Yet his continuous advocacy of an alternative to the destructive turmoil of the metropolis and his belief that the Berlin-type apartment blocks were a poor substitute for the one-family home did have an influence on future German planning.

Throughout World War I and the anarchy, occupation, and inflation that followed, virtually no major planning of any type was undertaken. However, beginning with the currency stabilization in 1924, the nation again began to plan new communities. These new communities were to affect the entire world.

The Weimar Republic. The Weimar Republic ushered in a new spirit of social well-being. The heavy boot of Prussia had been lifted, and a sense of change had swept the nation. This new feeling stimulated great changes in city planning as well. Nowhere was this more evident than in the development of new communities.

Germany in the mid-1920s had an overwhelming housing shortage caused by increased population and over 15 years of preoccupation with war. To overcome this shortage, drastic measures were necessary. The federal government, saddled with enormous reparation debts, could offer neither financial nor technical assistance to the cities. Thus laws were passed to enable cities to undertake their own planning and finance their own housing. With the power to raise funds, plan, and implement within one organization, several cities took the opportunity to develop small satellite towns on their fringes. Of particular note were Frankfurt-am-Main and Berlin.

In Frankfurt-am-Main small settlements were to surround the city. They were to be separated from the city and from each other by a greenbelt. Each was designed at the lowest construction cost possible without sacrificing sunlight, air flow, green space, farmland, and easy access to the central city. The new settlements had all the characteristics of satellite new towns, including small shopping centers, schools, recreational areas, and community centers. However, the planners saw a much stronger relation between the new areas and the central city than normally existed in satellite towns. In fact, the planners referred to them as "daughter towns," for they were conceived, nurtured, weaned, and developed by a parent city.[17] Perhaps more importantly, these settlements were designed to serve as the nucleus for a new concept of living called *wohnkultur*—that is, the new settlement programs were not designed merely to aid in the housing shortage, but also to serve as symbols of a new society. Ernst May, chief planner in Frankfurt-am-Main, summarized this point as follows: "Our new era must create new forms for both its inner and its outer life . . . and this new style must find its first concrete expression in city planning and in housing."[18] Again, as in the Bismarckian Era, one can point to ideology as being an important criterion in the development of new settlements. May was not alone in his advocacy of this approach.

Indeed, Gropius, Taut, and Le Corbusier were urging similar approaches as well.

One project stands out in the Frankfurt experience as being unique. Called the *Römerstadt*, it is considered by Mumford as one of the best examples of planning in the first 35 years of this century.[19] For the first time in German urban planning, a series of new phenomena was combined to create this unique settlement. The structures were prefabricated, standardized, and internationally styled. The setting was in a green agricultural belt where each dweller could have his own plot. The housing was designed to meet the essential living requirements of the dweller but nothing more. In fact, to minimize costs, even the interior was planned, and functional requirements such as the kitchen facilities and furniture were designed specifically for the project. It was an example of total planning. The new community soon became the object of European study, and in 1931 a course was developed to teach other planners the "Frankfurt System."[20] It also impressed the founders of the Congress of International Modern Architects to the extent that Frankfurt was selected as the meeting place for their conference on housing.[21] In time the Frankfurt experience became a model for similar settlements in Germany and elsewhere throughout the world.[22]

In Berlin during this period, new-town settlements also received great support. Indeed, the Frankfurt experience was both envied and copied by Berlin's urban planners.[23] The new settlements were conceived as satellite garden towns of three-story apartment blocks with extensive lawns and gardens throughout. Constructed along wide thoroughfares and carefully arranged space, the new towns managed subtly to integrate the life of Berlin and its hinterland. Of all the new settlements in Berlin during this period, the *Siemenstadt* (Siemen town), designed by Häring, Scharoun, Bartning, and Gropius, was considered to be the architectural achievement of the decade.[24] Essentially a company town for the Siemens industrial combine, the structures were the ultimate in *neue sachlichkeit* (new objectivity). Stark, flat-roofed, nonornamental, community-oriented, yet set in a garden atmosphere, these structures, built approximately 45 years ago, would still be considered modern today. The complex also represented the ultimate *zeilenbau* (superblock) treatment—a term used by German planners to describe communities in which the site planning and architecture reflected maximum consideration for sunlight, green space, and the free flow of air.[25] Otto

Friedrich summarized the work of these architects when he wrote, "Everywhere that young architects found an opportunity, they started erecting these bleakly rectangular houses and apartment buildings, with white walls and horizontal windows. . . ."[26]

With the coming of the National Socialists, these new-town settlements were labelled as products of a non-Germanic culture, a proletarian social policy, and a Bolshevist political program. Gropius' housing was described as reducing men to collective beings, while May's was described as being fit for geometric animals.[27] In time, the creators of the new *wohnkultur* and *neue sachlichkeit* were forced to flee to England, the United States, Africa, and the Soviet Union.

New Towns and The National Socialists. Hitler's reign brought new policies in the development of new communities. The most basic change was that community self-determinism was eliminated. All planning was nationally centralized. There was a Central Planning Board and a Reich's Research Institute. Regional planning authorities in each district were established to carry out the programs of the Central Planning Board. Experiments such as the Frankfurt *Römerstadt* and the Berlin *Siemensstadt* could no longer be determined by the local planners and their people.

From this change came many policy decisions, based primarily on the romantic medieval, Germanic-Teutonic writings of the ideologues mentioned earlier, designed to create a new Germany. The National Socialists initially attempted to stop the growth of large cities, thwart suburbanization, recolonize the agricultural lands, and create a "peasant class."[28] There was also a recognition of the need to create new settlements to further industrial production. Simultaneously, one could note an attempt to create a move to new village communities and new industrial towns. As with so many of the National Socialist programs, the intention never became a reality. They had focused large propaganda efforts against the *neue sachlichkeit* and initiated a new housing policy, which was supposed to be based upon radically different principles. This policy was short-lived, and the program was never implemented nationally. However, a survey taken in 1972 showed that 27 percent of the German people today still want to live in the type of settlement then proposed.[29] In contrast to May's satellite cities with their rows of apartments, the National Socialists advocated "homesteading," and instead of flat roofs, the open

floor plan, irregular fenestration, and balconies, they urged the re-creation of detached "candy-covered cottage" structures with steep, pitched roofs, shutters, and plain surfaces.

Settlements that were built were usually sited beyond the outer suburbs close to new defense plants. The houses were tiny, having approximately 600 square feet per dwelling. Yet they were placed on large lots where the settlers were expected to be, at least part of the time, truck farmers. One can note the differences between the Weimar and National Socialist approaches in the design of a new town called Goldstein, south of the Main River in Frankfurt-am-Main. The Weimar proposal, although monotonous, employed the latest principles of mechanization and modern technique. It was not implemented, however, because it was judged too expensive, due to the Depression and falling revenues. The design was replaced by a make-work, WPA-type project in which single, pitched-roof dwellings were created in a farm-like setting. If the National Socialist settlements are contrasted with those of the Weimar years, one cannot help but notice how one type has withstood the test of time and the other has not. In Frankfurt, for example, the satellite cities of the Weimar years are still intact and operating as healthy, vital communities. The settlements of the National Socialist Era are, in many instances, completely changed. With a large lot and a small home, the owners naturally started constructing additions to their cottages that were quadruple the size of the original home. The Hausern settlement in Frankfurt-am-Main is an example of this. A person looking at these settlements today would almost consider the basic cottage as the attachment rather than the original house.

Like the small settlements, new industrial towns were an integral part of the proposed resettlement program. The goal of these cities was threefold: to resettle the underpopulated areas of the nation, to further industrial production, and to create space for the development of a German sense of community. The ideal industrial new town was to house 20,000 inhabitants. Their planners believed that only at this size could economies of scale, rural advantages, and urban amenities combine for the benefit of all concerned. There was to be a formal arrangement of traffic and structures. Two main axes would cross in the cental core where the political and government structures would dominate. There was also to be a strict separation of functions. On one side of the axis would be industry, public utilities, and transportation terminals; on the opposite side would be recreational areas, formal plazas, medical facilities, and the cemetery. Housing would be located along the crossarm of the axes.[30]

The ideal would take on a squat, conical shape with a wide base. The importance of the various structures would determine the size and mass of the buildings. In essence, the planners were employing the *stadtkrone* (city crown) idea of Bruno Taut.[31] Each city would have a center to signify its relative importance—that is, the elements of each city would focus upon the center. This center would be scaled according to its importance as a local, county, district, regional, or national government focal point. The theoretical use of a circular instead of a gridiron form was of great significance to the theorists. Only through such an organically derived shape could a sense of community be derived. It united people in a readiness to help and participate in community life (*soziale grundfigur*). Such a concept was a direct repudiation of the row-on-row designs of the Weimar-era planners. Indeed, the National Socialist planners wrote that the straight row (*zeilenbau*) treatment oriented man toward himself, while the circle created communities (*kreisbildendes prinzip*).[32] While this ideal was not fully employed in any new town, elements of it could be found in the industrial new towns called the "Town of the Hermann Goering-Werke" at Salzgitter and in the "Strength Through Joy Automobile Works" town at Wolfsburg.

The Goering-Werke was to be an ideal, highly structured National Socialist community. Proposed ultimately to house 300,000 people, it was originally laid out with an elaborate center. Housing was located in satellite areas and was to be connected to work places by high-speed *autobahnen*. It was never fully implemented but was in part adapted to postwar conditions. Now called Salzgitter, it houses 30,000 people.[33]

The other totally new effort was the "Strength Through Joy Automobile Town."[34] Hitler, very early in his reign, became enamored with the idea of a people's car. He commissioned the automotive engineer Ferdinard Porsche to develop this vehicle, and in 1934 the basic design was ready. Hitler then decreed that a new plant and city be built in the underpopulated, underdeveloped, northern hinterland. Declaring that the city would be "one of the happiest and most beautiful in the world," he laid the cornerstone in 1938 of what was to be another model for a Fascist new town. Under the planning direction of Peter Kolb and advisorship of Albert Speer, the design was truly megalomaniacal in scope. It was to

have been dominated by a Fascist acropolis consisting of party buildings, theater, great hall, and cultural center. This complex was never built. The town did begin to take shape during the Third Reich, but the makeshift housing and barracks-like atmosphere did not meet the expectations of the master plan. The original plan was modified in the postwar period; only then did the Volkswagen city that we know today take form.

As war continued into the 1940s, the planning of cities and settlements of grandiose proportions became increasingly difficult. Plans and projects were constantly downgraded. The number of dwellings constructed dwindled from 115,000 in 1940 to 28,000 by 1944. By 1944 there was a shortage of 11 million housing units in East and West Germany combined.[35] Some Germans, with at least a degree of sarcastic levity upon recalling the government's promise of airy, sunlit homes, concluded: "Well now we have really got houses with plenty of light, air and sunshine!"[36]

The Postwar Era and the Bonn Republic.　The end of the war brought peace, but little else. The cities were wastelands; public and private institutions were destroyed; and little more than planning for food and shelter could be undertaken. Of 10 million homes in West Germany, over 2,300,000 were destroyed. Adding to the housing problem were the more than 13 million refugees who fled to West Germany from the Communist-occupied territories of Europe.[37] Without a fully operating government, legal framework, or sense of social order, meaningful planning became virtually impossible during the Occupation Period. Although the Allied Occupation governments did undertake some planning, the amount and extent were too little, too late. Of their attempts, the proposals of Blumenfeld and Gropius were notable. Blumenfeld's work focused mainly upon the planning process, while Gropius urged a new-town approach to solve the problem of overcrowded, urban-oriented regions. In fact, he advocated a series of new, decentralized, small towns that would be the satellites of other large new towns. These new towns were to be placed where transportation ganglia intertwined.[38] Although elements of both Blumenfeld's and Gropius' proposals have found their way into the German planning experience, there was no direct relation between recommendation and implementation.

Only after 1948 did planning begin in earnest. In that year the German economy began to revive due, largely, to the stimulus of the currency reform. At this time also the occupation governments began preparing to allow the creation of the *Bundesrepublik Deutschland* (Federal Republic of Germany). With the creation of a new government, a booming economy, and a new legal framework, conditions necessary for the need and support of planning were present. Yet very little modern planning of any type was implemented. In fact, the major focus of the planning that did occur was oriented toward restoration and replacement of bombed-out settlements. In terms of a modern approach, Hans Blumenfeld noted that it was as if the entire National Socialist era had not existed, and planning was being undertaken with principles created in the late 1920s.[39]

One key reason for this was that the German people had suffered greatly under a planned society and were quite distrustful of any state interference whatever. This feeling continues today. Indeed, as Wolfgang Pehnt recently wrote: "Any planning measure is regarded with distrust.... Instead of democratizing the planning procedures and replacing poor by better planning, it is planning as such which is condemned. The obvious consequence is not the absence of planning but poor planning."[40] Indeed, as Ernesto Rogers noted, European architects had abandoned hope that they could direct the evermore chaotic and empiric expansion of urban centers.[41]

It is little wonder then that the opportunity for drastic change was resisted. Factors such as haste, lack of building materials, costs, and cultural iconography permeated the planning process to the point that the results were mixed. The new towns that were built in this period owe their origin to the refugee problem. With the over 13 million people flooding the wasted nation, homes had to be found someplace. Military structures were converted to homes and in time to permanent new towns. Traunreut, Espelkamp, and even Sennestadt owe their existence to this beginning.[42]

From this set of conditions the various governments had to develop planning goals and objectives, programs, and funding procedures for an entire nation. The immediate needs of health, safety, shelter, and food had been met. The next step was to move from the recovery and restoration phase to short- and long-term planning. The results of this move represent planning as it is practiced today.

PLANNING

The major aspects of planning are found on four levels in the federal republic: federal planning (*bundesplanung*), state planning (*landplanung*), regional planning (*raumordnung*), and local or town planning (*städtebau*). All have competence in new-town planning, and all at various times have been active in it. The functions of the various levels were clearly and definitively explained in the Federal Physical Planning and Regional Planning Act of 1965 (*Raumordnungsgesetz*).[43]

Federal Role. The federal government's planning functions center essentially upon building and maintaining federal highways and railroads and creating balanced economic growth throughout the nation. While the planning for national auto and rail networks met with little resistance, the balanced growth program was initially quite controversial. This was due in part to the fears of centralized planning. However, the need for such measures was so great that this criticism was soon quieted. This program, called the Regional Development Program, was first developed in 1951. Its intent was to stop the flow of farmers and small-city dwellers from the East German and Czech borders to the big city.[44] From 1945 to 1955 this flow was so heavy that the areas were becoming either depressed or were not keeping pace with other regions. Thus the federal government established a policy to stimulate the economy of these areas by providing funds for the expansion of industry and service centers. The program has been quite successful to date; the flow to the big cities has been greatly slowed, and the smaller centers have been provided with an expanded industrial base and improved service capabilities.

Since 1968 the federal government has focused on single growth centers instead of broad regional development areas. In the 300 designated centers, the public pays up to 25 percent of private investment costs to the investor. This inducement is further increased by additional tax deductions, land cost subsidies, and transportation subsidies. Although no formal evaluation of the program has been made to date, there appears to be an increased sense of stability in the formerly depressed areas.

The performance of the federal government in stimulating the development of housing also has been quite successful through a comprehensive series of grants and subsidies to state, regional, and local governments for funding of approximately 33 percent of all annual housing construction. (In the early postwar years the amount reached 80 percent.) The net result of this participation has been to provide low-income families with acceptable, inexpensive housing.[45]

Unfortunately, the housing assistance programs

reflected a narrow approach to the needs of shelter and contributed to two key planning shortcomings. First, by not insisting on a regional or local planning program as a condition for obtaining housing assistance, large housing developments were allowed to be built without much forethought. In the early postwar years the result was that the cities were rebuilt along the same patterns as before the war. Thus the old town centers were filled in, followed by a ring of settlements at the cities' edges. These surrounding settlements increased to the point where, finally, small independent villages became part of the urban fabric. With little planning machinery and the government's unwillingness to direct or control development, the formerly ordered pattern of German city building was virtually destroyed. Only in 1965, with the passage of the *Rauordnungsgesetz,* was an attempt made to bring this situation under control. Many people believe it was too late.

Second, because of the nature of the approach, the opportunity to combine economic development and housing subsidies into a comprehensive new-community development program was lost. Instead, single programs for housing, industry, and population stabilization were allowed to operate irrespective of the overlapping character of each. Perhaps the key reasons for this were that such sweeping comprehensive measures violated German civic traditions and culture and represented the evil of centralized planning.

German civic traditions are strongly held in most areas of Germany. In fact, regardless of an increasingly mobile society, there is still a strong desire among the German people to maintain ties with the city where they have grown up. This is due mainly to the unique character and flavor of German communities and to the fact that family ties are still important there. Citizens have responded negatively to the absence of unique qualities and family ties in the new towns. Recent studies of the new communities at Neue Vahr in Bremen, Freilassing in Munich, and the Märkisch Quarter in Berlin support this view. The planners simply have not captured the desired flavor and atmosphere of the traditional city. In his study of urban change in Germany, Koschnik discusses the failure of the new-town planners to respond to the German sense of romance and nostalgia about what once was a place of positive memories as a key factor in the recent drift back to the cities.[46] He summarized this point by noting that the most pressing need in developing communities is not in building new ones and ignoring the old centers, but rather in developing the old and new in concert.[47]

Planning literature throughout the 1930s, 1940s, and 1950s regularly endeavored to present the city as a place where roots could not be maintained. This simply is not true. In fact, in a study of the role of "home" in German culture, Lenz-Romeiss found that the city does indeed allow the citizen to develop those attachments essential for community.[48] Further, the study debunked the idea that such proposals as the garden city resulted in improvement in the development of community. Hillebrecht, in fact, has noted that most German cities today have the same densities as those advocated by Ebenezer Howard. The result is a continuing scrutiny of new towns in any form as a means to improve the quality of life.[49]

The lack of a sense of community and belonging has also been noted in "user satisfaction" studies in German new towns. In essence the same "new town blues" syndrome of the British new towns has been noted in Germany, particularly among children.[50] With shaded pedestrian paths, large play areas, and modern equipment, the children still feel relatively bored, regimented, and isolated. Studies undertaken by the Institute of Psychology at the University of Erlangen-Nürnberg have shown that the key to happiness in these new communities is not the new facilities by themselves; it is the sense of freedom that one derives from them.[51]

The federal government has realized the desires of the citizen to live close to the place where he was raised and the importance of maintaining a symbolic, iconic relation between the citizen and his community. These feelings have been incorporated into policy, and thus there has been no attempt to create a large-scale, federally sponsored, comprehensive new-town planning program for unattached communities. Instead, the federal government has allowed the states, regions, and municipalities to decide whether new towns are necessary. State and local governments also decide whether the new towns created will be in the form of separate communities, satellites, or agglomerates. For the areas that desire new towns, the federal government will provide a large portion of funding and professional assistance. However, the major funding and sponsorship rests with the nonfederal agencies.

In the mid-1960s, there was much interest expressed in the Federal Ministry of Physical Planning, Building, and Town Planning concerning active federal participation in new towns. In fact, former Minister Paul Lucke, in explaining a proposed Town Development Act (*Städtebauförderungsgesetz*), which was finally passed in 1971, stated that one of the major tenets was to give active aid to the building of new towns.[52] Yet by late 1973 the then current minister, Dr. Hans Vogel, rejected the new-town idea because it did not relate to the German concept of home and community:

It has taken us a long time to understand that the value of a dwelling is not solely determined by the number of cubic meters in an apartment and that the social context is crucial also. For this reason, we are having second thoughts about satellite towns and about the rehabilitation of large areas. It is very difficult to plan and create a social structure. The Ministry of Town Planning will therefore advocate and fund the preservation and modernization of old buildings that are already imbedded in a social context.[53]

Another important fact that has affected federal policy is the desire of each German family to own its own home. Survey after survey has determined that most German families want to purchase a typical-family, detached dwelling constructed to make the best use of sunlight and to have a small garden and a fence. These desires run counter to the planning of the *avant garde* in the 1920s and the crisis planning following the war. Solving this problem has been a major concern of the federal government, and a solution is becoming even more important with the ever-increasing prosperity of the German people.

The implications of this problem have not become fully obvious to date. By rejecting the separate new-town idea, the federal government has become committed to assisting existing communities. Yet land prices and high-density requirements preclude the development of affordable low- and middle-income, single-family housing. In addition, to satisfy this desire, there would have to be a large increase in federal financial assistance to the municipalities for building infrastructure. This assistance does not appear to be coming. In fact, between 1964 and 1972 private real estate investment increased by 47 percent, while combined public investment increased by 11 percent. This is an ominous trend for the person desiring his own home. Unless there is a major allocation of funds to housing assistance, the possibility of obtaining such a dwelling will become less likely.[54]

The federal government has noted this trend. Minister Vogel's desire to improve and expand existing infrastructure was an attempt to mitigate the trend's negative effects; there is at once merit and question in his approach. On the positive side, the extreme shortage of housing, for the first time since before World War I, has been overcome. Also, in much of the existing housing, essential facilities are lacking.

Over 4 million units lack toilets, 6.3 million lack a bath or shower, 1.9 million have no sewer connection or sanitary waste disposal systems, and over 4 million are more than 75 years old.[55] Thus a switch from a growth program to a qualitative program appears to be quite timely. Yet the major metropolitan areas are expanding in population at a faster rate than other areas of the nation. Areas like Frankfurt-am-Main, Munich, and Stuttgart are expanding at an average of 30,000 to 60,000 people per year.[56] Because of this extreme growth in key areas, the federal policy appears, at least theoretically, to run counter to the need. In fact, the creation of new towns or new communities appears to be a logical answer to the overspill. Unless measures are taken to provide for overspill or to develop entire new towns, the chronic housing situation of the past could again become commonplace in the popular areas of the nation, overcrowding will occur, and all the lessons of the early twentieth century will have been lost.

The net results of the postwar federal policies have been, generally, quite admirable. In some areas, particularly in terms of the quantity of housing, the German experience has been unparalleled. Over 22 million units were built in the 25 years following the war. Further, the various programs of rental assistance and home savings mortgage provide a great stimulus to the home purchasing ability of the common man and to the availability of inexpensive dwellings.[57] Yet the haste with which this was done left deep scars throughout the nation. Opportunities for greatly improving existing cities, for coordinating industrial and home growth centers in depressed areas, and for building new towns to relieve pressures on existing cities while maintaining the established cities' psycho-social-iconic sphere were lost. The future of federal policy and participation is still uncertain. The move toward national qualitative improvement appears to have great validity. Yet unless equal attention is given to the rapidly expanding metropolitan areas and conurbations, the federal government will be ignoring one of the major problems within its jurisdiction.

States' Role. As in the United States, legislative jurisdiction over local municipal government is the responsibility of the 10 *länder* (states). As a result of the *Raumordnungsgesetz* of 1965, the federal government required the states to establish regional planning programs. However, it stopped short of totally imposing its will on the states and allowed them to determine the type, extent, and nature of programs according to their needs. Thus each state has set up its own planning program. For example, only two of the states established comprehensive programs, and only Nord Rhein-Westfalen made provisions for new towns. This is now changing, for as a result of the passage of the Town Development Act of 1971 (*Städtebauförderungsgesetz*), more of the states are taking an interest in new towns. Still there has not been any comprehensive move to focus upon the problems in terms of a combination of existing, agglomerated, and new community settlements. Each of the states, to varying degrees, has established planning goals, objectives, and criteria for the communities in their jurisdiction. Also, they have endeavored to help finance, on a revenue sharing-type plan, many of the projects in the municipalities,

which are accountable to the state through the regions for meeting the goals and objectives and complying with state directions on matters that are of regional and state interest.

Regional Role. Regional planning has long been a tradition in Germany. In fact, regional needs have been taken into account to a greater extent in Germany than in any other European nation. The nation, similar in size to the state of Oregon, is divided into 60 regional planning agencies. Some of these, like the *Siedlungsverband Ruhrkohlenbezirk* (SVR, Ruhr Coal Basin Settlement Association) have existed for over 50 years, while others are still in the planning stages.[58] These regional planning authorities

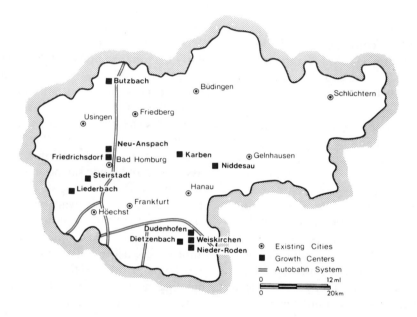

SETTLEMENT GROWTH CENTER	DWELLINGS 1969	PROJECTED 1970–1980	TOTAL CAPACITY
Dietzenbach	12.086	15.000	50.000
Karben	10.787	10.000	50.000
Niddesau	5926	10.000	40.000
Dudenhofen			
Weiskirchen	28.964	30.000	130.000
Nieder–Roden			
Neu–Anspach	5673	5000	30.000
Friedrichsdorf	14.353	10.000	45.000
Steirstadt	6912	5000	25.000
Liederbach	4396	10.000	40.000
Butzbach	10.763	5000	30.000
Total	99.860	100.000	440.000

Figure 2.   The Untermain region.

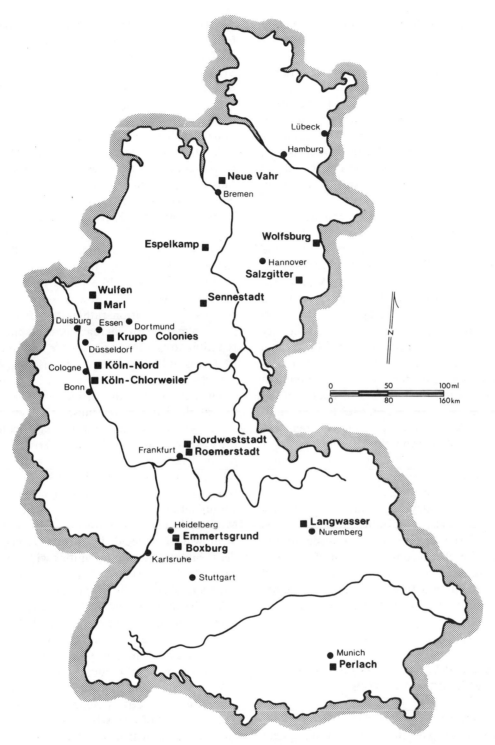

Figure 3. Exemplary new communities in West Germany.

vary in function, but all serve as critics of local planning. They have the right to veto any plan or proposal that does not meet state or regional objectives. This level of planning has been most active in developing new towns. For example, in the Ruhr region there are the new towns of Marl[59] and Wulfen.[60] In the Untermain region there are several growth centers that will become new towns (see Figure 2).[61] In the Westfalen region there is Sennestadt.[62] This level of government also has the greatest authority in legal administration and finance.

Local Planning. Unlike North America, the framework for local planning in the Federal Republic of Germany is uniform, as a result of the *Bundesbaugesetz* of 1960. Functions include zoning and subdivision control, uniform development procedures, and a bill of rights for the owner, buyer, and developer. Inclusive in the law are the procedures for the use, appropriation, consolidation, taxation, and development of land (see Figure 3). One of the key sections of the law is its careful explanation of what is and what is not developable land. Land is divided into three groups: built-up areas, developable areas, and outer areas.[63] In the built-up areas, conformity is the key to new development. A proposed project that conforms to existing construction and development will most likely be approved. Development areas are areas of land through which the city expands. New towns have been built mainly in these areas. The city determines that a certain area is ready for development; it then creates a development plan that specifies the major types of land use and the nature of the infrastructure and sends the plan to the regional office for approval. Outer areas are unsettled areas of the community. Sections of outer areas adjacent to developable areas often change function as time passes. However, those on the edge of the hinterland can only be developed for compatible uses such as forestry, agriculture, or passive recreational land. The resultant success of this program is ordered development. Unlike in the United States, the checkerboard pattern of development is prevented, community facilities and infrastructural requirements keep pace with development, speculation is at least moderated, and harmful land uses are avoided.

GOVERNMENTAL INTEGRATION AND THE FUTURE OF NEW COMMUNITIES

The federal government is not advocating the building of new towns as part of a national settlement policy; neither is it prohibiting their creation by other public planning agencies in the republic. In essence, the government's stand is that major problems have resulted from new towns, and a great degree of caution and study should be undertaken before new towns are built. It has not in any way held back financial aid from those state, regional, and local

agencies that are developing new settlements. Yet the future is uncertain because the *Stadtebaugesetz* (1971) conflicted with the views of Minister Vogel. The *Stadtebaugesetz* does allow the development of separated new and expanded settlements, although Vogel appears to view agglomeration as being of more importance and new communities as being of questionable value.

At the state level only Nord Rhein-Westfalen passed comprehensive new-town planning legislation. This state, through its regions, is now building the new towns of Wulfen and Sennestadt. Because of the lack of federal guidance and the lack of experience of the other states in new-town development, Nord Rhein-Westfalen is becoming a model for the other states as they become increasingly involved in new towns. Ironically, unlike the British experience, the impetus toward new towns is coming from the regions of the nation rather than from the national government. With increasing overspill in the metropolitan areas, the regions have had to employ rapid measures to house and serve thousands of new people per year.

The net effect of the national and regional policies is that the federal government is trying to create a stable settlement pattern in the east while the flow to the west continues. In the short term there will be disparities; however, should the federal policy become effective—and it already has to a degree—the westerly flow will diminish and the need for new communities will become less critical. At such a time Minister Vogel's move toward a qualitative improvement will be a decidedly advantageous measure. In the meantime new communities will continue to be a part of the German settlement fabric. Of these, however, there will be virtually no separate new towns because of the lack of federal support, the scarcity and high cost of land, and the psychosocial factors that create a strong relation between the citizen and his community.

Two forms of new communities appear likely: the growth center and the agglomeration. The federal government is actively supporting the improvement and expansion of infrastructure costs in existing communities. This will mean that it would be easier, in terms of cost, for a region to advocate the fusion of a new section to a city by expanding its water, transportation, and sewage facilities, as has been done in Nordweststadt at Frankfurt-am-Main[64] and in Perlach in Munich.[65] This policy also aids in the expansion of selected growth points. There are now throughout the nation more than 300 designated areas. Although this number at first glance appears large, most of the areas are in the east and are designed solely to stop outward migration. In that regard, perhaps the term *growth point* is a misnomer. However, in the west there are several designated growth points that will indeed take on the characteristics of new towns. For example, in the Untermain region the 10 selected growth points are expected to expand their number of dwellings from 99,000 to 440,000 by the turn of the century.[66]

If the federal growth point policy proves effective, if the regions can funnel their new citizens into carefully planned new or expanded communities, and if the German building trades can continue to build at their present rate of 500,000 units per year, there is reason to believe that an improvement in the quality of community will result. Whether the improvements will be undertaken depends largely on the financial and legal backing of the federal and state governments and the abilities of the regions to understand their needs and to plan accordingly. There are examples where the integration of the various governments, to varying degrees, has resulted in the development of new communities.

Although the integrative efforts of four levels of government to improve the quality of life through the development of various types of new towns is quite admirable, perhaps the unique aspect of the entire experience is the method of implementation. Since the end of the last century a large number of nonprofit companies have been active in building large communities.[67] They have been responsible for approximately 40 percent of all dwelling units built since the war.[68] These organizations are usually backed by a municipality, cooperative, or union group and are given a mandate to build according to the needs of the organization. For example, the *Neue Heimat* organization is financed by the Congress of German Unions,[69] which has authorized the firm to develop regional housing policies and to plan and build new towns. With this authorization, *Neue Heimat* then becomes at various times developer, planner, contractor, and manager of various community-oriented projects. Since the end of the war it has built over 400,000 homes, is managing 332,000 units, has a working fund of 10 million Deutsche marks for city planning, and has been building at the rate of 10 new units per day. The result of this wide base is that the firm is the largest participator in the mortgage market in Germany.[70]

Neue Heimat and other nonprofit building organizations are becoming increasingly involved with new-town planning. For example, when a municipality wants to develop a large satellite new-town project but does not want to increase its debt or raise revenues through taxation, it may select one of these firms to handle the project from conceptualization to implementation. In so doing, the new community is built without constant bureaucratic influence, the parent city is free of management and staff problems, and financing does not become a problem. Further, since these firms are backed by trade unions, cooperatives, and utility organizations and are nonprofit, the city can be sure that the housing will be built as inexpensively as possible and will be designed for the typical worker—the person with the greatest need for improved housing.

One criticism of the marriage between the nonprofit organizations and the city is aesthetic. Since low cost is an important criterion, the company has the mandate to build as cheaply as possible. This means that prefabricated, mass-produced housing is used. Many people are critical of this approach, for a sense of sterile monotony in each of these new settlements is becoming evident. Remarkably similar characteristics are seen on the fringes of formerly unique German cities.

Another criticism centers upon the loss of civic control once approval is given to one of these firms to develop a project. In the larger cities, unfortunately, there has been no choice. Migration has been so rapid and so extensive that they have had little choice but to turn over municipal control to private organizations. These organizations, with extensive financial and management capabilities, are able to undertake large projects with skill, speed, and efficiency. Quite often, when speed becomes critical, quality suffers.

SUMMARY

The development of new communities will be actively pursued in Germany for years to come. Its form will be determined by and large by the growth of the large cities and the success of the growth center strategy. There is no indication that large-scale, independent, self-sufficient new towns will be pursued by either public or private interests. There are indications, however, that satellite dormitory and office towns will continue to expand as a method to accommodate overspill.

One would have to give the German planners great praise for their successes to date. The fact that between 1945 and 1970 they built 13 million dwellings (while between 1918 and 1943 only 3 million were built) represents a great feat.[71] Such major efforts no longer are needed, however, and a switch to an increase in qualitative improvement, as opposed to quantitative improvement, appears quite likely. This switch will ultimately have major ramifications on existing towns and cities and will also serve as a continuing stimulus for new-community development. Whether it is accomplished will depend upon the success of the federal government in developing a dual system to provide assistance to the crowded cities while stabilizing and even increasing the population in the east, on the ability of the states to create comprehensive planning legislation, on the efforts of the regions to coordinate strategies for rural growth points and urban overspill, and on the success of the large cities to build new sections that satisfy demand while improving the quality of life. Although there are still major obstacles to overcome, the future German new-town experience is bright and will in the long run be a major contribution to an improved quality of life for the German people.

NOTES

1. C. B. Purdom, *The Building of Satellite Towns* (London: Dent, 1949), p. 486.

2. These new-town types are explained in detail in Akademie für Raumforschung und Landesplanung, *Handwörterbuch der Raumforschung und Raumordnung*, Vol. 3 (Hannover: Gebruder Janecke Verlag, 1970), pp. 3112ff.

3. See Klaus Bergmann, *Agrarromantik und Grossstadtfeindschaft* (Meisenheim am Glan: Anton Hein Verlag, 1970).

4. Koppel Pinson, *Modern Germany: Its History and Civilization* (New York: Macmillan, 1966), pp. 219ff.

5. These ideas are noted and explained in George L. Mosse, *Nazi Culture: Intellectual, Cultural and Social Life in the Third Reich* (New York: Grosset & Dunlap, 1966).

6. See Camillo Sitte, *City Planning According to Artistic Principles* (New York: Random House, 1965).

7. Theodor Fritsch, *Stadt der Zukunft* (Leipzig: Hammer Verlag, 1902, first published 1896).

8. Thomas Reiner, *The Place of the Ideal Community in Urban Planning* (Philadelphia: University of Pennsylvania Press, 1963), pp. 36–38.

9. Lewis Mumford, *Roots of Contemporary American Architecture* (New York: Reinhold, 1952), p. 351.

10. See Mosse, p. 112.

11. Leonardo Benevolo, *History of Modern Architecture: The Modern Movement*, Vol. 2 (Cambridge: The M.I.T. Press, 1971), pp. 380ff.

12. See P. Abercrombie, "Some Notes on German Garden Villages," *Town Planning Review* (October 1910): 246–250.

13. Thomas Adams described the poor living conditions in German cities in a discussion before the Seventh National Conference on City Planning, Detroit, 1915. He chastised the Germans for developing grandiose schemes while ignoring the living conditions of the masses. See Thomas Adams, "A Discussion on Some Aspects of City Planning Administration in Europe," *Proceedings of the Seventh National Conference on City Planning, Detroit, 1915* (Cambridge, Mass.: Harvard University Press, 1915), pp. 155–166.

14. Felicitas Lenz-Romeiss, *The City: New Town or Home Town* (London: Pall Mall Press, 1973), p. 17.

15. Ralf Dahrendorf, *Society and Democracy in Germany* (Garden City, Doubleday, 1967), p. 50.

16. Akademie für Raumforschung und Landesplanung, Vol. 1, pp. 877–888.

17. Ernst May, *Die Frankfurter Wohnungspolitik* (Frankfurt: International Housing Association, 1929), p. 9.

18. Barbara Lane, *Architecture and Politics in Germany, 1918–1945* (Cambridge, Mass.: Harvard University Press, 1968), p. 88.

19. Lewis Mumford, *The Culture of Cities* (New York: Harcourt Brace Jovanovich, 1970), photo legend 32.

20. Catherine Bauer, "Art in Industry," *Fortune* **3**, No. 5 (1931):95.

21. Gerd Albers, "West Germany," in *Encyclopedia of Urban Planning*, Arnold Whittick, Ed. (New York: McGraw-Hill, 1974), p. 468.

22. Dennis Sharpe, *A Visual History of Twentieth Century Architecture* (London: Heinemann/Secker & Warburg, 1972), p. 113.

23. Lane, p. 112.

24. *Ibid.*, p. 111.

25. Catherine Bauer, *Modern Housing* (Boston: Houghton Mifflin, 1934), p. 182.

26. Otto Friedrich, *Before the Deluge* (New York: Avon, 1973), p. 194.

27. Lane, pp. 164ff.

28. Arthur Schweitzer, *Big Business in the Third Reich* (Bloomington: University of Indiana Press, 1964), p. 202.

29. "Wie die Deutschen Hausen und Wohnen," *Bundesrepublik Deutschland*, 1971, unpaged mimeo.

30. See Christian Otto, "City Planning Theory in National Socialist Germany," *Journal of the Society of Architectural Historians* **24**, No. 2 (1965):70–74.

31. See Bruno Taut, *Die Stadtkrone* (Jena, 1919).

32. Otto, p. 72.

33. See "Town of Hermann Goering-Werke," *Journal of the Town Planning Institute* **26** (January–February 1940):36–39.

34. The entire development process is described in K. B. Hopfinger, *Beyond Expectation: The Volkswagen Story* (London: G. T. Foulis, 1962).

35. Richard Grunsberger, *A Social History of the Third Reich* (London: Weidenfeld & Nicolson, 1971), p. 218.

36. *Ibid.*, p. 219.

37. Robert Wertheimer, "The Miracle of German Housing in the Post-War Period," *Land Economics* **34** (November 1958):338. Also see Federal Republic of Germany, Federal Ministry of Housing, *Housing and Urban Development in the Federal Republic of Germany* (Bonn: Federal Ministry of Housing, 1961), p. 1.

38. Walter Gropius and Martin Wagner, "A Program for City Reconstruction," in *Programs and Manifestos of Twentieth Century Architecture*, Ulrich Conrads, Ed. (Cambridge: The M.I.T. Press, 1970), pp. 146–147.

39. Hans Blumenfeld, "A Review of *New Housing 1940–1950: Planning of Housing Projects*," Hermann Wandersleb and Hans Schossberger, Eds., *Journal of the American Institute of Planners* **20** (1954):48–49.

40. Wolfgang Pehnt, *German Architecture 1960–1970* (New York: Praeger, 1970), p. 11.

41. Ernesto Rogers, "The Phenomenology of European Architecture," *Daedelus* **93** (January 1964):361.

42. Albers, p. 481.

43. For a further explanation of the various planning levels in Germany, see Norman Perry, "The Federal Planning Framework in Germany," *Journal of the Town Planning Institute* **52** (January 1966):91–93.

44. Ulrich Pfeiffer, "Market Forces and Urban Change in Germany," in *The Management of Urban Change in Britain and Germany*, Richard Rose, Ed. (London: Sage, 1974), pp. 45–48.

45. *European Housing Subsidy Systems: An American Perspective* (Washington, D.C.: U.S. Department of Housing and Urban Development, 1972), p. 25.

46. Hans Koschnik, "Politics and Urban Change," in *The Management of Urban Change in Britain and Germany*, p. 211.

47. *Ibid.*

48. See Lenz-Romeiss, "Home: A Symbolic Attachment to Place in the Language of Sociology," in *The City: New Town or Home Town*, pp. 17–47.

49. Klaus Muller-Ibold, "Administration and Urban Change in Germany," in *The Management of Urban Change in Britain and Germany*, p. 174.

50. Lawrence Fellows, "Psychologist's Report Finds New Towns in West Germany Boring to Children," *New York Times* (May 9, 1971), p. 14.

51. *Ibid.*

52. Perry, p. 93.

53. "Federal Republic of Germany: New Minister Discusses Policies," *HUD International Series*, No. 25 (November 5, 1973):1–2.

54. *Ibid.*, p. 2.

55. U.S. Department of Housing and Urban Development, *European Housing Subsidy Systems: an American Perspective* (Washington, D.C. United States Government Printing Office, 1972), a pamphlet published by the HUD Office of International Affairs.

56. Pfeiffer, p. 51.

57. U.S. Department of Housing and Urban Development, p. 29.

58. See E. Kalk, "Regional Planning and Regional Autonomy in the Federal Republic of Germany," in *Regional Planning and Regional Government in Europe*, E. Kalk, Ed. (Den Hag: International Union of Local Authorities, 1971), pp. 223–228.

59. See Justus Bueckschmidt, Ed., *Marl: Geburt Einer Grosstadt* (Hamburg: Verlag der Werkberichte Bueckschmidt, 1957).

60. Fritz Eggeling et al., *Planung Neue Stadt Wulfen* (Stuttgart: Karl Kramer, 1965).

61. For a detailed review of the *Unter-Main* growth centers, see

Carsten Coordes, "Neue Städte nach dem Städtebauförderungsgesetz," *Bauwelt* **63,** Nos. 51–52 (1972):286–292.

62. Hans Reichow, "The Building of Sennestadt," *Annals of Collective Economy* **20,** No. 1 (1959):51–61.

63. Dean S. Rugg, "Selected Areal Effects of Planning Processes Upon Urban Development in the Federal Republic of Germany," *Economic Geography* 42 (1966):322–335.

64. Hans Kampffmeyer, *Die Nordweststadt in Frankfurt-am-Main: Wege Zur Neuen Stadt* (Frankfurt: Europaische Verlaganstalt, 1968).

65. See the section on Neu-Perlach in Shimon Gottschalk, "Citizen Participation in the Development of New Towns: A Cross National View," *Social Services Review* **45** (1971):194–204.

66. Coordes, p. 286.

67. See J. W. Werner, "Trade Union Housing in Western Germany," in *Public Housing in Europe and America*, J. S. Fuerst Ed. (Toronto: Wiley, 1974), pp. 67–87.

68. Heinz Umrath, "Our Housing Record: European Approaches," in *The Right to Housing*, Michael Wheeler, Ed. (Montreal: Harvest House, 1969), p. 288.

69. Werner, p. 70.

70. Josh Moskau, "German Giant with Foothold in Canada," *Globe and Mail* (July 6, 1974), p. 7.

71. Pfeiffer, p. 100.

BIBLIOGRAPHY

Aalto, Alvar. *Alvar Aalto*. Zurich: Verlag Für Architektur, 1963.

Abercrombie, L. "Some Notes on German Garden Villages." *Town Planning Review* (October 1910), 246–250.

Akademie Für Raumforschung und Landesplanung. *Handworterbuch der Raumforschung und Raumordnung*. 3 vols. Hanover: Gebruder Janecke Verlag, 1970.

Arndt, Hans J. *West Germany: The Politics of Non-Planning*. Syracuse, N.Y.: Syracuse University Press, 1966.

Bahrdt, Hans P. *Humaner Städtebau*. Hamburg: Christian Wegner Verlag, 1968.

Bauer, Catherine. "Art in Industry." *Fortune* **3**, No. 5 (1931), 94ff.

———. *Modern Housing*. Boston: Houghton Mifflin, 1934.

Becker, Horst. *Wohnungsbau und Stadtentwicklung: Demonstrativbauvorhaben*. Munich: Facher, 1967.

Berndt, Heide. *Das Gesellschaftbild bei Stadplanern*. Stuttgart: Karl Kramer Verlag, 1968.

"Bielefeld's Nascent Brother." *The Bulletin* (Germany) **6** (1958), 6.

Blumenfeld, Hans. "Notes Submitted to the United States Department of State on the German Housing Problem" (October 6, 1949), xerox copy.

Breckenfeld, Gurney. *Columbia and the New Towns*. New York: Ives Washburn, 1971.

"Bremen's Super Garden City," *The Bulletin* (Germany) **5** (July 1957), 4.

Bucholz, Hans. *Formen Städtischen Lebens im Ruhrgebiet*. Paderborn: Schoningh, 1970.

Bueckschmidt, Justus, Ed. *Marl: Geburt einer Grosstadt.* Hamburg: Verlag der Werkberichte Bueckschmidt, 1957.

———. "Salzgitter: Eine Stadtgründung Unserer Zeit." *Neue Heimat* **6** (1962), 1–12.

Burchard, John. *The Rise of the Phoenix.* Cambridge; The M.I.T. Press, 1965.

Burtenshaw, David. "Regional Planning in the Ruhr." *Town and Country Planning* **42**, No. 5 (1974), 267–270

Christaller, Walter. *Central Places in Southern Germany.* Englewood-Cliffs, N.J.: Prentice-Hall, 1966.

Conrads, Ulrich, Ed. *Programs and Manifestos of Twentieth Century Architecture.* Cambridge: The M.I.T. Press, 1970.

Coordes, Carsten. "Neue Städte nach dem Städtebauförderungsgesetz." *Bauwelt* **63**, Nos. 51–52 (1972), 286–292.

Dahrendorf, Ralf. *Society and Democracy in Germany.* Garden City, N.Y.: Doubleday, 1967.

"Das Raumordnungs Programm des Bundes Muss Politisch Entschieden Werden." *Frankfurter Allgemeine Zeitung* (February 26, 1974), 4.

Despo, Jan. *Die Ideologische Struktur der Stadte.* Berlin: Akademie der Künste, 1973.

Deutscher Verband für Wohnungswesen, Städtebau und Raumplanung. *Urban Renewal in the Federal Republic of Germany.* Koln: A. Etienne, 1966.

Eckardt, Wolf Von. *A Place to Live.* New York: Dell, 1969.

Eggling, Fritz. *Theorie und Praxis im Städtebau.* Stuttgart: Karl Kramer Verlag, 1972.

"Espelkamp-Mittwald." *Aufbau* **13** (1958), 42–49.

Eversley, D. E. C. "New Towns in Germany Too." *Town and Country Planning* **29**, No. 1 (1961), 39–40.

Federal Republic of Germany, Ministry of Housing. *Housing and Urban Development in the Federal Republic of Germany.* Bonn: Ministry of Housing, 1961.

"Federal Republic of Germany: New Minister Discusses Policies." *HUD International Information Series*, No. 25 (November 5, 1973), 1–2.

Fellows, Lawrence. "Psychologist's Report Finds New Towns in West Germany Boring to Children." *New York Times* (May 9, 1971), p. 14.

Feuerstein, Gunther. *New Directions in German Architecture.* New York: George Braziller, 1968.

Fleischer, Michael. *Bielefeld: Bauen und Planen.* Berlin: Landerdienst, 1967.

Friedrich, Otto. *Before the Deluge.* New York: Avon, 1973.

Fritsch, Theodor. *Stadt der Zukunft.* Leipzig: Hammer Verlag 1902.

Gelatt, Roland. "Volkswagen's Next Turn." *Saturday Review World* **1** (January 26, 1974), 12ff.

Giedion, Sigfried. *Space, Time and Architecture.* Cambridge: Harvard University Press, 1967.

Goshko, John M. "Amazing Story of Europe's Lost Nation." *Boston Globe* (August 4, 1974), p. A-3.

Gottschalk, Shimon. "Citizen Participation in the Development of New Towns: A Cross National View." *Social Services Review* **45** (1971), 194–204.

Gropius, Walter. *The New Architecture and the Bauhaus.* London: Faber & Faber, 1935.

———. *Town Plan for the Development of Selb.* Cambridge: The M.I.T. Press, 1967.

Gruen, Victor. *Centers for the Urban Environment.* New York: Van Nostrand, 1973.

Grunsberger, Richard. *A Social History of the Third Reich.* London: Weidenfeld & Nicholson, 1971.

Gutheim, Frederick. "Continental Europe Offers New Town Builders Experience." In *Taming Megalopolis*, Vol. 2, H. Wentworth Eldridge, Ed. Garden City, N.Y.: Anchor Books, 1967.

Hahn, Gerd. "Nürnberg-Langwasser." *Garten und Landschaft* **77**, No. 1 (1967), 15–20.

Hall, Peter. *The World Cities.* London: Weidenfeld & Nicolson, 1966.

Hamilton, Calvin. "If the Germans Can Do It. . . ." *Landscape Architecture* **62** (1972), 216–221.

Hanke, Erich. "Verkehrsplanung einer Neuen Stadt." *Garten und Landschaft* **73**, No. 7 (1963), 220–221.

Hemdahl, Revel G. *Cologne and Stockholm: Urban Planning and Land Use.* Metuchen, N.J.: Scarecrow Press, 1971.

Hever, Jürgen. "Das Wagnis der Neustädte." *Neue Heimat*, No. 8 (August 1959), 1–8, 10–14.

Hillebrecht, Rudolph. *Zwischen Stadtmitte und Stadtregion.* Stuttgart: Karl Kramer Verlag, 1970.

Hollatz, J. W. *Deutscher Städtebau 1968.* Essen: Richard Bacht Verlag, 1970.

———. "West Germany." *Town and Country Planning* **33**, No. 1 (1965), 421–423.

Hopfinger, K. B. *Beyond Expectation: The Volkswagen Story.* London: G. T. Foulis, 1962.

Hormann, Eckardt. *Wohnen in Neuen Gebieten.* Stuttgart: Karl Kramer Verlag, 1972.

"Inside Germany: New Lebensraum." *New York Times* (March 25, 1972), p. 9.

International Congress on Housing and Town Planning. *Die Stadt und Ihr Umland.* Vienna: International Congress on Housing and Town Planning, 1956.

Istel, Wolfgang. "Bundesraumordnungsprogramm: Bedeutung und Aufgabe." *Garten und Landschaft* **83**, No. 10 (1973), 489–492.

Jantzen, Fritz. "Geschaftsstadt Nord-Ein Zeitdokument." *Garten und Landschaft* **83**, No. 5 (1973), 241–244.

Kalk, E. "Regional Planning and Regional Autonomy in the Federal Republic of Germany." In *Regional Planning and Regional Government in Europe*, E. Kalk, Ed. Den Hag: International Union of Local Authorities, 1971.

Kampffmeyer, Hans. *Die Nordweststadt in Frankfurt am Main.* Frankfurt: Europäische Verlag, 1968.

"Karben 1970: Entwicklung der Neuen Stadt." In *Architekturwettbewerbe*, No. 65. Stuttgart: Karl Kramer, 1971.

Kennedy, Declan. "Experiments and Designs for Urban Dwelling in West Germany." *Ekistics* **33**, No. 196 (March 1972), 211–217.

Killus, Heinz. "Der Totalitatsgedanke im Neuen Städtebau."

Monatshefte für Baukunst und Städtebau **24**, No. 4 (1940), 85–88.

Krewinkle, Heinz W. *Heidelberg: Emmertsgrund.* Stuttgart: Neue Heimat, 1971.

Krupinski, Hans-Dieter. "Funf Gemeinden Werden eine Stadt." *Bauen und Wohnen* **26**, No. 9 (1971), 421–424.

———. "Verdichtung in Stadtteilen." *Bauen und Wohnen* **28**, No. 5 (1973), 197–200.

Lenz-Romeiss, Felicitas. *The City: New Town or Home Town.* London: Pall Mall, 1973.

May, Ernst. *Die Frankfurter Wohnungspolitik.* Frankfurt: International Housing Association, 1929.

———. "Kranichstein New Town." In *Planning and Architecture: Essays Presented to Arthur Korn*, Dennis Sharpe Ed. London: Barrie and Rockliff, 1968, pp. 43–48.

Mayhew, Alen. "Regional Planning and the Development Areas in West Germany." *Regional Studies* **3** (April 1969), 73–79.

Moholy-Nagy, Sybil. *The Matrix of Man.* New York: Praeger, 1968.

Mosse, George L. *Nazi Culture: Intellectual, Cultural and Social Life in the Third Reich.* New York: Grosset & Dunlap, 1966.

Mullin, John R. "Incinerator Heating Plant: Element in City Planning." *Military Engineer* **64** (November 1972), 418–421.

Mumford, Lewis. *Roots of Contemporary American Architecture.* New York: Reinhold, 1952.

———. *The City in History.* New York: Harcourt, Brace, and World, 1961.

Neuffar, Martin. *Städte für Alle: Entwurf einer Stadtpolitik.* Hamburg: Wegner Verlag, 1970.

"New Garden City Near Bielefeld." *The Bulletin* **6** (August 5, 1958), 6.

"New Town in Westphalia." *Town and Country Planning* **25**, No. 3 (1957), 117.

Ohl, Herbert "Wohnstadtsystem: Wohnstadt Saarlouis-Beaumarais." *Bauen und Wohnen* **27**, No. 9 (1972), 409.

Otto, Christian. "City Planning Theory in National Socialist Germany." *Journal of the Society of Architectural Historians* **24**, No. 2 (1965), 70–74.

Papageourgiou, Alexander. *Continuity and Change: Preservation in City Planning.* New York: Praeger, 1970.

Pawley, Martin. *Architecture Versus Housing.* New York: Praeger, 1971.

Pehnt, Wolfgang. *German Architecture 1960–1970.* New York: Praeger, 1970.

Pernice, Dietrich. "Raumordnerische und Städtbauliche Überlegungen zur Bildung der Neuen Stadt Bergkamen." *Raumforschung und Raumordnung* **25**, No. 3 (1967), 119–127.

Perry, Norman. "The Federal Planning Framework in West Germany." *Journal of the Town Planning Institute* **52** (January 1966), 91–93.

Petersen, William. "The Ideological Origins of British New Towns." *Journal of the American Institute of Planners* **34** (1968), 160–170.

Pinson, K. *Modern Germany.* New York: Macmillan, 1966.

Purdom, C. B. *The Building of Satellite Towns.* London: Dent, 1949.

Rave, Rolf. *Bauen Seit 1900 in Berlin.* Berlin: Verlag: Keipert, 1968.

Reichow, Hans B. "The Building of Sennenstadt." *Annals of Collective Economy* **20**, No. 1 (1959), 51–61.

Reiner, Thomas. *The Place of the Ideal Community in Urban Planning.* Philadelphia: University of Pennsylvania Press, 1963.

Rickett, Richard. "Die Nordweststadt." *Der Aufbau* **20** (1965), 329ff.

Rogers, Ernesto. "The Phenomenology of European Architecture." *Daedelus* **93** (1964), 337–358.

Rose, Richard, Ed. *The Management of Urban Change in Britain and Germany.* London: Sage, 1974.

Rossow, Walter. "Heidelberg-Emmertsgrund." *Garten und Landschaft* **83**, No. 2 (1973), 56–61.

Rother, Ewald et al., Eds. *Zwischen Rostock und Saarbrücken.* Dusseldorf: Droste Verlag, 1973.

Rowan, Jan C. "New German Town." *Progressive Architecture* **42**, No. 12 (1961), 132–137.

Rugg, Dean. "Selected Areal Effects of the Planning Processes Upon Urban Development in the Federal Republic of Germany." *Economic Geography* **42** (1966), 326–335.

Schlesier, Karl H. *Halle Neustadt.* Berlin: Verlag Für Bauwesen, 1972.

Schmidt, Hans. *Gestaltung und Umgestaltung der Stadt.* Berlin: Verlag Für Bauwesen, 1969.

Schmidt, Karl. *Multi-Story Housing.* London: Architectural Press, 1966.

Schussler, Karl W. "Planung einer Mittelstadt." *Bauen und Wohnen* **25**, No. 9 (1971), 402–404.

Schutz, Otto. *Die Neue Städte und Gemeinden in Bayern.* Hannover: Gebruder Janecke, 1967.

Schulz, Paul O. "The New Town of Wulfen." *Ekistics* **36**, No. 212 (July 1973), 64–66.

Schumacher, Fritz. "Von der Planung einer Neuen Stadt." *Die Neue Stadt*, No. 1 (October 1947), 5–6.

Schwagenscheidt, Walter. *Die Nordweststadt: Idee und Gestaltung.* Stuttgart: Karl Kramer Verlag, 1964.

———. *Die Raumstadt und Was Daraus Wurde.* Stuttgart: Karl Kramer Verlag, 1971.

Schweitzer, Arthur. *Big Business in the Third Reich.* Bloomington: University of Indiana Press, 1964.

Souchon, Fritz. "Espelkamp: Die Entwicklung einer Neuen Stadt." In *Neue Stadte und Slum Sanierung in Deutschland*, H. J. Seraphim, Ed. Koln-Braunsfeld: Müller Verlagsgellschaft, 1959.

Taylor, Robert. *The Word in Stone.* Berkeley and Los Angeles: University of California Press, 1974.

Teut, Anna. *Architektur im Dritten Reich.* Frankfurt: Ullstein, 1967.

"Towards Better More Spacious Homes: 'A Roof Over One's Head' No Longer Considered Sufficient." *The Bulletin* (March 2, 1965), 4–5.

"Town and Country Planning in a Free Society." *The Bulletin* (August 10, 1965), 7–8.

"Town of the Hermann Goering-Werke." *Journal of the Town Planning Institute* **26** (1940), 36–39.

Ulfert, Herlyn. *Wohnen im Hochhaus.* Stuttgart: Karl Kramer, 1970.

Ungers, Liselotte and O. M. "Nordwestzentrum." *Architecture Forum* **133** (October 1970), 31–36.

U.S. Department of Housing and Urban Development. *Country Report: Results of German City Planning.* Washington, D. C.: U.S. Government Printing Office, 1972.

———. Division of International Affairs. *Urban Land Policy: Selected Aspects of the European Experience.* Washington, D.C.: U.S. Government Printing Office, 1969.

U.S. House of Representatives Subcommittee on Urban Affairs. *Report on Housing Development and Urban Planning: The Policies and Programs of Four Countries.* Washington, D.C.: U.S. Government Printing Office, 1970.

Wendt, Paul. *Housing Policy—The Search for Solutions: A Comparison of the United Kingdom, Sweden, West Germany and the United States.* Berkeley and Los Angeles: University of California Press, 1963.

Werner, Johann W. "Trade Union Housing in Western Germany." In *Public Housing in Europe and America*, J. S. Fuerst, Ed. Toronto: Wiley, 1974.

Wheeler, Michael. *The Right to Housing.* Montreal: Harvest House, 1969.

Whittick, Arnold. *Encyclopedia of Urban Planning.* New York: McGraw-Hill, 1974.

"Wie Die Deutschen Hausen und Wohnen." *Bundesrepublik Deutschland*, 1971. Mimeo.

Wittwer, George. "The New Town of Wulfen." In *Financing New Towns: Government and Private Experience in Europe and the United States.* Washington, D.C.: U.S. Department of Housing and Urban Development, 1972, pp. 51–57.

———. "Planung und Realisation der Neuen Stadt Wulfen." *Bauen und Wohnen* **26**, No. 9 (1971), 385–392.

Zahn, Erich et al. *Planung Neue Stadt Wulfen.* Stuttgart: Karl Kramer Verlag, 1965.

CHAPTER 11

Urbanization in Switzerland

DIETER ACKERKNECHT AND WILLIAM R. TSCHOL

Planning tasks and issues and therefore the question of building new towns, do not expose themselves in Switzerland in the same way as in other industrialized countries. In this chapter the particular situation of Switzerland is described because of the different conditions for realizing new towns. Switzerland did not have to suffer the consequences of early industrialization (e.g., slums) and the damage of two world wars. The existing natural beauties and manmade inheritance of a dense settlement structure in a relatively small area led to the problem of ensuring economic and suitable use of the livable space.

Responding to the pressures of a quickly expanding population and economy, especially since World War II, Swiss settlements grew rapidly in an unorganized way in many areas. The need for a coordinated program of urban, regional, and national planning became increasingly apparent. The idea of founding new towns had reached this country following the movements in Great Britain, Germany, and Sweden. Several proposals and attempts to build new towns in Switzerland have been made with moderate success on a smaller scale than in England, France, or Sweden. Today new-town ideas and projects are no longer a point of discussion because growth tendencies have changed; the euphoric enthusiasm that prevailed during the 1960s has faded. Planning is beginning to focus more on the problems of renewal—a relatively late phenomenon in the Swiss context—than on new developments. To clarify the potentials of new-town planning in Switzerland, this chapter presents a few examples of new towns that have been proposed or built in Switzerland since World War II.

A brief background of the socioeconomic, physical, political, and legal conditions as well as planning in general and a short historic review are necessary. Starting from these general facts, we describe the theoretical basis for town planning and urban design, although we focus on the leading ideas and possibilities in Switzerland.

CHARACTERISTICS OF SWITZERLAND IN BRIEF

The Swiss Confederation consists of 25 cantons (states) and over 3000 communities located in a beautiful natural setting (see Table 1). The strong federal form of the state is necessitated by the extreme linguistic, cultural, and topographical diversity of the country. The four official languages, German, French, Italian, and Romanch, express the cultural relations deriving from Switzerland's central geographic location in Europe. For centuries transportation routes of European importance led through the country—for example, via the St. Gotthard Pass. The ideas that are the basis for structural development are influenced mainly by two factors: the cultures to which different parts of Switzerland belong and the special concept of personal freedom and its related responsibility. This concept is expressed, for instance, by the extended autonomy of the communities, particularly in questions of structural development and in the refusal to allow power to be concentrated in a single person or at one level of government.[1]

Table 1   Some Facts About Switzerland

Area Types and Land Use	Area (%) (41,293 km^2 total)
Forest	25
For settlement and intense agriculture	32
Water, mountain pastureland, wasteland	43
Mountain area	51
Valley	49
Built-up land	4

Population	Population (in millions)				
	1850	1950	1960	1970	1975
Swiss	2.33	4.42	4.85	5.19	5.36
Foreigners	0.07	0.29	0.58	1.08	1.04
Total	2.4	4.71	5.43	6.27	6.40

	Average Annual Change in Population (%)		
	Total	Swiss	Foreigners
1850–1950	1.0	0.9	3.1
1950–1970	1.6	0.9	18.7
1970–1975	0.4	0.65	−0.75

Short History of Swiss Settlement.   Before the foundation of the nucleus of Switzerland in 1291, most of its territory belonged to other European countries. The formation of today's existing federation concluded with the declaration of the constitution of 1848.

The country had already been settled around 2500 B.C. The remains of early dwellings are still found on the shores of the numerous lakes. The Romans, who occupied large parts of Europe, had also established towns and military camps in Switzerland. When the Roman Empire collapsed in middle and western Europe, the Teutons from the north conquered the area, and the flowering Roman culture was suppressed because Teutonic society did not favor the Roman lifestyle, and urban culture perished. The form of government did not demand a permanent residence of the ruler; hence a rural culture with single estates, housing groups, and fortifications of defense developed.

Only in the twelfth century were permanent seats of government established that gave the initiative for new urban lifestyles. With the establishment of secular and religious leadership and institutions—for example, seats of government and monasteries—and the development of market and craftsman traditions, the towns again began to play a dominant role. They developed in particular at strategic points on transportation routes. Often these were of Roman origins—for example, Zurich, Geneva, Lausanne, and Basle. In addition, different rulers founded new towns. For example, Berne and Fribourg, were both founded by the Counts of Zähringen.[2] Although we can find only 14 towns that existed at the end of the twelfth century in the German part of Switzerland, the number grew to about 88 towns by the end of the fourteenth century. (A town was defined by its rights—for example, to be a market place, to build fortifications, to coin money.) Many magnificent old downtowns from the Middle Ages can still be admired today, and efforts for their preservation must be expanded.

The form of towns changed essentially with the modifications of the fortifications because of the enlargement of the territory or a change of defensive techniques. The Renaissance and Baroque concepts of urban design had little influence on town planning in Switzerland. An attempt to build a new town named "Henriopolis"[3] in 1626 by the sovereign of Neuchâtel did not succeed. The increasingly democratic system of federal and civil governments in Switzerland favored the independent growth of many towns so that no one was predominant. Zurich, Berne, Geneva, Basle, Lausanne, Lucerne, and St. Gall grew rapidly to their dominant positions of today.

Economic Activity.   Switzerland contains almost no raw materials and relatively few areas are appropriate for intense agriculture. Because Switzerland is land-locked (the only access to the sea is through the Rhine), from the beginning of industrialization business had been concentrated mostly on producing goods that are not associated with high transport costs. Almost no heavy industry has been established. Textile, chemical, machine, watch industries, and construction as well as the service sectors of banking, insurance, and tourism are today's most important economic activities (see Table 2). The economic structure and economic growth in different parts of the country are diverse. In mountain areas tourism has the dominant role.

Recent intense economic growth in Switzerland would not have been possible without the high number of imported foreign working forces (see Table 1). This fact also has a great influence on the housing demand.

Housing Productions. High density building has been common from the time of industrialization. Such density is explicable by the tradition of the dense structure of European cities since the time of the Romans, especially during the Middle Ages with the restricted space inside fortifications. Speculation also played an important role in the nineteenth century. These tendencies were intensified through the ideas of some urban designers and planners, such as Le Corbusier, who glorified and propagandized high-rise housing as a machine for living. The low structural form of the single dwelling and row housing lost more and more importance as dwelling forms, particularly in cities, not only because of the ideologies of urban designers and planners, but also because of economic

and legal circumstances. This situation is changing today for social, economic, and psychological reasons. The dwelling form of the single-family or cluster unit and low structures up to three floors are again in demand. According to current opinion, the floor area ratio for residential areas should be between 0.4 and 0.75.

The configuration of settlements in Switzerland outside the urban centers are predominantly residential structures with one or two floors. Dwellings comprise 61 percent of all buildings, with an average of 2.4 dwellings per building, but most Swiss live in buildings with more than two floors. Only 20 percent live in single family houses.

The high standard of completion for dwellings and the required kind of massive construction partially explains high Swiss construction costs. The form of high-rise housing and the corresponding thinly built-up area do not help to save land compared to the denser but lower form of housing. Single- or low multifamily houses can offer an even better living quality for families.

The number of rooms per dwelling is rising, as it is in the United States. The tendency is toward large dwellings of five or more rooms. Of course, distinction must be drawn among the tendencies in inner cities, agglomerations, and rural areas. In inner cities and new tourist areas, many small dwellings are still produced, partly as second residences. Compared to the situation in the United States, direct dwelling ownership is not common in Switzerland: about 75 percent of dwelling units are rented. The main reasons for the few direct owners of dwelling units may be the high land prices and construction costs. Only with the

Table 2 Swiss Employment, Income, and Prices

Employment		1960 (%)	1970 (%)
Population employed		46.3	47.9
Occupation			
Primary sector (agriculture, forestry)		11.4	7.6
Secondary sector (manufacturing, construction)		50.2	48.3
Tertiary sector (distribution, services)		38.4	44.1
Income and Prices (in Swiss francs[a])	1970	1974	1975
Gross national product (in billions)	94	146	145
Per capita	15,000	22,700	22,600
Change (%)	100		151
Disposable personal income			
Per capita	9,300		14,100
Change (%)	100		152
Cost of living index	100		142

[a] 1 sFr = $0.4 (1976).

1965 and 1974 Federal Housing Acts was government assistance for housing introduced. This legislation should promote housing construction as well as direct dwelling and home ownership by residential financing.

The annual production of dwellings from 1960 to 1970 amounts, on the average, to 60,000 units. During the same period the net increase of dwelling units was 47,000. This could mean more than one new town a year (see Table 3). This high amount of dwelling production is partially due to the establishment of an industry for prefabricated housing. Considering the latest computations, the average annual increase between 1970 and 2000 will be only 23,600 units. The decline of growth in the number of dwelling units can be explained by several facts: slowed population growth, exodus of foreigners, small increase in real income, previous production of dwellings beyond the immediate demand in speculative anticipation of increasing construction costs, land prices, and interest rates.

Compared to those for households, the statistics for second residences are still incomplete. From the statistics on housing production for 1960–1970, we can conclude that the number of second residences per

Table 3   Swiss Housing: Number and Production

	Number of Dwelling Units		Persons per Dwelling
	Existing	Increase (%)	
1850	460,833	100	5.3
1950	1,275,688	176.8	3.7
1970	2,050,483	445.0	3.1
1974	2,468,089	535.6	2.7

1000 inhabitants increased from 13 to 21. Reasons for this tendency during the growth period were increased leisure time and real income of inhabitants from metropolitan areas and foreign countries, as well as the increasing prices of hotels. These investments decline particularly in tourist areas because of the changing economic situation and federal acts against expansion of real estate ownership by foreigners.

Cities and Metropolitan Areas.   As in other countries, we can observe growing urbanization in Switzerland. Metropolitan areas are more attractive than sparsely populated regions and can therefore register

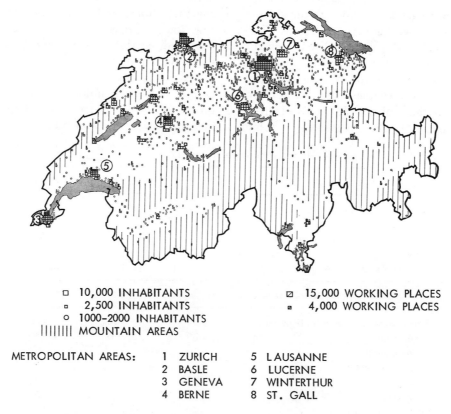

☐ 10,000 INHABITANTS   ☑ 15,000 WORKING PLACES
▫ 2,500 INHABITANTS   ▪ 4,000 WORKING PLACES
○ 1000-2000 INHABITANTS
||||||| MOUNTAIN AREAS

METROPOLITAN AREAS: 1 ZURICH   5 LAUSANNE
                      2 BASLE   6 LUCERNE
                      3 GENEVA   7 WINTERTHUR
                      4 BERNE   8 ST. GALL

Figure 1.   Switzerland: distribution of population and working places (1970).

Table 4 Urbanization in Switzerland

	Urban and Rural Population		
	1950	1960	1970
Cities[a] and agglomerations[b]	1,973,000	2,755,500	3,613,800
%	41.8	50.8	57.6
Remaining communities	2,741,800	2,673,500	2,656,000
%	58.2	49.2	42.2
Total	4,715,000	5,429,000	6,269,800

Density, 1970 (inhabitants per km^2)			
Switzerland		United States	22
Total	150	France	91
Urban areas	1007	Netherland	315
Rural areas	70		

Large Metropolitan Areas[b]
(estimated resident population, 1974)

Zurich	732,100	Lausanne	234,100
Basle	385,000	Lucerne	161,500
Geneva	327,300	Winterthur	110,800
Berne	290,900	St. Gall	91,900

Number of Cities	
Places of 100,000 or more	5
Places of 50,000–100,000	4
Places of 20,000–50,000	22
Places of 10,000–20,000	61
Total, 1974	92

[a] According to the federal statistical office, the statistical definition of a city is a settlement unit with more than 10,000 inhabitants.

[b] The statistical definition of an agglomeration is a physical (spatial) linking up of administratively different settlements, which conform to the following conditions: (1) The (nuclear) central city has at least 10,000 inhabitants, (2) between the central city and any suburban community exists a continuity of structures (buildings), (3) at least one-third of all occupied people of the suburban community commute to the central city, (4) the number of workers of the agricultural sector and their relatives are less than 20 percent of the residents.

the biggest increase of employed persons in industry, crafts, and building industry. Table 4 shows this growth of the population from 1950–1970 in urban centers and their fringes. While the growth in the urban centers themselves slowed down, the urban fringes continued to grow (1950–1970, 64 percent) as expected. This phenomenon has rapidly reduced the land available for recreation near the cities.

Intense growth concentrated in a few places has produced metropolitan areas of formerly economically independent communities. The discrepancy between the political autonomy and the economic dependence of many communities in metropolitan areas is one of the actual urban planning problems. In Figure 1 we can clearly distinguish that most of the agglomerations lie on the axis Geneva-St.

Gall and only a few are farther removed. If this tendency continues, the population living in metropolitan areas by the year 2000 could rise from 58 percent today to 80 percent. The threat of depopulation and its connected economic problems in several regions manifest that many communities lack the proper base for economic growth (see Figure 2). In addition to internal migration, the pressure on the metropolitan areas has increased because of a large immigration of foreigners (see Table 1). This high percentage of foreigners and the restrictive handling of naturalization in Switzerland poses the problem that with any change of the political and economic situation a sudden large emigration might occur. The possibility of a relatively quick decline or stagnation of the population carries with it the danger that the

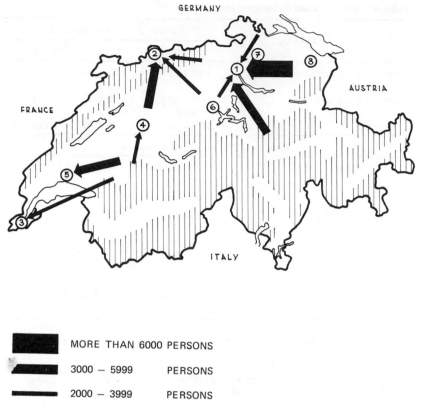

Figure 2.   Internal migration of native-born Swiss (1950–1960).

shortage of housing and the requirements for common facilities can suddenly reverse themselves to an oversupply of dwellings and insufficient use of existing or partially built community facilities. These problems are already acute, particularly in the metropolitan areas and the tourist centers.

PLANNING IN SWITZERLAND

Although a planning act for the whole of Switzerland has not yet been legislated and the authority to plan belongs still to the cantons and communities, the importance of permanent physical planning at all levels has been emphasized for some time.

National Planning.   A constitutional amendment demanding a federal law on planning, which is actually in preparation, was accepted by the people in 1969. This proves that pressures have been exerted from different sides to introduce meaningful land use and ordered development and to preserve nature and ancient settlements.[4] One impetus is the urbanization as a consequence of industrialization since the begin-

ning of the nineteenth century and the connected exodus from the rural areas as well as spoiling of the natural environment. At the end of the nineteenth century all forest land was placed under federal protection. In 1905 and 1909 the Swiss League for Preservation of Cultural and Architectural Heritage and the Swiss League for Protection of Nature were founded. The first basis for a federal urbanization law was created in 1920. This proposal included the most important points for general planning. At the same time a new awareness and concern for planning among certain groups of architects occurred.[5]

In 1932 there were attempts in parliament to introduce planning legislation. In 1943 a temporary National Planning Commission delivered the working paper "Schweizerische Regional- und Landesplanung." In the following year increasing activity occurred, especially in the communities, to plan their areas physically by controlling land use and by regulating building design. Zoning maps and building codes were applied as means to reach these goals. The main concepts for ordered and organized settlement structure are the creation of new towns at appropriate locations in the framework of a general plan and the development and completion of already existing towns of central importance.

During and after World War II different groups and societies advocated planning attempts; and in addition, since 1961 the Institute for National, Regional and Local Planning at the Swiss Federal Institute of Technology has done so. With town, regional, and national planning, the increasing conflict between the needs of different human activities, including housing, working, and leisure, became apparent; hence the main goal of planning was to coordinate and provide for these needs and to assure proper development for the country in caring for the welfare of populations in all regions.

As a basis for national planning, in 1970 the Swiss national development concepts were established at the demand of the Federal Department of National Economy, according to the 1965 Housing Act.[6] In their present form the development concepts are descriptions of different spatial organizations for Switzerland in the year 2000. There is not a single description of the future, but different alternatives depending on the goals one intends to achieve. The development concepts can already be considered as instruments for evaluating future decisions. It would nevertheless be valuable if the political authorities could make a choice for a particular direction in which development should be oriented, so that the investments influencing the physical development and the spatial organization policy could be channeled accordingly. However, the strong federal elements of the Swiss government system and different interest groups render decision making very difficult. The concept of a certain decentralization as one of the alternatives tallies with the traditional image of Switzerland; it promotes the federal state system and direct democracy and is therefore favored in the actual discussion. This alternative is a concept of equalizing the distribution of population and employment as well as the standard of living, with special regard to existing spatial distribution of dispersed settlements. The realization of the concept of regional centers would be very difficult within a reasonable time span, if the trend for population to concentrate in the metropolitan areas and to leave rural areas continues (see Figures 1 and 2). In times of economic recession, regional centers in depleted areas are rarely supported by private business activities due to lack of private investments. Migration to metropolitan areas will increase as the possibility to survive in the rural areas decreases. If we assume that there will not be much development outside the metropolitan areas in the near future and also that little area is left in the *Mittelland,* we have to ask ourselves if and where new towns could, in the real sense of the word, be realized. The national question is, therefore, no longer to create new towns, but to reinforce existing places of a medium central importance.

It is hoped that a future federal planning act and the acts of different states on planning lead to coordination of relevant planning policies by all governments.[7] More comprehensive planning than at present should achieve a better distribution of population and employment as well as the preservation of irreplaceable land and resources. Planning can have a strong impact on the development policies of the communities, particularly in the metropolitan areas.

City Planning.   Many of the cities that grew fastest in the relatively dense net of settlement in Switzerland in the middle of the nineteenth century were strategically located and were characterized by the medieval fortifications and densely built areas in their centers. As the cities grew quickly with industrialization and the increase of population, heritage of the past and questions of urban design were often neglected. Economic progress, particularly for the railroads and urban transports, was seen as most important. Only a few projects of urban design, such as the shaping of the lakeshores in Zurich and Geneva, were realized. The suburbs of that time grew generally without design concepts. Monumental buildings and complexes were rarely built; instead many important single buildings of architectural value were erected as products of a bourgeois culture.[8]

People used ideas of the French revolution to help develop new views and concepts about city planning and urban design. ("A perfect society in a perfect city.") New guiding principles, pilot concepts, and options for urban design were sought. The new city was to fulfill the needs of its citizens; new social, political, economic, and technical conditions had to be considered. The demand for healthy, agreeable employment was to be satisfied. The advancement and development of the common welfare found its expression in different public measures and safeguards, such as the introduction of building codes, which in addition to the regulation of technical and hygienic demands, gave a first basis for a foresighted regulation of land use in the public interest. Related to the implementation of building laws in different cantons, the concern of urban design and planning received added importance.

In that spirit the city of Zurich and some of the con-

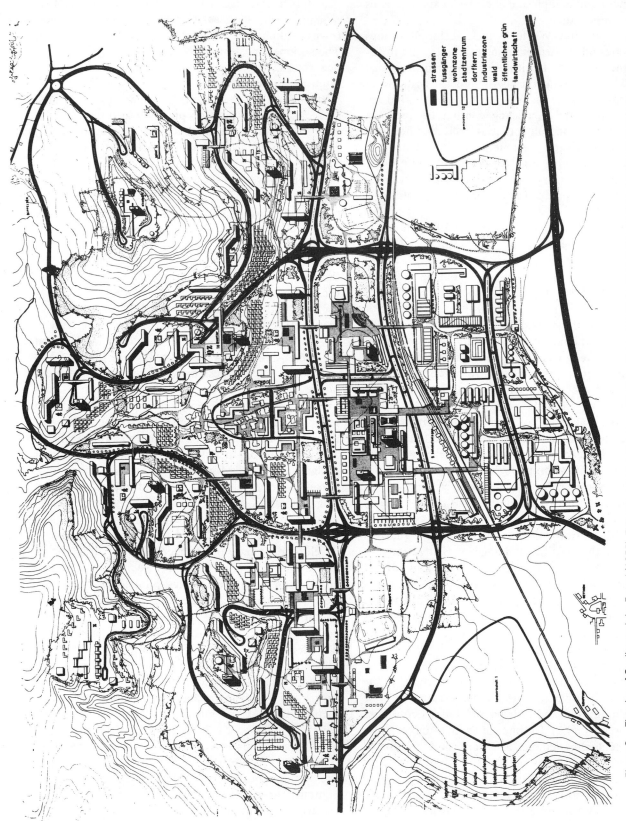

Figure 3. The plan of Studienstadt im Furttal (1955). This was a model city planned to serve as an example for three to five medium-sized new towns located along important transportation axes to absorb population growth and relieve large cities. The model was based on a scheme of organic structuring of the city: neighborhood, neighborhood group, small quarter, quarter, and city with corresponding inhabitants of 200, 600, 1800, 7200, and 28,000. This model was never realized. Architects and Planners: Ernst Egli, Werner Aebli, Eduard Brühlmann, Rico Christ, Ernst Winkler. Source and copyright: Ernst Egli et al., *Die Neue Stadt: Eine Studie für das Furttal.* Zürich (Zürich: Verlag Bauen & Wohnen, 1961).

nected suburban communities opened an international planning competition for the design of "Gross Zürich" in 1915. World War I interrupted this development, but the following period was a time of realization for different public facilities. Many professionals, such as architects and geographers, continued to pursue seriously the questions and problems of urban design and of city and regional planning (e.g., Meili, Real, Carol, Werner[9], influenced not only by Le Corbusier and the *Congres Internationaux d'Architecture Moderne*—CIAM, founded in Switzerland, La Sarraz, 1928—and by Bernoulli's book *Städtebau in der Schweiz, 1929*[10]).

After World War II, against all expectations, the economy grew with extreme speed, and good planning concepts that could have helped to handle and order this development were not nearly ready. Where theories and proposals existed, such as the proposal for the design of Swiss metropolitan areas presented in the example of the city and state of Zürich, political action was not taken because of the mistrust about intervention by the state authorities. Thus the opportunity of ordering and preserving free spaces within metropolitan areas was by and large lost.

Because of the sudden increase in traffic, the state authorities had trouble finding a long-term strategy for desirable allocation of development. City planning consisted mostly of street and highway planning for the needs of the car. A relatively high living density helped the public transportation systems to survive until today, and they are again extensively supported. After the shortcomings of the situation in the cities became obvious in the early 1960s, city planning and urban design were reconsidered; and regional, economic, social, and cultural aspects were integrated.

Nevertheless, in most communities general land use is determined by the zoning map and building regulations. The zoning plan divides the city into different

Figure 4. Aerial view of Volketswil. The impetus to develop this town came from an important enterprise for industrialized housing to provide residential relief to Zurich. The community consists of five villages, with a goal of 20,000 inhabitants. Developer: E. Göhner AG; Planner: Emil Stierli. Copyright: Swissair Photo & Vermessung AG.

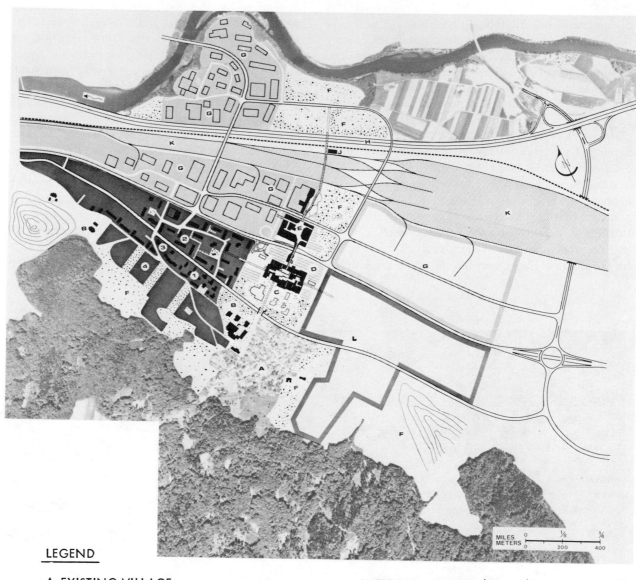

LEGEND

A EXISTING VILLAGE
B SCHOOLS
C CIVIC AND CULTURAL CENTER
D&E COMMERCIAL CENTERS (SHOPPING & TRADE)
F SPORTS AND RECREATION AREA
G INDUSTRIAL AREA, PARTLY BUILT UP

H FREEWAY ZURICH/BERNE/BASLE
J RAILROAD STATION
K FREIGHT AND SHUNTING YARD
 FOR EASTERN SWITZERLAND
L RESIDENTIAL AREAS
1,2,3 RESIDENTIAL, REALIZED
NEIGHBORHOODS
4 RESIDENTIAL, NEIGHBORHOOD, PROJECTED

Figure 5. Spreitenbach. This town was initiated in the early 1950s when the Swiss Federal Railway planned to locate its central freight yard here for the eastern region of Switzerland. Spreitenbach is a rare Swiss example of a town that has had some success in directing urban growth. Planner and copyright: Klaus Scheifele, Spreitenbach.

areas; allowed types of density and use, scale of buildings, and tolerated emissions are described in zoning ordinances. Normally state laws leave much freedom to communities for the establishment of their zoning size and building and planning regulations. During the 1950s and 1960s speculative construction activities and land procuring were favored through too many large zones. The result of this phenomenon were numerous projects of large-scale developments in metropolitan and tourist areas, but no real new towns. Through the instruments of the intended comprehensive planning it will become difficult for private investors to realize large-scale projects on any site for an acceptable short-term profit, even if the growth of population and economy will again intensify considerably. Due also to the stagnation of large-scale projects today, planning concentrates mostly on protecting the environment, the problem of separation of activities and population groups, particularly in inner cities, and the preservation of the use and appearance of existing buildings (housing).

Planning of New Towns.   As said before, for a long time Swiss planners and architects have had the intention of building new towns. By the creation of new towns, new and better planning principles should be demonstrated as allowing for good living quality.[11] They should also serve as an instrument influencing the entire urbanization pattern. They have precedents—for example, *Die Stadt der Zukunft* (1897) by

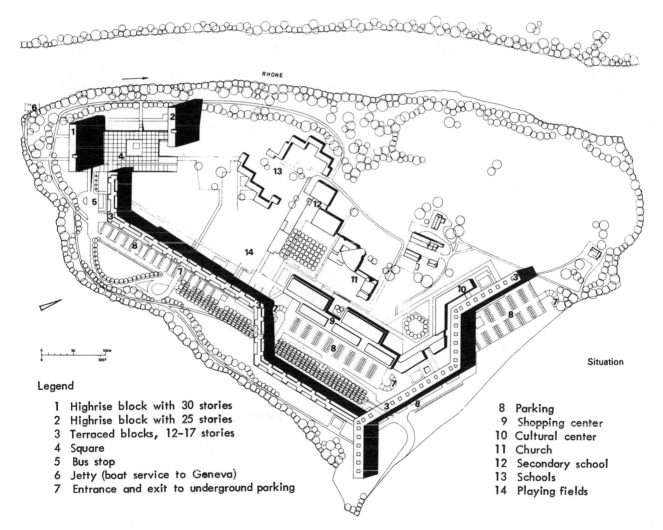

Legend

1 Highrise block with 30 stories
2 Highrise block with 25 stories
3 Terraced blocks, 12–17 stories
4 Square
5 Bus stop
6 Jetty (boat service to Geneva)
7 Entrance and exit to underground parking

8 Parking
9 Shopping center
10 Cultural center
11 Church
12 Secondary school
13 Schools
14 Playing fields

Figure 6.   Le Lignon. This is a satellite of Geneva located five kilometers from its center. Le Lignon has unique monumental residential buildings that have a housing capacity for about 10,000 residents, these structures are one kilometer long. Architects: Addor and Julliard, Geneva (1964). Source and copyright: H. Aregger/O. Glaus, *Hochhaus und Stadtplanung* (Zürich: Verlag für Architektur Artemis, 1967).

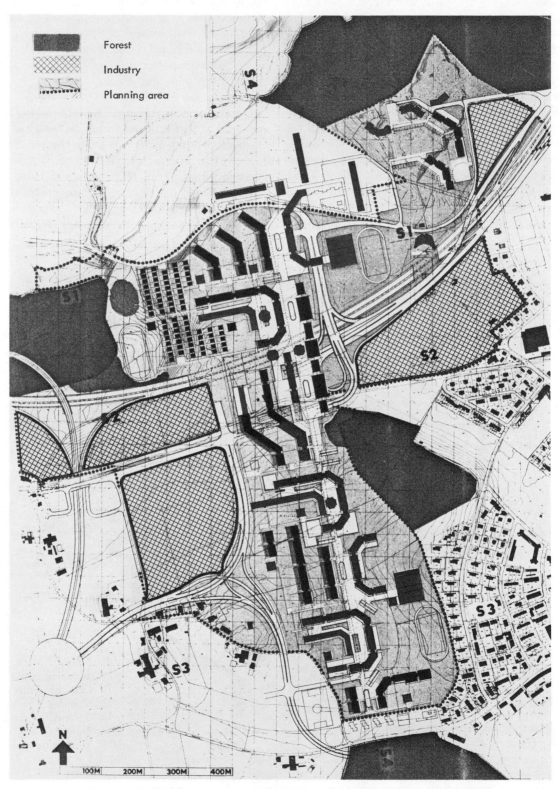

Figure 7. The plan of Brünnen. The territory of Brünnen belongs to part of Berne and includes an extension of about 84 hectares. Like Le Lignon. Brünnen is a type of extended suburban planning with the intention of becoming a settlement with urban character and the facilities to relieve central Berne. The realization has been postponed. Architects: H. G. Reinhard, Lienhard and Strasser, O. Lutstorf, E. Helfer, R. Ehrenberg; Engineers: Emch and Berger. Source: *Planning Report Brünnen* (Bern: AGK, 1972). Copyright: U. Strasser, Berne.

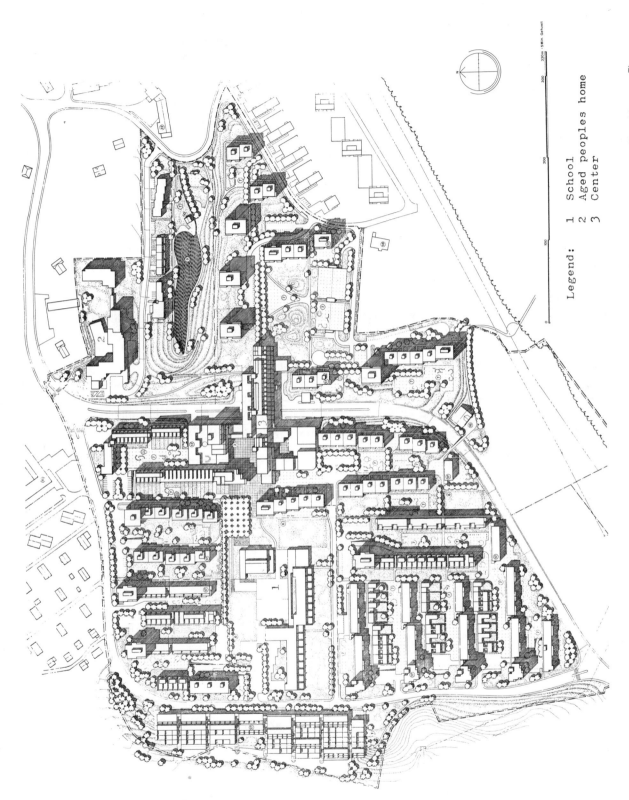

Figure 8. The final overall plan of the neighborhood Ruopigen of Littau. Planned for about 35,000 residents, by 2000 Littau is to serve as a satellite of Lucerne. The town is planned for an area of 530,000 square meters. The design of the neighborhood for 9000 inhabitants includes an administrative center for community authorities, schools, churches, a cemetery, a home for the aged, and a commercial center. Architects and copyright: Dolf Schnebli, R. Matter and partners, Agno, 1972.

Legend: 1 School
         2 Aged peoples home
         3 Center

Fritsch, *Garden Cities of Tomorrow* (1898) by Howard, "La ville radieuse" (1935) by Le Corbusier, *Broad-Acre City* (1947) by Wright, and *The New City* (1944) by Hilbersheimer.[12]

The meaning of new town should be defined in the framework of the Swiss situation before trying to describe the objectives and possibilities of new towns in Switzerland. The characteristics of a new town are: communal autonomy; central economic, social, and cultural functions for a certain region; a framework for an urban lifestyle; and a number and density of inhabitants that is clearly distinguishable from a rural community. In function, new towns are either new foundations or expansions of an autonomous urban nucleus. We would define as new foundations towns established where no or nearly no previous settlements existed. Towns of completion characterize places that are developed in connection with an already existing, substantial settlement, but where expansion in size and speed and change in function go comparatively beyond normal growth. Both kinds of new towns can be differentiated as either fully autonomous towns, in which an important part of its working population works and lives and has adequate services, or relief or satellite towns that have strong functional connections to the city to be relieved. They may be residential towns if they serve mainly as dormitories. The different definitions are not always easy to separate in practice. This is valid for new foundations and completion towns as well for the full residential town.

Considering the development in Switzerland previously described, it becomes evident that a long, existing, relatively dense net of settlements would not allow the creation of new towns in the sense of new foundations and full towns (see Figure 1). In addition, the conditions to realize such large-scale projects are different from other countries and have always been difficult because there are almost no strong government housing policies, initiative for construction is left to private forces, ownership of land is extremely varied, and lots are relatively small. Other reasons are: too few inhabitants who could be attracted to one place, no great internal migration to only one city to be relieved, strong local power of communities, a certain aversion of the Swiss toward new large projects, and the planning policy of communities and states not in favor of new-town projects. Nevertheless, several new towns were proposed, but seen as utopias[13] reflecting a certain resignation to the real situation, they often were left unrealized.

The situation and circumstances are different for mountain areas predestined for tourist use. There, particularly in the 1960s and beginning of the 1970s, several tourist settlements were planned and realized

Table 5   Descriptions of Some New Urban Settlements

	Volketswil	Spreitenbach	Le Lignon	Brünnen	Littau, Ruopigen
Located from (km)	Zurich	Zurich	Geneva	Berne	Lucerne
	12	15	5	6	6
Proposed land use[a]					
Forest	397	396			
Agriculture	438	90			
Open space	19	49	20	17	5
Settlement area	537	425	8	67	27
Covered	425	230	2		17
Circulation	57	94	4	14	5
Common facilities	55	101	2		5
Total area[a]	1,391	860	28	84	32
Population					
1960	2,170	1,927			
1970	7,463	5,969	10,000		
1975	10,044	6,770	10,000		
Goal	20,000	25,000	10,000	17,000–25,000	8,000
Employment					
1975	4,100	4,500	300		
Goal	7,800–11,000	15,000		14,000	

[a] In hectares.

that can be defined as new foundations but because of their seasonal tourist functions, are only temporarily full new towns.

Many places could be named as at least potential new towns if one computed the high capacities for inhabitants and working places of the zoning plans of these communities, mainly in metropolitan areas. However, we have also to consider the criterion of general systematic development within a certain time under the support of the community authorities and a few developers, which is not fulfilled in most cases.

In applying the mentioned criteria there are a few examples of new towns in Switzerland that could be compared with models in other countries. Also, the actual number of inhabitants is mostly around 10,000 and not like the normally considered minimal 20,000—30,000 for a new town. The production of dwellings is numerically high, partly due to industrialized construction; the large-scale projects realized are rather incomplete developments or new quarters added to existing settlements. (See Table 5 and Figures 3 to 8.)

CONCLUSION

Swiss settlements are realized differently in type and size from those in other countries. The reasons lie in the relatively strong partition of Switzerland into autonomous communities and in the small size of geographic and cultural regions and the relative lack of policies for development at the different levels of government. However, the following three types of new settlement forms can be distinguished:

1. Fringe communities around the big cities do not have a real new-town character; they are more or less large suburbs, integrated into the city structure except for their political jurisdiction.
2. New-town-like settlements can be found; they are not new foundations, but towns of a distinct central function, growth, and size.
3. New-town-type foundations have been built in the Alpine region. They are summer and winter sport centers for tourism.[14] These are relatively small in size and population, but because they are used temporarily, they have few inhabitants in the real sense of the word.

NOTES

1. See Jakob Maurer, "Städtebau und Stadtplanung," in *Handworterbuch der Raumforschung und Raumordnung* (Hannover: Editor Akademie für Raumforschung und Landesplanung, 1970), pp. 2864 ff.

2. See Ernst Egli, *Geschichte des Städtebaus*, Zweiter Band, Das Mittelalter (Erlenbach-Zürich und Stuttgart; Rentsch-Verlag, 1967), p. 152.

3. See Ernst Egli, *Geschichte des Städtebaus*, Dritter Band, Die Neuzeit (Erlenbach-Zürich und Stuttgart: Rentsch-Verlag, 1967), p. 119.

4. As a summary of national planning, see Ernst Winkler, "Raumordnung und Landesplanung," in *Handworterbuch der Raumforschung und Raumordnung* (Hannover: Editor Akademie für Raumforschung und Raumordnung, 1970), pp. 2854 ff.

5. Armin Meili, "Allgemeines über Landesplanung," in *Autostrasse* **2**, No. 2 (February 1933). Basel: Schweiz. Autostrassenverein.

6. See *Landesplanerische Leitbilder der Schweiz*, report in three volumes and a box of plans, Publication series of the Institut für Orts-, Regional- und Landesplanung No. 10A-D (Zürich: Institut für Orts-, Regional- und Landesplanung, 1971). Also see D. Ackerknecht, "Ansätze zu Landesplanerischen Leitbildern," in *Gedanken zur Landesplanung*, Festschrift für Prof. Dr. E. Winkler (Zürich: Institut für Orts-, Regional- und Landesplanung, 1967), pp. 63 ff.

7. See Dieter Ackerknecht and Willy R. Tschol, "Problemaspekte der kantonalen Raumplanung," in DISP Nr. 38, *Informationen zur Orts-, Regional- und Landesplanung* (Zürich: Institut für Orts- Regional- und Landesplanung, 1975), pp. 4–15.

8. See Maurer, pp. 2864 ff. Also see Jean-Pierre Vouga, "L'urbanisme et l'habitation en suisse," *L'architecture d'aujourd'hui* **35** (June 1965):AA 121.

9. Armin Meili, "Zürich Heute und Morgen, Wille oder Zufall in der baulichen Gestaltung," *Neue Zurich Zeitung* (1944); W. H. Real, *Stadtplanung, Moglichkeiten für die Aufstellung von Richtlinien am Beispiel der Verhältnisse in der Stadt Zurich* (Bern: Buri, 1950); H. Carol and M. Werner, *Stadte, wie wir sie wünschen: Ein Vorschlag zur Gestaltung schweizerischer Grosstadt Gebiete, dargestellt am Beispiel von Stadt und Kanton Zürich* (Zürich: Regio, 1949).

10. H. Bernoulli and C. Martin, *Stadtebau in der Schweiz* (Zürich: Fretz-Wasmuth, 1929).

11. L. Burckhardt and M. Kutter, *Wir selber bauen unsre Stadt*, Basler Politische Schriften Nr. 1 (Basel: Handschin, 1955).

12. See Ernst Egli, *Geschichte des Städtebaus*, Dritter Band, Die Neuzeit, p. 335 ff.

13. "Utopie, visionärer Städtebau Gestern und Heute," *Du* (January 1972);2–62. Justus Dahinden, *Stadtstrukturen fur Morgen, Analysen, Thesen, Modelle* (Teufen, Schweiz: Verlag Niggli, 1971).

14. For example, Henri Bonnemazou, "Thyon 2000: Creation et recherches estéthiques européennes," *Revue internationale d'architecture et de design*, No. 2 (December–January 1969–1970.)

CHAPTER 12

National Strategy for the New-Town Program in Israel

NATHANIEL LICHFIELD

Six categories of new towns have been identified according to the purpose for which they were founded:

1. To serve as capital cities.
2. To fulfill strategic or military needs.
3. To exploit natural resources or to develop the potentialities of the land.
4. To relieve congestion in large urban centers or to organize more rationally existing and future metropolitan growth.
5. To cope with population growth, movements of population, or special features of a population.
6. To be part of a national planning and development policy.[1]

For example, Canadian new towns were created to exploit some natural resource (e.g., Kitimat for aluminium). Most American and British new towns would fall into category 4. Only in Israel, however, has a new-town program been developed as a part of a national policy for urbanization and settlements (with single towns fitting also into other categories), and this element makes the Israeli experience particularly interesting.[2] This experience is of interest for another reason: the massive scale of the program in terms of the size of the country. In this connection a comparison can be made with the British program, which is also of impressive dimensions. Since 1946 Britain has initiated some 27 new towns with a net growth of population of some 700,000 by December 1971.[3] As Figure 1 shows, Israel initiated some 29 such towns with a net growth of 490,000 in 1969.[4] Thus in terms of absolute numbers of population growth the British program is the greater; but as Table 1 shows, the Israeli achievement is greater in terms of current new-town population as a percentage of 1950 population or of grown in population since 1950.

Recently I headed a large-scale study on the Israeli new towns, and various aspects of that study are the primary basis of this chapter.[5] Prior to this study, in addition to the innumerable articles, there were two other major, comprehensive reviews of the progress of the Israeli program. The first, in 1966, concentrated on the planning of individual new towns,[6] and the second, in 1970, analyzed the socioeconomic forces and characteristics of the towns as developed.[7] By contrast, our study reviewed achievements leading to the devising of alternative possible development strategies compared with those implicit in the then current national plans. More precisely, the terms of reference were to review the success and failures in the building of the new towns since 1948; to analyze the situation current around 1970 in terms of the socioeconomic conditions in particular; to identify possible alternative national new-town strategies; to make an evaluation of these strategies with a view to recommending a preferred approach; and to offer guidance based on the study and other experience on the planning, development, and management of the Israeli new towns in the future.[8]

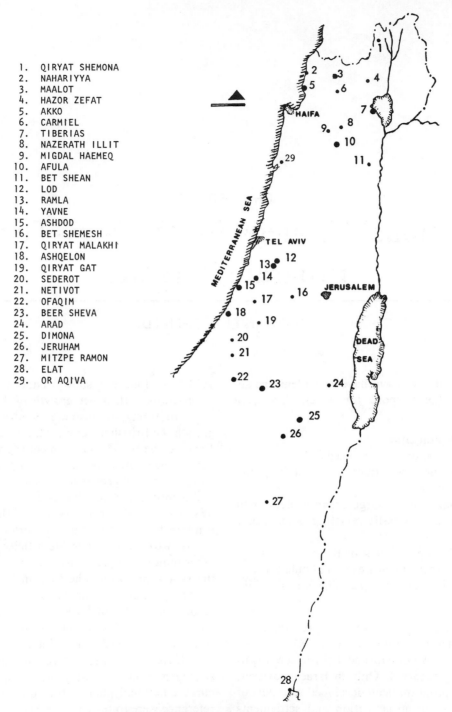

1. QIRYAT SHEMONA
2. NAHARIYYA
3. MAALOT
4. HAZOR ZEFAT
5. AKKO
6. CARMIEL
7. TIBERIAS
8. NAZERATH ILLIT
9. MIGDAL HAEMEQ
10. AFULA
11. BET SHEAN
12. LOD
13. RAMLA
14. YAVNE
15. ASHDOD
16. BET SHEMESH
17. QIRYAT MALAKHI
18. ASHQELON
19. QIRYAT GAT
20. SEDEROT
21. NETIVOT
22. OFAQIM
23. BEER SHEVA
24. ARAD
25. DIMONA
26. JERUHAM
27. MITZPE RAMON
28. ELAT
29. OR AQIVA

Figure 1.   The new Israeli towns of this study.

Only particular aspects from the large-scale study can be considered here: the primary objective is to show how the study set about the problem of formulating alternative development strategies for the future and then to make an evaluation among them as a basis for a recommended course of action.

However, before reaching this point, we must examine briefly the ideology behind, and the achievements and problems of, the new towns since 1948.

Goals in Urban and Rural Development.   In the period of Jewish immigration from the end of the nineteenth century to the creation of the state of Israel in 1948, there was a continuing conflict between ideology and reality. Great thought and attention were given to the problem of rural settlements;[9] hence the *kibbutzim* (the full collective) and *moshavim* (where the land may be worked privately but with cooperative marketing arrangments) were established.[10] Even though the country grew from 50,000 Jews in 1900 to 600,000 in 1948 and the rural life was emphasized, the proportion of Jews living in the cities remained much the same as in 1948 when it was 86 percent. The major towns had grown without any planning direction, but the agricultural villages were already highly planned in theory and practice.

The creation of the state fundamentally transformed the situation. There is the obvious point that direct control of the country's institutions gave the Jewish people direct control of policy, but simultaneously the authorities were faced with a massive wave of immigration of a radically different social composition from former waves. Among the immigrants were many refugees or displaced people or others incapable of resettling themselves in a strange country; it has been calculated that 85 percent of these immigrants depended on the government and official institutions for housing, employment, and other initial needs.[11] This immigration offered a unique opportunity for a planned geographic distribution of the new immigrants in accord with national goals designed to create an Israel that would provide refuge, security, and opportunity for all Jews who wanted to immigrate.

These goals were never definitively recorded, but there was enough discussion and thought to permit a generalization as to what they were. For example, Shachar has recently listed these goals as settlement in sparsely populated regions, which would overcome regional inequity of development; occupation of frontier regions for purposes of defense and for establishing national presence and sovereignty over those areas; opening of "resource frontiers," mainly natural resources in the desert areas in the southern part of the country; changing the primary structure of the urban system by limiting the growth of urban concentration in the central coastal plain and establishing the missing level of medium to small-size towns.[12]

The New Towns at 1970. Many new towns are in the sparsely populated regions, thus helping to fulfill the first goal listed by Shachar. New towns have been established near sensitive border areas, particularly in the north part of the country near the Lebanese, Syrian, and Jordanian borders. Several of the new towns have successfully exploited the natural resources of the area, simply by their presence, particularly in the south. These are established as small- and medium-sized towns.

Set against the terms of reference for the study,

Table 1 Population Growth in British and Israeli New Towns (in thousands)

Item	Great Britain[a]	Israel (Jewish Population)
1950 national population	50,000	760
Current national population[b]	55,000	2,500
Net growth in national population	5,500	1,740
Original new-town population	717	60
Current new-town population[b]	1,436	490
Net growth in new-town population[c]	720	430
Item 3 as percent of item 1	10	240
Item 6 as percent of item 1	1.4	56
Item 6 as percent of item 3	14	25

[a] Great Britain is England, Wales, and Scotland. Northern Ireland also has a significant new-town program.
[b] Current for Britain in 1971 and for Israel in 1969.
[c] Approximate only.
Sources: Derived by the author from sources in Israel: Nathaniel Lichfield, *Israel's New Towns: A Development Strategy*, Vol. 2 (Tel Aviv: Institute for Planning and Development Ltd.), Tables 2.1.2, 9.4A, 9.5.1; and in Britain from *Town and Country Planning* **40**, No. 1 (January 1972).

can the new-town program be judged a success? The whole concept of success or failure in planning is extremely difficult. Is the criterion the achievement of historic goals, or the meeting of problems that later emerged, or the seizing of possibilities for the capacity, opportunities, and the circumstances in which they worked?

The simple conclusion was this: that there were failures was obvious. As much was implied in the need for a thorough study in addition to numerous other studies that had analyzed particular problems. Although national goals such as population dispersal have been achieved, the social and economic cost has been considerable. (This is brought out in the report, and I mention it here only as information.)

The new towns have from the beginning accommodated many settlers of Afro-Asian, Oriental Jewish origin.[13] In the period 1957–1968, 57 percent of the immigrants to the new towns were of Afro-Asian origin, as against 38 percent of European/American origin,[14] even though this period was one when the total number of immigrants into the country was split almost evenly between the two groups. Emigration from towns has been great (between 1961 and 1967 total population increases in the new towns could have been three times higher than the actual increases with a factor much higher for single towns if there had been no emigration). Emigration has tended to be among the European/Americans, the middle classes, and the skilled workers, which has reinforced the social and ethnic homogeneity of the new towns.

Economic opportunities have, in general, been unsatisfactory.[15] The towns have been based primarily on manufacturing industries, and their role as service centers for the agricultural villages has not materialized. The *kibbutzim*, with their self-contained economies and their efficient marketing links with the major cities, have largely bypassed the new towns. Thus the planning theory on which they were based has been negated. However, even if there had not been an established pattern of village-city communication, the new towns probably would have been unable to provide the services demanded by the inhabitants of the *kibbutzim* because many of them were of small size. These problems have, in recent years, coincided with a period when immigration has substantially slowed and when those who do arrive (primarily from the Soviet Union and America) have been less inclined to settle in the new towns. This has not helped the towns to advance.

THE METHODOLOGICAL APPROACH

The rest of this chapter is a discussion of the approach taken toward formulating ultimate development strategies for the new towns, the basis of choice among them, and the implementation of the preferred strategy.

There is a logistical problem involved when dealing with a subject that has so many components and so many ramifications. Obviously, any long list of recommendations and proposals covering all aspects of housing, employment, population, administration, and other matters would become unmanageable. Hence I decided to focus attention on various hypotheses that are not directly dissimilar in every respect, but that offer differing perspectives that could guide policy makers for the future. Before these hypotheses could be designed, the constraints or foundations that conditioned the nature of the hypotheses had to be established.

Seven factors, or foundations, were identified: national goals, constraints on the solution, objectives derived from the analysis of the problems, assumptions as to population growth, influence of regional concepts being adopted in modern planning, assumptions about economic growth, and contribution of urbanization to socioeconomic development.

Taking the first foundation meant that the design of the hypotheses had to be consistent with the national goals. Without a definitive statement for the goals previously mentioned, there are enough official documents and reports to allow the formation of a consensus, at least as far as they affect the new-town program.[16] Nine national goals were identified, covering topics such as "reducing the country's dependence on imported capital," "achieving and maintaining conditions of full employment throughout the country" and "population dispersal." Similarly, analyses were undertaken for the rest of the foundations.

Need for Hypotheses. The hypotheses were designed to concentrate attention on certain key issues. The hypotheses had to be broad enough in scope to deal with most of the 29 new towns and discrete enough not to make them simply variations of a single theme. The hypotheses had to be visualized as part of the urban development of the whole country. For focus, they were arranged around theories of urban and regional form.[17] Each of the hypotheses carried within it certain key variables that could materially affect the resources devoted to, and the life within, the new towns.

Although all the relevant factors were taken into consideration when designing the hypotheses, two key related items were paramount: the lack of regional integration and the smallness of the new towns. They were originally conceived as regional or subregional centers for the surrounding agricultural villages. However, the villages already had a highly developed system of economic links with the large cities, and the towns stood outside this system. Another reason for this relates to the second of the items, the smallness of the new towns. While the topic is a thorny one, our conclusion from the survey was that towns below 20,000 people could not fulfill the current expectations of an acceptably urban system of commerce and services and had difficulty in establishing a new economy independent of great government support. Of the 29 new towns, 20 had a population of less than 20,000 in 1967. But because of the previously determined constraints to the solution, new towns could not be closed down, and new ones could not be opened.

The Five Hypotheses. Theories of urban forms have provoked a great deal of thought at either end of the practical-theoretical range. At the practical end, however, there seemed to be three basic theories that have relevance to the Israeli situation[18] (see Figures 2, 3, and 4).

The first hypothesis was urban clusters, the grouping of nearby towns into clusters for the establishment of urban regions of interdependent activities. The functional structure and physical arrangement of the constituent settlements would vary among the urban regions. Each, however, would act as an aggregation of the separate units to provide the advantages of a large town and to be able to divert activities from the coastal belt.

The clusters have been delineated, taking into consideration the broad geographic areas of the country, the use of existing settlements and their development, and the exploitation of the existing national infrastructure. Because each of the clusters would provide the services now available only in the three large cities (Haifa, Jerusalem, and Tel Aviv), the tendency in this hypothesis is toward the reduction of congestion in the coastal belt and the distribution of urban activities about the peripheral areas of the country. Almost all of the new towns are located in these areas, and therefore, the adoption of this

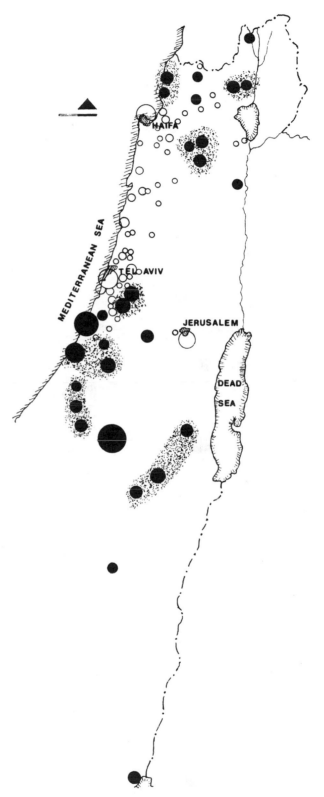

Figure 2. Hypothesis 1: urban clusters.

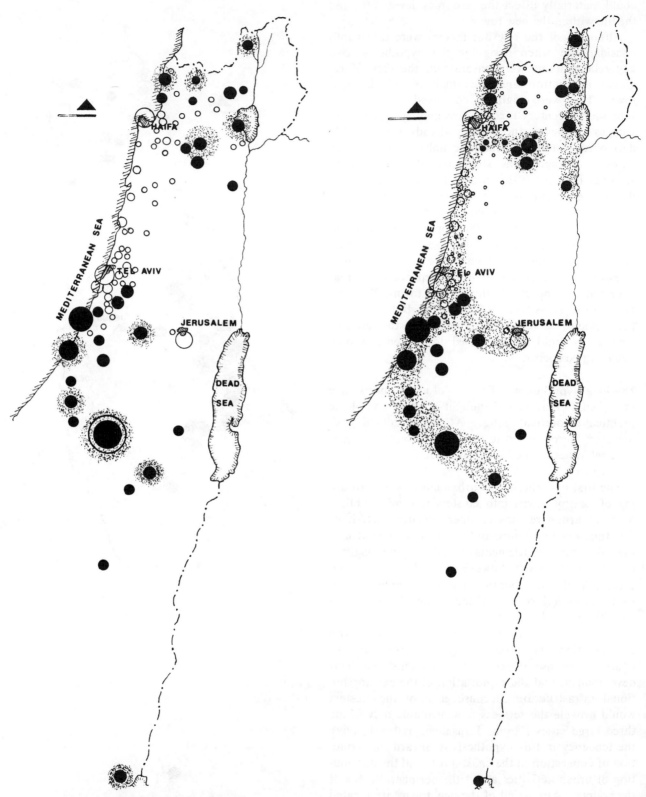

Figure 3. Hypothesis 2: growth centers.

Figure 4. Hypothesis 3: axial development.

hypothesis favors the development of these towns within the national urbanization pattern.

The second of the hypotheses chosen is based on establishing urban growth centers. From his study of relations among Israeli settlements, Berler, has made proposals for the country's urban pattern.[19] Finding that Beer Sheva fulfills a major metropolitan function for the settlements in the southern district of the country, he examined the north for similar relations and found that a metropolitan center is lacking there, but that the potential for its evolution exists in Nazareth. Examining the size of Israeli settlements with regard to certain assumptions about the country's development, Berler concluded that concentration should be upon medium-sized and large towns.

Berler proposed, therefore, that Beer Sheva be designated as a major metropolitan center for the southern district, and Nazareth/Nazareth Illit for the northern district, with populations of 200,000 and 150,000 respectively. In addition, he suggests development of six or eight medium-sized towns, scattered over the country to provide major urban centers for a maximum number of people.

The third of the hypotheses was axial development. The importance of transportation lines as the main skeleton for development is emphasized in this planning alternative. The spatial distribution of the population follows development axes, the major transportation routes, ending at major poles of development along these axes, where activities will be more intensive than in other parts of the country. The development axes in time will take the form of strings of urban concentration, smaller or larger according to local conditions.

This hypothesis is based on the assumption that urbanization takes the form most natural to socioeconomic forces. Economic activities and population would then be concentrated in an urban belt along the Mediterranean Coast from Ashqelon to Nahariyya with concentrations at Tel Aviv and Haifa. The concept thus envisages a major urban spine running north/south and fingers of intensive development projecting eastward into the country at points where major urban centers in the interior have an intense relation with the coastal belt. Intersecting lateral corridors of urban development would occur at Nazareth, Jerusalem, and Beer Sheva/Dimona. These towns would function as focal points for large areas of the hinterland.

Those settlements involved in the area of intensive urban development would show rapid growth,

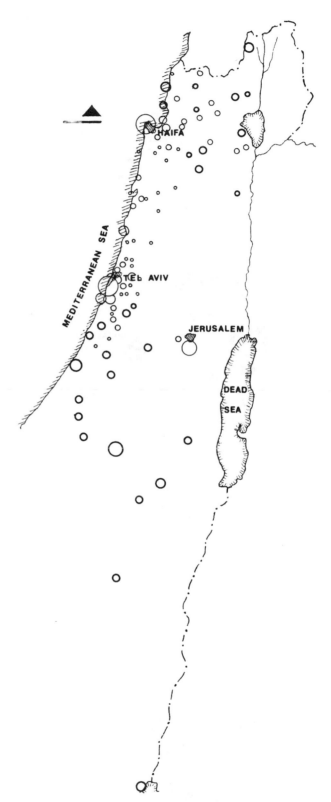

Figure 5. Hypothesis 4: Ministry of the Interior's plan.

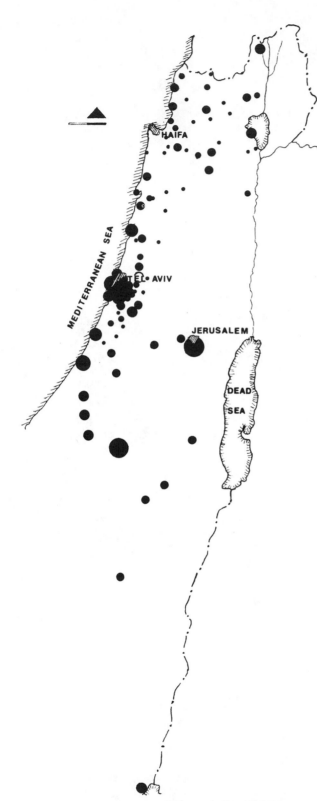

Figure 6. Hypothesis 5: existing trends.

whereas other new towns throughout the country would grow slowly. Thus the axial development concept provides a possibility of resolving the fundamental diseconomies of the program by concentrating infrastructure, services, and production along existing and planned transportation lines.

Two additional hypotheses were also chosen (see Figures 5 and 6). The first is the Ministry of the Interior's plan for a population of 4 million people by 1985, which was published in 1967. At the time of the survey this plan was the eighth in a series of plans revised periodically since 1949 (when the population target was 2 million) based on population forecasts.[20] It distributes urban centers over the country in hierarchically structured regional patterns. The plan was conceived to establish a continuum from small rural settlements to large cities. Although the largest population increases are proposed for the southern district, the plan does not make any attempt to equalize the distribution of population about the country. The majority of settlements are proposed for the central districts, with a high density of both urban and rural settlements in the intense agricultural areas. In many respects this plan is a variation of the growth-centers hypothesis, though perhaps the most important difference is the lack of emphasis placed upon developing major centers in the north and south.

A fifth hypothesis was the continuation of existing trends. It is not a "planned" hypothesis, being prepared solely from population forecasts on the assumption that the past and present development trends and implementation policies will not be altered and devised primarily to provide a basis for comparison with the other four hypotheses.

The detailing of these five hypotheses was not meant to present the decision makers with a "take A or B" situation. They are detailed as five hypotheses primarily to assist in the evaluation procedure. In addition, because there are bound to be some similarities in the treatment of the same town under different hypotheses, the preferred solution will probably have some elements of more than one hypothesis.

EVALUATION

Design cannot be considered as an isolated stage in the planning process; it is intimately bound up with considerations of evaluation, which are themselves ever-present considerations.[21] It is thus misleading to regard evaluation as a discrete stage after, say, design and before implementation even if, for purposes of exposition, this is the most logical place. For the New Towns Study, evaluation was conducted in three separate exercises. The first proceeded more or less simultaneously with design—testing the hypotheses against planning objectives. The second, feasibility, was carried out as a separate exercise. The hypotheses were then subjected to a comprehensive evaluation to see which offered the greatest net social benefits to the Israeli community.

Testing Against Planning Objectives. The planning objectives were derived from the study team's analysis of the problems facing the new towns. In that they are in accord with the national ubanization goals,[22] the planning objectives may be regarded as the operationalization of these goals. The goals were suggested by the study team; it was not practicable to obtain them from consensus in government. Thus the team put forward goals and objectives and intended them to become part of the debate on the report.

Three main objectives were selected: to establish growth foci to provide for all socioeconomic activities, to provide for a high standard of living, and to establish new planning concepts and systems. To make them operational, these vague general objectives were then broken down into specific ones. Thus "providing for a high standard of living" means, in the context of the problems facing the new towns at the moment, "Development of manufacturing activities with high paid employment and a wide variety of jobs, which also provides development of related services.

The testing was carried out by seeing whether the strategies achieved the objectives. It was not quantified in terms of units of measurement and thus by itself could never provide a realistic guide to the relative merits or demerits of particular schemes. However, testing kept the design process within practical limits, by keeping the strategies in line with the planning objectives.

Feasibility. Feasibility was defined in terms of being practicable with reference to possibilities of implementation and general acceptability to those concerned. For this there were various tests, as follows.

The strategies were reasonably feasible simply because they had been devised having regard (1) to national goals, constituents, and assumptions; (2) to the context studies of the new towns in terms of demography, physical constraints and opportunities, geography, economics, sociology, political science,

and law; and (3) to the problems and planning objectives that the study had raised. Then followed tests for economic feasibility, under three heads: economic demand for the new towns, economic base of the new towns, and critical resources in construction—that is, land, investment resources, public finance, and the construction industry. Demand is given by the fact that the hypotheses set out a certain population for each of the towns. It does not necessarily mean, however, that they will be able to pay their way, and therefore government subsidies may be necessary. To determine the economic base for the new towns, a model designed to allocate industry to them was developed.[23] The model took as constraints the participating labor force available (after deductions for those engaged in agriculture, the service trades, and building the new town itself) and the total amount of capital available, deduced from past experience and future expectations. Beyond these considerations it was necessary to ensure that the land, the investment resources, public finance, and the capacity of the building industry were up to the job of implementing the various strategies. Against all of these criteria, the strategies were shown to be feasible.

Planning Balance Sheet Analysis. Economic resources can be available, but whether the best use is being made of these resources, given the continued development of the new towns, is another question. There is, of course, no easy answer as to the nature of the term *best use*. This could be interpreted in terms of least financial cost and greatest financial returns for the government. However, if the study is taken as being substantially on behalf of the population as a whole, one must take into consideration all the social and economic costs and benefits as they affect all sectors of the population. The methodology used to deal with a problem of this scale was the planning balance sheet, which is an adaption of social cost benefit to the problem of choice in urban and regional planning.

Planning balance sheet analysis has a standard approach and methodology that can be applied to a whole range of situations.[24] I do not intend to expound the principles behind the method of the planning balance sheet, because they are fully described elsewhere,[25] but rather to show how it was adapted to deal with the issues posed by the five hypotheses. Certain critical features can be picked out and illustrated by reference to the actual balance sheet shown in Table 2.

The first stage was to identify the groups concerned and their instrumental objectives. Because

Table 2 Planning Balance Sheet[a]

Item	Sector and Instrumental Objective	Unit of Measurement	Comparison of the Alternatives — Hypotheses					Ranking — Hypotheses					Preferred 1–5	Preferred 1–4
			(1) Ministry of the Interior Plan	(2) Urban Clusters	(3) Growth Centers	(4) Linear Development	(5) Trends	1	2	3	4	5		
1.0	**Producers of New Developments**													
1.1	*Of New Urban Fabric in New Towns*													
	(a) Agricultural loss	—	Nil	Nil	Nil	Nil	0	—	—	—	—	—	—	—
	(b) Construction costs	M	+0.283	+0.335	+0.513	+0.242	0	3	4	5	2	1	5	4
1.2	*Of New Development in Other Urban Areas*	—				Uncertain								
1.3	*Of New Regional/National Infrastructure* Water supply Roads Drainage Electricity	M	+0.294	+0.248	+0.291	+0.193	0	5	3	4	2	1	5	4
2.0	**Consumers of New Developments**													
2.1	*New Residents of New Towns*													
	(a) Quality of premises	—	Nil	Nil	Nil	Nil	Nil	—	—	—	—	—	—	—
	(b) Environmental amenities														
	Physical environment	—				Uncertain								
	Sociocultural environment	—				Uncertain								

2.1	*New Residents of New Towns* (Ctd.)													
	(c) Accessibility													
	Job opportunities	Rank	2	4	5	3	1	2	4	5	3	1	5	1
	Shopping facilities	M	+0.190	+0.031	+0.149	+0.147	0	3	2	4	4	1	5	2
	Cultural/recreation					As for shopping facilities								
	Education and schooling	Rank	5	1	4	3	2	5	1	4	3	2	2	2
2.2	*New Manufacturing Enterprises*	M	−10828. Less (?)	−11559. Less (?)	10885. Less (?)	−10225 Less (?)	Uncertain	1	2		Uncertain		1	1
2.3	*New Commercial Enterprises*	—	Nil	Nil	Nil	Nil	Nil	—	—	—	—	—	—	
3.0	**Occupiers of Existing Developments**													
3.1	*Existing Residents*													
3.1.1	*Of New Towns*													
	(a) Quality of premises	—	Nil	Nil	Nil	Nil	Nil	—	—	—	—	—	—	
	(b) Environmental amenities													
	Physical environment	—				Uncertain								
	Sociocultural environment					Uncertain								
	(c) Accessibility													
	Job opportunities	Rank	5	2	4	3	1	5	2	4	3	1	5	2
	Shopping facilities	—				in Sector 2.1(c)								
	Cultural/recreation	—				As for shopping facilities								
	Education and schooling					In Sector 2.1(c)								
3.1.2	*Of Other Urban Areas*	—	Nil	Nil	Nil	Nil	Nil	—	—	—	—	—	—	
3.1.3	*Of Rural Areas*													
	Job opportunities	Rank	3	1	2	4	5	3	1	2	4	5	2	2
	Accessibility to shops		Uncertain		Uncertain		Uncertain			Uncertain				
	Accessibility to cultural/recreation		Uncertain		Uncertain		Uncertain			Uncertain				

Table 2 (Continued)

Item	Sector and Instrumental Objective	Unit of Measurement	Comparison of the Alternatives — Hypotheses				Ranking — Hypotheses					Preferred 1–5	Preferred 1–4
			(1) Ministry of the Interior Plan	(2) Urban Clusters	(3) Growth Centers	(5) Trends	1	2	3	4	5		
3.2	*Existing Manufacturing Enterprises*	—	Nil	Nil	Nil	Nil	—	—	—	—	—	—	
3.3	*Existing Commercial Enterprises*	—	Nil	Nil	Nil	Nil	—	—	—	—	—	—	
4.0	**Displacees**	—	Nil	Nil	Nil	Nil	—	—	—	—	—	—	
5.0	**Traveling Public**	Rank	4	1	1	5	4	1	1	3	5	2 and 3	2 and 3
6.0	**The Israeli Public**												
	(a) Economic objectives												
	Balance of payments	Rank	1	3	5	4	1	3	5	2	4	1	1
	(b) Dispersal of population												
	Settlement of land	—	Nil	Nil	Nil	Nil	—	—	—	—	—	—	
	Establishing Jewish presence	—	3	1	1	5	3	1	1	3	5	2 and 3	2 and 3
	Defense	—	Nil	Nil	Nil	Nil	—	—	—	—	—	—	
	Development of backward regions	Rank	3	1	1	5	3	1	1	3	5	2 and 3	2 and 3

[a] Hypotheses assessed against hypothesis 5. All money figures in Israeli Lira (IL) millions discounted to 1975 at 8% p.a.

the proposals have such wide ramifications, the consumers of existing developments, people displaced as a result of development, the traveling public, and the Israeli general public are identified in addition to identifying the producers/operators and the consumers of the new development. The most interesting category is the general public because in most evaluation exercises they would be ignored. However, if one takes as a basis for the study that the new-town program should meet various national goals, clearly one must admit the possibility that there may be a different effect with reference to these goals as a result of adopting one strategy rather than another. Thus the Israeli general public has improving the balance of payments as one of its instrumental objectives. This was determined by analyzing the effects on the cost and output scedules of manufacturing enterprises of the new towns.[26]

Obviously, in the formulation of these instrumental objectives the ideal would be to represent the expressed view of the people concerned. Difficulties of time and of finding an appropriate methodology to determine these objectives make this ideal rarely realizable, and thus the planners themselves, acting on the best advice available, must decide what these objectives would be. This is not necessarily so contentious as it appears because there are many factual and commonsensable objectives that single groups could not dispute. Thus, for example, *ceteris paribus,* one objective is assumed to be that residents generally prefer to be close to shopping facilities. Hence accessibility becomes an instrumental objective.

Then comes the essence of the evaluation, the comparison of the differences between the hypotheses in terms of the differences in social costs and benefits accruing to each sector of the community in terms of its own instrumental objectives. As far as possible the costs and benefits were measured in monetary terms, but various items could not be measured in money or even perhaps in other physical terms. These items were nonetheless identified and presented within the context of the planning balance sheet. The conclusions were drawn by ranking the hypotheses against the measurements made, and the conclusions and recommendations are now given in full.

Conclusions and Recommendations. The findings of this comparative evaluation of the four planning hypotheses set out in the previous section were as follows: hypotheses 1 (urban clusters and 4 (the Ministry of Interior plan) were preferred overall

compared with the other alternatives, although we could not say which of these two alternatives was superior. In addition, there seemed to be no reason for supposing that any one of the alternatives had special features in terms of the likely effect of the decision on the distribution of income within society or of marked effects for particular interest groups, so that the conclusion that these two hypotheses are preferred on the basis of the efficiency of the analysis of the planning balance sheet does not seem to be open to serious contradiction by any considerations of equity.

Broadly, the reasons the two hypotheses are preferred are as follows. Both hypotheses have advantages in terms of the value of the output of economic goods from the manufacturing sectors. This is because the alternatives allocate populations to areas of comparatively high productivity in the country, or because the manner of population allocations is conducive to high productivity.

The Ministry of the Interior plan has an advantage over the alternative of urban clusters for the balance of payments item. Because this item is more indicative of possible balance of payments difficulties than of precise estimates of the foreign exchange account, it cannot really be considered to be substantial.

In addition to the aspect of the output of economic goods, we have that of the new towns as residential environments. The urban clusters hypothesis has advantages for the new residents of new towns and their existing residents as well as the rural population. This is essentially due to the fact that this hypothesis brings to the new towns a better juxtaposition of work places and residences, along with shopping and other facilities for consumers, than the alternative hypotheses, including the Ministry of the Interior plan. Indeed the *raison d'etre* of this urban clusters hypothesis is mostly to provide for advantages of accessibility to residential groups—hence its superiority in this regard.

The hypothesis of urban clusters also has advantages over the Ministry of the Interior plan on items of interest to the general Israeli public relative to the country's settlement goals. Indeed it is as good as any other hypothesis for these considerations of settlement goals, especially in terms of establishing Jewish presence and the development of backward regions.

Both the hypothesis of the Ministry of the Interior plan and the hypothesis of the urban clusters have advantages in terms of the outputs of economic goods, but superiority is indeterminate. Urban clusters has certain advantages for the various residential sectors. It also has advantages in terms of the achievement of Israel's settlement goals but is less preferred for the balance of payments item. Whether the advantages to the residential sectors in terms of education and schooling and consumption of services in the urban clusters strategy is likely to outweigh any possible disadvantages of that hypothesis in terms of the total value of economic goods produced by the economy compared with the Ministry of the Interior plan is indeterminable. Nevertheless, these do seem to be the issues involved between these two preferred hypotheses.

Thus, neither one of these two hypotheses can be the preferred one. Both have advantages over the other alternatives and, for selected items, over each other. The conclusions of the evaluation of this study are that the Ministry of Interior plan and urban clusters are preferred overall and that urban clusters be subjected to more detailed planning study and formulation, to be put forward alongside the Ministry of Interior plan as a realistic alternative strategy for development of the new towns of Israel (see Figures 7 and 8).

Each town could develop within the cluster according to its locational, economic, or social characteristics. The existing characteristics of each cluster and the unclustered towns were analyzed in this study and can be defined as Table 3 shows (also see Figure 8). The unclustered towns could develop within their regional context according to their specific characteristics. In each town local services would be developed for the residents of the town and for the rural region. The main objective is to create an efficient local educational system, including primary and secondary schools, according to the reform that is already being implemented in some of the new towns. A regional synthesis would aid the erection of at least two comprehensive high schools in each town, to create the minimum necessary variety for the pupils and staff. Local shopping facilities, health services, and cultural activities should also develop according to accepted norms and standards.

Political Acceptability. The balance sheet analysis was more than a social cost-benefit analysis. By showing which groups would benefit and which would suffer, it offered a basis for political choice. This might not be so difficult in Israel as elsewhere, because there have veen various government policies that have persisted throughout the building of the state. At a more detailed level, those politicians concerned with specific groups or people (either by

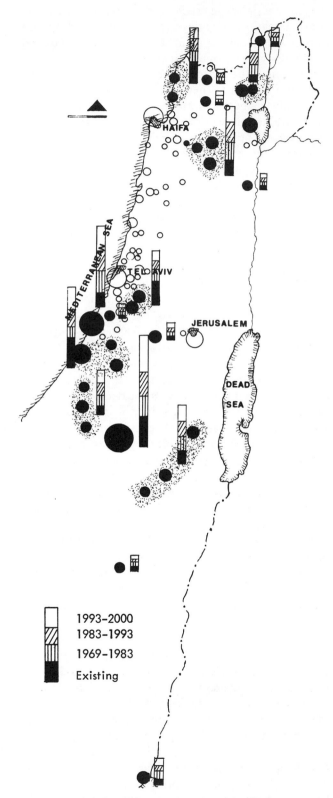

Figure 7.   Urban clusters: population growth.

interest or by location) or with specific issues will be able to trace the incidence of effects as set out in the planning balance sheet. It would be naive to imagine that all politicians and all groups will be equally happy; the most that can be hoped for is that points of issue be clearly indentified and that, in the final analysis, some concentration of the general interest predominates over sectional interests.

IMPLEMENTATION OF THE PREFERRED STRATEGY

Two problems have exacerbated the difficulties in implementing new-town development in Israel: planning concepts and legal procedures that are inadequate[27] and an organizational structure that inhibits coordinated decision making.

Planners unduly deferred to the classic theories of regional settlement hierarchies without considering the implications arising from the highly developed state and national economic organization of the agricultural settlements. The new towns themselves were planned under the only legal provisions available—an Ordinance of 1936, dating from the time of the British Mandate—and a new Planning and Building Law, produced in 1965, has done little to improve the legal and administrative machinery of new towns.

Perhaps, however, the most serious aspect is the lack of coordinated development for new towns. As the program grew, more agencies and ministries became involved. Initially the Ministry of Labor, through its Housing Department, undertook the responsibility for housing construction as well as certain aspects of transportation planning. The Ministry of Commerce and Industry became responsible for industrial development, and the Ministry of Development took charge of natural resources. The Ministry of the Interior assumed responsibility for the functions of physical planning and more recently (1968) responsibility went to the Ministry of Absorption for the immigrants. The bulk of public-sector housing is carried out by the Ministry of Housing.

The current division of responsibilities for the new towns prevents any one ministry from assuming overall control and thus taking into consideration the wider issues previously mentioned. Accordingly, the report suggested the establishment in one ministry enough financial and legal authority to be able to instill coordination on the planning and development

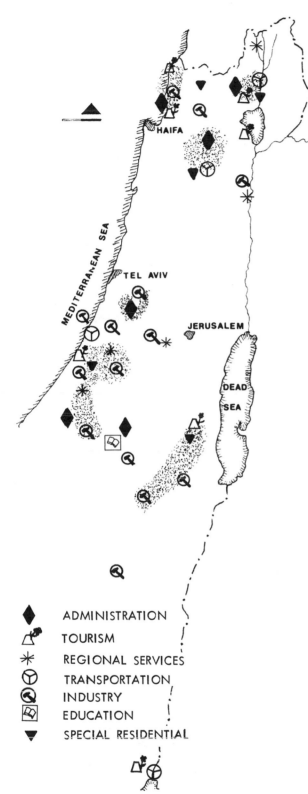

ADMINISTRATION
TOURISM
REGIONAL SERVICES
TRANSPORTATION
INDUSTRY
EDUCATION
SPECIAL RESIDENTIAL

Figure 8.   Urban clusters: specialized functions of towns.

Table 3   Characteristics of Clustered and Unclustered Development Towns

	Characteristic
Clustered towns	
Zefat-Hazor Cluster	
Zefat	Administration (subdistrict capital), higher education, health, and tourism
Hazor	Transportation center, industry, and services for rural settlements
Nazerat Illit-Afula-Migdal HaEmeq Cluster	
Nazerat Illit	Administration (district capital), higher education, tourism, industry, and commerce
Afula	Transportation center, health, and services for rural settlements
Migdal HaEmeq	Special residential area, vocational education, and some industry
Akko-Nahariyya Cluster	
Akko	Administration (subdistrict capital), industry, and tourism
Nahariyya	Tourism, health, and industry
Ramla-Lod Cluster	
Ramla	Administration (district capital), health, and vocational education (in joint area with Lod)
Lod	Industry, services to airport, and transportation center
Ashquelon-Qiryat Gat-Qiryat Malakhi Cluster	
Ashquelon	Tourism, administration (subdistrict center), health, and industry
Qiryt Gat	Industry and services for rural area
Qiryat Malakhi	Transportation center and services for rural area
Sederot-Netivot-Ofaqim Cluster	
Sederot	Services for rural area and industry, including regional council
Netivot	Administration and services for rural area
Ofaqim	Industry
Dimona-Yeruham-Arad Cluster	
Dimona	Industry, vocational education, and commerce
Yeruham	Extractive industries
Arad	Tourism, including health resort, and special residential areas
Unclustered towns	
Qiryat Shamona	Regional services and footloose industries
Tiberias	Tourism, including health resort, health, regional tourist, administrative, commercial, and cultural center
Bet Shean	Industry and regional services
Carmiel	Industry and regional services
Ma'alot	Health resort, services for rural area, and special residential quarters
Yavne	Industry

Table 3 (continued)

	Characteristic
Bet Shemesh	Industry and regional center
Ashdod	Industry and transportation (harbor)
Beer Sheva	Administration (district capital), commerce, industry, higher education, health, and communication
Mizpe Ramon	Industry and services
Elat	Tourism, commerce, transportation (harbor), and industry

of the new towns. However, something more is needed.

No institution on the lines of new-town development corporations or the New Towns Commission of Britain exists. Furthermore, the weakness in local government in the rural areas means that local involvement in the running of the new towns is not satisfactory. In a small country a corporation for each town may not be needed, and the report recommends the establishment of a new-towns commission or authority. To all these points the report suggested remedies or offered alternatives for further investigation and research. The precise findings are perhaps too localized to be of general interest, but one concept that has wide implications for new-town planning and development is amplified in conclusion.

The new-town goals of dispersal of the population have been largely achieved, but the price in terms of the living conditions in the new towns has been high. Therefore, now that the towns are established, it would seem appropriate to revise the emphasis and place priority on the successful development of the community living in the towns—at least to create a life that in terms of economic and social opportunity is the equal of that in the established towns. That is the role of community development. Going a stage beyond that, it might be conceivable to reintroduce some element of utopianism into the development of the new towns in the same way that element has been successfuly incorporated into the development of agricultural settlements. Unhappily for Israel and the world, there is no example of an urban *kibbutz*.

No one can disagree with such a goal, but in everyday administration of planning, realization of the goal is difficult. Among the accommodations made, two can be mentioned: first, a standing on its head of the conventional approach to the planning and development process. Just as planners consider the expectations for physical development of the towns, they should consider the relation of expectations for

human development to physical development. Consequently, recommendations are made for improvements in the comprehensive planning, comprehensive development, and community development of the new towns. The second recommendation relates to the practice of community development. In this respect the towns go through a series of socioeconomic stages—from subsistence through opportunity to security and takeoff. Throughout, some human development plan and program is needed comprising *inter alia* the towns' economic development, social development, and local government. Coordination of both the official and unofficial agencies is needed here just as in comprehensive planning and physical development. Also needed is meaningful participation by the public, seen in parallel to the maturing local government; and overall there is more than usual scope for monitoring, evaluation, feedback, and review. If the Israeli new-town movement can grasp this method of community development, it will add yet another dimension to its significance in the international new-town movement.

NOTES

1. Ira M. Robinson, "Small, Independent, Self-contained and Balanced New Towns: Myth or Reality?" in *New Towns: Why - and for Whom?* Harvey Perloff and Neil Sandberg, Eds. (New York: Praeger, 1973), pp. 3–27.

2. Lack of available data makes it impossible for me to comment on the east European experience, although the centralized nature of planning in those countries makes it likely that their new-town programs could fall into this category.

3. *Town and Country Planning* **40**, No. 1 (1972): entire issue.

4. Nathaniel Lichfield, *Israel's New Towns: A Development Strategy* (Tel Aviv: Institute for Planning and Development Ltd., 1971), to be published in 3 vols.; Vol 3 not yet published. The report was commissioned by the Minister of Housing and was undertaken by the author leading an interdisciplinary team of Israelis provided by the Institute of Planning and Development Ltd., Tel Aviv, and set up under the local direction of Shmuel Shaked, with Alexander Berler as consultant.

5. *Ibid.*

6. Erika Spiegel, *New Towns in Israel* (Stuttgart/Bern: Karl Kramer Verlag, 1966).

7. Alexander Berler, *New Towns in Israel* (Jerusalem: Israel University Press, 1970).

8. For a comparative account of the development process in British and Israel new towns see Nathaniel Lichfield, "The Development of New Towns: Britain and Israel Compared," in *Physical Planning,* Proceedings of the Third World Congress on Dialogue in Development (Tel Aviv: Engineers and Architects in Israel, 1974).

9. See, for example, D. Ben-Gurion, *Jews in Their Land* (London: Aldus, 1966).

10. G. Yalan, *Private and Co-operative Agricultural Settlements* (Rehovot, Israel: Rehovot Settlement Center, 1969).

11. E. Brutzkus, *Regional Policy in Israel* (Jerusalem: International Federation of Housing and Planning, Permanent Committee for Regional Planning, Israeli Section, 1969).

12. Arie S. Schachar, *The Development Towns of Israel: A National Policy of Urbanisation and Spatial Organisation* (Jerusalem: Proceedings of the Rehovot Conference on Urbanization and Development in Developing Countries, 1971).

13. See, for example, Berler.

14. Figures derived from data supplied by the Jewish Agency.

15. Nathaniel Lichfield, "Economic Opportunity," in *New Towns: Why and for Whom?* pp. 48–67.

16. The goals were derived principally from the directives to the Economic Planning Authority issued by the Ministerial Committee on Economic Planning and from the Economic Planning Authority itself.

17. Other approaches were discussed, but in each a major variable was the physical form of the towns, and thus it seems logical that this variable should be isolated.

18. See Lichfield, *Israel's New Towns,* Ch. 8 and 16.

19. See Berler.

20. See Lichfield, *Israel's New Towns,* Ch. 3 and 4.

21. Nathaniel Lichfield, Peter Kettle, and Michael Whitbread, *Evaluation in the Planning Process* (Oxford: Pergamon, 1975).

22. Lichfield, *Israel's New Towns,* Ch. 7–9.

23. A. Cohen, "A Model for an Optimal Distribution of Industries," in Lichfield, *Israel's New Towns,* Vol. 3 (unpublished).

24. For an account of planning balance sheet analysis (PBSA) see Nathaniel Lichfield, *Economics of Planned Development* (London: Estates Gazette, 1956), Ch. 19 or many other cases in PBSA cited in Lichfield, Kettle, and Whitbread, 1975. For a comparison with other methods see Lichfield, Kettle, and Whitbread, Ch. 4.

25. See case studies in Lichfield, Kettle, and Whitbread, Ch. 4.

26. See Cohen. The model was run on the basis of the populations allocated to the new towns, which vary in total between the hypotheses. Thus, the results of the model reflect not only the geographic locations of the population and industry in the new towns (the points primarily at issue), but also the differing total numbers of workers as well. It is difficult to separate the latter effect from the former, although a tentative conclusion (which preferred the urban cluster strategy) was reached.

27. See Lichfield, *Israel's New Towns,* Ch. 4.

CHAPTER 13

Social Policy for Israeli Development Towns

ALEXANDER BERLER

In Israel urbanization is congruent with the settling of the country as a whole. This process consists of two major factors that must be analytically separated: the background and direction toward towns of immigration and the process of urbanization occurring in rural settlements.

The people who founded the Jewish settlement in the country, from its beginning to this day, were in most cases city or town dwellers in their country of origin who demonstrated a wish to detach themselves from the urban way of life. The Jewish village in Israel was originally a creation of former city dwellers. It is therefore important to emphasize the unique urbanization processes in Israel, which result in an attitude toward the dichotomy of city versus village that is different from the one we find in most countries of the world, developed and underdeveloped alike.

POPULATION DISPERSAL AND REGIONAL DEVELOPMENT

The percentage of urban population in Israel is one of the highest in the world. At independence in 1948 the urban population of the country was 73.4 percent of the total, and by the end of 1974 its share had risen to 86 percent.[1] Such a large degree of urbanization, *per se* an insufficient indicator of overall development, has to be analyzed in the light of population dispersal patterns. If we were to examine countries with a large percentage of urban population, we would find that the existing pattern of population dispersal has occurred in two ways. In old nations that have undergone an industrial revolution, towns grew organically against the background of existing rural population with old traditions of its own; a whole hierarchy of urban settlements, small and big, has formed under such conditions. In countries of recent pioneer settlement, we find large tracts of land sparsely populated and extensively exploited by a small rural population, while proportionately large parts of the total population concentrate in a few urban centers with almost no intermediate urban settlements acting as links between the main towns and the countryside.

As early as 1948 Israel seemed to have a settlement pattern resembling the second type. If we consider the ratio of the population living in centers of 100,000 inhabitants and above to the total population as a measure of demographic concentration, we observe that the only center of this category existing at that time (Tel Aviv) already accounted for about 30 percent of the total. Table 1 shows this weight equalled the aggregate share of the other categories of urban settlements out the country's total.

Israel resembled countries of the polarized pattern in yet another phenomenon: the concentration of the population in maritime plains and in harbor towns. In 1948, the population of Tel Aviv, Haifa, and central districts, accounted for 60 percent of the country's total.[2]

Under conditions of a polarized settlement structure, characterized by direct links from the smallest

Table 1   Distribution of Settlements in Israel, by Size

	Over 100,000 Inhabitants			50,000–100,000 Inhabitants			20,000–50,000 Inhabitants			5,000–20,000 Inhabitants		
	N	Population (in thousands)	%	N	Population (in thousands)	%	N	Population (in thousands)	%	N	Population (in thousands)	%
1948	1	248	28	2	183	20	—	—	—	9	88	10
1961	2	350	16	2	145	0.07	16	492	22	33	348	16
1974	7	1,373	40	5	377	11	19	593	17	47	484	14

Source: *The Statistical Yearbook of Israel, 1975,* No. 26.

village to the major towns, the density of the rural population really determines the overall population density of the national territory. To a certain measure the *kibbutz* had reinforced this trend toward polarization. Enjoying direct access to the major towns due to its affiliation to national organizations, the *kibbutz* exerted a negative influence on the creation of regional concentrations and internal road nets, so that each of the settlements formed its own social and economic connections and usually did not relate to the smaller towns in its area.

The objections that this settlement pattern has aroused include, *inter alia,* the economic aspect: the sparsely populated countryside has either to maintain at great cost the modern services vital for its inhabitants or do without them, while the few major towns enjoy a considerable economic advantage, thanks to the concentration of many of the existing services in a relatively small area. Also, this type of settlement structure involves high transportation costs, both for agricultural products from the country to a small number of marketing centers and for the shipment of processed goods from towns to the single rural settlements. In Israel most rural areas are characterized by a great demand for modern services and amenities, due to a standard of living that is higher than the urban average, a clear departure from patterns found in many other countries.[3]

The influence of the existing major population concentrations became increasingly powerful and further emphasized the lack of interregional balance throughout the country. Such conditions resulted in a vital, urgent need for changing the geographic pattern of settlements in Israel. Therefore the new towns were a result of a national planning effort aimed at achieving a defined objective. Under the particular conditions of Israel, the following additional factors were also active:

1. The founding of towns was carried out in desert or sparsely populated regions where the various elements of infrastructure were virtually nonexistent.
2. National authorities directed the settling population to these new towns as part of an accelerated absorption of massive immigration.
3. Most immigrants who were directed to the new towns experienced an acute transformation that directly influenced each person economically, professionally, socially, culturally, and physically, with an effect more powerful than was ever experienced by those new immigrants who settled in the center of the country.

In recent years Israel's growing agricultural production has met the country's demands, and the emphasis has turned to industrial development. In this respect the importance of medium-sized centers became evident due to increasing prices of land in densely populated areas, to the need for a better distribution of population and employment opportunities throughout the national territory, and to the need to care for a more equitable allocation of resources in a country like Israel, chiefly based on immigration.

Against this background, the main elements that have influenced the planning policy of Israel were rapid demographic growth and the need for a comprehensive change in the settlement structure of the country. Eventual changes in the sociocultural and economic compositions of immigrating groups also contributed to the urgent need to establish a large number of new urban settlements. This policy of decentralization found its expression in the settlement of Israeli's new towns, mainly in the development zones of the southern and northern regions.

In this chapter the term *development town* is used in its broad interpretation to connote both brand new towns created since 1948 and those towns that have undergone a process of renewal and reconstruction with part of the population remaining or with a complete turnover of populations.[4]

During the period 1948–1967, 17 new towns were created. The term *development towns* is now applied to 27 urban centers, located all over the country. These towns in 1974 had a population of .5 million— 15 percent of the total population of Israel, or 17 percent of the Jewish sector. This policy of settlement did not fail to affect the overall dispersal of population, as Table 1 shows.

Table 1 also shows that the process of development of urban settlements during the period 1948–1974 has been intensive both quantitatively (from a total of 13 settlements in 1948 to 78 in 1974, an increase of 500 percent and qualitatively (from no settlements in the 20,000–50,000 size category to 19). However, the group including locations with more than 100,000 inhabitants shows the most significant increase, both in the absolute number of settlements (+ 600 percent) and of the population (+ 453 percent). If we consider the share of this category out of the total population of the country, as compared to the combined percent of the other categories, we observe that the ratio has remained almost the same: 0.93 in 1948 and 0.95 in 1974.

Settlement policy has also changed the relative weight of the development zones, where most of the development towns are situated, to the total Jewish population of Israel. This weight increased from 20.5 percent in 1948 to 25.4 percent in 1954 and 30.5 percent in 1964. Since then, however, the increase has been slower, to 31.8 percent of the total population in 1973.[5] A steady, continuous increase has occurred in the relative weight of only one district—the southern one—from 0.9 percent in 1948 to 12.4 percent in 1973. The increase of the northern district

was less significant: from 7.6 percent in 1948 to 10.4 percent in 1964 and then down to 9.7 percent in 1973.

On the whole, the development districts' weight in the total Jewish population in 1973 was 31.8 percent as compared to that of the central district, which alone accounted for the remaining 68.2 percent.[6]

The extremely polarized structure characteristic of the Jewish population during the period of the British mandate has gradually been replaced by a different pattern aiming at a more even distribution of the population over the national territory. The creation of a whole hierarchy of centers constituting a regional system has succeeded only in part and constitutes an increasingly vital concern for planners. In fact, objectives of overall development in terms of the creation of attractive, dynamic foci cannot be achieved by means of the mere creation of isolated centers. To fulfill the functions expected of it, a development town has to reach a minimum size as a condition of a viable system.

Unfortunately, most development towns were until recently still far from this target. Table 2 shows that at the end of 1973 more than a third of the development towns had populations of less than 10,000 inhabitants. This category accounted for 14 percent of the total population of the development towns; 36.9 percent of this population lived in places of less than 20,000 inhabitants. From 1964 to 1973 the percentage of people living in towns of more than 30,000, increased from 36 percent to 43 percent, but during the subsequent three years it increased by only 1 percent.

The whole issue of the Israeli development towns is complex. Before we proceed to an analysis of sociocultural issues, let us refer briefly to a few observations concerning a major condition of a successful process of absorption of new immigrants: the

Table 2   Distribution of the Development Towns According to Population Size

Size Group	Number of Localities			Total Population in Each Group			%		
	1964	1970	1973	1964	1970	1973	1964	1970	1973
Up to 10,000	13	12	11	81,700	70,300	71,800	22.6	15.9	14.1
10,001 to 20,000	8	8	8	126,800	114,800	115,900	35.2	26.0	22.8
20,001 to 30,000	1	3	4	23,400	68,300	99,800	6.5	15.4	19.7
30,001 to 40,000	2	2	1	66,700	71,500	35,500	18.5	16.2	7.0
40,001 and above	1	2	3	62,200	117,500	184,700	17.2	26.5	36.4
Total	25	27	27	360,800	442,400	507,700	100.0	100.0	100.0

Source: *Statistical Abstracts of Israel,* 1965, 1974.

problem of the number of professional people living in each locality.

Israel has been confronted with a pressing need to transform within a short period a great number of people who previously made their livings as petty traders and artisans or have been without any skilled occupation whatsoever into farmers, industrial workers, or government officials. These constituted occupations unfamiliar to the majority of the newcomers from Afro-Asian countries. As the latter differed considerably from the veteran population of the country, a three-fold process has taken place simultaneously since the establishment of the state.

1. The logistic transfer of the new immigrants into the country.
2. A resulting shift in the national economy toward the absorption of immigrants.
3. Great changes in the occupations, economic condition, and societies of the immigrants themselves.

These requirements resulted in adjustments along trends contrary to those prevailing in other countries—from the town to the countryside and from tertiary occupations to primary and secondary ones. The capacity to succeed in such changes depended on the sociocultural background of the various immigrating groups and their predispositions toward professional adaptation.

The most characteristic feature of Israel's labor force proved to be the polarity of its occupational structure. Alongside masses of immigrants coming from underdeveloped countries without the work tradition of a modern society and lacking in education and skills, other immigrating groups including highly qualified professional and skilled manpower arrived. This polarity found its manifestation in most development towns in a two-fold phenomenon: (1) a high local concentration of manpower with few skills and (2) only a few professional workers with qualifications needed for industrial development ready to settle in those areas.

As a result, development efforts came mainly from the central government with little local initiative. Small and medium-sized industries and commercial services did not develop on the whole according to goals. Under such conditions, industrialization means first and foremost professionalization. It is not sufficient, as has been customary for a long time in the writings of many authors, to point to industrialization and urbanization as the major determinants in modern social change, with only secondary reference

to the subject of professional activity as a factor influencing such a change. An approach that limits itself to the aforementioned factors prevents a sociological interpretation of social dynamics. Such an approach seems to be too narrow, because it is precisely the dynamics of professional activity that constitute one of the chief components of industrialization and urbanization. In the following sections the discussion is focused on the need for a rethinking of sociocultural factors, with a view to creating more favorable conditions for the attainment of major structural and professional objectives considered thus far.

DISPERSAL OF SOCIOCULTURAL ASSETS

The relatively rapid increase of population in the development towns was a result of the diversion of immigrants and a high birth rate. Some of them even tended to develop into attractions (attracting internal migration from other settlements) and showed a considerable decrease in emigration; it was also found that through the influence of veteran immigrants, mainly the younger generation who arrived from other settlements, the population characteristics (e.g., occupational cross section) were improved. With the development of local sources of employment, there occurred a transfer from unnatural work (relief works) and agriculture to permanent employment in industry and other sectors. Still the process of improvement influenced only a few of the employees who lacked education and skill.[7]

Therefore we must direct our planning ideas, which aim at decentralization of settlement in urban areas, into various channels, including those not in themselves concerned with physical decentralization of the population. Simultaneously we should encourage the decentralization of cultural amenities to avoid an additional increase of the existing gap between the investment in economic assets and demographic settlements in border areas[8] and the investment in cultural amenities[9] in these areas. This danger is imminent because the gap is not static but constitutes a self-propagating process. The self-propagating nature of the cultural system has many aspects: the existence of cultural amenities serves as an attraction of major importance for settlers whose occupational training allows them many choices. However, the presence of people whose cultural level is high becomes in itself a focal point of attraction for candidates for settlement who follow them. Thus a circle is created: the percentage of cultured people is conditioned by the concentration of cultural assets in the town, while constituting an element of those local cultural assets.

This process creates a second circle: the existence of a cultural focus improves the town's cultural level not only by causing an external demographic flow, but also by contributing to the improvement of the local population's cultural level, mainly that of children. As a result, people who have higher economic ability and level of ambition stay in the town, while the weaker ones are spared cultural backwardness. The same process, when moving the other way, is also self-propagating. When a regression starts, it becomes stronger by the very power of its acceleration. The lack of local assets will result in the desertion of those few with a high level of ability or ambition and will abandon the rest to a cultural decline. As the increased supply increases the demand and the demand increases the supply in the promotion process, a mutual decrease occurs in the inverse process.

Although it may appear in the short run to be competing with the sociocultural infrastructure and the allocation of resources, the economic system depends for its development in the long run on the level of education. A developed economy demands a high level of knowledge. However, it is the basis for raising the standard of living above the level of ambition, on which, again, depends the allocation of resources for cultural development.

The socioeconomic infrastructure's characteristic of motivating several self-propagating processes (in both directions) demands the review of the geographic decentralization of the national investment in cultural assets. An inappropriate geographic division of the national investment in cultural assets created a new image for the border settlements. This image has already acquired for itself an independent psychological entity, able to disconnect itself from the facts. When many people believe this image, the cancelling out of the fact that caused it would no longer suffice to cancel out the image, and people will tend to act and behave in accord with the image, as if its causes still exist. When people became accustomed to the fact that border settlements, in this sense, are lacking in cultural institutions and cultural assets, a psychological association was created between border settlements and cultural backwardness. This association may serve as an important, possibly a determining, factor for people's decisions not to settle in such places—or even to desert them.

The image is even more rigid than the facts themselves. To change the image, a new image must be created that will be strong enough to replace the rooted one. Any retarded investment in this objective will necessarily be an increased one.

Figures indicate the existence of a cultural gap between settlements in development regions and the national average.[10] (As a result, the gap between those settlements and their veteran, well-established counterparts, with which they are compared, is much bigger.) Moreover, a long-term comparison verifies the assumption that a gap in the sociocultural infrastructure tends to become wider.[11] If we allow this development to continue along these apparent trends, without initiated counteraction, the future picture will be considerably graver than at present. The necessary investment for halting this process is the kind of activity that should become an immediate concern of various authorities. The intention is not to claim that much is not being done. In fact, enumerating the various actions might convince us that the maximum is being done, and we may not demand more; however, there is no escape from the fact that an additional powerful push is needed. We must show that the nature of the needed activity constitutes a sound economic investment.

It is apparent that the need for accelerating the extent of investment in human potential in the long run is essential. The extent of investment in human potential—that is, the human capital of the population in a given place—is influenced by two factors: an additional investment in the existing population and an additional population, bringing the capital that was invested in it in some other place. These two factors are thus related: the "capital export" will not occur under conditions of pure, spontaneous demographic movement unless the existent capital level has reached its critical value. The presence of this critical level is at the same time a necessary and sufficient condition—that is, the flow of potential toward the focus will never occur unless the condition is fulfilled and will always occur if the condition is so fulfilled.

Moreover, inasmuch as the potential flowing toward the focus must start at some source and due to the fact that in places where the critical level has been achieved there always exists a flow toward the focus (positive flow), it is inevitable that places that are below critical level will constantly lose what little they have. Therefore, as soon as there are foci that are past critical level, polarization occurs. At the foci of attraction there is a constant enrichment in human potential, while other places decrease in resources due to their lag. This phenomenon exposes the qualitative nature of the distinction between city and town and indicates that urbanization (under conditions of spontaneous demographic movement) is a process of qualitative change. The manner in which this occurs in parts of Israeli society, where conditions are known to be far from spontaneous and undisturbed, is discussed later.

Why do we find an abstract illustration sufficient without quantitatively defining critical level, and what is the use of such an abstract model? The critical level's value depends on so many variables that even ranges of values cannot be evaluated without analyzing the problem, and for that this framework is too narrow. However, the abstract model is used in the development of an assumption that within a given society, where all the conditioned variables are taken to be constant, there is a threshold of educational capital under which any settlement will not continue to exist in the long run: its personnel resources, which carry a load of human capital, will be carried away, leaving behind an impoverished sediment, the extent of whose additional impoverishment is inversely proportional to the existing level. To this characteristic of the model a well-known fact may be related: in the framework of the most developed cultures and civilizations, foci of extreme retardation tend to occur.

Moreover, the model also indicates a recommended direction of attack that may overcome polarization: an intentional direction of human capital to counter the spontaneous flow (to be compared with an antiperiodic economic policy). Such a direction must be achieved through the aforementioned channel: directing personnel to embryonic foci of decline by way of planning a system of incentives and directing other resources that will increase the educational capital of the original population.

Educational level is not only the foundation of the employment structure; education is one of the factors that determines the population's image in the eyes of potential settlers. The lower the existing educational level of the population, the more difficult it is to motivate settlers with a higher educational level to settle there (or in other words, the bigger the necessary incentive required for such motivation). Thus the educational level index acquires a weight proportional to its size and may accordingly, in extreme cases, dominate all other variables. Due to that, the sociocultural infrastructure is a cause for rigidity in settlements, where this infrastructure remains difficult to change even when considerable resources are allocated for the attempt. The poorness of the infrastructure and its poor chances of recovery may create a situation (and in the Israeli experience many such instances may be illustrated) where considerable resources are lost because their rate flow is insufficient to generate an adequate change that will increase the foundations's value to a level higher than the critical threshold. Whenever this value is still less than the critical value, the process of decline goes on (even though it may temporarily slow down); and at the end of a period, the length of which is a function of the insufficient investment, the settlement regresses to its point of departure. This dynamic process seems to have no solution other than the operative conclusion that is derived from the knowledge of its nature—that is, only a push powerful enough to transfer the settlement immediately to a level higher than the critical threshold may be considered a profitable investment, and therefore, when carrying out public policy, only a policy thus directed is normatively justified by any rational criterion of resources allocation.

The model's characteristic that indicates an inverse proportion between the existing level and the rate of impoverishment also indicates the urgency of the problem for every developing society, due to the fact that the necessary means for halting the polarization increase by the same proportion.

We must give thought to an appropriate dispersal of cultural assets—that is, to a just division of nonmaterial assets that in their turn may establish conditions of equal opportunities for all people in all regions. The assumption is reasonable that decentralization may be of assistance in imparting modern urban values to new development towns. Frontal implementation of long-term plans—in fields like economy, administration, education, and culture—may become the cause of reversing the cultural trend in development towns.

An appropriate geographic decentralization will have a considerable influence on the population's living conditions and its ability to participate in cultural functions; differences in the level of decentralization among settlements and regions are a cause for establishing and even widening social gaps.

It would be dangerous to let cultural assets flow through channels that are dictated by the rules of supply and demand. Though these are no less universal than the rules of physical entropy, channels of development that are dictated by universal rules may still be changed by means of an appropriate investment: just as the biological system can reverse the trend of natural disorder by means of an investment of energy, so can the social system counter the trend of distribution of assets by means of an economic investment; if the direction of cultural assets against the natural channel of supply and demand may require an economic sacrifice, so the avoidance of it will require a social sacrifice. To determine which of the two different costs is more worthwhile, one must know the rate of exchange.

When we compare the economic assets system to that of the cultural assets, using as a criterion their tendency for increasing or decreasing polarization, it becomes apparent that cultural assets are more diffuse and tend to divide themselves to blunt polarization: when an economic investment is made in a social unit, the profits, as unequal as they may be, will also reach the fringes of the society, while more selective cultural assets tend to divide themselves to increase polarization. Infusing a society with cultural tools is in itself insufficient for distributing the profits beyond a core that is conditioned to absorb them; and the fringes of the society will find themselves dispossessed and in a state of higher relative disadvantage, which will contribute toward the increase of polarization both in the original cultural facet and in the economic one.

Furthermore, where the distribution of assets of both kinds is concerned, the rate of polarization is decisively influenced by the extent of existing polarization. The higher it is, the more it is resistant to change and the bigger the investment required to counteract it, by both absolute and relative accounting. Apparently, the problem should be attacked as early as possible during the development of polarization and according to long-term needs, and at the same time not disregarding the unavoidable short-term requirements.

An optimal integration of long- and short-term requirements is truly the essence of a desirable development policy. Such policy will avoid the pitfall of regarding the economic and the social goals as two different and separate components; development, as distinct from economic growth, must incorporate those two terms simultaneously: development means growth combined with change.

The change is social and cultural as well as economic; it is qualitative as well as quantitative. When the social results of various economic and technological changes are being discussed, regarding them always as independent variables is illogical; actually, the manifestations of both changes in so-

ciety are correlated and tend to alternate in the roles of cause and effect. As a matter of fact, any economic activity and its successes or failures may be properly understood only when associated with sociocultural background, cultural structure, scale of values, and so on. The social aspect, therefore, is both a result of economic activities that are universally recognized as causes for social change, and a prior condition for economic activities and, even more important, for the ability for economic activities.

This generally valid distinction is especially valid under conditions where the development policy's objective is not only constructing new towns but also constructing a new society, most of whose members have undergone a sharp change in their modes of life. A development policy in a society where the requirements for physical construction (under conditions of extreme differentiation of development between different regions) converge with the need to absorb a demographic increment (the members of which, although closely and powerfully linked, still suffer from considerable gaps in living patterns and cultural heritages) should therefore pay close attention to the relations between the investment in creating human and other components. The relation exists, if you wish, on two levels: the basic universal level (due to the fact that in the society and production methods that are specific to our time, personal well-being is almost categorically dependent on an educational level that only a few decades ago was typical of certain classes of the elite) and the level specific to conditions of constructing a country and a people.

We are not concerned only with raising the level but with homogenizing two very distinct levels: that of a country, part of which is developed and part of which requires development, and that of a people, part of whom has achieved modern patterns of life and production, while the rest is carrying a heritage of backward patterns of life and production. The objective of the two-fold development policy must be to close both gaps. One is dependent on the other: the human pools that one may use for tasks of physical development cannot help relying on the demographic addition resulting from immigration, and the arena where this metamorphosis of the nation's living patterns may take place in those same regions that require development. This essential simultaneity in the implementation of two tasks (due to their mutual dependence) seems to be the problem of Israeli development policy. Its solution is certainly not independent of the imponderability that accompanied the process of Zionist realization from the start; but in this age of overconsciousness of the need for explicating objectives and means (and possibly explicating irrational elements in rational terms), one should indicate the possibility of explaining the actions of the Israeli people to achieve simultaneously a regeneration of itself and of its country as an intuitive understanding of the mutual dependence.

As for the present and future, when we may be facing needs the size of which will not be sufficiently predicted by means of intuitive understanding, it is necessary to emphasize the need of formulating a conscious rational policy, based on the understanding of that mutual dependence between productive economic and technological changes and social, educational, and cultural ones.

As a result of integrating the requirements of immigrants with those of the urban population as a whole, a considerable similarity in countries of origin and veterancy in the country is to be found in the new towns. This similarity became a disturbing factor when causing an additional similarity between country of origin and local leadership. One may question whether concentrating a population consisting of large homogeneous groups (from the point of view of country of origin) is either desirable or efficient for the requirements of reconstruction of an immigrant population. Such a settlement pattern encumbers the integration and the fusion of different ethnic groups, as it prepares the ground for internal community separatism in terms of political power; however, whether a forced process of integration accompanied by a planned mixing of population would compensate for the loss of mutual support in terms of alternative social solidarity is doubtful.

By stating the question as a dichotomy, it becomes apparent that extreme solutions on both sides may carry imminent social dangers that are sufficient to eliminate them from the range of recommended social experiments. To look for alternative solutions in the middle of the range of possibilities is therefore desirable; that is to say, one must avoid populating by means of uniform demographic transfusions of settlers from one country of origin and equally avoid the complete abolition of various communities.

The same, and even more, is to be said about the integration of the educational system. We may hope for only limited success in integrating the existing layer of initial adult settlers with their new counterparts. When we come to the integration of young people, there is a well-grounded hope that the im-

pulse for social mobility will push the development towns' youth into acquiring an education. These impulses require proper assistance and channeling that will enable young people to identify climbing the rungs of the social ladder with staying in their home towns. Such a tendency makes it necessary, even as planning is in its initial stages, to narrow the cultural gap of the second generation of immigrants—a task that will be decisively influenced by the factors of physical planning and location of educational institutions. Due consideration must also be given to the need for preliminary thinking about long-term planning of social, cultural and educational aspects, as an inseparable part of the overall plan.

The planning of development towns must therefore balance the requirements of the development itself with the needs of social dynamics. It must aim at extracting the benefits that are to be found in a rational distribution of resources throughout settlements using the criteria of national requirements within the limits of the expected social restrictions.

While exploiting the maximum possibilities in this subject, we must expect peripheral pressures, allot them their legitimate place, spare citizens frustrating experiences, and prepare the ground for the integration of central and peripheral requirements. This is not at all simple and cannot be put in the narrow form of a miraculous formula; but being an unavoidable lesson derived from the experience of quite a few development towns, it demands the close attention of social planners.

CONCLUSIONS

The building of development towns in Israel and the rehabilitation of existing ones in the development zones following the establishment of the state have been the outcome of a national policy aimed at developing the country's territory economically and socially. At the base of this policy was the need for decentralization and land settlement, with a view to decreasing the demographic concentration in the central regions, especially the maritime plain.

The considerations underlying the foundation of the development towns have undergone numerous alterations since 1948. The emergence of the concept of new urban settlements may be traced to a social and economic approach toward the creation of urban frameworks based on productive occupation. Thus during the early stages, the building of new neighborhoods for agricultural workers was predominant in new urban settlements. However, as the rate of economic growth increased and emphasis turned to services and industry, a new approach toward the planning of urban settlements was adopted.

This new approach led to the creation of a considerable number of development towns. However, some of the considerations later proved to be unrealistic. The main deficiency turned out to be the unjustified dispersal, expressed in the relatively large number of new localities, and the resulting dispersal of the means that were directed toward the consolidation and extension of the development towns. Also, the fact that an effective policy with regard to a balanced, selective direction of the population—from an economic and social point of view—to these settlements, led to a certain lag in the rate of development of these towns, compared with the entire country.

The time that has elapsed since the foundation of most of the development towns or since the beginning of rehabilitation and extension of the other towns covered in this chapter seems to be sufficient for arriving at several conclusions.

The building of new urban settlements in Israel undoubtedly has been dictated by the country's vital needs and has formed an integral part of a comprehensive policy aimed at the development of the entire country. Despite the fact that the percentage of urban population in Israel is one of the highest in the world, it still was of utmost importance to encourage urbanization further under the peculiar conditions prevailing in the country. Population was concentrated in the central regions and the maritime plain, including the Tel Aviv conurbation, which has grown beyond any acceptable proportions, while the major part of the country remained unpopulated. This may be further emphasized, if we take into consideration the existing drawback that faced any additional expansion of agriculture—drawbacks that are the result of both physical and climatic factors and of the characteristics of the immigrating groups that arrived in the country. Owing to demographic pressures, especially in periods of mass immigration, a need for space has emerged where many could be absorbed, a need that dictated the foundation of new settlements. This was accompanied by an undesirable phenomenon: under such demographic pressure, due attention for a comprehensively planned approach could not always be given; hence part of the development towns were built before a plan for local industrialization could be prepared. This amounted,

then, to quantitative demographic urbanization without an economic urban aspect.

There is no doubt that a remarkably positive change has been realized concerning the planning concepts in the sphere of developing main employment branches. The mere provision of a technical infrastructure is not sufficient for viability in a new, planned town. Hence substantial efforts and numerous investments have been diverted out of public funds to most of the development towns to activate the cycle of production, albeit the absence of a simultaneous process of investment in skilled manpower retards the process toward modernization because the locally available labor lags behind the demands of modern industrial plants.

The analysis of the settlement structure in Israel leads to the conclusion that its pattern is considerably lacking in compactness and integrity. National policy then should aim at strengthening the existing hierarchy. Considerations about optimum courses of development seem to indicate that in relation to production plants in new settlements, their order of magnitude should be adaptable to that of the size of the given town.

The pattern of our settlement structure generally lacks development of the medium-sized towns, which are often considered to be the backbone of a sound settlement structure. To develop the towns that have already come close to medium size seems desirable.

The analysis of the functional structure of the small towns indicates lack of balance between their city-forming and city-serving functions. The serious lag found in most of the small towns regarding the development of their infrastructure should be eliminated to assure an appropriate demographic and economic development and a full use of their potential sources of growth.

In this issue of planning the settlement structure, Israeli conditions are unlike those prevailing in other countries. In our country the existence of well-developed agriculture, based mostly on intensive cultivation, has a bearing on the main direction of the settlement policy, which is not geared toward the modernization of rural areas. Our main settlement planning effort is geared toward the urbanization of whole regions. This involves two tendencies: to detract from the preponderance of the central region of the country and to create an urban hinterland. However, experience has shown that the planned role of the small towns—that is, regional centers for their agricultural hinterland—has not justified itself from the beginning.[12] Furthermore, it cannot be seen as a long-range solution. A town that remains small-sized, both numerically and in its attraction for the environment, has no *raison d'etre* in a modern society. Among other things. it remains a locality devoid of an urban character in every respect. Because in most cases those towns are also far from the main centers, they are not even satellites.

A change in the planning concept of the settlement structure, then, may be contemplated: the small towns should be increased and turned into urban centers, with social and cultural services that will naturally lead the agricultural hinterland. Also, the creation of an additional focus—as a counterbalance to the country's major urban centers—out of one of the development towns may be considered. In the southern region Beer Sheva could be developed into such a focus with relative ease. In this case it should be thoroughly reinforced. The policy of decentralization could be successful and effective if we develop a series of medium-sized towns (50,000 to 80,000 inhabitants) of a characteristically urban appearance that will serve as an intermediary link between the two settlement structures: the agricultural and the metropolitan.

NOTES

1. *Statistical Yearbook of Israel,* 1949 and 1975.

2. *Ibid.*

3. See S. Pohoryles and A. Szeskin, *FAO Research in Contemporary Changes in Agrarian Structure, Case Study: Israel* (Tel Aviv: The Tel Aviv University, Department of Geography Agrarian Structure Research Project, 1973), Tables 35 and 37 and Figure 6, pp. 81–84.

4. For a detailed discussion of the concept of "development towns," see A. Berler, *New Towns in Israel* (Jerusalem: Israel University Press, 1970), pp. 58–62.

5. *Statistical Abstracts of Israel 1957/58, 1965, 1974.*

6. *Ibid.*

7. See A. Berler, *Strengthening Absorption in Development Towns and Their Rural Hinterland,* Publications on Problems of Regional Development, No. 10 (Rehovot: Settlement Study Center, 1972), Introduction.

8. The term *border areas* as used here is not limited to the customary defensive interpretation of the term and is to be understood as embracing every region in the country that constitutes an objective or a potential objective for population movement to increase the demographic decentralization.

9. *Cultural amenities* is used here to mean the physical and material complex of installations and institutions for cultural and educational activities as well as the cultural and educational level of the population.

10. See Berler, *New Towns in Israel.*

11. *Ibid.*

12. Berler, *Strengthening Absorption in Development Towns.*

CHAPTER 14

The Concept and Method of New-Town Development in Japan

KISHO KUROKAWA

When one considers new-town development in Japan, one cannot ignore the process of how the emphasis in housing policy has shifted from the construction of housing projects to the development of new towns. Even today, like housing project construction, development of new towns plays an important role in solving housing shortages, coping with population and household increases, meeting the demand for replacement, and maintaining the optimum rate of vacancies.

Housing Policy and New-Town Development. Following the Public Housing Act in 1951 and the Japan Housing Corporation Act in 1955, the national government took the initiative in solving postwar housing shortages. The Public Housing Act encouraged the prefectural and municipal governments throughout the country to build public housing with subsidies from the national treasury, and the Japan Housing Corporation Act was aimed at providing housing in large metropolitan areas where housing shortages were the most severe due to population concentration. The advantage of the Japan Housing Corporation over prefectural and municipal governments is that it has been empowered to transcend prefectural and municipal boundaries to solve housing problems on a broad, regional basis.

In these housing projects the main purpose was to provide at the least possible cost a large quantity of minimum-space houses that guarantee a decent level of living. The construction of community facilities, such as primary and junior high schools, kindergartens, nurseries, retail stores, and clinics, was not incorporated in project plans; these facilities were left to develop themselves spontaneously outside the projects.

The *laissez-faire* policy with regard to provision of community facilities, however, was of necessity gradually changed, partly due to the demands of those who came to live in the projects and partly due to the demands of local governments that had to bear most of the expenses for providing community facilities for new residents in the projects, and the construction of these facilities came to be incorporated in project plans. Because housing projects were built on the principle that the ultimate consumers should pay the total cost of the projects—land costs, construction costs, and overhead expenses—additional costs in building community facilities were passed on to the ultimate consumers: new residents in the projects. There was, however, a limit to the increase in costs for community facilities because the projects were part of public housing programs. Often the Japan Housing Corporation and local governments did not agree on who should build and pay for the construction of community facilities. Later national coordination among the Ministries of Construction, Finance, Home Affairs, Health and Welfare, and Education was worked out as "The Understanding Concerning the Construction of Convenience Facilities and The Development of Community Facilities Related to Residential Land Development and Housing Construction";[1] but the problem was far from being solved.

Under these circumstances, planning for the development of Senri New Town was begun in 1957. This marked the evolution of housing policy from housing project construction to new-town development. Senri New Town, planned in the suburbs of Osaka, the second largest city in Japan after Tokyo, was to have an area of 1160 hectares and a population of 150,000. Since then large-scale new towns, not housing projects, have been planned in rapid succession in many parts of Japan.

As to the necessity of the evolution from housing project construction to new-town development, there are various opinions. Each new town has some contingent factors in its development, but it has been marked by an increasingly large scale. Table 1 shows the evolution of new-town development.

As the number of housing projects increased and the amount of experience with life in such projects accumulated, their residents came to demand the construction of community facilities within or near the projects. Some community facilities, however, could not be built without a sustaining population. Therefore, the larger the scale of housing projects, the easier the provision of a larger variety of facilities demanded by the residents. As long as the principle that the ultimate consumers should pay for the construction of facilities was observed, sites for projects were sought in places increasingly distant from the existing city centers, where the land price was low and the problem of land acquisition was not very difficult, so that the land cost, accounting for a large proportion of the project cost, could be reduced.

It became imperative to develop the infrastructure, including roads, water supply system, sewerage, and railroads, as well as community facilities. Such large-scale investment for the infrastructure became possible only when the scale of new-town development grew much larger so that the cost per capita for facility construction could be lowered.

The disorderly expansion of residential areas in large metropolitan areas—that is, sprawl—resulted in the deterioration of the living environment. But housing projects created, at least within their boundaries, carefully planned, orderly living environments. Planning for the projects drew from the British experience in new-town development, urban planning theories of CIAM and Team Ten,[2] the Radburn system of the

United States, and others. In due time the housing projects came to be planned as strategic points in the areas, the influence of which should go beyond their boundaries. To make the housing projects function fully as strategic points it became necessary to plan for much larger ones.

Many additional factors have contributed to the emergence of new-town development out of housing project construction. New-town development is now aimed at community formation.

Mr. Satoshi Mifune of the Japan Housing Corporation defines a new town as a new community with a population of 50,000 (the minimum population size required of a municipality to be elevated to the status of city) or more or with an area of 300 hectares (an area that can provide an urban service center) or more.[3]

New-Town Construction and Urban Policy. Most of the residential land development projects that can be called new-town developments were started after 1965. At present people live a full-fledged community life in only a few of them, (Senri New Town was completed in 1970, but shopping and office areas in its center have not yet been finished.) People have begun to live in many new towns, although construction work is still going on in some areas of them. Data and experience accumulated so far are not sufficient to enable a comparison between new towns as a residential environment as conceived by planners and an actual community life as led by residents in the completed new towns.

Many new towns under construction are confronted with various problems: some are behind the construction schedule; others have been forced to modify the original plans. The new towns that are being constructed on schedule are rather few in number. Among the causes that delay the construction schedule are a difficulty in land acquisition and a funding problem due to a sharp rise in construction cost, but the problem facing almost all new-town projects is the lack of successful coordination among developers, residents living in or near the areas planned as new towns, and local governments. The reason for the lack of coordination is the failure among those concerned to translate the concept of new-town development as community formation into a concrete principle for construction. The Japan Housing Corporation, Japan's biggest developer, and other agencies concerned with new-town development projects are still exerting their main efforts to provide houses and residential land in the form of housing projects and consider the community formation project as something they are not really interested in doing but are forced to do by circumstances. They are not community builders in a positive sense. They do want to establish the principle by which they can protect themselves from the demands of local governments.

As the scale of new-town development becomes larger and the number of community facilities increases, local governments make more strict demands of new-town developers than before as to the construction and management of community facilities. Furthermore, as the living environment changes in a short period of time due to large-scale development projects failing to improve the surrounding areas of new towns, residents in the surrounding areas have negative reactions to new-town development. In fear of traffic problems arising from an increase in mass transportation and in private cars, of floods, and of water pollution, the residents often resort to demonstrations shouting, "Down with new towns!"

New towns are being constructed without any basic agreement reached between developers and local governments about the classification of urban service facilities and who should pay for their construction. As a result, local governments, the jurisdictions of which are urbanized overnight due to new-town development, are faced with the need for direct investment in facility construction and for tremendous overhead expenditures for the maintenance of the constructed facilities. Once people begin to live in new towns, local governments must perform public services for new residents, such as garbage collection, water supply, sewerage, and administration; and their financial burdens increase enormously. The cost of facility construction must be paid for by taxes on residents in new towns, but the need for public services comes earlier than does the tax money. Even if a small number of people settle in new towns, local governments must begin to perform public services for them. Strong financial pressures on local governments are not reduced even if their direct investments in facility construction are subsidized by developers or the national government because overhead expenditures for the maintenance of facilities are so large.

According to an estimate of the costs of constructing public facilities of a model housing project of 100 hectares prepared by the Ministry of Construction on the basis of the present fiscal system of local govern-ments, the balance sheets of local governments will not be favorable for 10 years after the construction of public facilities.[4] The breakdown of costs by public facility and payer of cost is outlined in Table 2. Another estimate on recent large-scale new-town development (700 hectares with a target population of 100,000) prepared by the Japan City Center says that the balance sheet of a local government will not be favorable for 25 years.[5]

To cope with such a situation, some local governments have formulated guidelines for development to be followed by developers engaged in residential land development. These guidelines provide that developers offer land for the construction of public facilities and pay for the construction cost, and they also specify the development standard so that developers may not lower the quality of development because of its increased cost. The guidelines do not have legal binding powers, but with the support of local public opinion that once cried, "No more danchi (housing projects)!" and taking advantage of all the administrative procedures local governments are authorized to use under the City Planning Law (the City Planning Law provides that local governments negotiate with developers before they issue development permits), they are making their influence felt on new-town development now. Some examples of the development guidelines appear in Table 3.

When the development standard is maintained (which means restrictions on the amount of developed land at the disposal of developers) and the cost of facility construction increases, housing supply programs are sometimes seriously affected with regard to the number of housing units and the price or rent. When new towns are developed by public agencies with a view to providing low-income housing, the increase in the cost of facility construction may give rise to social problems. Because there is a limit to the ability of developers to pay for facility construction, coordination between developers and local governments tends to drag. The establishment of a general principle concerning facility construction is very difficult because the problem is too complex or too specific a matter.

New-town construction now needs to be reexamined within the entire framework of urban policy. New-town development in Japan has been criticized in terms of the British concept of developing self-contained new towns. We need, however, to formulate a new concept of new-town development in view of the present state of urbanization in Japan and

Table 1 New Towns in Japan

Name of New Town	Area Development (hectares)	Target Population (10,000)	Method of Development	Developer	Start Planning (year)	First Occupancies (year)	Completion of Work (year)
Tama Den'en Toshi (26 divisions in 4 areas reapportionment)	4,300 (2,000)	40.0 (20)	Site reallocation	Tokyu Electric Railway Co.	1953	1961	—
Senri New Town	1,160	15.0	Housing estate New housing	Osaka Prefecture	1957	1962	1969
Kozoji New Town (region for which work has been decided)	850 (702)	8.7 (6.8)	Site reapportionment	JHC	1960	1968	—
Tama New Town	3,014 (2,770) (244)	41.0 (38) (3)	New housing Site reapportionment	JHC TMHPC TMG	1962	1972	1971
Itabashi Area	332	6.0	Land reapportionment	JHC	1963	1972	1971
Tsukuba Academic City	2,700	12.0	Housing estate; government related buildings New housing Site reapportionment	JHC	1963	1972	—
Senboku New Town (3 divisions)	1,518	18.8	New housing	Osaka Prefecture	1964	1967	—
Heijo New Town	609	7.5	Site reapportionment	JHC	1965	1972	—
Kohoku New Town (2 divisions for site reapportionment)	2,530 (1,324)	35.0 (22)	Site reapportionment	JHC	1966	—	—
Kita (North) Chiba New Town (3 divisions)	2,912	34.0	New housing	Chiba Prefecture	1966	—	—
Fujisawa City West	425	4.5	Site reapportionment	Fujisawa City	1967	—	—
Atsubetsu Shimonotsuboro (4 divisions)	373 (242)	5.8 (3.3)	New housing	Sapporo City	1967	1971	—

Project	Population	Area	Purpose	Developer	Year 1	Year 2
Kita (North) Hiroshima	441	3.3	New housing	Hokkaido Prefecture	1968	—
Kaihin New Town	1,272 (834) (438)	24.0 (16) (8)	Land reclamation	Chiba Prefecture Chiba City	1968	—
Narita New Town	487	6.0	New housing	Chiba Prefecture	1968	1972
Suma New Town (6 divisions)	900	11.3	New housing Site reapportionment Housing estate	Kobe City and others	1968	—
Hokushin (North Kobe) New Town (5 divisions)	871	13.0	Site reapportionment New housing	JHC (Kobe City) Kobe City	1968	—
Hokusetsu New Town (4 divisions)	1,244	12.8	New housing Industrial estate Industrial estate	JHC Hyogo Prefecture JHC	1969	1975
Atsugi New Park City	312	2.0	Housing	Long-term credit Bank of Japan	1969	—
Den'en Toshi Hashimoto New Town (6 divisions)	830	6.0	Housing	Nankai Electric Railway Co.	1969	—
Chiba City South (2 divisions)	976	13.0	Site reapportionment	JHC	1969	—
Seishin (West Kobe) New Town (2 divisions)	4,900 (892)	35.0 (7.0)	New housing	Kobe City	1969	—
Momohanadai High Town	322	5.4	New housing	Aichi Prefecture	1970	—
Sen'nan New Town	2,000	20.0	New city improvement program	Osaka Prefecture	1970	—
Hokuryudai District	330	4.0	Site reapportionment	JHC	1970	—
Izumi City New Town	1,060	5.0	Housing (and industry)	Mitsubishi Estate Ltd.	1970	—
Biwako (Lake Biwa) New Town	685	5.0	Housing	Siga	1970	1975

Table 1 (Continued)

Name of New Town	Name of Cities	Population in 1970 (persons)	1965–1970		Area (hectares)	Population density (persons/hectare)
			Population Increase (persons)	Rate of Increase (%)		
Tama Den'en Toshi (26 divisions in 4 areas reapportionment)	Kawasaki City	973,486	118,620	13.9	13,001	74.9
	Yokohama City:					
	Kohoku Ward	221,511	63,464	40.0	4,207	52.7
	Midori Ward	147,156	76,941	109.6	7,779	18.9
	Machida City	202,801	86,883	75.0	7,315	27.7
	Yamato City	102,706	37,769	58.1	2,860	35.9
Senri New Town	Suita City	259,619	62,954	32.0	3,660	70.9
	Toyonaka City	368,498	76,448	26.0	3,660	100.7
Kozoji New Town (region for which work has been decided)	Kasugai City	161,835	44,451	37.9	9,303	17.4
Tama New Town	Tama City	30,370	11,994	65.3	1,871	16.2
	Inagi City	30,817	11,472	59.3	1,761	17.5
	Hachioji City	253,527	45,774	22.0	18,819	13.5
	Machida City	202,801	86,883	75.0	7,315	27.7
Itabashi Area	Tokyo MG: Itabashi Ward	471,777	5,230	1.1	3,190	147.9
Tsukuba Academic City	Ibaragi Prefecture:					
	Yatabe Town	20,134	41	0.2	7,952	2.5
	Toyosato Town	10,409	88	0.8	3,212	3.2
	Tsukuba Town	21,308	783	3.5	7,708	2.3
	Ohba Town	10,856	97	0.9	3,403	3.2
	Sakura Village	8,942	3	0.0	3,495	2.6
	Kukizaki Village	6,461	208	3.3	2,747	2.4
Senboku New Town (3 divisions)	Sakai City	594,367	127,955	27.4	13,209	45.0
	Izumi City	95,987	11,216	13.2	8,545	11.2
Heijo New Town	Nara City	208,266	47,625	29.6	21,191	45.0
	Kyoto Prefecture:					
	Kizu Town	10,731	83	0.8	2,317	4.6
	Seika Town	10,929	1,311	13.6	2,563	4.3

Project	Municipality					
Kohoku New Town (2 divisions for site reapportionment)	Yokohama City: Kohoku Ward	221,511	63,464	40.2	4,207	52.7
	Midori Ward	147,156	76,941	109.6	7,779	18.9
Kita (North) Chiba New Town (3 divisions)	Chiba Prefecture: Inzai Town	16,114	749	4.4	5,303	3.0
	Funabashi City	325,426	101,437	45.3	8,178	39.8
	Shiroi town	10,509	2,204	26.5	3,519	3.0
	Inba Village	7,331	308	4.0	4,658	1.6
	Motono Village	4,566	486	9.6	2,283	2.0
Fujisawa City West	Fujisawa City	228,978	53,795	30.7	6,963	32.9
Atsubetsu Shimonotsuboro (4 divisions)	Sapporo City	1,010,123	188,906	23.0	111,798	9.0
Kita (North) Hiroshima	Hokkaido Prefecture: Hiroshima Town	9,746	1,724	21.5	12,105	0.8
Kaihin New Town	Chiba City	482,133	142,283	41.9	24,807	19.4
Narita New Town	Narita City	42,514	107	0.3	13,050	3.3
Suma New Town (6 divisions)	Kobe City: Suma Ward	111,123	7,614	7.4	2,416	46.0
Hokushin (North Kobe) New Town (5 divisions)	Kobe City: Hyogo Ward	269,639	15,563	6.1	26,121	10.3
Hokusetsu New Town (4 divisions)	Mita City	33,090	825	2.6	21,190	1.6
Atsugi New Park City	Atsugi City	82,888	21,505	35.0	9,284	8.9
Den'en Toshi Hashimoto New Town (6 divisions)	Hashimoto City	33,334	527	1.6	10,786	3.1
Chiba City South (2 divisions)	Chiba City	482,133	142,283	41.9	24,807	19.4
	Ichihara City	156,016	42,779	37.8	36,663	4.3
Seishin (West Kobe) New Town (2 divisions)	Kobe City: Taremizu Ward	207,899	59,908	40.5	17,069	12.2

Table 1 (Continued)

Name of New Town	Name of Cities	1965–1970			Area (hectares)	Population density (persons/hectare)
		Population in 1970 (persons)	Population Increase (persons)	Rate of Increase (%)		
Momohanadai High Town	Komaki City	79,606	18,729	30.8	6,300	12.5
Sen'nan New Town	Kishiwada City	162,022	18,312	12.7	6,994	23.2
Hokuryudai District	Ryugasaki City	37,267	2,350	6.7	7,490	5.0
Izumi City New Town	Miyagi Prefecture: Izumi City	33,190	14,129	74.1	14,545	2.3
Biwako (Lake Biwa) New Town	Ohtsu City	171,777	14,017	8.9	30,274	5.7
	Kusatsu City	46,409	8,081	21.1	4,755	9.8

Note: *Method of development* refers to the applicable law or framework used for the project. *New housing* refers to a law for promotion of new housing development, and *site reapportionment* refers to a law for adjustment of property lines and transfer of ownership to permit more effective utilization of land.

Source: S. Mifune, *Modern Urban Policies*, Vol. 7, pp. 188–192.

Table 2 Cost of Public Facilities Required for a Model Housing Estate (Scale, 100 hectares—ha) and Allocation of Costs

Facilities	Total Costs (mil/yen)	Site Development (mil/yen)	Housing Development (mil/yen)	National Government Express (mil/yen)	Local Government and Local Public Bodies — General Account (mil/yen)	Local Government and Local Public Bodies — Debt (mil/yen)	Private Sector (mil/yen)	Total (mil/yen)	Unit Cost at Site (yen/sq m)
Housing site	1,980	1,980	—	—	—	—	—	—	10,000
Subdivision roads	486	486	—	—	—	—	—	—	—
Subdivision main roads	196	196	—	—	—	—	—	—	—
Residential area roads	276	183	44	88	—	—	—	132	—
Neighborhood public space	184	184	—	—	—	—	—	—	—
Children's play area	171.5	171.5	—	—	—	—	—	—	—
Parks	96	96	—	—	—	—	—	—	—
Elementary schools (2)	432.8	198	—	71.2	35.5	128.1	—	234.8	5,000
Junior high school (1)	271	126	—	65.9	19.8	50.8	—	145	5,000
Kindergartens (4)	78	36	—	7	4.2	9.8	21	42	6,700
Sewer system	350	210	84	56	—	—	—	140	—
Refuse disposal	150	37.5	22.5	30	—	60	—	112.5	—
Riparian improvement	90	30	—	30	(Prefecture 24)	(Prefecture 6)	—	30 (Prefecture 30)	—
Water supply system	225	50	—	—	—	175	—	175	—
Gas mains and lines	53	—	21	—	—	—	32	53	—
Power lines and facilities	23	—	—	—	—	—	23	23	—
Public facilities	344	306.5	—	2	5.2 (Prefecture 24)	15.8	12.5	35.5 (Prefecture 2)	Child care center 6,700
Regional arterial roads	194	—	32.5	129	22.7	9.8	—	194	Others 10,490
Miscellaneous construction costs	152	152	—	—	—	—	—	—	—
Reserves	288	288	—	—	—	—	—	—	—
Research and office costs	302	302	—	—	—	—	—	—	—
Interest on loans	1,425	1,425	—	—	—	—	—	—	—
Total	7,767.3	6,418.5	204	479.1	87.4 (Prefecture 26)	457.8 (Prefecture 6)	88.5	1,316.8 (Prefecture 32)	Average 9,328

Note: 1. Housing site development costs are 6418.6 million yen; housing development costs are 204 million yen. The total, 6622.6 million yen, is distributed over the entire area. Areas that may be developed are the following—expressed in hectares—ha:

Housing site	55 ha
Elementary and junior high schools	9 ha
Kindergarten and child care centers	1.6 ha
Public facilities sites	5.4 ha
Total	71 ha

Average cost of development 9,328 yen/sq m

2. Shares to be borne by prefectures (indicated in parentheses) are approximate.
Source: Planning Bureau, Ministry of Construction; data as of June 12, 1967.

199

Table 3 Comparison of Compendiums of Guidelines for Housing Developers As Adopted by Five Cities[a]

	Kawasaki City, Kanagawa Prefecture	Kawanishi City, Hyogo Prefecture	Yokohama City	Kobe City	Musashi City, Tokyo
Name	Implementation Standards for Formation of Housing Estates	Compendium of Guidelines Related to Formation of Housing Sites	Compendium of Regulations for Development of Housing Sites in Yokohama City	Compendium of Development Guidelines for Kobe City	Compendium of Guidelines
Date of publication	August 1965 (enactment) October 1970 (revision)	May 18, 1967	August 1968 (enactment) May 1973 (revision)	January 1971	October 1971
Purpose	Improvement and expediting (sic) of public facilities and utilities to be provided by the developer	1. Provision of guidance for rational implementation of housing site formation 2. Prior to following legally-prescribed procedures, to provide developer with necessary guidance on the basis of discussion with the mayor 3. Improve self-supporting ability of public facilities	1. Prevention of sprawl 2. Provision of public facilities and public service facilities (matching population densities) by developer	1. Planned development and formation of balanced, sound urban areas 2. Phased improvement of public facilities in urban areas	1. Prevention of sprawl by housing development 2. Elimination of inconveniences and nuisances to region's residents caused by construction of medium- and high-rise buildings
Object of application	Creation of a housing estate of 0.1 ha or more	Housing site development of 0.5 ha or more	0.1 ha or more used for creation of housing sites, development or equivalent	1. Activities for improvement of urban facilities (housing facilities for one estate) 2. Development of 0.1 ha or more 3. Landfill operation	1. Development of housing sites of 0.1 ha or more 2. Buildings of 10 m or more in height.

Land that developer must set aside for public use	1. Public facilities area: 3% of site area (4% in case of development by a public body) and/or more than 3 sq m per capita: no payment 2. Public service facilities area: 5% (plus 0.5% for every 150 persons/ha above 150 persons/ha): 3,000 yen/sq m	(Same as Kawasaki City)	1. All public facilities required by law must be constructed at developer's expense and turned over to the city free of charge. 2. Public service facilities such as water supply and sewer systems, schools, kindergartens, nursery schools etc. must be provided and turned over to the city free of charge or through purchase.		1. Public sites: 3% or more: no payment 2. Public service sites: for up to 150 persons/ha, 5%; more than 150 persons/ha, 7%; 5000 yen/sq m	1. Public sites: 6–10%: no charge 2. Public service sites: one primary school per 1000 residents, 1 junior high school per 2000 residents: no payment
Other obligations of the developer	Citizens of Kawasaki to be given preferential treatment in rental and sale of home sites developed by public bodies		1. Municipal inspection required for facilities that would belong to the city 2. Prior agreement required in regard to facilities for compulsory education and mass transit	Preference to be given to persons designated by the city for rental or sale	1. When water mains must be laid or expanded or water must be pumped up: electric power charges for 5 years 2. Parking facilities must be provided in medium- and high-rise housing units.	1. Consent of nearby residents in event of deprivation of their sunlight, loss of good TV reception, or noise and vibration during construction 2. Priority to be given to city residents when construction is by a public body

[a] As of October 1, 1972.

Source: R. Hirose and S. Iwasaki, *Modern Urban Policies*, Vol. 7, pp. 106–107.

with measures for solving future urban problems in mind.

The location of new towns in Japan has been determined to a great extent by contingent factors. Developers sought land for new towns at places not necessarily favorable for development. The areas that included sites of proposed new towns had to accept land-use plans that centered on residential land and were imposed suddenly from above. New-town developers, however, cannot take responsibility for all the changes arising in the areas from such land-use plans. The financial problem of who should pay for facility construction is one of the problems over which developers and local governments confront each other. In Great Britain, however, new-town development designed as a measure for containing the population growth of large cities, especially London, is smoothly proceeding in accordance with the Town and Country Planning Act of 1946, and many new planning instruments based on actual experience with new-town development are being invented. The developers of British new-towns do not suffer from the kind of problem experienced by Japanese developers. It is imperative to specify the functions of a new town and to build it in the most appropriate way at the place best suited to such functions. However, the functions and roles of a new town need not be the same as those of British new towns.

First, it is necessary to examine the current urban situation in Japan and to establish the concepts of functions and roles of new-town development as community formation. Second, in Japan where the density of activity per square kilometer of inhabitable space is extremely high, precautions must be taken to avoid the friction that may arise when a new town is a new tight spatial order. Then, to establish the concept of new-town development as a method for avoiding such friction, it is necessary to study the process of spatial changes Japanese cities have experienced and to find out the kind of spatial order and problem that new-town development, one of the strongest forces now pushing Japanese urbanization, is creating.

Once we understand the problem and concept of new-town development, we have to design a new town as a tangible living environment. Our design method will be based on that concept and will be unique to each new town.

On the basis of such thinking, I present in the following sections the concept and method of new-town development that I am convinced are effective.

We will take Fujisawa New Town, which I designed, to serve as an example of the physical planning of a living environment. The design method employed there is explained in relation to the concept of new-town development.

THE CONCEPT OF NEW-TOWN PLANNING AS A RESPONSE TO MODERN SOCIETY

If we understand that new-town construction is to develop urban areas in a planned manner, it is not a development project but urban planning itself. At long last new-town construction has come to be considered as part of urban planning.

Physical and Social Planning. When the term *urban planning* is mentioned, most people immediately think of the physical planning of the city. The city is, however, a place for human life and a container of human society. In other words, the city is a means for man to conduct his social life. The city, a container, and man's social life, its contents, influence each other, and so physical planning (for the container) and social planning (for the contents) must be related to each other. The basis of social planning in relation to urban planning is a theory of the structure of urban society.

The key concept in the structural theory of urban society is that of community. It played a crucial role in the theories of human ecology developed at the University of Chicago in the 1920s.[6] Since then it has played a gradually differing role in the transformation of urban sociology, and yet it has remained a key concept in urban sociology throughout.

Physical planning in Japan has been much too preoccupied with the model based on Western social planning. The neighborhood unit plan has been dominant both in urban redevelopment and new-town development. It has become obvious, however, that neighborhood units do not either conform to the functions of new towns or prove congenial to new-town dwellers. The reasons are that Japan has never had the historic social situation in which the Western concept of neighborhood is applicable, and the concept of neighborhood is becoming increasingly difficult to identify in modern society.

The structure of community has two aspects—spatial and temporal—and the dynamics of community are also explained from these two aspects. Man's collective life is led under a given temporal system. In a modern open society what happens in other communities such as work places and amusement quarters characterizes the spatial rhythm of community. In other words, man's movements (commuting, shopping, etc.) become conspicuous and mobility more and more diverse.

Urban community is a component of the social system and must be understood in the framework of the total society. Community is an informal small group. It is not community, however, but systems outside it (such as factories, shops, banks, and churches) that maintain structural relations as units in the social system. Community finds it increasingly difficult to maintain its boundaries. Many theories of community in urban society continue to be formulated, but we find the main feature of community in the mobility of modern Japanese society.

Two Aspects of Mobility. Mobility may be considered from two aspects. One kind of mobility is a person's movement through life, from birth to death. It is changes of address. In recent years, 8 to 9 percent of the Japanese population have changed their addresses every year. In other words, every Japanese changes addresses every 12 or 13 years. This phenomenon indicates the rapidity of Japanese urbanization. It also indicates the collapse of community based on the spatial and spiritual links a given population formed by living together in a given area for a long period of time, because the quick turnover of residents is not conducive to the formation of such links. An old community could satisfy all the demands of people living within it, but now the demands of people with regard to social life have become so diverse in family composition, social strata, houses, and occupations, that a single community cannot meet them. Helped by market flexibility and the great mobility due to advances in the transportation system, people move themselves to satisfy their diverse demands. In such circumstances, physical planning for community as a standard static image will no longer be effective.

The second kind of mobility is the movements of a person in the 24 hours of a day. From getting up in the morning until going to bed at night, the modern person has many chances to move around, and the radius of one's daily mobility is rapidly expanding. In metropolitan areas such as Tokyo and Osaka many salaried employees and students commute 30 to 50 kilometers to their work places and schools, spending one to one-and-a-half hours one way. Even

housewives spend an increasingly large amount of time in their daily movements for shopping and leisure activities, such as theater going and parties, leaving their communities behind.

The mobility phenomenon makes community more and more open, and community finds it difficult to maintain its boundaries. The basic factor accelerating mobility is the availability of means for mobility in making society, and now social planning based on mobility can be linked with physical planning based on very good information networks.

The *En*-System as a New Community. In the social structure with rapid mobility, what will happen to human relations or a sense of solidarity implied by the term *community* in an old sense? Here we would like to present a new concept: *en*-system (*en* is the Japanese word meaning connection, tie, or link). To put it differently, the *en*-system is a temporal community. The traditional community theory concentrated on analyses of the spatial structure of community, but my theory focuses on the temporal structure of community. In the traditional theory, the temporal structure was regarded as something that disturbed a community equilibrium and was given a negative value in community formation, whereas in our theory of temporal community, the temporal structure as a unit of the social system distinguished from the spatial concept, gives unity to and emphasizes the human relations that may arise in any given place.

A temporal community may be formed on the basis of residences, work places, or any other place where voluntary activities occur. These voluntary activities may include educational activities such as study meetings and seminars, leisure-time activities, and hobbies in which new human relationships may be formed. Participants in the voluntary activities need not live or work in the same place; their human relationships are formed at a certain place at a certain time. The totality of these may be called a temporal community.

In Europe and the United States this kind of relationship may be found in clubs. Most of these clubs serve to maintain the social status of their members. In Japan, where such clubs do not exist, human relationships in a temporal community will be those characterizing groups striving to express individuality or hobby groups—that is, marked by extreme volunteerism. People belong, at different times of a day, to different groups whose standards of human relationships are different from each other. A person is a member of the work group at his work place at a certain time of a day; at another time he is a member of a group that is formed by those who are away from their work places. Both the number and kind of these human relationships increase and diversify. By developing human relationships outside the work place, a person can manage to be liberated spiritually from the organization and extend the circle of human emancipation. Thus around one person are formed many groups that are related to each other.

We call the temporal community thus formed *en*-system because it serves as a medium connecting each person with society and the private with the public in modern urban society. In the process of urbanization Japanese society has expanded both private and public spaces, the boundaries of which were ambiguous in a closed community, without developing any connecting medium. The conflict between each person and society, between the private and the public, has intensified. In Japanese cities, for example, the maintenance of public spaces such as roads and parks and of street trees is extremely bad. City parks are far from being used effectively. In the traditional closed community, the space round one's house was regarded as communal space. Now one regards the space outside one's house as the public space other people, local government, or the national government should maintain and concentrates on maintaining the space inside the house as the place for keeping private property. Thus the separation between the public and the private in one's mind has sharpened. Without doing something about this separation, it will be impossible to find a proper place in modern urban society for the space that is semiprivate and semipublic in the sense that it is used exclusively by voluntary groups in mobile society. We call this kind of space semipublic space. It is the space for connecting people's movements in mobile society; sometimes it is private space used jointly with other people; sometimes it is the space whose use and expense people share. The space used for drinking companionship, study meetings, seminars, hobby groups, and all other activities in the *en*-system is semipublic space. It is there that new human relationships are created, a place satisfying life goals, a connecting point for mobile people in mobile society.

Semipublic space is a node. Making as many nodes as possible in society and developing human relationships formed in them we call *en-zukuri* (connection-making). In this sense we call community building in response to mobility *en*-system.

An Image of the Network City and New-Town Planning. In response to mobility we have established the concept of urban community as nodes. Next we need a theory in which community, a part, is integrated into the total social system. The basis of the traditional city was the territory within which a person's daily life was contained. This was true at the time when community and city completely overlapped; it is also true today when community is either expanding in size or declining. When the sphere of a person's daily activity has expanded, this activity can be contained within the city simply by redefining or expanding an urban area. Grouping several villages into a town, several towns into a city, several cities and their suburbs into a metropolitan region, and several metropolitan regions into a megalopolis is the redefinition of urban area on the basis of the expanded sphere of man's daily activity in mobile society.

The urban theory centering on the Tokaido Megalopolis is based on the concept of a huge urban belt connecting the three metropolitan regions of Tokyo, Nagoya, and Osaka and containing man's and groups' daily activity within an integrated single urban area.

Opposed to the concept of megalopolis is the concept of network city proposed in the New Comprehensive National Development Plan formulated in 1969.[7] The plan called for the creation of information networks connecting regional nuclear cities, local cities, and large metropolises and of the activity-oriented environment based on high interurban mobility. A person's activity for 24 hours or a much longer cycle will be contained in a number of cities.

The information networks include transportation networks (a national network of new express railways and a national network of expressways), communication networks (a network of data communication connecting major cities of the country and networks of telegraph and telephone), and energy networks (pipelines). The completion of these networks throughout the Japanese Archipelago would, the plan assumed, create throughout Japan the environment that would guarantee the basic standard of social life. The information networks are the basic cause of increased mobility and will further accelerate interurban mobility and activity.

The principle for network city formation is to place cities in complementary relation to one another. According to this principle, the city is not self-contained. According to traditional thinking, the city was the area within which all the necessary elements for man's social life must be contained. Even the Tokaido Megalopolis is simply an expanded urban area within which the elements necessary for man's activity are contained. In the network cities, however, people satisfy their demands by moving; single cities provide only the basic element for satisfying personal needs as well as the geographic and historic elements peculiar to them; when people cannot satisfy some of their demands in one city, they will move to another where they can satisfy them. Every city will have the specialized elements that other cities cannot provide, and all the cities will complement one another.

The concept of network cities must be applied to the planning of a new town. New-town development policies in various countries of the world are more or less variations of the British model, which aims at the construction of self-contained residential environments, complete with all the elements for social life, including work places. It is doubtful, however, whether the concept of a completely self-contained residential environment will be acceptable to people who live in an extremely mobile society. In the society where diverse communities with semipublic spaces as *en*-systems have developed and where people can use information networks efficiently, the values of people will shift toward a greater range in the choice of lifestyles. The self-contained new town can offer nothing but a small range in the choice of work places, amusements, and so on, for people who live in it. With increased mobility, people increasingly use facilities outside the new town. As a result, some facilities are underused, while other facilities are overworked and are in short supply. All this suggests that it is not proper to provide identical facilities in every new town and that in constructing facilities the special characteristics of an area where a new town will be constructed should be considered.

A new town in the framework of network cities should complement the existing cities that should retain and reinforce their special features. However, the deficiencies of the existing cities should be identified, and a new town should emphasize new functions as well as complement the deficiencies of the existing cities. This concept of new town is different from either that which has so far prevailed in

Japan—complete interdependence of central city and dormitory new town—or that in Great Britain—the completely self-contained new town.

The kinds of facilities to be built in a new town will be diverse, depending on the kind of role the new town should play within the network cities. The problem of who should construct what facilities and who should pay for them will not be decided according to the uniformly established principle, but according to the concensus of all those concerned, including the beneficiaries of such facilities.

The facilities thus constructed probably will be faced with a need for renovation, or entirely new facilities will be required as the new town transforms itself. Pressures for renovation come not only from the transformation of the new town but also from changes in the cities in complementary relation to it.

Spatial plans for facilities in new towns should take various forms, taking into account the conditions of areas where the new towns will be constructed, and at the same time they should be flexible to accommodate the need for renovation after construction. The method of new-town development planning should be based on such a concept of new town.

NEW-TOWN DEVELOPMENT AS SUBURBAN DEVELOPMENT

New-town development emerged as housing projects turned to large-scale community building. In the search for inexpensive large tracts of land, new-town developers moved into more and more distant suburbs. They resorted to all the available development instruments to consolidate land holdings as the scale of development grew larger and larger.

Large-Scale Developments in Suburban Agricultural Areas. The land consolidation was possible in the first half of the 1960s when many of today's new towns were planned in areas where large tracts of forested and agricultural land existed in suburbs. In large-scale developments (more than 1000 hectares) started in the latter half of the 1960s, the area of one project site ranged from 300 to 500 hectares—that is, one new town consisted of several scattered project sites. For example, in Semboku New Town in the southern suburbs of Osaka, three project sites are completely separate from one another; in Tama New Town in the western suburbs of Tokyo, too, there are large isolated tracts of land. To achieve the integration of a new town, a railway connecting several isolated project sites is planned (see Figure 1).

As the scale of new-town development has grown larger, the project sites have taken on the character of strategic points of growth for surrounding areas; at the same time new towns have come to include the existing built-up areas and agricultural land. It has become impossible to plan for new towns without

taking into consideration conditions and changes in their surrounding areas. Now, from the beginning, new-town development plans take into account the surrounding areas and their possible changes.

A new town is developed at a given place as an environment with a territory. New towns are rarely built in a vacuum; more often they intrude on some kind of human activity. In planning for new-town development, it is important to incorporate the new

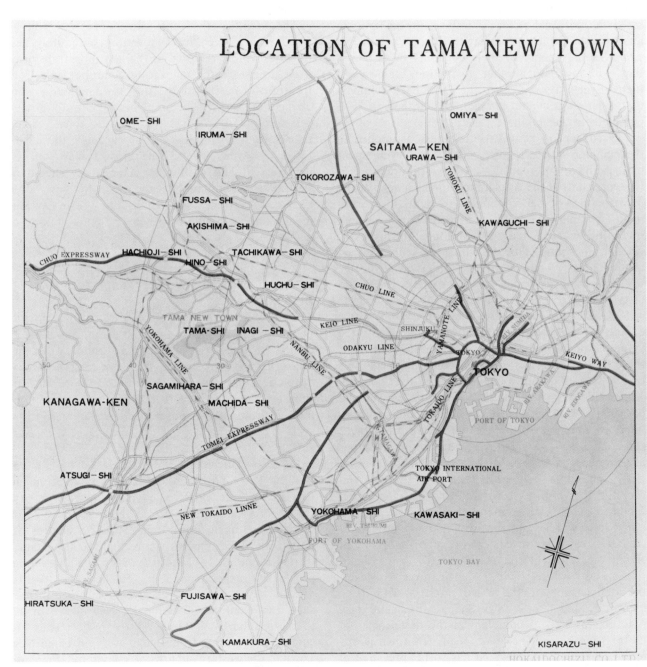

Figure 1.   Tokyo metropolitan area.

town into the existing order of the place as well as to identify new functions the new town should perform in the area. Harmony with the existing order is an important element for community formation.

New towns located in the suburbs of large metropolitan areas are always faced with the problem of how to cope with suburban agricultural land. Such land is being rapidly turned into urban use. Sprawl rather than new-town development is responsible for the conversion of farmland into urban use. Often new-town development has to deal with the problems created by sprawl.

The rate of farmland conversion differs markedly among the regions of the country; it is extremely high in Tokyo, Aiichi (Nagoya), Osaka, and their neighboring prefectures. The main reason for farmland conversion is growing demand for residential land due to the increase in urban populations and for industrial land by factories seeking relocation due to congestion in the built-up areas. It is quite natural that the rate of farmland conversion is conspicuously high in the Tokaido Megalopolis where urban populations and industry are concentrated.

During a boom for investments in plants and equipment throughout Japan in 1960–1962, the proportion of farmland converted into industrial land was highest everywhere except the Tokyo Metropolitan Perfecture. In the 10-year period from 1953 to 1962, 86 percent of the applications for farmland conversion and 52 percent of the land covered by the applications were for residential use in Tokyo; this means that pressures from the population increases were far greater than those from industrial relocation in Tokyo. In Kanagawa and Saitama, the neighboring prefectures of Tokyo, farmland conversion for residential use became greater than that for industrial use around 1963–1964. In the Nagoya region, in the five-year period from 1962 to 1966, 51 percent of converted farmland was for residential use and 23 percent for industrial use. In the suburbs of large cities large-scale farmland conversion for residential use began in the mid-1950s when the Japan Housing Corporation, local public corporations, and business firms started building collective housing.

The amount of farmland converted for school construction was also considerable in the metropolitan suburbs. This was because local governments built many schools to accommodate students whose number increased due to the construction of housing projects. However, most responsible for suburban farmland conversion for residential use

were private investors, not new-town developers. These people were agents for urban sprawl and hindered large-scale planned development.

As farmland became unsuitable for farming due to the pressure of urbanization, farmers were forced to reduce the area of land they cultivated; some farmers sought new farmland in fringe areas less influenced by urbanization to maintain the scale of their operations. Some farmers lost working morale, and some could not find their successors. Natural selection of farmers is still taking place. To secure stable income many farmers converted their farmland into residential land and built houses and apartment houses there for sale and rent. Since they did not consolidate their land holdings for the purpose of building houses together at the same places, their houses were scattered at many different plots. Furthermore, residential land development proceeded in a leapfrog fashion in search of cheap land. This way suburban agricultural land was invaded, and unplanned and disorderly urbanization proceeded with the result that urban sprawl rings the large cities of Japan.

Problems Arising from the Urbanization of Suburbs. In new-town development it is necessary to understand what kind of social life is going on and what kind of order is maintained in the suburban agricultural areas confronted with urban sprawl and on the basis of such understanding to draw up appropriate project plans.

The first problem to be considered is the marked decline of agricultural production in the areas. When farmland is converted to urban land use, the prices of the surrounding farmland as well as of the converted land increase. This is because the surrounding farmland is considered to be potential urban land and is so evaluated. Interest on the money from the sale of converted farmland is far higher than the income from agricultural production if the land remained cultivated. All this leads to the loss of working morale on the part of farmers. Many farmers abandon farming, resort to extensive farming, or leave farmland uncultivated and wait for the opportunity to sell their land at great profit.

The second problem is the outflow of the agricultural labor force from the areas. In the suburbs the gap between agricultural and industrial wages is strongly felt, and many farmers seek urban jobs as subsidiary work. In many cases urban jobs become primary and farming is done part time. The development of transportation such as railways and roads further accelerates the increase in the number of part-time farmers and expands the areas where the agricultural labor force outflows.

The progress of urbanization also causes the deterioration of the agricultural environment. Untreated sewage from houses and factories pollutes agricultural water and damages paddies and fields; harmful insects propagate in abandoned farmland. Full-time farmers suffer great loss because of the deterioration of the agricultural environment. In the areas where houses and farmland are mixed, urban dwellers suffer from obnoxious odors caused by stock farmers, and eventually these farmers must leave the areas.

The decline of agricultural production leads to changes in the environment of suburban agricultural areas and in rural society. Delays in infrastructural development due to disorderly urbanization not only cause inconveniences to those who move into suburbs but also lead to the deterioration of the living environment for farmers. Water supply, sewerage, roads, and schools are the minimum public facilities even for rural life. The development of these facilities in the mixed areas requires far greater investments than do programs for agricultural development. In the face of a need for such investments, local governments in former agricultural areas are in financial difficulty. Even before large-scale new towns are constructed, local governments in the suburban agricultural areas have experienced the need for greater investments in public services generated by urbanization.

There is also a clash between rural and urban society, leading to a problem of neighboring that defies quantitative analysis. Shozo Yamamoto observes that suburban rural society affected by urbanization will not transform itself into urban society overnight and that instead of the disintegration of tradition, the neighborhood solidarity, which once prevailed in purely rural society, tends to gain importance.[8] *Burakukai* (rural neighborhood associations) strengthen rather than weaken in the face of urbanization. Nonfarming households, however, lack parochialism and usually remain cool to the *burakukai*. Often there occurs a confrontation between old (farming) and new (nonfarming) residents, bringing their heterogeneity and incompatibility into sharp focus. When new towns are developed, urban people move into the suburban areas *en masse* during a short period of time. Unless something is done about their heterogeneity, a confrontation probably will oc-

cur between new residents and old ones who form the *burakukai*.

We have examined various aspects of suburban agricultural areas. Their characteristics will be changed with the development of new towns. This kind of problem will differ according to the specific factors affecting each new town and to its relation with the network cities, but every new town will be faced with the problem of how to cope with agricultural areas. New-town developers must incorporate into their development plans measures for dealing with agricultural areas—before the problem arises.

FUJISAWA NEW TOWN

In the course of preparing concrete plans on the basis of the analyses and concepts discussed, I have developed many planning tools. My plans for new towns took various forms, taking into account different locational factors and employing different planning tools. I tried throughout to develop the concept of new-town planning in modern urban society and the designing method. In the following section I introduce my concept and methodology of new-town development, taking as an example Fujisawa New Town, the development and planning of which I have participated in from its inception.

Locational Factors of Fujisawa New Town. Fujisawa New Town is located in the western part of Fujisawa City, and its western boundary adjoins Chigasaki City. Fujisawa City has an area of 70 square kilometers and a 1970 population of about 240,000. It is located at the western edge of the Tokyo metropolitan area (an area within a 50-kilometer radius of central Tokyo). Its population has been increasing annually by more than 10,000. The city is connected with central Tokyo by the Tokaido line (national railway) cutting across the city from east to west and with Shinjuku, Tokyo's largest subcenter, by the Odakyu line (private railway) running through the eastern part of the city from south to north and intersecting the Tokaido line at Fujisawa Station. Travel times to central Tokyo and Shinjuku by train are 50 and 60 minutes, respectively. Fujisawa is a typical dormitory city (see Figure 2).

Industrial location took place along the Tokaido line in the second half of the 1950s. Industrial estates, the development of which was begun in the early

Figure 2. A model of Fujisawa New Town.

1960s in the northeastern part of the city along the Odakyu line stations, have now been almost completed. Early urbanization in Fujisawa was led by industrialization. The population increase caused by industrialization and the emigration of population from Tokyo in recent years have brought about sprawl in the area south of the Tokaido line (where suburbanization began in the 1930s) and in the area along the Odakyu line. Before industrial location took place, more than half of the city area was paddies and fields. Now factories and houses have invaded both farmland and forested land. Table 4 lists changes in land uses.

In 1965 Fujisawa City prepared a comprehensive development plan with the motto "from industrial development to social development." Social develop-

Table 4   Land Use in the Area of Fujisawa City (%)

	Paddies	Fields	Residential Land	Forested Land	Other (including public land)
1960	11.3	35.3	13.8	16.5	23.1
1965	10.4	29.3	19.4	14.2	26.7
1970	9.3	25.2	24.4	12.3	28.4

ment meant the development of public facilities and community formation.

Against such a background Fujisawa City drafted a plan for Fujisawa New Town. Fujisawa City as a local government should be commended for its farsightedness in that it included new-town development in its comprehensive plan. In many cases local governments had to deal with urban planning not before but after plans for new towns emerged out of the blue.

The area designated as Fujisawa New Town is the western part of the city with Tsujido Station of the Tokaido Line, next to Fujisawa Station to the west, as its core; it is also the starting point of the urban axis extending toward another residential area to the north.

When in 1967 Fujisawa City decided to develop Fujisawa New Town, its guideline for development was as follows:

By respecting favorable natural conditions, conserving the greenery, constructing adequate public facilities, we will develop Fujisawa New Town as a high-amenity and cultural environment. The policy for realizing this new town will be based on a comprehensive plan to be formulated by the city. We will invite not only the national and the prefectural government but also private business firms to invest in the development of Fujisawa New Town and ask for government-business cooperation.[9]

The area consists of large tracts of forested land and farmland almost untouched by urban sprawl. Since it is located at a distance of less than four kilometers from Tsujido Station, it has strong potential for becoming an excellent urban area when large-scale developments, including roads, water supply, and sewerage, are undertaken. It is a suburban agricultural area where, in view of its potential for urbanization, many farmers have already become part-time farmers.

The Policy and Concept of Fujisawa New Town. About half of the development work in Fujisawa New Town has been completed, and houses have been built in some parts of the town. Fujisawa New Town has been faced with some problems that have troubled other new towns. The biggest problems have been financial, but they have been solved one by one, according to the basic principle that new-town development is part of the city's urban policy. The development of Fujisawa New Town is not merely residential land development; it also is part of the

work aimed at developing a new urban axis in the city. The construction of water supply and sewerage systems and roads in the town is the development of the infrastructure for a new urban area and is to be realized by stages in the conventional framework of city planning projects. The construction costs of these projects are shared equally by the national government, the prefectural government, and the developer (Fujisawa City)—about one-third each. Other public facilities are constructed as part of the projects incorporated in the city's comprehensive plan. Since Fujisawa New Town and the old built-up areas of Fujisawa City are in complementary relation, a project for the latter is included in that for the former, when the schedules or both projects fit each other.

In Fujisawa new-town development is incorporated into the urban policy of a local government. The conservation of greenery and the construction of the basic public facilities is emphasized; and the positive participation of the national government, the prefectural government, and private developers is sought if they understand the basic plan of the city. Actually, Chigasaki City, Fujisawa's neighbor, Kanagawa Prefecture, and three private developers are participating in housing construction and land development in Fujisawa New Town. This case suggests a direction future new-town development should follow.

Sprawl, disorderly groups of small residential plots, is conspicuous in the north-south urban axis in the eastern part of the city, where redevelopment to improve public facilities is impossible. If the western part of the city is left to itself, similar sprawl will take place. The basic policy for Fujisawa New Town is planned development of an urban area, including the development of public facilities, taking into account the future development of the surrounding areas, so that sprawl cannot occur. By developing the compact urban axis toward the north and forming a low-density residential area, the disorderly invasion of farmland will be avoided, and the suburban agricultural area will be given the time for reorganizing itself in response to urbanization. Fujisawa New Town will provide living space for 40,000 to 50,000 people, a community congenial to modern society.

Fujisawa City is ringed by a large variety of cities: cities of over 1 million such as Tokyo, Yokohama, and Kawasaki, industrial cities such as Atsugi, and dormitory cities such as Hiratsuka, Chigasaki, and Kamakura. Fujisawa and these cities are closely connected by networks of national and private railways and national prefectural highways. People in Fujisawa go to these cities for commuting to work places and schools, for shopping, and for leisure-time activities. The basic approach was that Fujisawa New Town should be connected with Tsujido Station of the Tokaido line, one of the most efficient networks (efficient in terms of high density activity); it should form part of the network cities; and it should complement the existing cities connecting by networks and with the existing built-up area of Fujisawa City.

Fujisawa New Town should offer the other cities, by means of networks, the facilities that would take advantage of favorable natural conditions of the area. First, a cultural property park, the largest of its kind in the Tokyo metropolitan area, was planned. The 10-hectare park is located at the place where both houses built during the paleolithic and the neolithic ages and a castle built during the Kamakura period (1192–1333) were excavated; it is designed to preserve the archeological ruins and protect forests of the area. The land for the park has been acquired by the city, and the park construction work is now going on as part of the city's project. When completed, the park will attract a large number of visitors from other cities in the Tokyo metropolitan area because it is located within the range of one-day round trips.

Second, in view of the shortage of graveyards in the Tokyo metropolitan area, a 50-hectare cemetery park was planned. Situated on low hills in the southwestern section of the town, the park has been completed and is accepting applications for plots from Fujisawa citizens; it will accept applications from people in other cities in the future.

The kind of function Fujisawa New Town should perform in its complementary relations with the existing built-up areas in Fujisawa City in particular and in Kanagawa Prefecture in general had to be considered. In the built-up areas it is becoming increasingly difficult to construct public facilities matching a new form of social life, although the degree of difficulty depends on the history of each built-up area. In view of the development of efficient networks of transportation, it is no longer necessary to locate new public facilities close to the place where people live; the location of new public facilities should take into consideration the complementary relations between the new town and other cities. We thought that the public facilities Fujisawa City had already decided to construct should be incorporated in the plan for the new town. Eventually, however, some of these facilities were built elsewhere outside the new town, and some others were not constructed at all, due to delays in the project plans before the completion of the new town. The initial list of a large variety of facilities planned for construction in Fujisawa New Town, given in Table 5, included a hospital, old people's home, and various kinds of facilities for children that would be used by people from the built-up areas of Fujisawa and from Fujisawa's neighboring municipalities.

Table 5 Facilities Planned for Fujisawa New Town

Cultural property park	About 10 ha; includes museum and youth center
Cemetery park	About 50 ha
Shopping area	Includes department stores, supermarkets, shops, and leisure facilities
Old people's home	1
Children's center	1
Meeting halls	6
Clinics	2
Community center	Includes branch office of the city government, citizen's hall, library, new-town management center, post office, police station
Hospital	Includes colony for physically handicapped
Prefectural senior high school	1
Junior high schools	2
Primary schools	4
Kindergartens	11
Nurseries	7

The facility construction program is now being planned, but it will undergo some modification when houses are built and people begin to live in the new town. Recently in many new towns developers tried to secure as much reserve land as possible on which to build the public facilities that are needed after people begin to live in the new towns. Such an approach to facility construction will exert a considerable influence on land use in new towns.

Suburban agriculture will also influence land use in new towns. Table 6 lists present land use in the area of Fujisawa New Town. An overwhelmingly large proportion of the planned area in Fujisawa New Town is farmland, forests, and wasteland. As for land use in the three districts of Oba, Ishikawa-Nambu, and Endo, in which the planned area of Fujisawa New Town is included, paddies accounted for 11.5 percent, fields 43.3 percent, forests 39.3 percent, residential land 3.4 percent, and other 2.4 percent; combined paddies, fields, and forests accounted for 82.6 percent when planning work for the new town started. The breakdown of employed persons by industry shows those employed in primary industry accounted for 29.3 percent in Oba, 44.6 percent in Ishikawa-Nambu, and 41.2 percent in Endo. Furthermore, 54 percent of those employed in primary industry were full-time farmers, while more than 30 percent were second-class, part-time farmers (farmers whose incomes from nonagricultural side jobs are larger than agricultural incomes). This shows that the area is a typical suburban agricultural one. Although the size of farmland owned by farmers is relatively large, the agricultural labor force is rapidly becoming feminized due to the emigration of male workers seeking nonagricultural jobs. The farming households that suffer from the labor shortage resort to intensive but small-scale farming, and the amount of uncultivated farmland is also increasing.

This kind of situation confronts almost every new town. In many cases farming households lose their land and become urbanized overnight. Farmers who lose their land have no time to adjust themselves gradually to urban life, and many of them lose even the money they get from the sales of their land and find themselves in distress. Abrupt changes in the environment facing the farmers tend to destroy the basis for harmony with new residents in new towns.

In Fujisawa New Town the choice and volunteerism of farmers are respected. Those who want to give up farming and seek urban jobs in the new town are encouraged to do so. The plan is designed to fulfill their wishes.

The largest proportion of land in the planned area of Fujisawa New Town is farmland, and about one-half of this is reserve land exempted from development. Farmers in the area will spend 5 to 10 years to adjust themselves gradually to urban life, and in the meantime, they will continue farming, assured of their land. Fujisawa City has bought one-half of the farmland in the planned area of the new town and all other land, including forests, in the area and is now executing the land readjustment program, separating mixed land into farmland blocks and residential land blocks. Urban facilities are being developed outside farmland blocks.

A similar method is now being employed in the development of Kohoku New Town by Yokohama City. Those who want to continue farming and those who want to seek an urban lifestyle will live in physically separate zones in the new town; the work to create these separate zones will be achieved through the land readjustment program. The farming zone will be designated the urbanization-controlled area where all activities other than farming will be restricted. This method will be very effective in dealing with the problem of suburban agriculture in future new-town development. The features of agricultural land remaining in Fujisawa New Town are as follows: it is farmland within the city planning area, adjoining the built-up area. It will remain farmland temporarily (for 5 to 10 years after the completion of the new town). Those who want to continue farming will sell their land and move to the agricultural area to the north. Agriculture will be intensive, taking advantage of the area's proximity to mass consumption markets. While it remains farmland, an agreement to restrict nonagricultural use of

Table 6   Current Land Use in the Area of Fujisawa New Town

	Paddies	Fields	Forests and Wasteland	Residential Land	Public Land	Other	Total
ha	44.2	160.2	149.1	12.0	37.3	14.4	417.2
%	10.6	38.4	35.7	2.9	8.9	3.5	100

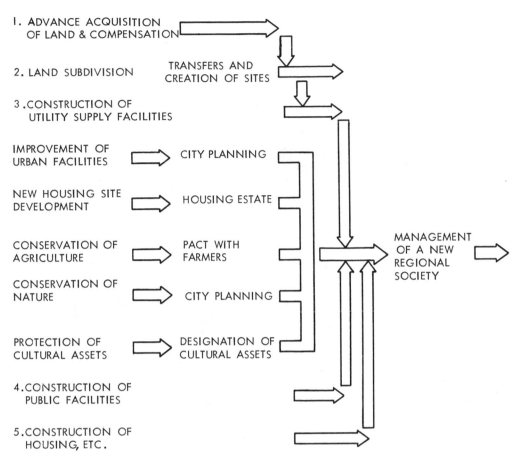

Figure 3. The development schedule of Fujisawa New Town.

farmland so as to prevent disorderly sprawl will be signed by farmers in the area. The city's comprehensive plan provides that financial and technical assistance be extended to the farmers in the area. Figure 3 gives the project schedule based on the development guideline.

Blocks Formed by the Linear, Central, and Ring Roads. The conditions and problems facing community formation in Fujisawa New Town on the basis of the development guideline may be summarized as follows: Fujisawa New Town is located at the southern edge of the north-south urban axis projected in the city's comprehensive plan, and an urban area will be extended to the north of the new town in the future. The mixture of urban and rural living environment in the same new town will prevent the formation of a homogeneous community spirit and of an integrated physical structure. The construction of public facilities, educational facilities, and facilities for shopping and leisure activities will undergo modifications because the

needs of the residents are expected to change after they have begun to live in the new town. Facilities needed in the new town will not be limited to those required of the traditional neighborhood units because the new town is planned in relation to the network cities. The new town will be affected by changes in the existing cities, and its facilities must be planned to be able to meet new requirements. Through traffic in the residential areas of the new town must be prohibited to create safe pedestrian spaces.

A physical plan that would meet requirements for growth, pedestrian spaces, flexibility, and urbanity was necessary for Fujisawa New Town (see Figure 4). We proposed a plan for residential areas, surrounded by a linear central zone accommodating public facilities and by ring roads, and in which only minimum public facilities such as kindergartens and nurseries would be built. The traditional neighborhood unit plan includes educational, shopping, and other service facilities in an area where 5000 to 10,000 people live. Almost all public facilities are

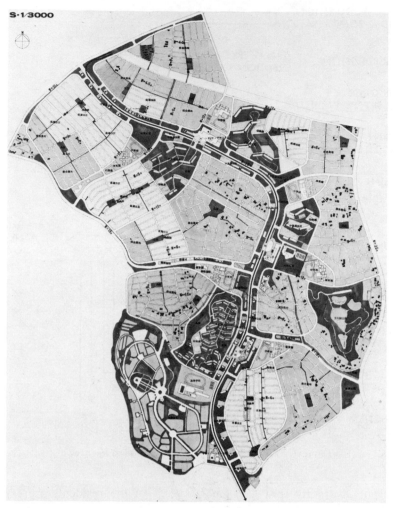

Figure 4. The master plan of Fujisawa New Town.

concentrated in the linear central zone; residential areas are planned as cul-de-sac residential blocks surrounded by ring roads (the cul-de-sac system is also employed for farming blocks that are expected to become urban residential areas in 5 to 10 years), and each block is connected with the central zone.

Each residential area surrounded by a ring road is not a community subunit; people living in it are directly connected with what they need in the central zone or outside the new town. Within the area surrounded by a ring road, complete separation between vehicular and pedestrian traffic is maintained through the cul-de-sac system, providing pedestrian space for residents. The size of the residential block formed by a ring road is quite flexible up to a certain limit (the limit is determined by the amount of vehicular traffic generated in the block) because the

block is not designed for any fixed community; within the block a great degree of flexibility in design is permitted: low-rise housing, middle- and high-rise collective housing, farmers' houses and farmland, and mixtures of all these—each block can be planned independent of other blocks.

Blocks differ in size, character, and spatial layout. By creating the linear central zone that is directly connected with each block and concentrating public facilities with the high density of activity on this zone, the urbanity of the new town as a whole in both spatial and social terms will be enhanced.

In Fujisawa New Town there are large agricultural blocks as open space. To enhance the urbanity of the new town as a whole and to accentuate the spatial features of the central zone, the construction of high-rise housing as well as of public facilities is planned.

To provide spatial variety in the central zone, encircling public facilities with abundant greenery have been considered.

In Fujisawa New Town old residents will continue to live in agricultural blocks, and new residents will move into residential blocks. If they are left to themselves, the old and the new residents will develop a sense of alienation from each other. Through the joint use of public facilities in the central zone, they should come to understand each other's lifestyles and become friendly to one another.

In the physical layout in which residential blocks and the area of public facilities are not mixed, a balance can be maintained between the varying needs of people and the public facilities meeting such needs when the direction and speed of growth change. Changes in land use in the central zone will also be possible without affecting the neighboring residential blocks, and the central zone will be able to provide the facilities that will have become necessary on a broad regional basis in its complementary relation with the system of network cities, as well as to meet the changes within the zone itself.

Our plan for the physical layout based on the linear central zone and independent blocks provides a system for the development of a new north-south urban axis projected in Fujisawa City's comprehensive plan. The planned area of Fujisawa New Town is only part of a larger urban community to be developed in Fujisawa City in the future. We hope that Fujisawa New Town will provide all the necessary conditions for modern urban life that we have examined in this essay.

New towns in Japan will be constructed on an increasingly large scale in the suburbs of large cities to provide housing. The situation confronting new-town construction will be more and more complex. However, no matter how complicated or perplexing the situation may be, our concept and method of new-town development can be applied if the conditions peculiar to each one are considered.

NOTES

1. The notes were entered into an agreement on July 1, 1966.

2. The aim of Team Ten has been described as follows: Team Ten is a group of architects who have sought out each other because each has found the help of others necessary to the development and understanding of his own personal work, but it is more than that. The group has met at Aix-en-Provence (July 1953), Paris (July 1955), La Sarraz (September 1955), Dubrovnik (1956), La Sarraz (Autumn 1957), and Ottero (September 1959). Main members of the group are J. B. Bakema, Aldo van Eyck (Holland), G. Candilis (France), and A. & P. Smithson (England).

3. Satoshi Mifune, *Modern Urban Policies*, Vol. 7 (Tokyo: Iwanami, 1973), p. 187.

4. Japan, Planning Bureau, Ministry of Construction, *The Annual Report of Research and Studies for Housing Development* (Tokyo: July 12, 1967).

5. Japan City Center, *New Town and Finances*, (Tokyo: Japan City Center, 1970).

6. The Chicago Group was R. E. Park, E. W. Burgess, and R. D. McKenzie. See R. E. Park and E. W. Burgess, *Introduction to the Science of Sociology* (Chicago: The University of Chicago Press, 1921).

7. Ministry of Economic Planning Bureau, 1969.

8. Shozo Yamamoto, *City and National Land* (Tokyo: Kashima Institute, 1971), pp. 197–198.

9. Fujisawa City, *Concept for West-North Area of Fujisawa City Development*, January 1967.

CHAPTER 15

A Proposal for Transportation Systems in a Residential New Town

SAKAE IEMURA

In every metropolitan area of Japan, rail transport is still prevalent and active against floods of cars. I intend to discuss planning of a residential new town and its transportation systems, focusing on rail systems.

DISTINCTIVE FEATURES OF JAPANESE NEW TOWNS

Almost all new towns in Japan are residential satellites built by governmental authorities such as the Japan Housing Corporation; they depend on a mother city or metropolis and have no industrial functions. They have large planned populations and high population densities of over 100 persons per hectare. New towns are usually provided with rail transport connections with the mother city. The government involvement indicates that obtaining a large area of land in Japan is difficult for anyone or any private corporation, so construction of new towns in our country is not work suitable for private business.

Urban and residential growth in Japan is strongly influenced by economic growth. Before World War II we already had urban planning study on the problems of metropolitan areas, but various disputes about them occurred after 1955 when the economy of Japan began to make rapid progress.

Approximately 112 million people live within the little islands of Japan, which total 372,000 square kilometers. Four-fifths of these islands are mountainous. Consequently, the flat lands suitable for urban areas are only one-fifth of Japan, or 74,000 square kilometers; and population density in these flat lands is some 1500 persons per square kilometer. In 1955 when the population of Japan was some 89 million, there was almost no place for a new town independent of any metropolis, excluding the Hokkaido region or northern territory of Japan.

Prior to becoming a modern nation and society, Japan was a condensed society with numerous population on the small islands, so zoning of land use and ownership of property were extremely divided. Governments have owned only small properties, and most land was privately owned. Moreover, as one of the democratic policies, large farms were subdivided into many small properties by law after World War II. As a result, much land suitable for urbanization is extremely divided by use and ownership and scattered all over Japan. Today the first step of new-town construction is dominated by obtaining large sites. Because of these reasons, location, size, territory and shape of a new-town site are generally decided by factors beyond proper planning concerned with obtaining sites.

Residential new towns are necessary to provide homes for people, especially in metropolitan areas. Of course, it is often said that the economic, industrial, government and cultural functions of the Tokyo metropolitan area should be dispersed to avoid excessive concentration; and as an adequate method to resolve these problems, an innovative industrial new town should be made by improving an old rural town. However, the new town is used today to supply numerous residences in every metropolitan area. As a result, large new towns exist mostly in the three great metropolitan areas: Tokyo, Osaka, and Nagoya.

SELECTION OF A TRANSPORTATION SYSTEM IN A NEW-TOWN REGION

Because most of our new towns are part of a vast residential zone in a metropolitan area including a mother city, most of the residents in these towns are accustomed to having employment outside the new town or in the mother city. In this case, the problem of transportation within the new town and between it and the mother city is very important. We usually use the following transportation systems for commuters:

1. Private cars,
2. Bus transit,
3. New transportation systems such as personalized rapid transit (PRT), automatic controlled transportation (ACT), dasher-bear,
4. Rail transit.

The appropriate one differs according to each social situation, life of the people, regional condition, size of the new town, and so on.

Because our population is concentrated in limited areas, it is difficult for us to use private cars as the main conveyer of commuters, particularly in the Tokyo, Osaka, and Nagoya metropolitan areas. Providing sufficient parking lots in the central business district of the mother city is a greater problem than constructing highways with adequate capacity for commuters from the new town.

New transportation systems such as PRT, ACT, dasher-bear, and so on have many future possibilities, but today they still have many faults, including large initial equipping costs and considerable operating costs. The new transportation system—bus transit, and rail transit in the future—is expected to substitute for many private cars, but today these modes of transport are unavailable in most new towns.

The best transportation system for commuters in a residential new town is either transit by bus or rail.

Making a detailed examination, we can sort these systems as follows:

1. Bus transit.

   a. Walking and local buses.
   b. Walking, local buses, and express buses.
   c. Private cars and express buses.

2. Rail transit.

   a. Walking and rail transit.
   b. Walking, local buses, and rail transit.
   c. Private cars and rail transit.

Local buses mean that intervals between bus stops are short (400 to 600 meters), and average operating speed is slow. Express buses mean that intervals between bus stops are usually longer than 800 meters, and average operating speed is rapid. These buses are rather better substituted by any new transportation system with middle capacity in the future.

The advantages and disadvantages of the six cases are as follows: transportation system combining walking and local buses is common; but as traffic volume on the highways or streets increases, time necessary to reach some destination does also, and certainty of arrival at some scheduled hour decreases. The number of persons transported by one operating man is very few—that is, the productivity of transportation is very low. So in any advanced country with high wages for general laborers, the costs to operate buses have a tendency to become higher and higher according to increasing wage level. This problem is economically important.

A system with express buses is similar to the preceding one, but it is not more desirable than the first system because commuters to a mother city need to transfer from a local bus to an express bus on many occasions. We should scarcely use this transportation system, but we can use it in a new town that is suited to providing any express bus routes along principal roads or freeways toward a mother city.

The third system of private car and express buses is used in a new town with bus stops sparsely scattered for some reason. This system needs numerous parking lots for commuters around every bus stop so it probably disturbs a residential zone that needs to preserve a favorable, quiet environment. If we can place the bus stations or stops in the new town directly along the freeway and connect the new town closely to the central business district of the mother city through the freeways on which express buses are operated, this system is profitably applied.

In the case of walking and rail transit the new town area is limited within the pedestrian radius centering at the railroad station, and we need not provide a great number of parking lots for commuters. Confusion of traffic does not happen on the main streets in the new town, so this system is usually very good. In the case of a new town expanding beyond the pedestrian radius we can add local buses to the system. It will then have the disadvantages already mentioned concerning buses.

The sixth transportation system, using private cars between every home and the railroad station nearest to those homes, generally requires many parking lots for commuters in the vicinity of the railroad station, like around the stations in the BART system in the San Francisco metropolitan area. Numerous parking lots in the center of the new town are never desirable for maintaining a favorable environment. If we use mainly the "kiss and ride" system and subsidiarily the park-and-ride system, these faults shall become relatively fewer.

Transportation Systems for Commuters Between a Residential New Town and Its Mother City. How to transport commuters between the residential new town and its mother city is always a big problem in the town's planning. Since in Japan, it is not suitable that commuters mainly use private cars, we have practically no choice but to use rail or bus transit.

A transport system organized around a rail system has the following advantages:

1. High speed and certainty of schedule. Railroad trains can easily maintain an average speed, including stopping time, of over 50 kilometers per hour, although the speed of the trains differs according to the station intervals, rail conditions, and so on. Therefore, supposing that the distance between a new town and a central business is 25 kilometers, running time of a train is only about 30 minutes.
2. Widely variable transporting capacity. In rail transit, transporting capacity can be varied by arranging the running train intervals and the number of coupled passenger cars on each train.
3. A possibility of manpower saving. This area can be improved, and accordingly, increasing wage

levels do not necessarily mean increasing overall costs.
4. Feasibility of rail terminal facility in the central district of the metropolis. It is comparatively easy to equip rail terminal facilities in the central district of a metropolis when railroads are built underground or connected with any existing old railroads.

The disadvantages of rail systems are as follows:

1. The huge initial facility investment. Rail transit is suitable only for a new town with a large demand from commuters because it is inevitably accompanied by a huge initial facility investment.
2. Means to reach railroad stations. This is no problem when the area of a new town is limited within the pedestrian radius centering at the railroad station, but if the new town has many residents outside the pedestrian radius, numerous parking lots are needed in the vicinity of the railroad station, or bus routes should be provided for these residents. In this case people have the inconvenience of transferring to a train from a bus or private car at the station.
3. Transferring at the station in the central district of the mother city to reach work places.

If we use bus transit as the main system between a residential new town and its mother city, the situation differs remarkably when buses are operated on a freeway or a principal road provided with one lane reserved for the bus only from the situation of no reserved lane. In the latter case bus traffic is confused by general car traffic, so the running speed of the buses is often extremely reduced. Consequently, fewer people ride the buses. Bus transit without a reserved bus lane is not suitable as a transportation system between a residential new town and its mother city and is feasible only for a new town with a population below 50,000 persons.

If the freeway or the principal road is provided with a reserved lane for buses, its advantages and disadvantages are as follows:

1. Remarkably flexible transporting demand. If we arrange a suitable network of bus routes and adequate frequency of operation, we have a great probability to realize a transportation system closely matched to transporting demands. Residents of new towns can arrive in many places

in the central district of a mother city by bus without transferring from everywhere in the new town. Besides, bus transit is fit for every residential area, irrespective of population density.

2. Variable transporting capacity. Increase and decrease of capacity in bus transit are freely variable according to transporting demand.

3. Very small initial investment. Because the initial investment for facilities is very small in bus transit, it is available for a small new town with a population below 50,000 people.

4. Impossibility to maintain high speed and certainty of schedule. Buses can maintain high speed and certainty of schedule on freeways provided with the reserved bus lane. However, because buses use the general streets in a new town and the central district of the mother city, the confusion of traffic causes lowering of speed and uncertainty of schedule.

5. Impossibility of manpower saving. There is almost no room for saving of manpower in bus transit, so increasing wages means increasing transporting cost.

6. Difficulty of operating buses in the central district of the mother city. The buses use bus stops on general streets or the bus terminal provided for the bus in the central district of the mother city, so operation of numerous buses in the central district crowded with cars is difficult and is accompanied by considerable increase of operating costs.

The advantages and disadvantages of buses operating on any highway or freeway without reserved bus lanes, especially in a new town with a population below 50,000, are as follows:

1. Variable transporting capacity. The capacity varies according to transporting demand, which is considerably smaller in a new town with a population below 50,000.

2. Very small initial investment. Because the initial investment for facilities is very small in bus transit, it is especially suitable for a small new town with a population below 50,000 people.

3. Difficulty to maintain high speed and certainty of schedule. As the population of the new town grows larger and larger, it becomes more and more difficult to run buses smoothly on any freeway without a reserved bus lane because of the confusion of traffic caused by increasing numbers

of commuters using private cars. Even if the population of the new town is below 50,000, when the ratio of bus passengers to all commuters is less than some number, floods of private cars disturb the smooth running of buses.

4. Difficulty with savings of manpower and operation in the central district of a mother city. The conditions here are exactly the same as those for a system with a reserved bus lane.

5. Confusion of traffic on the freeway. Even if a transportation system is mainly organized by bus transit, traffic on the freeway is quite similar to the condition that occurs in the case of using mainly private cars for commuting in the new town.

Efficiency of Each System. An essential problem for the planners of a residential new town is how to organize its transportation system, especially how to transport commuters smoothly between the new town and its mother city. I analyze three cases: rail transit, bus transit, and private cars. Using data of actual results in the metropolitan areas of Japan, the demands of transportation for commuters between a residential new town and its mother city are calculated approximately as Figure 1 shows.

If we research how all demands for commuters distribute to each transporting means (rail transit, bus transit, private cars, and so on), the conclusion differs according to the society, economy, and habits of each country and the geographic conditions of each metropolitan area. Here, to simplify the analysis, I assume the distributions given in Table 1, using average data for the metropolitan areas in Japan. These percentages are the ratios for commuters in the morning rush hours. Subsequently, I assume the details of each transporting means listed in Table 2. In the case when commuters mainly use private cars, I suppose that a reserved bus lane is not provided on the freeway. If I calculate a transporting number for each case, the results are listed in Tables 3 and 4.

It is evident from Table 3 that in the case of a

Table 1 Distribution of Commuter Demands (%)

	Rail Transit	Bus Transit	Private Cars
Mainly rail transit	90		10
Mainly bus transit		85	15
Mainly private cars		40	60

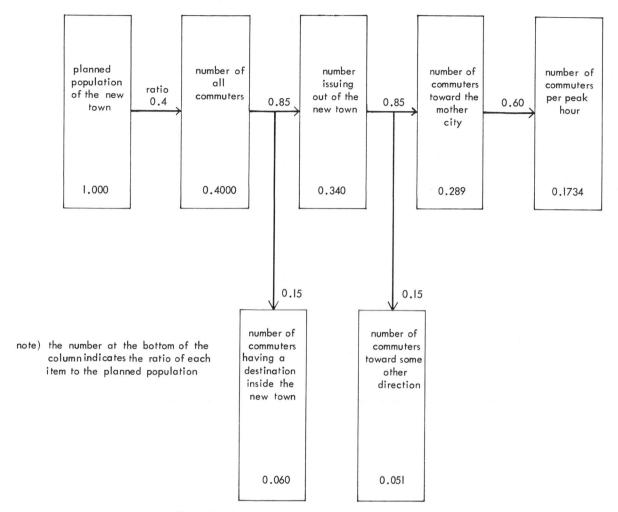

Figure 1. Commuter demand from a residential new town.

transportation system mainly organized by rail transit, one line of double-tracked railroad and two freeways with two or three lanes for one direction can transport all commuters even for a large new town with populations of 400,000 to 500,000 people.

In the case of a system mainly organized by bus transit, only one lane reserved for buses can easily transport all commuters using bus transit even for a large new town with a population of 500,000 people, although there are many problems in the operation of these buses in the central district of the mother city. In this case two freeways provided with three lanes for one direction is adequate for all commuters using private cars in the new town with a population of 400,000 people. However, if the condition of competition of bus transit is not equivalent or superior to private cars concerning speed, operating frequency, cost, certainty for schedule, and so on, the share of

bus transit decreases; as a result, the volume of traffic for private cars increases extremely, and the volume of all traffic may exceed the capacity of the freeway.

In the case of a system mainly using private cars I assume that the reserved bus lane is not provided on the freeway, and buses run on the general lanes being mixed among other vehicles (see Table 5).

In the case of private cars the new town with a population of 200,000 needs four freeways provided with three lanes for one direction, or three freeways provided with four lanes each way. To prepare three or four freeways is practically a limit for one new town. In addition, running speeds of buses are expected to decrease according to the increase of all traffic; as a result, commuters will change from buses to the private cars because these freeways do not have a reserved lane.

Table 2   Details of Each Means of Transport

Rail transit

(a) Double-tracked and electrified railroad
(b) Standard capacity per passenger cars: 140 people
(c) Minimum operating intervals of trains at peak hour in the morning: 2.5 minutes
(d) Passenger efficiency ratio

$$= \frac{\text{average number of passengers per car}}{\text{standard capacity per car}} : 1.7$$

(e) Number of transported passengers per car and per hour

$$140 \times \frac{60}{2.5} \times 1.7 = 5712 \text{ people}$$

(f) Maximum numbers of passenger cars able to couple on a train: 16 cars

Bus transit

(a) Freeway with limited access and provided with a lane reserved for buses only
(b) Practical traffic capacity per lane and per hour: 1500 vehicles
(c) Average number of transported passengers per bus: 60 people
(d) Maximum number of transported passengers by buses per lane and per hour: 1500 × 60 = 90,000 people

Private cars

(a) Limited access freeway
(b) Practical traffic capacity per lane and per hour: 1500 vehicles
(c) Average number of passengers per car: 1.2 people
(d) Maximum number of transported passengers by private cars per lane and per hour: 1500 × 1.2 = 1800 people

EXCELLENCE OF A TRANSPORT SYSTEM ORGANIZED MAINLY BY RAIL TRANSIT

If we compare the three transportation systems (rail transit, bus transit, or private cars), we can conclude the following according to the size of the new-town population. For a new town with a population of 50,000 to 100,000 people, one or two freeways can easily transport commuters mainly using private cars and subsidiarily buses. However, rail transport is not suitable for a town of this size because transport demands are very low, making the efficiency of investment for facilities inferior. A reserved bus lane must be provided in a system mainly organized by bus transit, but in a new town of this size the transport demands for bus are very few, so the percentage of buses using the reserved lane to its full capacity is very low. However, I do not think that the efficiency of investment for facilities is as important as other considerations, because only one additional lane reserved for the buses is needed.

When the planned population rises to 150,000 to 300,000 people, we need three to five freeways, if using private cars is the main conveyor for commuters and this method is not practical. Using rail transit as the main conveyor for commuters has few problems for a new town of this size, and efficiency of investment for facilities is comparatively good.

In using bus transit as the main conveyor, the percentage of buses using the reserved lane to its full capacity is about 25 to 50 percent, so efficiency of the reserved lane is comparatively good. However, as

Table 3   Number of Users in a Transportation System Organized Mainly by Rail Transit

Planned Population of the New Town (A)	Number of Commuters Toward the Mother City per Peak Hour (B) = (A) × 0.1734	Rail Transit		Private Cars	
		Number of Commuters to Use the Rail Transit (C) = (B) × 0.9	Number of Coupled Cars Needed to Transport	Number of Commuters to Use Private Cars (C) = (B) × 0.1	Number of Freeway Lanes Needed for Smooth Run
50,000	8,670	7,803	2 (1.4)	867	1 (0.5)
100,000	17,340	15,606	3 (2.7)	1734	1 (1.0)
150,000	26,010	23,409	5 (4.1)	2601	2 (1.4)
200,000	34,680	31,212	6 (5.5)	3468	2 (1.9)
250,000	43,350	39,015	7 (6.8)	4335	3 (2.4)
300,000	52,020	46,818	9 (8.2)	5202	3 (2.9)
350,000	60,690	54,621	10 (9.6)	6069	4 (3.4)
400,000	69,390	62,424	11 (10.9)	6936	4 (3.9)
450,000	78,030	70,227	13 (12.3)	7803	5 (4.3)
500,000	86,700	78,030	14 (13.7)	8670	5 (4.8)

Table 4 Number of Users in a Transportation System Organized Mainly by Bus Transit

Planned Population of the New Town (A)	Number of Commuters Toward the Mother City per Peak Hour (B) = (A) × 0.1734	Bus Transit		Private Cars	
		Number of Commuters to Use the Bus Transit (C) = (B) × 0.85	Number of Buses Needed to Transport	Number of Commuters to Use Private Cars (D) = (B) × 0.15	Number of Freeway Lanes Needed for Smooth Run
50,000	8,670	7,370	123	1,301	1 (0.8)
100,000	17,340	14,739	246	2,601	2 (1.5)
150,000	26,010	22,109	369	3,902	3 (2.2)
200,000	34,680	29,478	492	5,202	3 (2.9)
250,000	43,350	36,848	614	6,503	4 (3.7)
300,000	52,020	44,217	737	7,803	5 (4.4)
350,000	60,690	51,587	860	9,104	6 (5.1)
400,000	69,360	58,956	983	10,404	6 (5.8)
450,000	78,030	66,326	1106	11,705	7 (6.5)
500,000	86,700	73,695	1229	13,005	8 (7.3)

the number of commuters using buses increases, problems develop concerning the network of bus routes, operating frequencies, and flexibility corresponding with periodic changes of commuters. In addition to these difficulties, very difficult problems often happen for the treatment of buses at terminals or bus stops in the central district of the mother city.

Even if the planned population rises to between 350,000 and 500,000 people, we need only one double-tracked railroad if rail transit is the main transportation system for commuters. Using bus transit as the main system in this case is problematic because arranging the network of bus routes, operating frequencies in the new town, and treatment of buses at

terminals or bus stops in the central district of the mother city are extremely troublesome. Therefore, excluding the case when the network of streets and other conditions of traffic in the central district of the mother city are especially suitable for buses, bus transit is not applicable for a new town of this size.

Combining these various discussions I come to the following conclusions:

1. A transportation system mainly using private cars is applicable only for a small residential new town with a planned population below 100,000.
2. A transportation system organized by bus transit is applicable for every size new town, but this

Table 5 Number of Users in a Transportation System Organized Mainly for Private Cars

Planned Population of the New Town (A)	Number of Commuters Toward the Mother City per Peak Hour (B) = (A) × 0.1734	Private Cars		Bus Transit		Total Number of Private Cars and Buses Needed to Transport	Number of Freeway Lanes Needed for Smooth Run
		Number of Commuters to Use Private Cars (C) = (B) × 0.6	Number of Private Cars Needed to Transport	Number of Commuters to Use the Bus Transit (D) = (B) × 0.4	Number of Buses Needed to Transport		
50,000	8,670	5,202	4,335	3,468	58	4,393	3 (3.0)
100,000	17,340	10,404	8,670	6,936	116	8,786	6 (5.9)
150,000	26,010	15,606	13,005	10,404	174	13,179	9 (8.8)
200,000	34,680	20,808	17,340	13,872	232	17,572	12 (11.8)
250,000	43,350	26,010	21,675	17,340	289	21,964	15 (14.7)
300,000	52,020	31,212	26,010	20,808	347	26,357	18 (17.6)
350,000	60,690	36,414	30,345	24,276	405	30,750	21 (20.5)
400,000	69,360	41,616	34,680	27,744	463	35,143	24 (23.5)
450,000	78,030	46,818	39,015	31,212	521	39,536	27 (26.4)
500,000	86,700	52,020	43,350	34,680	578	43,928	30 (29.3)

system inevitably develops extreme difficulty with the treatment of buses in the central district of the mother city, according to the increase of population.

3. In a transportation system mainly organized by rail transit the efficiency of investment for facilities tends toward remarkable improvement according to increasing population in the new town, and this system is most suitable for a huge residential new town. In this system we can smoothly transport commuters in the central district of the mother city by connecting directly with some existing railroads or subways or by construction of a new terminal underground.

All concentrated metropolitan areas in Japan have very few existing freeways, and construction of new freeways is very difficult in those areas. If we research how completely the network of freeways is equipped and how many parking lots are provided in the central district of metropolises in the United States, we find immediately that every metropolitan area in Japan is inferior in each respect. So rail transit is surely the most suitable transportation system in the residential new town, and every large one depends on the transportation system mainly organized by rail transit, although the degree of dependence varies.

Extent of a Residential New Town Served by Rail Transit. It is very desirable to find the most suitable extent for a residential new town where rail transit is used as the main transportation system. If we restrict the approaching measures for every railroad station to walking only, the most suitable extent is deduced as follows. The distance for an easy walk is generally 1.2 kilometers in Japan. How long a distance is suitable for the intervals between adjoining stations is

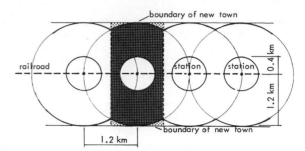

Figure 2. Model A.

discussed in various ways, but from personal experience I assume the average intervals between adjoining stations as 1.2 kilometers. Here, I recommend two models.

Model A assumes the following:

1. The new town extends 1.2 kilometers from both sides of the railroad serving the new town.
2. The density of population is 300 persons per hectare in the vicinity of the railroad station (within the 0.4-kilometer radius centering at the station), 120 persons per hectare between the 1.2 kilometer radius and 0.4 kilometer radius, and 100 persons per hectare outside the 1.2-kilometer radius (see Figure 2 and Table 6).

Model B assumes the following:

1. The new town extends 2 kilometers from both sides of the railroad serving the new town.
2. The density of population is the same as in Model A (see Figure 3 and Table 7).

In Model A every inhabitant can reach the railroad station by walking, but in Model B two-thirds of all residents can reach the station by walking, and the other one-third must use private cars or buses.

Table 6   Model A

	Area		Density (persons per ha)	Population	
	ha	%		Number of Inhabitants	%
Within walking distance					
To 0.4 km	50.24		300	15,072	
0.4–1.2 km	225.18		120	27,022	
Total	275.42	95.6		42,094	97.1
Outside 1.2 km	12.58	4.4	100	1,258	2.9
Total	288.00	100.0	150	43,352	100.0

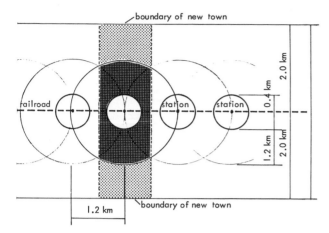

Figure 3. Model B.

However, the width of 2.4 kilometers is too narrow and unpractical, and Model B is better than Model A in this respect. The residental new town served mainly by rail transport should have a population of 250,000 persons if investment for facilities is to be efficient. Table 8 shows the most reasonable extent for residential new towns based on Models A and B with populations over 250,000.

The limit of extent for one residential new town is seven units joined to form one town while each station has dominant influence in its district. Consequently, for Model A the most reasonable extent for a new town has a width of 2.4 kilometers, a length of 8.4 kilometers, an area of 2016 hectares, and a planned population of 303,000 persons (see Figure 4 and Table 8). In this case, most of the new town lies within walking distance of the nearest railroad station so there is no problem about the transportation system for commuters.

For Model B, the most reasonable extent of the new town is a width of 4 kilometers, a length of 8.4 kilometers, an area of 3,360 hectares, and a planned population of 438,000 persons (see Figure 5 and Table 8). If we provide local bus routes for the area outside a radius for reaching railroad stations by walking and distrubute bus stops at adequate intervals along the bus routes, transporting services are adequate for the residents in the case of Model B.

Location of Residential Areas Around Railroad Stations. If I research in detail one unit of the district where each railroad station has dominant influences, organization of a residential unit is as follows. In Japan each residential unit is organized mainly considering arrangement of elementary and junior high schools. We usually provide one elementary school per residential unit, and one junior high school for two or three units. The standard planned population in one unit is 7000 to 10,000 persons. In the case of Model A one residential district consists of six residential units each with a planned population of some 7200 persons (see Figure 6 and Table 9). In the case of Model B one residential district consists of four residential units with some 7200 persons in each unit as planned population and another four residential units with some 8400 persons per unit as planned population (see Figure 7 and Table 10). Combining these results gives one residential district of six residential units in Model A and eight residential units in Model B. All residential units are separated by the railroad, main streets, or principal roads with wide greenbelts.

Facilities Related to Railroad Stations. In the residential new town using rail transit as an arterial transport means, essential functions of the residential district are concentrated around the railroad station—that is, shopping centers, banks, the post office, physicians' offices, other public facilities, and so on are provided in the vicinity of the station. Consequently, the layout of routes to the railroad station

Table 7   Model B

	Area		Density (persons per ha)	Population	
				Number of Inhabitants	%
	ha	%			
Within walking distance					
To 0.4 km	50.24		300	15,072	
0.4 to 1.2 km	225.18		120	27,022	
Total	275.42	57.4		42,094	67.3
Outside 1.2 km	204.58	42.6	100	20,458	32.7
Total	480.00	100.0	130	62,552	100.0

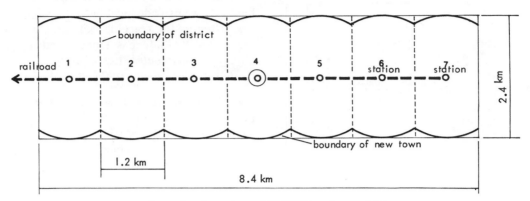

Figure 4. A new town of 303,000 based on Model A.

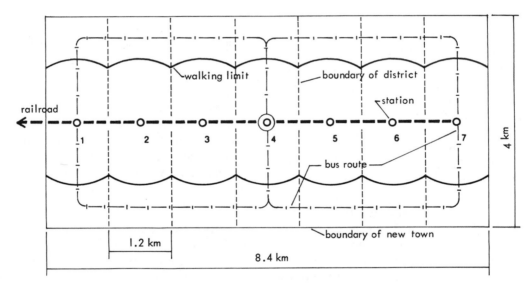

Figure 5. A new town of 438,000 based on Model B.

Table 8 Population, Extent of New Towns, and Number of Stations for Two Models

Planned Population (in thousands)	Model A				Model B			
	Number of stations	Area (ha)	Population (in thousands)	Width and length (km)	Number of stations	Area (ha)	Population (in thousands)	Width and length (km)
150–200	4	1152	173	2.4 × 4.8				
200–250	5	1440	217	2.4 × 6.0				
250–300	6	1728	260	2.4 × 7.2	4	1,920	250	4.0 × 4.8
300–350	7	2016	303	2.4 × 8.4	5	2,400	313	4.0 × 6.0
	8	2304	347	2.4 × 9.6				
350–400	9	2592	390	2.4 × 10.8	6	2,880	375	4.0 × 7.2
400–450					7	3,360	438	4.0 × 8.4
450–500					8	3,840	500	4.0 × 9.6

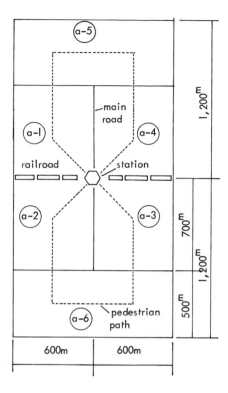

Figure 6.   Residential units in Model A.

from all places within the residential district is important because those routes are often used by pedestrians or private cars in ordinary daily life.

Every arterial pedestrian route to the railroad station should be provided straight through residential areas, be built as the pedestrian promenade independent of general streets, and be planned to underpass or overpass principal streets. If the pedestrian routes have excellent landscapes, the residential districts are attractive to residents.

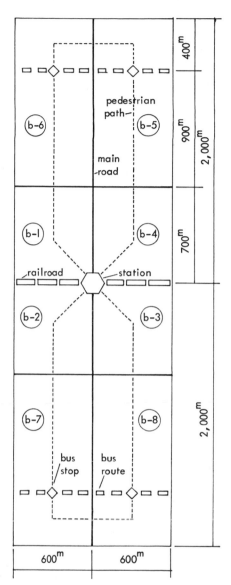

Figure 7.   Residential units in Model B.

Table 9   Dimensions of Residential Units Related to Populations (Model A)

Designated Residential Unit in Figures	Area (ha)	Width and Length (km)	Planned Population	Population Density (persons per ha)
a-1	42	0.6 × 0.7	7,238	172
a-2	42	0.6 × 0.7	7,238	172
a-3	42	0.6 × 0.7	7,238	172
a-4	42	0.6 × 0.7	7,238	172
a-5	60	0.5 × 1.2	7,200	120
a-6	60	0.5 × 1.2	7,200	120
Total	288		43,352	150

Table 10 Dimensions of Residential Units Related to Populations (Model B)

Designated Residential Units in Figures	Area (ha)	Width and Length (km)	Planned Population	Population Density (persons per ha)
b-1	42	0.6 × 0.7	7,238	172
b-2	42	0.6 × 0.7	7,238	172
b-3	42	0.6 × 0.7	7,238	172
b-4	42	0.6 × 0.7	7,238	172
b-5	78	0.6 × 1.3	8,400	108
b-6	78	0.6 × 1.3	8,400	108
b-7	78	0.6 × 1.3	8,400	108
b-8	78	0.6 × 1.3	8,400	108
Total	480		62,552	130

Arterial routes of cars should be arranged completely separate from pedestrian routes and should not pass through residential areas, even though cars are forced to make a detour. Main routes of cars should be planned so that those with a destination outside the new town can bypass the railroad station.

The areas near stations are important places. Table 11 lists principal facilities located in these areas. When both types of facilities are integrated they are more efficient and profitable than if they were separate.

CONCLUSION

Rail transit is the most appropriate system for a new town consisting of compact residential districts with high population density such as we have in Japan. Although this system has various difficulties for residential districts with low population density, such as in the United States, Canada, and Australia, if we use bicycles between residences and the railroad station, 1.2 kilometers maximum distance by walking

Table 11 Facilities Located Near Railroad Stations

Related to Transport	Serving Residents
Pedestrian plaza	Shopping center and other retail facilities
Terminals for arriving and departing cars	Banks, security corporations, etc.
Parking lots	
Taxi stands	Post office
Platform for "kiss-and-ride" commuters	Police station
	Fire department
Bus terminal	Medical facilities

can easily be increased to twice the maximum distance by using bicycles. (I have not discussed bicycles in this chapter because they are not suitable for rainy regions like Japan.)

Certainly a transportation system mainly using rail transit has characteristics that require walking between each residence and the nearest railroad station and between the railroad station and the working office in the central district of the metropolis. However, recently the general maximum distance for walking has tended to become longer in Japan because of current public opinion in favor of walking.

Walking and cycling eliminate confusion of traffic on streets and tremendous equipment for parking lots in the central district of a metropolis, and they save fuel and energy. In the transporting volume per energy unit, rail transit is the most efficient system, bus transit is second, and private cars are extremely inferior to either.

A habit of walking between homes and the nearest railroad station will certainly be difficult to form in regions where people have stopped using rail transit and networks of freeways and highways for cars have been completed, as in many metropolitan areas in the United States. However, efficient use of energy and change from cars to mass transit are strong movements in the world today, and limitation of traffic volume in cars decreases air pollution. In addition, walking within a distance of 1.5 kilometers in fine weather is very healthful, and time lost is insignificant.

Most Japanese people consider that a transportation system that mainly uses private cars and eliminates walking is not healthful and is uncomfortable, and such a system will lead people to unbearable conditions in a central business district that is occupied by many large buildings and gloomy parking lots.

After the oil panic in 1974, rail transport systems for commuters are becoming predominant in metropolitan areas all over the world. The system that is successful in the metropolitan areas of Japan will also be fundamentally successful in the United States, although there are some differences in the organization of metropolitan areas. Human nature is essentially the same everywhere, and the people of the United States will like walking as well as the people of Japan when they are trained to do it. Ultimately, rail transit is the most reasonable and profitable system for metropolitan areas all over the world.

CHAPTER 16

Indian Policy on Industrialization, Urbanization, and Industrial New Town Developments

DEBAJYOTI AICHBHAUMIK

In India the symptoms of urbanization are startling. The rate of growth for large cities is so great that coping with the increasing problems related to physical growth has become impossible. A number of cities have experienced more than 100 percent increase in population in only one decade. The cities with populations between 50,000 and 100,000—called medium-sized cities in India—are not growing at quite the same pace as the large cities, but a number of them, particularly the ones with an industrial economic base, have followed closely. New towns are being developed in large numbers for economic, administrative, or even political reasons, but ultimately they will provide accommodation for only the increasing urban population. Hundreds of new towns, ranging in size from 5000 to 100,000 in population, have been developed in India during the past two and a half decades. Most of the major industries have grown 10-fold during this same period; considering that industrialization is a strong generator of urban growth, this can be considered a significant cause of urbanization.

A superficial observation of all such indications has led to a widespread belief that the current rapid rate of urbanization in India, as in most other developing countries, is unprecedented in the history of urban development. Factual analysis, however,

does not support this notion. A simple examination of the figures of urban and rural population as percentages of the total population of India for each decennial census period (see Table 1) shows a picture diametrically opposed to the symptomatic indications. No doubt the percentage of urban population is undergoing a steady increase, but surely that increased rate is far too slow to be correlated in any way to the booming growth of the large cities.

Why this contradiction between the symptoms and the statistics? Are these symptoms false? The answers to these questions are not simple. Analysis of the symptoms shows that the pressing forces of urbanization in India are either kept intentionally uncontrolled or the potential of such forces is not transformed into overall ordered urbanization due to unfavorable policy decisions and an apathetic attitude on the part of the administration. The symptoms are not false; they are very real and indicate an urgent need for fast, comprehensive national urban development programs.

THE NATURE OF URBANIZATION

Rural-Urban Migration. Without exception, all large old cities in India have become victims of the

Table 1 India's Urban and Rural Population (% of Total Population)

Type of Settlement	1921	1931	1941	1951	1961	1971
Rural	88.8	88.0	86.1	82.7	82.0	80.1
Urban	11.2	12.0	13.9	17.3	18.0	19.9

Source: The Research and Reference Division, Ministry of Information and Broadcasting, *India 1975* (New Delhi: Government of India), p. 12.

country's postindependence rural-urban migration and have beome strangled by problems. Cities with populations of more than 100,000 account for almost 80 percent of this total shift of population (see Figure 1 and Table 2) and are facing catastrophe. A study of the growth of the nine largest cities of India, as shown in Table 3, indicates a steady, high rate of growth. The whole rural-urban migration has almost a unidirectional flow—making large cities larger at the expense of small cities. No significant change is observed in population in the rural areas, because the total rural population is so large compared to that of urban areas, and the 2 percent annual growth does not noticeably affect such a huge population.

The nine metropolitan cities shown in Table 3 were established and had grown until recently without any plan or control over their growth and therefore were burdened with problems even before the significantly large influx of population started in the late 1940s. Obviously, the migrating rural population, with a futile hope of finding better employment and better living conditions in these already overburdened cities, has only accelerated their rapid deterioration.

Planning officials quite often take the data on large cities (which is systematically compiled and readily available) and interpret them as indicative of

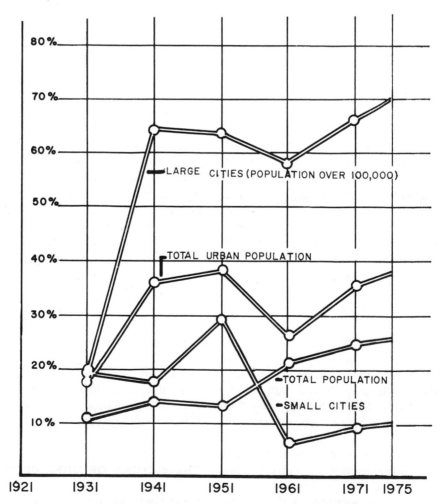

Figure 1. Rate of population increase on each decennial census in India.

Table 2   Population of Urban Areas

Year	Total Population of India (in millions)	Urban Population		Urban Areas with 100,000 Population or More		
		Total (in millions)	%	Number of Cities in this Catagory	Population Living in these Areas	
					Total (in millions)	%
1921	251	28	11.2	28	8.0	28.4
1931	279	33	12.0	31	9.6	28.7
1941	319	45	13.9	46	15.8	36.1
1951	361	62	17.3	71	25.8	41.7
1961	439	79	18.0	112	40.5	51.2
1971	548	109	19.9	147	67.0	61.4

the total urban picture and of the process of urbanization. Because there is a large discrepancy between the big and small cities in sharing the migrant population, inferences drawn from the study of any one of these categories will most likely give a rather distorted view of the total picture. In this case the total rural-urban migration, which can be considered a major indicator of urbanization, comes close to only 2 percent of the total population. Considering India's current population of 600 million (the 1971 census figure was 548 million and added to that are approximately another 13 million each year), the annual migrating population becomes 12 million. As we have already seen, almost 80 percent of this migrant population moves to large metropolises (the 147 cities in India that have 100,000 or more population). These cities absorb more than 9 million of this migrating population; the remaining 3 million are being shared by 2000 cities, of sizes ranging from 10,000 to 100,000 in population.

Table 3   Percentage of Increase in Population of Nine Major Metropolitan Cities of India

City	1921	1931	1941	1951	1961	1971
Calcutta	4	12	30	68	26	58
Bombay	20	− 1	46	67	46	48
Delhi	12	15	30	107	63	57
Madras	2	23	20	82	22	44
Bangalore	24	28	32	90	29	32
Ahmedabad	26	15	30	90	33	46
Kanpur	21	13	45	99	45	35
Poona	24	15	30	70	50	36
Nagpur	43	48	40	49	54	61

Industrialization and Urbanization.   The other most important indication of urbanization is industrialization. Statistics of industrial growth can also be deceptive. Compared to any international standard, India's industrial development is expanding rapidly. An important feature of this growth in the country after its independence has been the rapid expansion of the public sector. In 1951 there were only five public-sector undertakings, investing about $40 million, whereas by 1972 the number of such undertakings had increased to 401 with an investment of $650 million.

An annual survey of industries for 1969 showed 13,084 registered factories in India—an increase of about 2.5 percent over 1968, with an increase in productive capital of 10 percent over the same period of time. By contrast, the rate of urbanization for the same year was less than 1 percent.

From Figure 2 we can see the direct relation between industrialization and urbanization. Even with such an insignificant rate of urbanization along with a strong rate of industrialization, we can see their inseparable relation to each other. In studying the coefficients of urbanization and industrialization for different degrees of urbanization and industrialization for different states of India, we find that the states that have high coefficients of urbanization also have high coefficients of industrialization. A comparison of coefficients for 1961 and 1971 shows that almost the same states that were highly urbanized and industrialized in 1961 have also advanced in both areas in 1971.

The coefficients established here indicate achievement of a state in the areas of urban and industrial

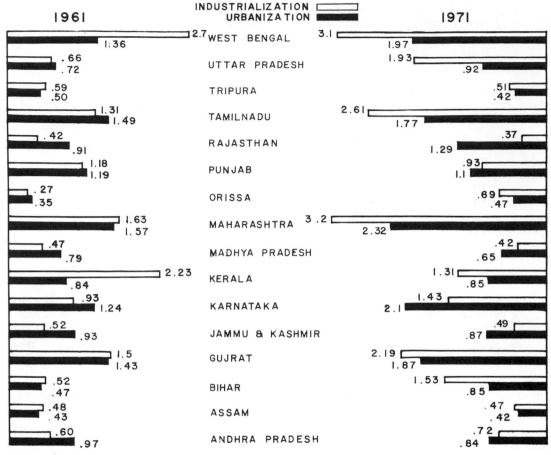

Figure 2. Coefficient of industrialization and urbanization of large states in India.

development in comparison to total national achievements in the respective areas. The ratio of urban to total population of a state, when divided by the ratio of total urban to total population of India, gives the coefficient of urbanization for that state. A figure higher or lower than 1.0 denotes a concentration of urban population in a state higher or lower than the national average. One interesting observation shown in Figure 2 is that the coefficients of industrialization for already industrialized states have gone much higher in 10 years without any significant change in the coefficients of urbanization. This probably suggests that many industries that are still nonurban in character have been established in such areas and reflects the decision of economic planners to establish industries without considering urbanization as a simultaneous task (see Figure 3).

Industrialization has undoubtedly been the basic cause of urbanization throughout the world since the beginning of the Industrial Revolution. Today in India, reflecting the typical attitude of a developing country toward economic advancement, crash pro-

grams for industrial development are being launched without recognizing the inseparable association of the process of industrialization and urbanization. While concentrated efforts are being made for industrial developments—the other facet of the same process— proper urban development is in most cases neglected and only taken up later as a peripheral task.

For the past two decades basic industries had been established to create a self-sustaining, self-reliant economy. Wherever industrial developments took place in the country, they caused a strong demand for the development of urban centers around them. A village faced the pressure of changing into an urban center, and a small urban center was subject to transforming itself into a large city—all within extremely short periods of time. This resulted in the creation of a large number of chaotic and problem-burdened industrial towns throughout the country. The huge industrial conglomerations and industrial new towns such a Ranchi, Durgapur, Rourkela, Bhilai (see Figures 4, 5, and 6) are examples of how fast urban growth has taken place wherever major industrial projects have been located. India's industrial implementation policies show no evidence of realization of the following facts:

1. The potential of industrial developments to create strong and healthy urban centers and to initiate balanced regional development of the country.
2. The inseparable relation between industrialization and urbanization—particularly in fulfilling the social and economic objectives set before the country through the Five-Year Plan.[1]

We always find in industrial new-town developments that the urban development program is secondary to the industrial development. In most cases the two are considered as completely unrelated functions, and their planning and implementation are carried out in complete isolation from one another.

For centuries India's economic base has been agricultural. Today even with rapid industrialization, India is still a predominantly agricultural country; but with the current rate of industrialization, it is on the threshold of entering the international industrial race. This is the time to formulate a well-coordinated policy for both industrial and urban development.

Industrialization indirectly stimulates growth in other areas of the economy, creates opportunities for employment, and most importantly, attracts people from rural areas to urban centers. Irrespective of the primary purpose for an industrial location, development of one industry acts as a catalyst and attracts more industries to select locations nearby, and the

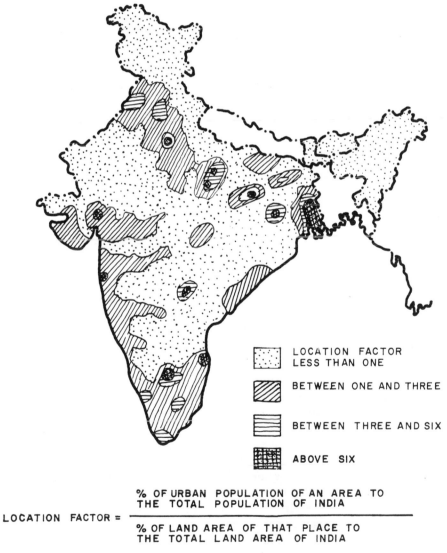

LOCATION FACTOR LESS THAN ONE

BETWEEN ONE AND THREE

BETWEEN THREE AND SIX

ABOVE SIX

$$\text{LOCATION FACTOR} = \frac{\text{\% OF URBAN POPULATION OF AN AREA TO THE TOTAL POPULATION OF INDIA}}{\text{\% OF LAND AREA OF THAT PLACE TO THE TOTAL LAND AREA OF INDIA}}$$

Figure 3. Indian areas of urban concentrations.

Figure 4. Indian states and metropolitan cities.

area gradually becomes very industrial. Such industrial agglomeration is a basic process through which industries flourish—in isolation they usually just survive and do not get the advantages of a highly specialized labor force, large market, and subsidiary industries. Agglomeration of industries is, therefore, a healthy sign for the economy. The work force, people associated in commerce, and technical, professional, and educational service people all create a large population concentration in these industrial agglomerations; and each complex starts developing as a self-sustaining urban, industrial growth area.

The same phenomenon also occurs when new industry is established in an existing urban center. The urban center grows larger and creates further advantages for industrial development. This cycle

continues until the urban center reaches a point where everything is chaotic, facilities are overburdened, and the population is maximum. Ultimately a process of decay starts, which Patrick Geddes termed "conurbation." At this point industries also gradually become more and more inefficient.[2]

We may confirm our earlier statement that industrialization is very closely associated with urbanization and that the relation of these two processes is so close that they may be considered absolutely inseparable. Furthermore, both processes induce strong regional concentrations. Proper balanced development in both areas will, therefore, need well-coordinated planning for both economic and physical reasons. Indiscriminate concentration of industries will be ultimately harmful to both industrial and urban development; consequently, the country will fail to achieve its social and economic objectives.

A decision on how much concentration or decentralization would be beneficial for the country demands close cooperation between economists and urban planners. Discouraging such cooperation, however, are India's different professional groups— economic planners, urban planners, and social planners—who work in almost complete isolation. Although they work under the same government, they follow separate objectives, concepts, and procedures. Attitudes of these professional groups have remained unchanged since India adopted its five-year plans in 1950. Indian urban planners have a general knowledge about processes like capital layout, fiscal planning, and long-term budgeting and about the social implications and impacts of various development programs; but also limited in knowledge are the other professional groups who are involved in land planning, the conception of three-dimensional physical forms of urban areas, or simply in the techniques or methodology of creating a livable urban environment. In this regard, comments made by Professor L. R. Vagale almost 10 years ago are still valid:

Urban and Regional planners are hardly consulted by the central, state and local governments regarding the location and planning of industries, formulating industrial development policies and programs and examining their physical consequences. The town and country planners have mostly confined themselves to studying the problems of towns and cities, which have local area dimensions only. The urban development plans prepared by them have, therefore, failed to reflect national aspirations, national policies and programs, and yet the national decisions regarding industrial locations, power installations, port developments, roads and railway constructions etc., create formidable urban and regional problems, which might be avoided or considerably minimized, were they considered and dealt with well in advance.

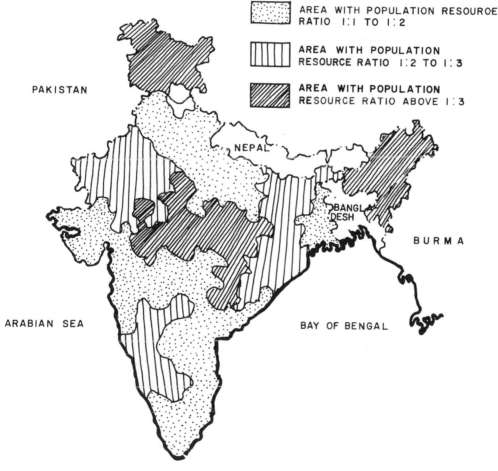

Figure 5. India: population resource ratio.

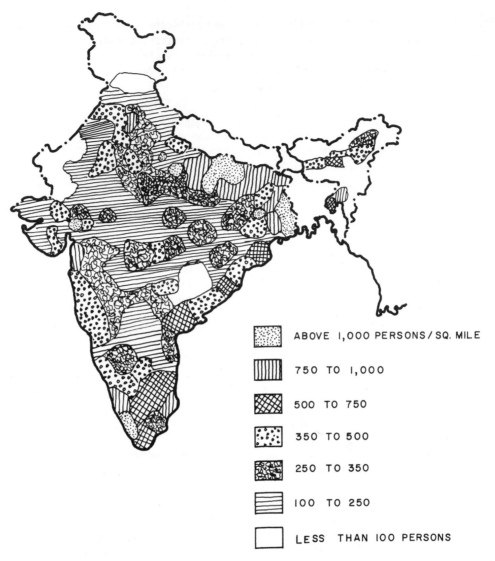

░░░	ABOVE 1,000 PERSONS / SQ. MILE
▥▥▥	750 TO 1,000
▨▨▨	500 TO 750
⁛⁛⁛	350 TO 500
▩▩▩	250 TO 350
☰☰☰	100 TO 250
☐	LESS THAN 100 PERSONS

Figure 6.   India: population density.

At best, the town and country planners have been brought into the picture to assess the undesirable consequences of the industrial policies and to suggest physical remedies.[3]

New-Town Developments.   The third major indicator of urbanization is new-town development. Both for meeting the challenge of urbanization and for minimizing the adverse effects of urbanization on the existing cities, new-town development provides a satisfactory answer. Along with concentrated, exhaustive efforts to shape the existing large cities, attempts are being made in India to develop new towns to relieve major metropolises from the continuous pressure of migrating population. However, such efforts so far have been only sporadic and unsuccessful because of an inadequate policy and

poor planning decisions. Kalyani, a new town developed during the 1950s, and Salt Lake City, developed a decade later, were both intended to relieve the metropolis of Calcutta; they are two perfect examples of unsuccessful new-town developments.

Many new towns have been developed in India since her independence in 1947, and even more are now being developed for purposes other than saving the big cities. These new towns can be classified according to their purpose of development: new towns for administrative purposes and new towns for economic purposes. New towns of the first category, under which come some new state capitals and a few company housing towns, are not often developed. Compared to the towns of the second category, which are large and small industrial towns, port cities, mining towns, and so on, administrative towns are far too few in number. However, the many towns of the second category—mainly industrial townships—do not reflect a figure even close to the national need. Industrial new-town developments fall far short of coping with the volume of industrial developments taking place in the country.

The administrative townships were the earlier of the two new-town development programs in India. Because their development has always begun solely for the purpose of administration, their plans are more comprehensive and successful than those of industrial towns. At least two of the towns of this category, Chandigarh and Gandhinagar, have been internationally acclaimed for their rich, imaginative physical planning and for their significant contribution to India's new-town development. Therefore, the expectation was that the success of these towns should have inspired and influenced the much handicapped industrial new-town plans and helped in the creation of a more livable environment than has been created in these industry-dominated cities. Instead, we find the total absence of any influence from them, either in physical forms or in land use plans. Why have these outstanding examples failed in developing any strong planning direction in India's new town development? They lack the functional viability of a traditional Indian town—the plans for which were generated not by the whims of an administrator or by the dreams of an architect to create a "Taj Mahal," but by realizing the desires and aspirations of the people who would be living there, by creating the right environment for all social and cultural activities and, above all, by adopting age-old methods of coping with the tropical climate.

The world-renowned administrative new towns of Chandigarh and Gandhinagar are the products of Western urban design concepts on Indian soil, with minimum modifications. Such towns are luxuries that a poor country like India can ill afford. However, the successes or failures of administrative or satellite cities are not going to influence all urban development as strongly as would the industrial new towns. Consequently, this is the category that demands more serious consideration from social, economic, and physical planners toward the development of a design solution most appropriate for Indian conditions. For balanced progress, many such towns must be developed, almost on a mass scale within a short period of time. Therefore an all-out effort for the development of some flexible prototypical

designs to suit India's special cultural, economic, and social needs is necessary.

NATIONAL PLANS FOR INDUSTRIALIZATION AND URBANIZATION

India's five-year plans have always been prepared after taking an overall view of the country's resources and need to achieve rapid, balanced growth within the framework of well-defined national priorities. In the four five-year plans so far formulated and implemented, rapid industrialization of the country has always been the main priority. As for urbanization, the policy has never been clearly articulated. In fact, the attitude of the policy makers toward urbanization seems to be somewhat negative. The most significant influence in the government's planning activities was the report submitted by the Bhore Committee in 1946. This report, notable for its progressive thinking, made some constructive recommendations toward environmental protection and urban and rural planning. Following those recommendations, planning agencies with advisory capacity were then established in the central government and a few state governments. These agencies have since provided the government with some guidelines in urban and regional planning developments. During the post independence period, the role of the central planning agency—the Town and Country Planning Organization—has still remained primarily advisory in formulating policies and programs at the national level as an integral part of the national five-year economic development plans. This organization is endeavoring to obtain maximum coordination in development programs within a framework of resource-based spatial planning. However, it has as yet been unable to produce any positive results. A brief review of the objectives, achievements, and failures of the Indian five-year plans for national economic development in the area of industrialization and urbanization will enable us to understand the extent and trend of these two activities.

The Five-Year Plans. In principle, the First Five-Year Plan (1951–1952 to 1955–1956) accorded the highest priority to agriculture, but in reality it made great efforts toward industrialization, spending 45 percent of its total outlay for that period (nearly $7.5 billion) on irrigation and hydroelectric projects. The Second Five-Year Plans (1956–1957 to 1960–1961) and Third (1961–1962 to 1965–1966) aimed at rapid industrialization, with particular emphasis on the development of basic heavy industries, such as steel, chemicals, fuel, and power, and the establishment of machine-building capacity, so that the requirements of further industrialization could be met within a period of 10 years or so from the country's own resources. The Fourth Five-Year Plan (1969 to 1974) did not have such a clear statement about industrialization, but one of its major goals was to increase industrial production by 8 to 10 percent during the plan period. Obviously, such a high target can be achieved only by establishing new industries and by expanding existing industries simultaneously.

What were the achievements of these five-year plans in the area of industrialization and national economic development? As the government reports claim, the first two five-year plans were very successful, but the third and fourth fell behind the targets set. The first and second plans, which both indirectly and directly aimed at rapid industrialization with particular emphasis on the development of basic heavy industries, spent $6 billion in the public sector and $4 billion in the private sector. This increased the national income by about 28 percent. During the Third Five-Year Plan these investments increased to $10.5 billion and $5.2 billion, respectively. Despite occasional setbacks, 15 years of planned development resulted in general economic progress. There was a notable expansion in basic facilities such as irrigation, power, and transport. Valuable mineral deposits were opened up to feed small and large industries. The net output in organized manufacturing industries nearly doubled during the first two plans. The share of the public-sector industries increased from 1.5 percent at the beginning of the first plan, to 8.4 percent at the end of the second plan. Much of this increase was in key industries such as steel, coal mining, and heavy chemicals. During the third plan the production of organized industry increased by 8 to 10 percent annually during the first four years but was only 5.3 percent the last year of the plan. The average growth of organized industries was 8.2 percent during the period of the third plan, against the target of 11 percent. All the same, there was continuous increase and diversification of production capacity, especially in steel and aluminum, machine tools, industrial machinery, electrical and transport equipment, fertilizers, drugs, pharmaceuticals, and petroleum products. All these increases contributed to the strengthening of the industrial structure. The fourth plan aimed at raising the standard of living of the people through programs that at the same time were designed to promote equality and social justice. The average annual growth rate during this period was only 5.4 percent, far short of the 7.7 percent target.

Observing that the Fourth Five-Year Plan was not a complete success, guidelines for the Fifth Five-Year Plan were set with primary stress placed upon the attainment of economic self-reliance, balanced development of different regions of the country, extension of the benefits of economic progress to less-developed regions, and diffusion of industry.[4]

Although there is no direct mention of any predetermined target toward industrialization, it is safe to assume that "launching of a frontal attack on unemployment" and "removal of poverty" could not possibly be achieved without further increase in industrial development.[5] Achievement of broad objectives such as laid out in the approach statement of the fifth plan, particularly in balancing development of different regions of the country and for extending economic progress to less-developed regions, would call for more extensive planning and programming and closer coordination than before in the areas of industrial and urban development.

The Role of the Five-Year Plans in Urbanization. Unfortunately, all these plans have always remained virtually uncommitted to urban development and confined primarily to fiscal programming and project planning. All of them so far have ignored the importance and need for integrated socioeconomic and physical planning. They have categorically ignored the spatial distribution of economic activities and their impact on urban growth. The objective statement of the Fifth Five-Year Plan expressed concern about concentration of industrial and urban developments in specific areas of the country, but unless a clear policy for industrial dispersal and urban growth is formulated, such a realization will remain useless. Balanced, uniform development of all regions of the country can be successful with the following considerations in the final plan:

1. The strong, direct relation of industrial development and urban growth.
2. The combined effects and influences of spatial economic structure, local and regional land use pattern, social processes affecting land use, and land value.

3. Identification of areas with growth potential.
4. A proper balance between rural and urban growth.

Because of the direct influence of industrial location on the development of new urban centers as well as on the growth of existing urban areas, future location and distribution of all major industries should be carefully analyzed in accordance with the decision of building new towns versus expanding existing cities. This is important for the fulfillment of the national objective of the Fifth Five-Year Plan in ensuring a balanced regional economy for the country. Since the end of the First Five-Year Plan, except for the recognition of the role of industrial estates as a tool for economic progress, these principles do not seem to have attracted any attention from the economic planners. Although the public-sector industries had considered partial dispersal (not based on the factors of urbanization but rather on political and economic considerations), the private-sector industries had completely disregarded this consideration because initially it would have been detrimental to their financial interest and efficient functioning. Unless they are compelled by the government to locate their industries where the government wants them, private investors will inevitably place industry in existing large urban centers. As a result, we find that almost 50 percent of the total industries established during the periods of the five-year plans have been located in the few large metropolitan areas of India. These cities account for only 12 percent of India's total population, and still they attract almost 50 percent of all new industries. Such cities have long been overcrowded with industries, their infrastructures have long been disastrously incapable of handling their load, and overcrowding has brought these cities to the verge of being almost entirely slums. Cessation of further industrial growth within such metropolitan areas and relocation of many of their already established industries to the underdeveloped regions should be seriously considered and formulated in long-term plans for obtaining balanced national development and for saving the metropolises from total collapse.

The central government, the state governments, and various planning agencies realize the desperate condition of the large cities brought on by overcrowding and overindustrialization, but so far governments have taken only limited steps toward any systematic dispersal of such population or in-

dustry by creating alternative urban centers in specific backward regions.

The Attempt to Save Calcutta.   The only example in this direction is probably the effort of the state of West Bengal to rescue Calcutta, and even this was a halfhearted attempt. Of the nine major metropolises in India, Calcutta, a city of vital national importance, suffers the most. Despite its size, its significance in the national economy, and its being the center for a vast region, Calcutta grew without any plan or control since its inception 200 years ago until 1960, when the Calcutta Metropolitan Planning Organization was established in collaboration with the Ford Foundation. Subsequently, a few more planning agencies were organized to assume various aspects of planning. A decision was made by all these agencies to develop systematically some alternative urban centers to save the city:

It is immediately evident, given the existing pattern of urbanization in eastern India and in West Bengal, that effective relief from the current population pressure on Metropolitan Calcutta will be found only in the development of other urban centers in the various states and regions in eastern India—centers having the necessary amenities of urban living, including adequate educational and cultural stimulus, to be regarded not as back waters but as major cities of genuine importance in the life of the state and the region.[6]

The purpose of going into a discussion of this venture, even though the decision did not seek a solution completely through the development of industrial new towns, is to show why industrial new towns, when they are not planned with a determined purpose, fail to function.

The state government and the planning agencies decided to develop three alternative urban centers: Siliguri, a small-sized old city in the northern tip of the state; Durgapur, an industrial new town in the initial stage of its development; and Haldia, a proposed port city to be located south of Calcutta. Of these three, only Haldia, which was a proposed new town to be developed by the central government as a major national port, had the opportunity to be modified on the drawing board to make its plan suitable as a regional urban center. Lack of coordination between the authorities and the planning agencies for the expressed objective of promoting that proposed new town into a regional urban center made this proposal unsuccessful. A broad, flexible, comprehensive plan was necessary to make that city work as a regional urban center. Instead, the city's planning and land-use decisions were aimed primarily toward serving the port's activities. This is an example where the objectives of economic planning dominated the causes of urbanization.

Durgapur New Town. Durgapur is interesting for its unique planning concept (see Figure 7). This city was initially laid out to provide housing for the employees of the huge steel plant, Hindusthan Steel Ltd. After the Calcutta Metropolitan Planning Organization's declaration on developing Durgapur into a dominant regional urban center, immediate priority was put on industrial development without the preparation of an appropriate physical plan to guide its growth in a rational, systematic way. Through government incentive, Durgapur started to develop giant chemical, rubber, and fertilizer industries; encouragement was given for quick growth of heavy engineering and industries ancillary to coal mining and for increased output as quickly as possible by al-

ready established industries. However. township and housing development responsibilities were left solely to single companies for their own employees. Prospective industrial developers were allotted factory sites in the peripheral belt of the initial 28-square mile area made available for the layout of the city, along with another block of land within the city adjacent to their factory sites for employee housing. The objective was to create a number of self-sufficient industrial towns joined together into a total urban complex. As a concept for large industrial new-town developments in countries where public finances for that purpose are extremely limited, the unique appropriateness of this plan cannot be denied. Durgapur could have become the pioneer in a successful application of this concept, had its authority conceived a measure to integrate the small towns developed by single companies into a unified urban entity. These company townships were all intended to be self-contained communities, and while most of the industries did actually bring reasonably good planning ideas into their respective towns, a lack of

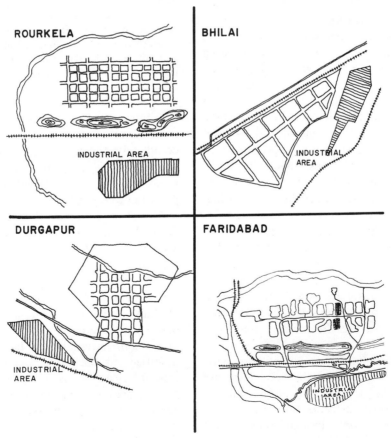

Figure 7.   Diagrammatic sketches of four of the major industrial new towns developed in India.

integration and positive direction for creating uniformity in them resulted in haphazard, irrational urban growth. According to K. C. Shivaramakrishnan, ex-chief executive officer of the Durgapur Development Authority, "Durgapur is a collection of townships and colonies that are yet to become a city."[7]

While most modern new-town developments, with their rigid master plans and imposition of strict legislative controls, have become machine-made places of monotony, Durgapur, with its unconventional development approach, had the opportunity to bring in a variety of design ideas unified by a few strong guidelines and to create a diverse, exciting, yet unified urban environment.

Siliguri New Town. A perfect example of a nonindustrial city having agriculture as one of its significant functions, Siliguri's importance in northern West Bengal is as a marketing, collection, and distribution center for that region's agricultural products. Long before its selection as a third regional urban center, Siliguri was growing in importance because of the improvement and increase in highway and railroad facilities. Even with such importance and its large population, Siliguri had never really developed into a complete urban environment. It could be characterized as a "rurban city," a term for a city that is partly urban and partly rural. Because this type of "rurban" city is quite common in India, attempts made to develop Siliguri are significant in regard to national application. Efforts made by the Siliguri Planning Organization to improve the urban character of that city and to bring it to a required standard for serving as a strong metropolitan core have so far not been fruitful. The many reasons for this are complex. However, without the establishment of appropriate large industries, the urbanization attempts obviously cannot be successful. Because of its unique cultural, social, and political organization, India cannot blindly follow the pattern of urbanization that has been emerging during the past century in the economically advanced and culturally different Western nations. The West has already reaped the horrible harvest of haphazard industrial development. In introducing large-scale industries in cities like Siliguri, extreme caution should be taken to prevent the complex destruction of the "rurban" character. If necessary, these cities should be spared from being developed into large urban centers at all. India should learn from the mistakes made in the past 100 years in the West and profit by careful planning for industry and industrial new towns now.

Other Industrial New Towns. Due to the segregation of industrial and urban planning activities, industrial new towns solely for housing the employees of major industries without any expressed purpose of inducing concentration or dispersion in either industrial or urban development have also not been able to conceive a successful plan. This attitude is conspicuous in the physical layouts of most large industrial new towns developed during the past two decades, where physical isolation of industries from the towns gives the impression of two completely divorced functions (see Figure 7). Vast areas of unproductive open land cannot be justified as a buffer zone—they are too large even for that. Faridabad, Rourkela, Bhilai, and Durgapur, the major industrial new towns of the period, have all their industrial areas completely isolated from residential and commercial areas. The industrial planning decision in each case has dictated the physical form of the town. All four towns are now experiencing severe transportation and communication difficulties due to such unrealistic separation of two major functions. Depending on the type and operation of an industry, sometimes a limited amount of physical separation might be desirable, and a minimum area of land could create the desired buffer between the living and working areas in industrial towns. However, employees need to be located as close to their workplace as possible for the sake of minimizing pressure on transportation facilities, reducing building of costly roads, and saving valuable land for more productive purposes. This is more important psychologically. Such closeness allows employees to identify with their places of work, gives their children an understanding of where their parents work and what they really do to earn their livelihood, and supplies a feeling of security to all. Recommendations by Le Corbusier in his last book, *The Three Establishments,* are quite appropriate, because he wrote this book with special reference to India:

Man has the right to a 24-hour day in which he should be able to work in comfortable surroundings, he should have a reasonable amount of leisure, and he should not spend an unnecessary amount of time in getting to and from his work.

Habitation and work—lodging and factory situated in such a manner, in relation to each other, that it will be superfluous to envisage mechanical means of transport for persons (for employees and for workers) but very nicely arranged roads will welcome these masses on foot at four kilometers per hour from their lodgings to their work, and vice versa.[8]

After all, both industry and township depend fully on each other for their existence in an industrial complex. Why then should the physical form not reflect that totality?

INDUSTRIAL GROWTH IN THE SMALL- AND MEDIUM-SIZED CITY

The tremendous disruption that takes place in a small city with a population of 50,000 when it is charged with the responsibility of accommodating a new industry employing 15,000 people can be easily imagined. For fulfilling the objective of industrial dispersion, decisions to do this are not uncommon in India's recent industrial development. Without developing a new industrial town for this purpose, preference is given to locating them in existing small- or medium-sized towns either for political reasons or for saving the initial trouble and capital investment needed to develop a new industrial town.

We have already seen that India's economic and industrial planners make their decisions based primarily on industrial location. Because of the absence of any regulation, the majority of industries are located in existing big cities and have become detrimental to India's progresss by deteriorating the cities' living conditions, by adversely affecting industrial production, and by creating unbalanced urban development over the country. The result has become even worse when indiscriminate decisions in the name of industrial dispersion have been made to locate large industrial complexes in medium or small cities. Due to this enterprise, whether public or private, these cities have had a sudden population boom, and the result has been almost devastating. (see Table 4). Ranchi, in Bihar state, which was a small city of only 60,000 until 1947, suddenly jumped to a population of 107,000 with the establishment of some major industries there. With the location of a few more industries every year, Ranchi has been growing at an almost constant annual rate of 30 percent. For a small city that never had any planned development prior to such industrial growth and was unprepared to accommodate such population influx, the impact of growth at this rate brought catastrophic problems in housing, transportation, sani-

Table 4.   Percentage of Increase in Population of Cities with Industrial Economic Base, 1941–1961

	1941–1951	1951–1961
Group I: Cities of 100,000 to 500,000 population		
Baroda	37.2	41.2
Surat	31.2	29.2
Coimbatore	51.6	44.8
Ludhiana	37.8	52.1
Bhopal	25.0	104.8
Ranchi	71.0	31.0
Kotah	37.4	84.6
Group II: Cities of 50,000 to 100,000 population		
Firozabad	61.3	50.8
Devangere	76.4	39.8
Sangli	32.2	47.0
Bhadravathi	117.0	55.0
Mandya	86.0	57.5
Tinsukia	47.0	133.0

tation, and water supply. No matter how hard the planning organization of that city now tries to solve the problems and make the city habitable, their efforts are bound to be futile. The planners cannot even cope with the rate at which the problems are continuously multiplying.

The same thing has happened to Ludhiana, Baroda, Surat, and Coimbatore. Bhopal and Ludhiana increased 100 percent within a period of only 10 years around the late-1950s. Although of much smaller size than the previous examples, Firozabad, Bhadravathi, Mandya, and Tinsukia, had the same devastating fate with the establishment of large industries in a short time.

The government has a negative attitude toward urbanization, which is one of the primary forces deterring planned urban growth in India. Forcing industries into small cities without considering the effects are an indication that deliberate attempts are being made by the leaders of the country to have the country industrialized, without having to be carefully urbanized at the same time. This attitude among Indian leaders of excluding planned urbanization from the process of industrialization is obvious:

Actually many or most Indian leaders are indifferent to the city, or indeed have anti-urban bias. They live in the cities, at least during their working hours. But the importance of the city or its social adequacy and excellence for labor productivity, for example, is by no means clear or compelling yet. Most nostalgically and theoretically their hearts are in the village, and it is a sort of article of faith that the villages are vastly superior to and more ethically habitable than the city. The city must be tolerated, but there is, generally speaking, no creative concept or sense of urgency or sense of identification.[9]

The reasons behind the anti-urban attitude can probably be traced to the Indian tradition of lust for land. Moreover, people living in any of the large cities in India find chaotic, unplanned, congested, unhygienic conditions; consequently, people acquire a feeling of repugnance for urban living. The city in India means the conglomeration of a large number of dilapidated housing units along narrow, crooked streets, absence of any land-use control exemplified in the display of obnoxious uses of land and buildings, the rarity of open spaces, overcrowding, overburdened and insufficient transportation facilities, lack of community facilities—the list could be endless. The questions are, Why then are industries still being located in old cities to enhance economic progress? How can these old cities, which are choking with problems of their own, provide conditions for industries to flourish or even to survive? Least of all, how can one expect that the establishment of new industries in old industrial towns will ever revitalize these dying cities?

CONCLUSION

In the foregoing discussion suggestions have been made that, if adopted, would provide some definite direction toward the development of effective national policies and programs needed for unified, balanced, progressive industrialization and urbanization in India. Because it is beyond the scope of this chapter to analyze thoroughly all the issues; only a few salient, most pertinent points have been presented.

India is moving toward industrialization rapidly through well-planned steps, but the tremendous locational impact of industries on all aspects of life has not yet been seriously considered. Thorough, systematic research in this area is immediately needed because the findings would certainly influence the final policy decisions.

Although urbanization and industrialization are inseparable functions, they have not been treated in a comprehensive way, and this attitude has been responsible for irrational, haphazard growth in existing cities as well as in industrial new-town develop-

ments. Lack of coordination among professionals of different planning areas and the government's indifference to spatial planning as a whole have also been responsible for such undesirable urban growth. Remedial measures are self-evident and should be accomplished starting with composing a planning body, representing all related areas, that will draft the initial all-encompassing strategy for dealing with the country's industrial and urban development.

Industrial agglomeration for the industries' benefit and the resulting inducement of growth in the urban centers have not been advantageously directed or controlled toward achieving the goals of industrial dispersal and balanced regional development. For better industrial production and an urban environment desirable for living, industries should preferably be located in industrial new towns planned for them (see Figure 8). Locating large, medium, or small industries in an existing city has proven to be detrimental to both the city's normal functioning and the productive efficiency of the industries. As an integral part of the national plan for industrialization, a comprehensive plan is needed for nationwide urban development with special emphasis on industrial new-town development. To increase the speed and efficiency of such town development projects the central planning agency should develop some prototypic designs and dimensional standards for certain elements of the new towns (e.g., types and sizes of streets, land-use relations of various major functions and their minimum and maximum standards, etc.). Some innovative concepts, like the one tested in the development of Durgapur, could be realized in detail for quick development of the new towns without encumbering the authority with much of the financial burden. India's special social, cultural, and economic characteristics and traditions and its special climatic conditions have not always been fully considered in developing industries or new towns. Industrial and urban developers should be encouraged to be sensitive in their designs to all these special conditions. Western examples and standards should not be indiscriminately applied without even making the minimum necessary modifications, which certainly do more harm than good to India's industrial development endeavors. Industrialization and urbanization should be guided in order not to disturb the country's agriculture-based economy. Agro-based manufacturing industries should be required to be directed for semi-urban locations, such as the "rurban-city" of Siliguri mentioned earlier. These "rurban cities" are marketing and distributing

Figure 8.   Eastern India: location of mineral resources (areas of potential industrial growth) and four urban centers.

centers in rural areas and already possess some of the basic facilities, including transportation routes providing adequate connections with their hinterland and also with at least one larger urban center. If development of industrial new towns is found to be more suitable for industrial development in an area evaluated in a long-term perspective against development of an existing semi-urban pocket, the latter should not even be considered as a temporary measure. The money, energy, and time spent in establishing a major industry in an existing city might be comparatively less in the beginning, but in the long run several times more will be spent just to combat the problems generated in that old city by such industrial development.

In establishing a national policy and program

toward industrial new-town development, the economic base as well as the size and number of industries for every industrial new town must be determined and strictly enforced. Otherwise, advantages generated by the initially established major industries will start attracting more industries, both subsidiary and major, and in a short time, the fate of such industrial new towns will be the same as that of the existing cities where major industries have been imposed: the demand on their facilities will far surpass the designed capacity.

After almost 25 years of working toward industrial progress, India has now come to a stage when industrial location should no longer be determined entirely by economic gain. During the initial stages of the developing economy, national emphasis was more on rapid growth and quick increase of national income. Now, however, the time has come when attention to the locational impact of industries for social gain must be given priority. Industries should not be allowed to choose locations that can provide all the desired conditions for efficient production; rather, the permission to locate must be given on the basis of how much economic improvement such industrial establishments can bring to an economically backward region. Location of industries in underdeveloped states or regions should be most leniently considered if the basic conditions are not adverse.

Each state in India is exerting pressure on the central government to have locational decisions for all major industries made in that state's favor, more often as a symbol of prestige than for real economic justification. For the sake of national interest, such political pressures from the states should be prevented. This can be done by determination of the potential growth points for every type of major industrial development and by a thorough analysis of all relevant factors and strict adherence to such selections.

Last, but not least important, is the impact of the unpredictable natural population increase of the country on urbanization and industrialization. India's population, which is multiplying geometrically, can easily upset all plans of industrialization, urbanization, or even the most competently prepared five-year plans for economic development unless such plans are based on a reasonably accurate projection of population. Under the present circumstances, it is extremely difficult to predict the population figures for the near future. The success of the measures being taken by the government of India to curb the population boom cannot be evaluated immediately. The situation is not, however, as grim as it appears. Demographers still are in a position to predict population figures that are acceptable for such long-term planning for each decade in the future. For broad-based policy decisions such as those discussed here, the exactness of the population figures is not so important as the indication of the trend or rate. The plans can make provision for an expected large population.

NOTES

1. A national long-term development program instituted in 1950 to create strong foundations of economic and social growth.

2. Patrick Geddes, *Cities in Evolution* (New York: Howard Fertig, 1968) (original publication, 1915).

3. Professor L. R. Vagale, head of Department of Town Planning, School of Planning and Architecture, Delhi, India. Comment made during the 13th Annual Town and Country Planning Seminar of the Institute of Town Planners, India (unpublished).

4. "Towards an Approach to the Fifth Plan," Planning Commission of India (May 1972).

5. India, The Research and Reference Division, Ministry of Information and Broadcasting, "India 1974" (New Delhi: Government of India, 1974).

6. *Basic Development Plan,* Calcutta Metropolitan District 1966–1968 (Calcutta: Calcutta Metropolitan Planning Organization, 1966), p. 4.

7. K. C. Sivaramakrishnan, chief executive officer, Durgapur Development Authority, "Durgapur a New Town," Paper presented to the Institute of Town Planners, India, 1966 Annual Meeting.

8. Le Corbusier, "The Three Establishments," unpublished manuscript.

9. Albert Mayer, "Some Operational Implications of the Delhi Plan," Paper given at the Seminar on Urbanization in India, Berkeley, California, June 1960.

BIBLIOGRAPY

Aichbhaumik, D. "Decentralization of Industries: a must for West Bengal." *Journal of the Institute of Town Planners,* India, **42** and **43** (1965):43–46.

———. "Durgapur: A Case Study of Housing and Tranportation Problems in New Town Developments in Developing Countries." *Proceedings of the International Conference on Housing and Tranportation.* Detroit, 1975.

Alexander, P. C. *Industrial Estates in India.* Bombay: Asia Publishing House, 1963.

Asansol Planning Organization. "The Growth of Asansol Urban Area," Unpublished report, 1974.

Bhagwati, Jagdish, and Padma Desai. *Indian Planning for Industrialization.* London: Oxford University Press, 1970.

Bhattacharjee, K. P. "Observations on Performance of Chandigarh, Lessons for Future Indian Cities." *Journal of the Indian Institute of Architects* **39**, No. 3 (July–September, 1973):11–16.

Calcutta Metropolitan Planning Organization. *Basic Development Plan,* Calcutta Metropolitan District—1966–1986. Calcutta: Government of West Bengal, 1966.

City and Industrial Development Corporation of Maharashtra Ltd. *Draft Plan Report for New Bombay,* 1974.

Chaudhury, M. R. *Indian Industries: Development and Location,* Calcutta: Oxford Book Co., 1970.

Durgapur Development Authority and Asansol Planning Organization. "Industrialization and Pollution Hazards to Our Resources." Unpublished report, 1973.

"Gandhinagar." *Journal of the Indian Institute of Architects* **39**, No. 3 (July–September 1971):16–17.

India. "Report of the Working Group on Housing and Urban Development in the Third Five Year Plan." New Delhi: Ministry of Works, Housing and Supply, 1960.

———. "Problems of Housing in India." New Delhi: Ministry of Works, Housing and Supply, 1967.

———. *Draft, Fifth Year Plan—1974–1979.* 2 vols. New Delhi: Planning Commission, 1973.

India Planning Commission. *The First Five Year Plan.* Delhi: Manager of Publications, 1952.

———. *The Fourth Five Year Plan.* Delhi: Manager of Publications, 1970.

———. "Report on Industrial Townships." New Delhi: Building Projects Team, Planning Commission, 1963.

———. *The Second Five Year Plan.* Delhi: Manager of Publications, 1956.

———. *The Third Five Year Plan.* Delhi: Manager of Publications, 1961.

India Registrar General. *Census of India, 1971.* New Delhi: Government of India, 1973.

Karanjgaokar, D. G., and K. Kaplish. "Master Plan for Bhopal." *Journal of the Institute of Town Planners,* India, **33–34** (1963):4–11.

Lewis, John P. *Quiet Crisis in India.* Bombay: Asia Publishing House, 1963.

Manickam, T. J., L. R. Vagale, et al. "New Towns in India." New York: United Nations, 1962.

Mayer, Albert. "Some Operational Implications of the Delhi Plan." Seminar on Urbanization in India, Berkeley, California, 1960.

Rao, V. K. R. V., and P. B. Desai. *Greater Study in Urbanization: 1940–1957.* Bombay: Asian Publishing House, 1965.

Vagale, L. R. "Indian Cities and Industries: Impacts and Relationships." *Journal of the Institute of Town Planners,* India, **42–43** (1965):31–42.

———. "New Towns in India and Other Asian Countries: Physical Planning Design Principles." *Journal of the Institute of Town Planners,* India, **52** (1967):34–37.

CHAPTER 17

New Towns in the Developing World: Three Case Studies

ALAN TURNER

In countries such as the United States and Britain, new towns are carefully planned, and their inhabitants are wealthier than the average person in an older city. In the Third World they may be created spontaneously by the poor in response to the pressing need for work and shelter. There is absolutely no doubt that new towns and expanded communities based on existing villages will continue to be created in the rapidly developing countries over the next few decades, whether they are planned or not.

The decision of an industry to locate a plant on a vacant site would gradually attract another factory nearby . . . the settlements would soon begin to spread . . . and an unplanned new town would result. Planning new towns should be part of the growth process, but the motivations and principles that applied to Britain and Europe were too often irrelevant for other parts of the world. . . . The planning of the British and European new towns presupposed a steady rate of social and economic change. . . . In contrast the less developed nations are experiencing sudden population inflows . . . and . . . are acting more directly to spur production and investment.[1]

Problems and Needs. Developing countries share a number of characteristics that combine to create social and economic problems requiring solutions quite different from those that have sufficed for the rest of the world. These characteristics include (but are not limited to) the following:

1. Low income per capita, often accompanied by extremes of wealth and poverty.
2. Large land area often with difficult topography and extreme climatic conditions.
3. Small populations in relation to areas, but extremely rapid population growth (as a result, the populations are young, and the demand for services is high).
4. Low educational standards.
5. Poor infrastructure.
6. Lack of regional balance.
7. Little technological development.
8. A need for labor-intensive industry.
9. Inadequate professional resources for development needs.
10. Unexploited natural resources (sometimes in abundance).

There are exceptions to some of these, but by and large, developing nations suffer from the first nine factors; some of these nations, however, can look forward to the opportunities suggested by the tenth. Developing nations also suffer from a compression in time scale brought about by the self-reinforcing developments in technology and communications that have been so well described by Alvin Toffler.[2] This acceleration means that people in central Africa, Latin America, and Asia must adjust in a few short decades to changes from primitive subsistence agriculture to familiarity with modern methods and machines, an adjustment that we in the West had several hundred years to make. In Europe or the United States towns grew slowly in response to social and economic needs; in the developing world, the process must be given a push, for which enormous investments are required.

Attempts to cope with the situation often take the form of large physical planning projects that may not be called new towns but have a remarkable tendency to generate settlements, if only as a result of the migration of hopeful settlers. Where there are widespread, scattered populations at very low overall densities living in small villages, as in some parts of Africa, we are dealing with a population implosion rather than an explosion. The need is for centers, large and small, to provide good social services and facilities and to increase the number of job opportunities, but at the same time to develop the agricultural base.

Three Experiments. The separate case studies that follow illustrate three approaches taken to the prob-

lem over almost a decade in three countries: Venezuela, Angola, and Malaysia. I make no apologies for the choice of these particular case studies except that I have been involved as a consultant in each case and can write with some knowledge of the specific problems. Many other countries could have been chosen to illustrate the problems described, but these particular ones clearly exhibit three modes of action taken in different parts of the world.

In Venezuela the approach was to plan large new cities to serve as regional growth poles. The first of these was Ciudad Guayana, which has been extensively described in various publications.[3] This was followed by plans for a new city of about 400,000 to the south of Caracas and another for 300,000 in the west of the country near to Maracaibo (see Figure 1). Each had a different industrial base, and each was intended to be at the focus of migration patterns. By creating counter-attractions, they were intended to reduce migration to Caracas. As Charles Abrams wrote over a decade ago, "Caracas, Venezuela, . . . is so crowded with squatters, traffic and people that un-

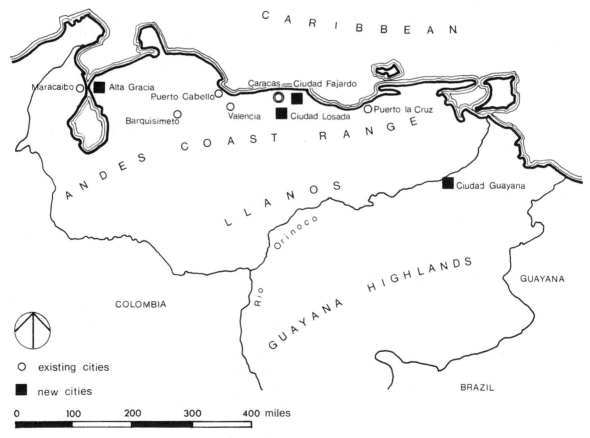

Figure 1. Map of Venezuela showing the location of new towns at Alta Gracia, Ciudad Losada, Ciudad Fajardo, and Ciudad Guayana.

less other cities are built or at least expanded, the continual inflow of people and automobiles will throttle it."[4] The situation is much worse today.

The second approach, typified by the Angolan example, is to plan and develop large-scale industry and to some extent let urbanization take care of itself. The concept of the large industrial estate is by no means new, but to locate one in a region with a very dispersed, poor population largely dependent on subsistence agriculture is a fairly certain way of attracting a large number of unskilled people to an unfamiliar urban life. The quality of that life may be open to question and will depend to a large extent on the availability of social development services, job training, and educational programs as well as new housing, public buildings, and roads.

The third approach, in Malaysia, is one that turns away from the single large-scale development to a multiplicity of small centers conceived within a social, economic, and physical regional master plan. The aim is to scale down development and to create a complete infrastructure of villages, small towns, agricultural developments, and road networks. At a conference on developing countries in 1974, Barbara Ward, Schweitzer Professor of International Economic Development, Columbia University, said, "If we really are heading in the next 20 or 30 years to a severe crisis in our energy supply, anything which reduces unwanted mobility or scales activities to where more human energy is supported, not dominated, by machines, we shall be more able to see the societies through this very dubious period."[5]

Perhaps one of the most important books regarding scale written in the past few years is *Small is Beautiful* by E. F. Schumacher. He argues persuasively for intermediate technology and appropriately scaled development:

The heart of the matter as I see it, is the stark fact that world poverty is primarily a problem of two million villages, and thus a problem of two thousand million villagers. The solution cannot be found in the cities of the poor countries. Unless life in the hinterland can be made tolerable, the problem of world poverty is insoluble and will inevitably get worse. . . . The aid givers—rich, educated, town-based—know how to do things in their own way but do they know how to assist self-help among two million villages, among two thousand million villagers, poor, uneducated country-based? They know how to do a few big things in big towns; but do they know how to do thousands of small things in rural areas? They know how to do things with lots of capital, but do they know how to do them with lots of labour—initially untrained labour at that?[6]

Barbara Ward, in a plea for the development of appropriate technology, wrote, "The overriding need is for decentralized labour intensive, highly skilled, small-scaled operations; and here the type and size of settlements can make the differences between success and failure."[7] She went on to say that development must be concentrated in the village, the market center, and the intermediate town. The message is that small is indeed beautiful and that a number of villages can house as many people as a large city, while the use of human energy aided by simple technology can increase agricultural production. The Malaysian program is an important example of development premised on this fairly new argument.[8]

VENEZUELA

Venezuela is not a poor country. Its wealth is from oil, which forms roughly 20 percent of the gross national product (GNP), and its income per capita of about $1000 (in 1969) is high by the standards of developing countries. It is not a densely populated country. In 1967 the population was about 10 million in a total area of 352,150 square miles. It is, however, a country of great extremes of wealth and poverty, despite the efforts of successive governments to achieve some redistribution. About 44 percent of Venezuelan families have an income too low to afford normal market housing or even the worst public housing. This is the section of the community that builds and lives in the improvised housing of the *barrios*. For them, oil does not represent a solution, although they may benefit indirectly from the heavy taxes paid by the oil companies. As a capital-intensive industry, the increased production of oil will provide a mere handful of jobs in relation to the need. The degree of urbanization is high (about 70 percent), and migration to the major cities shows no signs of slowing. John Friedman has described the serious lack of regional balance and the dominance of Caracas in the life of the country and has suggested policies of regional development to counteract this.[9] During the past 16 years a number of important steps have been taken to create major new developments, and these have met with varying success. In chronological order they are as follows:

1. Ciudad Guayana. Sited at the confluence of the rivers Orinoco and Caroni in the east of the country, Ciudad Guayana is part of a vast regional development plan created in 1959 by

President Betancourt. The region is rich in iron ore, bauxite, and other materials; and Ciudad Guayana is firmly based on extractive industry. The Corporacion Venezolana de Guayana, formed to develop both the region and the city, has been able to achieve spectacular progress in the growth of the city. Less than 10 years after its inception, Ciudad Guayana had a population of over 100,000, although a great many of these people had migrated in hope, had little chance of obtaining employment in the new industries, and will remain for a long time in the informal sector of the economy. Like many other planned cities in poor countries there is a striking difference between the sterility of some of the carefully planned areas and the lively squalor of the popular *barrios*, where semirural people are carving out a way of life.[10]

2. Ciudad Losada. The idea of a new city in the valley of the Tuy Medio, some 30 miles to the south of Caracas, was first conceived in 1957, although very little action was taken until 10 years later when consultants were appointed to prepare a development plan.[11]

3. Alta Gracia. This is the third new city, previously known as El Tablazo. It is situated directly across the lake from Maracaibo in the heart of the oil-producing region of Zulia. Plans for this city were prepared in 1968 by the same consultants.[12]

4. Ciudad Fajardo. This fourth new city in 1976 was still in the early stages of planning. It will be located near Guatire-Guarenas, directly east of Caracas.

Because Ciudad Guayana has been so well documented, this case study will deal solely with Ciudad Losada and Alta Gracia.

New-Town Strategy. To understand the basic reasons behind the locations of these new cities, it is necessary to know a little about Caracas itself. Situated in a long, narrow valley about 15 kilometers by 5 kilometers, Caracas had a population of approximately 2 million in 1967; this number is expected to reach 4.5 million by 1990. The Caracas-Valencia subregion is expected to have a population of 9 million by 1990, or roughly the equivalent of the total population of the country in 1961. The conclusion reached by the government was that it was essential to locate at least half a million people in the Tuy Medio by 1990. Consequently, an expropriation area for the projected new city was gazetted as early as 1957, although the land had not been purchased by the government as late as 1968.

The basic objectives of the development were:

1. To relieve pressure on Caracas.
2. To provide a countermagnet for migration.
3. To provide a more even distribution of population within the central region.
4. To provide sites for industrial development, which can no longer be found in Caracas.
5. To satisfy a large percentage of the increasing demand for consumer goods in a growing economy by providing new centers of development for industry.
6. To reduce the reliance on heavy industry in the country as a whole.

In the case of Alta Gracia, quite different problems arose. The site is directly across the lake from Maracaibo, the capital of the oil-producing state of Zulia. Unemployment in the region is high (in 1961 only 22.7 percent of the population of Zulia was classified as remuneratively occupied), and a high rate of population increase is forecast. In an attempt to provide more jobs, the government of Venezuela decided in 1967 to establish a new petrochemical complex at El Tablazo (a few miles north of the old town of Alta Gracia). Unfortunately, this is another capital-intensive industry, and it was estimated that the complex would support a town of only about 25,000 people. Obviously this was an insignificant contribution to a region with such high unemployment, and the plans were modified to include within the town a diverse range of labor-intensive industries related as far as possible to the secondary products of petrochemicals. In this way the city may eventually reach a population of about 300,000 by the time Maracaibo has grown to 1 million. Given good transport services across the lake (hydrofoils have been operating there for many years), the two cities could form a lakeside city-region with probably a great deal of commuting between them.

The strategy behind these ideas was that a large new city at Alta Gracia with new industries would attract many of the jobless inhabitants of Zulia who would otherwise migrate either to Maracaibo or to Caracas and that Ciudad Losada would attract many of those who migrated from all regions to the central one.

Planning Principles. The basic principles adopted in the formulation of plans for the two cities were as follows:

A Social Development Plan That Would Involve Incoming Migrants in the Planning Process. It was recognized that the original goals formulated by the planning team were made by proxy, as it were, on behalf of a future community, which may have quite different priorities.

Flexibility in the Physical Plan. By adopting a main road grid (1½ kilometers apart at Ciudad Losada and 1 kilometer at Alta Gracia) giving fairly uniform accessibility to the whole urban area and by taking a relaxed view about land-use zoning, planners thought that unforeseen changes in land use would not destroy the integrity of the basic infrastructure. By distributing industry in many parts of the city, huge tidal flows to and from industrial areas could be avoided. In terms of planning control, it was suggested that some areas would need fairly rigid control, but that other areas could be "soft" and controls could be very lenient.

Areas for Sites and Services. The planners thought it essential to include reception areas for those immigrants who would be too poor to afford even the rents of subsidized housing. These areas would be divided into lots, and roads would be leveled but not surfaced. Water supply points would be installed. Self-help construction (whether assisted or not) was to be an essential part of the housing program.

In addition, it was recommended to the government that new development corporations responsible to the Ministerio de Obras Publicas (MOP) would be essential to carry out these tasks and that public and private investment would be essential to ensure successful development.

Ciudad Losada. The site for Ciudad Losada is in the valley of the Tuy Medio, some 45 minutes by road to the south of Caracas, skirted by the main national motorway linking the capital with the west of the country. It is a low-lying valley, some 300 meters (984 feet) above sea level, in contrast to Caracas at 880 meters (2900 feet). Historically the valley has been an agricultural area served by six small market towns. It is separated from Caracas to the north by the mountains of the coastal range. The government in 1957 expropriated some 6900 hectares between the small towns of Santa Teresa and Santa Lucia in the eastern extremity of the valley (see Figure 2). When work began on the development plans in 1967, five alternative regional development strategies were assessed. These ranged from expansion of the existing

towns to a population of 500,000 people in 1990, with no new city, to a new city to take all the estimated population, allied to a policy restricting growth in existing towns (see Figure 3).

After assessing the various strategic alternatives, a plan was devised by which industry and population would be attracted to a new city in the initial stages. This would allow a period for the existing towns to carry out major improvements to their substandard services infrastructure, which would in turn stimulate limited growth (see Table 1).

An earlier project to continue the main national highway through the valley to link the east of the country with Caracas and the west was revived, and the highway was relocated to form the southern limit of the city. Thus the city would be situated at the fulcrum of Venezuela's national road network with easy access to all the major ports and markets.

The valley's estimated total population of half a million by 1990 was based on demographic projections and migratory tendencies into the central region, which allow for an estimated population for Caracas of 4.5 million inhabitants by 1990. The employment structure of the new city was conceived in relation to the number of jobs needed to support such a population and the type of light industry that would wish to locate in the Tuy to take advantage of its proximity to the main consumer market, available cheap land, and the possibility of establishing a stable labor force by providing new housing close to the sources of employment. To reduce pressure on the capital the city was designed to be as self-sufficient as possible and to provide a wide range of work opportunities and a choice of housing types and locations. Given these new facilities and inducements in terms of social, recreational, and educational services, which would become gradually difficult to use in Caracas itself, commuting between the two cities could be cut to a minimum.

The city, sited in two parallel valleys, was designed to expand outward from Santa Teresa and Santa Lucia to use existing roads as development spurs and make the most economical use of existing services. The structure of the city was determined by a main road network in the form of a loose 1½ kilometer grid related to the topography. Within each environmental area created by the grid, a residential population of some 25,000 people was divided into units of 5000 to 6000 persons.[13] The main road network had limited access and was designed to aid cross-town movement; a secondary road system carrying public transport fed into and across the environmental

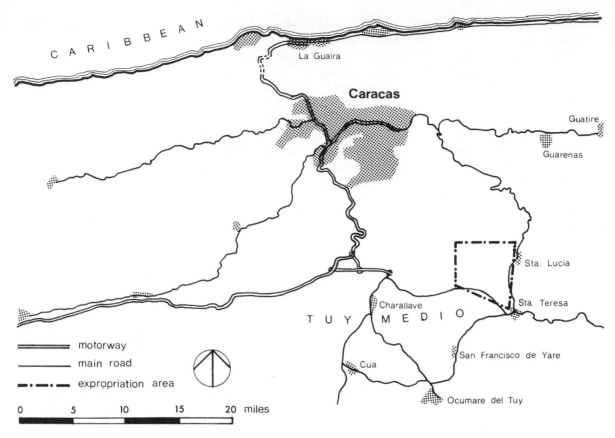

Figure 2. Tuy Medio in relation to Caracas.

areas, serving local centers and residential population (see Figure 4).

The central business district of the city was sited on the ridge that separates the two valleys and was intended to be visible from the whole area of the city. This district was to begin on a district-center scale between 5 and 10 years after construction of the city commenced. Its service potential was to be rein-

forced by three new district centers, each located to serve some 80,000 people, and the redeveloped centers of Santa Teresa and Santa Lucia would serve as additional district centers (see Figure 5).

To create the greatest possible flexibility and to safeguard against the formation of large, single-income areas within the city, development sites for specific groups were kept as small as possible. The estimate was, that of the incoming population (a growth rate of 20,000 a year was predicted), 20 percent would be able to afford housing built by the private sector, 60 percent would be served by public agencies, and the remainder would have to be settled in reception areas, where plots for improvised housing were to be available.

A number of policies, including progressive improvement and self-help schemes, were suggested in the plan to provide for the needs of the great numbers of immigrants with the lowest incomes who would migrate to the new city. A development corporation was suggested under the quinquennial fiscal control of MOP. It was considered a fundamental strategic consideration that, to show confidence in the project, a planning team should be set up on the site at the earliest opportunity.

Table 1   Existing and Proposed Populations for Towns in the Tuy Medio Valley

Town	Population in 1967	Population in 1990
Ciudad Losada	11,300 (Santa Lucia and Santa Teresa)	417,000
Ocumare	28,250	86,000
Charallave	8,700	48,000
Cua	10,000	33,000
Rural Area	31,700	11,000
Total	89,950	595,000

Source: Ministerio de Obras Publicas.

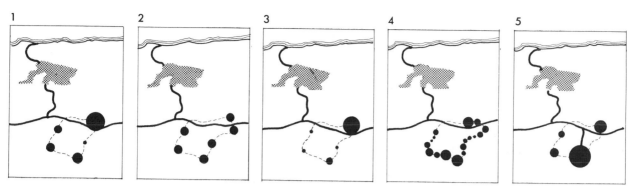

Figure 3. Alternative development strategies. (1) New city of 400,000 in the expropriation area, coupled with controlled development of the existing towns. (2) Expansion of the existing towns with no new city. (3) A new city of over 500,000 with no induced expansion of the existing towns. (4) A low-density polynuclear development spreading throughout the valley. (5) A new city for up to 1 million at Ocumare, together with development in the expropriation area. This proposal was made before the appointment of the consultants.

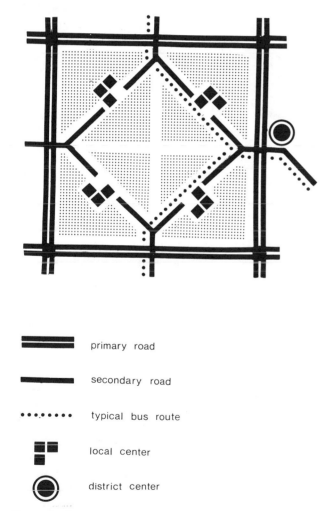

primary road

secondary road

•••••••• typical bus route

local center

district center

Figure 4. Diagrammatic layout of an environmental area, showing local centers served by the secondary road system. Buses would use the secondary system and would be given an advantage over private cars by means of "bus only links" through the local centers. A district center situated at the junction of primary and secondary systems would serve a population equivalent to approximately two environmental areas (although in practice the users would be drawn from two or more such areas).

Alta Gracia. In 1966 as part of the national policy of industrial diversification, the government decided to site a major petrochemical complex at the mouth of Lake Maracaibo. The site had ready access to cheap supplies of natural gas from the neighboring oilfields and to deepwater shipping lanes. The plant, located on a 834 hectare site, some 6.5 kilometers (4 miles) from the old colonial town of Alta Gracia (population 12,000), was planned to be highly mechanized, providing only about 1800 direct jobs. Apart from the production economies to be gained by this location, the government chose the site to provide new opportunities in an area where employment in oil has dropped steadily as the industry became increasingly automated (see Figure 6).

It was estimated that the population along the northern shores of Lake Maracaibo would double from 1 to 2 million over the next 20 years. A detailed survey of the oil towns and of Maracaibo itself showed that, owing to the lack of services, it would be extremely difficult and expensive to settle this population within the existing urban areas. In Maracaibo in 1967, about 35 percent of the population lived in shacks without utilities, and other towns with high unemployment could support only a limited influx of population.

Even assuming that they could provide for a reasonable number of migrants, these towns would not account for some 300,000 people. Thus it was decided to create the conditions under which they might settle around Alta Gracia, assuming as a basis the government's intention to induce subsidiary industry to locate near the petrochemical plant and create a major new source of employment.

The design requirements resolved themselves into the need to plan for a town that could be implemented by both the public and private sectors and

Figure 5. The plan for Ciudad Losada, 1990. Industry is located in various parts of the town to avoid heavy tidal flows. The configuration of the city is largely determined by the topography. The large area of housing to the east is an existing development.

that could accept incoming population at varying rates and still retain its viability, should the development be retarded or stopped for considerable periods. A one-kilometer-square unit, housing a population of approximately 10,000, was proposed. Within this

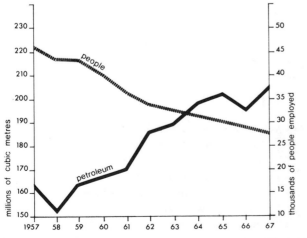

Figure 6. The relation between increasing oil production and decreasing employment.

unit, areas requiring varying degrees of control were specified to safeguard the main road network (see Figure 7). Shops, schools, and other facilities were sited on the periphery of the environmental areas so that interaction between adjacent units could be simply achieved, breaking down any rigid neighborhood concepts. Public transportation, except for the ubiquitous *por puesto* (shared taxi), was routed on the main roads.

The overall urban form at the target population of 330,000 in 1990 was derived from a study of land uses, transport, and the topographic constraints of the site. The climate is hot, and proximity to the lake has considerable advantages. Access by road was restricted to the north and west, and there was a strong directional pull toward the bridge connection with Maracaibo. It was proposed that the city have a linear form in its early years, gradually spreading to higher land in the final stages of development. Three alternative urban forms were studied: linear, rectangular, and T-shaped. Using the criteria of accessibility, journey-to-work time, and road and transportation costs, the EGTAC program[14] clearly indicated that the T-shape had distinct advantages (see Figure 8).

To avoid a low-income, one-class settlement, a varied employment structure was designed to attract a range of income and family groups. Land allocation within the city was programmed to allow wide choice of location for all uses to absorb the changes that would inevitably occur during the development period. To ensure mobility for all incomes, a bus system running on the main roads was proposed, giv-

ing good service in the early years, but allowing for a wider use of private cars in the future. Rail systems were considered in relation to the linear alternative, but the corridor volumes were too low for efficient use, and the capital cost was too great.

The climate, land form, and predicted family structure in which young families with children predominate, were all considered in arriving at a policy for density and housing. Following comparative cost studies, it was decided that the bulk of the population

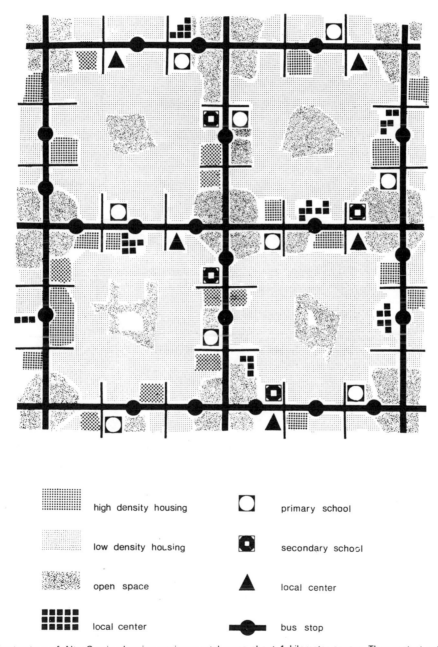

::::: high density housing	◯ primary school
::::: low density housing	◉ secondary school
open space	▲ local center
▮▮▮ local center	⬤— bus stop

Figure 7. The basic structure of Alta Gracia showing environmental areas about 1 kilometer square. The greatest activity is situated near the primary roads (but not fronting on them). Relatively less controlled, lower density "self-help" areas are toward the centers of the environmental areas.

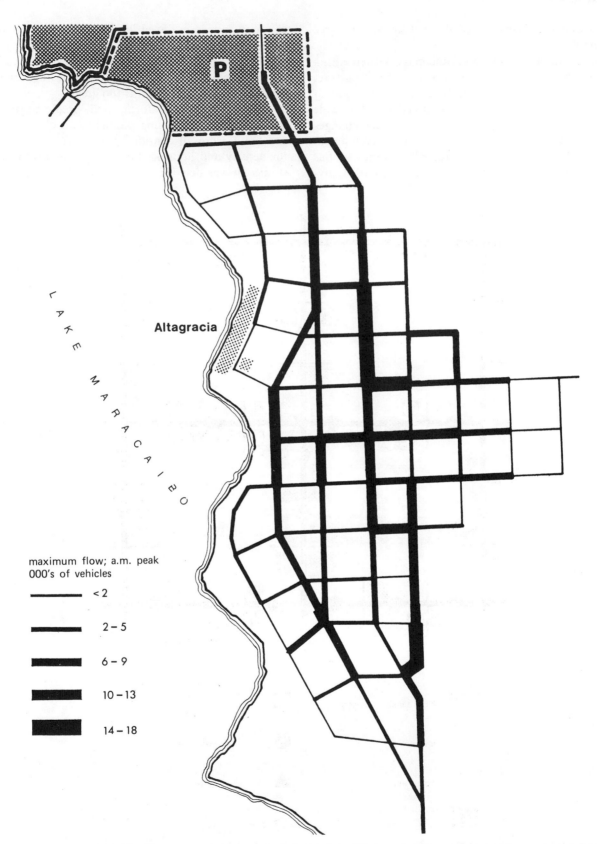

Figure 8. Predicted traffic flows at Alta Gracia. The design of the network and the location of housing, centers, and employment is intended to create fairly even flows throughout the systems.

was to be housed as close to the ground as possible and that only single people and small families were to be located in apartments adjacent to activity centers. Within the housing areas there would be a mix of density, tenure, and income groups as well as large reception areas for subsidized self-help housing. Figure 9 shows the proposed development plan for 1990.[15]

Today, ten years after the preparation of these plans, it would be encouraging to record that great progress has been made with the implementation of the proposals. Unfortunately, this has not been the case, and there has been very little development of either of the cities. In the case of Ciudad Losada, the government decided to go ahead with the project in 1972 and set up a development corporation. This was governed by representatives from the Ministerio de Obras Publicas; the economic planning body, Cordiplan; and the housing agency, Banco Obrero. The development corporation has built an office in the area of the new city; some houses have been built; and there has been minor development in some of the industrial zones; a number of studies on drainage, water supply, and transportation have been undertaken, but to all intents and purposes the plans have not been implemented. The situation is similar at Alta Gracia where, despite the growth of the petrochemical complex, little development has taken place in the new city.

The original concept for the new cities was to reduce population pressure in Caracas and to provide alternative magnets for migration, but it is obvious to any visitor in Caracas that this has not been the case. Within the last few years there have been enormous developments in the city, including vast new housing and commercial complexes; enormously expensive road-building projects, including the double-decking of part of the main autopista through the city; and no doubt a large increase in the number of improvised houses. Although I have no current figures, I would estimate that the population of Caracas has probably increased by over 0.5 million people since 1967 but that the populations in the designated areas of the two new cities have only increased by a few thousand.

These results are extremely disappointing, especially in a country as wealthy as Venezuela—wealth that is even greater now that oil prices have risen. If this is the situation in a richer developing country, what hope is there for creating large new cities in the poorer countries? Can the lack of progress be explained simply by saying that the projects were too large and complex for a developing country to un-

dertake, or is it merely a case of lack of political will? If the studies were undertaken today, would the general consensus among planners have been that a number of small developments should have been proposed?

However, despite the loss of several years in the implementation of these projects, there is still a desire in the government that they go ahead. According to the present director of the development agency, funds may become available for a major building program in Ciudad Losada within the next year or so. If this is the case, a really concerted effort by both the public and private sectors could, to some extent, catch up with the urgent need.

ANGOLA

Angola is a very large country (481,351 square miles) with a very small population of 5.7 million, over half a million of whom live in the capital city, Luanda.* The port of Lobito has one of the largest harbors on the southwest African coast, and the Benguela railway is a vital link with Zambia and the copper belt (see Figure 10). Potentially one of the wealthiest nations of Africa, Angola is a sad country torn by civil strife. Most of its people are poor subsistence farmers to whom a pair of shoes is a mark of affluence and a bicycle is a dreamed-of luxury, taking a little of the hardship out of a 10-mile walk to sell a basketful of vegetables.

Luanda itself has grown rapidly, doubling roughly every 10 years since 1940 when its population was 61,000. During this time many Africans have migrated to the city in search of employment, and there are now 300,000 to 400,000 living in and around Luanda. Most of them live in musseques, or shanty towns (the word is Kimbundu and means "a sandy place," which is descriptive of the red earth on which they are built). The musseques are a relatively new phenomenon, having existed in Luanda only for the past 20 years, following increases in coffee growing, a "fever of building construction," and expansion of the market of Luanda.[16] Their average density is 202 persons per hectare (499 per acre), ranging from 10 persons per hectare (24 per acre) in new musseques on the outskirts, to 541 persons per hectare (1336 per

* The section on Angola was written after the Portuguese revolution of April 1974 and before the outbreak of civil war in Angola. Therefore some of the figures will have changed—particularly the number of whites living in the country. However, the general thesis remains valid; despite war and changes in government the basic problems and opportunities will remain.

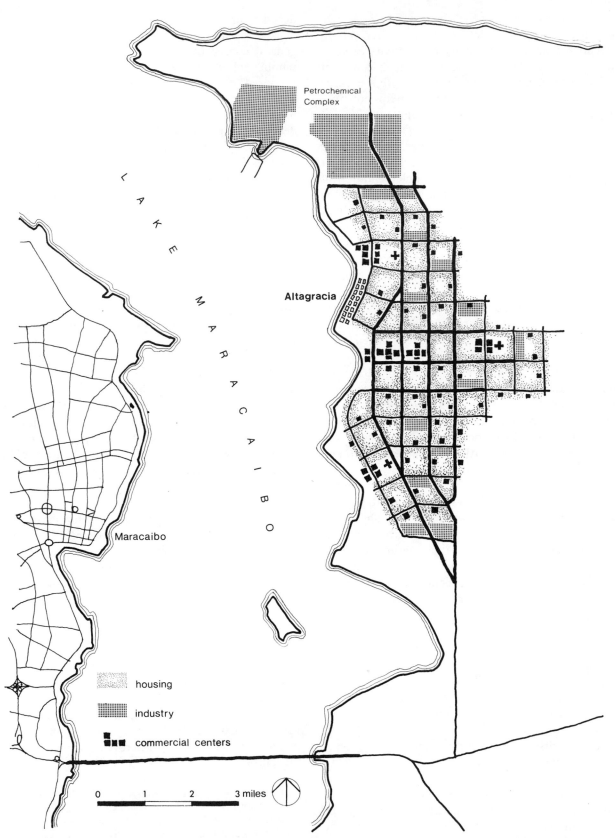

Figure 9. The plan for Alta Gracia. The petrochemical complex will not employ a large labor force; other industries are dispersed throughout the town to achieve a good relation with housing areas.

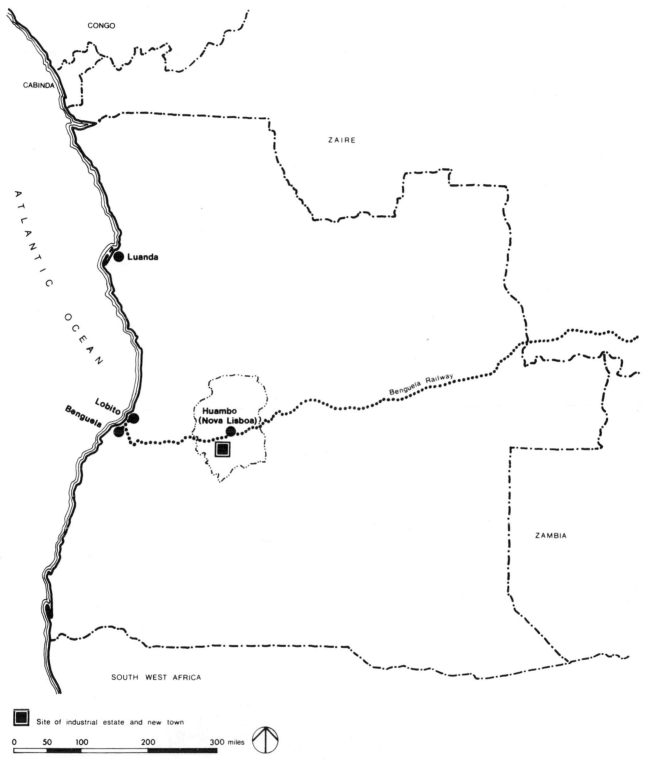

CONGO

CABINDA

ZAIRE

ATLANTIC OCEAN

Luanda

Benguela Railway

Lobito

Benguela

Huambo
(Nova Lisboa)

ZAMBIA

SOUTH WEST AFRICA

Site of industrial estate and new town

0   50   100   200   300 miles

Figure 10.   Map of Angola showing the District of Huambo and the town of Nova Lisboa, now renamed Huambo.

acre) in the inner *musseques*.[17] They are the direct equivalent of the *barrios, barriadas*, or *favelas* of Latin America, exclusively formed of huts (*cubatas*) of make-shift construction, using materials such as mud and sticks (*pau-a-pique*), corrugated zinc, and scrap wood or metal (see Figures 11 and 12).

They have almost no sanitary facilities or communications network. About 80 percent of heads of families in the *musseques* were born in rural areas, and a small proportion (about 3.7 percent) are Europeans.[18] As usual in areas of this kind, there is a high proportion of owner occupiers; 51.4 percent of houses are owner occupied, and of this group, 85 percent live in houses they built themselves.[19]

Employment for men is in a wide variety of trades, usually unskilled or semiskilled, and over 55 percent earn between 1000 and 2000 *escudos* (U.S. $36 to $73) per month. The median income per capita is 428 *escudos* (U.S. $16) per month. The largest employment for women is washing clothes, but the next highest group, the *quitandeira* or street vendor carrying a large basket of fruit or vegetables on her head, has a higher social status. Essentially a single entrepreneur (they seldom if ever form cooperatives), the *quitandeira* earns about 875 *escudos* (U.S. $33) per month.[20] From these incomes the *musseque* dweller must find between 100 *escudos* and 500 *escudos* (U.S. $3.8 to $19) per month for rent, which explains the great preference for living in a self-built house.

This is a very brief picture of the lifestyle of the typical urban African in Angola; his country cousin is different. In the central plateau (5570 feet above sea level), the Huambo district with 837,000 people is, after the Luanda area, the most populated in the country. The regional capital, Nova Lisboa (now named Huambo), has a population of about 60,000, but the vast majority of Africans live in hundreds of small villages dotted about the countryside in incredible profusion (see Figure 13). Their houses are usually built of sun-dried mud bricks with palm thatched roofs, and their living is from subsistence farming, employment on a few large estates, or seasonal migration to the coffee-growing areas north of Huambo. In the latter case as many as 60,000 men are known to migrate annually, leaving their families

Figure 11. Part of typical *musseque* in Luanda with a density of about 66 houses per hectare. The population density in this case may be as high as 400 to 450 persons per hectare (160–180 per acre).

Figure 12. Typical *musseque* houses showing, even at this density, the need for small yards for animals, for washing, and even for growing food. (The two papaya trees visible provide both shade and fruit.) The construction of the houses is mud and sticks with corrugated metal or tiled roofs.

behind them and creating social problems at both ends of their journey.

Industrial Estate in an Agrarian Region. During recent years the work of the Agricultural Expansion Program has succeeded in teaching many villagers to grow cash crops and to organize the sale and processing of their produce on a cooperative basis. As a result, fewer people than before are needed to work the land, and there is a need for alternative employment. To provide an alternative, the Portuguese government decided to develop a major new industrial estate in the Nova Lisboa region, and a consortium of British consultants, led by Ward, Ashcroft and Parkman, Consulting Engineers, was set up to carry out a study and prepare development plans.[21] The terms of reference called for the creation of an industrial estate, related mostly to the processing of agricultural produce, with associated urbanization. Calculations showed that if the estate were to be developed successfully at normal industrial employment densities and if supporting service employment

and an informal sector formed by those who migrate in hope were allowed for, the resulting total population could be anything from 30,000 to 100,000 people, depending on various assumptions. The emphasis, therefore, became quite different; as well as the creation of an industrial estate with all the infrastructure required by modern industry, it would be necessary to develop at the same time a new town that might approach the predicted size of Nova Lisboa by 1990. After a locational study had been made, a site was selected at Caala, 25 kilometers from Nova Lisboa, and preliminary development plans were produced (see Figure 14).

Self-Help Housing Program. The urbanization plans were based on moderate densities of about 100 people per hectare (40 people per acre), with great emphasis placed on walking distances to school and work places. Most Angolans in rural areas walk great distances to work or to sell vegetables; a bicycle is a great step up on the ladder of progress. The path network through the town is, therefore, conceived as be-

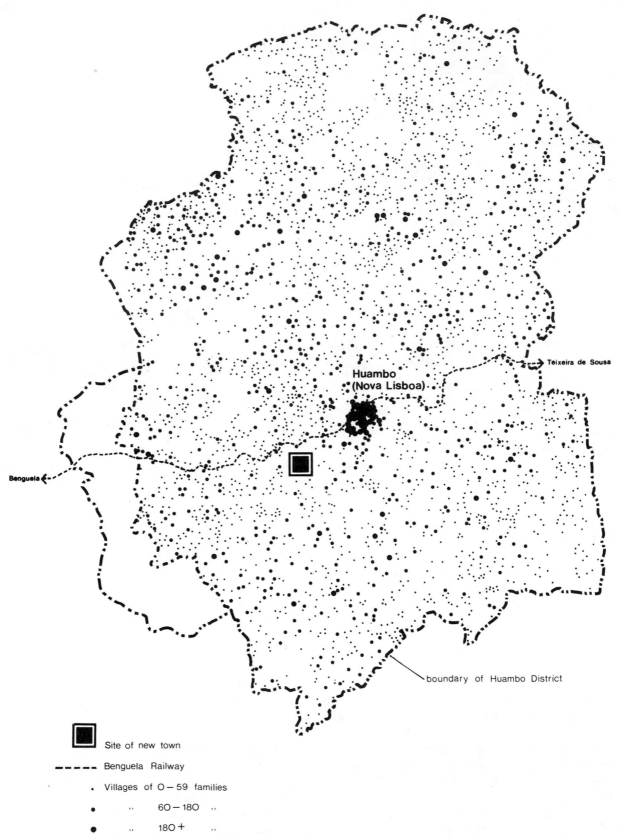

Huambo
(Nova Lisboa)

→ Teixeira de Sousa

Benguela ←

boundary of Huambo District

☐ Site of new town

━ ━ ━ Benguela Railway

. Villages of 0 — 59 families

• ,, 60 — 180 ,,

● ,, 180 + ,,

Figure 13. The dispersed pattern of villages in Huambo makes the distribution of social services extremely difficult. Even with migration to new urban centers there will be a need for a large increase in rural employment opportunities. Source: Profabril and Camara Municipal do Nova Lisboa. Huambo, Angola. n. d.

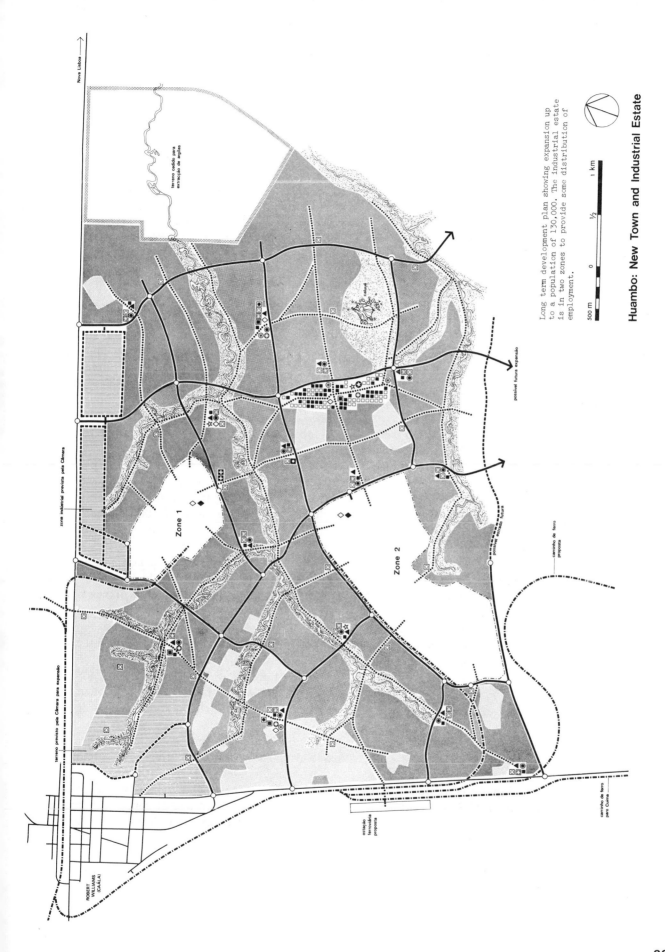

Figure 14. Long-term development plan, Huambo New Town and Industrial Estate. The dark areas are new housing located in relation to a network of shaded pedestrian routes along river valleys. The road network is designed for upgrading as the need arises.

Long term development plan showing expansion up to a population of 130,000. The industrial estate is in two zones to provide some distribution of employment.

Huambo: New Town and Industrial Estate

ing for both walking and bicycling. The main roads at about 1-kilometer intervals are constructed for heavy traffic, but housing roads have a simple topping, which can be upgraded as funds become available.

The most difficult problem is to provide housing, and a wide range of policies will be needed to cope with the projected need of about 1500 dwellings per year.[22] During the period 1969–1972, the Junta Provincal de Habitacão (Housing Authority) built an average of 586 dwellings per year in the whole of Angola and about 23 per year in the Huambo district.[23] Even with a really dramatic increase in the number of public housing units, it seems extremely unlikely that conventional contract building could meet the need or that sufficient funds would be available. It was recommended, therefore, that an important part of the program be self-help housing, including sites and services, core houses, materials depots, and small loans.

There is experience in Angola with these techniques, and much can be learned from the pioneering venture of the city of Lobito. Lobito, with an urban population of 60,000, has a serious housing problem with large African musseques. Aware of the impossibility of building enough houses by conventional means, the city council selected an area known as Alto Liro for a self-help project. Today there are 1500 houses on 68 hectares of land, with a total population of over 7500. The process involved public relations programs with models and radio broadcasts, interviews of applicants, and selection of eligible families (income less than 2500 escudos per month), and instructions to the new occupants of their obligations. A site office was established to process applications for bank loans for the purchase of materials. The loans were made largely by the Totta-Standard Bank of Angola and were the first experience for most people of the banking process. (An amusing side effect is that the name "Totta" has come to mean "bank" in local parlance.) Materials depots were set up for blocks, cement, asbestos sheets, doors, windows, hardware, stone, and sand, and the bank checks were restricted to the purchase of these materials. The land was rented for 50 centavos a square meter or about U.S. $3 a year for an average site of 155 square meters.[24]

The houses were of two basic types:

1. Walls built by contractors employed by the city and the house completed by occupants.

2. Complete house built by occupants, but sometimes employing skilled labor.

According to the city council, the total house cost was about U.S. $920, whereas the average cost of conventional public housing in Angola is U.S. $2281 per unit. Even allowing for the element of hidden costs referred to by Abrams, this represents a considerable saving of public money and makes possible spreading the benefits of improved housing to a much larger number of people.[25]

There are defects: the layout is unimaginative—all the houses are in straight lines; there is no planting in public spaces; the houses are minimal and not entirely suited to the climate; the only sanitary accommodation is in blocks, each serving about 250 people. The project must, however, be counted as an improvement over conventional public housing and represents an intermediate stage in development that should form an important component of housing policy in the new town in Huambo.

The new town, if carried out according to plan, will radically alter the relation of Huambo to the rest of the country. Nova Lisboa is projected to reach 90,000 population by 1990, and with the population attracted by the new town from the rural areas, the Nova Lisboa/Caala area will become an urban agglomeration of perhaps 200,000 people by the 1990s.[26] If present trends continue, Luanda will be a city of over 1 million people and will be about five times as large as the Nova Lisboa/Caala complex. At present Luanda is nearly eight times larger than Nova Lisboa, and the development of new industry will help toward gaining regional balance to some extent. There is little doubt that dependence on Luanda will be reduced to the benefit of the region (see Figure 14).

I do not think, however, that the creation of the industrial center will by itself solve the problems of the majority of rural Africans in Huambo. It will also be necessary to develop new village centers based on agricultural hinterlands, with some form of processing plant available on a cooperative basis, and this has been recommended to the government for its consideration.[27] These small centers would be able to support, in addition, a range of community facilities such as clinics, schools, and shops, which are now totally lacking in rural areas. A policy of taking jobs and services to the people is essential. It is far better to let them adjust gradually to new methods, ways of life, products, and social and political aspirations in the known environment of their own villages than to be plunged too soon into an alien urban situation where the rapidity of change will cause new social pressures.

MALAYSIA

The Federation of Malaya was formed in 1957, and in 1963 it joined with Sabah and Sarawak to make up the Federation of Malaysia. It is a much smaller country than either Venezuela or Angola, with a total land area of 129,864 square miles, but with a relatively large population of approximately 12 million. The capital city, Kuala Lumpur, now has a population of 707,000. The main racial groups are Malay (45 percent), Chinese (36 percent), and Indian (9 percent). Traditionally, the Malays have been rural people engaged in agriculture, and the Chinese have been active in business and live mostly in the large towns. This difference in economic status between the two races was responsible for the racial riots of 1969, which in turn caused the government to establish its new economic policy. This policy aims to bring Malays into the modern urban economy by eliminating the identification of race with economic function. The first prong of the strategy is meant to eradicate poverty and emphasize the agricultural sector where the bulk of the population works and to open up land for agricultural production. "The second prong is aimed at restructuring society to correct racial, economic imbalances . . . [and to] establish new urban centers in the less developed areas by introducing industries and other facilities."[28]

As part of this policy, special new development authorities were set up with boards that include federal and state politicians, businessmen, and civil servants. They have direct routes to the highest levels of government, and their powers are more extensive than those of even the British new-town development corporations. The boards are able to reach their own aid and loan agreements with international financing agencies and employ their own staff and consultants. The boards are also able to set up companies, raise capital, dispose of land, and provide housing and infrastructure.[29]

The Regional Plan for Pahang Tenggara. Authorities of this kind exist in the neighboring states of Pahang and Johor, and regional plans have recently been prepared in both cases (see Figure 15). The re-

gional plan for Pahang Tenggara was carried out in 1972 by a consortium of Canadian firms.[30] The objectives of the plan were the creation of efficient enterprises in agriculture and forestry, the promotion of industry and urbanization, the prevention of income levels from slipping below the national average, and the provision of means for acquiring new skills and new employment opportunities. A proposal was made to settle 500,000 people in the Pahang Tenggara region by 1990. As a base for employment, logging operations would proceed at the rate of 60,000 acres per annum up to 1980, and 500,000 acres would be developed for oil palm. In addition, there would be the creation of new forest complexes, conservation areas, and mineral exploration.

As part of the policy, the regional plan proposed that 36 new towns, based mainly on oil palm production but with other forms of employment, should be built throughout the Pahang Tenggara region (see Figure 16). These new towns were to be a hierarchy by function and size with five stages as follows:

1. Resource-based settlements of less than 5,000 people each. By 1980 less than 10 percent of the population would be living in settlements of this size. They were considered to be a consequence of remote hinterlands, pockets of existing population, or awkward access due to physical barriers.
2. Processing and basic service communities. It was projected that by 1980, 17 of the new towns would be in this category. This will be 50 percent of the regional population and will probably decline to about 35 percent by 1990. The population of these towns would be about 10,000, which does not necessitate the division of the town into smaller units. The focus would be on the center of the town, but at this point the first significant threshold in public services and increases in commercial activities may begin.
3. Service and supply towns. These towns would have a population of from 15,000 to 30,000. By 1980 there will be two towns in this category, with 15 percent of the total regional population, and about seven towns by 1990. Eventually the majority of workers will be in nonprimary activity.
4. District centers with 30,000 to 50,000 people. Two towns of this size are expected by 1980, with a quarter of the total regional population. One will develop into the regional center by 1990.
5. Regional center. This town, Bukit Ridan, is the only settlement projected to have a population

THAILAND

SOUTH CHINA SEA

WEST MALAYSIA

● Kuantan

PAHANG TENGGARA

● Kuala Lumpur

MELAKA STRAITS

JOHOR TENGGARA

SINGAPORE

0   50   100 miles

Figure 15. Map of west Malaysia showing the areas of the regional plans for Pahang Tenggara and Johor Tenggara.

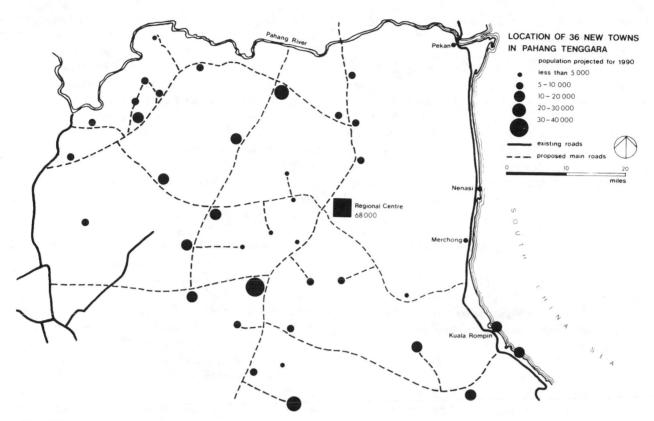

Figure 16. The regional plan for Pahang Tenggara proposed up to 36 new towns of varying sizes as a means of opening up a new region.

over 50,000. It should approach 70,000 by 1990. Only about 15 percent of the population will be involved with primary resources, and the majority of employment will be in service industry.

The size and location of the towns were determined by a number of factors. The steeply rolling terrain, flood-prone areas, forest reserves, and marshlands were major constraints. The consultants' view was that because of the pioneering nature of the projects, more infrastructure than normal would be necessary to attract settlers.

To understand the nature of these proposals, it helps to know something of the FELDA villages, which have been created during the past 20 years. The Federal Land Development Authority is a quasi-governmental agency and the biggest agricultural development organization in Malaysia. It was started in 1956, and by 1972 it had settled 23,000 families in reclaimed equatorial forests, and 356,000 acres of rubber and oil palm have been planted in 100 land settlement projects. In addition to land clearance and reclamation, FELDA operates retail businesses, trucking services, processing plants, bulk storage facilities, and kindergartens.[31] FELDA projects have

contributed considerably to Malaysia's total production. Rubber production was estimated to have reached 1.5 million tons in 1973, and small-holder production accounted for 53 percent of the total, compared with 47 percent in 1972.[32] Altogether, FELDA has been a great success.

In 1970 the targets for land development were 50,000 acres a year with jobs for 5000 people and housing for 25,000. The process is fairly standard: the jungle is cleared, and a new village is built in the center of an agricultural area, with about 500 to 1000 wood-framed houses on quarter-acre lots allowing people room to grow some food for their own purposes. There is usually a mosque, a primary school, a FELDA office, a few shops, and a reserve area for future facilities. Normally provided services are a water standpipe for every six houses and a pit latrine for each house; electrical power is also provided in most cases. Roads are usually laterite, owing to the relatively light traffic, and buses are provided for children to attend secondary schools.[33]

In a typical FELDA scheme at Bukit Goh there are 635 houses and a total population of about 3800. All the houses are identical but are able to be extended; and in fact, FELDA has a design for house extension. Of the 635 houses, a total of about 100 are now being extended. The settlers are shareholders in the FELDA scheme and receive incomes related to the production of oil palm. In this particular village the average income is about 1500 Malaysian dollars a month, and out of the income the settler pays mortgage installments on his house. After 15 years he will become the owner of his house, but the particular form of ownership is restrictive. The settlers will not be allowed to dispose of the house, except to their wives or children, and they cannot sell the property; as yet the eventual pattern of disposal seems to be uncertain. If a settler leaves the FELDA scheme, he surrenders his home, and there is no provision for the second generation. In this way, although the FELDA villages provide enormously improved income for rural Malays and although they have contributed greatly to the national production of oil palm and rubber, it cannot be said that they will produce stable new communities, and indeed many settlers in these projects have always tended to maintain a base in their original villages.

Industrial New Towns. In addition to the FELDA villages, Malaysia has built a number of urban communities and industrial estates in the last two decades; the best known of these is Petaling Jaya, located on the outskirts of Kuala Lumpur. Started in 1957, Petaling Jaya had a population of 93,000 by 1972 and now occupies 6000 acres of land with 700 acres of industry and 300 factories. Its success led the government to plan a series of industrial estates. Among these were Syah'alam, 10 miles north of Petaling Jaya, which occupies 5000 acres with 1200 acres of industry; Port Klang, which is a reclamation of 2155 acres of mangrove swamp; and Sungei Way/Subang, which is seven miles from Kuala Lumpur and covers 104 acres. There are a number of other industrial developments of this nature, most of which are fairly near Kuala Lumpur and which, conceptually, are "industrial areas with associated urbanization" as described in the Angolan example.[34]

Special Problems of Pahang Tenggara. The physical and institutional design of the new communities in Pahang Tenggara must break away from the patterns set by both the FELDA settlements and the industrial new towns. Neither of these precedents provides a suitable model for the new towns that are intended to form stepping stones to urban conditions for large numbers of rural Malays.

Development plans for the first of these new towns were begun in 1974 by the Pahang Tanggara Development Authority (DARA), and early in 1975 a group of British and Malaysian consultants started the detailed planning of six towns.[35] Implementation began in 1976, and rapid development is expected up to 1980, by which time the towns should have reached their planned populations. There are many (myself included) who think that this is an unduly optimistic projection and that it will take longer to build up the towns and attract migrants, but the short time scale gives a measure of the importance that the state government gives to this project.

The Regional Plan for Johor Tenggara. A regional study carried out in Johor Tenggara in 1971 came to somewhat similar conclusions about the need to create new agriculture-based communities.[36] Johor Tenggara is a region of about 750,000 acres, two-thirds of which is covered by primary and secondary forest. Approximately half the forest area has been exploited or is currently being logged, and in addition, there are extensive developments in rubber and oil palm. However, there is still enormous potential for exploitation, and the master plan seeks to maximize this. The region has about 135,000 people, including three small aboriginal settlements and the two large towns of Kluang (61,000) and Kota Tinggi (8,000).

The existing population is predominantly agricultural, with an unemployment level in Johor state similar to that of West Malaysia as a whole (between 8 and 10 percent of the labor force). Agriculture, if not the sole source of employment, is the largest prospective source, and no development plan can succeed without recognizing this fact. However, employment in agriculture has little appeal, particularly to young people, and attempts to improve this must depend on the provision of good social facilities and infrastructure in rural settlements.

The main recommendations of the master plan are as follows:

1. Clearance of 250,000 acres of forest and the development of oil palm, rubber, and other agricultural activities, including a dairy cattle breeding unit.
2. Establishment of an integrated logging and timber complex to obtain maximum value from lowland forest.
3. Creation of a tourist complex.
4. Conservation of forest trees on steeply sloping

land, catchment areas, land unsuitable for agriculture, and land containing biological communities of special interest.

5. The building of 30 to 40 new villages, six larger central villages, two new towns, and the expansion of Kluang and Kota Tinggi. The total population increase by 1990 would be over 300,000; the urban population living in the new towns and villages is projected to be 94,000.

Detailed proposals in the report indicate 26 new villages, ranging in size from 2000 to 4000 people, and six central villages, each with about 6000 people. The two new towns will be Bandar Lebam (44,000) and Bandar Tengah (13,000). Kluang is planned to increase to 180,000 and Kota Tinggi to 21,000, making a total regional population of over 450,000.

The concept of the basic settlement as described in the master plan is 300 to 700 families on 200 to 300 acres, the precise number depending on "the size of the agricultural area served, the labour requirement of the crops, and the income and employment policies of the production agencies around the village."[37] It is thought that villages of this size will give families easy access to work and social facilities and will allow the growth of some shops and commercial activities. Over a period of 15 years, natural growth would probably increase the size of the village to 4000 people.

The central villages should become minor service centers located between five to eight miles from the smaller villages; they should be large enough to contain banking, insurance, and marketing facilities. The expanded town of Kluang will become a major regional center analogous to Bukit Ridan in the Pahang project.

If these two major regional plans in Pahang and Johor are fully realized, there will be a total of 80 or so new towns in the underpopulated and underexploited eastern region of Malaysia. This will make a considerable difference to the urban structure of the country. According to the Pahang master plan, there is evidence that Malaysia is underurbanized for its state of development, but the lack of regional balance is not so great as in some other developing countries because there is one growth center in each region ex-

Figure 17. A typical *kampung* on the east coast of Malaysia. The trees are vital to comfort but also provide a scene of great visual quality.

Figure 18. Current commercial clearance procedures leave behind complete desolation. Conservation areas will be essential when building the new towns.

Figure 19. A typical government housing project in Malaysia. The timber houses are excellent; but even when the debris of construction has been cleared, it will be many years before the site will be softened by shade trees.

272

Figure 20. The sketch shows how the layout in Figure 19 might have been improved with sensitive conservation procedures.

cept the east coast. These plans should contribute greatly to the lessening of that lack of balance even if they fall short of the targets set in the master plans. This may well be the case because to a large extent they are competing for the same national resources for development costs and for the same migrant populations.

Environmental Concerns. In environmental terms there is one overriding problem that must be solved to attract settlers to make permanent homes in the new towns and villages; this is the problem of "landscrape." One of the outstanding qualities of Malaysia is the great beauty of the traditional village or *kampung*, where simple timber houses rest in the shade of tall palm trees. The houses rise about four feet off the ground on stilts, which help to keep the house cool and free from crawling insects; the surface of the ground is covered with goat-mown grass, unbroken by fences and crossed by narrow winding footpaths; the height of the palms allows the cooling wind to circulate. In every way the *kampung* is a testimony to the skill men have in adapting to their environment when allowed to do so over many generations. Except for the introduction of sanitation and water supply, it would be almost impossible to design a better habitat in the Malaysian climate (see Figure 17).

However, what happens when large-scale housing projects are built *for* people instead of *by* them? The undulating hills are first stripped of their commercial timber—useless trees are left strewn on the ground (see Figure 18). Then the hills are flattened into plat-

forms to suit the limited abilities of professionals who can think only in terms of straight lines in section or plan. The result is a red desert of laterite on which nothing will grow for years, where erosion will fill streams and drainage courses, and where rows of standard houses will bake in the piercing midday sun (see Figure 19). It is hardly surprising to hear of instances where workers on estates have left such housing to fend for themselves in the nearby jungle where there is that simple requirement of all people in the tropics—shade.

Obviously, policies of selective clearance, conservation, and slope protection coupled with sensitive layout and design are essential, and this may be one of the most important facets of the physical plans for the new towns (see Figure 20). At least if they succeed in creating environments that approach the qualities of the *kampung* (but with better services and facilities), they will have gone a long way toward ensuring the success of the regional objectives in terms of attracting settlers to a new frontier.

CONCLUSION

Although we cannot draw any generally valid conclusions from three examples, there are certain points emerging that may help to show the way for new-town development in the developing world. In Venezuela the emphasis was on large, new industrially based cities. Of these, the one that has so far been successful is based on extractive industry and is in an isolated, developing region. However, the attempt to create a new city near the capital based on manufacturing industry has not been implemented after almost 20 years of effort. In Angola the development of the industrial estate will boost the importance of the region and will provide employment for many thousands of people, but in my opinion, its influence will hardly be felt in the outer agricultural areas. In Malaysia, where it is too early to judge the success of the new-town program, a great deal can be learned from the earlier FELDA projects, which have been enormously successful, largely because they are small-scale and based on agricultural resources.

I have already quoted E. F. Schumacher several times. His book *Small is Beautiful* is one of the most significant of the past decade for the people of the Third World. It is subtitled *A study of economics as if people mattered*, and one has only to look at some of the chapter headings to see that Schumacher's concerns are different from those of the more conventional economist. He demonstrates that neither money nor high technology can be an answer to the problems of the developing countries. He shows that the total of western aid spent on development, and divided by the number of people in the developing countries, is less than $5 a year per person. He regards this as derisory but suggests that even if it were possible to double it, this would still be laughably inadequate.[38] He concludes that the best aid to give is intellectual, rather than material, and he illustrates the points as follows:

Give a man a fish, as the saying goes, and you are helping him a bit for a very short while; teach him the art of fishing and he can help himself all his life. On a higher level: supply him with fishing tackle; this will cost you a good deal of money, and the result remains doubtful; even if fruitful, the man's continuing livelihood will be dependent on you for replacements. But teach him to make his own fishing tackle and you have helped him to become not only self-supporting, but also self-reliant and independent.[39]

Money is in itself no solution, but neither is high technology. The failure of technology in the field of housing has been very well demonstrated by I. D. Terner, who describes a case in Latin America in the 1960s where, after feasibility studies, a European housing manufacturer imported expensive equipment to provide public housing.[40] As soon as the project commenced, serious problems arose. It was almost impossible to find anyone in the country with the right kind of experience in management, repairs to machinery took weeks and sometimes months, and

there was a general lack of back-up services. Gradually, the operating company tried to become a self-sufficient island, but it could not be divorced completely from its general social setting. Terner describes many other problems, which were mostly related to the lack of an infrastructure of support services, and points out that high technology of this kind must create, or re-create in miniature, many of the supporting services that are taken for granted by producers in developed countries.

However, even if these difficulties—and some of them were no doubt due to bad management—were overcome, the cost per unit would still be far too high to have any meaning for the vast majority of people in most developing countries. It would be a question once again of providing relatively high standards for a few people, which is no solution.

For these reasons, the views put forward by Schumacher about intermediate or appropriate technology are particularly attractive. It makes no sense to leap straight from primitive subsistence agriculture and mud huts to industrial production and prefabricated concrete houses, but the benefits of modern technology should be available to the subsistence farmer at the level at which he can both comprehend and make use of them. If we accept this argument, and it seems to be the only one with real hope for the future, what is the corollary in planning and urbanization? How should the planner fit in with the ideas of appropriate technology, and what form should his plans and programs take? What is the equivalent in physical planning of the bicycle or cable-drawn plough driven by a small internal combustion engine, instead of a large, relatively inefficient oil-intensive tractor? It seems to me that the answer must lie in making use of whatever form of development is appropriate and avoiding rigid theories. There are always experts who want to adopt a single solution. For some, self-help is now the cure-all for housing, and nothing but complete participation and control by tenants and users can have any meaning at all. For others, all urban development seems suspect, and high-density buildings are held to be responsible for crime and a host of urban ills. Some conservationists would have us preserve all old buildings whether or not they are beautiful or useful; they are used to what has been there for a long time and fear anything new, whether it be good or bad.

In developed and developing countries alike, the typical housing authority has an almost missionary desire to bulldoze and redevelop. At various times officials have expressed to me the need to clear the *barrios* in Caracas, the *gechekondu* housing in Istanbul, or the *musseques* in Luanda, without a hint that they are aware of the social problems they would create if they could do so, and to replace them with expensive and dull public housing. However, some professionals now seem to believe that all public housing is a social evil and that everyone would be better off if they could build their own accommodation, either singly or cooperatively.

I do not believe that such extreme views are very useful in practical situations; they are usually held by people who want a nice, neat, tidy theory that will cure once and for all this or that set of problems. Those who hold strongly that self-help is the only way would be at loggerheads with the officials I have described who want to put everyone into public housing, and the officials themselves would regard the self-helpers as impractical romantics. In fact, they are both needed. The provision of housing in developing countries is a war against deprivation. It will not be won unless it is fought on all fronts and full use is made of every available weapon.

A balanced view is needed to select the best from a whole range of approaches and use what is appropriate in a particular case, without worrying too much about whether it fits closely with received theory. Self-help housing, core-housing, sites and services, public housing, and conventional private housing are all necessary, and none will have enough effect alone. To experiment with simple industrialized public housing using rationalized traditional methods may be as important as it is to encourage the use of improved sun-dried mud bricks or new ways of using waste materials in self-help construction. In a similar way it can be argued that a full range of programs is essential at the scale of the community; it is not a case of building or not building cities, because they will continue to grow, with or without planners or planning, until presumably the world's population evens out at some dim and distant point in the future and no further cities are needed. Both new cities and new villages are essential, and in fact, one may lead to the other. If an attempt to develop a new region is based on a single large city, it may fail for many reasons; but if 20 or 30 small resource-based communities are planned, some of them may fail, but one or more may grow into larger towns with all the services that large scale makes possible. It is for this reason that I have high hopes for the Malaysian program. Planners should be willing to follow the lead of the new generation of intermediate technologists, and intermediate urbanization should be their goal.

There is, however, a basic dichotomy that advisers from developed countries should not ignore. We should not fall into the trap of transferring irrelevant ideas and technology to developing countries, which must inevitably be a disservice; but it is often difficult to say to less fortunate people, "You don't want what we already have." They may not agree, while the West goes on using so much of the world's supply of energy and food. It may seem hypocritical to say to people in Africa or Asia that the benefits of modern technology are not for them. They may retort that they too want cars, roads, modern machinery, and the advantages we have derived from them. We can say to people that they should not migrate to the large cities, but they may still feel better off if they do; if you are hungry, atmospheric pollution is not a major priority. We may preach population control, but to a subsistence farmer whose sons will work his land and look after him in his old age, a large family is his only social insurance, and our arguments will be meaningless. With these reservations in mind, however, planners should be prepared to do many small things in many places rather than concentrate on the single big gesture, as has been their tendency in the past.

NOTES

1. Charles Abrams, *Housing in the Modern World* (London: Faber & Faber, 1966), p. 135.

2. Alvin Toffler, *Future Shock* (New York: Bantam Books, 1972).

3. See, for instance, Lloyd Rodwin "Ciudad Guayana: A New City," *Scientific American* **213,** No. 3 (1965):122–132 or Anthony Penfold, "Ciudad Guayana: Planning a New City in Venezuela," *Town Planning Review* **36,** No. 4 (January 1966):225–248.

4. Abrams, p. 137.

5. Barbara Ward, "The Urban Process in Developing Countries: the Problem Stated," *Proceedings of the Town and Country Planning Summer School*, University of Exeter, September 7–18, 1974.

6. E. F. Schumacher, *Small is Beautiful* (London: Blond & Briggs, 1973), pp. 178–191.

7. Barbara Ward, "The Triple Crisis," *RIBA Journal* **81,** No. 12 (1974):13–19.

8. I say new because 10 years ago one of the world's greatest experts on development planning, Charles Abrams, had not considered this alternative. He favored satellite new towns or, if distant from a large city, towns with a diversity of industries. See Abrams, pp. 138–139.

9. John Friedman, *Regional Development Policy: A Case Study of Venezuela* (Cambridge: M.I.T. Press, 1966).

10. An excellent description of life in the *barrios* of Ciudad Guayana is contained in Liza Peattie, *The View from the Barrio* (Ann Arbor: University of Michigan Press, 1968).

11. Llewelyn-Davies, Weeks, Forestier-Walker & Bor, and Nathaniel Lichfield and Associates, *Planning Proposals for the Tuy Medio, Venezuela* (Caracas: Ministerio de Obras Publicas, March 1968).

12. Llewelyn-Davies, Weeks, Forestier-Walker & Bor, and Nathaniel Lichfield and Associates, *Development Proposals for a New City at El Tablazo, Estado Zulia,* (Caracas: Ministerio de Obras Publicas, February 1969).

13. This term was probably first used in the report *Traffic in Towns*, the Buchanan Report (London: Her Majesty's Stationery Office, 1963). The glossary defines an environmental area as "an area having no extraneous traffic and within which considerations of environment . . . predominate over the use of vehicles."

14. The Transport Network Theory Unit of the London School of Economics in conjunction with the British Ministry of Housing and Local Government and the Joint Urban Planning Group designed this program (Elementary Generation of Traffic and Computation).

15. For a detailed description of these projects and further illustrations, see Alan Turner and Jonathan Smulian, "New Cities in Venezuela," *Town Planning Review* **42,** No. 1 (1971):3–27; and Walter Bor, M. Corao, A. Penfold, J. Smullian, and A. Turner, "Venezuela," *Architectural Design* **39,** No. 8 (1969):425–447.

16. Ramiro Ladeiro Monteiro, *A Familia Nos Musseques de Luanda* (Luanda: Funda De Accão, 1973), p. 61.

17. *Ibid.*, p. 94.

18. Franz-Wilhelm Heimer, Ed., *Social Change in Angola* (Munich: Weltforum Verla, 1973), p. 214.

19. Monterio, p. 251.

20. *Ibid.*, pp. 222–233.

21. The other consultants included L. H. Manderstram & Partners, Inbucon International, and Alan Turner and Associates.

22. By comparison the average rate of building in the British new towns has been about 1000 houses per year. At Milton Keynes it is proposed to build up to 3000 per year.

23. Angola, *IV Plan do Fomento* (Luanda: Government of Angola), p. 250.

24. *Programa do Fomento da Habitac*ão & Reordenamento Urbano no Lobito, Ano II, No. 15, Camara Municipal do Lobito.

25. Abrams, p. 173.

26. *Plano Director De Urbanizac*ão De Nova Lisboa. A report by the consultants, Profabril, 1972–1974.

27. During discussions in Nova Lisboa, I was interested in suggestions made by Herman Possinger of the Rural Extension Service, for what he called "primary transformation centres" where the first steps in the processing of produce could take place for later transportation to bigger processing plants.

28. *National Unity Through Development.* The Second Malaysia Plan 1971–1975. Speech by the Prime Minister Tun Haji Abdul Razak bin Hussein, July 12, 1971. Motion presented in Davan Ra'ayat (Parliment), Kuala Lumpur.

29. David Walton, "A Rural Economy and an Urban Way of Life," *Journal of the Royal Town Planning Institute* **61** (April 1975):133–138.

30. Pahang Tenggara Regional Master Planning Study. Consultants: Foundation of Canada Engineering Corporation, Ltd., Van Ginkel Associates, Ltd., S. G. Gardiner Engineering Services, Ltd., Charrell International Consultants, Ltd., June 1972.

31. *FELDA.* A brochure published by the Federal Land Development Authority, Malaysia, 1972.

32. *Malaysia* (London: Economics Department, National & Grindlay's Bank, Ltd., March 1974).

33. Walton, p. 135.

34. *New Industrial Estates* (Kuala Lumpur: Selangor State Development Corporation, October 1972).

35. Freeman Fox and Associates, Akitek Bersekutu Malaysia, Tahir Wong Sdn. Bhd., Roger Tym and Associates, and Alan Turner and Associates.

36. Hunting Technical Services, Ltd., Overseas Development Group, University of East Anglia, Binnie and Partners and Shankland Cox Overseas, *Johor Tenggara Regional Master Plan* (Johor: Johor Regional Development Authority, August 1971).

37. *Ibid.*, p. 84ff.

38. Schumacher, p. 182.

39. *Ibid.*, p. 184.

40. I. D. Terner, "Technology and Autonomy" in *Freedom to Build*, J. F. C. Turner and Robert Fichter, Eds. (New York: Macmillan, 1972).

Acknowledgments: The illustrations were drawn by Lucy Wynne Turner. The photograph in Figure 18 is by David Walton; all others are by Alan Turner.

CHAPTER 18

National Growth Policy and New Communities in the United States: An Overview

FREDERICK A. McLAUGHLIN, JR.

The Ebenezer Howard view of new towns as a setting for new lifestyles away from the congestion
and evils of the industrialized city would seem to be
reason enough to warrant a national policy supporting the development of new towns, or "new communities" as they are labeled in the United States. Cou-
pling these presumed benefits with the popular belief
that large-scale, comprehensive development is the
most effective tool of a nation's growth policy would
seem to make new communities leading candidates
for government support. Yet the United States has
lagged far behind most developed countries in adopting a federal new communities program, and it is
even further behind in articulating a growth policy to
guide the inevitable process of urbanization.

The first purpose of this chapter is to trace the
development of the American interest in a national
growth policy, including the constraints that slow its
formulation. The second is to use the concept of a
growth-policy framework to gain a perspective on the

progress—and problems—of the federal New Communities Program.

THE DEVELOPMENT OF NATIONAL GROWTH
POLICY

Policies Versus Goals. One of the most often cited
approximations of a major component of national
growth policy is found in the Housing Act of 1949:
"the realization as soon as feasible of the goal of a
decent home and a suitable living environment for
every American family." Actually, of course, this
phrase states a goal rather than a policy. A few
sentences later in this 1949 Declaration of National
Housing Policy, the policies to govern the achievement of this goal are stated. These include that "(1)
Private enterprise shall be encouraged to serve as
large a part of the total need as it can; (2) governmental assistance shall be utilized where feasible to
enable private enterprise to serve more of the total
need. . . ."[1]

The question of what is a goal and what is a policy is
not a major concern here (we freely use the words
interchangeably), but it is important to point out that
means (policies?) are as important as ends (goals).
This early expression of the policy of the maximum

This chapter is a revision of a paper originally published in
Strategy for New Community Development in the United States,
edited by G. Golany, © 1975 by Dowden, Hutchinson and Ross,
Inc., Stroudsburg, Pennsylvania. This paper represents the personal views of the author and does not necessarily reflect those of
the United States Department of Housing and Urban Development (HUD).

use of private enterprise has been a guide (some would say a constraint) to all national legislation since. The primary, if not sole, government role in achieving national goals, as a realization of this policy, has been to assist the private system, especially by helping to eliminate impediments to its effective operation. This policy decision on the proper role of government is why a federal new communities program took several years to pass congressional muster. Legislative proposals during the early 1960s, which emphasized a strong government role, faded away rather quietly under congressional and interest-group scrutiny. However, Congress finally approved a strong private role when it passed the New Communities Act of 1968, which established a program featuring a federal guarantee for loans to private new-community developers.[2] A familiar phrase appeared in the Urban Growth and New Community Development Act of 1970, which expanded the program established in 1968:

It is, therefore, the purpose of this part to provide private developers and State and local public bodies and agencies ... with financial and other assistance necessary for encouraging the orderly development of well-planned, diversified, and economically sound new communities ... and to do so in a manner which will rely to the maximum extent on private enterprise. ...[3]

As Americans, we seemingly continue to hold to the belief that government should be as benign as possible in getting things done. The benign role seems hardly adequate when one begins to define a national growth policy[4] or to understand its purposes. The all-embracing scope of a growth policy becomes apparent by reading the purposes listed by Congress in the 1970 act:

The Congress further declares that the national urban growth policy should—

(1) favor patterns of urbanization and economic development and stabilization which offer a range of alternative locations and encourage the wise and balanced use of physical and human resources in metropolitan and urban regions as well as in smaller urban places which have a potential for accelerated growth;

(2) foster the continued economic strength of all parts of the United States, including central cities, suburbs, smaller communities, local neighborhoods, and rural areas;

(3) help reverse trends of migration and physical growth which reinforce disparities among States, regions, and cities;

(4) treat comprehensively the problems of poverty and employment (including the erosion of tax bases, and the need for better community services and job opportunities) which are associated with disorderly urbanization and rural decline;

(5) develop means to encourage good housing for all Americans without regard to race or creed;

(6) refine the role of the Federal Government in revitalizing existing communities and encouraging planned, large-scale urban and new community development;

(7) strengthen the capacity of general governmental institutions to contribute to balanced urban growth and stabilization; and

(8) facilitate increased coordination in the administration of Federal programs so as to encourage desirable patterns of urban growth and stabilization, the prudent use of natural resources, and the protection of the physical environment.[5]

If growth policy is expected to be, among other things, a key to reversing migration, maintaining economic stability, and providing for the wise use of resources, one would wonder whether government can be assigned only a supporting role. Yet a resistance to any centralized, pervasive direction from government was evidenced in the president's first report under the 1970 statute:

There is no place in our country for any policy which arbitrarily dictates where and how our citizens will live and work and spend their leisure time. Our plans for national growth must rather seek to help individual Americans develop their unique potentials and achieve their personal goals.[6]

The growth policy goals cited previously obviously do not provide a working definition of such policy. One difficulty of grappling with the substance of a national growth policy is that, like the proverbial blind men and the elephant, each interest group sees the policy as being the solution to its own problems. The policy expands into an amorphous mass of motherhood principles and multiple goals. The long list of objectives contained in the 1970 act, including "to treat comprehensively the problems of poverty and employment," only adds to this difficulty.

The basic purpose of a national growth policy, although not the only one, is to create balance and order in any growth. The policy, as it evolves, will be strongly oriented toward the geographic distribution of people and economic activities or, expressed another way, toward the distribution and patterns of urbanization within the nation and its cities and regions. This purpose embraces the related problems of decline in rural areas, rapid growth in suburban communities, and decay in urban centers.

Are balance and order primarily physical? Perhaps the visible results of applying a policy will be physical—changes in the patterns, densities, sizes, and locations of communities. However, as the painful experience in massive public housing projects has taught us, physical housing and communities are valid only if they are consistent with social and economic goals and constraints and are responsive to human needs. Thus a national growth policy, although it may be expressed mostly in physical terms, must help to achieve social and economic policies.

If balanced and orderly growth is a principal objective, we may define a national growth policy as a bundle of policies, programs, and activities that attempts to guide the forces of change and growth into a preconceived pattern of development that will be most responsive to citizens' desires for good and rewarding lives. Such policy is an attempt to create an orderly process—to direct growth, as well as the multitude of public and private decisions affecting it, toward some common goals.

The Historic Background in the United States. Most proposers of new-community legislation in the United States have astutely avoided using foreign experience too closely as support, if that experience might create a socialistic image. (Thus legislation in the United States used the term "new communities" to avoid the public-approach, socialistic stigma of British new towns.) Indeed, the American heritage of private initiative and private property and a tradition of placing government decisions close to the governed (reaffirmed in the concept of new federalism) have determined the legislative concepts and administrative procedures of past national programs intended to affect growth or ameliorate its consequences. Out of this heritage and tradition were created the policies, programs, and activities that have made up our changing national growth policy, although it has hidden influences and must still be clearly articulated.

Perhaps the historic roots of American growth policy began with the homesteading acts and railroad grants in the 1800s. Certainly these conscious efforts to settle the West and spur the expansion of the nation were the epitome of an early growth-policy concept. However, they were really running with the tide, appealing to a land-hungry immigrant population, and

required little reallocation of resources because the land was basically free. These actions hardly apply to later growth pains resulting primarily from a reversal of the tide, a flow back from the land to the urban centers (see Figure 1).

During the 1930s the first real foundation stones of our present policy were laid. Typically, these early policy decisions dealt with symptoms—the distortions of growth—rather than with root causes. Some major legislative and program milestones in the 1930s through the 1960s and their contributions include the following:

1. The National Housing Act, 1934, established the program of federal mortgage insurance, led to more liberal amortization terms for private mortgage loans and improved design of subdivision developments, and confirmed a national policy favoring home ownership.
2. The United States Housing Act of 1937 created the federally assisted local public housing program, with emphasis on slum clearance as a by-product.
3. The Housing Act of 1949 set forth national housing goals and policies, provided federal grants to assist local slum clearance and urban redevelopment projects, expanded a national interest beyond housing to "a suitable living environment," and required local redevelopment projects to (a) include a relocation plan for displaced people and (b) conform to the general plan of the locality as a whole.
4. The Housing Act of 1954 broadened urban redevelopment to a concept of urban renewal (including conservation and rehabilitation as well as slum clearance), established a policy of conditioning federal aid on evidence of local effort to help themselves, and provided federal grants for comprehensive metropolitan and local planning (commonly known as the Section 701 Program).
5. The Highway Act of 1956 established the program and financing for a national system of interstate and defense highways. As it was constructed, this system helped establish highways as the favored transportation mode; helped make the automobile the focus of the American dream; and by vastly improving mobility, was a primary cause of the decentralization of urban areas.
6. Grants for open-space land and basic facilities for water and sewer had as one underlying purpose the promotion of the efficient, orderly development of communities and urban areas.[7] Grants

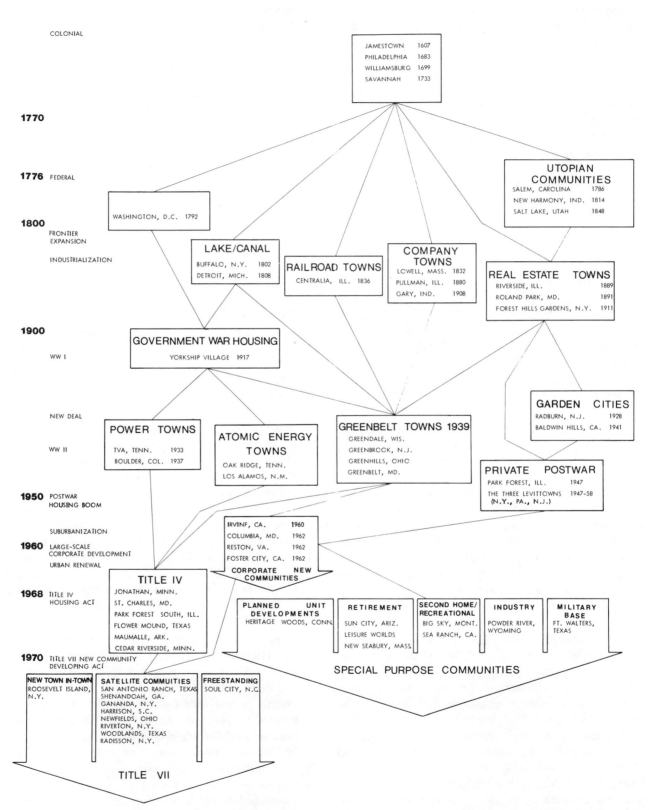

COLONIAL

JAMESTOWN	1607
PHILADELPHIA	1683
WILLIAMSBURG	1699
SAVANNAH	1733

1770

1776 FEDERAL

UTOPIAN COMMUNITIES

SALEM, CAROLINA	1786
NEW HARMONY, IND.	1814
SALT LAKE, UTAH	1848

1800

FRONTIER EXPANSION

INDUSTRIALIZATION

WASHINGTON, D.C. 1792

LAKE/CANAL

| BUFFALO, N.Y. | 1802 |
| DETROIT, MICH. | 1808 |

RAILROAD TOWNS

CENTRALIA, ILL. 1836

COMPANY TOWNS

LOWELL, MASS.	1832
PULLMAN, ILL.	1880
GARY, IND.	1908

REAL ESTATE TOWNS

RIVERSIDE, ILL.	1889
ROLAND PARK, MD.	1891
FOREST HILLS GARDENS, N.Y.	1911

1900

WW I

GOVERNMENT WAR HOUSING

YORKSHIP VILLAGE 1917

NEW DEAL

WW II

POWER TOWNS

| TVA, TENN. | 1933 |
| BOULDER, COL. | 1937 |

ATOMIC ENERGY TOWNS

OAK RIDGE, TENN.
LOS ALAMOS, N.M.

GREENBELT TOWNS 1939

GREENDALE, WIS.
GREENBROOK, N.J.
GREENHILLS, OHIO
GREENBELT, MD.

GARDEN CITIES

| RADBURN, N.J. | 1928 |
| BALDWIN HILLS, CA. | 1941 |

PRIVATE POSTWAR

PARK FOREST, ILL.	1947
THE THREE LEVITTOWNS	1947-58
(N.Y., PA., N.J.)	

1950 POSTWAR HOUSING BOOM

SUBURBANIZATION

1960 LARGE-SCALE CORPORATE DEVELOPMENT

URBAN RENEWAL

IRVINE, CA.	1960
COLUMBIA, MD.	1962
RESTON, VA.	1962
FOSTER CITY, CA.	1962

CORPORATE NEW COMMUNITIES

1968 TITLE IV HOUSING ACT

TITLE IV

JONATHAN, MINN.
ST. CHARLES, MD.
PARK FOREST SOUTH, ILL.
FLOWER MOUND, TEXAS
MAUMALLE, ARK.
CEDAR RIVERSIDE, MINN.

PLANNED UNIT DEVELOPMENTS

HERITAGE WOODS, CONN.

RETIREMENT

SUN CITY, ARIZ.
LEISURE WORLDS
NEW SEABURY, MASS.

SECOND HOME/ RECREATIONAL

BIG SKY, MONT.
SEA RANCH, CA.

INDUSTRY

POWDER RIVER, WYOMING

MILITARY BASE

FT. WALTERS, TEXAS

1970 TITLE VII NEW COMMUNITY DEVELOPING ACT

NEW TOWN IN-TOWN

ROOSEVELT ISLAND, N.Y.

SATELLITE COMMUITIES

SAN ANTONIO RANCH, TEXAS
SHENANDOAH, GA.
GANANDA, N.Y.
HARRISON, S.C.
NEWFIELDS, OHIO
RIVERTON, N.Y.
WOODLANDS, TEXAS
RADISSON, N.Y.

FREESTANDING

SOUL CITY, N.C.

SPECIAL PURPOSE COMMUNITIES

TITLE VII

Figure 1. A geneaology of new communities in the United States. Adapted from an illustration by Barton-Aschman Associates, Inc.

were conditional to the consistency of the proposed projects with a program for a unified or coordinated areawide system as part of the comprehensively planned development of the area.

7. The Public Works and Economic Development Act of 1965 affirmed a national policy of assistance to regions, mostly rural in character, of persistent unemployment and underemployment, and provided public works grants and business loans to such regions.

8. The National Environmental Policy Act of 1969 expressed a national concern in conserving the quality of the environment and established a requirement for environmental impact statements to be formulated in connection with major federal actions.

These are only a few of the federal laws and programs established during this period aimed at alleviating the problems of declining rural regions and burgeoning urban areas. By 1973 some 400 federal programs budgeted for $37 million were providing aid for one problem or another. In the 1960s especially, a whole rash of programs was created by a simple legislative formula of reasoning: local problem plus federal money and requirements equals solution.

Calls for a National Growth Policy. By the late-1960s many urbanists perceived that each federal program had its own objectives and was sometimes in conflict with other programs. The aggregate of programs was not successful, and one reason seemed to be that the nation had no overall set of common goals and strategies to guide these separately enacted, separately administered programs.

In the meantime the evidence continued to build that the forces of growth were about as strong as ever, that these forces were increasing an already distorted national settlement pattern, and that the consequences were undesirable.

The total population of the United States in 1970 stood at 203 million people, up by 33 million over 1960 and 128 million over 1900. More important, the trend toward an increasing concentration of people in urban areas continued: in 1900, 40 percent of the population was urban in character; by 1970 the urban percentage stood at 74 percent. The continued decline of the rural hinterlands was confirmed by the 1970 census revelation that almost one-half of the counties in the United States had lost population

during the 1960s. The census also revealed the continued rapid suburbanization of metropolitan areas and a corresponding decline of urban centers. These kinds of statistics and trends were often used to support opinions that the national and regional development patterns were unbalanced or distorted. Although the terms were ill-defined, they seemed to mean to many people that human desires were being thwarted or that urban problems were being exacerbated, or both.

Public-opinion polls seem to show that there is still an innate human desire to live in a small community. A Gallup poll in 1972 disclosed that 55 percent of the people interviewed desired to live in small towns or on farms, 31 percent preferred suburban life, and only 13 percent chose city living.[8] The validity of these figures is somewhat suspect because other similar polls have indicated that many people may vote for small-town life as long as they retain metropolitan services and conveniences,[9] and the actual decline in rural towns seems to contradict the stated desire for this kind of lifestyle.

At the other end of the rural-urban shift of population, many people were concerned that this migration pattern contributed unnecessarily to the congestion and sprawl of the metropolitan regions. This was a rather simple deduction; these regions were already overcrowded and sprawling outward in a ticky-tacky way; immigration from rural towns and farms made matters worse. Many problems were physical and fiscal in character (ugly and expensive sprawl); others were of a social nature (increasing separation of the races and of economic groups).

The emergence of environmental protectionism in the late 1960s and, later, energy conservationism increased the national concern over the size and location of growth. The warnings of Rachael Carson, Dennis Meadows, and others and the Commission on Population Growth and the American Future cast strong doubt on whether the resources and ecology of the nation or the earth could sustain uncontrolled or unlimited growth.[10] Concern over the consequences of a distorted, unbalanced growth pattern was compounded by the realization that no one was really running the growth railroad. Growth patterns resulted from thousands of private and public decisions, mostly in response to the marketplace. Formal national planning, by the National Resources Planning Board, was abandoned in the early 1940s, and planning at the national level was still a "dirty word."

However, toward the end of the 1960s, a number of prestigious organizations and people called for a national growth policy.

The Advisory Commission on Intergovernmental Relations. In its landmark 1968 report, *Urban and Rural America: Policies for Future Growth*, the commission found evidence that an increasing concentration of people in large urban centers would make public and private consumption more costly and might well take a net social and psychological toll in urban living conditions. The commission recommended the development of growth policies at both national and state levels and a reexamination of the role of multistate planning. The recommendation with respect to a national policy was as follows:

To help assure the full and wise application of all governmental resources consonant with the economic and social health of both rural and urban areas and of the Nation as a whole, the Commission recommends the development of a national policy incorporating social, economic, and other considerations to guide specific decisions at the national level which affect the patterns of urban growth.

The Commission recommends that the President and the Congress assign executive responsibility for this task to an appropriate executive agency. The Commission also recommends that the Congress provide within its standing committee structure a means to assure continuing systematic review and study of the progress toward such a national policy.

The Commission further recommends that the executive and legislative branches, in the formulation of the national policy, consult with and take into account the views of State and local governments.[11]

The commission also recognized a strong role for new communities in the components of a national growth policy and recommended consideration of a federal program of low-interest loans and tax incentives for new-community development.

National Committee on Urban Growth Policy. This prestigious committee, composed of high federal, state, and local public officials, made an extensive study of European experience in carrying out growth policies. A principal recommendation was the following:

The Committee further recommends that the Executive branch and the Congress, with the assistance of the new mechanism, mold a national policy which coordinates a range of programs designed to assure more rational patterns of urban growth and development in the United States. These programs should include new measures to further assist existing cities to redesign and rebuild, to organize new growth on the peripheries of metropolitan areas, and to strengthen and expand smaller communities in rural areas designated as "accelerated growth centers."[12]

In addition, the committee recommended that the federal government extend financial assistance to enable the construction of 100 new communities averaging 100,000 population each, and 10 new communities of at least 1 million population each.

Daniel P. Moynihan. In a 1969 speech at Syracuse University Daniel P. Moynihan, then assistant to the president for urban affairs, called for a nine-point national urban policy, ranging from attacking the problem of the poverty and social isolation of minority groups in central cities to instituting a sustained urban research program.[13]

National Goals Research Staff. A report by the National Goals Research Staff of the White House, issued to the president in July of 1970, contained few policy recommendations.[14] Rather, it discussed the issues and options of various facets of a growth policy. One chapter of the report was devoted to an analysis of population growth and distribution.

President Richard M. Nixon. In his 1970 State of the Union address the president clearly stated the case for a growth policy:

The violent and decayed central cities of our great metropolitan complexes are the most conspicuous area of failure in American life today.

I propose that before these problems become insoluble, the Nation develop a national growth policy.

In the future, government decisions as to where to build highways, locate airports, acquire land, or sell land should be made with a clear objective of aiding a balanced growth for America.[15]

The Ashley Hearings. In 1969 and 1970 Congressman Thomas L. Ashley chaired a series of hearings held by the Ad Hoc Subcommittee on Urban Growth of the House Committee on Banking and Currency. Many professional urbanists and others representing professional organizations such as the American Institute of Architects (AIA) testified on the nature and consequences of urban growth and made recommendations for control measures. Indicative of the general theme of the hearings was the AIA's reference to the policy statement adopted in 1969 by its board of directors. It said in part, "We hereby resolve actively to seek a national policy for urbanization. The purpose of this policy will be to direct the Nation's expansion and development in a balanced effort to match our needs with our resources."[16]

The Urban Growth and New Community Development Act of 1970.

Title VII of the Housing and Urban Development Act of 1970 finally articulated a congressional mandate for the development of a "national urban growth policy." Part A of Title VII (to be cited as the Urban Growth and New Community Development Act of 1970) called for the development of such a policy; part B authorized an expansion of the federal New Communities Program as enacted in 1968. The act did little to clarify the substance of a national growth policy, nor did it set forth national policies. However, the act did state the eight objectives of a growth policy quoted previously.

Indeed, the opening congressional declaration established the procedural orientation of the act, an orientation of many previous calls for a policy: "It is the policy of the Congress and the purpose of this title to provide for the development of a national urban growth policy. . . ."[17]

As one way to "provide for the development," the act directed the president to use an adequately staffed "identified unit" of the Domestic Council (the successor to the Urban Affairs Council) as one means of enabling him to transmit a "Report on Urban Growth" to the Congress in February of every even-numbered year. The act required the report to include the following:

(1) Information and statistics describing characteristics of urban growth and stabilization and identifying significant trends and development.

(2) A summary of significant problems facing the United States as a result of urban growth trends and developments;

(3) An evaluation of the progress and effectiveness of Federal efforts designed to meet such problems and to carry out the national urban growth policy.

(4) An assessment of the policies and structure of existing and proposed interstate planning and developments affecting such policy;

(5) A review of State, local, and private policies, plans, and programs relevant to such policy;

(6) Current and foreseeable needs in the areas served by policies, plans, and programs designed to carry out such policy, and the steps being taken to meet such needs; and

(7) Recommendations for programs and policies for carrying out such policy, including such legislation and administrative actions as may be deemed necessary and desirable.[18]

Reports on National Growth and Development.

In July 1971 the president appointed the Domestic Council Committee on National Growth as the "identified unit." Most federal departments were represented as well as independent organizations such as the Office of Economic Opportunity and the Council of Economic Advisors. George Romney, then secretary of the Department of Housing and Urban Development (HUD), was named chairman.

The committee met shortly after its appointment and began outlining the work to prepare the first report, due in February 1972. The Domestic Council staff was assigned the responsibility of gathering material for the report, much of which was expected to be delivered by member departments and agencies. In October the staff focus for writing the report was shifted to HUD. The several tentative chapters of the report, generally following the specifications in the statute, were assigned to specific personnel, mostly in HUD, or to agencies. Senior staff members of the most critically involved departments were made available to HUD for assisting in and coordinating the work. In January, Secretary Romney transmitted a committee draft of the report to the staff director of the full Domestic Council. The committee's recommendations were subsequently discussed in at least one meeting of the council.

The final printed report, without new recommendations for congressional or executive actions and considerably condensed from the January draft, was transmitted to the Congress on February 28, 1972.[19] The report did more to describe the administration's philosophic views on the concept of a national growth policy than to make substantive policy recommendations. These views and reminders included the following:

(1) The task is not the work of a day; rather it must be the work of a generation.

(2) It cannot be done according to neat blueprints; rather it must grow out of an ongoing process.

(3) The policy cannot arbitrarily dictate how our citizens will live and work; it must build on our heritage of freedom in choosing among various styles of life.

(4) It must respect diversity and pluralism.

(5) The Federal Government cannot dominate growth policy; ours is a Federal system.

(6) The biennial reports to the Congress, as specified in the statute, are to assist in the development of policy not to enunciate it.[20]

The response to the report was unenthusiastic to say the least. The *New York Times* editorial about it was headed, "Missing: One Policy."[21] Testimony before subsequent hearings of the Ashley Subcommittee recorded similar concern over the lack of specific policy directions in the report.[22]

The president's 1974 *Report on National Growth and Development* was almost a year late in being delivered to Congress.[23] Oversight hearings on the report were held in September 1975. A staff summary of these hearings concluded that "the 1974 growth report was an improvement over the 1972 version, but there is still much more to be desired."[24] More specifically, the summary cited the report's failure

To discuss the implications of the data it presented;

To make substantive policy recommendations or even discuss policy options or alternatives;

To draw conclusions about how new population trends should be managed;

To present the policy implications of increased rates of household formation and urban density;

To advance either answers or substantive recommendations to questions it posed;

To come to grips with the difficult intergovernmental issues related to growth policy, to involve State, regional and local governmental officials in the preparation of the report; and

To fully address the issues of critical importance for regional development—issues such as the development of western energy resources.[25]

The 1976 report,[26] which was delivered on time, responds to many of the criticisms of the 1974 report. Public participation was emphasized in writing the report; it is comprehensive in scope; discusses a wide range of urban, rural, and intergovernmental issues; and attempts to describe policy implications and op-

tions. It still may be considered to be lacking substantive recommendations.

The report discusses a relatively new trend in federal aid to state and local governments, a trend away from categorical grants. The concept of revenue sharing—federal aid with no requirements attached—after years of debate, was finally enacted in the State and Local Fiscal Assistance Act of 1972, which authorized the distribution of $30.2 billion over a five-year period. One-third of the funds goes to states; two-thirds go to localities. The concept of block grants—federal aid with only a few requirements attached—is illustrated by the Community Development Block Grant program, enacted as part of the Housing and Community Development Act of 1974. This program substituted a single grant for aid previously provided under seven categorical programs.

Both the programs of revenue sharing and block grants are founded on a belief in the desirability of giving maximum flexibility to local governments to set their own spending priorities. An emerging debate involves a counterbelief that federally raised revenues should be spent in the national interest, presumably including the objectives of national growth policy, and that more federal control and direction is therefore required.

The Rough Road to a Growth Policy.   The search for a national policy is fraught with elusive multiple goals, enormous requirements for wisdom and facts, and probable requirements for changes in our traditional ways of not minding the nation's growth business. The following is a brief summary of the frustrations facing the developers of a national growth policy.

Comprehensiveness.   The eight objectives listed in the 1970 statute cover the entire spectrum of the country's domestic affairs. This comprehensiveness is fine in principle, but is probably not feasible in practice.

One key to developing the policy will be a realistic sorting of the possible from the impossible. Decision making in government can absorb only a limited number of variables; although it would be desirable to be assured that the solution to every domestic problem would fit into a grand scheme of things, a limited approach is much more pragmatic. The dilemma, of course, is that being comprehensive is a chief function of a national growth policy. Indeed, a large share of the support for such a policy rests on a conviction that present government urban policies represent piecemeal, uncoordinated efforts that cannot produce a desirable growth pattern.

The Jungle of Interests. Policies and legislation theoretically will have wider support and more chance of success, if they have something for everyone rather than for a few. Omnibus housing legislation has used this principle for years. Yet the comprehensive substance of the growth-policy concept, and the vast number of interests it seemingly must represent, may be more of a burden than a benefit. The players in the growth-policy game include the following:

1. Several executive departments and agencies and their bureaucracies.
2. The White House, Domestic Council, and Office of Management and Budget complex.
3. Public-interest groups representing the states, cities, counties, and regions—and their Washington staffs.
4. Professional societies, such as the American Institute of Architects and the American Institute of Planners.
5. Associations representing housing, real estate, and farm groups.
6. Congress and its committees, subcommittees, and staffs.
7. Political parties.
8. The media.
9. Conservationists.
10. Academia.

The scope of a growth policy will certainly affect these groups, who often have completely opposite objectives. Whatever pleases one group will probably raise the ire of others.

The Peter-Paul Principle. To cure the lack of distributive balance in the nation's economic development and population concentrations would seem to require a shifting of resources. Thus if we truly desire to turn growth away from massive urban regions toward other places, we shall probably need to reallocate some federal investments. This means taking from the urban Peter to pay the less urban Paul—an extremely difficult principle to get legislators to adopt in practice.

For example, every consultant to the Economic Development Administration recommended that loans, grants, and projects be concentrated in a single growth center within each Economic Development District. But in most cases, these "goodies" were spread over all parts of the District to help the local Congressman gain support from all his constituents—in spite of the diluting impact that often nullified the basic growth center concept.[27]

Expressed another way, balanced growth is embraced by almost everyone, but the idea aborts as soon as the definition of balance is articulated and the losers and winners begin to be sorted in the reallocation planning.

Traditions and Heritage. America was founded with an innate suspicion of government and a reverence for private property and initiatives. It is easy to conclude that an effective growth policy will require more government and fewer private rights in property than exist now. The best policy, of course, would be one that somehow channels or limits the forces of growth with the least public interference, but this kind of magic has yet to be discovered.

A New Mood. The report of the Rockefeller task force on land use begins "There is a new mood in America."[28] The mood is one that questions the value of growth. Indeed, many communities and states have gone beyond the questioning stage and have adopted policies to limit growth severely or to try to stop it altogether. There is both promise and danger in the new mood. If it is channeled into serious efforts to develop a meaningful national growth policy sensitive to the nation's needs and to human rights, the promise is encouraging. The danger is, of course, that it may take the familiar form of community protectionism and exclusionism, which tries to force the problems of growth to go somewhere else. For example, in February 1976 the Supreme Court denied a review of a lower court's decision upholding the Petaluma, California, ordinance that limited construction of subdivision housing to 2500 dwelling units during a five-year period.[29]

With a national growth policy facing these kinds of negative odds and remaining mostly a statement of lofty objectives, one might question the effectiveness of the new-community tool of growth policy.

NEW COMMUNITIES AND NATIONAL GROWTH POLICY

The link between the new-community process of development and the objectives of a national growth policy was implied in the statement of purpose in the New Communities Act of 1968, but the Urban Growth and New Community Development Act of 1970[30] had to articulate clearly the goals of a policy and at the same time to provide an expanded role for new communities as a principal means of realizing that policy. In this section we discuss how well the fledgling federal New Communities Program has begun to realize national growth policy.

Characteristics of the New-Community Process. Benefits flow essentially from four basic characteristics of a new community, which serve to define it:

1. Large scale. A new community is a large-scale development. There is no magical number of acres at which a traditional tract development automatically becomes a new community because size is only one measurement of "new communitiness," but new-community sites are relatively large. In the federal New Communities Program the average size of the sites of 16 communities approved as of January 1976 was about 5700 acres. The size, of course, is smaller for new towns in-town, which are constructed on the expensive, intensely developed land within built-up cities.
2. Balanced development. Title VII requires assisted new communities to be characterized by "well-balanced and diversified land use patterns." Actually, balance has come to mean more than this physical characteristic. Balance especially means that a new community, by contrast to unbalanced bedroom suburbs, must contain a range of employment opportunities and housing for low- and moderate-income families.
3. Unity of planning and process. A new community is developed under one plan, in one program, by one developer. This unity of the development process is in sharp contrast to the usual process of piecemeal development of land areas fragmented into a multitude of single parcels owned by different developers with different objectives and development schedules. The loose guides of public zoning and planning cannot equal the benefits from a single ownership and plan.
4. "Packaging" concept. The federal New Communities Program is in part built on a packaging concept similar to the earlier model cities program.[31] Both the 1968 and 1970 new communities statutes provided for the supplementary grants, to be administered by HUD to serve especially as catalysts for packaging a wide range of federal

aids for new communities. Even in the absence of a federal program, however, the balance and comprehensiveness of a new community represent a potential ability to deliver an entire package of urban facilities and services to a site.

A Brief Legislative History. The characteristics of the new-community pattern of urban development stimulated a number of federal legislative proposals for new-community programs during the early 1960s. As early as 1961 the proposed Open Space and Urban Development Act of 1961 included a provision authorizing 10- to 15-year loans to state and local public agencies for the purchase of open land for later disposition for private development, including new communities. The provision failed to pass. The administration's proposed Housing and Urban Development Acts in both 1965 and 1966 included authorizations for 15-year loans to state land-development agencies to finance the acquisition and development of land for new communities. Congress deleted these authorizations before passing the legislation.

Although care was taken to avoid comparing these proposals to British new-town policy, they were opposed, at least in part, as undue government intrusion into the private land-development system. They also were opposed or ill-supported by some of the urban public-interest groups, usually advocates of new ideas for planning and development, as potentially diluting both the economic life of the cities and the federal urban aids.

The most that Robert Weaver, administrator of the Housing and Home Finance Agency and first secretary of HUD, could get in the form of new-community legislation was Title X, a 1965 addition to the basic mortgage insurance statute, which authorized insuring loans for large-scale development.[32] The terms of Title X insurance apparently were not attractive enough to private developers; by 1967 the program was still almost unused.

In 1967 President Johnson appointed a Task Force on New Towns comprised of senior officials from several federal departments and agencies. Charles M. Haar, HUD's assistant secretary for metropolitan development, was named chairman. With consultant and in-house staff help, the task force soon arrived at these conclusions:

1. The new communities system of development represented an advantageous way of accomplishing many national goals and providing a superior environment.

2. An effective, and most legislatively feasible, federal program should use private developers.
3. The chief impediment to the successful use of private developers was a lack of sufficient patient money from normal lending sources.

In its report submitted to the president in October 1967 the Task Force recommended, "A program of Federal guarantees of the financing of entrepreneurs who spur the development of new communities; and Grant and loan incentives to public bodies participating in the development of new communities."[33]

The task force also recommended a special program of assistance for moderate-income housing.

The New Communities Act of 1968. In February 1968 President Johnson's "Message on Housing and Cities" announced a proposed New Communities Act of 1968:

For the lender and developer, this Act will provide a major new financing method.

A federally guaranteed "cash flow" debenture will protect the investment of private backers of new communities at competitive rates of return. At the same time it will free the developer from the necessity to make large payments on his debts, until cash returns flow from the sale of developed land for housing, shops and industrial sites.

For the local and State government, the Act will offer incentives to channel jointly financed programs for public facilities into the creation of new communities. The incentives will take the form of an increased Federal share in these programs.[34]

The act was introduced in Congress as Title IV of the administration's proposed Housing and Urban Development Act of 1968. In hearings on the act, the new communities title was supported by organizations such as the American Institute of Planners, the American Institute of Architects, and Urban America. It was opposed as a further government invasion of the private sector by the U.S. Chamber of Commerce and the National Association of Real Estate Boards. In a rather neutral position were the National Conference of Mayors, the National Association of Housing and Redevelopment Officials, and the National Association of Home Builders.

Although Senator John G. Tower of Texas introduced an amendment to strike Title IV from the bill during the Senate floor debate, the amendment failed to carry, and Title IV was passed by the Senate. In the House Committee, however, new communities had rough sledding. Title IV passed in the subcommittee by one vote, but failed to get through the full committee. Title IV was, however, saved in conference. The conference committee agreed to include the Senate version of Title IV with a minor modification; in late July 1968, both House and Senate agreed to the conference report on the 1968 HUD act.

Title IV authorized two basic aids for new-community developments:

1. Federal guarantees of the obligations issued by private new-community developers up to $50 million per community. The repayment of these loans could be geared to the cash flow of the project—that is, repayment of principal could be deferred during the early planning development years when outgo exceeded income.
2. Supplementary grants to increase the federal share of the costs of certain basic facilities. These grants, plus the basic grants for projects such as water, sewer, and open space, would be made to the local government jurisdiction covering the new-community site.

The statute placed the administration of the new program in a Community Development Corporation in the Department of Housing and Urban Development.

It was a little over a year before HUD announced its first commitment to guarantee the debt obligations of a new community. In February 1970 Secretary Romney announced a guarantee of $21 million for Jonathan, a satellite new community planned on 5000 acres 20 miles southwest of Minneapolis, Minnesota. By the close of the year, HUD had approved four other new-community projects.

The Legislative Marriage of New Communities and National Growth Policy. Although the legislative history of Title IV placed it within the context of broad national community-development goals, the Urban Growth and New Community Act of 1970 had to clarify the relation of new communities to specific objectives of a national growth policy. We traced the development of the growth-policy aspects, part A of this statute, in the first section of this chapter; part B created a new statutory base for the federal New Communities Program.

The Urban Growth and New Community Development Act of 1970 became Title VII of the Housing and Urban Development Act of 1970. The basic guarantee authority and supplementary-grant concept in the 1968 statute were incorporated in Title VII, but it also provided the following additional incentives and support for new-community development:

1. Interest grants to public developers to compensate for increased interest charges for the issuance of taxable bonds.
2. Interest loans to assist developers in paying interest costs during early development years.
3. Special planning grants to developers to help develop plans concerning social or environmental problems or for the use of new and advanced technology.
4. Public service grants to cover the costs of providing essential public services during the first three years of the development period.

The statute stated a set of requirements for eligibility for federal assistance. In brief, a Title VII supported new community was required to:

1. Provide an alternative to disorderly urban growth or to help reverse migration from existing cities or rural areas.
2. Be economically feasible.
3. Contribute to the welfare of the entire area.
4. Be physically and socially consistent with comprehensive planning.
5. Have all required state and local approvals.
6. Be well-balanced, with diversified land-use patterns and adequate public, community, and commercial facilities.
7. Provide an appropriate proportion of housing for low- and moderate-income families.
8. Make use of advances in design and technology.

As of January 1976 a total of 16 new communities had been approved for federal assistance, including those previously approved under the 1968 Title IV program. At maturity these communities were to contain almost 900,000 people on a total of 91,793 acres of land (see Table 1).

The Potential of New Communities to Achieve the Objectives of National Growth Policy. The Title VII legislative linking of the New Communities Program with a mandate to begin developing a national policy of urban growth indicates the perception of a strong role for new communities in achieving the objectives of the policy. In the following discussion of why this perception seems logical, we condense national growth policy into two basic objectives: a good balance in the national or regional distribution of populations and orderly growth in metropolitan regions.

Balance is not defined, but it is commonly understood to mean increasing the growth of rural regions or smaller cities while slowing the growth of large urban areas. Congress restated this objective in the Agriculture Act of 1970: "The Congress commits itself to a sound balance between rural and urban America. The Congress considers this balance so essential to the peace, prosperity, and welfare of all our citizens that the highest priority must be given to the revitalization and development of rural areas."[35] Attempts to create balanced (rural) growth certainly cannot overcome the demographic facts of life: natural increase plus foreign immigration will continue to expand most existing metropolitan regions, but this process should be orderly, unlike the sprawl of the past.

The potential of new communities—either as freestanding communities or as major additions to "growth center" existing towns or cities—to redress the lack of urban-rural balance is derived from the capacity of new communities to deliver comprehensive urban facilities and services, many of them drawing on federal aid. A new community can deliver housing, infrastructure, social services, and amenities that can attract and hold the economic development that is the life blood of any program for rural development. In the competitive world of industrial development, a manufacturer can be offered both industrial sites and the real promise of supporting housing, adequate public facilities—in brief, a total community.

A description of the potential use of new communities to develop our rural areas should not obscure the reality of how difficult it would be to use new communities to produce any significant shift in economic activity and population distribution away from the large urban centers. To build a freestanding new community requires the resolution of complex problems of finance, market, timing, and sponsorship, problems that are not encountered to the same degree by the satellite new community.

At any rate, recent population trends indicate that the lack of urban-rural balance may be redressing itself. Estimates of the U.S. Bureau of the Census disclose:

By mid-1974 the population in metropolitan America is estimated to have reached 155 million. This is an increase

Table 1 New Communities Approved Under The Federal New Communities Program, March 1976

Name	Type	Location (nearest city)	Size (acres)	Projected Population	Projected Dwelling Units	Projected Employment
Cedar-Riverside	New town in-town (NTIT)	Minneapolis, Minnesota	100	31,250	13,039	4,609
Flower Mound	Satellite	Dallas, Texas	6,156	64,141	18,326	16,454
Gananda	Satellite	Rochester, New York	5,847	55,808	9,500	12,890
Harbison	Satellite	Columbia, South Carolina	1,734	23,558	7,362	7,071
Jonathan	Satellite	Minneapolis, Minnesota	8,914	50,000	15,504	14,143
Maumelle	Satellite	Little Rock, Arkansas	5,221	33,131	10,863	22,937
Newfields	Satellite	Dayton, Ohio	4,032	40,000	12,218	5,643
Park Forest, South	Satellite	Chicago, Illinois	8,163	110,000	38,214	28,633
Riverton	Satellite	Rochester, New York	2,434	25,632	8,010	11,180
Shenandoah	Satellite	Atlanta, Georgia	7,200	69,000	23,000	24,000
Soul City	Freestanding	Raleigh/Durham, North Carolina	5,287	44,000	13,326	8,200
St. Charles	Satellite	Washington, D.C.	7,600	79,145	27,730	14,890
Woodlands	Satellite	Houston, Texas	16,937	150,000	49,160	40,000
Radisson[a]	Satellite	Syracuse, New York	2,700	18,300	5,000	12,614
Roosevelt Island[a]	NTIT	New York, New York	147	18,000	5,000	5,300
San Antonio Ranch[b]	Satellite	San Antonio, Texas	9,318	87,972	29,476	17,990
Total			91,793	899,937	285,728	246,554
Average			5,737			

[a] Publicly sponsored projects by the New York State Urban Development Corporation. No Title VII guarantees were requested.
[b] No Title VII guaranteed loans have been issued.

of 5 million or 3.4 percent since 1970. Almost three-quarters of our population (73.2 percent) now lives in metropolitan areas compared with 56 percent in 1950.

During the 1970–1974 period the nonmetropolitan population by comparison grew 5.5 percent. This is a rare period in recent American history when nonmetropolitan America has grown faster than its metropolitan counterpart.[36]

Some nonmetropolitan growth seems destined to take place in connection with the development of energy resources, especially in the sparsely settled coal and uranium regions of the Rocky Mountain states. The building of small new communities would seem to be a logical way to deliver the needed housing, infrastructure, and urban services required by

the influx of construction and operating personnel that will otherwise overwhelm the existing small towns.

The Objective of Orderly Growth. Although most of the concern over a lack of a national growth policy to guide the development of metropolitan regions has focused on the sprawling growth at the suburban edges, the interdependence of city and suburb requires an equal concern over the decline of urban centers. Policies intended to create orderly growth must reflect an objective for the redevelopment and revitalization of the inner city.

Two types of new communities can be used to carry out plans for the rational growth and redevelopment of metropolitan areas: satellite communities and new towns in-town.

Satellite New Communities. The basic genius of a new community as a growth-ordering device flows from the unity of its process for planning and development—one large site, one plan, one developer, and one integrated development program. The integrity of this process stands in sharp contrast to the alternative process for the same area of land—piecemeal, haphazard development by a multitude of owners under a multitude of plans unrelated as to scheduling and only loosely and ineffectively coordinated by public planning.

Unity of process and the scale of new communities foster an ability to achieve many desirable growth-policy subobjectives within the context of orderly growth.

1. Capturing growth and creating well-ordered, attractive communities, which should engender great concern for, and participation in, the well-being of the communities.
2. Making efficient use of land and reducing the costs of facilities and services. Various studies (including studies of Reston, Virginia, and Howard County, the county in which Columbia, Maryland, is located[37]) have provided estimates of local savings and tax benefits derived from a pattern of new-community development. A study of several different types of development, *The Costs of Sprawl*, estimated considerable savings in the capital costs of producing planned development versus sprawl.[38] For example, the study estimated the capital costs of land acquisition and development to be $10,613 per acre less in a planned-mix development, which is comparable to a new community, than in typical low-density sprawl. These benefits, of course, are made possible by the densities, scale, and sound planning in new-community developments.
3. Providing balanced development, which means, first, a balance of housing types and prices that are marketed in complete conformity with fair housing objectives. Some 28 percent of the housing planned for Title VII new communities will be for low- and moderate-income families. Second, it means providing a complete community in the sense of balancing housing with industrial, commercial, and other development, which offers a range of employment opportunities. Plans for the

16 approved Title VII new communities* projected 246,500 jobs within the communities. The balance between housing and other land uses contributes to a saving of metropolitan transportation costs and provides an opportunity to walk to work for those who desire to do so. This has obvious implications for energy-saving policies.

Because satellite new communities basically capture the strong growth operating in the burgeoning urban regions of the nation and therefore enjoy relative certainty of continuing markets for residential, industrial, and commercial land, such new communities are most prevalent. In the Title VII program 13 of the 16 approved communities as of January 1976 were satellites.

New Towns In-Town. The rapid growth of suburbia may have contributed to sapping the strength of urban centers. The suburbs have attracted people and jobs. In congressional testimony, Anthony Downs referred to an analysis in the *New York Times* of October 15, 1972, which showed that between 1960 and 1970 the suburbs of the 15 largest metropolitan areas gained a total of 3.1 million new jobs, whereas their central cities lost 836,000 jobs.[39] Decay, abandoned buildings, and a weakening tax base have impeded the city's effort to renew itself.

New-community development might help achieve for the cities some of the same benefits that satellites achieve for the suburbs. Although having similar objectives as suburban-growth new communities, new towns in-town must be developed on more limited sites and at much higher densities than satellites. New communities within cities may be effective in creating strong nodes of balanced residential, commercial, and industrial growth on vacant sites in cities and also may exert a strong influence on the stability and rehabilitation of adjacent neighborhoods. The federal Surplus Land Program will contribute to the development of some new towns in-town, as in the case of Fort Lincoln in Washington, D.C. Approved Title VII new communities include two new towns in-town: Cedar-Riverside in Minneapolis and Roosevelt Island in New York City.

Related Objectives. Although it is helpful to consider balance and order as the two basic objec-

---

* In this article, "Title VII new communities" or "Title VII program" includes Title IV approved projects.

tives of a national growth policy, it is also an oversimplification of the complex requirements for such a policy. The new-community process of development offers a potentially effective way to achieve other objectives or subobjectives of a growth policy. These are summarized in the following paragraphs.

Protecting the Environment. The sprawled growth of metropolitan regions created by tract development is especially destructive to land and other ecological resources. Tract developers bare the land to erosion, silt the streams, unknowingly cover aquifer recharge areas, and fill the wetlands necessary to an ecological balance. Again, the integrity and scale of the new-community process permit realization of a carefully planned design that preserves the land and valuable areas of natural resources. The scale of development provides a flexibility in design not feasible for a tract developer.

The plans for the approved 16 new communities call for the preservation of some 24 percent of the land in open space. Some of it will be devoted to active recreation; other areas will provide passive recreation while preserving areas of environmental significance.

Encouraging Innovation. One of the most valuable resources—which must be fostered by a national growth policy—is the ability of our decentralized system of government and entrepreneurship to be creative. The extreme of disorderly, piecemeal growth by a multitude of developers, however, severely limits innovation. By contrast, development of large sites for *new* communities offers a superior potential for devoting a part of the efforts to experimentation, which may be social, financial, governmental, or technical. Because they "start from scratch" and are often free of restrictive codes and zoning—and rigid attitudes about social institutions—new communities represent a promising framework for advancing the art of community building and living.

Innovations being considered for approved Title VII new communities include wide-band cable television, tertiary sewage treatment and water recycling, special health services, a heating plant using solid waste for fuel, a carless community, and a central vacuum solid-waste disposal system.

The Record. As Table 1 shows, 16 new communities have been approved for assistance under the federal New Communities Program. They range in size from 100 to almost 17,000 acres. Two of the projects are new towns in-town, one is a freestanding new community, and the remainder are satellites to existing cities. The satellite communities are projected to contain a considerable amount of basic employment, a requirement under the federal program.

There are, of course, many other non-Title VII, large-scale projects in various stages of development. In 1974 the Urban Land Institute published a "New Community Checklist" of 143 new communities. Many of these probably would not qualify for Title VII assistance because of a lack either of housing for low- and moderate-income families or a strong employment base.[40] A recently completed survey of 141 U.S. new towns disclosed a current population of 984,863.[41]

Potential versus Harsh Realities: The Moratorium. By 1974 the potential of the Title VII-aided new communities to demonstrate one way of achieving the objective of national growth policy—especially in ordering metropolitan expansion—had encountered the realities of an economic recession that most severely affected the land development, housing, and construction industries. In April 1975 Otto G. Stolz, general manager of the New Community Development Corporation,* reported to HUD's Appropriation's Subcommittee in the Congress that

Three projects currently have a zero or nominal cash balance in their escrow account, and, absent refinancing, it is currently projected that 7 out of the 13 financially assisted new communities will exhaust their available cash in the next 6 months. These existing projects constitute an aggregate financial commitment by the Federal Government of $354 million. Thus, a major effort must be made with the owners and financial institutions to refinance these projects. However, despite all of our efforts, the serious mistakes of the past and the present economic conditions may result in substantial financial losses to the Federal Government due to the failure of some of the new community projects.[42]

The "serious mistakes of the past" include a number of planning and management deficiencies of both the project developers and the New Communities Administration (NCA) in HUD. These defi-

---

* The Community Development Corporation was changed to the New Community Development Corporation by the Housing and Community Development Act of 1974.

ciencies include (1) projections of development costs that were far below those actually incurred, in part due to high inflation rates, and (2) projections of revenues based on unrealistically optimistic estimates of land sales, even if the recession had not occurred. The squeeze was compounded by the costs of carrying the debt and other overhead created by the large front-end expenditures for the facilities and amenities thought to be needed to support sales of land for housing. Thus the precarious condition of many of the projects was not a result solely of the state of the economy, but was due in some significant measure to other factors—either human errors or flaws in the structure of the Title VII program itself.

At any rate, the troublesome financial condition of the Title VII projects led HUD, in January of 1975, to declare a moratorium on new applications for assistance. This action permitted NCA staff resources to be focused on the existing 16 projects, of which 13 had Title VII guaranteed debt. (Two of the other three approved projects were sponsored by the state of New York and did not request a federal guarantee; the third project had not issued guaranteed debentures.) The moratorium also would give the staff time to determine which of the most troubled projects might be acquired by HUD in order to restructure the financing or change the physical plans.

Program Evaluations.   The new-community concept and the Title VII program have been evaluated in a number of studies since 1974. The most thorough analysis of the concept was made at the Center for Urban and Regional Studies at the University of North Carolina. The study, funded by the National Science Foundation, gathered information, primarily through personal interview surveys, from 36 communities including 17 new communities, two of which are in the federal program. The basic support for the study findings was derived from a comparison of conditions and perceptions in the new communities with those in conventional, control communities. The major findings of the advantages of new communities were summarized as follows:

The outputs of new community development processes were in many respects superior to those of conventional community growth. The advantages in favor of new communities included: (1) better land use planning and access to community facilities; (2) reduction in automobile travel; (3) superior recreational facilities; (4) enhanced community livability; and (5) improved living environments for low- and moderate-income households, blacks, and the elderly.[43]

Other aspects of the community environment, such as satisfaction with the quality of life and the provision of some community services—often beyond the control of the developer—were found to be essentially the same in both new and conventional communities.

An evaluation of the New Communities Program by a staff of HUD reached different conclusions about the benefits of new communities from those of the North Carolina study, even though the staff had access to preliminary data of the latter. The HUD staff report, the "PD&R Report" concluded that new communities produce environments only "marginally more satisfying than that provided by less-planned development," and that any additional federal assistance should be directed at increasing innovative activity in new communities.[44]

The innovative potential of the program was one focus of recommendations made by the staff of a congressional appropriations committee. The staff report[45] calls for turning the current Title VII projects into government supported "living urban laboratories." The overall tone of this report, however, was similar to the PD&R report:

In total, new communities have not reached the high expectations of their proponents. Many of the areas in which new communities have done well have been matched by other forms of urban development, with less cost and risks to the developers, less Federal involvement, and fewer administrative problems. The concensus appears to be that new community development on a national scale is not feasible as originally envisioned, and that alternative forms of urban development should be explored and encouraged, including planned unit development and improved State and local government land use planning.[46]

In a criticism of the report, Stolz remarked that the subjective nature of some of its findings were inaccurate and misleading.[47] In his general comments he noted that the report emphasizes the negative aspects of new communities, overlooks the positive achievements, confuses Title VII with non-Title VII new communities (which do not have the same goals), and does not adequately document many of its assertions. As an example of his criticism, he questioned why the report reaches a conclusion that new communities are only "marginally superior" when a number of seemingly substantial achievements are also cited. These criticisms are also generally applicable to the PD&R report that had been extensively used as a reference source by the appropriation's committee staff.

Although it is not an evaluation of new towns, *The Costs of Sprawl* provides substantial evidence of the economies and environmental benefits that are derived from the planning and densities achievable in a new-community pattern. The comparison of a development pattern of planned mix for a 6000 acre site of 10,000 dwelling units, a pattern comparable to a satellite new community, with a pattern of low-density sprawl, comparable to conventional urban sprawl, produced estimated differences such as the following:

1. The capital costs of development of planned mix, including land, are 30 percent less than those required for low-density sprawl.
2. Energy consumption (gasoline, natural gas, and electricity) is 26 percent less.
3. Air pollution (from automobiles and residences) is 35 percent less.
4. Auto travel time is 38 percent less.
5. Traffic accidents are 40 percent less.

Oversight Hearings. These and other program evaluations—and rebuttals—were considered at congressional oversight hearings in September 1975.[48] The House subcommittee heard testimony from people representing research and academic interests, financial institutions, developers of Title VII and non-Title VII projects, and HUD officials. In general, the witnesses seemed to accept the benefits of new communities as givens and concentrated instead on problems and solutions. The proposed solutions to the admittedly severe financial difficulties of the projects were varied. They include the following:

1. Reduce the size of projects to overcome the financial strain of carrying the heavy front-end costs of acquiring large land areas and building community type facilities.
2. Establish public land banking.
3. Fund all of the authorized financial aids in Title VII.
4. Provide federal grants for infrastructure facilities.
5. Convert the Title VII program to an experimental or demonstration program.
6. Develop housing and national growth policies as prerequisites for the success of a new-community policy.

The Key Issue. The solutions serve to identify the problems. In sum they raise the key issue of whether the current concept of the Title VII program is valid, assuming that the 1974–1975 recession, which was especially severe in the land development industry, was not the sole cause of the problems. Basic to resolving this issue is the question of whether Title VII properly allocates costs between the public and private sectors. Most of the solutions seem to involve shifting some of the costs—such as for land and basic infrastructure—from the private developer to some level of government.

Shifting costs, of course, raises the question of who benefits. Public provision of water and sewer lines increases the private developer's land values, and this benefit is not necessarily passed along to the public either as consumers or taxpayers. The point is that no balance sheet of benefits and costs has been developed that equitably relates these to the receivers and payers. Even to identify all the beneficiaries is a difficult task.

Therefore, it is not enough to conclude simply that under Title VII the private sector is being called upon to shoulder an excessive share of new-community costs and that more of the costs should be paid from public funds. It would seem reasonable to ask whether increased public costs should entitle the public to additional benefits—or some of the profits, if and when they ocur. Congressman Thomas Ludlow Ashley has suggested the answer in noting the probable need for governments to buy and hold land for future development and to finance the costs of basic infrastructure. He notes that this will "insure that the community will benefit from the land values created by the process of developing the new town."[49]

The dilemma is that these kinds of solutions are greeted by public apathy, perhaps because they are politically unacceptable. Ashley acknowledges that, with one or two notable exceptions, federal, state, and local governments have shown "little or no interest in large-scale development and even less concern about the need to develop a national growth policy."[50]

In this vein, perhaps James W. Rouse, the developer of Columbia, Maryland, has identified the cause of public apathy and the real reason new communities in the United States have not worked: "Truly, it is because they haven't yet been really tried."[51]

NOTES

1. "Housing Act of 1949," Public Law 171, Section 2, *United States Statutes at Large* 61 (1949):413–444.

2. "Housing and Urban Development Act of 1968," Public Law 90-448, Title IV, *United States Statutes at Large* 82 (1968).

3. "Urban Growth and New Community Development Act of 1970," Public Law 91-609, Title VII, *United States Statutes at Large* 84, Part 2 (1970). This act later became Title VII of the "Housing and Urban Development Act of 1970."

4. The terms *national urban growth policy*, and *growth policy* are used interchangeably in this chapter.

5. "Title VII, Housing and Urban Development Act of 1970," Section 702(d).

6. United States, Executive Office of the President, Domestic Council, *Report on National Growth 1972* (Washington, D.C.: U.S. Government Printing Office, 1972), p. xi.

7. The program of federal grants for state and local acquisition of parks and other open-space lands originally was provided in Title VII of the Housing Act of 1961. Grants for basic water and sewer facilities were authorized in Title VII of the Housing and Urban Development Act of 1965.

8. I recall reading (in an unidentified source) the results of a "choice-of-living" poll of the residents of Paris. Surprisingly, 54 percent of the interviewed Parisians expressed a desire to live elsewhere, if they could earn the same incomes.

9. Glenn V. Fuguitt and James J. Quiches, "Residential Preferences: Implications for Population Redistribution in Nonmetropolitan Areas," in *Commission Research Reports*, Vol. 5, *Population Distribution, and Policy*, Sara Mills Mazied, Ed. (Washington, D.C.: U.S. Government Printing Office, 1972).

10. Rachel Carson, *Silent Spring* (Boston: Houghton Mifflin, 1962); Donella Hager Meadows, D. L. Meadows, J. Randers, and W. W. Behrens III, *The Limits to Growth: A Report for the Club of Rome's Project on the Predicament of Mankind* (New York: Universe Books, 1972); The Commission on Population Growth and the American Future, *Population and the American Future* (New York: New American Library, 1973).

11. U.S. Advisory Commission on Intergovernmental Relations, *Urban and Rural America: Policies for Future Growth* (Washington, D.C.: U.S. Government Printing Office, 1968), p. 131.

12. National Committee on Urban Growth Policy, *The New City*, Donald Canty, Ed. (New York: Praeger, 1969), p. 172.

13. Daniel P. Moynihan, "Toward a National Urban Policy." Address on the occasion of the Annual Honors Convocation, Syracuse University, May 8, 1969.

14. National Goals Research Staff, *Toward Balanced Growth: Quantity with Quality* (Washington, D.C.: U.S. Government Printing Office, 1970).

15. Richard M. Nixon, The State of the Union Message, January 22, 1970.

16. *The Quality of Urban Life*, Hearings before the Ad Hoc Subcommittee on Urban Growth, Part 2, Committee on Banking and Currency, House of Representatives 1969-1970 (Washington, D.C.: U.S. Government Printing Office), p. 2.

17. "Housing and Urban Development Act of 1970," Title VII, Section 701(b).

18. *Ibid.*, Section (703(a).

19. United States, Executive Office of the President.

20. *Ibid.*, pp. ix-xii.

21. "Missing: One Policy" (editorial), *New York Times*, March 29, 1972, p. 42L.

22. *National Growth Policy*, Hearings Before the Subcommittee on Housing, Committee on Banking and Currency, House of Representatives, 92nd Congress, Second Session, June 1972.

23. *National Growth and Development*, Second Biennial Report to the Congress Submitted Pursuant to Section 703(a) of Title VII, Housing and Urban Development Act of 1970, prepared under the direction of the Committee on Community Development, the Domestic Council, December 1974.

24. *Staff Summary Report on the Oversight Hearings on the President's 1974 Report on National Growth and Development*, Subcommittee on Housing, Committee on Banking, Currency, and Housing, House of Representatives, 94th Congress, Second Session, February 1976.

25. *Ibid.*, pp. 13-14.

26. *1976 Report on National Growth and Development: The Changing Issues for National Growth*, Third Biennial Report to the Congress Submitted Pursuant to Section 703(a) of Title VII, Housing and Urban Development Act of 1970, prepared under the direction of the Committee on Community Development, the Domestic Council, February 1976.

27. Anthony Downs, "Testimony of Anthony Downs on National Public Works Investment Policy," presented to the Committee on Public Works, House of Representatives, November 1, 1973 (Washington, D.C.: U.S. Government Printing Office, 1973).

28. Rockefeller Brothers Foundation, *The Use of Land: A Citizens' Policy Guide to Urban Growth*, A Task Force Report Sponsored by the Rockefeller Brothers Fund (New York: Thomas Y. Crowell, 1973).

29. *Construction Industry Association of Sonoma County v. City of Petaluma*. In January 1974, the U.S. District Court for the Northern District of California invalidated the Petaluma plan. The U.S. Court of Appeals for the 9th Circuit overturned the lower court and upheld the plan.

30. Later became "Housing and Urban Development Act of 1970," Title VII.

31. "Demonstration Cities and Metropolitan Development Act of 1966," Public Law 89-754, Title I, *United States Statutes at Large* 80, Part 1 (1966):1255.

32. Title X of the National Housing Act, as added by Sec. 201 of the "Housing and Urban Development Act of 1965," Public Law 81-117, *United States Statutes at Large* **79** (1965). More liberal terms were provided by a 1966 amendment.

33. "Summary, Report of the Task Force on New Towns," Washington, D.C., October 16, 1967, unpublished.

34. Lyndon B. Johnson, *Message on Housing and Cities*, February 1968.

35. "Agriculture Act of 1970," Title IX, *United States Statutes at Large* 84, Part I (1970-1971):1358-1384.

36. Department of Commerce, Bureau of the Census, "Estimates of the Population of Metropolitan Areas, 1973 and 1974, and Components of Change Since 1970," in *Population Estimates and Projections*, Series P-25, No. 618 (Washington, D.C.: U.S. Government Printing Office, 1976).

37. The study of Reston was done by the management consultants Booz, Allen and Hamilton, Inc., Washington, D.C.: the Howard County study was done by the Howard County Planning Commission.

38. Real Estate Research Corporation, *The Costs of Sprawl* (Washington, D.C.: U.S. Government Printing Office, 1974).

39. Downs, p. 4.

40. "New Community Checklist," *Urban Land: News and Trends in Land Development* **30**, No. 4 (1974):17–19.

41. *New Towns and the U.S. Postal Service: Some Guidelines for Postal Officials and New Town Developers* (Washington, D.C.: U.S. Postal Service Headquarters, June 1975).

42. U.S. Congress, House, "Department of Housing and Urban Development: Independent Agencies," in *Hearings* before a Subcommittee of the Committee on Appropriations, House of Representatives, 94th Congress, First Session, 1975, p. 714.

43. Raymond J. Burby and Shirley F. Weiss, *New Communities USA* (Lexington, Mass.: D.C. Heath, 1976).

44. U.S. Department of Housing and Urban Development, Office of Program Analysis and Evaluation, Office of the Assistant Secretary for Policy Development and Research (PD&R), *Evaluation of the New Communities Program*, Evaluation Report number 1, April 1975. The report contained the following caution: "The analysis and conclusions are those of the Office of Program Analysis and Evaluation and do not necessarily reflect the opinion of the Department of Housing and Urban Development."

45. U.S. Department of Housing and Urban Development, Independent Agencies Appropriations for 1976, *Hearings* before a Subcommittee of the Committee on Appropriations, House of Representatives, 94th Congress, First Session, Part 5, 1975, pp. 740–797.

46. *Ibid.*, p. 740.

47. Department of Housing and Urban Development Independent Agencies Appropriations for 1976, p. 797.

48. *Oversight Hearings on the New Communities Program*, Hearings before the Subcommittee on Housing and Community Development of the Committee on Banking, Currency and Housing, House of Representatives, 94th Congress, First Session, September 23, 29 and 30, 1975.

49. Burby and Weiss, p. xx.

50. *Ibid.*, p. xviii.

51. *Oversight Hearings*, p. 98.

CHAPTER 19

Canadian New-Town Policy

NORMAN E. P. PRESSMAN

Urban settlements throughout Canadian history were most often started by deliberate design. In a country as young as Canada, where few settlements were built until the nineteenth century (with the exception of several small outposts of seventeenth- and eighteenth-century New France), the vast majority of urban centers can hardly be considered old, and in many respects they are still in the infancy of their development. In that they have all been founded and created during the past few centuries, with the major cities experiencing rapid growth only during the past 100 years in previously rural or unsettled landscape, all Canadian urban areas can be considered new towns.

New towns as planned urban centers, in the modern sense, claim honorable antecedents. As lands were opened up for settlement during the eighteenth and nineteenth centuries, town sites were usually laid out by military surveyors, who took little account of probable future development but often chose methods that allowed them to settle as quickly as possible. As a result, many communities today are based upon rectangular or gridiron patterns and plans. Farmlands were usually cleared in 150-acre units. Both French and British surveyors laid out waterfront lots as thin, rectilinear strips, the French

strips half as wide as the English. Because the standard measure of the surveyor, the chain, was 66 feet long, lots were often divided accordingly. Many towns in Upper Canada—for example, Kingston, established in 1784—were ruled off in lots 66 feet wide and 132 feet deep.

A few of the country's earliest communities were laid on a radial plan. The French king, upon his instructions to Intendant Jean Talon of New France, decided that the radial form would be more appropriate than the strip or ribbon plan for settlement in Quebec; and the villages of Charlesbourg, Bourg Royal, and Auvergne, all a few miles northwest of Quebec city, were created from a large square about a mile and a half on each side. These sides were then divided into 10 parts, and lines drawn from each of the division marks to the center cut the square into wedge-shaped lots of about 34 acres each. The radial plan followed the traditions of French village life and served a defensive purpose: while working in their outlying fields, settlers who were attacked by Indians could rush to the center of the village and ward off the invaders together.

If the owners of each lot were to follow their property to the center of town, they all would meet in a tight circle at the convergence of the radial properties, but before doing so they would have come to the edges of a smaller square surrounded by a road. Inside were the church, the cemetery, and the mills—the heart of the community. The settlers built their houses on both sides of this road, which was called the *trait-quarré*.

Most of the ideas for this paper were published in *Planning New Communities in Canada* (Urban Paper A.75.4), Ministry of State for Urban Affairs, Ottawa, Canada, August, 1975. They represent the views of the author and not necessarily those of the Ministry. The Canadian Council on Urban and Regional Research assisted the study through a grant awarded to the author.

Two English communities based on the radial plan were Guelph (1827) and Goderich (1829). These towns were both crucial to the development of the Canada Land Company's Huron Tract. Places like Niagara-on-the-Lake and Ottawa were founded in advance to serve as capital cities. New cities, such as Regina and Saskatoon, were models of town planning and landscape organization in the midst of virgin frontier prairie. Calgary and Vancouver were laid out on a gridiron system far in advance of westward migration.

Many of these planned communities have not experienced rapid growth, and indeed, some have even declined, but all retain traces of their original planning. Others, which were well-conceived and strategically located, have grown quickly in such a manner that their planning has long been forgotten, and their novelty has given way to a conventional look.

THE ROLE OF NEW COMMUNITIES AND URBAN GROWTH POLICY

Canadians, like people of all the developed nations, have become and will probably continue to be not just an urban, but a metropolitan people. The advantages that result from this metropolitan life can be summarized as diversity of opportunity, and they have already attracted to the metropolis a large, growing share of the Canadian people (nearly a quarter of all Canadians live in two metropolitan areas).

Some experts have suggested that the problems of metropolitan planning arise from rapid growth, rather than from absolute size. A deliberate policy goal to retard or control growth in metropolitan areas can be accomplished in only two ways:

1. To encourage other urban centers (of smaller size and growth rates) to grow to the point where they can act as effective countermagnets to already established metropolitan centers. Such a policy could both ease metropolitan growth pains and provide a stimulus to underdeveloped regions. This would entail a coherent approach to regional development based on a clear concept of federal planning, carefully integrated with provincial policy.
2. To disperse portions of metropolitan growth to new or existing satellites within the metropolitan

region: physically separate new or expanded communities, functionally linked to the central metropolis. This solution applies especially in provincial plans and is in effect embodied in Ontario's plan for the Toronto-centred region.

In this context, N. H. Lithwick mentions that future expansion must be fully integrated into the urban system. At the same time, it must not add to the land-use problems of the large metropolitan areas. This requires the siting of new development beyond the urbanized area. These two superficially conflicting requirements—integration with spatial divorce—lead to only one solution: the sequential development of new communities.[1]

A policy of new community development requires at least the following supporting programs:

1. Limiting sprawl at the pressure points.
2. Assisting growth where viable.
3. Developing new communities.

The Toronto-centred region (TCR) plan is a bold provincial policy statement concerned with the orderly distribution of population from the crowded, rapidly growing Toronto area. The strategy selected has been the designation of sites for expanded communities—in addition to the commencement of a new community—while settling basic guidelines for regional land use. Obviously, the vehicle of the new community alone is not the answer to problems of urban regions. It must be employed in conjunction with methods already in use—redevelopment, expansion, and infilling of existing centers and continuing suburbanization on the urban fringe close to existing development. However, new communities, whether used in regional, provincial, or national strategies, can achieve a number of important goals for Canada:

1. The addition of pleasing, comprehensive urban environments that emphasize aesthetics and natural surroundings. New communities stress unity of environment, and they usually contain more space than do conventional subdivisions.
2. The addition of massive numbers of housing units to the residential market in an ordered, properly phased manner.
3. The provision of spillover population from congested central cities.
4. The provision of a healthy alternative to urban sprawl, piecemeal development, and congestion.

5. The revival of declining areas and the balancing of rural/urban areas in terms of population numbers and distribution of human resources, expertise, and economic-base activities.
6. The provision of great, varied employment opportunities.
7. The recapturing of appreciated land values—and their recycling to recover the costs of infrastructure and of essential community services and facilities.
8. The aiding of central city renewal and rehabilitation. By building new communities as companion pieces, in addition to urban rebuilding, we can begin to absorb those people frequently displaced in the redevelopment process and to redevelop at higher densities than usual. A new-community policy might thus help in slowing down or, in reversing migratory trends to the large metropolitan areas, relieving certain inherent pressures.
9. The provision for innovation and experimentation, which could provide a basis for social and physical progress in the hope of attracting both private and public entrepreneurial leadership and imagination.
10. The establishment of entirely new, independent cities to act as growth poles of development (in urbanized regions or on the northern resource frontier) or to assist in the reorganization of small urban and rural settlements into large units, in which many good facilities may be provided.

Legislation for New-Community Development. There was no stated federal policy dealing with the founding of new communities in Canada until the 1973 amendments to the National Housing Act that have made provision for the New Communities Program. The province of Alberta has been the only one of Canada's 10 provinces to have passed a new towns act. Created in 1956, it was originally conceived as a flexible instrument to assist in the creation of new communities in both developing resource regions, such as the areas of some of the remote oilfields, and in urban-centered regions.

The act gives authority to the lieutenant governor in council, under the recommendation of the Provincial Planning Board, by order, to form a new town, "describe the boundaries . . . and state the date upon which the order becomes effective."[2] It requires that information be placed before the Provincial Planning Board to determine that the town is necessary, practical, and in the public interest. Generally, the act provides for initial capital front-end outlay, professional planning assistance to the proposed communities, and government and administrative handling and management of the entire process of new-town building from inception through implementation. Provisions are made to pay monies as required to meet all authorized current and capital expenditures for the development and operation of the new town through the means of grants, loans or advances, and purchase of debentures of the town. The act has found considerable application in the planning of such new communities as St. Albert and Mill Woods.

Spiralling costs and short supply of land in urban centers have prompted the call for an intergovernment land strategy to deal with immediate and long-range aspects of such dilemmas. A federal commitment of at least $100 million per year over a five-year period for the public assembly of land (land banking) and assistance for new communities was made available. Amendments in 1973 to the land assembly provisions of the National Housing Act encourage government participation in land assembly and introduced a new communities section to assist in the accommodation of urban growth and promote the development of regional growth centers. Section 45 of the act makes assistance available through the Central Mortgage and Housing Corporation (CMHC), by way of cost-sharing agreements or through its participation in the acquisition of lands for such communities, which are defined as follows:

A "new community" is an area of planned urban growth having all the facilities of a self-contained community. Spatially separated from an established community, it may be independent in its economic base or integrated with an existing urban centre. In addition, the new community must provide a provincial response to one or more of the following objectives: (1) To promote means of urban growth other than by the continued expansion of existing major centres; (2) To provide a mechanism for the establishment of new regional growth centres; and (3) To facilitate the balanced development of resource-based new communities.[3]

The term *new community* seems appropriate to the type of developments now being proposed and constructed in Canada, and because this term is used in the National Housing Act, it is used for the remainder of this chapter.

The lending arrangement for land assembly,[4] which expired by statute on March 31, 1972, has been broadened and established as a continuing program with 90 percent loans available for any purpose having to do with housing. A loan may be made to a province, a municipality with provincial approval, or a publicly owned housing agency. The loan amount may not exceed 90 percent of the cost of acquisition, clearance, planning, and servicing of the land, as determined by the CMHC. The new arrangement provides for debentures, as well as mortgages, to be used as security for the federal loan. In addition, where the province or municipality intends to lease the land and thereby keep it in public ownership, the term of the loan will be extended to 50 years from the normal 25 years. Repayment is possible during the term of the loan or as the land is disposed of, according to agreed terms.

This legislation makes it possible to assist provinces by either a loan and forgiveness mechanism or a partnership cost-sharing agreement. Loans are available to public agencies for 90 percent of the cost of site selection and acquisition of land, including linking corridors with other communities, open space, and planning and servicing.

To encourage the rapid development of recreational and social facilities, CMHC may forgive up to 50 percent of that portion of the loan covering acquisition of land for these purposes. A forgiveness of an amount not exceeding 50 percent of the part of the loan used for initial planning costs may also be approved. This would include salaries, accommodation, and expenses of the new-community development corporation and necessary consultants to provide overall administration, site investigations, surveys, background research, conceptual plans, overall development plans as may be required by the provinces, and detailed phasing of layout and urban design. As an alternative to borrowing, a province may enter into a federal-provincial partnership under which the federal government would share up to 75 percent of the capital costs and profits or losses.

In parallel with this new program, the Ministry of State for Urban Affairs is expected to promote the coordination and channeling of the appropriate programs and aids of other federal departments and agencies in the direction of new-community development. Additional grants are available through the Ministry of State for Urban Affairs and through the National Housing Act for both the loan and cost-sharing agreements. These facilitate new-community experiments in fields such as urban transportation and communications, mixed land-use concepts in contrast to traditional zoning practices, endeavors to reduce urban pollution, and new management techniques in community development. The New Communities Program is intended to complement the land assembly program now available under the National Housing Act.

The New Communities Program contains certain conditional features that must be satisfied prior to the acceptance of an application:

1. A province must establish an agency or corporation to run the program.
2. The new community must be decided in the context of a provincial urban growth strategy.
3. The public must receive any economic benefits derived from the disposal of land to the private sector.

New Towns and the Quality of Life. New problems emerged during the massive exodus from the city centers after World War II. Urban sprawl devoured the land and endless rows of houses—produced in cookie-cutter fashion—were situated in the landscape. This result produced a monotony that offended the eye and troubled the human spirit. More land was taken up for single-family houses than was necessary, and property values rose unrealistically. The resulting low population densities have limited the amount of land that could have been used to generate good tax income and provide community services. The suburban homeowner was being taxed heavily for low-density living, while the need for community services was on the rise.

As evidenced by the advent of recent federal new communities programs, urban problems and rural difficulties are not separate. The cities, where initial emphasis was placed, were merely reflecting and reinforcing the problems of the rural areas. These national issues were to create the need for national policies for urban growth, as embodied in the recent legislation. The new amendments to the National Housing Act directly imply that new-community development can be considered one possible, effective tool in the achievement of national urbanization policy to improve the overall quality of life for Canadians. Such stated policy, combined with forms of new-community development, should attempt to attain the following goals:

1. Favor patterns of urbanization and economic development and stabilization that offer a range of

alternative locations and encourage the wise, balanced use of physical and human resources in metropolitan regions, as well as in small urban areas that have the potential for accelerated growth.

2. Foster the continued economic strength of all regions of Canada, including central cities, suburbs, small communities, local neighborhoods, and rural areas.

3. Assist in reversing the trends of migration and physical growth that reinforce disparity among provinces, regions, and cities.

4. Treat comprehensively the problems of poverty and employment (including the erosion of tax bases and the need for better community services and job opportunities), which are associated with disorderly urbanization and rural decline.

5. Develop means for encouraging good, innovative housing for all Canadians.

6. Refine the roles of federal and provincial governments in revitalizing existing communities and encouraging planned, large-scale new developments.

7. Strengthen the capability of government institutions to contribute to balanced urban growth and stabilization.

8. Encourage desirable patterns of urban growth, the prudent use of natural resources, and the protection of the environment and its enhancement.

If they are to be all that the term connotes, rather than mere glorified subdivisions, new communities should provide a major array of public and social services. This implies that the new community itself is not simply a grandiose and romantic reconfiguration of a basic land-use form, but an emerging new social, government form as well. It must provide for fulfillment through access to public facilities and services of high orders and varying types, while allowing for effective means of expression.

Although the resolution of our social and economic ills will not necessarily follow from seeking to establish, in microcosmic form, profiles within new communities similar to those found within the urban regions, one of the fundamental reasons for establishing these new communities has very much to do with this thing we refer to as the "quality of life"—that is, a high standard of living in the form of access to various amenities, an opportunity to fulfill personal and group goals, and relief from many undesirable aspects of urban life.

Quality of life may also imply a certain time that accompanies new-town development. The level of

services in association with the scale and composition of population at any given time may have as much to do with a successful quality of life as would be the case at ultimate development. Considerable thought must therefore be given to early development and its impact on personal and overall community life.

TYPES OF NEW COMMUNITIES

Modern Canadian new communities can be classified into several distinct categories:

1. Independent (freestanding) communities developed
   (a) For nodal strategy or communications reasons
   (b) For public or administrative functions
   (c) For resource exploitation (single-enterprise)
2. Satellite towns (of limited function and entirely dependent)
3. Suburban cities
4. Expanded new communities (regional growth centers)

Independent Communities. Most Canadian new communities are independent or single-enterprise, based upon resource exploitation. These resource communities tend to be specific point developments, and in many instances have limited futures and functions. Canada's huge undeveloped areas and their various primary resources have resulted in many somewhat small, company-town communities to serve the labor needs of the resource extraction industry. A 1953 survey indicated that Canada had more than 166 single-enterprise communities with a combined population of some 189,000 inhabitants. Sixty towns had been built since 1945, and in the period of 1953–1972, approximately 20 additional communities were founded. Rex Lucas estimates that there are approximately 636 single-industry communities in Canada, with a combined population of 903,401. These tend to be small, with only a handful having populations exceeding 8000. Nevertheless, nearly 1 million people in Canada are directly affected by the qualities intrinsic to communities of single industry.[5]

Resource-Based Single-Enterprise Communities. The common characteristic of all these towns is that they have been created by the fiat of a single authority, usually a private industrial company but on occasion government agencies. The majority have been planned *ab initio* and have been for the most part the products of industrial entrepreneurs in Canada and the United States, who have had to face the fact that the creation of a new town in the wilderness is often a necessary evil if the Canadian forest, minerals, oil, fish, and hydroelectric power sources are to be exploited.

Unfortunately, the single-industry community, despite its best intentions, has inherent weaknesses that are often difficult to surmount. The normal functions, responsibilities, and civic freedom of an organized municipality are often lacking; company paternalism takes the place of personal responsibility and initiative in a wide range of social and political activities. The company, by necessity or by choice, is employer, landlord, storekeeper, town council, recreation director, and education supervisor. In most towns the company also provides the fire department, maintenance services, and even the police service. As a result, the towns tend to be economically and physically unstable, with a high turnover rate for professionals and other employees.

In many towns the sites are so isolated geographically and the terrain is so unfavorable for road building that no roads lead to outside settlements. Often automobiles are brought in on railway flat cars or even aboard ship even though their utility is strictly limited.

There has been an increased interest in the creation of model planned industrial communities embodying concepts held to be desirable by most modern planners and urban designers. Prominent examples are Kitimat, British Columbia; Terrace Bay, Ontario; and Fermont, Quebec. Many companies, however, consider that planning is none other than surveying of housing lots, streets, and sidewalks in the traditional housing subdivision of rectilinear block design. Their own engineering departments prepare their planning studies. Recently a noticeable trend toward cooperation by industrial companies with provincial governments and agencies is occurring in the establishment of new-town sites.

Some companies have abdicated their control and operation of townsites because their once remote locations have become readily accessible due to improved communications and transportation. Others still continue to open up new sites in areas where the scarcity of existing populated centers of either an urban or rural nature permit no alternative to the creation of new communities through single enterprise—industrial development requires the establishment of townsites within a period of a few

months, instead of the traditionally gradual transition from hamlet to village to town to city. Nevertheless, the once all-powerful paternalistic company dictatorships common to the history of new company towns in the first three to four decades of this century have all but vanished in Canada. Among the causes are the counterbalancing power of the labor unions, the churches, and the provincial government and the impersonal nature of the present large-scale industrial corporation in which ownership is separated from management. Usually industrial companies proposing to pioneer in the resource frontier are encouraged by the provincial authorities to join with one or more other enterpreneurs, as well as with the provincial agencies, in the creation of multi-enterprise, instead of single-enterprise communities.[6]

The strong interdependence among the resource, the production plant, and the community has functioned to weaken the ability of single-enterprise towns to survive for any appreciable length of time. Their chance for long-term viability is often weakened by a number of external forces, such as (1) resource depletion, causing progressively acute unemployment; (2) decreasing competitive advantage of some Canadian primary resources in international markets; (3) demand for resources and various raw materials, which is strongly influenced by prevailing national and international economic climates, changes in technology, consumer preferences, and so on. Such factors contribute to economic instability in the towns, reflected in the willingness of residents to remain only temporarily. Such impermanence also places heavy financial burdens on the parent companies.

The usual location of the site will be determined by the location of the particular resource to be extracted (see Figure 1). Due to isolated location and the absence of competing land uses, land costs are usually low. Because large tracts of land are often under single ownership, the land is easily acquired. These factors are in part offset by high construction costs necessitated by transportation factors and the need for skilled labor. Until rather recently, the private company financed all site servicing and works.

Company housing rental policies have potentially reinforced the company town and created antagonism toward it. Rapidly rising costs of building have caused some companies to sell rather than rent accommodation and to divest themselves of retail store ownership in favor of separate, private, commercial operations.

Canada lays claim to an exceedingly large number of small, specialized, planned, new company towns that can be found in almost all frontier regions. Some, like Kirkland Lake, Ontario (1911, gold mining) or Coniston, Ontario (1934, nickel) are now in locations that pose a number of problems after these regions have been woven into the fabric of overall settlement. Significant differences between the planned community size and actual population of new towns illustrate a phenomenon that is, with few exceptions, characteristic of single-enterprise communities. Prince Rupert, British Columbia (1909) provides an example. The town was originally conceived on a grand scale, as a "doorway to the East," with a target population of 100,000. However, a subsequent failure of the port facilities to develop on the scale anticipated resulted in stunted growth, with the 1966 population barely exceeding 15,000.

Many of these communities have become important elements within their regions, with considerable guidance of the related pattern of communications and settlement by senior levels of government. Some examples are:

1. Kitimat (British Columbia)—some 400 miles north of Vancouver, providing a major employment base for the Nechako-Kemano power scheme. Built by the Aluminum Company of Canada (ALCAN) with advice from Clarence Stein, the town is based on principles of the Radburn plan. This is one of the country's successful ventures, and the community has been integrated into the regional settlement framework. It is considered one of the most significant of North American modern contributions to planning principles and practice, and one of the few examples on this continent to compare in scale and character with the British new towns.[7]

2. Arvida (Quebec)—founded by ALCAN in 1926 to exploit the Saguenay River's power for aluminum production.

3. Thompson (Manitoba)—a rapidly growing nickel-mining town, with a population close to 10,000.

4. Grand Prairie (Alberta)—planned to serve as a regional center.

5. Elliot Lake and Manitouwadge (Ontario)—built

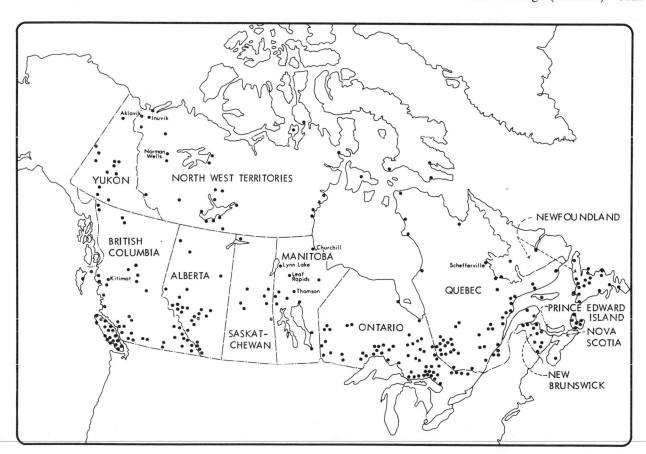

Figure 1. Communities of single enterprise in Canada.

respectively for uranium mining and smelting, these are fine examples of government planned and controlled towns, which have transposed metropolitan suburbia to the wilderness.

6. Churchill (Manitoba) and Moosonee (Ontario)—essentially abortive attempts to create major ocean ports on Hudson Bay and James Bay, respectively.

7. Labrador City and Sept-Iles (Quebec)—founded on the north shore of the St. Lawrence River in response to the need for iron ore.

8. Lanigan (Saskatchewan)—an expanded new town created to cope with potash resources.

9. Corner Brook (Newfoundland)—created in 1915 as a pulp and paper town.

10. Churchill Falls (Labrador)—a response to the need for power.

11. Deep River (Ontario)—developed in 1945 in reply to the needs of the Canadian atomic energy and heavy-water production program.

These are only a few of the significant developments. Most of the planned communities of single enterprise exhibit layouts that appear typically suburban. Pine Point in the North West Territories (1961) is characteristic of some of the well-organized, single-family, suburban types, with some multiple dwellings for single workers. The community has a licensed motel, service industries, supermarket, a school, a public park, and buildings. Some, like Lynn Lake in Manitoba, have had to be entirely relocated when the basic function declined. Nearly all are vulnerable to drastic changes in economies and frequently have limited futures. Some of the choice situations have potential roles as future growth points, and few resource towns are deliberately built for ultimate removal, although government intervention has been called for in cases of severe hardship.

The future growth and stability of such communities will depend to a large extent upon their becoming a closely integrated part of their regional settlement networks, with refined and coordinated systems of transportation and communications. This regional approach requires that broad changes be made in public and private decision making, which has resulted in the proliferation of a large number of small, vulnerable, disconnected settlements in what is basically an *ad hoc* and unplanned manner.

Because the responsibility for new-town development in Canada is fragmented, falling largely within the jurisdictions of federal and various provincial authorities, it is not possible to present a coherent view of the public policies and planning that have directed the development. Instead, examples have been discussed with the hope of fostering an understanding of the past and current course of independent new-community enterprise.

New Communities for Strategic Communications. Generally in the independent, freestanding model, new communities for strategic communications have usually served a single function. In this respect they are not very different from single-enterprise resource-based towns, although their functions and locations are of an entirely different nature.

Many of the early railway towns serve as examples. Terrace, British Columbia, combines both rail and road nodality with supply functions. Nelson, British Columbia, at the outlet of Kootenay Lake, has used its strategic location in its transformation from a mining-smelting function to add administrative and university activities. Dawson Creek, Alberta, was created to serve the Peace River region. Kenora and Geraldton, Ontario, emerged as major regional centers, due to their nodal locations and purposes.

Newly planned towns have been founded for essential services and activities related to transportation and communication. Military townsites such as Clinton and Summerside on Prince Edward Island have encountered problems relating to changing military needs and policy. Some, such as Shearwater Naval Air Station in Dartmouth, Nova Scotia, have enventually been absorbed into the metropolitan tissue. Others—for example, Newfoundland's Goose Bay—have served extremely limited roles. Stephenville, Newfoundland, a town planned by the Strategic Air Command with public facilities and hospital, generated critical problems when abandoned; but it also serves as ready-made infrastructure systems for new industries that may locate in such places.

One of the best examples of a town left in the wake of technological change is Gander, Newfoundland. This town of about 5000 people was founded on a curvilinear plan in 1953 in response to the need for a transatlantic air terminal. The advent of the jet engine made the town obsolete as soon as it had been completed because the longer flight range of aircraft negated the importance of this town as a stopover and refueling point.

Problems of this type of settlement are well illustrated by Canso, Nova Scotia, built on an isolated peninsula as the terminal point of the transatlantic cable, which is no longer needed for this purpose. Although other industry has been attracted, the functional obsolescence of this planned new community has yet to be resolved.

Settlements Planned for Administrative Functions. Inuvik, in the North West Territories, is a new community in Canada's far north, a mere 60 miles from the Arctic Ocean. Building began in 1954, when a decision was made to relocate the Aklavik regional school, airport, and administrative facilities; the site was found to lie upon difficult permafrost conditions. Here basic public utility services are provided by pipelines (termed "utilidors") above grade, and research continues in the areas of arctic building and related technologies for moving basic resources, such as gas and oil, south.

Gagetown-Oromocto, New Brunswick, is a military training complex, with an associated civil townsite southeast of Fredericton. The town, however, is situated so close to the capital that it can hardly be considered independent.

Regional relocation of population has been exhibited in some parts of the country. The best example is the creation of the new communities of Cardinal, Iroquois, Morrisburg, Ingleside, and Long Sault—all on the St. Lawrence Seaway between Brockville and Cornwall—to replace those towns that were drowned by the floodings brought by the seaway project. These display no innovative qualities whatever because most of the existing houses were physically relocated from their original settings.

The outports of Newfoundland have been relocated, to some extent, by moving houses and partially by creating planned communities whereby fish plants, schools, and other needed elements are provided. This undertaking has met with its share of social dilemmas, but it has alleviated the disadvantages of isolated areas now reorganized into local new towns integrated with historic sites, such as St. Anthony, Port Saunders, Deer Lake, Bonavista, and Grand Bank.

Expanded new towns, which are rarely found in the modern idiom, do exist and relate to the creation of new centers of regional administration in the north. Yellowknife, designated the capital of the North West Territories, has been replanned as a modern town, one in which office buildings and apartments are constructed today. In the Yukon, Whitehorse, a poorly served community, was replanned since the 1950s to weave together Lower Townsite, the army Camp Takhini, Royal Canadian Air Force and Canadian National telecommunications townsites, and

to provide new engineering works and facilities. By 1967 the site included a hospital, library, museum, town hall, prison, a new airport, and several hotels.

Towns of this type are essential in the huge land mass of Canada. As additional resource frontiers or depressed regions concentrate and urbanize their populations, this experience probably will be repeated.

Satellite Towns. This type of new community can best be described as a planned growth unit created spontaneously and linked to the urban field of an existing center. Satellite towns exhibit a full range of housing, social, and other facilities, and normally have a limited employment function. In many instances, the chosen site is untouched, but a self-contained town seldom develops. Due to its dependence upon the existing, usually larger, more dominant center, a considerable degree of commuting occurs.

Satellite towns are perhaps the most common type of new planned unit found in the southern urbanized areas of Canada, although such towns may be related to the metropolitan growth of any city of relative importance within a region. In addition to expanding the housing stock of their "parent" settlements, these new communities are also designed to order urban growth. In a setting such as Toronto, order has been urgently needed: the regional land market has suffered from serious inflation and instability; to a large extent sprawl has characterized area land-use patterns since as early as the 1950s; and the city has seen an area population increase of some 20,000 people annually for the past 10 to 15 years.

Although differentiating between satellite and suburban new communities situated within urban-centered regions may not be easy, the assumption can be made that the satellite version is more dependent on the existing metropolis for a variety of employment opportunities and high-order services than is the suburban community. Although the suburban city may also rely to a large extent on such facilities and services, its larger population and area allow it eventually to be more self-sufficient than satellites, despite substantial commuting in the journey-to-work. In some cases the satellite town is a form of dormitory suburb that has provided accessible, minimal basic services required by the immediate population. These towns have almost invariably been financed and developed by private enterprise. A refined evolution of the garden-city tradition is frequently observed, and in some cases they have established a physical form and identity that is quite distinct in the Canadian urban landscape (see Figure 2).

Don Mills: A Quasi-Urban Satellite. The community of Don Mills, Ontario, was perhaps the first early Canadian new town of considerable size. Although originally planned for a diverse population, housing was largely oriented toward the well-to-do classes of modern suburbia. With a large industrial area constructed (Flemingdon Park, a related office-commercial and industrial area including high-density forms of housing later augmented this successful venture), a planned central shopping town center, and innovative diverse housing types, Don Mills exerted a strong influence upon most subsequent large-scale Canadian development. It was postulated that the majority of inhabitants would both live and work there; however, because it was so close to downtown Toronto and linked by excellent transportation routes, this did not happen.[8]

Land acquisition, begun in 1946, was relatively simple because block purchases were made from some large estates. The Canadian Equity and Development Corporation conceived the formal project in 1952, and the scheme was planned to take from 6 to 10 years and house 35,000 persons on 2056 acres. The community is barely distinguishable from the city that has surrounded and absorbed it, and what the land would be used for was not known at the time of assembly.

An unusual amount of planning expertise served in many ways as a prototype for subsequent, recently built new communities in the Toronto region and elsewhere, using modified Radburn principles in the siting of roads and buildings. The gradual integration of Don Mills into the metropolitan Toronto fabric has posed the question of whether, despite extensive planning, there will be an eventual blending of other privately sponsored new communities into urban areas.[9]

Other Urban Satellites. Kanata, Ontario, a privately planned but still uncompleted community west of Ottawa, stands out as a design *tour de force* and demonstrates the opportunities for shaping the elements of the built environment, when development is on a large scale based on the principle of the planned integration of the parts of the city. Begun in 1966 and in the secondary stages of its growth, Kanata is an example of suburban satellite expansion that is leapfrogging Ottawa's extensive greenbelt system. It

demonstrates the notion that a greenbelt in itself is not sufficient to contain urban growth. Further growth of the National Capital Region is expected to be accommodated outside the greenbelt and will probably be concentrated in a limited number of nodes, each of which will depend on the capital and be connected to it by rapid mass transport and expressway networks. Kanata is planned to house a population of about 70,000 people, on the basis of some 14 neighborhood units combining varying housing types. The employment base is expected to provide 17,750 jobs, with 20 percent being filled by residents of the community. The overall viability of such satellites is predicated on three major factors: provision of mass rapid transit connecting the satellites to Ottawa, expansion of federal government opportunities to provide further jobs, and successful integration of the communities within the capital region. Two key points in the Kanata plan for the 3200 acre site are the preservation of space and the enhancement of natural beauty.

A similar example is well under way at Montreal's Nun's Island, in the midst of the St. Lawrence River. This satellite city might best be described as a downtown new town or new town in-town. The community, to be developed over the next 15 years, is planned to provide rental housing for about 50,000 people, along with a town center, park-school campuses, resort motel complex, golf course, marina, recreational facilities, and areas for institutional and commercial development. The different areas will be linked by a landscaped parkway on which an around-the-island bus system will operate and will also connect the island with Montreal's downtown. Utmost care has been taken to preserve the natural beauty of the site, with contributions made by town planners, economists, engineers, architects, land planners, and traffic and design consultants. The land acquired by the Quebec Home and Mortgage Corporation, an agency of the provincial government, was leased to Metropolitan Structures of Canada, Ltd. for 99 years. However, with rents averaging in the $300 to $400 per month category, an integrated social mix is unlikely. The project will probably serve as a well-designed, optimally located, middle-class dormitory.

Other Montreal regional satellites are Pointe-Claire and Ville d'Anjou, large-scale suburban developments, and Ste. Therese-en-Haut, a planned suburban extension of Ste. Therese, north of Montreal. Bromont, Quebec, instituted in 1966 in the Eastern Townships near Granby, is to serve as a residential and tourist center for the subregion, with 1100

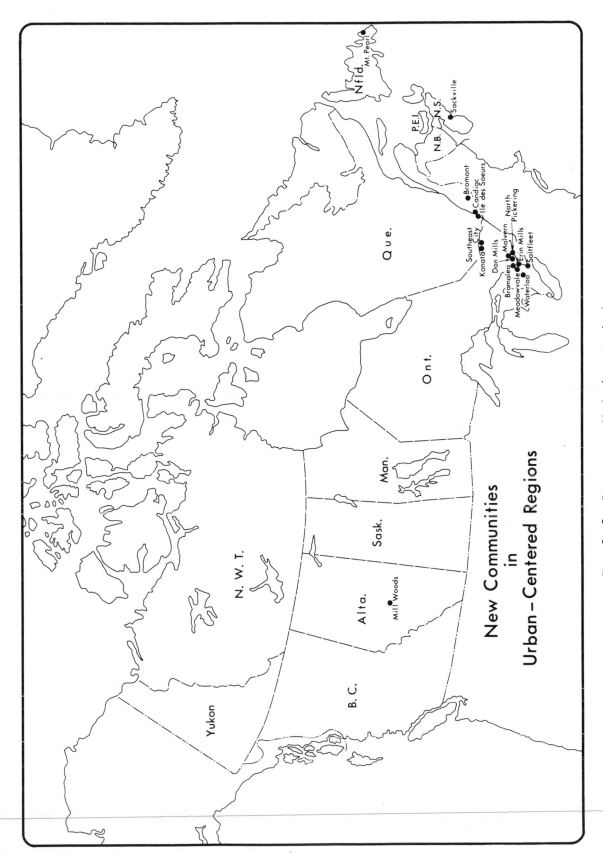

Figure 2. Canadian new communities in urban-centered regions.

residents as of 1971. Candiac, less than 10 miles southeast of Montreal and in its metropolitan region, is a parcel of 4000 acres and had about 5200 population in June 1971. In general, these communities (10,000 to 40,000 population) are predominantly dormitory towns housing various elements of the regional populace and concentrating on managerial, executive, and professional groups. The degree of home ownership is high, with a predominance of single-family dwellings. These satellites have resulted chiefly from the speculative efforts of private developers, with site selection closely related to availability of reasonably priced, suitable land.

Mount Pearl New Town, Newfoundland, in the St. John's conurbation, is an excellent example of a type of town sponsored to a great extent by government departments. CMHC and the Department of Regional Economic Expansion (DREE) have played major roles in the financing of this planned community. The former agency has supplied funding for land assembly for general residential purposes, while DREE was required to fund industrial lands to the sum of some $4 million.

The Edmonton District Planning Commission of Alberta, forced to control growth during the oil boom after 1947, channeled some of this into satellites using a regional approach. Under this plan, Jasper Place grew from 4000 to around 30,000; the former coal-mining center of Beverly grew from 1000 to 10,000; St. Albert was to undergo a similar increase. This is one of the few examples in Canada of regional planning and a strategy of growth diversion. The New Towns Acts of 1956, enacted by the province of Alberta, was instrumental in assisting this form of growth and stands alone today as the only example of its sort in the country.

Suburban Cities. Humphrey Carver spoke of the potential of using both public and private forms of enterprise to assist in the creation of "cities in the suburbs," which have come to fruition in many large Canadian centers.[10] This type of new community will often be on development sites of 2000 to 6000 acres, and population will be from 60,000 to 200,000. They are large enough to act as self-sustaining urban settlement units and support all of the facilities and activities normally associated with independent cities anywhere. Suburban cities are a function of rapid growth and assist in absorbing some of this expansion and in ordering fringe development. They also bear significant links to new regional shopping, commercial development, industrial parks and basins, expressway systems, seaports, and airports.

The prime Canadian examples are to be found in urban-centered regions. Bramalea, Meadowvale, and Erin Mills are excellent cities, all located in the Toronto-centred region (TCR). They will accommodate populations of 150,000, 250,000, and 250,000, respectively, and will act as major nodes in the restructuring of regional growth patterns. Another major new suburban city, now in its initial stages, is Mill Woods, Alberta, located close to Edmonton and planned for a population of 120,000.

The planning for Mill Woods has involved great foresight in publicly sponsored, major land assembly and development. The selected site of 6500 acres is 68 percent owned by the Alberta Provincial Housing Corporation, with a further 660 acres acquired outside the planning area to act as a buffer zone between the development project and the city of Edmonton. The project is the realization of a concept that regional growth should assume the form of a rapidly expanding central city comprising continuous growth areas and communities situated within a reasonable distance from the city along major transportation corridors. Such a scheme has been made possible through the vision of the Edmonton Regional Planning Commission, which applied regional zoning to avoid premature subdivision outside the city limits. Use of the land around the new community is subject to strict controls that prevent competitive urban development. As a consequence, land values in and around the planning area have been steady or have declined, and speculation has thus been avoided. Progressive servicing of land in the area will occur to provide good public and private housing at minimum costs. Suggestions made in the plan deal also with the city of Edmonton, using the funds of the Mill Woods project to establish a specific land acquisition program that will bear direct relation to the public works programs of the city.[11]

Mill Woods will be a new city in a suburban environment. This project represents a major breakthrough in North American practice—public sponsorship on a large scale. The economics affecting land and housing markets should be significantly controlled while creating an urban milieu of the highest order. The concept presents exciting possibilities for innovative development processes in the future. Mill Woods will be a most interesting Canadian experiment to ascertain whether the problems characterized by privately sponsored new communities will be avoided. Public land assembly, intervention, and coordinated regional planning make this undertaking uniquely Canadian.

Another recent form of the large, comprehensively

planned addition to an area is the proposed master plan that will radically change the form of an existing rural area to an urban node. One such major proposal is Mississauga City, west of downtown Toronto. The developer held large parcels of land in a checkerboard pattern, with fragmented ownership between the parcels and desired to plan for the overall area to be capable of coordinating his own holdings. The Mississauga city center covers 4000 acres east of the Credit River. This city is largely commercial in nature; it is unstructured in a planning sense, with no long-range plans for the entire assembly now available, and it is not set within regional planning frameworks. The aim of the development will be to channel Mississauga's urban growth into an area several miles north of the present center in Cooksville. Mississauga's municipal offices have already moved to this new area, and the developer hopes that most of the town's urban growth will follow. The city center is to include a huge shopping complex and four residential quadrants—in privately sponsored new-community fashion—around the center, with industrial development farther north.

Another similar proposal is that of Runnymede, in Pickering Township, northeast of Toronto on 3960 acres of land held in one holding. This constitutes a proposal for the TCR plan's subregional settlement of Ajax, in which a rural area will be transformed into an urban node, calling for a target population of 175,000 by 1986, and for 19,200 jobs. To this end, Runnymede suggests the establishment of a provincial development agency to oversee and guide progress.

The provincial government through the Ontario Housing Corporation (OHC), has three planned ventures into new-community building in southern Ontario: Malvern, northeast of Toronto; Saltfleet, southeast of Hamilton; and Kitchener-Waterloo. All have been designed to increase the housing stock, especially family and moderate-income housing. Relatively less attention was paid to their potential for stimulating or directing regional development.[12]

PUBLIC POLICY AND REGIONAL PLANNING STRATEGY: THE TORONTO-CENTRED REGION

Canada differs, in many respects, from the United States where respect must be given to the constitutionally derived powers of home rule on the part of the various central cities and their suburbs in dealing with uncontrolled urbanization. There has traditionally been an absence of such an attitude in

Canada with respect to provincial authority. Such an absence of home rule in Ontario has enabled the provincial government to assume leadership in local government affairs and to initiate promising, if not yet adequately tested, programs of metropolitan-regional planning reforms and strategies. It is this provincial power that precisely forced the introduction of metropolitan planning in Ontario in 1953 with the establishment of the Municipality of Metropolitan Toronto, North America's first true metropolitan government.

Employing the growth-pole concept, the Ontario provincial government, in its regional development program, has drafted economic development plans for designated regions of Ontario. These plans will identify urban centers eligible for governmental incentive grants and will recommend strategies for achieving particular sets of socioeconomic objectives. Without much doubt, the most important development region is the Toronto-centred region, and one of the key components of the plan is that of population distribution and its supporting development infrastructure.

The temptation to equate the quest for a regional growth strategy or policy with new-town development is almost too great to resist. Indeed, the new-community concept has proven itself a key component, although by no means the only one, in the structuring and reordering of metropolitan growth—especially where the concentrations of population and life-support services are major factors. The planning and building of new towns and satellite communities will in the end greatly assist the implementation of the Toronto region planning strategy for regional development.

The concept of the Toronto-centred region, presented as government policy in May 1970, was the outgrowth of the Metropolitan Toronto and Region Transportation Study (MTARTS).[13] This study conceived a regional restructuring of the urban settlement systems by deflecting growth from the metropolitan Toronto core in a network of closely interacting cities distributed in two tiers along 100 miles of Lake Ontario's shoreline. One of the objectives of the concept was to channel economic growth and development to the lakeshore area east of Metro Toronto, because historically the major thrust of growth in the region has been to the west of Toronto, accompanied by undesirable urban sprawl. The emphasis is to be on the creation of a network of cities, new and existing, set along a transportation corridor that would constitute a single labor market as well as a single leisure and recreation market. To stimulate orderly growth eastward, the concept of the Toronto-centred region proposed further development of existing communities along with the planning of a series of new communities in the second tier. The two tiers of cities will, to the maximum degree possible, be separated by a parkway belt system to incorporate efficient transportation facilities, trunk services, electric transmission lines, and other services that will be needed to integrate the system properly. The new cities will have a distinct role and community identity within the region but will not be self-sufficient in employment.

Essentially the plan of the Toronto-centred region is a statement of provincial urban policy for southern Ontario's growth, linking regional development and local government reorganization.[14] Its main concern is the orderly distribution of population from the already crowded, rapidly growing Toronto area, which is economically booming and straining at the seams.[15] Although the province's intentions toward specific places in the province are expressed in terms of population allocations, the major effort will be devoted to structuring the growth already occurring, rather than to initiating new growth.

New Communities in the Metro Toronto Region. There are several new communities in the Metro Toronto region. Some of these have been built within the past 10 to 15 years; others are under construction (see Figure 3). Since development is proceeding at such an accelerated pace, the TCR document provides a framework within which new development proposals can be reviewed and others encouraged. It is also intended to act as a guide in coordinating and assisting development insofar as it is influenced by public policy and strategy adopted by the many affected agencies as well as by private entrepreneurs. The new communities of Bramalea, Erin Mills, and Meadowvale conform in general terms with the TCR plan's final views and with its implementation priorities. Three private new-community schemes for the area have already been ruled out by the plan, with reports concluding that the proposed lands were best suited for agricultural and recreational uses and that serving these lands for urban development and providing transportation infrastructure would be difficult and costly.

Eight new communities in the Toronto region are built, proposed, or under construction. The proposed

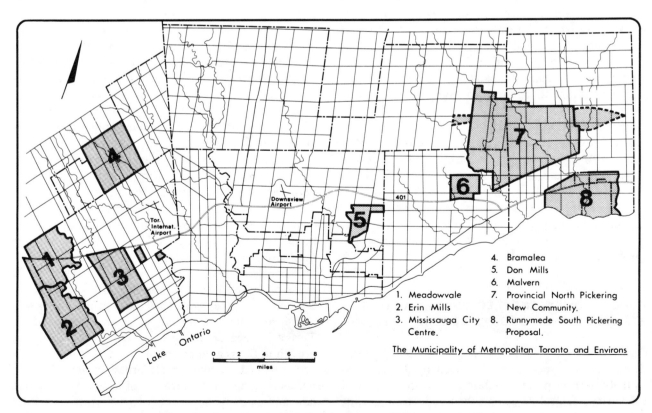

Figure 3. Comprehensively planned developments (Toronto centred region).

combined target population is about 900,000, or about 15 percent of the projected planned figure for the year 2000, which is estimated at close to 6.5 million. The following general remarks may be advanced about the Toronto region's new towns:

1. The majority of the new communities will be satellite to Toronto and will represent large-scale enterprises relative to that city. Combining comprehensive planning techniques, they will present a broad choice of living units, a cross section of socioeconomic population types, access to public and private services and facilities, and on-site employment in many instances.

2. The communities are directed at the private sector, which is the designated vehicle of implementation for public policy.

3. Provincial government bodies will play a more aggressive role than they have done in the past through powers of land assembly, provision of basic infrastructure, or expanded assistance to municipal and regional jurisdictions.

4. The new communities will be looked upon as instruments and catalysts of provincial/regional development strategies.

5. Growing awareness of environmental consequences of development form will seriously affect new-community studies, especially as these concern pollution control, environmental protection, and architectural conservation.

6. The new settlements will both explore effective land-use forms and provide for innovative social and governmental roles offering great access to public facilities and meaningful tools for personal and group involvement.

7. Citizens' aid will be recruited in determining plans and policies at all stages of the developments, which will usually require from 15 to 20 years for completion.

8. One of the fundamental goals in the establishment of new communities will be the achievement of a high standard for the quality of life: good access to improved facilities and amenities; fulfillment of personal goals; relief from the unpleasant aspects of urban living; and broad choice in housing, recreation, and employment.

9. Economies of scale must be attained through the successful attraction of certain minimum numbers of inhabitants so that worthwhile value will be obtained for required levels of public improvements. This is to be achieved through rational concentration of large populations within several new regional cities, in lieu of the well-known phenomenon of surburban sprawl.

10. Open education and cable television designed for schools will aid the trend toward flexible methods of teaching and communication. Eventually there will be two-way transmissions to the central commercial cable from various community and educational institutions.

11. Pedestrian and vehicular traffic separation will be encouraged, and a major emphasis on landscaping will assist in achieving this objective.

The Toronto-centred region plan has been put forth by the Ontario government as a statement of its broad provincial policy regarding regional planning for the future. The plan declares the basic directions and alternatives for an area generally encompassing a 90-mile arc around Toronto, and it provides a basis for public reaction to the implementation of the development concept and to the means of making the broad proposals specific. This document sets a pattern of development and acts as an umbrella of provincial policy within which refinement of transportation concepts, precise regional land-use systems, and special policies for urban areas can proceed.

Clearly on the list of available alternative strategies is the development of new cities, some of which are already underway. The province may see fit to use the opportunity of a new-community policy to stabilize the unstable land market in Ontario, because concurrent development of a large number of such cities could stabilize such a market.

Expanded New Communities: Regional Growth Centers. The new procedures of regional planning, typified by recent provincial policies such as those of Ontario and Alberta and by DREE inducing and assisting regional development in declining regions, have created yet another type of new community: the expanded version or designated regional growth centers. Because these are relatively recent concepts only a few examples can be cited.

Lorneville in New Brunswick is proposing a new deep water port that will likely evolve into a new community in terms of the facilities and sheer volume of services needed; at the Straits of Canso in Nova Scotia a new complex is emerging in the area of Port Hawkesbury, using the sheltered harbor created by the Canso Causeway and built on the economic base of the oil refining and petrochemical industry.

MTARTS developed several alternative strategies

of future development and proposed new communities (arc cities) of target populations of about 200,000 in locations such as Alliston, Guelph, and Orangeville. The TCR concept, however, suggested the building of expanded towns in growth centers such as Midland, Barrie, Cobourg-Port Hope, and Orillia. Although a policy of expanded new communities has not yet been firmly established, the federal government, through the Federal Ministry of State for Urban Affairs, is pursuing research with the intent of initiating just such a program for the expansion of existing communities in strategically located growth areas. Although implementation techniques are still in the development stages, these new communities will essentially constitute a modified version of the satellite and suburban concepts previously described.

CONCLUSION

Canada is still in an enviable position compared with crowded countries in Europe and Asia. It is a nation that has a fairly high standard of living, although there is some pollution and poverty, and by international standards Canada is relatively underpopulated. However, the absence of official federal or provincial policies for population distribution allows the inevitability of cities such as Toronto and Montreal to continue to dominate urban development. In Ontario the winds of change have arrived. A restructuring of metropolitan and regional growth forms is underway, and the scale of involvement—public and private— promises an improved settlement pattern for all destined to live in the province in the future. Will a policy of creating new communities work? The answer is, partially. In addition, population growth will have to be shifted to smaller communities— 100,000 to 500,000 in population, for example. Urban redevelopment will continue, and rehabilitation will probably become important in preserving older areas of the existing central cities, and existing cities will expand at their fringes.

New-community planning and development in Canada usually has not been directed by coordinated national growth policy. In many instances the governments have been responsive, but until recently they have not assumed the role of leadership. The response has also been mostly uncoordinated, fragmented and *ad hoc*. Governments have, indeed, been involved; funds are available under the National Housing Act for land assembly, and a new community program has been activated. DREE, with

its aid to encourage growth in economically undeveloped and declining regions has provided funding, but this has not been a major factor in the development of satellite, urban-fringe communities. With the exception of the legislation enacted by the province of Alberta, most of the provinces have responded almost randomly to the new-community idea, although Ontario, with its Toronto-centred region plan for development, may be setting a pattern for the country. Serious national efforts are currently emerging through the energies of the Ministry of State for Urban Affairs and CMHC, which are trying to aggregate and coordinate federal urban policy. Such directives require close cooperation of all levels of government in Canada, so that inter- and intraprovincial concerns mesh with federal concerns regarding distribution of settlement patterns.

New communities policy has always been seen as a complement of the urban growth strategies of countries that have undertaken the formidable task of building such settlements. Urban sprawl has been substantially checked by deflecting some of the anticipated growth of population and employment from existing cities to new communities, coupled in many cases with open space policies. New communities are an essential alternative to peripheral development.

New communities are a deliberate attempt to create balanced development in urban regions. The aim of judicious intervention is to promote points of concentration within a developing urban area. The case for new communities will lead to a good, rich urban life. By focusing and concentrating development in an urban region, new communities make possible the retention of large tracts of open space within manageable reach of the city for recreational and agricultural uses. In offering opportunity for experiment and in demonstrating the potentials of urban living in the future, the new community is an event of the utmost public and political importance.

Canada has an extensive, varied, and even distinguished record in the field of new-community development. It is, however, uniquely Canadian and has been different from the new towns of highly developed and extensively urbanized European nations. Canada is young and vigorous. Its growth potential and undeveloped regions are huge. Canada has some of the best creative forms of leadership and some of the highest levels of professional skill and experience to be found. Given its vast resources, this nation should be able to build some of the finest new communities in the world, thereby eliminating much of the waste and duplication that have resulted from a lack of control and a failure to encourage and initiate good planning. Only the next few decades will tell whether the country will be successful in choosing to channel some of its growth into well-planned new communities.

metropolitan core into a two-tiered urbanized area, (ii) encourage growth in selected communities beyond easy commuting range of Metropolitan Toronto, and thus help to decentralize the region and to prevent a swollen growth within and near Metropolitan Toronto, and (iii) set basic guidelines for regional land use.

NOTES

1. N. H. Lithwick, *Urban Canada: Problems and Prospects* (Ottawa: Government of Canada, 1970), p. 230.

2. The initial legislation can be found in the Statutes of Alberta, "An Act to Provide for the Development and Planning of New Towns in the Province," Chapter 39, 1956. Subsequent amendments in 1959 and 1968 have resulted in later documents, but these have been brief. The 1956 Act was repealed and replaced by The New Towns Act, Code 81, Chapter 258, 1969.

3. See Roland G. Cooper, "Land and New Communities" in *New Communities in Canada: Exploring Planned Environments,* special issue of *CONTACT* **8,** No. 3 (1976):113–116.

4. Section 42, National Housing Act, Government of Canada. Originally proposed in 1964, revised in June 1969, terminated in March 1972 and reinstated in 1973.

5. Rex Lucas, *Minetown, Milltown, Railtown* (Toronto: University of Toronto Press, 1971), pp. 17–18.

6. Harry W. Walker, "Canadian New Towns," *Community Planning Review* **4** (1954):80–87.

7. See Nigel H. Richardson, "The Kitimat Region," *Resources for Tomorrow Conference Background Papers,* Vol. I (Ottawa: Queen's Printer, 1961), pp. 445–454.

8. The new community characterized by "labour market closure" has all but disappeared. The folly of this phenomenon, under modern conditions, has led planning authorities almost to dismiss this concept.

9. The lack of distinguishability may be a problem for present and future new-community building, for it makes the new area less of an ordered contribution to regional growth. Controlling urban sprawl between present development and new communities will be a real challenge in regional plan implementation.

10. H. Carver, *Cities in the Suburbs* (Toronto: University of Toronto Press, 1965).

11. Edmonton City Planning Commission, *Mill Woods* (Edmonton: City Extension of Edmonton, City Hall, 1971).

12. Industrial land use averages only 10 percent of total uses in these communities. Single-family detached housing accounts for 50 percent of housing stock in two of the three, although this will almost certainly be revised. The HOME (Home Ownership Made Easy) plan of buying the house and leasing the lot will be used extensively in these projects.

13. Metropolitan Toronto and Region Transportation Study, *Choices for a Growing Region* (Toronto: Department of Municipal Affairs, Ontario, 1967).

14. For details, see *Design for Development: The Toronto-Centred Region,* coordinated by the Regional Development Branch of the Department of Treasury and Economics (Toronto: The Queen's Printer and Publisher, Ontario, May 1970).

15. The main purposes of the TCR as stated in *Choices for a Growing Region* are to (i) shape the growth of the region's

BIBLIOGRAPHY

Alberta. *The New Towns Act,* Code 81, Chapter 258, 1969.

Alonso, William. "The Mirage of New Towns." *The Public Interest,* No. 19, (Spring 1970), 3–18.

Archer, Hilary M. "A Classification and Definition of Single-Enterprise Communities." M. A. Thesis. University of Manitoba, 1969.

Bureau of Municipal Research. "The Toronto Region's Privately Developed New Communities." *Civic Affairs,* No. 2. Toronto: Bureau of Municipal Research, 1972.

Carver, Humphrey. *Cities in the Suburbs.* Toronto: University of Toronto Press, 1965.

Central Mortgage and Housing Corporation. "Single Enterprise Communities in Canada." Ottawa: Institute of Local Government, Queen's University, 1953.

Clapp, James A. *New Towns and Urban Policy.* New York: Dunellen, 1971.

Cooper, R. G. "Land and New Communities." *New Communities in Canada: Exploring Planned Environments,* special issue of *CONTACT* **8,** No. 3 (1976), 113–116.

Dietz, S. H. *The Physical Development of Remote Resource Towns.* Ottawa: Central Mortgage and Housing Corporation, 1968.

"Don Mills, the Planned Industrial Community near Toronto, Is a Good Place To Live, But Its Workers Don't Live There." *Architectural Forum* **114** (January 1961), 63–66.

Edmonton City Planning Commission. "Mill Woods." Edmonton: City Extension of Edmonton, City Hall, 1971. Mimeo.

Eichler, Edward P., and Marshall Kaplan. *The Community Builders.* Berkeley and Los Angeles: University of California Press, 1967.

Fraser, Jack B. *Vital Questions—New Towns: What Architects Should Know About Them.* Washington, D.C.: American Institute of Architects, 1969.

Gertler, L. O., "The Process of New City Planning and Building." Waterloo: School of Urban and Regional Planning, University of Waterloo, March 8, 1971. Mimeo.

Howard, Ebenezer. *Garden Cities of To-Morrow.* London: Faber & Faber, 1970.

"Kanata: New Design for Living." *Canadian Building News,* Issue I, (1966), 2–5.

Keilhofer, P., and J. W. Parlour. *New Towns: The Canadian Experience.* Ottawa: Ministry of State for Urban Affairs, 1972.

Lithwick, N. H. *Urban Canada: Problems and Prospects.* Ottawa: Government of Canada, 1970.

Ontario. *Design for Development: The Toronto-Centred Region.* Toronto: The Queen's Printer and Publisher, May 1970.

———. Metropolitan Toronto and Regional Transportation

Study. *Choices for a Growing Region.* Toronto: Department of Municipal Affairs, 1967.

Osborn, F. J., and Arnold Whittick. *The New Towns.* London: Leonard Hill, 1969.

Pearson, Norman. "New Towns: The Canadian Experience." Paper prepared for the Ministry of State for Urban Affairs, Canada, for the O.E.C.D. Secretariat Urban Sector Group, Publication No. 57, Ottawa, February 1972.

Pressman, Norman E. P. "New Towns." Occasional Paper No. I. *Contact* (Bulletin of Urban and Environmental Affairs). June 1972.

———. *A Comprehensive Bibliography of New Towns in Canada.* Exchange Bibliography No. 483. Monticello, Illinois: Council of Planning Librarians, September 1972.

———. Ed. *New Communities in Canada: Exploring Planned Environments.* Special issue of *CONTACT* **8,** No. 3 (1976).

Princeton University School of Architecture and Urban Planning.

Innovation and New Communities. Report of the Princeton University Conference of September 28 and 29, 1970.

Richardson, Nigel H. "The Kitimat Region." *Resources for Tomorrow Conference Background Papers,* Vol. I. Ottawa: Queen's Printer, 1961.

Robinson, Ira M. *New Industrial Towns on Canada's Resource Frontier.* Research Paper No. 73. University of Chicago, 1962.

Saturday Review. New Communities Special Issue, May 15, 1971.

Sidenbladh, Goran. "Stockholm: A Planned City." *Scientific American* **213** (September 1965), 106–118.

Town and Country Planning. British New Towns, **43,** No. 2 (February 1975).

United Nations. *Planning of Metropolitan Areas and New Towns.* New York: United Nations, 1969.

Walker, Harry W. "Canadian New Towns." *Community Planning Review* **4** (1954), 80–87.

CHAPTER 20

New Cities in Australia: The Australian Government's Growth Center Program

"The adoption of a program for growth centres is a major component of the Government's effort to accommodate future growth in an efficient and equitable manner, responsive to the changing needs and life styles of Australians."[1] In its 1973–1974 budget, the Australian government allocated $33 million for the first year of a program for growth centers. This chapter discusses the rationale underlying the commitment of funds to new-city development, the actual content of the program, progress in its implementation, and concludes with some perspectives on the implications of the program for the future of urban and regional development in Australia.

The program was initially conceived and proposed as a program of new cities, encompassing developments within the major metropolitan regions and others at major rural centers. A plethora of terms, including *new cities, growth centers, system cities, regional cities, metro-towns, satellite cities,* and so on, sprang into vogue as attempts were made to describe and popularize the intentions of the government and the contents of the first year of the program, which in fact was significant for the diversity of the projects it encompassed. By 1974, however, the terminology had been clarified, with *regional growth center* and *metropolitan growth center* emerging as the accepted descriptors of the projects involved. Nonetheless, the growth centers program began as a diverse program of widely differing development projects, each of a character specific to the area in which it was located, and each reflecting the planning policies of the government of the state in which it was located. It was very much a federalist or cooperative venture.

This diversity is well-illustrated by the nature of the projects supported during 1973–1974, the first year of the program. Australian government support was offered for one literal new city—Monarto, to be developed on a "green-fields" site in South Australia. Funds were included to support the development of regional growth centers—Albury/Wodonga and Bathurst/Orange. Funds were also provided for the development of four metropolitan centers—Holsworthy/Campbelltown,* Gosford/Wyong, Geelong, and the northwest corridor of Perth. Funds were included to allow the protection of areas to the southeast of Melbourne against urban development, to overcome backlogs in social and physical infrastructure in the major centers of the Fitzroy region on the central Queensland coast, to support land acquisition and institutional development in Townsville and the Moreton region, and to support the activities of the newly established State Planning Commission in Tasmania. Figure 1 shows these projects.

Not all of these projects came to fruition, largely because of the failure of some of the state governments and the Australian government to reach ap-

* Now known as Macarthur.

propriate agreements on the terms and conditions under which finance would be made available. Only four projects for growth centers have actually received significant expenditure, and of the $33 million allocated in 1973–1974, only $6.6 million were actually spent on such development (see Table 1).

Nevertheless, as Table 1 shows, the level of expenditure on growth centers increased during the years of the Whitlam government, to some $60 million in 1975–1976, 7.8 percent of total Commonwealth assistance for urban development, housing, and related programs, or 53.3 percent of urban development assistance. This compares with 1.7 percent and 45.2 percent, respectively, in 1973–1974.

The first budget of the new Liberal-Country party government, elected in December 1975, under the leadership of Prime Minister Malcolm Fraser, saw major reductions in expenditures on growth centers as well as other urban and environmental programs. The final 1976–1977 figures for expenditure on growth centers are somewhat higher than the $19.4 million indicated in Table 1.[2] Government reviews of the program resulted in a commitment to support for the major projects (Albury/Wodonga, Bathurst/Orange, and Macarthur) for at least the next five years and sought a greater involvement of the private sector in the projects, as well as significant state government contributions, to substitute for reduced Commonwealth assistance. The willingness of the states and the private sector to play a greater role than before in growth centers will be a profound influence on the possible scale and effectiveness of what is the most ambitious attempt since colonization to influence the development of Australia's urban system.

BACKGROUND

The long-standing movement toward decentralization is the main social and political progenitor of the growth centers program. Originally the rationale for decentralization was primarily expressed in terms of stopping the "rural-urban drift of population," although as early as 1944 the Commonwealth Housing Commission urged the then Commonwealth government to decentralize industry and create satellite towns because of the deteriorating living conditions in the major cities.

The unplanned development of towns has led to unplanned transport and to an excessive amount of travelling between different parts of large towns. This in turn has involved high costs of transport to the community as a whole, as well as to the individual who pays this cost not only in money but in time fatigue. . . . The rising price of land . . . has driven people to the outer areas where land is cheap, but the location has forced them to pay high fares, often leaving them worse off than before. The decentralization of industry and the possibility of establishing satellite towns will need to be considered.[3]

Between the early 1940s and the mid-1960s various moves were made to encourage decentralization. Single state governments offered a wide range of incentives to industrialists to relocate to or locate in country centers. Government departments were established in a number of states officially to implement state government policies on this matter. The major effort was made in New South Wales, but even there the achievement has been modest.

Reviews of progress on decentralization by academics as well as government agencies criticized this general lack of achievement. One of the main criticisms was that because decentralization policies were not selective, little could be achieved because adding small increments to numerous small towns did not achieve any substantial agglomeration of activities, which could rapidly bring towns to a size where they could perhaps become self-generating or spontaneous growth centers. This led to the advocacy in the mid-1960s of selective decentralization.[4] Little was done to pursue policies along selective lines, although the Victorian government in 1967 accepted a recommendation from a select committee on five centers to be chosen for accelerated growth in that state.[5]

Throughout the 1950s and early 1960s, successive Commonwealth governments did relatively little to assist decentralization. However, in 1964 at the annual premiers' conference, it was agreed that there should be joint discussions among the Commonwealth and states about the issue. A joint committee was formed, which conducted a number of studies in following years and presented a final report to the governments involved in June 1972.[6] The report advocated selective decentralization and proposed ways and means of achieving this as a joint policy.

A further catalytic event in the evolution of present policies, involving a significant change in emphasis, was the publication in August 1972 of the report *New Cities for Australia,* prepared by the Australian Institute of Urban Studies (AIUS).[7] The report advocated the creation of a number of new cities throughout Australia to meet the needs of an expected population growth from 13 million to between

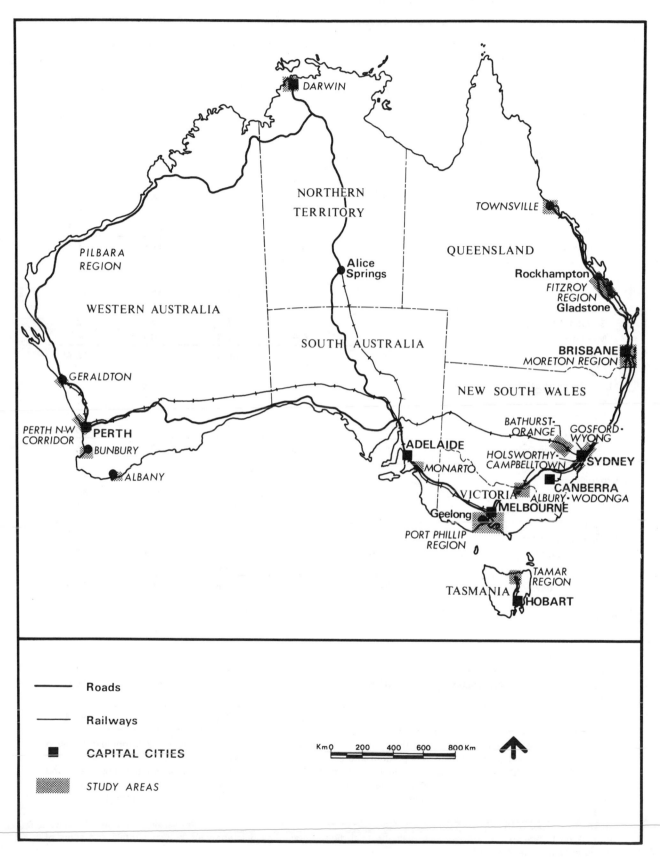

Figure 1. Areas of Australia assessed for the development of growth centers.

Table 1 Commonwealth Funding of Urban Development Assistance Programs, 1972-1973 to 1976-1977[a]
(in millions of Australian $)[b]

Program	1972–73	1973–74	1974–75	1975–76	1976–77 (budget) estimate)
Urban Development					
Land commissions/urban land councils					
New South Wales	—	—	0.8	11.2	2.6
Victoria	—	—	8.7	14.5	2.5
South Australia	—	8.0	18.6	16.9	6.0
Western Australia	—	—	11.7	6.1	3.0
Tasmania	—	—	—	—	0.3
Unallocated	—	—	—	—	0.8
Total	—	8.0	39.8	48.6	15.1
Growth centers					
Albury/Wodonga	—	2.2	42.3	35.4	15.3
Macarthur	—	—	6.7	15.7	2.0
Bathurst/Orange	—	—	5.0	8.4	2.0
Monarto	—	4.4	5.4	0.7	—
Total	—	6.6	59.5	60.1	19.4
Moore River (WA) study	—	—	—	0.5	—
Tasmanian strategy study and Tamar open space	—	—	0.4	0.5	0.1
Holsworthy project	—	—	3.4	3.0	0.1
Total Urban Development		14.6	103.1	112.7	34.6
Urban renewal	—	5.3	16.7	7.1	10.6
Urban water services	—	27.9	122.1	124.1	60.8
Environment and conservation	0.3	1.3	13.1	11.0	8.6
Housing	59.6	300.1	524.6	471.7	497.7
Community assistance	—	8.8	18.7	21.4	11.7
Sport and fitness	0.6	1.7	2.9	2.8	1.1
Not allocated	11.0	18.9	24.6	15.5	13.2
Total Outlay	71.5	378.6	825.8	766.5	638.4
Receipts					
Interest					
Growth centers	—	—	—	—	0.2
Water and sewerage authorities	—	—	2.3	11.2	21.0
Australian Housing Corporation	35.5	36.1	38.1	66.0	70.0
Other receipts	0.6	0.6	0.8	0.4	—
Total	36.2	36.7	41.2	77.6	91.3

[a] The program of expenditures included in the table are the responsibility of the Department of Environment, Housing and Community Development, which was brought into being in December 1975 by combining and rationalizing elements of the former Departments of Environment, Tourism and Recreation, Housing and Construction, and Urban and Regional Development. In preparing details of outlay and receipts in recent years, the assumption has been that the Department of Environment, Housing and Community Development existed in this configuration prior to December 1975.

[b] 1 $Aust. = 1.26 $US.

Note: A dash indicates nil or less than half the final digit shown. Any discrepancies between totals and sums of components are due to rounding.

17 million and 22 million by the year 2000. Two types of cities were advocated—new "system cities," which would be established close to the major metropolitan areas, would be substantially self-contained and would result in the creation of polycentric rather than monocentric metropolitan development; and new "regional cities," which would be a substantial distance from the existing metropolitan areas.

These ideas were largely taken up by the Commonwealth government under Prime Minister McMahon in 1972 and were expressed in the establishment of the National Urban and Regional Development Authority (NURDA), later called the Cities Commission. NURDA was established in October 1972 with the statutory responsibility to report to the prime minister in relation to Commonwealth participation in a national program of urban and regional development.[8] The concept of Commonwealth participation was based on fostering the two types of new cities envisaged by AIUS and earlier advocates of selective decentralization—metropolitan growth centers (or system cities) and regional growth centers. The intention of this policy was to develop alternative locations for population growth to the major metropolitan areas, and to assist in consciously structuring the growth of the metropolitan areas.

Following the election of the Australian Labor party to government in December 1972 under the leadership of Gough Whitlam, the Department of Urban and Regional Development was created to carry out the government's urban and regional program. NURDA was renamed the Cities Commission, and its responsibilities and structure were somewhat redefined.[9] The Whitlam government agreed that the Cities Commission should fulfil NURDA's statutory responsibility and advise the government, through the minister for urban and regional development, on a program of Australian government assistance for regional and metropolitan growth centers. This advice formed the basis of the growth centers program.[10]

RATIONALE

The main thrust and purpose of the growth centers program, from the viewpoint of the Australian government, has been to serve as a means of providing substantial Australian government assistance for, and involvement in, the process of accommodating the nation's anticipated future population growth in ways that would be more efficient, more equitable, more diverse, and more environmentally attractive than during most of the postwar period.

In the period since 1947, as Table 2 shows, Australia's population grew from 7.6 million to over 13 million in 1974, due to high rates of natural increase and to immigration from overseas, with a net gain of

Table 2 Population Distribution by Settlement Size for Australia, 1947–1974

Settlement Size	1947	1954	1961	1966	1971	1974
Number of persons (in thousands)						
500+	2711.3	3889.6	5223.6	6500.5	7372.1	8104.9
Sydney	(1484.4)	(1863.0)	(2197.0)	(2447.2)	(2807.8)	(2898.3)
Melbourne	(1226.9)	(1524.1)	(1858.5)	(2108.4)	(2503.5)	(2620.4)
100–499	1184.5	1010.3	882.1	620.7	837.0	1036.4
50–99	76.6	258.6	253.7	371.3	320.7	481.4
Rest of population	3608.4	3827.9	4148.6	4057.9	4225.7	3715.5
National Total	7580.8	8986.5	10,508.0	11,550.5	12,755.6	13,338.3
National total (%)						
500+	35.8	43.3	49.7	56.3	57.8	60.8
Sydney	(19.6)	(20.7)	(20.9)	(21.2)	(22.0)	(21.7)
Melbourne	(16.2)	(17.0)	(17.7)	(18.3)	(19.6)	(19.6)
100–499	15.6	11.2	8.4	5.4	6.6	7.8
50–99	1.0	2.9	2.4	3.2	2.5	3.6
Rest of population	47.6	42.6	39.5	35.1	33.1	27.8

Source: Australian Bureau of Statistics, Census of Population and Housing, 1947, 1954, 1961, 1966, and 1971 and Yearly Estimate 1974.

close to 2.5 million people directly from immigration throughout this period. Immigrants and their children contributed about half of Australia's postwar population growth.

Most of that growth occurred in the largest cities, particularly in Sydney and Melbourne. Australia has only 10 metropolitan areas with populations in excess of 100,000 (in the total built-up areas, not just the central city municipal district), and by 1974 almost 70 percent of the national population lived in these areas. This compares with only 51 percent in cities of over 100,000 people, in 1947 (see Table 2).

Sydney, with almost 3 million people, and Melbourne, with 2.6 million, dominate Australia's urban system. The quality of life in these two cities and the other large centers really is a reflection of living conditions for most of Australia's population.

As described before, there has been a growing political awareness of the many varied social, physical, and economic problems that exist in Australia's major cities. Some of these problems can be tackled directly through increased government funding. Improving public transport, overcoming sewerage and other infrastructure backlogs, assisting in the expansion of social opportunities in underprivileged areas of Sydney and Melbourne, government intervention in the land market—all these activities represent steps to tackle identifiable urban problems in the most direct way. The 1973–1974 and 1974–1975 Commonwealth budgets contained funds for all of these activities (see Table 1).

These problems are problems of the existing cities, affecting present populations. The existing cities continue to expand, and the Australian government believed that such expansion should be anticipated, planned for, and guided in directions and into urban forms that would represent a substantial improvement over existing conditions, would improve the efficiency of the urban development process, and through careful planning, would improve the quality of the urban environment—hence the support for metropolitan growth centers as part of the program.

However, some if not all of the problems of the metropolitan areas (particularly Sydney and Melbourne) are compounded by their size and absolute annual growth. The addition of about 50,000 new residents each year to both Sydney and Melbourne during the 1950s and 1960s put substantial pressure on resources of land, housing, major physical infrastructure, and social facilities. To the extent that a reduction of the rate of growth of the metropolitan areas could be achieved, significant improvements could be made in the quality of life for metropolitan residents.

One approach to achieving a reduction in rates of growth is to support the development of regional growth centers away from the present metropolitan areas. A substantial effort would be needed to begin the long-term task of building alternative centers outside the metropolitan regions to provide new worthwhile opportunities for people who prefer nonmetropolitan living, but who at present find insufficient facilities outside metropolitan areas to meet their needs for employment, education, and a full social and cultural life. Regional growth centers could be developed in such a way as to begin quickly to offer opportunities as varied as possible and either attract population away from the metropolitan regions or intercept previous nonmetropolitan residents who might otherwise have migrated to a metropolitan area. Albury/Wodonga was seen as the main center, with support being offered for the New South Wales government's Bathurst/Orange proposal, and for Townsville in Queensland (see Figure 1).

The program was intended to affect much more than metropolitan structure and the distribution of population and other activities. It also involved a substantial effort to change processes of urban development in Australia. Each growth center was to be planned, developed, and managed by a development corporation, on land acquired by the governments involved, at prices fixed at market value at a date set by legislation. Leasehold land tenure was originally proposed, although residential freehold was later adopted as a result of discussion following a report arising from a government inquiry into land tenure policies, directed by Justice Else-Mitchell.[11]

This process, with the development corporation as the central agency, was seen as a major step toward reform in urban development in Australia. It would serve to eliminate predevelopment speculation and windfall profits, to aid efficient and equitable provision of services, to aid conscious environmental planning, and to reduce the total expense of land development and thus permit affordable land prices. This aspect of the growth centers program was as important as its other basic goals.

This proposed approach to Australia's urban future was not unique to the Australian government. Some of the state governments were as firmly committed to similar philosophies and actions. The South Australian government, for example, took the initiative when it announced in 1971 that the future population of Adelaide should not exceed 1.4 million, and additional growth would be directed to a new city at Monarto, near Murray Bridge, 50 kilometers east of Adelaide.

The New South Wales government announced, via the state planning authority's Sydney Region Outline Plan, that 500,000 people from Sydney's expected future population would have to be located outside the metropolitan region, that a further 500,000 would be located at Gosford/Wyong to the north, and that Sydney's expansion would be catered for in major growth corridors with substantial activity centers intended to create local self-containment.[12] In 1972 the New South Wales government announced its intention to develop a growth center at Bathurst/Orange and later agreed to support development at Albury/Wodonga.

The Victorian government also actively supported the Albury/Wodonga project and later committed itself to the future development of Geelong as a growth center. These were all commitments with the same long-term objective—to improve community well-being through well-located, well-planned, and well-developed urban areas.

CONTENT OF THE PROGRAM

Because of NURDA's statutory obligation to report to the prime minister by June 1973 on a program of urban development projects for Australian government support (an obligation the Whitlam government agreed should be fulfilled by NURDA and then the Cities Commission), the first actions taken late in 1972 were to identify, in association with the state governments, a number of centers that were either regarded as having significant potential for accelerated growth, had already been nominated by various governments, or were projects to which they were politically committed.

Twelve areas, involving 16 localities, were chosen for study (see Figure 1). During the first few months of 1973 consultants carried out economic, social, physical, and planning studies in varying depth for each of these areas. On the basis of the results of these studies and its own considerations, the Cities Commission prepared a five-year program of expenditure on growth centers throughout Australia, which was passed to cabinet for consideration in June 1973.[13] A few centers were selected for immediate financial support, and further studies were commenced to plan for the development of these selected centers,

to affirm recommendations on other centers previously studied but not recommended for immediate development, and to identify possible new sites with growth potential.

Cabinet considered the five-year program and from it derived the budgeted program for the first year, 1973–1974. The following are some of the details of that first year's allocations.

The Australian government made $9 million available to support development of Albury/Wodonga. These funds were to be spent primarily on land acquisition, with some set aside for selected public works and for social infrastructure. Initial studies indicated that a population of 300,000 by the year 2000 could be a viable proposition for Albury/Wodonga.

In the case of Bathurst/Orange, $2 million were provided for assistance to the growth center. This project was seen as primarily the responsibility of the New South Wales government. Studies were commenced to define the further growth potential of the area, after initial studies assessed the feasibility of increasing population to around 250,000 to 300,000.

A total of $7.4 million was allocated for developments at Gosford/Wyong, north of Sydney, and in the Menai/Holsworthy/Campbelltown corridor to the south. These were primarily funds for land acquisition and site development.

In Victoria a total of $5 million was set aside for expenditure at Geelong and to the southeast of Melbourne. Again this was primarily money for land acquisition, but with emphasis in the latter case on acquisition of critical areas for recreation and conservation as a means of guaranteeing their continued protection against urban development.

Some $1.25 million were provided for assistance to the South Australian government for its project at Monarto, while $3.5 million were budgeted for the development of Salvado in the northwest corridor of Perth. These were primarily funds for land acquisition. An allocation of $0.5 million was made to assist the Tasmanian government in preparing state strategic plans and developing state and regional planning organizations.

Provision was made for a total of $4.5 million to be extended on projects in Queensland, consisting of $2.0 million for the development of Townsville, $1.25 million for social and other infrastructure in the Fitzroy region, and $1.25 million primarily for land acquisition in the Moreton Region (Brisbane).

The total budget for the program in the first year, $33.1 million, was seen as rapidly accumulating over the following five years to about five times the allocation of the first year. This was the order of capital believed to be necessary for a successful, continuing program.

The funds were offered to state governments under Section 96 of the Australian Constitution, which states, in part, that "the Parliament may grant financial assistance to any State on such terms and conditions as the Parliament sees fit."[14]

The terms and conditions that the Australian governments sought as part of its provision of assistance under the growth centers program were broadly that for each project assisted under the program there should be

1. Public acquisition of the necessary land.
2. State legislation establishing controls on land price for those lands to be publicly acquired.
3. State legislation establishing a development corporation or at least a single planning, development, and management agency for each project.
4. Agreement and, if necessary, supporting legislation to provide for leasehold tenure within growth centers, at least for most nonresidential land uses.
5. Commitment by the state governments that growth centers would receive priority in the state's own planning and budgeting.

Development funds would be provided to the states by the Commonwealth as 30-year loans, with interest tied to the long-term bond rate, 10-year deferment for commencement of loan repayments, and a guarantee that the states would be indemnified by the Commonwealth for losses incurred on growth center development. Incomes from the sale or lease of developed land were expected to be adequate in time, for loan repayments and sufficient for growth center projects to become self-sustaining through reinvestment of development profits.

These terms were acceptable to some of the state governments, but not to others, which was reflected in the differing degrees of progress made in reaching agreement with the states to proceed with the projects for which the Commonwealth budgeted funds. Only four projects became the subject of formal intergovernment agreements—Albury/ Wodonga, Bathurst/Orange, Macarthur, and Monarto—involving three states: New South Wales, Victoria, and South Australia. Tasmania received grants for state strategic studies. No projects were agreed upon in Queensland or Western Australia.

PROGRESS

Five major projects have commenced: Albury/ Wodonga, Bathurst/Orange, Macarthur, Monarto, and Geelong.

Albury/Wodonga. The Albury/Wodonga project has two main aims. Through accelerated growth to establish it as an alternative to metropolitan areas, the government intends that the project affect the long-term growth of Sydney and Melbourne. Accelerated growth will result in greater employment, career, education, living place, and other social opportunities than currently exist for communities in the hinterland of Albury/Wodonga.

A number of factors have been identified as central to the potential of Albury/Wodonga to achieve these aims. The center is located on the major communication network between Sydney and Melbourne and is especially well served by rail and road links. The greater Albury/Wodonga district is one of the most versatile primary producing areas in Australia. The two cities constitute a major service and distribution center. Secondary industry is well established, and both cities have attracted a significant number and range of industrial activities. Even before growth center proposals, the growing economic base of Albury/Wodonga had singled it out as an exceptional rural center in growth terms.

The governments of the Commonwealth, New South Wales, and Victoria formally decided in January 1973 to develop Albury/Wodonga as a growth center with a target population of 300,000 by the year 2000. The Cities Commission authorized an initial investigation of the area. The Commission's first five-year report summarized the results to the government on June 30 1973. The initial investigation mostly concerned establishing the physical, economic, social, and environmental factors and constraints that would influence the achievement of the target population.

Following the initial investigations, major studies of land use, economics, water resources, and the environment commenced. These studies culminated in the designation of 54,000 hectares of land surrounding the two cities for the development of the growth center. Negotiations progressed among the three governments on the nature of the arrangements for the development of the growth center and the institutional framework to carry out the development. The agreements reached between the three governments were set forth in the Albury/Wodonga Area

Development Agreement, which was signed October 23, 1973, and was subsequently approved by acts of the parliaments of the Commonwealth and the two states.[15]

The broad objectives of the project set forth in the preamble to the Albury/Wodonga Area Development Agreement are as follows.

And whereas the intentions of the three Governments are:

that a Development Corporation will bring about in the Area, by the development of the growth complex, the creation of a city with a high quality of environment, appropriately planned and developed having full regard to human requirements and the involvement of the public. . . .

The basic purposes of the corporation include (1) the promotion and economic development of the growth complex and its region and the mobilization and maximization of private-sector confidence and growth and (2) the coordination of public- and private-sector investment in accord with a firm development strategy.

In the context of the population target of 300,000 people by the year 2000, the development corporation has carried out planning and set growth targets for the next 10-year period. In March 1975, the development corporation published a report outlining a range of alternative short- and medium-term plans for physical development over the next 5 to 10 years. In August 1975 the three governments, in a ministerial council, approved the adoption of the southern development strategy outlined in the report and involving

1. The first major greenfields development in the growth center at Baranduda to the south and east of Wodonga for commencement in 1976–1977 (see Figures 2 and 3).
2. A second greenfields development in Thurgoona to the north and east of Albury for commencement in 1977–1978.

3. Concurrent with the preparations for the greenfields development, the development corporation would continue development in the designated areas contiguous to the existing urban areas of Albury and Wodonga.

The medium-term (10-year) development strategy is based on the attaction of an additional 50,000 people to the growth center to bring the total population to 96,000 by about 1986. The development corporation's five-year plan for the period 1975–1976 to 1979–1980 is based on an increase of about 16,000 people and 9000 jobs during the five-year period. This involves an average growth rate of about 6 percent per year compared with a rate of about 3 percent prior to the commencement of growth center implementation.

Table 3 indicates estimated physical achievement to June 1976 in Albury/Wodonga and the other growth center projects. Much of the development site has been acquired, and construction has commenced for housing, infrastructure, and nonresidential building (including offices).

The former Labor government under Prime Minister Whitlam had decided to transfer significant numbers of government agencies and their employees to Albury/Wodonga to boost its initial development. The agencies proposed for either establishment in or transfer to the growth center would have provided a total of 1900 new jobs over a five-year period commencing 1976–1977. The Fraser government rescinded these transfer decisions both as a part of its total review of government structures and as part of its review of the growth centers program. In October 1976, however, the government opened the way for a future government transfer program by deciding that growth centers could be considered as suitable locations for government employment.

The private sector has also expressed considerable interest in the development of Albury/Wodonga. Information is available in relation to growth of

Table 3 Estimates of Physical Achievement, to June 1976

	Albury/Wodonga	Bathurst/Orange	Monarto	Macarthur
Land acquired (ha)	23,941	3,631	15,400	5,225
Land developed into residential lots	711	405	—	—
Industrial (ha)	75	31	—	260
Homes started/completed	408	145	—	—
Other building (m^2)	4,600	5,400	—	500
Commonwealth expenditure (in thousand $)	83,834	13,613	10,286	26,712

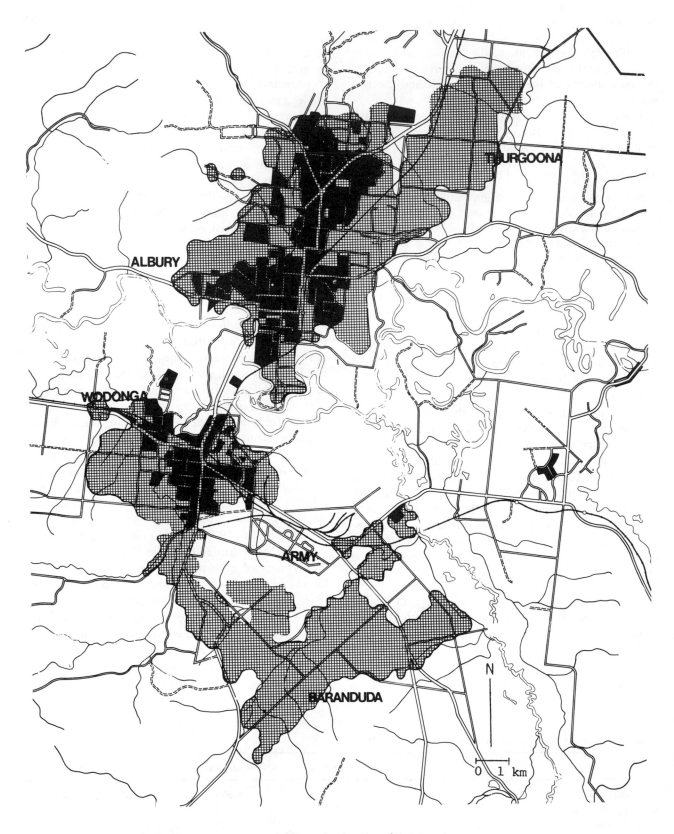

Figure 2. Medium-term—the next decade or so—development plan for Albury/Wodonga. The black shows the existing cities of Albury-Wodonga. In hatching are the areas to be developed in the 1980s.

Figure 3. The beautiful Middle Creek valley, about eight kilometers southeast of Wodonga, is the site for the proposed new city of Baranduda, part of the Albury/Wodonga accelerated development project. Baranduda is expected to reach a population of 30,000 in the 1980s. The Albury/Wodonga target population is 300,000 by the turn of the century.

private-sector employment in 1975. The 1976 annual survey of private-sector establishments, which takes place as part of the preparation of the forward development plan, involves all firms in Albury/Wodonga with more than 20 employees and 20 percent of those with less than 20 employees. Results show that private employment in Albury/Wodonga in the calendar year 1975 increased by 7.5 percent from 12,030 to 12,930. For the fiscal year ending June 1976, employment was expected to increase by 12.8 percent from 12,460 to 14,050.

Albury/Wodonga has enjoyed relatively low unemployment compared with other nonmetropolitan centers. At the end of March 1976, there were 1434 persons unemployed. This is estimated to represent an unemployment rate of some 4 percent or less, compared with rates of 6.4 percent, 7.05 percent, and 6.25 percent for nonmetropolitan Australia, New South Wales, and Victoria, respectively. This suggests that the development program may have saved Albury/Wodonga from the generally depressed economic conditions applying in Australia as a whole, and in nonmetropolitan areas in particular.

In relation to employment growth over the next few years, the Albury/Wodonga Development Corporation has provided information on firms likely to establish on land held by the development corporation (see Table 4). This does not include possible new relocations and expansion of existing firms on private freehold land within the built-up areas of Albury and Wodonga. The corporation is confident that most of the 23 firms would establish on corporation estates, given an assurance of firm government support for the growth center. These firms would employ about 1270 people, corresponding to an equivalent population increment of about 3500. Active negotiations are

being pursued with another 20 firms with a possible total employment potential of between 1000 and 1500 people. If these negotiations are successful, the associated direct population increment could again be about 3500. The corporation has also had discussions with an additional 20 firms.

Also indicative of the effect of the growth center program is the increase in private-sector investment in Albury/Wodonga. Table 5 gives information available in 1974–1975.

Considerable doubt was cast over the future of Albury/Wodonga by the lack of commitment from the newly elected Conservative Commonwealth government led by Prime Minister Fraser. However, the government in October 1976 decided to continue to support the project for the next five years, provided the state governments share the cost with the Commonwealth on a dollar-for-dollar basis. Other changes would include less emphasis on land acquisition and a greater role than before for the private sector in development of the project. The position is now being negotiated among the three governments.

Bathurst/Orange. The Bathurst/Orange growth center (present population 54,000) is situated 220 kilometers west of Sydney. Development within the

Table 4   Establishment on Albury/Wodonga Development Corporation Estates

Sector	Number of Firms	Direct Employment
Manufacturing	12	1020
Service	7	200
Semigovernment	4	50

Table 5   Increase of Private-Sector Investment, 1974–1975

	Albury/Wodonga		National	
	$ (in millions)	Increase on Previous Year (%)	$ (in millions)	Increase on Previous Year (%)
Dwellings	10.6	−19.2	2456	−1.4
Nondwellings and civil works	9.6	+74.6	1986	+24.7
Vehicles, plant, and machinery	18.7	+110.9	4435	+17.3

growth center is currently occurring around the existing townships of Bathurst, Orange, and Blayney. These existing urban areas do not have sufficient land with urban potential for expected future demands for residential and industrial land. For this reason a new city is proposed about midway between Bathurst and Orange to accommodate anticipated future growth of about 100,000 by the year 2006. No development on the proposed new city area is contemplated in the next five years. Development will continue to focus in and around the existing town centers during these years.

In March 1974, Bathurst/Orange was designated as a growth center under the New South Wales Growth Centres (Development Corporations) Act 1974. The development corporation for Bathurst/Orange was subsequently established in July 1974 with a full-time chairman and five part-time members of the board. Later two Commonwealth government nominees were appointed to the board.

The objectives of the Bathurst/Orange growth center are best illustrated by the projected population targets for the year 2001, given in Table 6.

Under the arrangements of the development program the Bathurst/Orange Development Corporation was required to prepare and submit for consideration by the ministerial conference each year a forward plan for the development of the growth complex based on a rate of growth agreed to by the ministers.

Table 6   Populations for Bathurst/Orange

	1975	2001
Bathurst	18,060	44,600
Orange	24,824	54,600
New City	—	78,000
Blayney	2,479	9,100
Rural Area	8,056	9,800
Total	53,419	196,100

Commonwealth funds have been made available ($5 million in 1974–1975, $8.6 million in 1975–1976) to the Bathurst/Orange Development Corporation and the local government authorities in the growth center for land acquisition, development, and municipal works backlog in accordance with approved programs. Table 1 shows direct expenditures for the growth center.

Commonwealth and state ministers noted a five-year development program at a conference in October 1975, and they agreed to consider an up-dated five-year plan at their next conference. Decisions made in October 1976 by the present Commonwealth government mean, however, that the ministerial arrangements and the need for consideration of a development program will be discontinued, at least as far as the Commonwealth is concerned. From 1977–1978, the Commonwealth will simply provide loan funds to match expenditures on agreed activities of a capital nature by the New South Wales government on a $1 for $2 basis. This position is now being negotiated with the New South Wales government.

Table 3 shows physical progress to date in Bathurst/Orange. In early 1976 the New South Wales government transferred its Central Mapping Authority with some 350 employees to Bathurst and has announced its intention to transfer its Soil Conservation Service to Orange and the NSW Police Academy to Bathurst. The previous Commonwealth government had planned to locate some 1000 public employees in Bathurst/Orange, but the present government rescinded these decisions.

The Bathurst/Orange Development Corporation has had inquiries from about 50 private firms since its establishment in July 1974. Two manufacturers have already commenced construction of factories and another ten have indicated serious intentions to relocate. The estimated total employment associated with these 12 firms is in the vicinity of 900. As a direct result of the government transfers and the increased private-sector activity in the growth center, at least five local firms are known to have expanded their operations resulting in staff increases of some 65 employees.

The development corporation states that its objectives are related in an overall sense to attracting people to the center and retaining those already living there as well as providing an alternative lifestyle to that found in the metropolis. Specifically, its objectives can be summarized as follows:

1. To promote and coordinate the orderly and economic development of the center.
2. To enhance the quality of the center.
3. To optimize the efficient use of all resources.
4. To provide an efficient, adequate land use/transportation system.
5. To develop the growth center at the minimum feasible financial cost with the maximum social benefits.
6. To establish systems to aid the coordinated implementation of public- and private-sector plans.
7. To develop the growth center as a regional center adequately serving the region.
8. To provide opportunities, freedom of choice, variety, equity, and participation to all members of the community.

In March 1975 the Commonwealth and New South Wales governments exchanged documents comprising the formal intergovernment agreements for development of Bathurst/Orange, including specific arrangements for ministerial consultations, and for consideration of rolling five-year development programs for the project. The ministerial arrangements provided for a ministerial conference of Commonwealth and state ministers to meet formally at least two or three times each year and possibly more frequently during the initial phase of the development of the growth centers. The function of the ministerial conference involved a process of consultation and negotiation to arrive at agreed development and financial programs based on agreed proposals concerning growth, planning, and organization.

Macarthur. The Macarthur growth center, lying some 60 kilometers southwest of Sydney, is virtually an extension of the development of the Sydney metropolitan area. The project has existed under various titles during the past few years (Sydney South West Sector, Holsworthy/Campbelltown), but it was formally established in March 1975, through both an intergovernment agreement on the project and the creation of a development board having

powers similar to those of a development corporation but not existing as a separate statutory authority.

The Macarthur Development Board was established under the New South Wales Planning and Environment Act 1973. It powers have been formally delegated to the board by the NSW Planning and Environment Commission. The board has a part-time chairman, appointed by the Planning and Environment Commission, and a full-time deputy chairman and general manager. In addition, the board has two state and two Commonwealth nominees, and each of the four municipal councils within the development area of the growth center is represented.

The project's objective is to develop a series of relatively self-contained cities instead of dormitory suburbs. This is intended to relieve pressures on metropolitan communications and to provide greater opportunity for balance and diversity in homes, jobs, community services, and recreational facilities than would be provided by suburbs.

The new cities of Campbelltown, Camden, and Appin will be grouped around a major new regional center being incrementally developed to offer metropolitan services and commercial facilities for a population of up to 500,000. Each new city is designed to have a separate identity.

The planned capacity and time span for the new cities are set out in Table 7. However, actual development is tailored to the short-term future rather than these long-term projections.

The concept was first made public in the *Sydney Region Outline Plan Strategy Report,* published by NSW in 1968. Before the publication of that plan the state purchased about 4000 hectares of land to secure control of some key areas (commercial and industrial) to assist in influencing the development of the project.

Until the signing of the Growth Centre Agreement in 1975, the state had invested about $170 million in the area. The headworks for water and sewerage capable of serving a population in Campbelltown City of about 100,000 people had been installed; industrial estate development was in progress, and a large

Table 7 Development Strategy, Macarthur Growth Center

Location	Population	Time Span
Campbelltown	230,000	1972–1985
Camden	100,000	1978–1990
Appin	170,000	1984–2000
Total	500,000	

public housing program was substantially underway, with a forward program of dwelling construction committed to 1980.

In 1968 the population of the growth center was about 30,000. It has now reached 70,000. On the basis of committed public housing programs plus continued private-sector involvement, the population is anticipated to reach 100,000 during 1978 and 125,000 by 1980.

The development strategy pursued by the Macarthur Development Board concentrates on the following:

Production of Industrial Land. Industrial development work is essentially concerned with installation of basic infrastructure to enable industrial sites to be turned on. To meet employment targets in the area, at least 60 hectares per year over the next five years are required. Current indicators of demand point to present shortfall of 150 hectares of industrial sites.

Development of the Regional Commercial Center. The focus of the regional center is the provision of basic infrastructure such as roads, bridges, servicing, and drainage to enable the first stage of this project (50,000 square meters) to be completed in 1978. A private company is to develop the building and related facilities that make up the center.

Construction of a Government Office Center. A site is available for construction of this center. Some infrastructure installations are required to enable building construction. The intention is for the private sector to construct the office center on a build/lease basis to accommodate about 2000 employees.

Production of Residential Land and Housing. The strategy of the Macarthur Development Board is to leave the production of residential land and housing construction substantially to the NSW Housing Commission and to the private sector.

University. The Commonwealth and state have agreed that Sydney's next university will be located in the regional center at Campbelltown. A site has been agreed upon and is available. The aim is to begin preliminary planning and design work at the earliest opportunity.

Table 3 shows details of progress in the physical development of Macarthur in recent years. There are already some 95 industrial firms in the growth center. These firms now employ some 2700 workers. Of these firms, 20 are only partly established; completion of establishment would lead to a creation of some 1000 further jobs.

Fifteen establishments, including important firms such as Pirelli (300), Unilever (250), Arnotts (3000), Johnson and Johnson (100), and Bowater Scott (250),

have made the decision to relocate since the previous Commonwealth government became associated with the growth center. Establishment of these firms would add some 4500 employees to the area.

Restrictions on the level of funds during 1976–1977, imposed by the Commonwealth government, will reduce the pace of public investment, but the Commonwealth has decided to continue financial support for the project in the future, on the basis of loans to the state of $1 of Commonwealth funds for each $2 of state funds spent on agreed-upon activities.

Monarto. Monarto was announced as a state initiative by the South Australian government in March 1972 as a major development initiative to syphon off population growth from metropolitan Adelaide to avoid the problems that confront Melbourne and Sydney. It is a metropolitan growth center in that it will develop within the influence of the Adelaide metropolitan area, but Monarto will be a self-contained entity.

The Monarto Development Commission was established under state legislation in January 1974 to plan and develop the new city. One member of the three-man commission is a nominee of the Commonwealth.

The project was formulated within the context of 1961–1971 population trends, which fixed a population figure of between 1.4 million and 1.6 million for Adelaide by the year 2000. Based on these projections, initial proposals for Monarto envisaged a population of 150,000 by the turn of the century, and initial development planning was based on this target.

South Australia also envisaged Monarto as a special project to be promoted and financed outside the constraints of time and cost imposed by state works budgets. There was an explicit assumption in the development strategy initiated by the Monarto Development Commission that the new city project would be accorded top priority by the state and Commonwealth governments, with the latter providing the bulk of development capital during the establishment phase of the project.

Commonwealth funds have been provided for the project under the Urban and Regional Development (Financial Assistance) Act (1974), on terms and conditions specified from time to time in annual financial agreements between the Commonwealth and state governments. Financial assistance is for the most part by way of repayable loans at the long-term bond rate payable over 30 years with a 10-year deferment of repayments.

The most recent forward development plan prepared for Monarto in November 1975 envisages a first stage geared to a population target of 15,000 by December 1985. The plan relates to the official state population projections, which assume an annual increment of 10,300 people for the decade ending 1985. The actual rate of increase since 1971 census has consistently exceeded this and suggests that an average annual increase of at least 14,000 is more likely to occur for the next 10-year period. The 1974–1975 increase was 17,000 people. Monarto, as it is now conceived, would take no more than 20 percent of forecast population increase and provide less than 10 percent of the demand for served residential land.

The growth path of Adelaide since 1971 is obviously sufficient to sustain and justify an alternative urban node. The contentious issues at present are not whether the revised growth target for Monarto stage 1 is technically feasible but whether (1) the state government will order its priorities to ensure that the priority for Monarto and the priority accorded to other major metropolitan subcenters are consistent and the allocation of resources is coordinated, and (2) the new stage-1 building block of 15,000 is large enough to secure efficient viable delivery of basic urban services.

The main thrust of expenditure in the 1973–1974 and 1974–1975 fiscal years has been toward the acquisition of the designated site of approximately 16,000 hectares and locations for basic headworks in the area adjoining the designated site. A total of $7.8 million has been spent on essential land acquisition, and this stage of the project is now virtually complete.

The stated reason for accelerated acquisition has been to constrain land speculation in the area adjoining Monarto and limit the effect speculation would have on compensation claims from vendors within the designated site itself. This objective has been achieved to the extent that the designated site has been purchased for the relatively modest sum of $7.8 million. This figure is quite small in terms of total investment expenditure, and the cost of raw land in final marketing costs for serviced residential land will be small enough to enable the development commission to offer sites to prospective residents at attractive prices. Table 3 summarizes physical progress to date.

Next to land acquisition, the most important activity undertaken by the Monarto Development Commission has been project investigation. A conceptual plan has been formulated and a viability study concluded for the original concept aiming at a population target of more than 150,000. A number of studies are also in progress connected with the shape and form of Monarto.

The Commonwealth government has not committed itself at present to any future support for the Monarto project, and it is therefore probable that its development will be long-term.

Geelong. Geelong is a metropolitan growth-center project in that its aim is to structure, in a strategic sense, future growth within the Port Phillip region, by promoting Geelong as an alternative center to Melbourne for employment and population. To achieve this in the medium term is primarily a task of regional economic development to avoid the probability of social and economic decline of the Geelong region that would arise without action to stimulate growth.

Analysis of unemployment figures since 1960 shows that under the most favorable economic conditions Geelong still suffered from a persistently high unemployment, rarely below 2 percent. The sudden structural changes that affected the Australian economy in recent years have worsened this persistent structural unemployment. This and the continued depressed state of the Australian economy have kept the overall rate of unemployment in Geelong at more than twice the national rate.

In October 1974 a steering committee of officials was established to carry out a program of studies to investigate the general social, physical, and economic means by which the growth center objectives could be achieved and the existing and emerging needs of the Geelong region accommodated. From the study program it emerged that the strategy should have two broad themes—growth and conservation. In relation to the growth theme, the need for strong policy actions to foster new employment in the region is paramount.

The key elements of the proposed strategy can be summarized as follows:

1. Population growth in the region to be confined mainly to existing urban Geelong, a few rural towns, and major new city development southwest of and close to the present city so as to be integrated with it.
2. The central business district of existing Geelong to be enhanced as the regional focus in function and identity.
3. Permanent population growth in the coastal towns to be curbed as far as possible so that they may retain their resort character.

4. Preservation and enhancement of the special conservation and recreational assets in the region.

5. A mixed policy of economic development that broadens the economic structure through the injection of new public and private tertiary employment (to provide employment opportunities for the young and lead to an increase in the opportunity for work force participation by females) and that restructures the Geelong manufacturing sector through selective expansion so that it is not so dependent on several major cyclically sensitive industries and is an alternative manufacturing location to Melbourne.

In December 1974 the then prime minister and the premier of Victoria made arrangements that provided for a ministerial committee to oversee future policy developed for the project. The committee considered a document proposing the future management of development in the region (including the structure of the development organization), but formal agreements between governments was not reached. No financial arrangements were concluded for Geelong's development.

Notwithstanding that the former Commonwealth government did not formally make a commitment to Geelong, the government did make a number of investment decisions that reflected its support for Geelong as a growth center:

1. 1973–1974 budget allocation of $3 million (not taken up).
2. 1974–1975 budget allocation of $20 million (not taken up).
3. Funding of 1974–1975 Geelong Study Program by Cities Commission: $0.6 million.
4. Support for establishment of a new university at Geelong.
5. Cabinet decision to transfer National Animal Health Laboratory to Geelong.
6. Cabinet decision to transfer National Biological Standards Laboratory to Geelong (later rescinded by the present government).
7. Cabinet decision to negotiate with developers for provision of office space to accommodate 1000 office employees (later rescinded by the present government).

The Victorian Parliament has passed enabling legislation for a Geelong Development Authority. Unless guarantees of financial assistance are forthcoming, the Victorian government probably will not be prepared to proceed with these special institutional arrangements to manage the future planning and development. The present Commonwealth government has decided not to allocate funds for assistance to Geelong in 1976–1977 and to review its future commitment at some later time.

Other Projects. In the three years after June 1973 the Commonwealth and states undertook joint planning studies for economic, social, and physical development in Townsville, the Fitzroy region, Moreton region, Gosford/Wyong, Southeast Sector of Melbourne, and Perth, but the governments did not formally agree to any funding of development. The present Commonwealth government, after its review of the growth center policy, will probably again offer state governments the opportunity to propose further projects for Commonwealth support in the future, so that the studies undertaken to date will provide a useful basis for presenting project proposals.

PROSPECTS

The growth centers program was originally formulated at a time when national population projections indicated that Australia could anticipate a total population of between 17 million and 23 million by the year 2000, an increase of between 4 million and 9 million over present levels.[16] However, recently Australian fertility rates have declined, as has net immigration.

The First Report of the National Population Inquiry suggested that if the decrease in the birth rate continues and stabilizes at low levels for the rest of the century, it would result in a national population of only 15.9 million at the year 2001, excluding any immigration after 1973. If immigration continues to add an average of 50,000 settlers to the population each year, the national total, with a continued low birth rate, would be some 17.6 million by the year 2001, or the lower end of the range envisaged at the time the growth centers program was planned. Even if higher levels of fertility were in fact to apply, a national total population of 20 million probably would not be exceeded.[17]

In June 1973, when the growth centers program was initiated, Australia's population was estimated to be 13.132 million. Growth to 17.6 million would represent an increase of 4.5 million. The growth centers now in the program will provide for a total population of around 1.15 million, or a growth capacity approaching 1 million people (see Table 1).

Albury/Wodonga and Bathurst/Orange are the only growth centers at all distant from a major metropolitan complex. Together they provide a planned growth capacity for around 400,000 people in major urban areas outside the metropolitan regions (see Table 8). This would represent roughly 9 percent of an anticipated national population increase of some 4.5 million. Canberra alone over recent years has absorbed around 7 percent per year of the total national population growth, while Albury/Wodonga and Bathurst/Orange have together accommodated somewhat less than 1.5 percent of national growth.

Monarto and Macarthur provide capacity for 580,000 people, or almost a further 13 percent of anticipated national population growth. If, as expected, Sydney continues to absorb a significant share of national growth, there seems every likelihood of Macarthur developing to capacity over the remainder of the century. Monarto will probably not achieve its target population until the next century without firm, specific policy decisions relating to its priority with regard to other possible developments in South Australia.

Delivering the Walter Burley Griffin Memorial Lecture in Canberra in 1972 prior to the election of the Labor party to office, Tom Uren, then Labor spokesman on urban affairs spelled out his party's objectives as follows, advocating a population policy that would ensure a national population not exceeding 18 million by the end of the century:

Our natural annual increase in population during the last 23 years has been 1.1 per cent. Immigration has added another 0.8 per cent. As a result we have had an annual overall increase of 1.9 per cent over the period of the present government's administration. With a 1.1 per cent growth rate our population would be 17.3 million at the end of the century. . . . If we can put one million people into our new cities in regional areas in Australia by the end of the century we will be making real progress. . . . If the population increases by 1.1 per cent annually until the year 2000 and we put one million people in new cities and regional areas we will have 3.3 million people left who will live in the existing large cities and system cities.[18]

In these terms the growth centers program is still seen as a fundamental part of policy, even in the context of relatively slow rates of national population growth. It is tempting to take the view that slower national growth, implying a smaller population at some chosen year in the future, obviates the need for such a program. This is, however, a precarious position. First, population projections are only projections—the factors that control population growth are only partly predictable. They are strongly influenced by social attitudes, and some are subject to policy intervention. It would be foolhardy to abandon a program with significant long-term implications for the accommodation of future growth on such uncertain grounds. Second, the long-term advantages of a growth centers program are substantial, as the Canberra experience already demonstrates. On the grounds of both efficiency and equity, the creation of new nodes of substantial urban growth away from the existing metropolitan centers can be justified. The population of those regions, for example, would be provided with a far wider range of opportunities than at present, and others would face a greater choice of locations in which to enjoy the advantages of living in a medium to large urban center.

Nonetheless, it would be equally foolhardy to pursue a substantial growth centers program ignoring national population projections. Obviously, decisions such as the number, scale, and timing of projects must be related to such projections. This is in fact being done in each instance where the Commonwealth government is providing financial assistance. As a basis for long-range planning, target populations for each growth center for the year 2000 are set and assessed in terms of feasibility. Actual year-by-year expenditure is geared to five-year rolling programs, which in turn are related to short-term targets and projections. In other words, a mechanism is established for ready review of programs based on realization of actual population growth and on short-term projections but set against long-term objectives.

Another argument against growth centers arises from the assumption that slower national growth means slower growth throughout the nation. This argument is untenable because the factors affecting

Table 8   Australian Growth Centers: Current and Projected Population

	Estimated Population, 1975	Assumed Target Population	Increase, 1975–2001
Albury/Wodonga	46,000	300,000	254,000
Bathurst/Orange	54,000	200,000	146,000
Monarto	—	150,000	150,000
Macarthur	70,000	500,000	430,000
Total	170,000	1,150,000	980,000

aggregate national population growth are different from and only distantly related to the factors affecting population distribution. Where people choose to live will be related to their particular aspirations and the opportunities in the alternatives they consider. The growth centers will offer attractions that will compete with other locations as realistic options among people's choices of living areas, and these choices will be influenced by considerations about quality of life. There is little reason why the growth centers could not be expected to capture their needed segment of the market in conditions of declining rates of population growth, zero population growth, or population decline. The distribution of population can be in a continual state of flux under any of these conditions, and there are international examples of this happening.[19]

An associated common fallacy is to assume that the metropolitan regions must continue to expand under conditions of slower national growth at the expense of other parts of the nation. In particular, the continued growth of Sydney and Melbourne is widely regarded as a foregone conclusion. Nonetheless, Sydney's share of national population growth has declined from 22 percent between 1966 and 1971 to 21 percent in 1971–1972 and 15 percent in 1974–1975. Lower birth rates and lower international net migration are contributing factors. However, net internal migration away from Sydney has become increasingly significant in recent years. Each year between 1966 and 1971 Sydney had an average surplus of departures over arrivals of around 2000 people, aged five years or more. By 1973–1974 Sydney's net loss to other parts of Australia was estimated to have reached almost 41,000 people, of all ages.

Melbourne's share of national population has also declined, but less dramatically than Sydney's, from 24 percent in 1966–1971 to 22 percent in 1974–1975. Melbourne is still gaining through net internal migration, but between 1971–1972 and 1973–1974 the estimated gain fell from 14,000 to less than 200.[20]

In other words, there are marginal trends that cast doubts on the validity of assuming unchecked natural growth for the major metropolitan areas—trends that suggest that people may be seeking nonmetropolitan opportunities and that the growth centers policy, particulary the regional growth center, may be extremely apposite in its timing for meeting a growing social need.

A related, important aspect of slower national population growth is, of course, the extent to which this will reduce the effective demand for land, housing, and urban services, a component of which would be provided under the growth centers program. There are indications still being studied that the age structure of the Australian population is now such that the rate of family formation will continue to be relatively high, despite a decline in the rate of aggregate growth, and that smaller families will account for part of the aggregate change. This implies that there will be a continual, great demand for urban accommodation for some time into the future, and changes in the age structure will not affect the demand for land, housing, and services for several decades.

In other words, simplistic interpretations of the relation between slower rates of national population growth and growth center policy will continue to be inadequate. There is certainly a need for careful, long-term, willful, positive planning—not simply a reaction to the demand for accommodation of trends.

The prospects for attracting economic activities to metropolitan growth centers appear to be excellent. One recent study of the locational preferences of business activities in Melbourne showed clearly the importance of the simple availability of land and premises as a major factor in their choice of intrametropolitan locations. The metropolitan growth centers should provide adequate supplies of competitively priced land and premises.[21] In regional growth centers the prospects are less obvious, the issue is more controversial, and the steps that will need to be taken will be more substantial than in metropolitan centers. These steps, however, will be realistic.

Growth center theory, the geographic evolution of Perroux's growth pole concept, argues that if they are to grow, geographic centers of economic growth must contain "propulsive" economic activities, or in other words, growth poles.[22] Obviously, if policy is to create substantial economic growth in regional growth centers, the government should seek activities that are rapidly growing or are likely sources of innovation, new products, and new capital.

Traditional locational theory has much to say about the way in which firms engaged in "propulsive" economic activities might emerge and might choose to locate. In particular, M. J. Webber's treatise on the effect of uncertainty on location indicates a preference, in the context of a spatially neutral economic policy, for metropolitan locations.[23]

Two assumptions can be questioned: first, why the economic policy should be assumed to be spatially neutral, and second, the assumed adequacy of traditional locational theory in explaining the locational behavior of modern corporations. In relation to the first assumption, Australia is accustomed to patterns of economic growth that occur within a policy that rarely differentiates between locations. Certainly there are rural subsidies, and there are programs of incentives to industry to locate outside the metropolitan regions. However, as Alonso has argued, these direct spatial policies are often completely insignificant beside the massive spatial impact of other economic policies that in a *de jure* sense are spatially neutral.[24] Policies for tariff, taxation, public investment, communications, pricing, and many others are not explicitly spatial, but do have the effect of constructing an economic framework that favors metropolitan locations. The spatial effects of such policies should be subject to scrutiny and the policies themselves reviewed in accord with the objectives of policy for urban and regional development.

It is also desirable to question the second assumption of the applicability of traditional locational theory as a means of describing or predicting the locational behavior of modern multiproduct, multiplant, multinational corporations, as opposed to the behavior of privately owned, single-product, single-plant firms on which the theory is based. The former corporations, particularly large ones, have far more diverse objectives than simple cost minimization or profit maximization with respect to each plant they operate. Their motives appear to be directed toward corporate growth, profits, and security. They are demonstrably capable of complex cost and income substitution across the corporate structure and of sustaining long-run suboptimal operations—for example, to exclude competitors from a given market and thereby achieve long-run security. They are therefore likely to be relatively "footloose" in terms of their choice of single plant locations.[25]

Economic base theory which underlies the assumption that employment growth precedes population growth in developing urban centers, can also be questioned. Richard Muth cast substantial doubts on this in his study "Migration: Chicken or Egg," and recently a study on internal migration and economic growth in Australia by John Paterson Urban Systems for the Cities Commission, concluded that increased metropolitan dominance could be avoided by the provision of attractive labor markets together with developed social and physical infrastructure in selected locations.[26] In other words, investment in infrastructure will serve to attract population and

economic activities, and the simple linearities of the model of the economic base need not apply.

In general these issues should not be viewed from too simplistic a position and the *status quo* in terms of the framework of economic policies that influence private-sector decisions should not be simply accepted. The economic prospects for regional growth centers cannot be predicted *a priori,* but ways of positively influencing those prospects can be examined and evolved, possibly with better results than anticipated. The relocation of some public activities to growth centers is underway. Substantial progress could be made over the next few years, which will have a strong influence on progress and development and on private-sector decisions.

CONCLUSION

Growth-center policy is necessarily an evolving policy. A sound start has been made, but there are still many real, practical problems to be studied, analyzed, and overcome. It may be far more successful than might be intuitively anticipated, but it will take some time for the success to be evident. In the meantime, however, there are sufficient indicators of changing social preferences in terms of the quality of urban environment that people want to justify its continued strong support.

NOTES

1. T. Uren, "Urban and Regional Development 1974–1975: Budget Paper No. 8" (Canberra: Australia Government Printing Service, 1974), p. 23.

2. In October 1976 the Commonwealth cabinet decided to offer the states a further $6 million for Albury/Wodonga, $2 million for Bathurst/Orange, and $3 million for Macarthur in addition to the funds already allocated in the 1976–1977 Commonwealth budget.

3. Commonwealth Housing Commission, *Final Report* (Canberra: Ministry of Post-War Reconstruction, 1944), p. 27.

4. G. M. Neutze, "Economic Policy and the Size of Cities" (Canberra: Australian National University Press, 1967), especially Chapters 7 and 8; and Development Corporation of New South Wales, *Report on Selective Decentralisation* (Sydney: Development Corporation of New South Wales, 1969).

5. Decentralisation Advisory Committee, *Report on the Selection of Places outside Melbourne for Accelerated Development* (Victoria: Victoria Government Printer, 1967).

6. Australia, *Report of the Commonwealth-State Officials Committee on Decentralisation* (Canberra: Australian Government Publishing Service, 1972).

7. *First Report of the Task Force on New Cities for Australia* (Canberra: Australian Institute of Urban Studies, 1972).

8. Australia, National Urban and Regional Development Authority Act, 1972, No. 117 of 1972.

9. Australia, Cities Commission Act, 1973, No. 41 of 1973.

10. *Report to the Australian Government* (Canberra: Cities Commission, June 1973).

11. Australia, *First Report of the Committee of Inquiry into Land Tenure* (Canberra: Australian Government Publishing Service, 1973).

12. "Sydney Region Outline Plan 1970–2000 A.D." (Sydney: New South Wales State Planning Authority, 1969).

13. *Report to the Australian Government.*

14. The Constitution of the Commonwealth of Australia, Section 96.

15. Enabling legislation for the Albury/Wodonga project was passed by the three governments involved, as follows:

Australia: Growth Centres (Financial Assistance) Act 1973
Australia: Albury/Wodonga Development Act 1973
Australia: Albury/Wodonga Development (Financial Assistance) Act 1973
New South Wales: Albury/Wodonga Development Act 1974
New South Wales: Growth Centres (Land Acquisition) Act, 1974
Victoria: Albury/Wodonga Agreement Act 1973
Victoria: Wodonga Areas Land Acquisition Act 1973
Victoria: Development Areas Act 1973
Victoria: Lands Compensation Act 1973

16. *Report to the Australian Government,* p. 13.

17. Australia, *Population and Australia: A Demographic Analysis and Projection,* First Report of the National Population Inquiry, vol. 1 (Canberra: Australian Government Publishing Service, 1975), pp. 280–292.

18. T. Uren, MP, Walter Burley Griffin Memorial Lecture, November 3, 1972, pp. 4–6 (mimeo).

19. William Alonso and Elliott Medrich, "Spontaneous Growth Centers in Twentieth Century American Urbanisation," in *Growth Centers in Regional Economic Development,* Niles Hansen, Ed. (New York: Free Press, 1972), pp. 229–265.

20. Australia, Bureau of Statistics, *"Internal Migration" 1969–1970 to 1974–1975,* Reference No. 4:26 (Canberra: Australian Bureau of Statistics, 1976).

21. Lyndsay Neilson, "Business Activities in Three Melbourne Suburbs" (Canberra: Urban Research Unit, Australian National University, 1973).

22. Tormed Hermansen, "Development Poles and Related Theories: A Synoptic Review," in *Growth Centers in Regional Economic Development,* pp. 160–203.

23. M. J. Webber, *Impact of Uncertainty on Location* (Canberra: Australian National University Press, 1972).

24. W. Alonso, "Problems, Purposes and Implicit Policies for a National Strategy of Urbanisation." Paper prepared for the National Commission on Population Growth and the American Future, August 1971 (mimeo).

25. A. Pred, "Industry, Information and City-System Interdependencies," selected extracts from A. Pred, "The Growth and Development of Systems of Cities in Advanced Economies" in Gunnar Tornquist and Allan R. Pred, "Information Flows and Systems of Cities: Two Essays," Lund Studies in Geography, Series B40 (Stockholm; University of Lund, 1973).

26. Richard F. Muth, "Migration: Chicken or Egg," *Southern Economic Journal* (1971):295–306. See also John Paterson Urban Systems, "Models of Internal Migration: Australia" (Canberra: Cities Commission, 1975).

CHAPTER 21

New Towns in Poland: Policies, Development, and Current Trends

CHARLES Z. SZCZEPANSKI

At the end of World War I the 1000-year-old nation of Poland was freed from its century-long occupation by three neighbors (see Table 1). For 400 years Poland was the largest country in central and western Europe, one of the mightiest,[1] and the only one able to stand against the Turkish armies. She was resurrected in 1918 with greatly reduced frontiers, access to the Baltic Sea, but left without a seaport. By 1922, still involved in the war on its east frontier, Poland started construction of its first new town since the beginning of the twentieth century. The small village of Gdynia in Gdańsk Bay was selected as a location for a new port on the Baltic.

Gdynia grew very fast; by 1939 it was the largest seaport on the Baltic with a population of 125,000.[2] This harbor was designed as the main outlet of Poland in overseas commerce. A new direct railroad line from mining districts of Silesia in the southern part of the country aided the flow of coal, one of the main export products. Despite extensive commercial harbor activities, Gdynia located in the middle of a summer resort seashore district, maintained an attractive overall environmental quality.

The second major event stimulating new-town construction between the world wars was the development of the Central Industrial Region (GOP).

It was initiated in 1936, in large part as a new region for the defense industry. Centrally located near the sources of essential raw materials in an area with excess labor force, the region was properly conceived and rationally developed. Many factories were finished when the war started in 1939. The most significant new town in the region was Stalowa Wola. In 1938 about 10 percent of the town area was completed, with 6000 residents settled there. The master plan for approximately 2000 acres was designed for 30,000 residents. In 1964 the town had 25,000 population, with local employment of 9000 in metallurgy and machine-building industry.[3]

Between World Wars I and II necessary basic methods of regional and local planning were developed in Poland. Enough planners were trained to provide a steady supply of specialists in later stages of regional and urban planning. The chair of city planning was established at Warsaw Polytechnic in 1915. Since then Professor Tadeusz Tołwinski has led training of many generations of planners and educators. The program, equally balanced among social and cultural requirements, technology, systems engineering, environmental considerations, and historical preservation, has assured a sound theoretical basis for several decades of planning. In 1927 John Chmielewski prepared the first regional plan for long-range development of the popular summer and winter tourism in the area of Zakopane in the Tatra Mountains.[4] The plan, partially implemented before

This chapter represents the personal views of the author and does not necessarily reflect those of the United States Department of Housing and Urban Development.

Table 1   Changes in Population and Area of Poland

Year	Population	Area (mi^2)
1000	1,500,000	120,000
1620	9,000,000	382,000
1938	35,000,000	148,000
1945	25,000,000	120,000
1975	34,000,000	120,000

1939, contained features, such as the transportation system, which remain valid among planning objectives in sophisticated plans of the 1970s. The "Functional Warsaw" regional plan for the capital of Poland was completed in 1936 by John Chmielewski and S. Syrkus. An exhibition visited by many thousands followed. This regional plan, innovative through its rigorous functional analysis, contributed broadly to formulation of planning theory, creation of permanent development trends, and genuine involvement of the population in planning (see Figure 1).

In the late 1930s regional studies were completed for nine key areas, covering half of the country; and in 1936 the preparation of a national plan was initiated (see Figure 2).

OUTLINE OF PLANNING SINCE WORLD WAR II

During the period 1939–1945 as a result of the German invasion and the Polish resistance struggle, the Warsaw insurrection in 1944, and the fight between the German and Russian armies, 40 percent of all buildings were destroyed and about 20 percent of the Polish population was killed.[5]

National Plan Study, 1947. Immediately after the war, on the basis of the Decree on Spatial Management of the Country of 1946, urban, regional, and national planning studies in all regions of Poland were simultaneously initiated.[6] In 1947 and 1948 two volumes of national plan studies were published.[7] The methodology resembled that used in prewar market economy times. It consisted in large part of the analysis of regional natural and human resources and principal transportation flows in long-range transit and in the interurban exchange—main flow directions were considered as growth corridors. Physical growth studies indicated the direction of development corridors, and study of local conditions defined in-

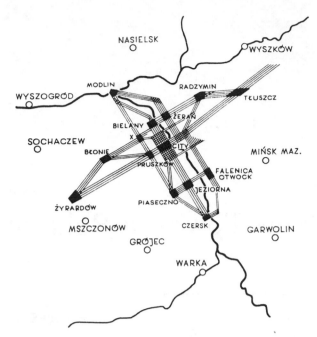

Figure 1. Diagram of "Warsaw Functional" metropolitan regional plan of 1936 by J. Chmielewski and S. Syrkus. Source: *Problematyka Przestrzennago zagospodarowania Kraju)*

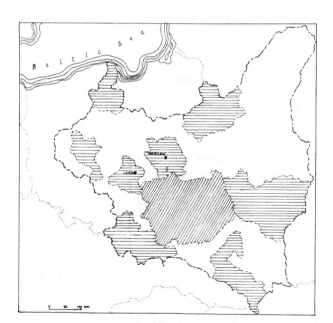

⎯ ⎯ ⎯   Poland's boundaries in 1937

··········   Boundaries of other states in 1937

•   Towns above 500,000 inhabitants (in 1938)

≣≣≣   Areas covered by regional planning

///////   The Central Industrial Area

Figure 2. The areas covered by regional plans in Poland between the wars, 1938. Reprinted from Jack Fisher: *City and Regional Planning in Poland.* Copyright 1966 by Cornell University. Used by permission of Cornell University Press.

dustry and other locational recommendations, which together with considerations of environmental preservation requirements indicated the width of development corridors. A general principle of decentralization of industrial activities was followed in an attempt to reduce further growth pressures in Silesia and the Warsaw area. Three major industrial growth areas were defined: prewar (GOP) Central Industrial Region; Region Piła in the north; and Region Wizna, near Białystok in the northeast. Three development periods were indicated: (1) reconstruction—up to 1950, including completion of resettlement resulting from major changes in the outline of national frontiers, and basic housing and industrial reconstruction; (2) industrialization—up to 1965, with concentration on development of significant industrial potential; (3) urbanization—up to 1980, with concentration on further strengthening the network of utilities, consumer goods, and provision of adequate services. Population and employment were predicted for 1950—24 million with 35 percent urban population, and employment of 50 percent in agriculture, 25 percent in industry, and 20 percent in services; for 1965—28 million population, with 50 percent urban residents, and employment of 40 percent in agriculture, 30 percent in industry, and 25 percent in services; for 1980—32 million population, with 62 percent urban residents, and employment of 27 percent in agriculture, 30 percent in industry, and 33 percent in services. Despite being prepared with incomplete statistical data and using simple calculations, these estimates fall close to actual levels that occurred during the 25 years following preparation of the studies of the 1947 National Plan (see Figures 3, 4, and 5). Only the process of industrialization in 1965 was faster than predicted, with 6.6 percent more of the population employed there than expected (see Table 2).

As planned during the period 1950 to 1960 the industry in Silesia, Warsaw, and other established regions was growing, but at a slower rate than in

EXIST.	PROP.	
+++++	+++++	RAILROADS
=====	=====	AUTOROUTES
-----	-----	OTHER MAJOR ROUTES
		AGRICULTURAL AREAS
		FORESTS
		AREAS WITH GOOD TRANSPORTATION SERVICE
		POTENTIAL ECONOMIC GROWTH AREAS
		EXISTING METROPOLITAN AREAS
		PROPOSED METROPOLITAN AREAS
-----	-----	EDGE OF INTENSIVE DEVELOPMENT
....		MAJOR TOURISM AREAS

Figure 3. Land-use zoning of Poland in the national plan of 1947. Source: *wg Atlasu GUPP.*

other regions. Consequently, the proportion of the output in old centers was reduced significantly. For example, the centers of Katowice (Silesia), Wrocław, and Łódz between 1946 and 1959 dropped from 60.7 percent of total industrial production of Poland to 45.8 percent. Least industrialized areas, such as Białystok, Olsztyn, Koszalin, Szczecin, Lublin, and Rzeszów, increased their contribution from 6.3 to 11.6 percent in this period.[8] In the second interval

Table 2 Distribution of Basic Occupations and Residence

Year	Agriculture (%)	Industry and Services (%)	Rural (%)	Urban (%)	Total Population
1938			70.0	30.0	34,682,000
1950	47.1	52.9	61.0	39.0	24,824,000
1970	29.8	70.2	48.0	52.0	32,805,000

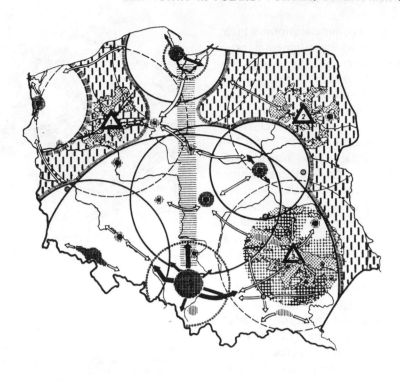

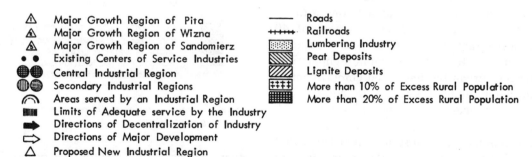

△ Major Growth Region of Piła
△ Major Growth Region of Wizna
△ Major Growth Region of Sandomierz
● ● Existing Centers of Service Industries
◉◉ Central Industrial Region
◉◉ Secondary Industrial Regions
⌒ Areas served by an Industrial Region
▦ Limits of Adequate service by the Industry
➡ Directions of Decentralization of Industry
▷ Directions of Major Development
△ Proposed New Industrial Region
⌒ Service Region of Proposed Industrial Region

─── Roads
+++++ Railroads
▦ Lumbering Industry
▨ Peat Deposits
▨ Lignite Deposits
▦ More than 10% of Excess Rural Population
▦ More than 20% of Excess Rural Population

Figure 4. Hypothesis of redistribution and location of industrial centers in the national plan of 1947 Source: *Atlasu GUPP: Studium planu krajowego,* 1947.

between 1960 and 1972 least developed regions had industrial growth rates of 308 to 442 percent, and previously mentioned districts increased their overall share to 15 percent of the national production. The most developed region, Katowice, had only 189 percent growth rate and reduced its input to national totals from 36.5 percent in 1950 to 18.9 percent in 1972. The efforts to balance the distribution of industrial activities followed the objectives closely. The concepts of the national plan studies of 1947 have been implemented satisfactorily.

Early Regional Plans and the New Towns. Regional plans supporting preparation of the national plan

study of 1947 were initiated just after the war in 1945. Basic concepts were ready to feed into the national plan in 1947, but further studies continued until the early 1950s.

Typical of the early regional plans, and one of the most important, is that of Silesia for the GOP, centering at Katowice. State authorities did not formally approve the plan until 1953, but the fundamental ideas for restructuring this coal mining and industrial center were relatively clear around 1950[9] (see Figure 6). The most active core of 930 square miles, with 12 towns of 1,400,000 total population and many coal mines, was named area A and designated for rehabilitation, protection against further development, and residential decentralization.[10] The outer belt of the core, covering 270 square miles, was called B—still covered by woods and lakes, it had a good environment for the location of housing communities. Surplus population from area A, which could not be provided with a good living environment

and social facilities, as well as most of new residents of the region, were designated to move to area B. Several locations were selected for new or extended towns. Nine small old towns were selected: Pyskowice, Rokitnica, Radzionków, Tarnowskie Góry, Grodziec, Gołonog, Knurów, Halemba, Nowe

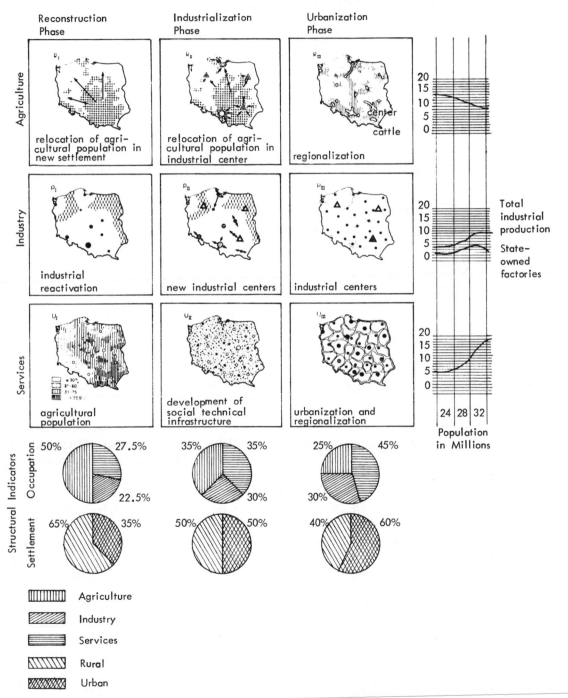

Figure 5. The outline of basic principles of the national plan of 1947. Source: *Atlasu GUPP: Studium planu krajowego,* 1947.

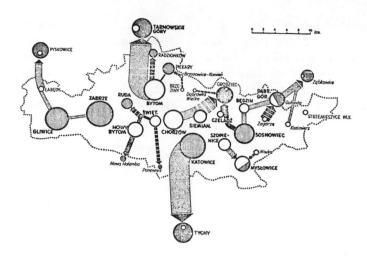

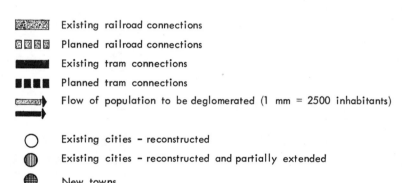

········   Boundary of zone "A" – determined by first phase of regional plan

    Existing railroad connections

    Planned railroad connections

    Existing tram connections

    Planned tram connections

    Flow of population to be deglomerated (1 mm = 2500 inhabitants)

○   Existing cities – reconstructed

◍   Existing cities – reconstructed and partially extended

●   New towns

Figure 6.   GOP deglomeration plan, prepared in 1953 (scale of cities by thousands of inhabitants). Reprinted from Jack Fisher: *City and Regional Planning in Poland.* Copyright 1966 by Cornell University. Used by permission of Cornell University Press.

Tychy, and Kedzierzyn further away. Not all of these towns were developed during the first 25 years, when approximately 300,000 population was expected to settle in area B. The basic principle in locating these towns was the possibility to reach the work place by rapid rail in less than 20 minutes (see Table 3).

Rehabilitation of the towns and cities in area A aims at renewing the living environment. It consists of rehabilitation of housing and provision of social infrastructure, community centers, shopping, open space, kindergartens, and so on. One of the outstanding examples of rehabilitation of industrial wasteland took place between Chorzów and Katowice in the middle of area A. A 1500-acre area of slag piles was transformed into a recreational center, with a sports stadium for 100,000 people, zoological park, amusement park, exhibition area, and a public park.

Nowe Tychy is the largest new town in this region. It had to satisfy a great need for a completely new,

healthy, residential environment located near the capital of Silesia: Katowice. Mining and industrial congestion in this area created inadequate conditions for a large portion of housing. Nowe Tychy, according to the 1945–1950 regional plan, was designated to fill a large part of these needs (see Figure 7).

In 1951 a national competition was organized to select the concept of the town plan and the chief planner for its implementation. The team from Warsaw Polytechnic Planning Institute directed by Professor K. Wejchert and Mrs. H. Adamczewska-Wejchert, won the competition. They have managed the planning and implementation of the town since then. The population of 130,000 was a growth objective to be achieved by 1980. Development of the town from an initial 10,000 population is progressing closely to schedule: it reached 61,000 in 1964 and 75,000 in 1972. Current discussion on continuation of town development concerns extending initial figures

Table 3   Population Statistics of New Towns Built After 1950

Town Name	Beginning		Planned				Existing			Town Type	
	Year	Population	1960	1970	1980	Later	1955	1960	1972	Use	Location
Nowa Huta	1950	2,000	100,000	120,000			70,000	100,000	120,000	With employment	Satellite
Nowe Tychy	1952	10,000	62,000	100,000		200,000	28,000	51,000	75,000	Residential	Freestanding
Pyskowice	1953	6,000	35,000	40,000			16,000	22,000	23,000	Residential	Satellite
Radzionków	1950	7,000	24,000	60,000			13,000	24,300	28,500	Residential	Satellite
Kędzierzyn	1950	10,000	28,000	60,000			21,000	21,000			Freestanding
Gołonóg	1955	1,500	20,000	40,000			1,500	14,000		Residential	Satellite
Swidnik/Lublin	1951	1,000	20,000	26,000			7,000	12,700	24,100	With employment	Satellite
Knurów								14,800	31,500	Residential	
Jastrzębie	1960	2,900	2,900		60,000	150,000			45,900	Residential	Freestanding

Source: *Town Planning in Poland, City and Regional Planning in Poland,* and *Mały Rocznik Statystyczny.*

to 200,000 population largely because of the location of an automobile factory in one of the areas designated for industrial activities (see Figure 8).

Three elements of the physical form of the town are especially worthy of mention in detail: (1) transition from the old town to new developments; (2) early-stage housing community B with the curvilinear street patterns; (3) Community E2 with irregular site plan and softened building shapes (see Figure 9).

In the largest coke yielding coal-mining district near Rybnik south of Katowice, construction of another freestanding new town was started in the early 1960s.[11] Jastrzębie expanded from its early population of 2900 to 21,000 in 1965. The initial objective for 1980 was 60,000, but it was later extended to 150,000. Construction of this town is now progressing vigorously.

Kraków Region. Directly to the east of Silesia the Kraków region offers two prime features: the perfectly preserved historic area of the city of Kraków and the southern part of the region, the rocky Tatra Mountains. Kraków was the capital of Poland between the tenth and sixteenth centuries, and the mountains include the most popular and fashionable summer and winter resort and sports region. The middle part of the region is industrial and the northern part agricultural. Regional planning was initiated here in 1927, with a series of studies prepared in 1938, 1945, 1949, and 1952.[12] The plan for 1961–1980 is a current basis for management of long-range growth. The employment of current excess rural population and of the natural increase of population, changing from 2,550,000 to 3,400,000, is planned in the same region. Except for Kraków, which grew from 240,000 in 1939 to 509,000 in 1964, the largest percentage of growth is expected in Oświęcim, which should grow from 24,000 in 1960 to 100,000 in 1980.

The city of Kraków resembles a giant museum, with its impeccably restored, preserved, and maintained royal castle, hundreds of old churches, and thousands of private buildings dating from the eleventh to sixteenth century. The prewar city of his-

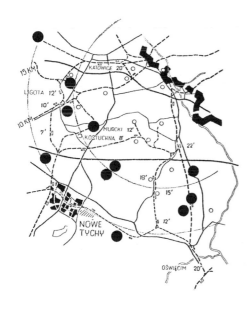

——— Main roads

● Location of mines

10 KM or 15 KM – Distance from Katowice

- - - - Railroad line

22', 15' – Number of minutes by train from Nowe Tychy

Figure 7. Rapid rail travel time from Nowe Tychy to surrounding mines and other employment centers. Source: *Nowe Tychy.*

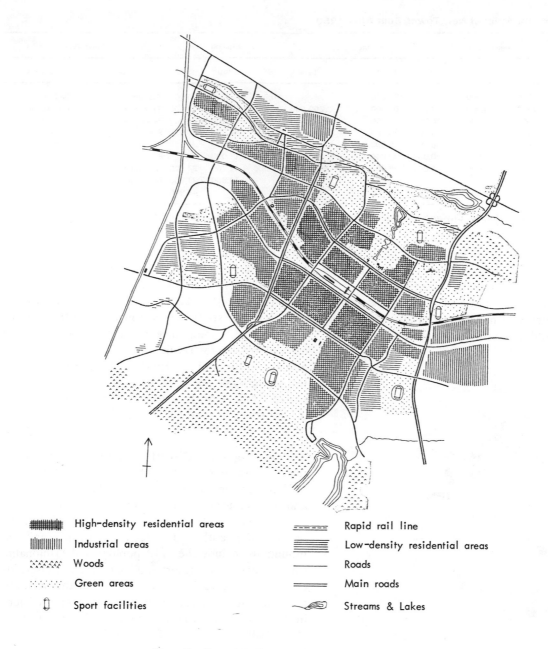

High-density residential areas   Rapid rail line

Industrial areas   Low-density residential areas

Woods   Roads

Green areas   Main roads

Sport facilities   Streams & Lakes

Figure 8. General development plan of Nowe Tychy. Source: *Nowe Tychy.*

toric monuments has been expanded significantly since World War II. Its old functions of historic symbol and intellectual and cultural center have changed by large extension of the university and construction of new, large, industrial sectors. More life has come to the city, but significant environmental problems have appeared. The population in the city increased from 344,000 in 1950 to 610,000 in 1972.

Thirteen new communities were built in the metropolitan area to house and serve increased population. Most of the communities are located east and north of the old town near the roads leading toward Nowa Huta, a new gigantic steel mill (see Table 4 and Figures 10 to 13).

Average size of these communities is close to 20,000, and the density varies between 50 dwelling units per acre to 140 dwelling units per acre with corresponding floor area ratios (FAR) of 2 to 4. Such density compares with medium housing density used in Washington, D.C., where FAR 6 applies. Tables 5 to 7 list the basic services required by regulations at the completion of the projects in an average community. The major employment centers were not in-

cluded in these purely residential communities. They are located within walking distance or a 30-minute ride by public transportation.

Twelve communities listed in Table 4, excluding Nowa Huta, were systematically evaluated by B. Bartkowicz for their qualities in location, internal

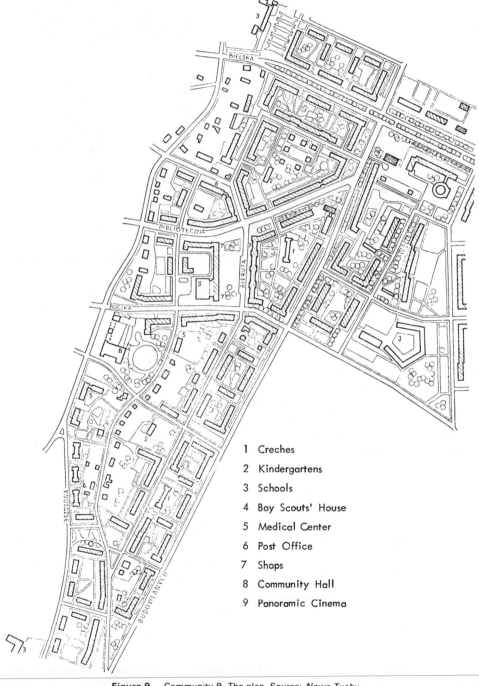

1 Creches

2 Kindergartens

3 Schools

4 Boy Scouts' House

5 Medical Center

6 Post Office

7 Shops

8 Community Hall

9 Panoramic Cinema

Figure 9.   Community B. The plan. Source: *Nowe Tychy*.

Table 4 Planned Population of New Communities

Community Name	Population
18th Stycznia	30,000
Wrocławska	8,000
Azory I	12,000
Azory II	12,000
Prądnicka	6,000
Olsza Wiśniowa	7,000
Wieczysta Ugorek	5,000
Nowogrzegorzecka	6,500
Na Kozłówku	14,000
Bieńczyce	40,000
Wzgórza Kreslawickie	14,000
Nowa Huta	100,000
Dąbie	7,000

Source: *Wypoczynek Codzienny Mieszkańców Nowych Osiedli na Przykładzie Krakowa.*

functional arrangement, physical design, open space, and design of recreational grounds.[13] Detailed criteria used in evaluation included the following requirements.

For locational analysis:

1. Public transit connected to place of work and sociocultural centers within a 30-minute journey.
2. Walking distance to local and district shopping centers of less than 10 minutes.
3. Public transit access to large open space areas and to major sports parks within a 30-minute journey.
4. Provision for equipped and maintained neighborhood open space areas.
5. No disturbance by surrounding industrial activities.

For community functional arrangement:

6. Major traffic arteries not bisecting the community.
7. Provision for a good, internal pedestrian traffic pattern.
8. Separation of the garages from residential buildings.
9. Separation of major pedestrian ways from mechanized traffic, good landscaping.
10. Development plan satisfying the standards in provision of social infrastructure.

▭	Industrial zone
▥	Agricultural zone
▨	Recreational zone
▧	The area of intensive agricultural production
┅┅┅	Communication network
———	Boundary of Voivodship
━━━	State frontier
●	Health resorts
◍	Planned size of town

Figure 10. The plan of the Kraków region. Reprinted from Jack Fisher: *City and Regional Planning in Poland.* Copyright 1966 by Cornell University. Used by permission of Cornell University Press.

Table 5 Basic Services

Nurseries	1 for 119 babies
Kindergarten	1 for 480 children
Elementary schools	1 for 1660 students
Commercial space	18,000 ft²
Craftsmen shops	21,000 ft²
Restaurants	3,900 ft²
Administration	6,100 ft²

Source: *Wypoczynek Codzienny Mieszkańców Nowych Osiedli na Przykładzie Krakowa.*

Table 6 Cultural Facilities

	Polish Standards	Existent in Kraków, 1966
The libraries	1000 volumes/1000 residents	1170 volumes/1000 residents
Movie theaters	40 seats/1000 residents	20 seats/1000 residents
Theaters	8 seats/1000 residents	10 seats/1000 residents

Source: *Wypoczynek Codzienny Mieszkańców Nowych Osiedli na Przykładzie Krakowa.*

11. Location of social infrastructure elements on main pedestrian ways and proper landscaping of the surroundings.
12. Integration of the social infrastructure with the neighborhood and community open space pattern.

For physical design of the community:

13. Adaptation of the design to natural characteristics of the site.
14. Integration of residential, recreational, and open space elements of the community.

1. Housing, 7 to 11 floors
2. Housing, 5 floors
3. Housing, 1 to 2 floors
4. Community Services
5. Nurseries
6. Community Parks
7. Visually Incompatible Activities
8. Tramway Line and Stops

Figure 11. Plan of Nowogrzegorzecka Community. Source: *Wypoczynek Codzienny Mieszkańców Nowych Osiedli na Przykładzie Krakowa.*

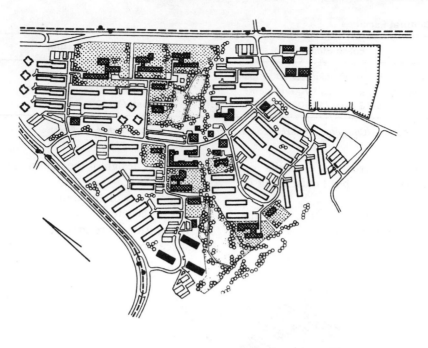

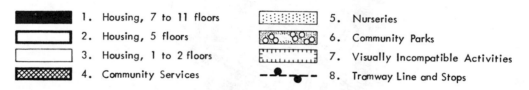

1. Housing, 7 to 11 floors   5. Nurseries
2. Housing, 5 floors   6. Community Parks
3. Housing, 1 to 2 floors   7. Visually Incompatible Activities
4. Community Services   8. Tramway Line and Stops

Figure 12. Plan of na Kozłówku Community Source: *Wypoczynek Codzienny Mieszkańców Nowych Osiedli na Przykładzie Krakowa.*

15. Aesthetic quality in urban design of large ensembles—scale, proportion, and so on.
16. Interesting views and perspectives among the buildings of the project, quality of views from the buildings toward the community and toward the city.
17. Appealing architectural design of residential and service buildings.

For the quality of open space and recreational facilities:

18. Design of playgrounds for small children up to six years old.
19. Parks and play areas for seven- to eleven-year-old children.
20 Sport facilities for teenagers and adults.

Table 7 Open Space in Kraków (ft^2/person)

Type	1965	Planned for 1970	1980	Polish Standards
Downtown parks and squares	53	77	187	165
Large parks	143	146	231	—
Metropolitan woods	19	38	186	—
Vegetable gardens	42	69	83	83
Sport parks	26	36	52	44

Source: *Wypoczynek Codzienny Mieszkańców Nowych Osiedli na Przykładzie Krakowa.*

21. Recreational areas for adults and elderly.
22. Percentage of well-landscaped and maintained areas.
23. Percentage of unfinished and damaged landscaping.
24. Percentage of the terrain that was not cleaned after construction.
25. Percentage of the area not integrated in community project.

The analysis of 12 communities, made after a 1967 survey, produced ratings in accordance with the listed criteria (see Table 8). Several of the analyzed communities were still in the early stages of construction.[14] The results range for project design from 77 percent to 46 percent and for implemented facilities as used by the residents in 1967, from 68 to 38 percent. The small difference between ratings for community design and project implementation indicates that the design usually is faithfully executed.

New town Nowa Huta (new steel mill) was hastily started immediately after World War II to implement economic growth objectives of the new political regime. At this time Kraków's prewar regional plan was not yet adapted to the entirely new postwar situation and assumptions that included large industrial activity. The new steel mill was initially designed for production of 1.5 million tons of raw steel per year. Later the mill was considerably enlarged producing close to 6 million tons per year, nearly 1 percent of world production. The impact of new activities on the old city, including air quality problems, were not taken into consideration. Nowa Huta was built for the 100,000 people necessary to meet the labor demand in the first phase of operation of the mill.

The plan selected from a planning competition follows a baroque pattern, unusual for Polish planning tradition at the middle of the twentieth century. A one-kilometer-wide greenbelt separates the town

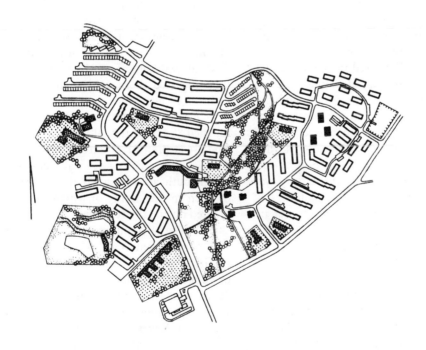

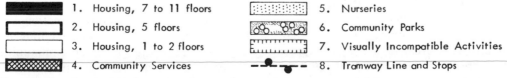

1. Housing, 7 to 11 floors	5. Nurseries
2. Housing, 5 floors	6. Community Parks
3. Housing, 1 to 2 floors	7. Visually Incompatible Activities
4. Community Services	8. Tramway Line and Stops

Figure 13. Plan of Wzgórza Krzesławickie Community. Source: *Wypoczynek Codzienny Mieszkańców Nowych Osiedli na Przykładzie Krakowa.*

Table 8 Rating of 12 Communities[a]

High Rating		Low Rating	
For Project Design	Developmental State, 1967	For Project Design	Developmental State, 1967
11 very good	11 very good	2 very good	1 very good
8 adequate	2 adequate	4 adequate	1 adequate
4 usable	10 usable	15 usable	21 usable
1 not included	1 not included	3 not included	1 not included
Out of 24 factors	23 out of 24	21 out of 24	23 out of 24
23 were evaluated			
Requirements satisfied			
77%	68%	46%	38%

[a] 3 = very good, 2 = adequate, 1 = usable; nonexistent features not evaluated.

from the steel mill. Building such an industrial complex and town four years after the end of the war (in which Poland theoretically was victorious, but lost 20 percent of population, 20 percent of her territory, and 40 percent of all buildings) was an enormous effort. During 10 years of intensive work, the new-town construction crew, housed in newly erected buildings, varied between 5000 and 10,000 people. In 1954 the combined construction crew for the town and the steel mill counted 26,000, all housed in newly erected, permanent buildings. Residential densities strongly fluctuated in yearly construction programs and different parts of town. In the next housing construction period in section C the density increased to 240 persons per acre in five-story, monotonous, historically imitative buildings. In construction of section D, the last part of the program, the density was reduced to 180 persons per acre, with buildings of various heights, good modern design, and proper integration with the landscape.

New town Bieńczyce for 40,000 people, which is a continuation of Nowa Huta, has a completely different character expressed by imaginatively varied building heights and irregular plan patterns.

Nowa Huta was without a doubt a great achievement for its time, dramatically increasing the industrial potential of reconstructed Poland. The steel mill output allowed the doubling of prewar steel production. The mill also was an important experimental ground for new construction methods, organization of production, and evaluation of social effects of various forms of town planning. However, many environmental problems created in the development rush remain to be resolved. Installation of equipment to control air pollution from the steel mill is one of the most expensive and urgently needed.

Warsaw Region. The region in which the national capital has been located since the end of the sixteenth century covers an area in which the traces of the first settlements date from the tenth century B.C. The thirteenth-century seat of the Prince of Mazovia became the meeting place of the Congress of the Polish Lithuanian Commonwealth in the middle of the sixteenth century. In 1564 Warsaw's population was about 14,000; in 1792 it was 100,000 with 500 industrial buildings. In 1828 a large iron smelting factory operated there, and steam engines were used in eight factories. An international railroad network was built between 1844 and 1861. In 1914 the population reached 884,000, and 600 factories were located there. In 1916 a plan of Greater Warsaw was prepared by Tolwinski, indicating several elements such as a new north-south artery, railroad networks, and a pattern of open spaces, many of which were gradually implemented during the following 50 years.[15]

In 1939 the population of Warsaw was 1,300,000. The "Functional Warsaw" Plan of 1934 remained an inspiring regional plan concept for a long time. Its principle of two linear chains of towns crossing each other was confirmed later by many plans,[16] and various portions were progressively implemented (see Figure 1). Several nodes of growth of this plan, primarily those later interconnected with rapid rail transit, became new towns (Ursus, Legionowo) or extended towns. Table 9 gives population predictions for such towns.

Warsaw region concentrates national administrative, educational, and cultural functions in the central city. Several towns or outer communities are the places of large industrial operations, including a steel mill; auto and trucks factory; and manufacturers of mechanical, electrical, and electronic equipment.[17]

Reconstruction and development plans were prepared for Warsaw in 1945, 1965, and 1970. Between 1939 and 1945, 80 to 85 percent of all buildings in Warsaw were demolished. The decision to rebuild the city at the same location was based on historic and economic factors. Reconstruction of historic buildings was essential to assure continuation of national tradition, and it was less expensive to repair damaged sewer and water systems, streets, and bridges than to start everything anew for a city of 1,300,000 population (see Figures 14 and 15).

In addition to rebuilding the city, the 1945 plan indicates limited industrial activities and clear formulation of residential communities along existing transportation lines. More open space is introduced, including a new corridor cutting the city from north to south as well as an enlargement of the green corridor along the Vistula River.

The 1985 plan provides further clarification of major directions of growth (supported by computer analysis of the cost of development of various urban patterns), extension of industrial centers, delimitation of the communities with complete town centers, and the addition of a circumferencial road and bypassing roads, with clarification and extension of green wedges.

Since 1945 residential communities, rebuilt and new, have grown in a form of new towns in-town, but without inclusion of major places of employment, which usually were located (except in unusual cases) within a 30-minute journey by public transport. A large part of travel to work is being provided by rapid rail transit. Tramway and bus lines, overloaded for several years after the war, now contribute an essential part of a very well-balanced, fast travel system. Pedestrian traffic takes care of a large percent of displacement. An adequate fleet of taxis

and private cars, assisted by new expressways, have provided effective means for rapid personal transportation since May 1976. Between 1950 and 1965, 15 residential communities were completed, including Muranow, Wierzbno, Praga II and III; 17 communities were planned to start between 1964 and 1970; in 1965, seven of them were under construction.

Wierzbno Housing Community is located in the southern part of the city in Mokotów; it houses 23,000 people in 6950 dwelling units on 158 acres, with a density of 48 dwelling units per acre. The construction was initiated in 1955 and completed in 1965. The social infrastructure includes two nurseries, five kindergartens, three high schools, a health center, shopping, and other services. Principal community open spaces are located in the middle of the project. A pedestrian system connects the entire area. The pattern of internal driveways discourages fast driving and through traffic. Many buildings are four stories high and, regardless of a quite ingenious site plan, frequently tend to look monotonous.

The community of Szaserów, a small community with only 3300 population, was initiated in 1957 and completed in 1965. Due to various building heights and a more imaginative designer, the impression is much more lively than Wierzbno.

The communities Praga II and III are located on the eastern shore of the Vistula River near a large community park, the National Zoological Park, and a large sport center. The communities connect these three open space elements and benefit from views from and toward the river. It is an experimental project with varying architecture, mostly tall buildings; imaginative design makes it one of the most attractive new communities in Warsaw. The project houses 27,000 people on 145 acres with 6450 dwelling units and a density of 45 dwelling units per acre.

Table 9   Population of Selected Communities in Warsaw Metropolitan Region

	1950	1964	1972	1985	2000
Otwock	18,000	38,000	40,800		
Ursus		22,000	32,000		
Pruszków	28,000	38,000	44,000		
Wołomin	14,000	23,000	24,400		
Mińsk Mazowiecki	12,000	21,000	25,400		
Legionowo		21,000	21,000		
Warsaw City	804,000	1,232,000	1,355,900	1,550,000[a]	
Total in Metropolitan Region	1,181,000				2,911,000

[a] *Warsaw* (Plan) 1971, p. 64.

Source: *Mały Rocznik Statystyczny* 1965–1973.

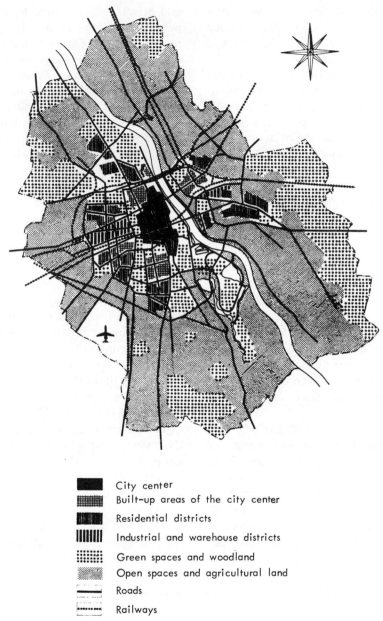

City center
Built-up areas of the city center
Residential districts
Industrial and warehouse districts
Green spaces and woodland
Open spaces and agricultural land
Roads
Railways

Figure 14. Warsaw reconstruction plan, 1945. Source: *Warsaw* (Plan), 1971.

Social infrastructure includes six elementary schools, six kindergartens, four nurseries, a large health center, a dental clinic, a shopping center, and other services (see Figure 16).

Located in the southwest part of Warsaw along the main artery going to Okęcie airport is Szosa Krakowska Community, designed for 40,000 population on a total area of 450 acres. The community is divided into six residential superblocks, each with its own set of complete social services situated in the middle. Green areas form continuous bands across the entire community. Construction started in 1957;

three superblocks were completed in 1964, and the project was planned for completion by 1967.

Directional long-range plan studies of Warsaw now aim approximately at the data of growth estimated in 1962 for the year 2000. These figures are used, but the directional plan does not intend to set the growth of the city at a certain limit; it is oriented toward indicating a general pattern and direction of possible development of the city (see Figure 17).

Predicted population for Warsaw's metropolitan region is 3 million to 4 million. Three alternatives of the directional plan considered the range of 2.5

million to 3.3 million. Central-city capacity is assumed to be 1.5 million. Therefore, approximately 1.5 million people have to be located in suburban corridors of growth. Many residents are expected to move to existing low-density communities along the rapid rail lines going to Żyrardów, Prószków, and Otwock. Similar lines of rapid rail are planned for several other directions. The population of each existing suburban community gradually will be increased to approximately 35,000, with relatively high density in the core delimited by an eight-minute walking distance. Each community core will contain complete social infrastructure; each two neighboring communities within 15-minute travel distance will

have employment and cultural and recreational facilities that will reduce the frequency of travel to central Warsaw. Travel-time objectives for the metropolitan region, including the eight-minute walk to station, range between 35 and 45 minutes, counting the access to main employment areas or cultural districts in central Warsaw. The major growth corridors are contained in a 20-mile radius.

Two independent new towns were proposed in the directional plan, both growing out of present towns of approximately 10,000 population, situated roughly 25 miles from Warsaw. One was Nowy Dwór-Modlin in the northern growth corridor at the junction of the Vistula and Bug Rivers, with a population objective

City center and groupings of services

Residential areas (high density)

Residential areas (low density)

Industrial and warehouse areas

Public green spaces and woodland

Figure 15. Warsaw development plan, 1985. Source: *Warsaw* (Plan), 1971.

Figure 16.   Praga II Community: view across Vistula River. Source: *Plan Generalny Warszawy*.

of 260,000; and the second was Góra Kalwaria in the southern growth corridor at the Vistula bank with a population objective of 140,000.[18] A computer analysis of development costs of the metropolitan region, which indicated that a pattern of four growth corridors was most advisable, also suggested forming two additional large new towns: one in the western development corridor at the present location of Pruszków on an existing rapid railway and the second in the eastern development corridor at the location of Wołomin on an existing regular railroad line[19] (see Figure 18).

The principles maintained in planning the region are rational patterns of utilities and their expected capacities and rigorous protection of certain environmental resources. Water supply is the most restrictive and growth-guiding resource. Therefore, there will be no settlements in forest, forest growth areas, wetlands, and on best agricultural lands. Green wedges will continue to separate each growth corridor and will be extended as green strips cutting central city areas. The experience in planning and developing Warsaw since 1916 allows one to have confidence that these principles will be followed, although modified at times to meet unique conditions.

Application of Analytic Technology to Housing and Planning of Towns and Cities. Since the early 1960s simple economic calculations as well as complex computer analyses were introduced to plan and design urban communities in Poland. Professor B. Malisz is the best known among early innovators in this area. He developed the threshold theory in 1963, for application in planning of large developments and small cities.[20] This theory is based on the observation that many elements in community construction have capacity thresholds. For example, an eight-inch water pipe may serve only a defined number of people. If used below capacity, its exploitation is unreasonably expensive. If demand exceeds maximum capacity of a utility system, large investment is necessary to serve even a small increase in population. The cost of service may depend on the length of utility line, type of soil it is going through, elevation, and so on. When adding regular costs and threshold considerations for all elements of utilities and services on each lot that can be available for development, the appropriate location for the project can be selected rationally. This method was used in several hundred towns in Poland. Using this experience, in 1973 the Scottish Development Department in

Edinburgh published a manual for application of threshold analysis and recommended its use for the communities between 5000 and 100,000 population.[21]

In 1964 S. Broniewski and B. Jastrzębski evolved a more sophisticated method from the threshold theory approach. The Warsaw optimization is primarily based on the cost per capita of housing community depending on physical location, design pattern of utilities, and yearly cost of service, including interest on capital and amortization. This method considers all steps of community program development, planning, utility system design, and operation of a city. Environmental evaluation is included in this process as well. A final decision is based on the analysis of 100 development alternatives ranged by cost per capita. The advantage of the method is that operations are performed by machine or by people, whichever is more able and efficient in a certain part

High density

Low density

Industry and Warehousing

Science centers

Urban parks

Vegetable growing

———— Main routes

Figure 17. Warsaw "Directional Plan." Source: *Plan Generalny Warszawy*.

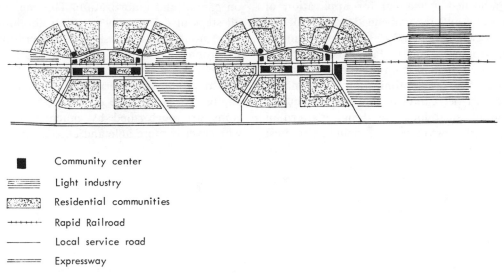

■ Community center

▤ Light industry

▦ Residential communities

+++++ Rapid Railroad

——— Local service road

═══ Expressway

Figure 18. Development scheme of a suburban growth corridor. Source: *Plan Generalny Warszawy.*

of the process. Final selection of the solution is human and political, once the predicted cost of a selected development plan is known. The selection seldom goes to the least expensive answer; it is the highest environmental quality of one reasonably priced alternative that leads to the decision. The Warsaw optimization method was applied primarily in large cities and metropolitan areas of up to 3 million population. These included Warsaw city in 1964; Skoplje, Yugoslavia, in 1965; Warsaw region in 1968; Gdynia, Sopot, Gdańsk region in 1967–1969; Łódz in 1968–1969;[22] Poznań and Częstochowa in 1972. Dr. J. Kozłowski in the Kraków Institute of Town Planning is conducting further research to combine thresholds and optimization.[23]

The Institute of Organization and Mechanization of Building Construction (IOMB) in Warsaw conducts the studies on application of optimizing analysis in design of housing communities. In 1965 Brzozowski published a study that proposed a method quantifying all expected costs in the program development phase and in preparation of detailed working drawings.[24] It considers the cost of all outside utilities and is based on national design standards and qualitative and quantitative characteristics of all elements of the construction program. In 1970 Pietraszkiewicz et al. from the Kraków office of IOMB completed the work on a mathematical model for optimization of housing communities design.[25] This model considers the requirements of national standards and regulations, the environmental requirements such as sun exposure, the cost of municipal utilities, project construction costs, and cost of land

that includes the loss of productive capacity resulting from the change of use. It also takes into account the selection of the set of typical buildings, minimization of used terrain, and several other elements.

The product of analysis may be adapted to the economic conditions of a particular year and specific economic development condition, of a defined geographic area, types of buildings, and topographic conditions of the site. The analysis also includes amortization of investment and project maintenance. Computation can be geared toward the general, executive level of decision making and to project design requirements. Preparation of this method was based on the experience of quantitative analysis on several projects such as the East Wall of Palace of Culture Square in Warsaw in 1958, the communities Zubardź in Łódź, Bederowiec in Katowice, Sas Axle in Warsaw, and Bieńczyce in Kraków.

CURRENT TRENDS AND THE NATIONAL DEVELOPMENT PLAN 1976–1990.

In March 1974 the Polish government approved the conceptual project of the National Physical Development Plan and recognized it as the basis for the 1976–1980 Five-Year Economic Plan.[26] Several studies were prepared in the 1930s, in 1947, and later, but never before were they officially approved by the government. The Planning Commission of the Council of Ministers with the cooperation of the National Academy of Sciences and of the entire national network of regional planning prepared this plan simultaneously for the nation, its macroregions, and metropolitan areas. The plan's basic philosophy aims at a policy of moderate concentration of multicentric growth. Twenty-three major growth centers were selected, out of which six are now only small cities with large growth potential and are needed in their location as major socioeconomic and cultural service centers. A design principle accepted in preparation of the national plan was the ability to serve any place in the country with the medical, commercial, educational, and cultural services with traveling time not to exceed 45 to 65 minutes.[27] The development program follows the principle of balanced growth with acceleration of economic and physical development at present, less active areas. It includes rational use of existing natural and mineral resources, development of processing industries in the regions with excess rural population, and consideration of limited labor supply through gradual transition to automated production. In physical form of growth the program supports further formation of a hierarchical network of national, regional, and local growth centers. Selected cities to become national and regional growth centers are named in the plan; prevailing growth rates of development in expanded cities and towns range between 200 and 400 percent during a 15-year period; creation of completely new towns is anticipated in only exceptional cases. Environmental protection receives primary attention in the entire development process through the ecologic approach in design limitation of used resources and application of best available technology to produce by-products instead of wastes (see Figure 19 and

Tables 10 and 11). Six potential major metropolitan areas included in the plan are Zielona Góra, Legnica-Głogów, Kalisz, Tarnów, Olsztyn, and Koszalin.

New Towns versus Extended Towns. The principle of extending cities and towns as major growth centers instead of creating entirely new towns or cities is based primarily on sociological and (sometimes) utility infrastructural elements. It appears more useful to develop existing sociocultural values and characteristics of an existing community, usually with hundreds of years of traditions, than to start a new social entity out of rather unpredictable components. A complex route is usually needed to create a self-generating center of social dynamism based on community values and pride, those being developed on social, esthetic, and physical qualities of a slowly growing new place. If certain areas were subject to environmentally devastating industrial development or lack of any centers with an adequate existing sociocultural core, completely new towns or cities are justified and are planned there.[28]

The lowest growth rate between 1970 and 1990 for other than rural areas is planned for the Katowice Metropolitan District, the heart of Silesia and most industrially developed region in Poland with a growth rate of only 115 percent, because it is difficult and expensive to provide a good living environment for the new population in this area. The highest growth among the cities is planned for Piła in Poznań Voievodship, a regional growth center with a national role and a growth rate of 295 percent. A densely populated rural region next to an inland canal, it has a

Table 10   Distribution of the Population in Various Elements of Community Systems in the National Plan, 1976-1990

	1970	1990 (in millions)	Growth Rate (%)
Major Metropolitan Concentration Areas (23)	11.6	15.2–16.7	Average 131 to 143 Range 115 to 220
Developed (10)	9.2	11.7–12.6	127 to 137
Developing (7)	1.7	2.5–2.9	144 to 164
Potential (6)	0.7	1.0–1.2	151 to 181
Regional centers with national role (15)	0.9	1.7–1.9	Average 181 to 203 Range 139 to 295
Other towns	4.6	7.8–6.9	Average 135 to 170
Rural settlements	15.6	12.7	Average 81 (decrease)
Total	32.7	37.4	Average 115

Source: "System Osadniczy w Koncepcji Planu Przestrzennego Zagospodarowania Kraju."

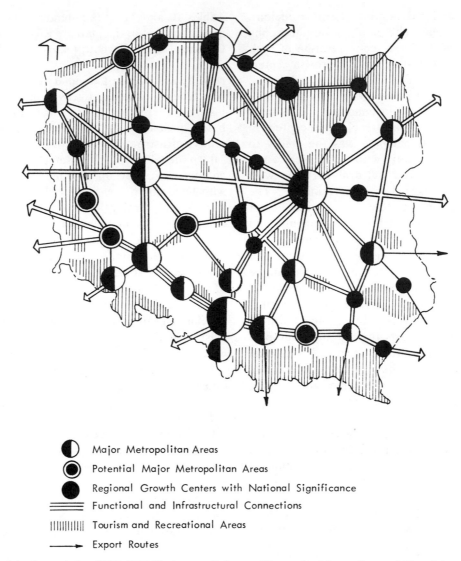

◐ Major Metropolitan Areas

◉ Potential Major Metropolitan Areas

● Regional Growth Centers with National Significance

═══ Functional and Infrastructural Connections

|||||||||| Tourism and Recreational Areas

———▶ Export Routes

Figure 19. National development plan, 1976–1990 (final proposal). Source: "System Osadniczy w Koncepcji Planu Przestrzennego Zagospodarowania Kraju."

large excess population easily adaptable to industrial occupations.

The major potential metropolitan concentration areas (see Table 10) and the regional centers with a national role, according to completed studies[29] and past Polish experience, can be treated as the best opportunity for orderly growth. These two groups of towns and cities with growth potential between 139 and 295 percent of their 1970 population can be treated as a classical extended towns program. Such a program, together with the potential advantages, also contains dangers and problems to resolve. To meet the expectations after careful selection of location in national and regional planning studies, these cities need early preparation of local growth plans as

well as development programs and schedules. These have to include estimation of infrastructural utility systems and prediction of their long-range capacities, pattern, cost, and necessary delivery time for various segments of the systems. Timely development of industrialized housing plants and early consideration of the needs for qualified technical staff and labor are equally important. In the past when decisions of industrial location were not considered in the perspective of regional planning analysis, or other of the previously mentioned preparatory development steps, planning and development processes were delayed, and serious difficulties developed.

Because of current intensive use of utility systems, the rate of investment in most of the systems during the period 1970–1990 must be high (see Table 12). The cost of all planned utility infrastructural systems is expected to take close to 9 percent of the gross national product. Such cost is high, but it is considered a reasonable expense in view of expected benefits.

Housing needs in the period 1970–1990 are composed of demand resulting from population increase, replacement of substandard housing, and the necessity to maintain some housing reserves[30] (see Tables 13, 14, and 15).

Table 11   Summary of New Development of Urban Centers and Their Types

New Towns	Past Population (in thousands)		1972 Population (in thousands)	Notes
Freestanding[a]				
Gdynia (harbor city)	2	(1920)	200	The triple city Gdańsk-Sopot and Gdynia contain 700,000 population.
Nowe Tychy (in Silesia)	10	(1945)	75	Despite its closeness to Katowice (15 miles), it's ultimate population is 200,000. It will include a university and many cultural facilities.
Jasrzębie	2.9	(1946)	46	Ultimate population 150,000. 20 miles from Katowice.
Satellite towns[b]				
Nowa Huta	0	(1945)	125	4 miles from Kraków
Bieńczyce	0	(1945)	20	Near Kraków and Nowa Huta. Ultimate population 40,000.
New town in-town[c]				
32 New Communities				In Warsaw
12 New Communities				In Kraków
Extended towns[d]				
6 Major Metropolitan Concentrations			100 to 200 60 to 130	To be developed as part of the national plan 1976–1990. The metropolitan centers are to contain 100,000 to 200,000 and the regional centers 60,000 to 130,000.
15 Regional Centers				
Rehabilitated towns and cities[e]				All old Polish cities and large towns belong to this group.
Warsaw	100	(1956)	1356	85% destroyed during the war.
Gdańsk	195	(1950)	378	80% destroyed during the war.
Wrocław	309	(1950)	542	60% destroyed during the war.
Łódź	600	(before WWII)	774	It was a major textile center. Modernized city.
Katowice	225	(1950)	308	Capital of industrial megalopolis in Silesia. Effectively modernized.
Lublin	117	(1950)	249	Historic site. Major metropolis with 2 universities.

[a] New Town relatively independent of other urban centers and cultural systems.
[b] Dependent on others for cultural services.
[c] Large residential communities with complete set of secondary social facilities. Several hundred of those have been built since World War II.
[d] The development of a hierarchical network of major cities in the national plan (1976–1990) follows previous trends and uses extensively the approach of expanding existing towns.
[e] These are old cities heavily damaged during the war and totally modernized in reconstruction.

Table 12   Expected Rate of Expansion of Selected Utilities for Poland (%)

Water supply	410
Sewer network	297
Sewage treatment	1290
Streets	
Length	117
Pavement area	299
Public transport (per 1000 residents)	
Trips	104
Seats	136
District heating	371
Solid waste	
Collection	200
Treatment	5000
Urban open space	266
Hotel rooms	437

Source: "Wstępna Hypoteza Rozwoju Komunalnych Gałęzi Techniczno Infrastructuralnych do 1990 r."

Northeast Macroregion. The northeast area of Poland, except for the Warsaw region, is the least developed in the country. It includes the regions of Olsztyn, Białystok, the northeast part of the Warsaw region, and a large part of the Lublin region. Agriculture is the primary occupation of close to 64 percent of the population. Productivity is modest: 34 percent of national agricultural lands produces 31 percent of national agricultural products. Urban network is sparse, and technical and social infrastructure of the region and the towns are inadequate. The need to bring this macroregion to the pace of activities and level of services similar to other parts of the country was recognized as a high national priority in preparation of the national plan. However, acceleration of the level of development cannot occur at the price of destroying its touristic values, such as large forests and numerous beautiful lakes in an unspoiled environment.

At the beginning the entire country will assist in acceleration of the macroregion's development, but the progress of implementation of the plans has to assure an increase of productivity in the very near fu-

Table 13   Housing Needs (1970–1990)

	Total	Cities	Country
Population increase	4,300,000	3,600,000	700,000
Replacement	2,850,000	1,150,000	1,700,000
Reserves	350,000	250,000	100,000
Total	7,500,000	5,000,000	2,500,000

Table 14   Proposed Housing Standards (m^2/unit)^a

	Housing Type			
Year	Multifamily	Single Family	Rural Multifamily	Rural Single Family
1971–1975	46	86	56	82
1976–1980	54	90	63	80
1981–1985	65	98	70	98
1986–1990	70	100	75	105

^{a} Used in preparation of the national plan.

ture. Development assumptions contain rational use of natural qualities and productive resources including acceleration of forest and agricultural production; development of facilities to serve domestic and international tourism; development of mineral resources, with a primary role of the new mining basin near Lublin with coal deposits similar in extent to Silesia (second largest in Europe). Regional development will use existing local labor resources and prepare for exchange of natural and human resources among the regions of the area and for exporting a significant part of the production to foreign countries.

The macroregion will include four metropolitan growth centers: Warsaw with 3 million population and technical, educational, research, and industrial resources supporting the entire macroregion but not expected to grow industrially in the near future; Lublin and Białystok with population objectives close to 300,000 each; Olsztyn and Ostrołęka-Łomża each with population below 200,000. This macroregion also includes four regional growth centers with national significance (each close to 100,000), and 16 regional centers of about 30,000 population each. Leading industrial activities will include electrochemical and chemical processing, manufacturing, and light industry. Several towns and cities will double in population before 1990.

Locational principles for productive activities will lead to concentration of key industries in major

Table 15   Utilities Supply (% of total number of housing units)

	1970	1990
Running water	75	98
Watercloset	56	92
Bathtub	50	88

metropolitan regions and in other regional centers, location of supporting industrial activities in subregional growth centers (primarily county seats), and location of light manufacturing in small towns and rural centers. Environmental protection and maintenance of ecological and sociological balance will influence industrial location, expansion of the towns, and use of mineral and natural resources. The industry locating in this macroregion will be applying best available technology to satisfy environmental standards, especially for air and water.

Warsaw Metropolitan Region. What are the new trends in development of the metropolitan region? Basic differences, compared with previous plans, appear now in more complete integration of Warsaw's metropolitan development with national, macroregional, and regional plans and problems, more advanced integration of the growth plans of the metro community in the socioeconomic plan, and further development of its comprehensive scientific basis. A

significant change is expected in Warsaw's plan, from a previous intense increase of industrial activities to concentration on growth of primary specializations typical for a national capital, and of administrative, scientific, cultural, and international transport functions. The industry will undergo technological review leading toward automation and application of the best available technology.

Quantitative objectives for the region have remained almost unchanged since the plans of 1965 and 1970; the total number of the population in the metropolitan region is to be 3 million in 1990 and the capacity of the central city 1.5 million. Not to exceed central city capacity is considered important because it might inhibit adequate development of the north corridor: the Legionowo Modlin-Nowy Dwór axis planned for 300,000 population. According to the new studies, the new corridor has the best development potential. The plans propose a new international airport, a new university center, a large exhibition complex, and an adequate extension of in-

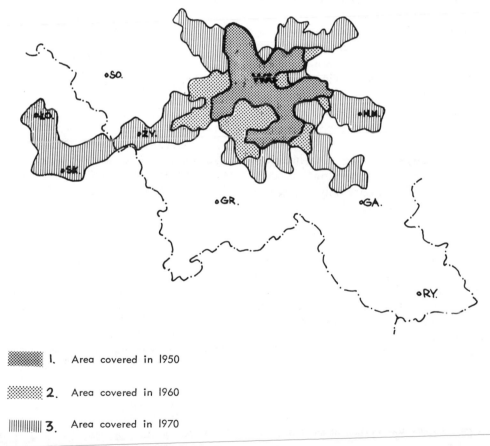

1. Area covered in 1950

2. Area covered in 1960

3. Area covered in 1970

Figure 20. Warsaw region development pattern 1950–1970. Source: "Rozważania nad Planem Rozwoju WZM."

dustrial activities that would limit as far as possible long-range commuting of area residents to central Warsaw.

The other three urban corridors, leading to Żyradów, Piaseczno, and Otwock, earlier developed in low-density patterns will continue to develop and rehabilitate its urban structure moving toward the objectives of the plan of 1965. The northeast corridor to Wołomin will be developed when adequate progress is achieved in construction of rapid railway as well as waterway and sewer systems (see Figure 20).

CONCLUSION

Through implementation of the National Plan 1976–1990, based on the long-range studies reaching into the twenty-first century, Poland is on the way to being transformed into a well-organized network of new cities and new towns (new in the sense of complete and contemporary structure of the physical plan of the community). In current development policies not many newly built towns in entirely undeveloped areas can be expected to start in the near future. A certain number of new towns, developed either from a small old community or from nothing, were started after World War II. They were initiated in most cases as a result of quickly—but as life is showing—properly conceived regional plans. Recent sophisticated plans support further development of these early new towns. However, in a relatively densely populated country with 250 people per square mile and a developed network of towns and cities, only in an exceptional case is a completely new town needed. Such towns are considered necessary only to assist in rehabilitation of large, hastily developed industrial regions similar to Silesia. It may also happen in the areas where enough good living space for the essential population cannot be found, even with energetic rehabilitation of existing towns and cities. New towns may also be needed in the areas of the northeast macroregion of Poland and in the Lublin region, where rapid industrialization will come very soon in selected districts.

NOTES

1. *Merit Students Encyclopedia*, Vol. 15 (London and New York: Crowell-Collier, 1967), p. 161.

2. J. C. Fisher, Ed., *City and Regional Planning in Poland* (Ithaca, N.Y.: Cornell University Press, 1966), p. 41.

3. B. Malisz, *Poland Builds New Towns* (Warsaw: Polonia, 1962), p. 113.

4. *Ibid.*, p. 50.

5. Most of these losses occurred in Nazi concentration camps, where one-half accounted for Polish citizens of Jewish origin.

6. B. Malisz, *Problematyka Przestrzennego Zagospodarowania Kraju* (Warsaw: Państwowe Wydawnictwo Naukowe, 1974), pp. 16–24.

7. Główny Urząd Planowania Przestrzennego, *Studium Planu Krajowego* (Warsaw: GUPP, 1947).

8. Malisz, *Poland Builds New Towns*, p. 24.

9. Fisher, p. 121.

10. Malisz, *Poland Builds New Towns*, p. 51.

11. Fisher, pp. 114, 131, and 132.

12. *Ibid.*, p. 314.

13. B. Bartkowicz, *Wypoczynek Codzienny Mieszkańców Nowych Osiedli na Przykładzie Krakowa* (Warsaw: Państwowe Wydawnictwo Naukowe, 1974), p. 48e.

14. *Ibid.*, p. 48d.

15. Planning Office of Warsaw, *Plan Generalny Warszawy* (Warsaw: City of Warsaw, 1965), pp. 19–25.

16. *Ibid.*, p. 45.

17. *Ibid.*, p. 48.

18. *Ibid.*, p. 173.

19. Teresa Swiecka, trans., *Warsaw 1970–1985* (Warsaw: Warsaw Town Planning Office, 1971), p. 47.

20. J. Kozłowski et al., *Thresholds Theory* (New York and London: Wiley, and Architectural Press, 1972).

21. Scottish Development Department, *Threshold Analysis Manual* (Edinburgh: Her Majesty's Stationery Office, 1973).

22. S. Broniewski et al., "Threshold Analysis and Optimization," (Edinburgh: University of Edinburgh, 1970).

23. Personal interview by author, 1972.

24. J. Brzozowski, *Metoda Optymalizacyjnych Porównań do Analizy i Ocen Planów Realizacyjnych Osiedli Mieszkaniowych* (Warsaw: Instytut Organizacji i Mechanizacji Budownictwa, 1965).

25. W. Pietraszkiewicz et al., *Metoda Optymalizacji Osiedli Mieszkaniowych* (Warsaw: Instytut Organizacji i Mechanizacji Budownictwa, 1970).

26. D. L. Kronika, "Państwowa Rada do Spraw Gospodarki Przestrzennej," *Miasto* 25, no. 12 (1974):31.

27. *La Politique de l'habitation de la construction et de la planification en Republique Populaire de Pologne* (Warsaw: Instytut Ochrony Środowiska, 1974), p. 25.

28. J. Koziński, "Rapidly Expanding Towns: Industrialization of Small Towns," Inter-regional Seminar on New Towns, London, June 4–19, 1973, UN/ESA/HBP, 9/35 (Warsaw: Planning Office of Warsaw, 1973).

29. A. Betka and B. Czechowicz, "Próba Przeglądu Problemów Realizacyjnych Kształtowania Systemu Osadniczego Polski," *Miasto* **25,** No. 3 (1974):1.

30. W. Nieciunski, "Prognoza Rozwoju Budownictwa Mieszkaniowego do 1990 r.," *Miasto* **24,** No. 7 (1973):1.

BIBLIOGRAPHY

Bartkowicz, B. *Wypoczynek Codzienny Mieszkańców Nowych Osiedli na Przykładzie Krakowa.* Warsaw: Państwowe Wydawnictwo Naukowe, 1974.

Betka, A., and B. Czechowicz. "Próba Przeglądu Problęmów Realizacyjnych Kształtowania Systemu Osadniczego Polski." *Miasto* **25,** No. 3 (1974), 1.

Broniewski, S., et al. "Threshold Analysis and Optimization." Edinburgh: University of Edinburgh, 1970.

Brzozowski, J. *Metoda Optymalizacyjnych Porównań do Analizy i Ocen Planów Realizacyjnych Osiedli Mieszkaniowych.* Warsaw: Instytut Organizacji i Mechanizacji Budownictwa, 1965.

Ciborowski, A. *Town Planning in Poland.* Warsaw: Polonia, 1956.

Czapliński, W., and T. Ładogórski. *Atlas Historyczny Polski.* Warsaw: Państwowe Przedsiębiorstwo Wydawnictw Kartograficznych, 1967.

Fisher, J. C., Ed. *City and Regional Planning in Poland.* Ithaca, N. Y.: Cornell University Press, 1966.

Grabowiecki, R., and S. Zawadzki. "System Osadniczy w Koncepcji Planu Przestrzennego Zagospodarowania Kraju." *Miasto* **25,** No. 1 (1974), 1.

Kozinski, J. "Rapidly Expanding Towns: Industrialization of Small Towns." UN/ESA/HBP, 9/35. Warsaw: Planning Office of Warsaw, 1973.

Kozłowski, J. et al. *Threshold Theory.* New York and London: Wiley, and the Architectural Press, 1972.

Lasik, J. et al. *Przegląd Prac Miastprojekt Nowe Tychy.* Nowe Tychy: Miastprojekt Nowe Tychy, 1965.

Ledworowski, B. "Wstępna Hypoteza Rozwoju Komunalnych Gałęzi Techiczno Infrastructuralnych do 1990 r." *Miasto* **24,** No. 1 (1973),1.

Malisz, B. *Poland Builds New Towns.* Warsaw: Polonia, 1962.

————. *Problematyka Przestrzennego Zagospodarowania Kraju.* Warsaw: Państwowe Wydawnictwo Naukowe, 1974.

Mały Rocznik Statystyczny. Warsaw: Central Statistical Office, 1973.

Nieciunski, W. "Prognoza Rozwoju Budownictwa Mieszkaniowego do 1990 r." *Miasto* **24,** No. 7 (1973), 1.

Pietraszkiewicz, W. et al. *Metoda Optymalizacji Osiedli Mieszkaniowych.* Warsaw: Instytut Organizacji i Mechanizacji Budownictwa, 1970.

Planning Office of Warsaw. *Plan Generalny Warszawy.* Warsaw: City of Warsaw, 1965.

La Politique de l'habitation de la construction et de la planification en Republique Populaire de Pologne. Warsaw: Instytut Ochrony Srodowiska, 1974.

Pyszkowski, A. "Makroregion Połnocno-wschodni." *Miasto* **26,** No. 1, (1975), 1.

————. "Rozważania nad Planem Rozwoju WZM." *Miasto* **25,** No. 11, (1974),1.

Scottish Development Department. *Threshold Analysis Manual.* Edinburgh: Her Majesty's Stationery Office, 1973.

Swięcka, Teresa, trans. *Warszawa 1970-1985.* Warsaw: Warsaw Town Planning Office, 1971.

Wejchert, K. *Elementy Kompozycji Urbanistycznej.* Warsaw: Arkady, 1974.

————. *Nowe Tychy.* Warsaw: Arkady, 1960.

CHAPTER 22

Development Policy of Polish New Towns

HANNA ADAMCZEWSKA-WEJCHERT AND KAZIMIERZ WEJCHERT

The task of creating new towns or new towns in-town is only one of the tasks of spatial and town planning in Poland. The situation in which Poland found itself after World War II demanded the fulfillment of other important tasks in the field of reconstructing destroyed towns of historic value (such as the Old Town in Warszawa (Warsaw) or Gdańsk), rebuilding and modernizing many towns (with Warszawa, Łódz, and Wrocław as top priorities), and activating small and average towns supplying the needs of agricultural areas. The growing processes of urbanization were the reason for the necessity of planning and rebuilding the dynamically developing city agglomerations.

All these tasks are solved on the basis of the resolution for spatial planning within the framework of a planned economy.[1] This resolution is also the basis for the development of spatial planning as a science and for the development of methods of planning.

A responsibility for the development of the living conditions of the population, a responsibility assumed by the community, has been imposed upon planning. This responsibility goes beyond the framework of a local, urban, or regional community to require decisions that affect the whole country. Decisions with respect to the construction of new towns are made on the basis of socially responsible national and regional planning decisions compatible with economic planning.

THE NEED FOR NEW TOWNS

Reasons for creating new towns can be classified into a few basic groups, which repeatedly occur in other countries as well. Most often the reason is the need to provide new housing facilities for areas with existing and expanding industries or near new industries creating new towns. Another reason is the need to disperse a too large, densely populated, and multifunctional area, either by means of creating virtually self-contained, small settlement links or the construction of modern settlement units. An agglomeration requires planned reconstruction for various reasons, such as transport and communication strains, the existing industrial microclimate, or negative technical and social features of residential building sites. Decisions with respect to the construction of new towns can also be made on political and economic grounds, such as the need to activate and improve neglected areas or those that are sparsely populated or urbanized.

Similar reasons have resulted in the creation of new towns and the development of completely new residential districts in quickly developing towns. Nowa Huta new town—today a great district of Kraków—was founded between 1949 and 1960 as the housing base for a big steel mill constructed simultaneously in its vicinity and changing the occupational structure and nature of the whole region. The decision to construct the town of Pyskowice was made as the result of a pressing demand for labor for the metallurgy and mining industries of the western region of the Upper Silesian industrial district (Górnośląski Okręg Przemysłowy—GOP), the greatest industrial region in Poland. The location of this new town on the site of the old medieval town partly situated on the boundary of the industrial and housing centers of the central GOP has also made it possible to counteract the tendency for further expansion of residential constructions in the existing towns and settlements of this zone, which are filled with smoke and bear the stamp of the unplanned economy of the nineteenth century. Pyskowice was also supposed to prevent the dispersing of small groups of buildings or separate houses in agricultural areas as well as in the greenbelts indispensable to the region.

Slightly different reasons were the basis for founding New (Nowe) Tychy in the southern region of the GOP. Its mines, which had rapidly expanded since 1950, substantially increased the demand for labor, and construction of this new town made it possible, in accord with the regional plan provisions, to relieve the overinvested central area of the GOP, both with respect to residencies and to planning the location of nonpolluting industries. Konin and Lubin were created because of discoveries of lignite and copper deposits; Jastrzębie in the Rybnik coal district—expanding at present at an extraordinary pace—was set up as a result of intensive mining of coking coal.

In Poland we consider towns as new when they are created not in virgin areas—*in cruda radice*—as in the Middle Ages, but in the vicinity of already existing small settlements or towns that provide a certain base, in the social sense, for the newly created organism, but do not influence the spatial pattern of the new part. The proportion of new inhabitants to the number of old inhabitants clearly points out that the towns are in principle "new." In Tychy the proportion of the "old" (population of the old village) to the "new" (new urban districts) is 8000 to the planned 160,000; in Jastrzębie, it is 10,000 to 150,000. New Lubin absorbed the old town—the latter constituting a part of its downtown. A new district of Konin with a population of 60,000 was founded on the other side of the river because of the unfavorable microclimate and physiographic conditions in the neighborhood of the old town of the same name. The refined spatial pattern and extensive social functions of old Konin, created in the Middle Ages to meet defensive requirements, were the reasons why at the beginning the new district was not treated as a new town. However, as the number of commercial and social services in the new part of the town increases, Konin is more and more frequently called a new town. At Tychy, in the first years of building, the name New Tychy was generally used. The tendency to underline the continuation of settlement traditions and the development of the existing settlement groups were the reasons the traditional name—Tychy—was chosen as the official name. People still use both names in everyday speech; when talking about new quarters the name New Tychy is used.

Reasons similar to these—a discovery of new deposits or initiation of the production of sulphur or coal—have been the causes of transforming old, neglected towns into new towns. Tarnobrzeg is expanding in this way, and additional new towns are planned in the new coal regions in the center and east of the country. The largest group, though of slightly different character, will be the new towns in-town. Like the new towns, the program of services is not fully realized and their independence is limited. However, many new towns in-town have been created and planned for 60,000 to 100,000 inhabitants or are already inhabited by that many people. These towns include Rataje in Poznań, Przymorze in Gdańsk, Brudno (80,000 inhabitants) or Southern Ursynów (150,000) in Warszawa. The realization of Southern Ursynów is planned for the near future.

POLISH EXPERIENCE IN THE CONSTRUCTION OF NEW TOWNS

The new-town experience should be analyzed in three stages: the period of planning and designing, the process of implementation, and the stage of operation. This analysis can look at technical, spatial, urbanistic, architectural, and social aspects as the basis of observation of life in new towns. Analysis of the final stage should observe the phenomena that were created by the construction of a new town in a given region and that clearly influence the community of that region, such as changes in people's attitudes, way of life, level of culture, and civilization.

Planning and Design. In discussing the experience of planning and designing, attention should be drawn to the period in which decisions about creating new towns are made. Drafting the master plan and designing projects of Nowa Huta were worked out at an unusually rapid rate under the pressing needs of 1948–1949 (see Figure 1). This period was characterized by clear tendencies toward geometric uniformity and "monumentalization." Contacts with town planning and architecture of western Europe were meager in those days. Problems of mass motorization were underestimated; however, the present critics of that period often forget about the existing (and obvious in the first years after the war) limitations of technical resources and building materials. The country—devastated during the war—had at its disposal only bricks, typical modest carpentry, and a few building machines. All these reasons clearly exerted their influence on the elaboration of the plan for Nowa Huta. The town was designed for a population of 100,000, and although six kilometers from Kraków, it was supposed to be a completely independent town.

It was planned as a whole, and then in detail, as a two-dimensional drawing, an "urbanistic work." The first groups of buildings, those bordering the central square and three symmetrical major axes of streets meeting at that square, were of a free pattern, somewhat romantic on a small scale to ensure good psychological conditions for their inhabitants. After the realization of the first groups of houses, the plan was corrected, and the spatial elements constituting the third dimension were monumentalized. The central fragments of the town were formed by introducing blocks of flats that touch, forming continuous walls.

It was as if the plan had been drawn in the third dimension. This principle was underlined by the then rigorously understood architecture, differentiated mainly by form of eclectic details. Only after 1956 was this principle abandoned, and freer structures appeared. However, the character of the town area so strongly and decisively defined in the central parts became, according to its inhabitants, so domineering that today it is a unanimous standard for the perception of the area of the whole town.

A similar method of designing and an inflexible method of implementation in its first years are responsible for the present appearance of Pyskowice. In this town one can also at first glance see the periods in which the particular groups of buildings were erected. Because the new quarters lie in the vicinity of a carefully reconstructed typical old town square, the method of spatial shaping reverted to the enclosed form of this historic square.

A different planning process was adopted in New Tychy, planned at the beginning for 100,000 inhabitants and built since 1950. The design and planned works following the initial competition for the master plan of the city are being continued in the same design office under the guidance of the city's general architects (see Figure 2). The principle of the crucial elements organizing the spatial pattern is consequently observed; however, single implementation plans for parts of the city or for particular buildings are subject to change due to existing housing standards, town planning norms, and increasing technological possibilities. Thus planning is sufficiently flexible while being subordinated to overall premises of the master plan and consequently observing the intended spatial structure of the town as a whole. The size of the town allows building separate complexes that avoid monotony and provide systems and views that are important to avoid spatial uniformity. The first residential complex, realized after ratification of the general plan (marked by the letter B), was located in the vicinity of the already existing old church village, Tychy, in an area partly occupied by small houses (see Figure 3). Therefore, a settlement was created in the character of an old development, with a romantic system of streets and provincial architecture. Thus from the beginning there was no tendency to monumentalize the forms of residential complexes.

The decision to build the town of Jastrzębie in the Rybnik coal district was made much later—that is, in the years 1965 to 1967. The town, which is now rapidly developing, was designed and projected in

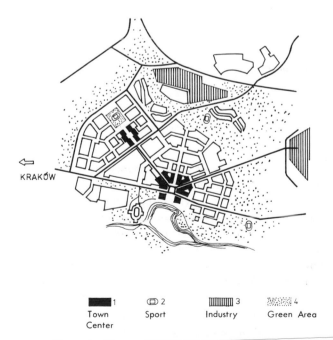

| 1 Town Center | 2 Sport | 3 Industry | 4 Green Area |

KRAKÓW

Figure 1. First master plan of Nowa Huta, Poland.

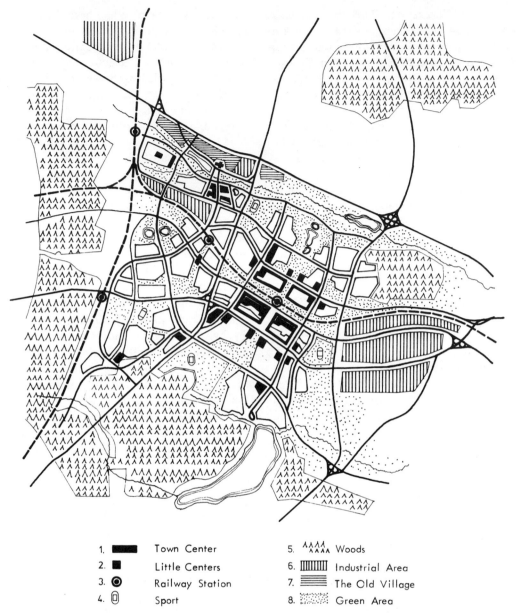

Figure 2.   Master plan of Tychy New Town, Nowe Tychy. After a figure in W. Ostrowski, *Urbanisme Contemporain.*

1. ▬▬▬   Town Center   5. ᴧᴧᴧᴧ   Woods
2. ■   Little Centers   6. ⦀⦀⦀⦀   Industrial Area
3. ◉   Railway Station   7. ☰☰☰   The Old Village
4. ◫   Sport   8. ⠿⠿   Green Area

view of the technological solution adopted—the technology of assembling the buildings from parts produced in housing plants. As in New Tychy, the draft master plan is a consistent framework, modified, however, to some extent in the course if implementation by taking into account the necessity of constructing buildings of definite, rather inflexible design. The impact of technology and differentiated topography requires spatial alignment of buildings parallel to contour lines (see Figure 4).

The Investment Service prepares programs of building new towns, and the local authorities ratify

them on the basis of valid urbanistic norms. New towns are not privileged. The urbanistic norm defines the amount of basic services according to the planned population, the intensity of development, and the density of population according to the height of buildings; the norm also defines the basic relations between above-ground buildings, greenbelts, and communication areas. The spatial living standards regulate the size of flats according to the number of family members. The urbanistic norms improve with time.

The program for creating a town or quarter does not change if the construction covers a short time. If

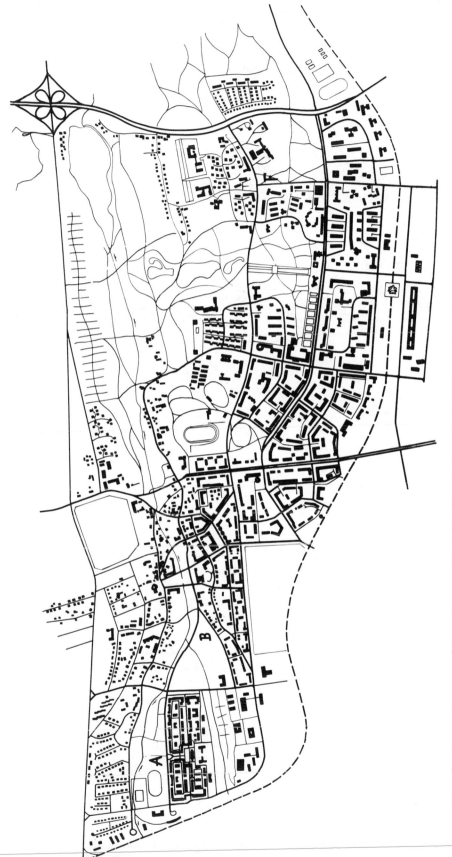

Figure 3. The spatial structure of the north quarter of Tychy New Town. At the left is the old village and at the bottom the town center. Source: *Wpływ Realizacji na Przemiany Planu Miasta.*

367

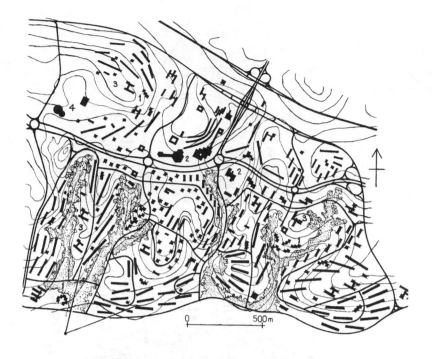

1   Services (neighborhood units)   3   Schools

2   Town Center   4   Sport Area

Figure 4. Jastrzębie in the Rybnik district. Source: *Elementy Kompozycji Urbanistycznej.*

the time of realization is prolonged, which is obvious in the case of towns of 100,000 population, the program is revised and the plan brought up to date. Thus a revision of the plan for New Tychy was made after the program was completed. The revised plan becomes possible because of reserves of land.

Decisions concerning the nature of the spatial form of a new town are made during the projecting stage. The period of elaboration of geometric plans (1949–1953) was followed by a virtually common tendency to shape new districts and new towns as spatially independent. The latter trend has become common under the impact of the theory of the neighborhood unit and of the structure of the organizationally and socially dominant unit of the settlement. The pattern of square and clearly defined streets and housing areas has disappeared. The necessity of the strict observance of town planning standards has led to schematic patterns and solutions. This development raises the question of new towns versus other forms of expanded settlements.

New quarters under construction, as in new towns in-town, lack urban atmosphere, which is important for their inhabitants, because half of them come to town from small towns and villages. "Street nostalgia" has also been felt by the inhabitants of these

new "settlements," which are not parts of the town organism.

The principle of building new quarters in expanded settlements may have negative influence on spatial structure, especially in medium-sized towns in which new quarters do not constitute new towns in-town (they are too small), and socially and spatially they become foreign bodies. This negative influence comes from big cities in which old and new buildings are incoherent.

Implementation. The most important problems of the implementation stage are those of investments and phases of construction, especially those of technical and social infrastructure. A positive feature has been a centralization of investment activities in the hands of a single state investor responsible for coordination and implementation of all projects and tasks in the city (see Table 1).

New towns are constructed on land expropriated under standard regulations. The state pays the owners for the land as well as for the buildings if they are to be demolished. Quite often, instead of financial compensation the owners receive land with buildings located outside the area of construction.

The process of implementation is swift in small

Table 1   Distribution of Costs for Tychy, 1951–1969 (%)

Housing estates	69.3
Installation of main services	18.4
Social facilities, service, and administration	10.2
Execution backround	1.7
Others	0.4
Costs of installation of main services	
Transport	26.7
Installation of industrial mains	22.6
Sewage and sewage filters	20.3
Thermal station and hot water main	17.1
Water piping	5.9
Gas piping	4.5
Electricity system	0.5
Sport and recreation facilities	2.4
Costs of housing estates	
Blocks of flats	72.7
Social and service buildings	9.9
Underground installations	10.8
Blueprints	2.3
Site preparation	0.3
Other outlays	4.0

Source: H. Kozubal, "Ekonomiczne aspekty bodowy Nowych Tych," *Architektura* 2 (1972).

cities. In cases of larger towns, however, for 100,000 or 150,000 inhabitants the problems of infrastructure become complex, sometimes resulting in serious complications. An example is the city of Pyskowice where difficulties of the connection between the new town and GOP railway network have led to giving up the initial plans, lowering the pace of construction, and modifying primary blueprints. A similar case is Tychy: delays in completing the construction of the railway connecting the town with work places— mostly mines—have led to the development of small settlements near the mines, a situation that may prolong the period of the town's development. These examples show that transport, especially that aimed at mass transportation of workers from their settlements to factories and plants, should be treated as the crucial element of the infrastructure, with implementation in advance of other projects. Priority to the whole infrastructure network over construction works in the strict sense is also necessary (see Figure 5).

Time phasing in cases of construction of a sewerage system and thermal station and the provision of electricity or gas results in development barriers, sometimes of minor nature, depending on decisions of various ministries, such as the ministry

of power industry or of municipal economy. Delays in investments for infrastructure result in technical and economic drawbacks. However, excessive advancement may be disadvantageous in certain cases. The construction of the thermal station prior to the

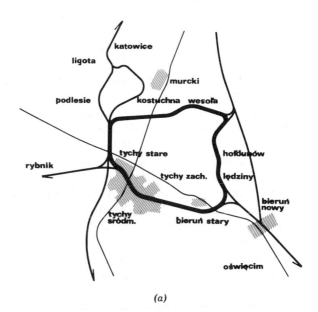

(a)

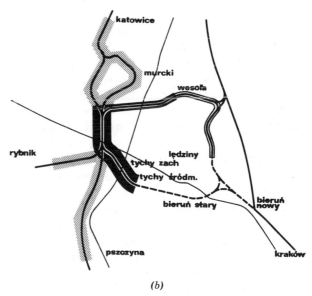

(b)

Figure 5.   (A) The Tychy railway circle, which is to link the town (shaded area) with the principal places of work: the coal mines at Wesoła, Hołdunów and Lędziny. This circle is also to connect to eastbound railway line to Oświęcim and westbound to the Rybnik coal region. (B) The Tychy railway circle in 1967. The broken line indicates a still incomplete section. Consequently, instead of going eastward to Lędziny from the central station, it was necessary to travel westward via Old Tychy and Wesoła, a much longer distance. The thickness of the black strip along the railway routes on the Tychy circle and a line shaded with short lines along the other routes indicates the intensity of passenger traffic according to the timetable of 1964–1965. The Tychy railway was completed in 1972. Source: *Town in the Making.*

construction of the housing estate (e.g., New Tychy) resulted in excessive production of heat during a certain period. To make this heat useful the authorities of the town accepted the construction of large greenhouses of a big horticultural facility. However, in the second stage of construction, this useful project caused considerable troubles because it took all the heat necessary for rapid construction of the town. The decision to accelerate the construction of the town was triggered by the plan to build a car factory and a factory for prefabricated housing units in New Tychy.

Road and street building prior to the construction of houses constitutes a considerable difficulty in Poland's economic conditions. Roads and streets are built during the implementation of projects and are often delayed. The building of several viaducts over the open tunnel crosstown railway line in Tychy is a favorable exception. These viaducts enable the workers to carry out the construction of two new quarters, northward and southward from the railway, nearly simultaneously. In the Lubin copper basin the advanced construction of outer roads was allowed in part to avoid heavy transportation across the site of the new town under construction.

To analyze social and psychological problems three periods can be distinguished in the course of the town construction. The first period may be called "heroic." It is marked by enthusiasm, improvisation, and spontaneity; however, it is prompted by propaganda. During this period various slogans appear— for example, "the most modern," "the newest," "the youngest," "Lubin—the city of copper"—as well as promises to achieve final goals by a given year. "The birth of the new" is favored by social confidence and benevolent expectation; if some new forms have been suggested in the project, they arouse interest.

The heroic period is characterized by the unavoidable clash between the old and the new. Everywhere in Europe new towns are built in areas that are already inhabited and functioning, usually connected with local communities that have been settled for generations. The conflict between the old and the new can manifest itself in a negative attitude toward anything that brings about change of the existing order, in a conservative resistance of social ecology, attitudes against expropriations or pulling down existing buildings, unfair criticism accepted by some newsmen as an objective voicing of so-called "public opinion." The inflow of strange population whose first part is composed of construction brigades—dynamic, sturdy, boisterous men—further intensifies

these conflicts. Then the conflict arises between people living in old towns (in the case of Poland always in worse conditions than those obtained by the newcomers) and inhabitants of new districts of the town. Conflicts among the newcomers living in different districts are also common. In the heroic period technical and construction processes go on fairly smoothly and efficiently; investor, design maker, and executor are all decision makers thoroughly acquainted with implementation plans.

After some time, when a part of the future shape of the town begins to appear, the period of "pressures" starts. These pressures, from administrative authorities or enterprises and various institutions, aim at modifications of original projects, changes of service locations, and other modifications of interests in each of these institutions. Because the part of the town does not give a clear idea of the entire project, imagination produces ideas inconsistent with or contradictory to the program and the planned shape. Protection of the plan against pressures becomes a necessity. The pressures can cause a quick management of sites reserved for future services, an excessive expansion of industrial and storage sites, or an unplanned development of single-family houses in suburbs encroaching recreational areas or arable lands.

This period is followed by psychological barriers. Social institutional imagination will be compelled to make further steps in town development, steps that at first could be treated as distant or not expected at all. Tychy is an example.

The open underground tunnel dividing Tychy into two districts—northern and southern—has become a psychological barrier. Instead of starting construction southward from the tunnel, the planners sought every possibility to build as many houses as possible in the northern districts so as not to start the construction outside the town—as the sites destined in the plan for the construction of the all-town center and downtown district are called.

The next period can be called the period of "maturity." The town is sufficiently large and has existed for a sufficiently long period to develop an integrated, uniform community. This is also true of the municipal authorities. Further expansion of the city takes place in an atmosphere similar to that of existing towns in which new housing estates are built.

There is a danger in an application of schematic patterns and spatial solutions based on models from districts of old towns. Chances for creating individualized forms are overlooked. Stagnation may find its expression in a lessening of the pressures for quick construction and in a desire to fill in all the actual or apparent gaps, either in areas reserved for particularly planned services or destined for greeneries.

The specific nature of the area and of the relation between exogenous and endogenous city-creating forces may result in variety within these social and psychological stages. Experience has shown that during each of the subsequent periods of town construction, appropriate measures should be formulated.

Operation.   Partial operation of the town starts with the arrival of the first inhabitants. However, problems start mounting during the maturing process of the town's form. Unlike old towns, in which the everyday routine of management—activities known for years, with centuries of tradition—is well developed, the new town faces a number of specific problems. The basic problem is ensuring the normal course of life in the completed part of the town and isolating the inhabitants from the inconveniences of neighboring construction sites. Transportation of building materials, pollution of streets, additional excavations, or the return of plastering works to tidy green surroundings of new blocks of flats—all create obvious inconveniences. Although they are essentially organizational problems, they also relate to planning of the location of independent construction capacities, projection of outlays for their proper management, and projected operation in subsequent phases.

Polish new towns did not manage to avoid clashes between the construction process and the already inhabited part of the town. This was handled relatively well in Nowa Huta and Lubin, in which the pattern of railway borders was advantageous (see Figure 6). The lack of means for lengthening sidetracks necessitated locating building depots too close to first settlements and expanding transport from the depots parallel to the implemented projects. A classical method of withdrawing this troublesome transport "to the depot" was used.

Another problem of exceptional importance is the steering of the growth of social infrastructure elements. The delay in the materialization of basic services—that is, schools, kindergartens, nurseries, or the most necessary shops in new districts of big towns—was troublesome for inhabitants because they had to travel to old districts to obtain these services. Small delays of that type ceased to be urgent as the methods of investments were improved.

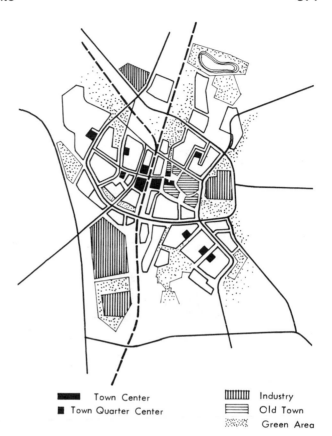

Town Center
Town Quarter Center
Industry
Old Town
Green Area

Figure 6.   The master plan of Lubin. After J. Suliga, *Lubin*.

New towns, lacking either an adequate old center—like that in Tychy—or convenient access to an old center—as in Konin—caused difficulties for programming infrastructure. This can be observed in the northern district of Tychy. In housing estates implemented in the years 1950 to 1955 and located in a neighborhood of the old town with small social potential, it was necessary to establish a provisional town center containing shops, restaurants, cinema, theater, and drug stores, until the proper all-town center had been constructed in the southern district. The provisional center was the only service center for many years. Because the construction of the town was slower than originally planned, similar facilities were constructed in other parts of the northern district as well because the all-town center was further delayed. The main street became a *strada vitale* and contained a number of shops and artisans' workshops, and the inhabitants felt much less inconvenience despite the lack of a proper center (see Figure 7).

The idea of localization of services along the main street was developed in a competition project of the new town of Pawłowice, which was to be constructed in a coal basin. In this project the main street of the

Figure 7. The town center of Tychy. Architect: M. Dziekoński.

town linked two stops of the railway connecting the town with major work places and offered all services. The street was to be built as a wide, moderately curved avenue, which would also serve the inhabitants of the towns as a promenade. The project was dropped and replaced by the new town Jastrzębie.

The period of construction of the new town and the period of its initial operation must be analyzed from the point of view of its inhabitants. They compare the promise, which is the town's master plan, with its fulfillment, which should be completed within a definite period. The smaller the divergence between promise and fulfillment, the higher the evaluation by inhabitants. Sociological studies undertaken in Tychy for five years clearly show this. Assuming that generations change every 28 to 30 years, the period of expectation for new living conditions cannot exceed (or can exceed only slightly) half of this period—that is, 15 to 18 years. Most inhabitants of new towns in Poland are young married people in their early thirties, who are in full productive capacities and have small children. If residents are not provided with a fully developed spatial environment (according to the plan) during this period, they may reach the retirement age spending their best years in an insuffi-

ciently organized environment and in an unstable mood resulting from the proximity of a construction site. At present one of the most bothersome but short-lived difficulties is the constant delay in providing paths, lawns, and local places of recreation.

The populous younger generation should be raised in fully developed urban agglomerations. Obviously, the impact of provisional conditions is negative. An inhabitant should be able to state: "This is my place. I am in my town—in my home: Here I feel happy." Citizens of new towns often say: "our house" or "in our building." A house should be distinguishable from others; the settlements should not be a "barracks." Another noteworthy expression may be "a nice view from our flat." There is a need for personal space; one singularly shaped building in a routine, schematic complex is insufficient.

There has been constant technological progress. Excavation works have been eased by heavy machines, and the construction of blocks of flats from heavy elements has been aided by assembly cranes of 45-, 80-, and 120-ton capacity. The dependence of the form of a building on technical means is revealed by a completed architectural project.

The years 1949 to 1956 brought brick architecture marked by window spaces typical of that technology.

The industrialized housing was started in the year 1955–1956. Tychy took the leading position with a series of cross-bearing walls made of large breeze concrete blocks as well as with outer walls made of gas concrete blocks. Urgent tasks of housing called for the construction of typical buildings in many towns. Town planning solutions must have been schematic under such limited means of spatial shaping. The next measure of easing the tasks of building enterprises was the introduction of the so-called *voivodship*[3] reproducible projects. This resulted in a rather minor improvement of design. On great building sites (Tychy included) local systems of prefabrication were expanded as open systems—that is, systems in which a standard set of units could have been used for the construction of buildings of singular character in accord with the town planning project. In 1970 a number of factories for housing units of the "W-70" system were constructed. It is an open system that has already proven itself flexible, providing a solution to attempted individualization of mass housing. This system allows for the construction of five-story buildings without elevators, as well as the construction of buildings as high as 11 stories. Taller units may be built using elevators.

Analysis of the time factor in a new town makes possible consideration of another problem—the attractiveness of flats and the durability of buildings, especially residential ones. The durability of buildings constructed at present in new towns can be evaluated at some 80 to 100 years. Spatial living standards applied are modest (see Table 2); they will certainly result in a rapid decrease in attractiveness of flats, which is likely to decline in 20 to 30 years or earlier.

Now if we plot on one diagram the building depreciation curve and the decrease in attractiveness curve and impose the curve reflecting the course of life of subsequent generations growing in the town, we can conclude that there is the necessity of projecting the reconstruction of housing stock in the period of the decrease in attractiveness—that is, when the first generation enters retirement age and the second reaches productive age (see Figure 8). This problem is not exclusive to Poland; however, there are no introductory scientific works on this subject, especially as far as technical and social aspects of the matter are concerned. The diagram allows one to assume that in new towns the sociodemographic prognosis may be close to that expected in the second, and perhaps in the third, generation of the inhabitants of the town.

New towns are centrally heated by thermal stations located on their outskirts. In the yearly period of their construction, first groups of blocks in Nowa Huta and Tychy were heated by local boiler houses. A few years later these boiler houses were liquidated, and the buildings became offices or artisans' workshops. In the early period of construction of the first groups of blocks, kitchens are equipped with gas stoves and gas heaters to assure hot water in bathrooms. Hot water is sent from central thermal stations to new quarters of big towns (see Table 2).

SOCIAL ISSUES IN NEW TOWNS

The formation of a new urban community is one of the most significant issues in the process of the construction of new towns. In new town in-town districts the problems of workers are not so difficult as they were in the early period of construction of Nowa Huta, Pyskowice, Tychy, or Konin. The inadequate manpower in these localities called for the employment of workers from other regions of the country. They lived in barracks, which were gradually replaced by workers' hotels with higher standards of living. Some of the workers wanted to stay in new towns and received new flats. The new towns were inhabited by people from all over the country, and in

Table 2   Obligatory Standard of Flats, 1954–1976

	Flat for 2 Persons	Flat for 3 Persons	Flat for 4 Persons	Flat for 5 Persons
	Room + kitchen	2 rooms + kitchen		3 rooms + kitchen
1954–1958	28–39 m^2		41–50 m^2	51–58 m^2
From 1959	24–30 m^2	33–38 m^2	42–48 m^2	51–57 m^2
From 1973*	35.5 m^2	45.5m^2	54.0 m^2	59.5 m^2
1976	30–35 m^2	44–48 m^2	56–61 m^2	65–70 m^2

* Maximum areas.

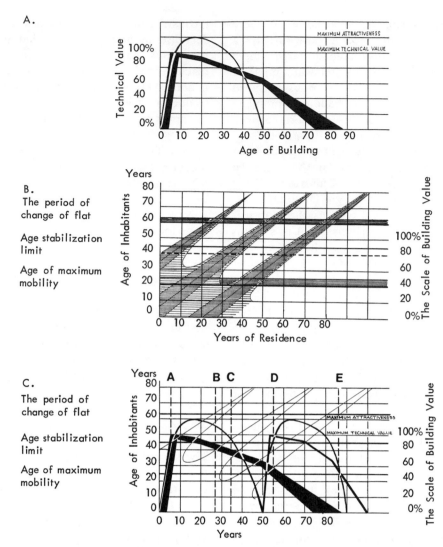

Figure 8. (A) A curve of depreciation of buildings and a curve of attractiveness comparing its dependence on depreciation. (B) The course of residence in a town for three generations. (C) The relation of depreciation of buildings, attractiveness of flats, and the course of residence for three generations. The broken vertical lines show the limits of social usefulness of buildings. After illustrations 162, 163, and 164 of *Town in the Making*.

the years 1950 to 1955 also by citizens returning from outside Poland.

A number of surveys were carried out on social composition, social status, and education of the inhabitants of new towns Płock, Nowa Huta, and Tychy. These surveys helped to show certain regularities: some 50 percent of newcomers come from the adjacent regions, and the next 10 to 15 percent come from central, southern voivodships with dense populations and a large number of petty farms. Some 50 percent of inhabitants come from the country; however, only 30 percent of them come to town indirectly from the country. Most of them, that is 70 percent, come from small towns that were larger

than country towns and smaller than the new town. Thus, before settling in a new town, some of the village dwellers are partly accustomed to an urban way of life.

Although the standards of living are not high, all the inhabitants of new towns regard their new conditions as decidedly better than the old ones. The destructions of the last war and the fact that newly married couples had not had their own flats before they came to new towns make this attitude very understandable. That is why the attitude of the inhabitants toward the new towns is positive, although in the period of difficulties resulting from the construction the attitude is often critical. This criticism is most often due to waiting for completion of the area surrounding blocks of flats as well as the poor selection of goods in local shops.

A poll carried out in Tychy in 1960–1965 showed that some 50 percent of inhabitants had no objections to the life in the town; some 35 percent had some objections; and only 5 percent expressed their dissatisfaction and would be willing to move to other towns. They mention mainly Warszawa, Kraków or Gdańsk—captial cities—as towns of their dreams. One of the objections of the inhabitants of Pyskowice, Tychy, and Nowa Huta and of inhabitants working in Kraków was the problem of transport from their residences to their places of work. In big towns workers who travel 30 to 45 minutes to their factories are regarded as employees working on the spot. It is so in Warszawa and other big cities. In Tychy, where a number of mines are located 10 to 15 kilometers from the town, workers who travel 20 to 30 minutes by an electric train are considered employees working outside the town, and journalists often call the town a bedroom.

A distinct increase of social mobility concomitant to the improvement of mass transport and the development of settlement systems and subsystems call for verification of classification of industrial enterprises as local, urban, or extraurban. This classification cannot be determined by administrative division. During the analysis of the directions of development of Lubin, for instance, a possibility of dotting the 70-kilometer route Lubin-Wrocław with housing areas was considered as well. This would call for modern means of mass transport, but it would allow the workers from Lubin the enjoyment of services and entertainments of the voivodship town of Wrocław. Similar projects of new towns of a chain-junction[4] type were made as one of the variants of the developing coal basin in the eastern part of the country.

A number of conclusions concerning projects and programs can be drawn from the evaluation of new towns by their inhabitants. Many of them point out an excessive density of housing estates (600 to 700 persons per hectare). Other remarks concern the uniformity of space and architecture. The need for interesting and rich spatial composition to allow the inhabitants identification of space is increasingly urgent, especially in the light of the lack of variety in the architecture of houses assembled from prefabricated units.

Integration of new-town communities progresses swiftly; however, family and professional relations dominate neighbor relations. The latter are established more swiftly in low, four- to five-story buildings than in those of 11 stories. The second generation regards a new town as the place they really belong. The atmosphere in which the new town is constructed and the everyday tangible progress of the work make the inhabitants interested in further development of the town, and their active participation in its expansion provides ground for local patriotism. It was due, perhaps, to such an atmosphere that a number of enterprises in Tychy are prized for their achievements: the pupils beat other schoolboys and girls in sport competitions; the design office wins numerous home competitions; and the young soccer players quickly take their place in the first division in Poland.

Rest and everyday recreation are important issues in a new town. In Sweden, Finland, or England this issue is not so difficult because of landscape variety and richness of environment. In Poland new towns and new settlements constructed on the outskirts of large towns usually lack sufficient natural green areas. Hence, the problem of providing and managing green sites in the vicinity of residential areas becomes especially important. Delays of these works are disturbing (housing estates in the vicinity of Kraków can be an example here).[5] Therefore, recreation areas should be provided prior to residential construction to "accelerate," at least partially, the slow natural growth of trees.

REGIONAL DEVELOPMENT

How do the new towns accommodate the regional complex, and what is the impact of the former upon the latter? Let us consider the example of Nowa Huta. This town has changed into a part of Kraków because of the growth of production in the steel mill necessitated the expansion of residential sites. This was possible only within the belt between Nowa Huta and Kraków. Improvements of transport made it possible to unify Nowa Huta district with old Kraków. For the whole complex, the center of Kraków has become the central part. Its role will grow still further after the expansion of the new center in the heart of the town (see Figure 9).

These two complexes have thus been integrated through cooperation and mutual relation. It is difficult to foresee whether these complexes will in the future develop into the chain-like system with a hierarchy of functions between the links. However,

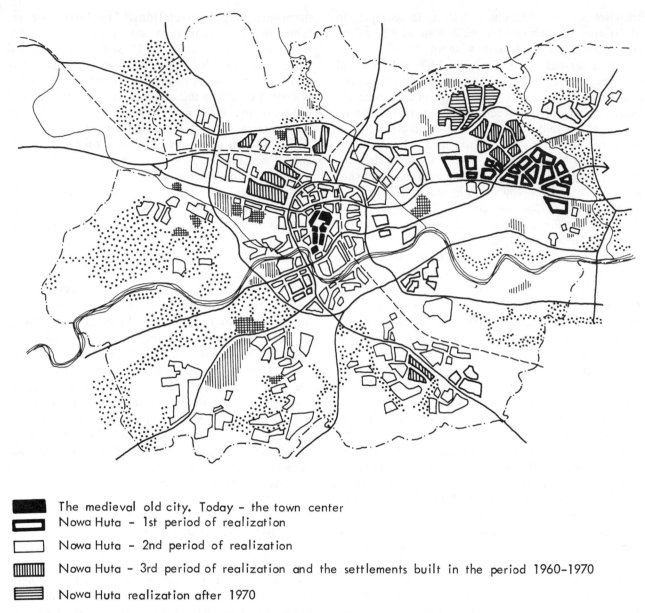

■ The medieval old city. Today – the town center

▭ Nowa Huta – 1st period of realization

▢ Nowa Huta – 2nd period of realization

▥ Nowa Huta – 3rd period of realization and the settlements built in the period 1960–1970

▤ Nowa Huta realization after 1970

Figure 9.   The location of Nowa Huta related to the master plan of Kraków, 1964.

the location of Nowa Huta at the eastern end of the complex makes it difficult, or in principle even impossible, to expand settlement areas in the eastern direction of Nowa Huta.

Lubin can be treated as an example of the complex expanding according to the regularity of such phenomena. This town expands into the Głogów-Lubin-Legnica chain agglomeration. This also is the pattern of development of the personal and commodity transportation network. On the basis of expansion of technical and economic infrastructure, full integration of the whole complex can be projected. Single sets of this infrastructure should be designed and implemented jointly; thus project and design decisions should be regional. This chain-junction complex expands automatically in a way. Its links—including Lubin with its large copper industry—should become the links of the purposefully organized settlement network. This town has, therefore, wide development prospects.

The location of Pyskowice and the lack of the regional expansion of transport joining the town with other agglomerations have produced technical and psychological barriers. A spatial pattern of the town

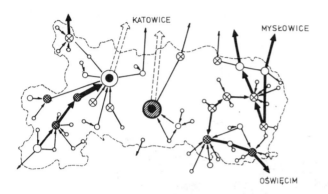

Figure 10. Relations in the region of Tychy until 1960. Source: *Wpływ Realizacji na Przemiany Planu Miasta.*

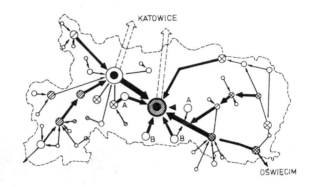

◉	MAIN TOWN (TYCHY)	⊗	VILLAGES
◉	LITTLE TOWNS – Second Center	○	VILLAGES
●	OTHER TOWNS	○	VILLAGES
◉	OTHER TOWNS	⊘	VILLAGES

Figure 11. Relations in the region of Tychy in the regional project after 1960. Source: *Wpływ Realizacji na Przemiany Planu Miasta.*

devoid of a dynamic nucleus is also responsible for such a state. Pyskowice consequently becomes a distant residential part of the western agglomeration of the GOP.

Jastrzębie, in the Rybnik coal district located in the vicinity of the old health resort Jastrzębie-Zdrój, becomes the main town of this industrial center. Conditions for projection and design of this complex extremely difficult because of unfavorable topography—rolling countryside punctuated by coal mines and work places. Even with costly expansion of technical and economic infrastructure, the desired developmental effects and the model spatial structure of this complex do not seem possible. Concentration of the building construction in Jastrzębie should be

judged as appropriate, but provision of the social infrastructure becomes the crucial problem. A new service center in this town and serving the whole region is required because of the location of Jastrzębie in the region and the large population agglomeration. Such a central service center has been designed; its quick and timely implementation should be postulated in line with expanding housing capacity of the region.

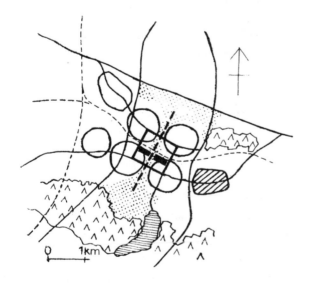

Nowe Tychy

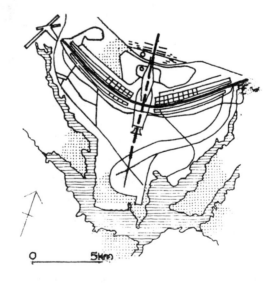

Brasilia

Figure 12. Brasilia and Tychy: the crystallizing elements of the town plans. Source: *Elementy Kompozycji Urbanistycznej.*

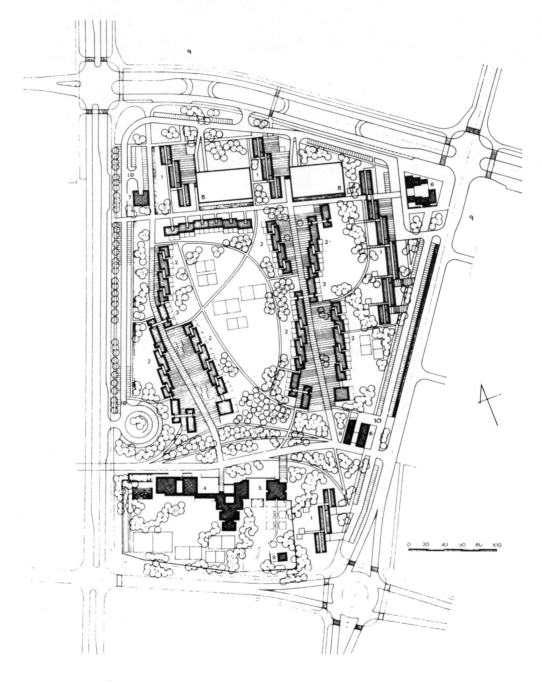

1	XI-Storage Buildings	6	Shops
2	V Storage	7	Bar (pub)
3	IV-Storage Buildings	8	Underground Garages
4	School	9	Locality of town-center
5	Kindergarten	10	Parking

Figure 13. Tychy New Town settlement "M-Magdelena." An example of spatial structure and organization. Source: *Architektura* 2 (1972).

Tychy was located in a developmental region, originally weighing heavily in its western part, toward the city of Mikołów (in 1950 having a population of 10,000), a town with old traditions dating from the fourteenth century. Because of the existing transport, the eastern part has been weighed heavily toward Mysłowice. The location of the town in approximately the geometric center of the region, as well as the projected railway connection with the central part of the country and with work places in expanding mines, permits one to foresee that it will soon become the true center of the region. This central role of the towns, begun in 1965, increases yearly (see Figures 10 and 11).

CONCLUSION

Considering the size of the town, one should keep in mind both technical and social aspects, including time needed for construction. In the chain-junction systems the biggest towns have 100,000 to 150,000 population. Towns of that size can constitute the links of the chain, creating possibilities for complete and all-round service of the population without the excessive inconveniences of big town life, and they are completed when smoothly constructed within the life span of one generation.

The introduction of crystallizing elements into the plan of the town can ease this construction and stimulate the imagination. In the Middle Ages they were market squares around which other buildings were constructed in a clearly planned way. A lack or exhaustion of such a gravitation pole has resulted in an unplanned and shapeless flood of construction. In the modern town such elements can be arteries (as in Brazil) or central streets (as in Tychy) (see Figure 12). While organizing the space, these elements make possible its flexible development and shaping. The current plans of new towns contain few crystallizing elements constituting the framework of the spatial structure of the town. The verification of a number of plans and the introduction of various crystallizing elements will allow for the singularity of the town that helps the inhabitants and newcomers identify with their surroundings.

A strong tendency in new-town planning is an attempt at a justified degree of separation of car and pedestrian traffic as well as the construction of streets and pedestrian paths to organize space and keep proportion and scale pleasant. Such streets,

closed or partly closed to car traffic, have been constructed in Tychy and are planned in Poznań and Warszawa. The experience gained during the construction of Tychy confirms the aptness of this way of shaping space.

Construction of new towns—this is a fascinating expression. Something new will be created, thus something better than previously existed; to create a new town is to create space constituting a natural environment organizing man's life. It will be created. We use the future tense, but we do not say at the same time that "the town of the future" will be created. This expression usually stands for utopian, fantastic visions based on an original idea: a floating town, underground town, or a town erected far above the earth. Such fantasies meet with bigger or smaller applause; they flourish for some time; they are written about; they fascinate and stir the imagination, especially of laymen, and are replaced by new ephemera. However, the systems proposed solve only the problems of setting the construction module of towns—they suggest a certain degree of freedom in expansion and flexible changes, which are difficult or simply impossible from the technological point of view. The essential carrying structure of these complex systems and their technical infrastructure would quickly become obsolete, more quickly than singly used units; and even from this point of view conflicts are unavoidable.

Spatial perception, people's impressions and feelings, must be considered. Space cannot be shaped only on the basis of exclusively technical and physical premises. However, towns constructed today and for today are usually towns for the future. That is why we think that they contribute much more to the future than the boldest visions and utopias. The only regret is that our economic and technical potentials are so limited. Nevertheless, we can draw still another conclusion: in constructing new towns the right of experimentation should be accepted, and experiments should concern both shaping the zoned areas and spatial architecture of the entire town (see Figure 13).

NOTES

1. A 1964 decree on spatial planning and a 1962 act on physical, spatial, regional, and local planning provide the basis for all planning.

2. Four architectural groups were invited to compete: Architect Ptaszycki, designer of Nowa Huta's plan; Architect Zielinski,

chief planner of the big projects office in Warsaw; Professor Todorowski of the Technical University, Gliwice; and Professor K. Wejchert and Architect Adamczewska of the Technical University, Warsaw. First prize and realization of the plan went to the group from the Technical University, Warsaw. Since 1951 Wejchert and Adamczewska, leaders of that group, have been the general architects and chief planners of New Tychy.

3. Voivodships are the largest administrative units in Poland. Since 1975 the country has been divided into 49 such districts; previously there were 17.

4. Chain-junction towns are placed along some linear transport route such as a road or railway line.

5 Barbara Bartkowicz, *Wypoczynek codzienny mieszkańców Krakowa* (Warszawa: PWN, 1973).

CHAPTER 23

Policies and Trends in the Development of New Towns in the USSR

V. N. BELOUSOV

Much attention is given to the problems of new town construction in the scientific planning and building activity of Soviet town planners. More than 1000 new towns have been created in our country during the period of Soviet rule. Among them are large-scale, diversified industrial and cultural centers such as Naraganda, Novokuznetsk, and Zaporozhje with populations exceeding 500,000 people, and smaller towns with populations of up to 10,000 inhabitants. However, the majority of new towns have populations of 30,000 to 150,000 (according to the data of the Central Research and Design Institute for Town Planning); these towns include the petroleum workers town of Almetjevsk, the glaziers' and tanners' town of Bor, the scientists' towns of Dubna and Pushchino, and the metallurgists' town of Temirtau.

During the period of Soviet rule the urban population of the country has increased from 26 million to 150 million, one-fourth of the whole population living now in new, comfortable towns.

POLICIES

The growth of urban areas and population as well as the construction of new towns in the USSR are the most characteristic manifestations of current urbanization, with the scientific and technological revolution and urbanization in the USSR inseparable elements of the integral process of the development of Communist society. At the initial stage new-town construction in the USSR is based on fundamental scientific investigations and practical developments for the field of settlement.

The System of Grouped Settlements. The transformation of the Soviet settlement system is based on the rational distribution of the productive forces facilitating the following:

1. Raising and equalizing economic development of different regions of the country; developing regions of Siberia, the extreme north and far east where basic raw materials, forest, fuel, water, and energy resources are concentrated; creating productive territorial complexes with regard to natural and economic conditions of the regions and the order of priority of their development; regulating growth of large cities, stimulating development of medium-sized and small towns, and also enlarging rural areas in systems of grouped settlements.
2. Transforming the urban environment in accord with new architectural, functional, scientific, technical, and hygienic requirements that arise from the socioeconomic tasks of society.
3. Preserving and developing the natural environment with due regard for its rational use for the benefit of all the people.

Directive documents of the party and government determine the tasks of the further transformation of the network of settlements of the country. They formulate the tasks of the development of the national economy, society, town construction, the safeguarding of nature, the rational use of natural resources, and a systematic approach to the complex solution of large-scale national economic problems.

Research is conducted in various directions of town planning. Particular attention is currently given to the investigations and elaboration of practical measures for creating basic directions of the distribution and development of urban areas and other settlements for a long-term plan for national economic development in the USSR. In 1975 the Central Research and Design Institute for Town Planning (TSNIIP) completed the elaboration of the general scheme of settlement over the whole territory of the USSR projected for the years 1990, 2000, and beyond. In addition to town planners, specialists of the most diverse professions from the Institute of Geography and Sociological Research of the Academy of Science, USSR; the Council on Productive Forces under Gosplan; and zonal, research, and design institutes for town planning in Leningrad, Kiev, Novosibirsk, and other cities participated in this work.

The general scheme of settlement is a long-range, scientifically justified concept of developing a network of settlements throughout the country, Soviet republics, and large economic regions. The scheme provides for the solution of the most important settlement problems connected with creating a material base for communism and increasing the standard of living of the Soviet people.

The general schemes of distributing settlements and productive forces, the comprehensive scheme of developing a transportation network, and different long-term branch plans are elaborated simultaneously. Further betterment of work on regional and town planning, renewal of existing urban areas, and construction of new ones is based on this general scheme of settlement. The formation of different systems of settlement linked in one way or another with the formation of large-scale national economic complexes is the principal direction of planned regulation and improvement of various settlement systems. These tasks are solved at three levels: territorially grouped, regional, and national economic. The following are the main tasks solved at the national economic level connected with improving the

development proportions of the existing network of settlements for the next 15 years:

1. The identification of about 25 regions and cities—regional centers, including economic regions of the Russian Soviet Federative Socialist Republic (RSFSR) and union republics.
2. The acceleration of the development of towns and settlements in eastern regions of the country to provide more regular population distribution between European and Asian parts of the Soviet Union.
3. The effective restraint of the growth of existing urban areas with populations of more than 500,000 people.
4. The extension of the network of large and larger cities and intensive construction of middle-sized and small towns of the European USSR with populations of up to 100,000 people.

The complex problems of transforming the existing network of settlements and of forming and developing systems of regional settlements in the union republics or economic regions are solved at the regional level.

The territorially grouped level encompasses the development of systems of grouped settlements formed in the following areas:

1. Zones of active influence of the existing largest and large cities and agglomerations.
2. Industrial regions with new towns as the main components of the system that are formed on the basis of territorially productive complexes created.
3. Regions of new exploration and poorly developed regions with unfavorable natural and climatic conditions covering extensive areas (taking into account the use of air transport and the availability of links with the largest and larger cities of inhabited regions of the country).

The inclusion of single urban areas, settlements, and their groups in systems of grouped settlements carried out on the basis of national economic, specialized working, and sociocultural links makes it possible to include towns and settlements of various sizes as well as rural areas. Thus more effective measures are taken for restraining the growth of the largest and larger cities and for developing smaller and middle-sized towns and to reduce irrational journeys of workers of mass occupations from the suburbs to the largest and larger cities.

The settlements included in the system should complement each other in productive, scientific, and cultural relations. They should have well-organized public services and amenities, domestic comfort, developed systems of transport and communication, and favorable conditions for the entire urban and rural population of the system, providing intellectual and physical development of the population and a choice of the sphere of work activity, which will contribute to accelerating the elimination of existing differences between town and country. The basic premises of the general scheme of settlement recommend a transition to interrelated settlements with the subsequent formation of large, middle-sized, and small grouped systems.

In the extreme north and in other regions of development, groups of related settlements with centers—basic towns or settlements—were identified, and the national economic base of each development group was established at the Leningrad Research and Design Institute for Town Planning.

Systematic creation of systems of grouped settlements based on new territorially productive complexes requires common planning and financing, with emphasis on national economic development and with centralization of resources for residential, cultural, service, municipal, and other forms of civic construction.

New towns can be established and developed in any region of a system of grouped settlements. The formation of large grouped systems is related first to the task of the successive, purposeful restraining of the growth of the largest cities, which are potential centers of such systems. This requires the priority growth of settlements in the outer system zones; new towns may be among these settlements. At the first stage small and medium-sized grouped systems are developed primarily by increasing the potential in their central cities. In most cases new towns act as centers of these grouped systems.

On the whole the creation and development of new towns assume organic combination of this phenomenon in Soviet town planning with the general process of the formation of systems of settlement involving the whole network of urban and rural areas (see Figure 1). The formation of systems of grouped settlements further opens perspectives for improving design, providing in particular the strengthening of regional planning and the compre-

hensive justification and longevity of general plans of the development of urban areas entering into a system.

The functional integrity of the system is expressed in its architectural and planning unity under definite natural conditions. This integrity results from the interconnection of general trends of spatial development of towns of the system (to avoid their unforeseen coalescence) and from clear-cut zoning of interurban open spaces.

At the suggestion of town planners, towns are linked by transportation infrastructure and by greenbelts of different designation that permeate the entire territory of the system and constitute a unity with urban green plantations. Adequate spatial exposures of urban development on water spaces, the inclusion of existing large green massifs into composition, and so on, are necessary while forming the grouped settlement system with due regard for natural landscape. All this should be carried out in accord with the unified architectural and planning scheme.

Possible viewpoints from which a vista of several towns of the system open, along with the availability of visual links between separate towns, are taken into consideration when forming the system. Town planners also consider the sequence of urban panoramas to be perceived when traveling on the river, flying up to an airdrome, and so on. All this is based on the organization of a "common (unified) interior" of the grouped settlement system; due to its great dimensions the interior is designed for uniform perception in correlation with different architectural and natural elements.

The scholars of TSNIIP[1] give particular attention to works on regional planning when forming local and regional systems. Sites are selected that are suitable for locating towns and villages, industry, residential areas, recreational zones, and transportation networks.

When selecting sites designated for industrial construction, the main task of the regional planning schemes is to provide comparative characteristics of various areas with respect to their regional distribution in relation to all settlements, communications networks, waterways, and so on. The most appropriate new construction site is selected with regard to various data so that an optimum solution can be obtained only by using a computer. Because of this, the practical introduction of quantitative simulation methods and correlation of natural, economic, and town planning factors of different quality with com-

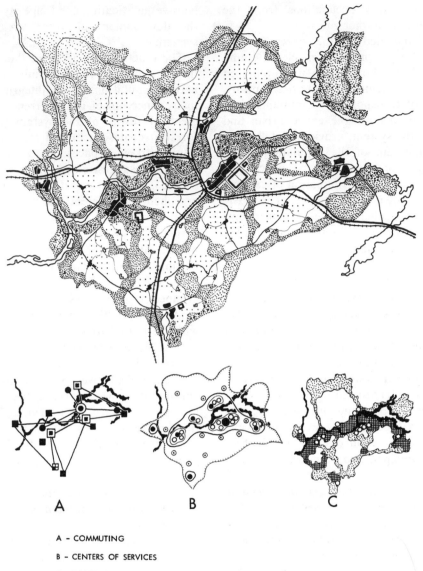

A - COMMUTING

B - CENTERS OF SERVICES

C - ZONES OF OPEN SPACE FOR RECREATION

Figure 1.   Experimental project of a system of grouped settlements (Russia).

parable results led to the quantification of solutions and to the wide use of computers.

Thus a considerable number of settlements and sites in Russia, the Ukraine, and Byelorussia that were identified during the examination of regional planning schemes were studied when choosing a site for the automobile complex constructed with the aid of Fiat. There were detailed data for evaluating conditions that were important for the distribution of the automobile plant—for example, the availability of labor and territorial resources, possibilities of use of the construction base, conditions of water supply, the provision or possibility of creating housing stock in a short period. All this allowed the most accurate choice of the most favorable area for new-town construction.

Therefore, we can determine the regions for new towns constructed during the tenth five-year plan (1976–1980) and indicate exactly their sites following the national economic plan. In addition, the planned national economy allows the rational distribution of housing, cultural, and service facilities constructed in urban areas; the plan of construction of new groups of house-building enterprises; and flexibility to account for increasing construction rates when planning and developing urban areas.

During the past decade the volume and rates of new-town construction in the USSR have increased sharply; dozens of large groups of house-building enterprises, plants of block-volume construction, and building materials industries have been put into exploitation and are being built. The powerful created building industry yearly provides about 2.3 million dwellings, making possible the development of towns by large-scale complexes and getting completed architectural ensembles in a brief period.

Architects and town planners pay particular attention to linking industrial and residential areas, community centers, and recreational zones in new towns, which results not only in the creation of a convenient transportation network between places of work, rest, entertainment, and residence of an urban population, but also in the creation of visual links and the integrity of scale and development character, as well as in the formation of a unique architectural image for a given town.

Specially designated industrial areas arranged to eliminate any negative influence on residential areas are characteristic of many new towns. In particular, when elaborating plans, special attention is drawn to the elimination or localization of noise in industrial areas. In many towns walking access to jobs or time savings of work trips are achieved when the *selitebnyi*[2] area is placed parallel to the basic industrial area and separated from it, if necessary, by a greenbelt. As a rule, recreational zones, created on the basis of reservoirs and existing woodlands or protected natural reservations, adjoin the residential area (see Figure 2). In new towns, public transportation provides good links between dwellings and places of work and recreation, allowing the possibilities of further improvement of transportation. Among many examples of towns with convenient combinations of places of work, residence, and recreation are Obninsk, Pushchino, Novosibirsk, Akadem-Gorodok, Angarsk, and Bratsk.

According to our norms and regulations of urban development, the total travel time of home-based work trips should not exceed 30 or 40 minutes in the largest cities.

85 miles to Moscow

An important place in the planning and development of new towns is given to the preservation, transformation, and development of the natural environment with regard to its comprehensive, rational use. Examples are the new towns of Protvio, Nurek, Amursk, Rustavi, Togliatti, and Sumgait.

The pattern of the new town of Sumgait, which arose on the basis of metallurgical and chemical

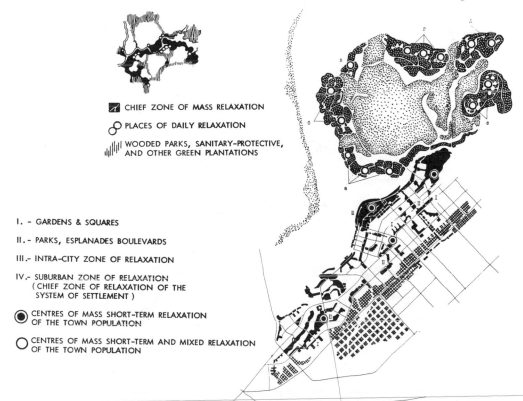

CHIEF ZONE OF MASS RELAXATION

PLACES OF DAILY RELAXATION

WOODED PARKS, SANITARY-PROTECTIVE, AND OTHER GREEN PLANTATIONS

I. - GARDENS & SQUARES

II. - PARKS, ESPLANADES BOULEVARDS

III. - INTRA-CITY ZONE OF RELAXATION

IV. - SUBURBAN ZONE OF RELAXATION (CHIEF ZONE OF RELAXATION OF THE SYSTEM OF SETTLEMENT)

CENTRES OF MASS SHORT-TERM RELAXATION OF THE TOWN POPULATION

CENTRES OF MASS SHORT-TERM AND MIXED RELAXATION OF THE TOWN POPULATION

Figure 2.   Centers of mass relaxation in the planned structure of a town and systems of settlement.

manufacture on the shores of the Caspian Sea in the northwestern part of the Apsheron Peninsula, is characteristic of many new maritime towns. Natural conditions of Sumgait were taken into consideration when elaborating its master plan. The seaside belt in the northeast part of the town is set aside for a town park and stadium, and the residential areas are designed to ensure convenient, fast access to the sea and to the industrial area. The system of urban landscaping unites the seaside park, regional and neighborhood gardens, boulevards, a protective greenbelt between the group of chemical enterprises and housing, and green plantations on the industrial sites themselves (see Figure 3).

Requirements and Standards.   The stringent normative requirements for clean air and water in towns and settlements and for the protection of nature and useful minerals help the architects and builders to solve all the town planning problems and to provide a systematic approach to science, planning, and construction.

A characteristic feature of Soviet town planning is a strict account of economic requirements. The

intensive use of land is one of the decisive conditions of construction economy. Before World War II this factor was not of great importance in new-town construction, and after the war economic requirements were not always taken into full account.

In many European countries the land for development is almost exhausted. In our country an area of 14.3 million square kilometers out of the total area of 22.4 million square kilometers is designated for the economic activity of business enterprises, organizations, and population. However, taking into account that in the next decades it will be necessary to assign to construction a large amount of new land, that 50 percent of the land fund consists of territories that have been frozen for many years, and that 20 percent of our territory comprises seismically dangerous regions, one can understand why the effective use of the land is sharply increased in new projects. At the present time special attention is given to the rational use of industrial and *selitebnyji* zones in new towns. In grandiose-scale housing construction the reduction of areas necessary for dwellings considerably decreased the street network and underground communications costs and released more improved green

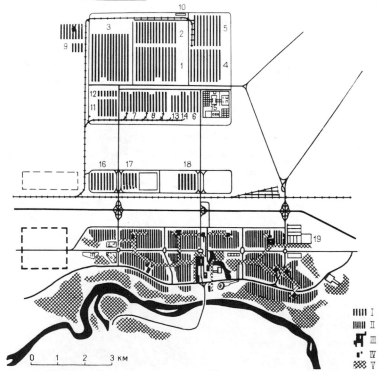

Figure 3.   Experimental scheme of the planning of a new town on the base of a petrochemical complex. I. industry; II. *Selitebnyi* zone; III. center of the city; IV. centers of the residential areas; V. green spaces. Composition of the complex: (1) petroleum refinery, (2) goods and raw material base, (3) petrochemical plant, (4) synthetic rubber plant, (5) goods and raw material base for the synthetic rubber plant, (6) synthetic fiber and textile plant, (7) plastics plant, (8) thermoelectric power station, (9) dumps, (10) purification installations, (11) store, (12) freight organization, (13) central repair and mechanical workshops, (14) administrative department of the material and technical supplies, (15) scientific technical center, (16) material and technical base of construction, (17) automobile base, (18) streetcar park, (19) light and food industries enterprises.

spaces for recreation. Naturally, in all the residential areas all the domestic and sanitary-hygiene requirements are observed, and a normative density of development is ensured. The scientifically justified standards of territorial use allow us to apply the development density that is economically most advisable and at the same time corresponds to the current complex requirements of town planning, providing the creation of comfortable and convenient conditions for the vital activity of the whole population.

New-town construction, as well as planning and development of all the other settlements of the country, is regulated by the national building norms and regulations (SNIP), prepared by research organizations and confirmed by the State Committee on Construction of the Council of Ministers of the USSR.

Planning and development norms provide for a differentiated approach to residential density; sizes of public building plots; and other essential indices for new towns, regions, and urban areas to be reconstructed. In particular, it is specified as necessary to take into account the concrete demographic composition of the projected town population when determining the total capacity of schools and children's institutions. SNIP favors better provision of new-town inhabitants, whose average age is considerably lower than in other settlements. The importance of new-town projecting, the complexity of the problems that arise in the process, and the desire to provide the best quality of projects, result, of necessity, in the inclusion of the following requirements in the state directions on the elaboration of planning and development projects: submission of all new-town master plans, regardless of their size, to the State Committee on Civic Construction and Architecture for approval.[3]

Architecture. The Soviet people make great demands for the architectural image, originality, and expressiveness of new towns. In many towns constructed near urban and rural areas that were destroyed during World War II, architects strive to preserve the features of the previous settlements. Continuity and innovation in architecture appear as basic qualities. Until now, 30 years after the Victory Day of the Soviet people in the Great Patriotic War,[4] this problem of our architecture has remained. One can understand it only by knowing our history and remembering the great destruction caused by the war: 1710 towns and urban settlements and about 70,000 rural settlements were destroyed by the Fascists. The war left in ruins Kiev, Minsk, Stalingrad,[5] and other large cities temporarily occupied by the enemy.

The architectural image of a new town causes the most frequent disputes and discussions among inhabitants, builders, and planners; the sharpest criticism seems to be caused by unattractive new development in some regions of mass standard construction, characterized by a certain monotony. The problem of architectural appearance is successfully solved in those towns the composition of which is based on the penetration into the structure of natural landscape, woods, reservoirs, and local relief, and on the creation of the architectural ensembles system (Nizhnekamsk, Monchegorsk, Volzhskij, and others).

Working on the solution of the current construction problems, the town planners look ahead. The architect is like a chauffeur: the faster a chauffeur drives a car, the further ahead he has to look—the faster the construction rates, the more accurately and distantly the architect must see the future of the towns. At the same time the extrapolation of present development trends in town planning is of no use. Therefore, new methods are required for forecasting great transformations in the social and spatial urban structure, caused by the scientific and technological revolution and social progress.

Plans for New Towns. An experimental new-town project was elaborated at the Central Research and Design Institute; the goal of the project was to determine the social conditions and theoretical principles of the physical planning pattern of the new town (see Figure 4). The work has two variants. The main variant was elaborated on the basis of socioeconomic, engineering, and technical characteristics of building for the nearest decade. The second experimental variant was attempted to approach the new-town model of the more distant future and to take into consideration the social transformations under the conditions of the advance of the scientific and technological revolution.

Taking into account these experimental projects, programs were elaborated for the actual construction of such large-scale, newly created towns as Togliatti and Naberezhnye Chelny, where many planning techniques and design indices processed beforehand in the experimental projects were applied.[6] The results of the experimental and actual construction are published in the monograph, "Generalnye Plany

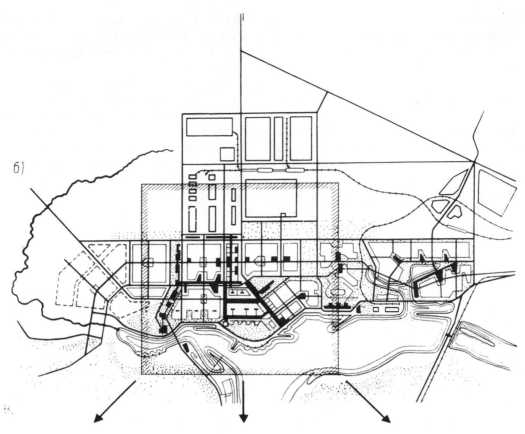

Figure 4. Planning structure of a new town.

Novyh Gorodov, M., 1973" ("Master Plans of New Towns, Moscow, 1973").

The future of our towns is created at research and design institutes. Architects are currently working on elaborating the development plan of the exemplary prospective residential area of Chertanovo Severnoe in Moscow that is to become the prototype residential area of the Communist town. The project provides for the creation of the healthiest and most comfortable living conditions that are equal for all. The architects suggested 16- to 24-story houses with apartments of different sizes and configuration, pedestrian alleys and sidewalks not crossing thoroughfares, underground garages, parking areas, and intrablock passages. The engineers prepared innovative utility services.

On the instructions of republic *Gosgrazhdanstroi* and *Gosstroi*, experimental planning of large residential areas of 60,000 to 100,000 inhabitants and single neighborhoods of 6000 to 10,000 people in various urban areas of the USSR is currently being conducted. These projects are based on new scientific achievements and successes in the practice of Soviet towns and settlement development.

In the extreme north architects are working on the problem of discovering new ways of housing organization—for example, by the creation of an artificial environment isolated from sharp temperature fluctuations and severe polar nights. Thus the construction of the covered town of Snezhnogorsk, which is so vividly described in the popular feature film *Lyubit' Cheloveka* (*To Love Man*), will become a town-planning experiment in the north. It will help to determine the character of influence exerted by the artificial environment on people (e.g., on their ability to work, their psyches, adaptation to specific northern conditions). This experiment will make it possible to justify and scientifically evaluate all new requirements in the creation of the best conditions for work, everyday life, and recreation of the workers in the extreme north.

The search for new solutions in the organization of developing new towns, residential areas and neighborhoods, and industrial centers helps today to build well and to introduce possible changes and improvements in the process of the practical implementation of the project. At the present time town planning in the USSR is directed more than ever before to the solution of important social, cultural, and economic problems. Addressing a meeting of the constituents of the Bauman electoral district of Moscow on June 14, 1974, L. I. Brezhnev said: "At the present time when millions of people have already improved their living conditions, the possibility arises to pay more attention to the quality of construction: to convenient planning of apartments, outward appearance of avenues, city blocks and public buildings. Our architects can and must finish with monotonous development and inexpressiveness of architectural decisions." These directives of Secretary Brezhnev mobilized the efforts of architects and builders for the improvement of the architectural quality and the perfection of town planners' skill.

Among the new constructions, the towns of Togliatti, Naberezhnye Chelny, Navoi, Shevchenko, and villages of Vertilshiki, Kodaki, and many others can be named among the most successful (see Figures 5, 6, and 7). Our towns, settlements, villages, and works of architecture are an integral part of the environment; and the degree of both their perfection and satisfaction of material and intellectual demands of the Soviet people considerably influences the full value, joy, and happiness of social work and life.

Scientific Methods and Agencies for New Towns. Such a trend of solving town-planning problems is greatly stimulated by research development. Scientific investigations and theoretical works in the field of town planning started as far back as the 1920s are connected with V. Vesnin, the first president of the Academy of Architecture of the USSR; G. Orlov, chairman of the Union of Architects of the USSR and an honorary member of the American Institute of Architects; A. Kuznetsov; B. Svetlichnyi; M. Leonidov; M. Ginsburg; N. Ladovskyi; V. Lavro; and others. At the present time, many expert architects, economists, sociologists, and geographers are concerned with the complicated problems of the creation, operation, and management of new towns. These professionals introduced a broad creative search for methods of planning towns and settlements under construction into present practice: zoning, a stepped system of public service, and integration of town and nature. The research forecasts are directed not at abstract innovations, but at the practical creation of a modern, progressive structure of new towns of various national economic profiles. Creative and scientific methodological work of research and design institutes is combined with various activities of state bodies for civil construction and architecture, local authorities for town planning, project organizations, and the Union of Architects of the USSR.

In the State Committee on Civil Construction and Architecture, the work on new towns is directed by Professor N. Baranov, the deputy chairman of the

Figure 5. Naberezhnye Chelny: model of high-density development of central neighborhoods.

Figure 6.   Navoi: fragment of high-density development.

committee, the people's architect of the USSR, and member of the American Academy of Architecture, and A. Kudryavtsev, chief of the Department of Urban Planning and Development, the honored builder of the RSFSR and chairman of the joint Soviet-American working group for enhancing the urban environment.

Projection and construction of new towns are conducted by various organizations. The planning and development projects of many new towns, such as Magnitogorsk, Novokuznetsk, Komsomolsk-Na-Amure, Karaganda, Temirtau, Togliatti, and Naberezhnye Chelny, were elaborated at the Central Research and Design Institute for Town Planning, which 10 years ago combined in itself the design institute *Gorstroiproekt* and the Research Institute for Town Planning of the Academy of Building and Architecture of the USSR.

The combination of researchers and qualified

expert planners immediately influenced the research and design work. Projects of many new towns were prepared at the institute, with researchers actively participating in the elaboration of almost every project. They are responsible for specific sections of the projects that require detailed investigations, such as prediction of town development in the system of grouped settlements and its influence on the system (the town of Naberezhnye Chelny), the choice of planning structural dimensions depending on local natural conditions (the town of Togliatti), air protection (the town of Temirtau), choice of development methods that ensure protection from heavy winds (the town of Balakovo), and so on. For all towns the urban transportation systems were elaborated by means of mathematical methods and computers. In their turn, the projects of new towns gave an additional impulse to conduct investigations and were a practical test of their vitality and effectiveness.

Figure 6. (Continued)

We place people at the apex of all our project proposals because all that we do is for people in the name of people. Proposals made in the field of a town of the future are alien to us because of their technicism and indifference to people.

The fact that the aesthetics of all these towns of the future is alien to us, the fact that any antihumanism in the urban appearance will be even more alien to our descendants does not mean, of course, the denial of the benefit of many structural and constructive ideas included in them, or skepticism on the possibility of their technical realization. We all know very well the feeling of great pride in mankind which we experience every time when we come across new technical achievements. I am convinced that the boldest ideas, including the chemical town of Katavolosa, are no more fantastic than the landing of man on the moon. However, the fact is that it is not technological development, boundless in its skill, that should dictate to man the forms of his surroundings, but it is man who should dictate

to building technology the directions of its development. This is a matter of principle, this is the essence of the town planning basis of the epoch of communism, and above all, we must apply this yardstick to any creative ideas for determining their progressiveness degree.[8]

Soviet town planning as a factor stimulating our social progress has become a sphere of state activity where the freedom of creative search and a wide range of scientific investigations are combined with the guiding principles of the state bodies.

PRESENT TRENDS

The town of Naberezhnye Chelny was used for the demonstration of modern tendencies for new-town planning and development. On the basis of scientific investigations it was decided to locate a heavy-duty truck plant, the largest in the world, and accompanying industries in the new town of Naberezhye Chelny.

Figure 7.   Shevchenko: panorama of high-density development.

The forecasts of the town development showed that its growth rate would be extremely high and by the end of the estimated period—that is, by 2000—its population would reach 400,000 people.

Naberezhnye Chelny.   Taking into consideration that the creation of a large-scale industrial node with Naberezhnye Chelny as its center creates objective conditions for effective development of urban areas existing within the given region and for the future construction of new ones, it was decided to elaborate the project of Naberezhnye Chelny as an integral part of the whole system of surrounding settlements. A special feature of the project was the proposition of creating a system of grouped settlements on the basis of new towns being built and the existing regional settlements (Naberezhnye Chelny, Nizhnekamsk, Elabug, Mendeleevsk, Menzelinsk, Zainsk, and Novyi Zai). The system formation is based on the close interrelation of towns involved and on their use of a common transportation network, places for mass recreation, and suburban agriculture.

Such a system possessing advantages of a large-scale city (highly efficient public production, sufficient services for the population, etc.) lacks many of its drawbacks (excessive congestion of the population, remoteness from the natural surroundings, etc.). The master plan of Naberezhnye Chelny includes the project "Grouped Settlement System," which is considered basic, and the essential text materials, describing the decision.

From the point of view of the scope of the territory (12,000 square kilometers) and the detailed nature of the study of the settlement pattern, the decision broadens considerably the range of tasks of the conventional project of a suburban area, required for the master plans; it also allows the simultaneous elaboration of the urban planning structure and common structure of the system of grouped settlements, taking into account and foreseeing their mutual effect (see Figure 8).

As the experience of projecting the master plan of Naberezhnye Chelny shows, such a town-planning approach allowed sound estimation of population and determination of trends of territorial urban development within the settlement system; the approach allowed planners to propose the tracing of lines and the siting of junctions of external thoroughfares with due regard for intragroup settlements, to establish the capacity and specialization of the main scientific and cultural centers, to include in the master plan scientific justifications for the town development for a distant perspective beyond the limits of the estimated period, and to increase the economic effect of the decision.

The elaboration of the system of grouped settlements as a part of the master plan of Naberezhnye Chelny became possible because simultaneous work was in progress on an independent project of planning the Naberezhnye Chelny industrial region, which encompassed the whole territory of the grouped system together with its external influence zone. The planning of Naberezhnye Chelny began in 1970, and today one can already stroll along the streets and squares of the automobile builders' city spread out on the banks of the river of Kama.

Togliatti. An analogous choice of site and construction was observed in Togliatti. In connection with the decree of the Central Committee of the Communist Party of the Soviet Union and the Council of Ministers of the USSR on the siting and construction of the Volga automobile plant in 1967–1968, the leading research and project institutes, together with 20 of the largest design organizations, elaborated a master plan of Togliatti and the project of its new part (see Figure 9). The master plan, as a basic town-planning document, determined the perspective of Togliatti's development for 30 years, taking into account the complex solution of all of its functional elements—that is, rational and convenient siting and solution of its industrial and residential areas, the center, areas for relaxation and sports, networks of public service, of amenities, and of urban transporta-

Figure 8. Naberezhnye Chelny: fragment of development.

Figure 9.   Togliatti: fragment of development.

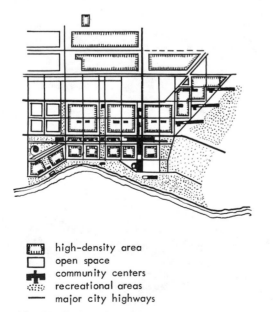

high-density area
open space
community centers
recreational areas
major city highways

Figure 10.   Distribution of production and settlement in the new towns of the metalworking industry and machine engineering industry.

tion. According to the master plan, the first phase of construction was assigned up to 1975 to finish the construction of residential areas and arterial roads and to create for the workers normal living conditions by the time the factory was in full production. This task has been successfully completed.

Both Naberezhnye Chelny and Togliatti belong to the group of industrial towns that includes numerous new towns based on heavy industry: machine manufacturing, instrument making and radio-electronics, and the extractive industries (see Figure 10). The towns of this group develop most intensely and quickly. The yearly increase of their population reaches 20,000 to 25,000 in the initial stage. The largest-scale new towns (e.g., Zaporozhje; Donetsk; Krivoi Rog and others based on the coal, metallurgical, and chemical industries) have been built during the years of the Soviet rule. Naturally, many new towns grow quietly and slowly, especially those that have been transformed into towns from settlements.

Other Towns. The past few years have been characterized by more intense development of the group of towns of scientific-productive and scientific profile. The emergence of the large scientific centers uniting dozens of scientific institutions is a characteristic feature of the union republics and developing regions of the country (see Figure 11). Many of them are being created within a radius of 100 kilometers from the large cities. For instance, during the past years 10 new towns of scientific and scientific-productive profile have been built and are being built around Moscow (e.g., Obninsk, Chernolovka, and Pushchino).

New towns are also built in the influence zone of the largest cities of Siberia and the far east. Akademgorodok, the complex, scientific center of Siberia located 25 kilometers from Novosibirsk, can be considered a characteristic example of such a town. In it there are 16 research institutes, a computing center, a university with 44 departments, a specialized physico-mathematical school, and a botanical garden of the Academy of Sciences of the USSR. The basic pursuits of the scientists concern mathematics, mechanics, chemistry, biology, geology, economics, and other disciplines. The management center of research activity of the largest region of the country—the Siberian section of the USSR Academy of Science—is also located in this town. The center coordinated the work of 51 scientific institutions, some of which are situated in Ulhan-Udé, Irkutsk, Krazsnoyarsk, and other towns.

The scientific town is built in accord with the master plan, providing a parallel distribution of main functional zones. The townwide community center, a part of the *selitebnyi* zone, has already taken shape in its essential features. It is up to one kilometer long. Cultural and service facilities are being distributed along the main town street—*Prospekt Nauki* (Science Avenue). The communications building, commercial center, and cinema have been built there. The community center perspective is enclosed by the university on one side and by the scientists' houses on the other.

The planning structure of neighborhoods is formed on a unified principle. The residential buildings are grouped around the neighborhood garden. Schools are situated on detached sites having an area of two and a half to three hectares. They adjoin either a garden or wood lots. Kindergartens and nurseries serve the groups of houses. The shopping and service

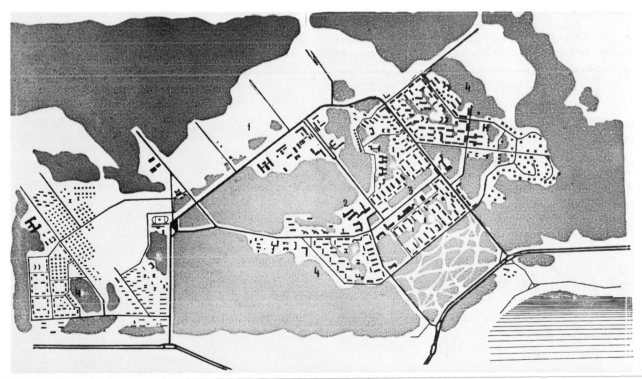

Figure 11. Example of the formation of the structure of a scientific new town: (1) science zone, (2) university, (3) community center, and (4) residential zone and zone of projected institute.

combines including food and manufactured goods stores are formed near the arterial roads or residential streets.

CONCLUSION

The town-planning principles that underlie new-town development in the USSR envisage the maximum possible and expeditious broadening of their national economic functions. At the same time the principles provide for improving the architectural images of towns under the conditions of modern methods of construction and with due regard for various natural climatic conditions of such a vast country as the Soviet Union. The development of new towns does more than simply provide the people with dwellings, services, cultural facilities, and the organization of leisure in the regions of new national economic development. In the process of new-town construction the social, economic, scientific, and technological progress of Soviet society is gaining in scope, with its basic goals being the overall satisfaction of material and intellectual requirements of the Soviet people.

NOTES

1. In the drafting of regional schemes and projects, highly qualified engineers of more than 20 specializations usually take part, and as a rule, an architect is in charge. In the series of works, especially in the large-scale industrial regions, it is necessary to enlist the services of up to 80 project and scientific research cotester institutes.

2. *Selitebnyi*: a term describing areas designated for the distribution of residential areas, public centers (administrative, research, educational, health and sports institutions), and public green plantations.

3. The State Committee on Civic Construction and Architecture is the highest Soviet organization concerning matters of town construction.

4. This term is used in the USSR for World War II after Germany invaded the country in the summer of 1941.

5. Now Volgograd.

6. The results of the experimental and real building are published in the monograph *General'nye Plany Novykh Gorodov, 1973* (Moscow: *General Plans for New Towns, 1973*).

7. Among our practical workers and town planners who are not working on the creation of large-scale new towns, it is worth mentioning the authors I. Orlov and N. Simonov (honored by the International Union of Architects with the Leslie Patrick Abercrombie prize in 1975), who built in the desert during the past few years the towns of Navoi in Uzbekistan and Shevchenko in Kazakhstan; the names of the architects V. Shkvarikov, B. Rubanenko, E. Kutirev, and V. Pliner, who were honored with the State Prize of the USSR for the architecture of the new town of Togliatti; M. Belyi and A. Mikhailov for the architecture of Novosibirsk Akademgorodok; Yu. Platonov, the director of the authors' collectives of many new-town scientific centers, and together with them I would also name the architect A. Shiphkov, who until now has not had the chance to build anything, but who persistently conducts work in the field of the construction of the covered town for the north. The expert practical workers, scientists, state officials, and builders work in close contact and complete mutual understanding, acknowledging the great responsibility that the people give them.

8. O. Shvidkovskii, *Scientific Forecasts of Soviet Towns Development and Formation on the Basis of Social and Scientific and Technological Progress*, issue 1 (Moscow: Central Institute of Scientific and Technical Information for Civil Construction and Architecture, 1968), p. 104.

CHAPTER 24

Soviet Policy for New Towns and Its Implementation, Achievements, and Problems

JACK UNDERHILL

The Soviet Union has undertaken one of the most massive centrally controlled, planned policies of human and industrial resettlement in history. Since 1926 the Russian government has built from 1000 to 1200 new towns (depending on definition) in which 40 million people live, work, and play. They plan to build during the next two or three five-year plans some 200 to 250 new towns (about 20 to 25 a year). In each of the past three five-year plans, 100 to 215 have been started.[1] In 1967 some 400 of the 791 new towns existing at that time were freestanding and had a population of some 10 percent of the nation's urban population. At that time 127 were in the Don-Dnieper region (southwest), 119 in the western-most portion of the Soviet Union, 90 in the "central chernozem" area, 85 in the Urals region, 46 in Kazakhstan, 59 in central Asia to the south, 77 in both western and eastern Siberia, and 42 in the far east.[2]

NEED FOR SOVIET POLICY AND ITS PRINCIPLES

To explain the pattern of industrial, new town, and urban development in the Soviet Union, I must describe some trends, events, and factors that have shaped Soviet growth and policy. The factors that I

The genesis and background of this paper lie in one attempt to implement a policy of reducing tensions with the Soviet Union through exchange of scientific and technical information and increased personal contacts under some 10 different agreements. In July 1974 I was a member of the U.S. New Towns Delegation, headed by Alberto Trevino, that visited the Soviet Union under the auspices of the US-USSR Working Team on the Enhancement of the Urban Environment. This team traveled about 3000 miles from Moscow to Leningrad and back; to Togliatti, the giant new town on the Volga River near Kuibyshev; the resort town of Sochi on the Black Sea; to 900-year-old Minsk, capital of the Byelorussian Republic; and back to Moscow to meet with the Central Research and Design Institute of Town Planning (TSNIIP).

In February 1976 a second new towns team went to the Soviet Union, this time under the auspices of the Housing and Other Construction Agreement. This team was headed by Assistant Secretary David Meeker, Jr. The team traveled from Moscow to Tashkent, the city of 1 million in Uzbekistan in Central Soviet Asia; to the new town of Navoi (also in Uzbekistan); the 2500-year-old city of Samarkand through which Alexander the Great, Marco Polo, and Genghis Khan had passed; Tibilsi, the capital of the Georgian Republic; nearby Rustavi; Donetsk, capital of one of the great coal producing regions in the world in the "DonBas" in the Ukraine; and Leningrad. This article reflects the detailed observations which were made from the first trip, general conclusions from the second trip, and considerable research between the two trips.

I made a third trip to the Soviet Union in October, 1976, and saw the new towns of Bratsk, Shelekhov, Novokuznetsk, Mezhdurechinsk, and Akademgorodok, plus the cities of Irkutsk and Novosibirisk.

This paper represents the personal views of the author and does not necessarily reflect those of the United States Department of Housing and Urban Development (HUD).

describe certainly do not exhaust the influences at work. One obvious factor has been the great centralization and strong state control. Among the other factors are the impact of World War II, the program of urbanization, and social policy.

Because of the terrible destruction of World War II, Minsk and Leningrad had to be restored. Leningrad had been besieged and bombarded for 900 days. During that period a large part of its population died of starvation, and the city was nearly destroyed. Minsk had a prewar population of some 270,000. In 1944 its population was only 45,000: it had been 80 percent destroyed.

These were not isolated cases: "1710 cities and towns were destroyed; Stalingrad, Minsk, and Sevastopol in utter ruins; Kiev, Karkov, Rostov-on-Don gravely damaged; 70,000 villages, 6,000,000 buildings, and 37,000 industrial enterprises demolished; 20 million people died; and 25 million homeless."[3]

There were at least three major consequences of the war. Soviet professionals and ordinary citizens seem to yearn for peace.[4] This feeling was reinforced by the broad influence of American music, dress, and styles in dance and entertainment. A second consequence was the movement of industry and the creation of new towns in the hinterland and all the way to the Chinese border. Finally, memorials to the war dead, such as that at Khatyn outside of Minsk, are everywhere (see Figures 1 and 2).

Soviet emphasis on industrialization has had a dominant impact on the amount of resources going to supporting services and housing in both old and new communities.[5] DiMaio argues that emphasis on industrialization starved resources going into housing until at least 1957.[6] A review of the location pattern of national new towns and growth centers indicates that raw materials needed for industry have been a major determinant of location.

Soviet achievements in industrialization have been commendable. Under a series of five-year plans beginning in 1928, Soviet policy has been directed to the achievement of the most rapid possible industrial development, particularly in heavy industries. "In less than 40 years in the period from 1928 to 1967, the production of pig iron rose from 3 to 75 million metric tons, of steel from 4 to 102 million tons, of coal from 26 to 595 million tons, of petroleum from 12 to 288 million tons, of natural gas from .3 to 159 billion cubic meters, and of electric power from 5 to 589 billion kilowatt hours. . . ."[7] New towns played a critical role in feeding this industrialization.

Figure 1. Part of Khatyn memorial near Minsk built to honor the dead in 186 villages completely destroyed by the Germans in Byerlorussia in World War II. The war had a strong, if not dominant impact on Soviet housing and national growth policy. Photo by Jack Underhill.

The Soviets have both a huge urban population and a huge rural population. The rural population in 1967 was almost the same as 70 years earlier in 1897: 106 million in present Soviet boundaries. By 1975 it had dropped to 100 million.[8] During the interim it increased sharply to a peak of 139 million in 1939.[9] This means several things. The first is that a large part of the population of the Soviet Union is engaged in relatively unproductive agriculture, causing a shortage of labor in the housing construction field and industry. Roughly one-third of the Soviet work force (which is 50 percent larger than the work force in the United States) in 1971 was engaged in agriculture, compared to an average of only 4 percent of the work force in the United States. Yet the Soviet agricultural output was only 80 percent of the United States production.[10] In the Soviet Union one farm laborer feeds only seven people; in the United States, one laborer feeds 46 people.[11]

The distribution of viable Soviet agricultural land has also had an impact. It is predominantly located in Europe and the middle zone of the Soviet Union: southern Siberia and northern Kazakhstan. Although the Soviet total land mass is 5.5 billion acres, 2.5 times larger than the 2.25 billion covered by the United States (including Alaska), only about one-fourth of the land is suitable for agriculture, compared with roughly half in the United States.

The huge rural population has settled largely in small villages. In 1969, of the 107 million rural population, some 92 million lived in the 581,542 villages of various sizes. Some 56 million lived in villages

Figure 2. Another view of the Khatyn memorial Photo by Jack Underhill.

ranging from 101 to 2000 people.[12] Considering the poor transportation facilities and the relatively low wages of agricultural workers, urban amenities are not accessible to a large part of the Soviet population. Instead of going to large cities, many collective farm residents migrate to small rural villages. The collective farm population declined from 76 million in 1955 to 53 million in 1968 while "other rural" (essentially small villages) increased from 31 million to 52 million.[13]

The urban population in 1930 was less than 30 million; it was 70 million in 1950 and 130 million in 1967.[14] In 1975, it was 153 million.[15] Much of this growth occurred during the 12-year period from 1926 to 1939: it grew by 113 percent at a rate of 86 percent per decade, or 6.5 percent per year. Only in one decade (1840 to 1850) has the United States approached this growth.[16] The Soviet urban population increased from 18 percent to 33 percent, which had required three decades in the United States (from 1856 to 1887) and probably about a century in most European cities. Of this total urban increase of 100 million from 1930 to 1967, an amazing 40 percent was in new towns, which is probably a record in the world.

Much of the growth has occurred in large cities. Of the 83 cities of more than 100,000 population in 1939, 36 had doubled their population in a decade. Only seven United States had reached the 100,000 mark and have grown so rapidly, and no more than three did so in any one census period.[17]

The Soviet Union is a nation of large cities. In 1969 it had 209 cities over 100,000, compared with 206 for the United States. The number of such cities increased from 31 in 1926, to 82 in 1939, and 146 in 1959. According to the 1959 census, about one-fourth of the urban dwellers in the Soviet Union lived in cities of more than 500,000 population, another fourth in cities of 100,000 to 499,999, another fourth in cities from 20,000 to 99,000, and about a fourth in cities of less than 20,000 population. Ninety-seven percent of these large cities are within what Harris called the "ecumene," that part of the Soviet Union in which climatic conditions are suitable for farming. The rural population average is 25 persons per square mile. Outside the ecumene the population is less than one person per square mile.[18] A large majority of the new towns are located in this populated zone.

In the absence of a new-town policy, it is highly probable that a much larger percentage of persons would be in the large cities, because most new towns are quite small.

Housing. To understand Soviet planning and new towns, it is necessary to understand housing policy, which applies to all developments, old and new. Housing is quickly and cheaply constructed and represents a great improvement over what previously existed. The Soviets claim great gains in housing consistently exceeding annual production in the West. They are justly proud of their housing achievements, particularly during the past decade, having built 2 million units every year since 1957. Average useful space (including all rooms) increased from 65 square feet at the end of World War II to 117.7 square feet per person by 1970. The ninth Five-Year Plan (1971 to 1975) calls for the average "net livable space" (excluding bathroom, kitchen, and hall) to be around 100 square feet per person and for the construction of 6 billion square feet of living space, the equivalent of 60 large cities of one million population each. Its estimated cost is 73.5 billion rubles, of which 43.9 billion will be government funds and the balance, private construction or condominiums. This should increase the average useful space to 127 square feet by 1975[19] (see Figure 3).

Achievements in housing are even more remarkable considering the relatively late start of progress in meeting the housing crisis. The period 1946–1960 alone saw the building of more housing than the entire period 1918–1946. The period 1956–1969 produced over 150 percent more housing than all of the housing built in the USSR from the time of the Revolution to 1955. For the first time in the development of the Soviet Union, the decade of the 1950s saw a serious attack on meeting housing shortages.[20] Thus, despite problems, Soviet citizens may not be discontented with housing because it is such an improvement from what they knew before, and satisfaction, in part, is a function of expectation. Another achievement of Soviet housing policy is the relative absence of problems of income and racial or ethnic differences. Soviet old and new towns are not divided into affluent sections and slums.

While the recent achievements have been substantial, there also are a great number of problems, primarily in the amount of space per person and in quality of construction. Further, even quantitative production (on a square-foot basis) has been outstripped by other countries, many of which were damaged by the war as badly as the Soviet Union.[21] These problems have led John Hart, a Soviet expert at the Library of Congress, to indicate that housing was the Soviet Union's most critical domestic problem.

According to a 1973 report, about 20 percent of all urban state housing was still without running water and sewerage, and for all housing, rural and urban, this figure probably exceeded 50 percent. The average waiting period for a person seeking an apartment in the Soviet Union ranged from one and one-

Figure 3. These highrise buildings are at 116 persons per acre in Togliatti, a half-million population new town on the Volga River. Photo by Jack Underhill.

half to three years.[22] It was worse in many Siberian cities.

Virtually every American housing delegation has commented on poor construction, but no one seems to have a satisfactory answer as to the cause. One detailed housing report indicated that the lack of skilled supervision and quality control on the job was a major reason for poor quality.[23]

The high degree of centralization and industrialization seems to be another source of problems. One Soviet writer indicated that of almost 800 standard designs available to architects and urban planners for apartment houses, scarcely 10 percent have been used and even more have been "dubbed alike as peas in a pod."[24]

The organization of the construction industry is another problem. Not until recent years were efficient construction "combines" created, replacing a multiplicity of small organizations of the different ministries. The creation of the combine represented a revolution in the Soviet building industry. This organization lowered labor expenditures by 35 to 40 percent and cut the time of construction by one and a half to two times.[25] However, even now quality does not rank high in these construction organizations. Inspectors have weak authority to require good construction. Because of the slowness in starting and completing repair work, many new buildings deteriorate quickly, and housing space is lost before its time. Between 1959 and 1961, 18 million square meters of housing became useless because repairs were not made on time. The reluctance of many tenants to be temporarily relocated during capital repairs was also a cause of problems. Not until 1969 was the decision made to increase the wages of a large category of construction workers and finishing workers because of the low quality of labor performance. However, overshadowing these construction industry problems is the emphasis on achieving production goals, rather than rewarding for good quality and punishing for poor quality.[26]

The members of the Central Research and Design Institute (TSNIIP) gave the United States team their own explanation for the poor quality of housing finishing, among which were the following:

1. Deficiencies in the industry that supplies interior finishing, such as plastic parts.
2. The fact that housing was built for people of all incomes, and there was an attempt to provide equal conditions for all.

3. The large cost of high quality interior finishing made it difficult to meet the basic housing demands for most people.
4. The acute shortage of skilled labor.

Whatever the causes, the Soviets probably will invest much time and money to improve the quality and space of their housing, just as they have tried to improve performance in other areas.

Social Policy. Although social policy is not directly in the scope of this study, it is worth mentioning because it has a profound impact on housing and community development. Virtually all housing viewed in the same size cities, constructed during the same time period is of a similar density and external appearance, although there are some variations in space.* Although party officials and other privileged groups may own a summer house or a *dacha*, this would typically be for temporary residence during the summer. There is also relatively little segregation in neighborhoods by incomes. In a typical new town there are no "gold coasts" for the rich and slums for the poor or lower-middle class.

This policy of equality in housing pervades other elements of society where money (beyond a certain point) is not important—certainly not so important as in Western society. Health care is free; education is free all the way up to and including college; vacations are partially free; housing is heavily subsidized for everyone; transportation costs only five cents a ride, and few people own cars. In each case services may not be very good, but basic service is open to everyone, and there are relatively few distinctions between rich and poor in terms of personal possessions.

All this is in fulfillment of a fundamental Communist goal of achieving a socially homogeneous (if not classless) society. In fact, in terms of incomes and physical possessions, the Soviets have reasonably approximated this goal, at least compared to western society. This observation is based upon the few existing limited income studies. The Soviets do not systematically publish income statistics by socioeconomic class. However, one study showed that in 1967 the average monthly wages of "salaried employees engaged in managerial posts" was 169 rubles, compared with highly skilled wage earners of

* Drabness and conformity are, of course, not a monopoly of any one country. It is merely a question of degree.

144, and on the bottom end of the range, "salaried employees without specialized education," 84 rubles, and "unskilled and low-skilled wage earners," 74 rubles.[27] Another study showed incomes were approaching equality in some sectors: in 1932 the workers earned 2.5 times less than specialists, but in 1964, only 1.5 times less.[28] A study done in Moscow in the early 1960s compared expenditures of a family with an income per capita of 44 rubles per month (probably a poorer worker household) and one with an income per capita of 113 rubles a month (probably upper working class or intelligentsia). There was only one ruble per capita expenditure difference between the two for housing and communal amenities: 1.5 rubles for the lowest income compared to 2.5 for the highest. The great variation in expenditures occurred for food (24.4 rubles compared to 45.4) and clothing (5.5 rubles compared to 45.5 rubles).[29] However, these figures may be misleading because influence and position are far more important than money in the Soviet Union. Hedrick Smith (who spent three-and-one-half years in the Soviet Union) in his book *The Russians* writes a whole chapter about the special privileges of the elite of the Soviet Union: their special stores, discount prices, country homes, and influence for getting their children into special schools and trips abroad.[30]

Despite the relatively small variations in income and housing characteristics, the Soviets have not achieved a classless society. After interviews with 100 emigrants from the Soviet Union in several countries, Katz points out that substantial "moonlighting"— supplementing income with extra jobs for extra income—exists. In addition, more and more sociological research is showing that, in fact, there are classes in the Soviet Union with different access to privilege and power. At the top of the Soviet pyramid are the *nachalniks* (managers) who constitute approximately 2 percent of the work force, intelligentsia (9 percent), and white-collar employees (service and technical employees) 6.5 percent.[31]

A similar debate and close examination should be accorded Soviet nationality policy. Nelson Foote was impressed with its achievement. He pointed out that lack of segregation by race or ethnicity in the cities he visited is in stark contrast to American experience and racial conflict.[32] The mayor of Togliatti was proud to point out that his young city (average age: 26) had 82 nationalities working side by side.[33] In his book on the Siberian people, based upon a three-month visit, Farley Mowatt praised Soviet treatment of native Siberians, in contrast to Canadian and American treatment of Indians.[34] Other experts have indicated that there is some natural ethnic clustering in older cities.

However, there is another observation that has a bearing on Soviet urban growth policy and urban development. Alex Inkeles commends the Soviet achievements in intergroup relations by saying that "the sum indication of such statistical evidence is that minority members (again with the striking exception of Soviet Jews) do not suffer from any discrimination insofar as educational training, economic opportunity, and social benefits are concerned."[35]

However, less than 55 percent of the Soviet citizens thought of themselves as Russian by nationality.[36] This percent is actually declining. Most of the minority people (80 percent or more) are located in the 15 national republics strung around the outer borders of the Soviet Union. A continuing chapter in Soviet history is unifying these people into a single nation and reducing separatist tendencies. The terrible purges of nationalist leaders, the dispersal of entire populations from four autonomous republics, interference with nationalist literature that seemed to show "bourgeois nationalism," and political domination of minority nationalities by the Great Russians are documented facts.[37] Inkeles concludes that despite the undeniable achievements in development of Soviet national minorities, "if these people had little part in choosing their path of national development, they have as little freedom today to alter it."[38] An excellent description of both the tragedy and supression of national yearnings for independence, along with substantial achievements in education, health, income, and industrial development appears in a series of books on Soviet Central Asia.[39]

Principles for Growth Policy. The Soviets have a host of acknowledged and unacknowledged principles for the new towns and national policy for urban growth. Among them are the concept of optimum city size, the need to eliminate differences between town and country, improvement in economic efficiency, exploitation of untapped natural resources, and political and social goals.

The concept of optimum city size is well grounded in the major textbooks or guidelines for town planning. A major work, setting standards in the field of town planning, *Principles of Town Planning in the Soviet Union*, and another book by a famous Soviet geographer, Davidovich, both include a strong defense of the concept of holding down the size of major cities on the grounds of both amenities and cost.[40]

Davidovich indicates that in 1955 there was a 2270 ruble difference in expenditures per capita in a town of 10,000 population and a town of 800,000.[41] These costs were 13,770 rubles for the small town compared to 16,040 for the large. Costs included residential and public buildings, services, and transportation. However, for the large towns, maintenance was cheaper annually (1120 rubles compared to 1215 for the small and large towns compared above). According to this calculation, there would be a savings of 2.2 billion rubles to provide for populations of 1 million new people in small towns rather than in large towns. Davidovich adds that excessive growth of a town leads to some undesirable results, such as deterioration in sanitary conditions resulting from pollution of air, noise of urban transportation, shortage of green areas, overcrowding of public transportation, little safety of street traffic, and large time losses on journeys. Twenty thousand is generally taken as the lower optimum size limit and 250,000 or 300,000 as the upper.[42]

There is some Soviet apology in the literature that among the errors of early Soviet new town planning cities such as Magnitogorsk grew much larger than originally contemplated. In addition, there is some counterargument in the Soviet literature that there ought to be more large cities. Lappo argues that his evidence "falls short of leading one to conclude that growth in big cities should be banned. The point is to control development. This means that the problem of regulation must, to a significant degree, be brought down to selection of those elements of the national economy which require the environment of the big city."[43]

A tenet of Marxism from the beginning of the revolution was that differences between town and country should be eliminated so that services would be equal throughout the country. Small rural villages are considered to be inefficient in providing adequate services for the rural population. A large number of the new towns were small developments serving rural areas. Davidovich shows that small settlements require high costs per capita and have poor services.[44]

Another basis for the new-town distribution is increased economic efficiency and reduced transportation costs, thus bringing the processing industry close to the mining industry, production near consumers, and related enterprises close together. Location of industry near raw materials, such as coal and oil as well as electric power, is a dominant theme in the location of many new towns. Some political objectives could conflict with this goal—a matter for further analysis.

The movement of population and new towns cannot be wholly explained by the economic and social factors already mentioned. There are other considerations that have been the driving force of industrial location, including geopolitical factors, which are difficult to document because they are scarcely acknowledged in the Soviet new-town literature. One such motivation is to reduce ethnic separatism in the border republics and to establish new towns and migration of Great Russians and other nationalities to encourage *zblezheniya* (rapprochement of nationalities). Also, there has been a strong move to try to fill the political vacuum of the vast less-populated areas of the east. Bernard points out that under the seven-year plan, at least 6 million workers would move to the eastern territories of the USSR; 60 percent of the labor force leaving their native region would go to the eastern regions.[45] This policy has been successful in part. The home nationalities in the Uzbek, Georgian, Moldavian, Turkmenian and Estonian Republics are less than 70 percent of the total republic population, less than 50 percent in the Kirghiz Republic, and less than 33 percent in Kazakhstan. The number of new towns in a region (or their proportion to old towns) seems to be directly related to the reduction in dominance of a home nationality.

Making the Soviet industry and population less vulnerable to attack certainly has been a driving force.[46] Bernard reports that "the impetus given to heavy industry was largely due to the war which led to the transfer east of 1200 large new industrial enterprises from the regions which had either been overrun or were threatened and to the building of a total of 2250 new enterprises."[47] Recent redoubled efforts have been made to establish a chain of towns and settlements along the southern border with China to fill up the vacuum[48] and to develop the BAM Line, an alternative railroad from Lake Baikal to the Amur River to decrease the vulnerability of the Trans-Siberian Railroad, which is right along the Chinese border. According to Foy Kohler, this defensive motive was supported officially by a 1971 party directive. The defense minister explicitly cited a possible nuclear attack and the need to disperse industry.[49]

IMPLEMENTATION OF SOVIET POLICY

The Central Research and Design Institute of Town Planning (TSNIIP) is the main intellectual and action center for planning of new towns in the Soviet Union. It is one of the research and design institutes within the State Committee of Civil Construction and Architecture (*Gosgrazhdanstroi*). This organization is, in turn, part of *Gosstroi*, which has the main organizational responsibility for nonindustrial construction and planning. The full name for *Gosstroi* is the State Committee on Construction Matters of the USSR Council of Ministers.

Gosstroi is responsible for executing the broad five-year plan directives established by *Gosplan*, the State Planning Committee of the USSR for economic growth, for town construction and housing. *Gosstroi* has regional counterparts that execute new-town planning and construction within their respective republics. Thus *Gosplan* will establish the five-year industrial growth plan; the republic *Gosplan* will establish the regional distribution and goals, and *Gosstroi*, working in cooperation with the various union industrial ministries, will establish the specific locations for this industrial development. *Gosstroi* works in conjunction with the *Mintiazhstroi* (Ministry of Construction for Heavy Industrial Enterprises), *Minpromstroy* (Ministry of Industrial Construction), and *Minsel'stroi* (Ministry of Rural Construction), which are responsible for construction in their areas of specialty.

The USSR Council of Ministers, the Supreme Soviet Presidium, and the Central Committee of the Communist Party coordinate all activities. Kosygin is currently chairman of the Presidium, and Brezhnev is general secretary of the Communist Party. This same organizational relation is duplicated in the republics, districts, and cities.

In theory, *Gosstroi* should have an easy job of locating and predicting the growth of the industrial base of the new towns, because industrial location is also controlled by government ministries. In fact, according to conversations with Soviet officials, it is not always an easy job to persuade the powerful industrial ministries to locate in a new town, because their primary job is production and they might not agree with decisions about new-town locations.

TSNIIP combines the functions in the Soviet Union that would be performed in the United States by planning consultants, the leading schools of planning, the Department of Housing and Urban Development, the General Services Administration, and private developers. TSNIIP is responsible for dealing with the following:

1. All of the scientific work relating to town planning, architecture, the spatial distribution of towns, regional planning, transport, sanitation, and housing.
2. Development of national standards for town planning and housing all over the Soviet Union, subject to more specific norms by related institutes.
3. Preparation of the master plans of new towns.
4. Assistance to design institutes in Leningrad, Kiev, Tashkent, Novosibirisk, Tbilisi, and Minsk, which are responsible for special problems in their own areas.

With a total 1974 staff of about 700 persons, TSNIIP consists of two major divisions: research (243 people) and design (433 people). There are also supportive and administrative sections. The research division has sections dealing with regional planning and the distribution of national settlement, town reconstruction, new towns, small towns' living areas and neighborhoods, industrial development, economics, urban and interurban transport, public facilities and engineering, landscape architecture, utilities, mathematical methods and computers, cultural systems and social services, design, and environmental problems including noise. The design department consists of various planning teams. A parallel institute is the Academy of Community Services, which deals with the functioning of cities once they are built.

Little distinction is made here between planning for new towns and old towns, primarily because the concept of new towns includes existing cities, and the same general principles apply to both. Any conclusions presented in this section are extremely tentative because American delegations have seen only eight new towns (Togliatti, Navoi, Rustavi, Bratsk, Shelekhov, Novokuznetz, Akademgorodok, and Mezhdyrechinsk) and several existing towns, including Leningrad, Moscow, Minsk, Sochi, Samarkand, Ivkutsk, Novosibirsk, Donetsk, and Tibilisi. The literature covered in the bibliography does not cover detailed urban plans with an objective assessment of them. Plans are only diagrammatic, because they appear to be classified information. The literature on new towns deals with prototypes, not the real thing, except in a few cases for illustrations. Therefore, I rely greatly upon secondary sources and the Soviet press as reported by Taubman, fortified by firsthand impressions.

Regional Planning. Leningrad, Minsk, and Byelorussia, in which Minsk is located; Togliatti, Tibilis, and Rustavi in Georgia; and Tashkent in Uzbekistan, are examples of planned regions. The literature reviewed covered only the subject of new towns and did not cover the subject in any depth. Therefore, I present little detail here.*

One of the major goals of the Leningrad plan is to organize the suburban areas of Leningrad, which comprise about 3.5 million acres. Included in this goal is the reorganization of agriculture, the creation of efficient urban settlements rather than small rural villages, and the concentration of population in fairly balanced developments mostly around existing communities, such as Pushkin, Pavlovsk, Petrodvoretz, Lomonosov, and Gatchina. These are existing developments that will be expanded into balanced communities.

A large percentage of the northern part of the Leningrad region will be preserved in open space, which will contain children's camps and other outdoor recreational areas. Large amounts of the other areas are not suitable for building and will be preserved in agriculture. This suburban zone is from 38 to 74 miles in radius. Within this suburban zone are some 15 cities, some 39 towns, and about 900 small agricultural villages.

Regional nodes of development seemed to me concentrated and integrated with open space and transportation. My impression is that this regional planning would compare favorably with any in Europe and was certainly better than that in the United States.

An examination of the special resource map of Shabad shows that Togliatti is located in a strategic location from a regional economic planning viewpoint.[50] It is adjacent to the giant Kuibyshev reservoir created by the 2.3 million-kilowatt hydroelectric dam, which was completed in 1957. The dam runs high voltage power lines, operating at 500 kilovolts, west to Moscow and eastward to the Urals. Massive oil deposits and oil fields are located within 100 miles of Togliatti at the new towns of Neftegorsk and Otradnyy to the southeast of Kuibyshev. Pipelines

run to Kuibyshev to refineries and to Syzran'. Within 150 miles to the northeast of Togliatti is the great oil field around the new towns of Almet'yevsk, Oktyabry'skiy, and others. From this center, both oil and natural gas lines run north across the Volga River to Kazan'.

Togliatti is also tied into the Volga River and rail transportation system and is located within the zone of not more than 10 percent above "minimum transportation effort."[51] Little information is available on the qualitative aspects of regional planning around Togliatti.

Towns in Byelorussia were not resource dominated and, therefore, had freedom of location. Maximum use was to be made of expansion of existing towns, as opposed to freestanding new towns. A series of factors were taken into account in determining the primary focus of future development for the region. Usually, major transportation arteries were a major consideration. They indicated the difficulty of controlling growth, regardless of what the plan says. The goal of Byelorussia is to increase to 12 million by the year 2000, compared with a current population of 9 million.

There is a complex interaction between economic and physical planning. *Gosplan* sets the overall production goals; these are translated into specific plant expansion schemes by the all union ministries and the republic ministries. The republic's planning bodies also suggest locations for industry, taking into account town planning factors. The goal of limiting population of Minsk to natural increase is followed as part of the regional plan.

Town Planning. The literature reviewed on national standards for new-town and city planning seems markedly similar from publication to publication. It would be familiar to most American planners as part of the mainstream of worldwide planning and presents few surprises. Extensive guidance is given as to neighborhood design, the size of open-space buffers between residential and industrial areas according to the degree of pollution emitted, the types of transport, permissible time to work, open space and utility standards, town centers, and other matters. It is virtually impossible to assess the quality of Soviet planning in these areas, due to the apparent unavailability of detailed actual plans and independent assessments of these plans: everything is shown in prototypes.

One special feature affecting the whole scale of overall urban planning is the extremely high

* Both of Smoliar's books on new towns have chapters dealing with regional clusters of settlements with both old and new towns. My impression is that Soviet planners have given careful attention to relations in regional clusters. However, so few examples of what has actually happened are given that these books provide a poor basis for judgment. Far more useful are the economic geography books of Harris and Shabad showing the relations between settlements, infrastructure, and resources.

densities, which run in the new towns anywhere from a low of 50 persons per residential acre (excluding open space, community facilities, streets, and squares) for Tayshet to a high of 116 persons per acre in Togliatti (see Table 1). This means that Soviet new towns as a whole are compact, easily accessible to transport and pedestrian traffic in neighborhoods, less consuming of the natural environment than American cities, and relatively cheap in terms of infrastructure.

However, before giving the impression of planning perfection based upon the theoretical plans and the special new towns and existing cities viewed, it would be useful to give some evidence of shortcomings directly from Soviet sources in the 1960s, including Kurcherenko, then chairman of the *Gosstroi*. Much of this list of shortcomings was covered in a June 1960 meeting in Moscow, which was designed to evaluate 43 years of Soviet urban development.

Based upon these sources, Taubman makes the following statement of problems in overall town planning:

As for urban plans—theoretically a must for every city—they were not to be found at all in a great many places in 1960. Of 1700 Soviet cities, half had no plan. Of 875 in the RSFSR, 350 lacked plans, as did 144 of 331 cities in the Ukraine and 48 of 64 cities in Byelorussia. Among those lacking plans were Kiev, Sverdlovsk, Novosibirsk, Gorky, Kharkov and Odessa.

Cities with plans found them more or less useless. Such plans were inaccurate, because *Gosplan* had not forecast economic prospects, thereby leaving town planners without essential data; insensitive, because the high level institutes that drafted them were too far away to comprehend local problems; and out of date in the time needed to prepare them (two and a half to three years for a city of 100,000 to 150,000). Not surprisingly city architects—functionaries with direct responsibility for planning—were in short and

Table 1   Residential Densities and Neighborhood Open Space in Soviet New Towns and Existing Cities

	Total Residential Area			Apartment and Neighborhood		Community Facilities		Open Space		Streets and Squares
	(in acres)	(persons/ acre)	Population (thousands)	(persons/ acre)	% of (1)	(persons/ acre)	% of (1)	(acres/1000 population)	% of (1)	% of (1)
New Towns										
Novokuznetsk	16,383	44.17	1525 (1967)	90.0	50.7	226.1	19.1	4.4	19.6	10.1
Temirtau	8,151	29.45	150 (1967)	78.3	48.9	251.3	17.9	4.4	17.4	15.8
Tayshet	7,434	30.4	226*	50.2	61.5	251.3	12	3.7	11.5	15
Angarsk	7,551	46.78	204 (1970)	107	43	251.3	18	4.9	24	15
Volzhskiy	7,595	40.1	114 (1967)	101.7	39	239.4	16	7.2	30	15
Novopolotsk	1,670	48.18	80*	95.9	50	814.2	6	6.14	30.2	13.8
Karaganda	15,326	36.02	565 (1975)	75.4	48	193.8	19	5.4	22	14
Chervonograd	1,235	49.89	62*	99	50.4	313.1	15.9	3.5	17.8	15.9
Novovolynsk	1,437	41.96	60*	78.6	53.6	238.2	17.6	3.4	14.4	14.4
Bratsk	2,719	37.00	122 (1967)	66.2	54.5	235.3	15.7	4.4	16.4	13.4
Togliatti	7,165	49.10	500 (1975)	116	41	270.4	18.6	3.3	19	21.4
Zelenograd	2,198	57.84	127*	110	52.7	297.1	19.6	2.3	13.8	13.9
Existing Towns										
Voronezh	11,142	48.45	611 (1967)	88.5	54.5	678.5	7.3	2.4	11.8	27.4
Irkutsk	7,602	40.11	420 (1967)	65.6	61.5	424.14	9.6	1.0	4.2	25
Volgograd	18,250	32.48	743 (1967)	66.76	53	646.1	5	1.3	5	37
Chelyabinsk	17,142	44.08	836 (1967)	71.5	61.6	667.3	6.6	.8	3.8	28
Cheremkhovo	4,174	29.7	109 (1967)	41.5	72	626.3	5	.98	3	20
Novorossiisk	2,769	36.36	123 (1967)	53.6	68	1696	2	.88	3	27
Kaluga	3,273	41.52	179 (1967)	63.6	64.5	904.6	4.6	.75	3.2	27.7

* Estimates made by multiplying persons/acre times acres.

Source: 1.   Smoliar, 1973, page 201, of original Russian text.

2.   Population *USSR in Figures*.

shifting supply. Only two education institutions trained town planners, and only 40 students matriculated in 1959.[52]

Much of Taubman's comment related to existing towns, at least in 1960. However, they do not exonerate new towns either. The problem is not so much the planning, which is not difficult, but the execution and financing of improvements to execute the plan in a quality manner:

Most new cities have been born and raised as Soviet style company towns in the shadow of one industrial establishment or with several establishments dividing responsibility or competing for control. The pattern was established in the 1930's. Central industrial ministries built not only factories but also housing and what meager services there were. City governments were an afterthought: they could do little more than ratify industrial actions—even when enterprises concentrating on production built insufficient housing and services or when several enterprises refused to coordinate their efforts so that well-off factories had an abundance of services and poorer plants had virtually none. . . .[53]

Thus, despite the apparent unitary government, where government and industry are one and the same, there is an underground pluralism with different ministries pursuing different directions and competing for scarce priorities between community building and industrial production.

Despite many problems of town planning reported in the Soviet press, the towns Leningrad, Tashkent, Togliatti, Samarkand, Akademgorodok, Donetsk, Navoi, and Minsk seemed well planned and well executed with good overall accessibility, little congestion, and balanced development. Execution of plans for specific buildings, such as sports palaces, hotels, selected public monuments, and recreational areas was also good. However, execution of plans for housing and other ordinary construction was poor, leaving a negative impression in many cases. In addition, even the planning had some weaknesses in that excessive centralization resulted in a sameness in all new neighborhoods and towns that I saw in the Soviet Union.

Poor quality construction can obscure to the visitor the overall structure of the plan. However, in Togliatti, Nelson Foote, an American sociologist on the United States team, remarked that he knew of few places in the United States where workers could live in decent housing, within 20 minutes of their place of work and a major recreational facility such as they did in Togliatti. The United States team received the same impression in Navoi on the 1976 trip in Uzbekistan.

Neighborhood Planning. One of the principal findings of the largest comparative study of new communities and small-scale development ever done was the importance of the neighborhood and home as a source of primary satisfaction or dissatisfaction.[54] Within the home and its immediate environment children are raised, daily recreation takes place, primary school is attended, and the housewife spends a good part of her day. The rest of the city is seen daily through the windows of a car (in the United States) or the bus (in the Soviet Union) in the journey to work, to and from recreational facilities, or on shopping trips. This situation places critical importance on the quality of neighborhood planning in determining life satisfaction outside the place of work (see Figure 4).

In 1958 the Soviet government decided to undertake the construction of an experimental section in the southwest borough of Moscow, with the aim of producing a national prototype for modern residential ensembles. That prototype is the *microraion* or microregion (neighborhood), which essentially is an evolution of the superblock concept of the 1930s.[55] This neighborhood formed the foundation for modern residential neighborhood planning, and Soviet guidelines require that "all new housing should be located in these large complexes." The essential Soviet city planning theory is that people do not live in homes but in communities, and the government encourages communal life in the neighborhood to reduce dependence on the home.

In Togliatti, Navoi, Tashkent, Rustavi, Minsk, and Leningrad, and presumably most other Soviet cities that are newly constructed or rebuilt, there is a uniform hierarchy of city building blocks. The basic unit is the *micro-raion*. In Togliatti this unit serves about 12,000 to 15,000 people. In both Leningrad and Togliatti these neighborhoods are served by schools located in the middle of the neighborhoods so that their 1000 or so students can walk to school without crossing major intersections. Shopping, playgrounds, and other local facilities are located from 440 to 550 yards from home. Although these neighborhoods are compact and convenient in all the cities I visited, typically (even in Moscow) they are drab, uniform, lacking in color, poorly landscaped, and lacking the type of variety that is apparent in European cities at comparable densities.

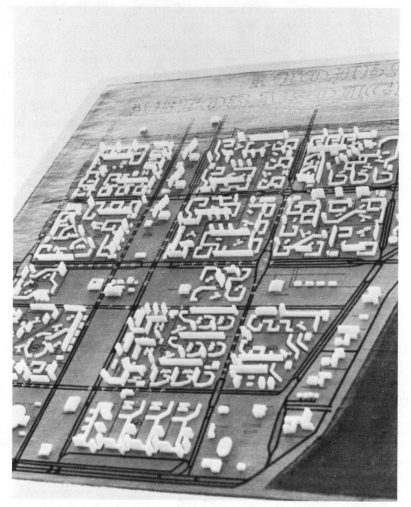

Figure 4.   This model of the new section of Togliatti shows typical neighborhood and section planning characteristic of most areas that the U.S. team visited. Photo by Jack Underhill.

At the next level is the residential district consisting of a population from 25,000 to 30,000 in Togliatti and 25,000 to 50,000 in Leningrad. Districts have better recreational and cultural and shopping facilities than the neighborhoods and are located within 1100 to 1650 yards of each home (15- to 20-minute walk). Several neighborhoods constituted a district. In Leningrad, each district is served by clubs, a theater, a community facility for the young, library, social and medical facilities, specialized food stores, and so on.

The next higher level in Leningrad is the planning district, which includes from 200,000 to 300,000 people (425 to 875 acres). In Togliatti the city is divided into the new town serving the automobile plant, which produces the Zhiguli's (modified Fiat), the old town around the existing town of Stavropol,

and the Komosomolsk region near the hydroelectric facilities.

How was the concept worked out in practice? Based upon systematic review of Soviet sources, DiMaio reports many problems in execution: by the end of 1966 certain critical comments were appearing in the Soviet press. Shops in the neighborhood were still half used while those near bus and subway stops were most often patronized. Timing of facilities and services was a critical problem. A report in *Pravda* indicated that the chief reason for the deplorable situation is that construction organizations consider trade and public catering enterprises secondary installations and "are unwilling to take on the construction. When they do take it on, they drag out the work for years."[56] Typically, one entity is responsible for housing and another for community facilities. Often there is money for the former, but not the latter. Thus the concept is good, but the execution has many problems.

High Density. The dominant Soviet philosophy has been toward high and higher densities in both old and new towns. Table 1 indicates two indices of density: residential density for the entire residential area and project or neighborhood density, which is the density of the actual dwelling area, minus open space, community facilities, streets, and squares. The table shows that project or neighborhood density ranges from a low of 50 persons per acre for Tayshet to a high of 116 persons per acre in Togliatti. The average for the 12 new towns was 88.7 persons per neighborhood acre. Surprisingly, this was considerably above the densities for seven older cities listed, which ranged from a density of 41.5 persons per acre in neighborhoods to a high of 88.5. The average for the seven older cities is around 51 persons per acre.[57]

Davidovich reports even lower densities in the older cities because of the existence of prerevolutionary single-family homes. It was 46 persons per acre in Gorkii, 44.4 in Kuibyshev, and only 20 in Omsk, assuming that there was the 100 square feet per person in the housing, which is roughly the national norm. Whether this was neighborhood density or residential density, which includes neighborhood parks and streets, is not clear.[58]

During the fifth Five-Year Plan (the early 1950's) the percent of single-family home construction throughout the Soviet Union was only 25 percent. It varies considerably from region to region.

Some of the figures on density may be understated or overstated, because most Soviet statistics on density are given in number of square meters per hectare. This must be converted into square feet per acre, then an estimate made of the number of square feet per person in a particular area. The space per person, in fact, will vary from city to city and from project to project. The point is that density is high and increasing.

There are various justifications for this density compared to a lower one, among which are the following: higher density is cheaper to heat in cold climates with efficient central heating serving whole building complexes. It is more efficient for use of industrialized methods with high-speed construction. It reduces transportation costs and permits journeys to work of less than 45 minutes in big cities. It saves large amounts of money in construction costs for infrastructure. Finally, it tends to emphasize communal rather than private life, and is cheaper to build than single-family homes.

Notably absent from this discussion of justification was consumer preference, which seems to play a very small role because there is virtually no choice in housing. Further, few sociological studies appear to have been done on the impact of this major decision affecting the quality of life for the average Soviet citizen. One Soviet study cited by Barbara Rosenfeld shows that peasants prefer their single-family homes with a plot to a better-equipped high rise. She also makes constant reference to the preference of Central Asians for the single-family homes which are all being bulldozed out of existence in Tashkent.[59] Even lovely two- and five-story buildings are slated for demolition in Minsk and Navoi on the grounds that the mistake of too-low density was made in earlier construction.

The real issue concerning predominance of high rises does not lie in costs, but in "quality of life" considerations. After a review of the literature on the social impact of density, I conclude that the policy of building only high-rise buildings in large new towns and extensions of existing cities could have negative social consequences and should be reexamined. The problem is not that there are some high rises, but that there is little or no choice to permit families of diverse interests, sizes, and lifestyles to choose the housing type that fits their own needs. The problem is primarily of families with small children or of crowding nonrelatives into the same structures, compounded by the very small room sizes. International studies have shown that there are problems of surveillance of a child's play from high-rise structures.[60]

There are other factors worth noting about Soviet housing. A fact of primary importance is that it is offered as a service to workers at a subsidized price. According to Soviet officials in towns I visited, rent averages only 5 percent of monthly salary, which according to one report, covered only 36 percent of upkeep and repair. The predominant form of tenancy was rental; however, in Minsk condominiums were offered with 40 percent down and low interest rates, at costs ranging from 5,000 to 6,000 rubles—the price of a new car.

The basic strength of Soviet housing is that all urban residents, regardless of ability to pay, have some sort of basic shelter that is safe and sanitary, although many units are overcrowded by United States standards. Rural housing is different. The weakness of Soviet housing is that there is little variety, choice, or diversity. There is little opportunity to make considerable improvements in housing regardless of achievement, and there is little difference between housing of different incomes. The state increasingly controls society by maintaining housing waiting lists. Repair and maintenance are poor; interior and exterior finishing is poor, and there is little space per person, even when compared with eastern European countries whose housing stock was also damaged by war.

Recreation and Open Space. Given the high densities of Soviet new towns and the high degree of control over the pattern of urban development, most Soviet cities probably have far more open space surrounding them within a short distance than do American cities. The material on the new towns revealed that information on what open space and recreation facilities actually exist is sketchy. Typically, goals and standards are shown, rather than what exists. According to Smoliar, the standard for recreation areas in new towns varies according to the size of the new town (see Table 2).[61] For new towns of less than 100,000 population, the standard (converted from metric measures) is 2.4 acres per 1000 persons within the housing project, 1.7 for the entire residential area, for a total of 4.1 acres per 1000 for the entire city. In addition, in the suburban areas the standard is 12.2 acres per 1000. Presumably, this latter measure would be equal to our regional parks. For cities of 100,000 to 250,000, the citywide norm would increase to 5.1 acres per 1000 persons, broken down to 2.9 acres for neighborhood space and 2.2 for total residential open space acreage.

Little detailed information is provided in the sources reviewed on standards for recreational facilities so common in American recreation, such as swimming pools, golf courses, and tennis courts. The probability is high that few of these facilities exist. Rather, the types of recreational facilities that are listed are places of culture, Young Pioneer (*Komsomol*) centers, theaters, dance halls, miscellaneous sports facilities, and suburban rest and recreational homes.[62] Some information about how much open space and how many recreational facilities is available, but not on a systematic basis in the sources reviewed. The only swimming pools I saw on the two trips were in Tashkent and Donetsk; the only tennis courts were in Donetsk.

Table 1 indicates that open space ratios are somewhat lower in the new towns than the ideal norm. In a few cases (Bratsk and Volzhskii), they are above the norm. In 12 of the large new towns the open space ran from a low of 2.3 acres per 1000 in Zelonograd to a high of 7.2 in Volzhskii. The average for the 12 was 4.42 acres per 1000. This was higher than the old towns, which ranged from a low of .75 acres per 1000 to a high of 2.4.

The Soviet new towns were endowed with better community facilities than were the existing towns, but varied enormously among themselves. The most generous was Karaganda, with 193.8 persons per acre. That with the least generous amount for a new town was Novopolotsk with 814.2 persons per acre. Ratios in existing cities listed in Table 1 ranged from a low degree of crowding of 424 persons per acre to a high of 1696. Thus the new towns represent an improvement in this area.

Transportation. In Soviet cities there is a relative absence of traffic congestion, consumption of scarce gasoline, expenditures on roads, parking problems, air pollution from cars, traffic accidents, and all of the negative consequents of the ubiquitous private automobile in the United States. Furthermore, public transit is cheap in the Soviet Union (5 or 6 cents a ride) and fairly convenient. Soviet officials argue that even at low rates, several of the major transit systems

Table 2   New Town Open Space Standards

City Size (in thousands)	Housing Project		Residential Area		Total		Outside City	
	Persons/ acre	Acres/1000 Population	Persons/ acre	Acres/1000 Population	Persons/ acre	Acres/1000 Population	Persons/ acre	Persons/1000 Population
Under 100	407	2.4	581.5	1.7	239.4	4.2	81.4	12.2
100–250	338.9	2.9	452.3	2.2	193.8	5.1	67.8	14.7
250–500	271.4	3.6	339	2.9	288.9	6.6	58.1	17.2

Note: Figures are converted from square meters per person in Russian text to acres per 1000 by author.
Source: Smoliar, 1973, p. 225 (Russian text)

(such as the Moscow subway) make money. However, this argument does not take into account capital cost, and I suspect, the true cost of labor is not paid by the transportation system. The true cost includes price of subsidized housing, health, and so on, which is paid in services, not wages. Thus the city absorbs part of the true cost of the transportation workers' wages because it probably furnishes their housing at low rents.

In 1970 there were 35.8 billion passenger trips on public transit in the Soviet Union and only 2.5 billion automobile trips. Of the auto trips, 1.1 billion were by taxi, 1.3 billion by private cars, and 78 million with official government cars. Bus was by far the most popular means of transportation, with 19.5 billion passenger trips; followed by tram, with 7.9 billion; subway, with 2.3 billion; and trolley, with 6.1 billion.[63]

The amount of long-distance travel, as a percent of all travel, has declined steadily since 1913 when long-distance trips formed 11.3 percent of all passenger trips, while city transit accounted for 83.9 percent. The percent of long-distance trips declined to only 1.7 percent in 1960, while city transit increased to 89.2 percent. Suburban passenger trips increased from 4.8 percent in 1913 to 9.1 percent in 1960.[64] On a per capita basis, the average annual number of trips on city transit in 1960 was 114.7 compared to 11.7 for suburban trips and only 2.2 for long distance.[65]

The reason for the high transit use is relatively simple: car production is a monopoly of the state, and heavy industrial production has taken precedence over production for consumer goods, especially the private automobile. Thus consumer choice is not affecting the transportation patterns, but rather a virtual public monopoly on public transit for virtually all uses—both for intra- and interurban use. There are only about 10 cars per 1000 population in the Soviet Union, as contrasted with over 400 per 1000 Americans.

Another constraining factor, at least for interurban traffic, is the poor road system.

The Soviet Union is twice the size of the U.S. but has a road system only one-fourth as long—847,500 miles excluding urban streets and roadways. Moreover, only 16 percent of the Soviet roads are paved with asphalt or cement and only 24 percent with gravel. The surfaced roads account for only 40 percent of the system. The remaining 60 percent are dirt roads that are frequently impassible in wet weather. Under the best conditions, these direct roads can handle loads of only seven tons, which means that they can support only the smallest model truck.[66]

Another reason for the high transit use is that the high densities are designed explicitly for minimizing the journey to work by transit. The main criterion for urban transportation systems is that travel time for one-way work trips should not exceed 40 minutes for 80 to 90 percent of passengers in cities of more than 250,000; it should not be more than 30 minutes for trips in smaller cities. In 1970 the tram, trolley, and bus traveled average speeds of 10.7, 6.86, and 7.7 miles per hour, respectively.[67]

The Soviet (transportation) systems, however, are subject to severe crowding, waiting lines, safety hazards, and considerable work to residence travel time in the large cities, although efforts are being made to reduce this to 20 to 30 minutes in the new cities. Rush hour traffic is handled by jamming passengers on board until every inch of space is occupied . . . the visit clearly showed that planning and centralized control over transportation are not sufficient by themselves to ensure an optimum level of transportation service and convenience. Although the Soviet 'metro's' are clean, aesthetically pleasing and efficient, much surface transportation equipment is old and appears inadequate to meet rush hour needs.[68]

Reports in the Soviet press also describe these problems. In 1966 an *Izvestia* correspondent surveyed urban transit in several provincial capitals; Krasnojarsk, Omsk, Perm, Sverdlovsk, Novosibirsk, and others. He discovered a crisis, analyzed its cause, and proposed a solution. He reported that the rush hour was the same in all cities: "The tram, covered with passengers like grapes on a vine, struggled along with great difficulty; those who failed to hang on are strung out along the bus stop. But overcrowded buses pass them by. Statistics showed that 2 percent of the Krasnojarsk labor force was regularly late for work." The reporter indicated that city repair facilities, depots, and garages were inadequate. When a bus broke down in Krasnojarsk, it had to be shipped halfway across the country to Leningrad for capital repairs. Similarly, there were problems in road construction. City road repair administrations lacked asphalt and construction equipment and had to rely upon the factories for equipment. *Izvestia* recommended that the central government must immediately spend 100 million rubles to liquidate the basic transportation mess in large cities of the Urals and Siberia alone.[69]

Sometimes the dominant urban enterprise operates urban transit. An *Izvestia* article of 1960 reported that the large industrial combine operated the transit system in Magnitogorsk. The system was desperately overcrowded because only 90 of the 268 vehicles were operating on the street, while others awaited repair at the overworked depot; but the combine refused to allocate money for a new depot. City officials were powerless to do anything about it, because threats would antagonize managers on whose good will so much hinged.[70]

The advantages and disadvantages of car ownership will change as Soviet automobile production increases. The current production is around 1 million cars a year, over 60 percent of which are produced in the single plant in Togliatti. Soviet officials said that they are contemplating an increase in private automobile ownership up to and above 200 cars per 1000 persons. American teams seldom failed to warn the Soviets of the possible impending problems that will face the Soviet Union with increased automobile ownership.[71] Soviet officials responded that the streets were of adequate size to handle future growth in car use, large multistory parking lots would be established near residential areas but would not disrupt them, and only a few people (20 percent) would actually drive cars to work due to the low cost of public transportation. However, use of automobiles may be more difficult to control than officials anticipate.

Pollution and Environmental Impact.   Because of the high density and highly controlled development, the Soviet cities probably have done much less to damage the environment directly through land pollution than do United States cities with their very low density. High density means fewer miles of asphalt to offer impermeable surfaces to increase water runoff, less disruption of top soil and trees, less distance to travel and therefore less pollution from vehicles, fewer building materials on a basis per unit, which means saving of energy resources in the production of these resources, and lower energy consumption on a direct per unit basis.[72]

However, both high density and low car ownership have been a matter of reducing costs and devoting emphasis to heavy industry, not consumer goods, rather than measures purposely taken to reduce consumption of natural resources and pollution. In fact, Goldman, who wrote a book on pollution in the Soviet Union,[73] raises a whole list of Soviet environmental problems, based primarily on reviews of the Soviet press:

1. Limited money for capital investment has limited investment in electrostatic precipitators for air treatment or for tertiary treatment plants for sewage controls.
2. Expenditures for water supply and sanitary treatment did not increase in any significant way until the 1950s.
3. Even then scant effort and resources were directed to solid waste disposal other than sanitary landfill and burning.
4. The Soviets have treated their forests carelessly. Woodlands in areas of 19 to 25 miles around most large cities in the north have been denuded; and because of the importance of timber exports, there has been bad overcutting in the European part of the USSR. The expectation is that by 1980 there will be virtually no forests left in the Ukraine.
5. Not until the 1950s was the decision made to bring in the higher quality coal to burn for Moscow, instead of the less expensive, but more polluting lignite. Thus the amount of particulate matter has not decreased greatly in the air over Moscow until the past decade.
6. At the present time premiums for Soviet plant managers depend almost entirely on their increased production or sales. This explains why it is so difficult to induce Soviet managers to spend money on the installation of pollution-control devices.
7. The total control over industry by the government has had an adverse impact on other areas of the environment as well. An environmental control industry like that of the United States, where firms are competing with one another to produce pollution-control devices has not been created.
8. Another factor working against conservation is the government ownership of all land and minerals. The extractor of ores does not have to pay for these resources, but labor is limited. Therefore, there is less incentive to conserve materials when additional labor costs are entailed. Recovery rates of 50 percent or less for mining of raw materials are not unusual. Coal, oil, potassium, and natural gas losses of 50 to 60 percent are reported in Soviet sources.

Because installation of pollution-control devices may reduce production, in the six years prior to 1967 no industry in the Russian Republic, Ukraine, Byelorussia, and Turkmenistan had fulfilled its plans for construction of purification equipment.[74]

Although progress has undoubtedly been made in the Soviet Union since Goldman did his research (before 1967), the United States teams confirm many of the findings today. The United States Working Group on the Enhancement of the Urban Environment reported as a result of its trip in 1973 that "while the objectives of the two nations are similar, the Soviets do not appear to be pursuing a solution to their waste disposal problems with great vigor, nor were particular innovations reported."[75] The team reported that, in general, environmental planning takes the form of separating people from the polluting source, rather than controlling pollution at its source. The whole literature on planning cities contains considerable emphasis on the size of the buffer to separate polluting industries from residential areas.[76]

In all probability, progress has been made in environmental control in the past several years that are not described in the literature. Of particular significance are the national norms for construction which apply uniform environmental standards to the whole country—unprecedented for such a large country! Variations in norms are made for different city sizes and climatic zones. These norms, which are quite stringent, apply both to existing development and to the new towns. They were passed in 1967. However, the point is that the Soviet Union shares the problems of the capitalist West in polluting the environment. The problems appear to have the same root: placing a value on jobs and production at the expense of the environment. The absence of the profit motive seems to have made little difference. What has made a difference in consumption of fuel and other resources has been a lower standard of consumption—particularly lower car ownership and higher densities in housing. Part of the environmental protection is historic preservation.*

Employment Base. One of the most important determinants of the location, internal plan, and quality of life in the Soviet new towns is the nature of the industry that forms their base: the Soviet new towns are created as the servants of industry. First, the decision is made to locate an industry in a particular area; then the new towns with necessary housing and support facilities to serve the workers are built around that decision. The degree of pollution determines the distance to the residential areas and the size of green buffer. The generosity of the firm or firms providing support for the new town also determines the degree of amenities and housing because

---

* According to the U.S. Historic Preservation team, the Soviets have done a truly outstanding job in this area. This is corroborated by my own trips to many parts of the Soviet Union.[77]

industry supplies such a large part of this base, in the absence of a powerful mechanism for raising funds to support city services.

Thus, a constant theme running through this chapter, based primarily on accounts reported in the Soviet press by Taubman (for community facilities and services) and DiMaio (for housing), is that Soviet new towns are, in effect, company towns. This probably would not be true for the large new towns where there is a diversified industrial base. However, it would be difficult to believe that the Volga automobile plant did not play a major role in Togliatti, or the Kama truck factory did not play a major role in Naberezhniye Chelny. Both of these cities are very large (see Figure 5).

An analogy between the Soviet new towns and the United States company towns may be useful:

Scores of little company towns, almost all of them drab wretched places, had been founded at isolated pitheads to supply housing for miners and their families. Clearly this type of town was unsuitable for modern enterprises. A few of the company towns did, however, show evidence of more careful and systematic planning. Among these Pullman, Illinois, stands out as a company town project more in the European tradition of enlightened paternalism. . . .

One characteristic of company towns that appears to have been widespread was the feeling, sometimes vague, sometimes strong, that the concept of a town in which an industry acted at the same time as employer, landlord, and governing agent somehow was contrary to American traditions. The failure of company towns to enlist sympathetic and vigorous support from their residents stems from this attitude. The history of these communities provided few precedents that we would care to duplicate in the future. American industry, for all its success in production, signally failed in its attempt to manufacture noteworthy communities.[78]

This is not to imply that all Soviet company towns are these same dismal places, but there is little doubt that a greater diversity in economic forces at the new-town level, larger size, and greater capacity of the local government to support itself from taxes than now exist would increase pluralism in the new towns and probably improve the quality of services. By the same token, the worker would have had better goods and a higher degree of choice if he were paid higher wages and given fewer free goods and services. Without being dependent upon his plant manager, he could afford decent housing and other necessities and have more choice than he does now. Great personal and corporate independence from the plant manager

Figure 5.   Heavy industry forms the base for many new towns. This is the auto plant built with Fiat assistance in Togliatti, which produces a substantial part of automobiles throughout the Soviet Union. Photo by Jack Underhill.

could be a good thing for the average citizen and town leader. However, while there may be disadvantages to company-dominated towns, particularly small towns, there are also advantages.

THREE GENERATIONS OF NEW TOWNS

I should point out that the definition of a new town is elusive. According to one Soviet source, a new town is any development converted from a rural settlement (typically less than 10,000 population) to an urban place (typically more than 10,000), a newly created town, or a rapidly expanding small- or middle-sized town. It has been difficult to identify the new towns on the map because many of them are, in fact, growth centers of existing cities. Table 3 is a selected list of new towns developed in three generations: from 1939 to 1959, from 1959 to 1970, and either before 1939 or often mentioned in the Soviet literature as prominent new towns, the development dates of which are not provided in the literature review.

The first-generation projects (including those which have grown to a significant size, even if established later, such as Togliatti) were obtained from a review of Harris and the Soviet literature on new towns and city building in general. These are described in Table 4. Ninety percent of the projects

referred to in the books reviewed for this study on Soviet new towns are limited to these few projects.

The second-generation projects were those discovered by Harris to have been created between 1939 and 1959. The third-generation projects were obtained from Soviet sources and cover up to 1970.[79] Yet this fairly comprehensive list covers only 223 projects, less than one-fourth of all new towns. I have seen no comprehensive listing of Soviet new towns; however, maps do exist showing all towns up to 1963, but the names of the cities were not used for the map and it cannot be cited here.

In fast-growing republics, new towns constituted a significant portion of all development even in 1963: 84 percent of all towns in Armenia, 75 percent of all towns in Kazakhstan, and 74 percent in the Kirgiz and Tadzhik republics.[80]

The locations of 223 new towns are shown in Figure 6. The numbers on the map correspond to the numbers in Table 3, with the prefix N designating towns developed from 1959 to 1970. The numbers without the prefix designate towns developed from 1939 to 1959. Large new towns and first-generation new towns that have grown to great size are listed by their names.

Figure 6 reveals a great clustering of major new towns. Figure 7 shows the reason for this clustering: the general oil, iron, and coal resource locations, as

Table 3   Selected List of Soviet New Towns to 1970 with Industrial Functions (Numbers keyed to Figure 6)

Third-Generation 1959 to 1970	Second-Generation 1939 to 1959	First-Generation and Other Large Cities

1.   *Donets Area* (E. Ukraine)   Total: 18

N1 Rodinskoye (1)	1. Kirovskoye	
N2 Dimitrov (1)	2. Novogrodovka	
N3 Ukrainsk (1)	3. Gornyak	
N4 Zorinsk (1)	4. Zhdanovka	
N5 Pereval'sk (1)	5. Verkhnedovannyy	
N6 Artemovsk (1)	6. Chervonopartizanski	
N7 Novodruzhesk (1)		
N8 Privol'e (1)		
N9 Schast'e (3)		
N10 Zimagor'e (1)		
N11 Molodogvardeysk (1)		
N12 Miusinsk (4)		

2.   *Balance of Ukraine and White Russia (Southwest) and Moldavia*   Total: 23

N1 Svetlovodsk (3)	1. Novovolynsk	Krovoyrog
N2 Zhovtnevoe (7)	2. Chervonograd	Zaporozh'ye
N3 Vol'nogorsk (2)	3. Valutino	Kishniev
N4 Vol'nansk (16)	4. Velikoya Danilovka	
N5 Igren' (16)	5. Oktyabr'skiy	
N6 Pivdennoe (16)	6. Novayakakhovka	
N7 Vishgorod (3)		
N8 Noviirazdol (6)		
N9 Sosnovka (1)		
N10 Svetlogorsk (4)		
N11 Soligorsk (6)		
N12 Zhodino (8)		
N13 Chashniki (3)		
N14 Novopolotsk (6)		

3.   *Northwest and North Central*   Total: 19

N1 Naueye Akmiane (9)	1. Kohtle Yarve	Noril'sk
N2 Olaine (6)	1a. Promyshelenny	
N3 Stuchka (3)	2. Severnyy	
N4 Zapolarnii	3. Komsomol'sk'iy	
N5 Apatity (13)	4. Gornyatskiy	
N6 Kovdor (1)	5. Vorkuta	
N7 Kirishi (6)	6. Inta	
N8 Mikun' (12)	7. Pechora	
	7a. Sosnogorsk	
	8. Severomorsk	
	9. Nikel'	
	10. Dudinka	

4.   *Central European*   Total: 12

N1 Zelenograd (14)	1. Skuratovskiy	Novomoskovsk
N2 Lobnia (8)	2. Lipki	
N3 Vidnov (6)	3. Severo Zadonsk	

Table 3 (Continued)

Third-Generation 1959 to 1970	Second-Generation 1939 to 1959	First-Generation and Other Large Cities
N4 Pushchino (14)	4. Sokol'niki	
N5 Ribnoe (12)	5. Kimovsk	
N6 Zheleznogorsk (1)		

5. *South Central*   Georgia, Armenia, Azerbaydzhan, and Black-Earth Central   **Total:**   29

N1 Tsimlyansk (1)	1. Gubkin	Volzhskiy
N1a Kotova (4)	2. Zherdevka	Sumgait
N1b Neftekumsk (1)	3. Gribanovskiy	
N2 Kaspiisk (4)	4. Kaich-na-Donu	
N3 Kisilyort (4)	5. Donetsk	
N4 Baksan (4)	6. Belaya Kalitva	
N5 Kaski (10)	7. Volgodonsk	
N6 Vale (1)	8. Akhtyrskiy	
N7 Rasdan (6)	9. Rustavi	
N8 Abovyan (7)	10. Marneuli	
N9 Sevan (8)	11. Mingechaur	
N10 Lusavan (4)	12. Barda	
N11 Ararat (9)	13. Kadzharan	
N12 Dzhermuck (15)		
N13 Naftalan (15)		
N14 Pushkino (16)		

6. *Volga-Urals Region*   **Total:**   31

N1 Novoulyanovsk (9)	1. Zavolzh'ye	Magnitagorsk
N2 Novocheboksarsk (6)	2. Kstovo	Naberezhnye Chelny
N3 Kachkanar (1)	3. Kirova Chepatsk	Orsk
N4 Gornezavodsk (9)	4. Togliatti	
N5 Chaikovskii (4)	5. Zhigulevsk	
N6 Neftekamsk (2)	6. Novokuykbyshevsk	
N7 Tuimazy (2)	7. Otradnyy	
N8 Nizhnekamsk (6)	8. Priyutova	
N9 Uchaly (1)	9. Oktyabr'skiy	
	10. Leninogorsk	
	11. Al'met'yevsk	
	12. Ivdel'	
	13. Volchansk	
	14. Tsentral'nyy Kospashskiy	
	15. Gremyanchinsk	
	16. Chebarkul'	
	17. Yuzhnoural'iy	
	18. Salavat	
	19. Kumertau	
	20. Kuvandyk	

7. *Soviet Asia*
    Kazakhstan and Border Area   **Total:**   44

N1 Shevchenko (13)	1. Nazyvayusk	Karaganda
N2 Novii Uzen' (1)	2. Bulayevo	Timirtau

Table 3 (Continued)

Third-Generation 1959 to 1970	Second-Generation 1939 to 1959	First-Generation and Other Large Cities
N3 Alga (6)	3. Rudnyy	Orsk
N4 Oktyabr'sk (11)	4. Tobol	
N5 Khromtau (1)	5. Kushmurun	
N6 Yesl' (12)	6. Krasnoarmeysk	
N7 Arkalyk (13)	7. Schuchinsk	
N8 Shakhtiisk (2)	8. Makinsk	
N9 Abay (2)	9. Aksu	
N10 Karazhal (1)	10. Bestobe	
N11 Yermak (4)	11. Zholymbet	
N12 Charsk (11)	12. Alekseyevka	
N13 Serebryansk (4)	13. Yermentau	
N14 Kapchagay (4)	14. Ekibastuz	
N15 Chu (11)	15. Novodolinskiy	
N16 Zhanatas (6)	16. Atasu	
N17 Karatay (6)	17. Nikol'skiy	
N18 Chardara (16)	18. Belousovka	
	19. Dzhusgly	
	20. Chiili	
	21. Chulak-Tau	
	22. Taldy-Kurgan	
	23. Korovskiy	

8. *Central Asian Republics* **Total**: 17

N1 Kungrad (12)	1. Talas	Dushanbe
N2 Akhangaran (9)	2. Mayli-Say	
N3 Gulistan (13)	3. Min-Kush	
N4 Kayrakkum (4)	4. Syrdar'ya	
N5 Sovietabad (11)	5. Pskent	
N6 Nurek (3)	6. Amalyk	
N7 Navoi	7. Krasnogvardeysk	
	8. Denau	
	9. Kubyshevskiy	

9. *Western Siberia (Novosibirsk Area)* **Total**: 15

N1 Ob'	1. Polysayevo	Kemerovo
N2 Berezovskiy (1)	2. Mezhdurechensk	Propop'yesk
N3 Kaltan (4)	3. Myski	Novokuznetsk
N4 Tashtagol (1)	4. Nazarova	Belovo
N5 Sorsk (5)		
N6 Divnogorsk (3)		
N7 Ak-Dovurak		

10. *Eastern Siberia (Baykal Region)* **Total**: 11

N1 Zheleznogorsk-Ilimskiy (1)	1. Maklakova	Bratsk
N2 Vikhorevka (12)	2. Uzhur	Angarsk
N3 Biryusinsk (12)	3. Nizhnaya Poyma	
N4 Skelikhov	4. Prozhskiy	
N5 Baikal'sk		

Table 3 (Continued)

Third-Generation 1959 to 1970	Second-Generation 1939 to 1959	First-Generation and Other Large Cities
11 *Other Siberia and Far East* **Total:** 6		
Mirnii (2)		Komsomol'sk na Amure
Susuman		
Pevek (11)		
Surgut (13)		
Nefteyugansk (1)		

Source: Third-generation new towns taken from map from Rasskazii O. Gorodokh, second-generation new towns from Harris (1970)

Industry Designations are as Follows:

1. Mining industry (excluding chemicals)
3. Electrical energy
5. Non-ferrous metallurgy
7. Machine building of all types
9. Production of construction materials
11. Transportation of all types
13. Administrative center
15. Resort center

2. Mining industry in combination with other branches of industry
4. Electrical energy in conjunction with industries
6. Chemical industry (including extraction of raw material) and oil refining
8. Machine building in conjunction with other industries
10. Production of construction materials with other industries
12. Transportation in conjunction with other industries
14. Scientific center
16. Miscellaneous

Table 4 List of Major New Towns of More than 100,000 in 1967 in Order of 1967 Size (Population in thousands)

City	Location	Dominant Econ. Base of Area	1920	1926	1939	1959	1967	1970	1975	Year Founded
Zaporozh'ye	Ukraine	Hydroelectric	50	56	282	435	595	658	744	1928
Krovoyrog	Ukraine	Iron ore	22	31	189	388	510	573	628	1926
Karaganda	Central Kazahstan (Desert)	Coal field and ore deposits	0	0	196	387	498	523	565	
Novokuznetsk	W. Siberia	Kuznetz Basin coal field	5	4	166	377	493	499	525	
Kemerova	W. Siberia	Kuznetz Basin coal field	6	22	133	278	364	NA	NA	
Magnitagorsk	Urals	Volga Ural oil field	0	0	146	311	357			1929
Dushanbe	Tadzhikistan	Ore deposits	NA	6	83	224	333			1930
Kiskniev	Moldavia	Construction	NA	115	112	216	302	356	452	

Table 4 (Continued)

City	Location	Dominant Econ. Base of Area	1920	1926	1939	1959	1967	1970	1975	Year Founded
Propop'yesk	W. Siberia	Kuznetz Basin		11	107	282	290			
Orsk	Urals	Volga ural oil field	16	14	66	176	215			
Komsomol'sk-na Amure	Far East	Iron and steel production	0	0	71	177	209			
Dzherzhinsk	Gor'ky Region	Chemicals	1	9	103	164	201			
Angarsk	Near Baykal in W. Siberia	Chemicals and oil refinery				135	183	204		1949
Temirtau	Near Karaganda	Steel			5	77	150			
Togliatti	Urals	Hydroelectricity and automobiles	11	6		61	150		500	
Bereznyki	Urals	Chemicals			51	106	134			
Noril'sk	Far North	Rare metals			13	109	129			
Novomoskovsk	Tula Region South of Moscow	Lignite chemicals	2	1	76	107	126			
Bratsk	E. Siberia Baykal Region	Hydroelectric power				51	122			
Novoshakhtinsk	Adjacent to Donbas	Coal		7	48	104	107			
Novokuykby-shevsk	Urals near Kuybyshev	oil refinery				63	107			
Sumgait	Azerbaydzhan				6	52	104			1939
Electrostal'	Moscow Region	Satellite			43	97	117	204		1938
Belovo	West Siberia	Kuznetz Basin coal field			43	107	116			
Volzhskiy	Near Volgograd	Electric power				67	114			

Source: (1) Growth to 67: Harris. (2) 70 and 75 population: *USSR in Statistics*. (3) Function: Harris.

well as the patterns of more severe climatic conditions. Comparisons of these two maps indicate the relation between resources, railroads, and climate in developing a national growth policy. The location of power stations (particularly hydroelectric) also had an influence. Figure 8 shows these power stations.

The significant fact is that most of the major new towns are along the major path of urbanization of the Soviet Union. They fill up the European Russia (336 in the Don Basin, southeast and central Black Earth part of European Russia in 1967), extend to the Urals, cover northern and western Kazakhstan and

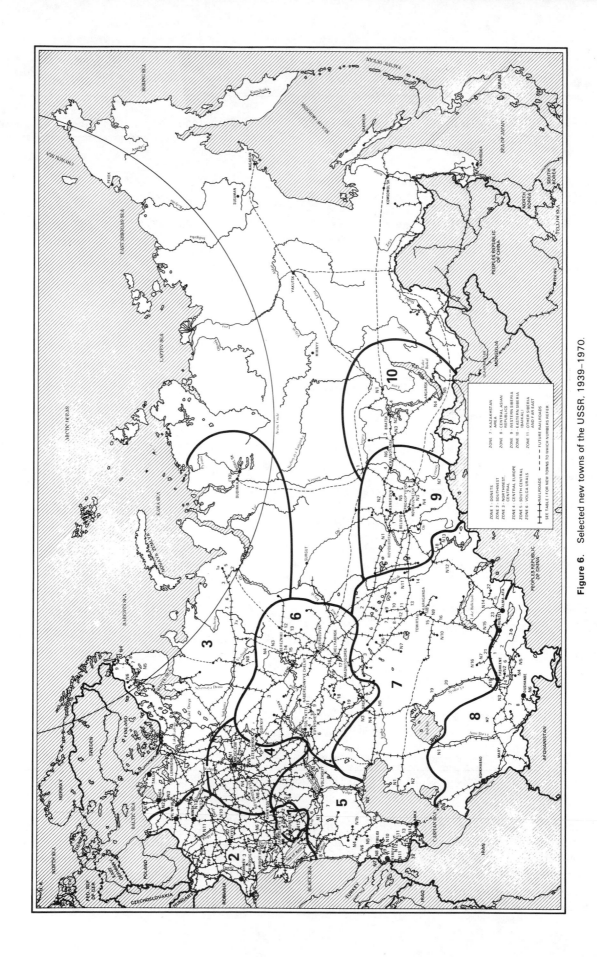

Figure 6. Selected new towns of the USSR. 1939–1970.

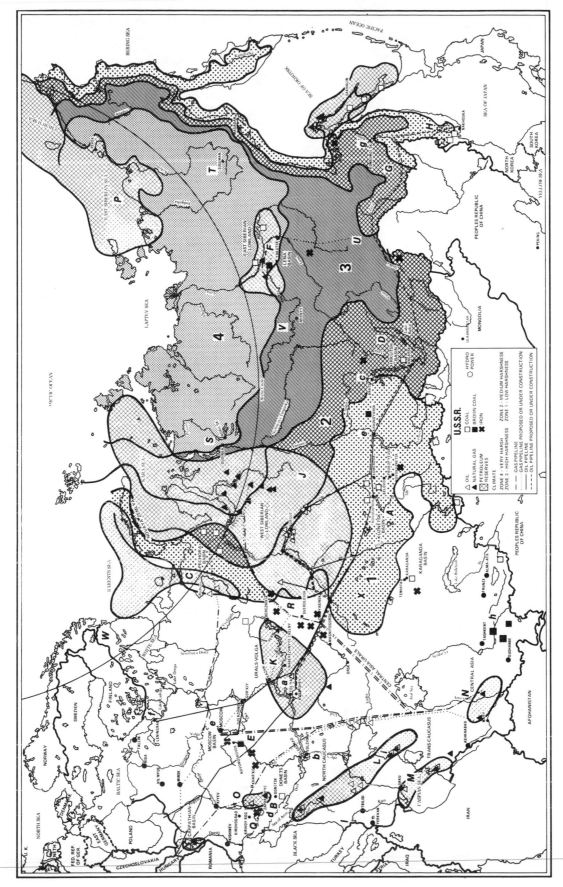

Figure 7. Natural resources and climate of the USSR.

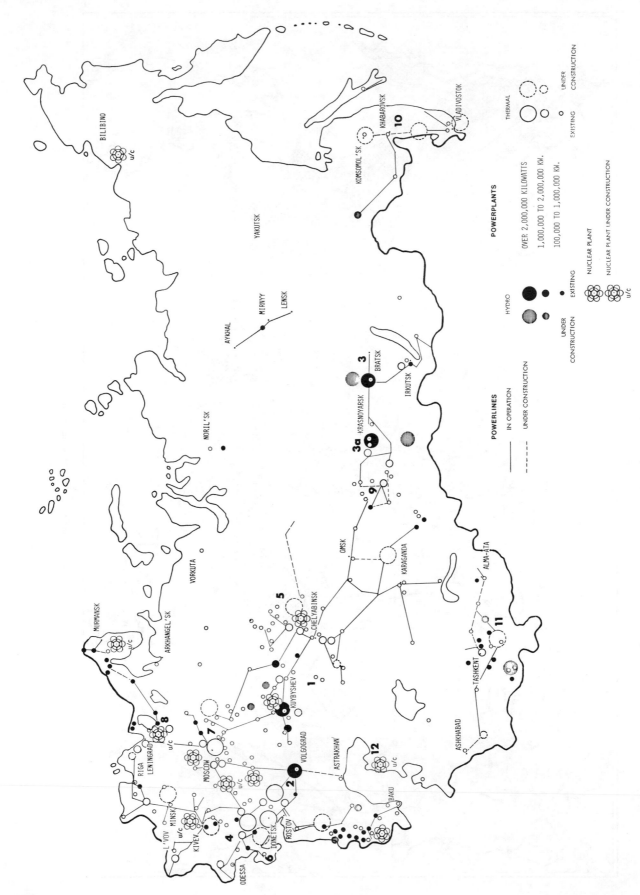

Figure 8. Electric power in the USSR. Source: U.S. Department of State, "USSR Summary Map," 1974.

the southern border in the central Asian republics (59), form a group on the Kuznetsk Basin in western Siberia and in the Baikal region of eastern Siberia (77 in both), and are found along the major arteries and mineral deposits of the far east.

Thus the new towns are not scattered at random, but are tied to the core central region and to the national rail system. The most important centers appear to be strongly related to coal, oil, and minerals, rather than transportation *per se*, as in America. The remarkable correlation between energy resources and minerals is apparent by comparison in the detailed resource maps in Shabad's excellent book on Soviet industrial resources.

Natural Resource Base.   The new towns of Togliatti (near Kuybyshev), Vollzhskiy (near Volgograd), Bratsk, and Zaparozh'e (shown as numbers 1, 2, 3, and 4 in Figure 8) were based primarily on hydroelectric power centers. In addition, the new town cluster in western Siberia is supported in part by the huge Krasnoyarsk station (3a in Figure 8). The coal and gas electric power stations form the power base structure for the Urals new towns (5), the Donets Basin new towns (6), the Moscow cluster development (7), the Leningrad area towns (8), and the Kuznetsk Basin new towns in western Siberia (9). In the far east, three great thermal power sources form the base for Komsomolsk, a large new town, as well as other new towns in the Vladivostok region. They were under construction in 1971, the date of this map (10). Also under construction were huge thermal and hydro power facilities in the central Asian republics, and a new towns center (11). Nuclear power is a base for the new town of Shevchenko on the Caspian Sea (12).

Figure 9 shows the coal, oil, and metal resources that appear to have a determining effect in the location of new-town clusters. The most important new-town clusters are grouped around the following:

1. The Kutznets Basin (1 in Figure 9), listed in Table 4 as the western Siberian area, where the major new towns of Novokuznetsk and Kemerovo are located.
2. The Donets Basin, the location of 19 middle- and new-generation new towns on Table 3 (2); the Karaganda Basin in central Kazakhstan.
3. The Pechora Basin (5) forming the northern chain in a series of new towns in the Komi Automous Republic, most of which are listed in Table 3 under "Northeast and North Central."

4. The Irkutsk Basin (4) forming the basis for a cluster of new towns in the Baikal region of eastern Siberia.
5. The Moscow Basin brown coal region (6) forming the basis for a cluster of new towns in the Tula region south of Moscow (listed in Table 3 as the Central European area).

Other small coal deposits are correlated with new towns not included in Table 3, but are in a more comprehensive map of Soviet new towns to 1963 prepared by the Central Research and Design Institute.[81] Small clusters of new towns are in the Lena Basin coal area in the far east near Yakutsk (7), the Burya Basin in the southern far east (9), the Vladivostok region (8), and the Batumi area in the Caucasus (10).

Oil and gas centers are also shown in Figure 9, with overlays of shaded areas showing major petroleum regions.[82] The vast petroleum resources of the Soviet Union are centered in the west Siberian lowland in the Tumen' Oblast' (11) with great natural gas fields southwest of Noril'sk and petroleum fields on the Ob' River that form the base for several new towns, Surgut and Nefteygansk, shown by name in Figure 6. The Volga Urals fields (12) to the east of Togliatti, support a whole cluster of new towns in the western Ural-Volga region with huge deposits of crude oil and also natural gas. The north Caucasus field west of the Caspian Sea extends under the Caspian Sea to the Mangyshlak fields (13). It contains both natural gas and petroleum and is the location of several generations of new towns listed in Table 1 under the south central region and Kazakhstan. The Transcaucasus fields, which extend from Baku underneath the Caspian Sea to Turkmenistan (14), serve a cluster of new towns listed in Table 3 (shown in Figure 6) and others not listed here.

The central Asian fields with large gas production (15) serve the large list of new towns in the central Asian republics listed in both Figures 6 and 7. The Shebelinka fields east of Kiev (16) and the Carpathian fields to the far west in the Ukraine serve a small cluster of new towns (17).

The Pechora Basin gas and oil deposits relate to a linear chain of new towns in the Komi region shown in Figure 6. The offshore and shoreline Sakhalin Island gas and oil deposits could be related to the new towns in Figure 7. The eastern Siberian lowland gas deposits near the Lena Coal Basin (7) serve a small cluster of new towns given in Figure 7. Finally, the

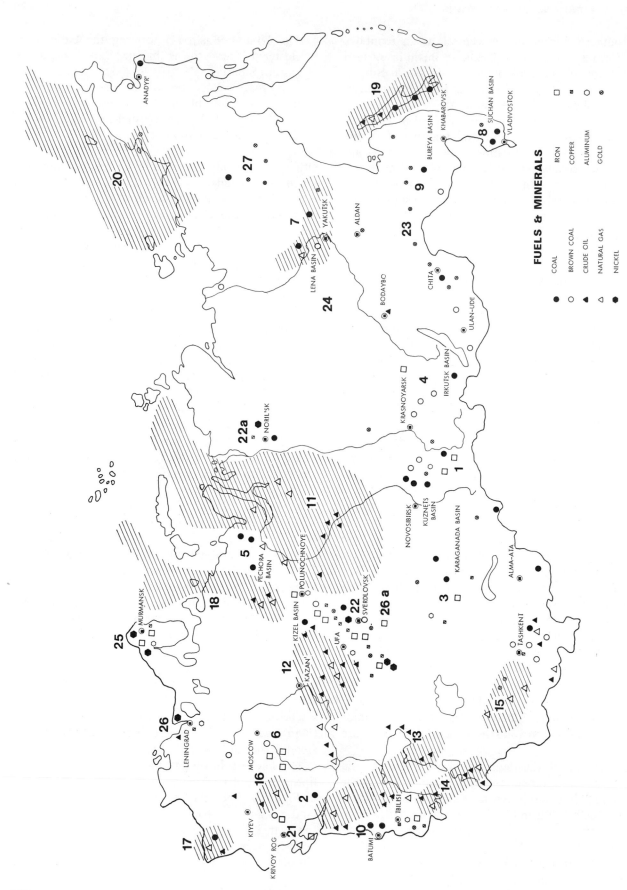

Figure 9. Fuels and metallic minerals in the USSR. Source: U.S. Department of State. "USSR Summary Map." 1974.

FUELS & MINERALS

COAL ●
BROWN COAL ○
CRUDE OIL ▲
NATURAL GAS △
NICKEL ⬣

IRON □
COPPER ⊡
ALUMINUM ○
GOLD ⊗

ANADYR'
MURMANSK
LENINGRAD
KIYEV
KRIVOY ROG
MOSCOW
TBILISI
BATUMI
KAZAN'
UFA
SVERDLOVSK
KIZEL BASIN
PECHORA BASIN
POLUNOCHNOYE
NORIL'SK
TASHKENT
ALMA-ATA
KARAGANADA BASIN
NOVOSIBIRSK
KUZNETS BASIN
KRASNOYARSK
IRKUTSK BASIN
ULAN-UDE
CHITA
BODAYBO
ALDAN
YAKUTSK
LENA BASIN
BUREYA BASIN
KHABAROVSK
SUCHAN BASIN
VLADIVOSTOK

424

east Siberian sea deposits are around the new town of Pevek (20) or the far north. Undoubtedly, the future development of new towns will serve as a basis for development of these oil resources—particularly the less exploited resources of the far north.

Iron ore (shown as large squares in Figure 9) formed the base for the older generation new town of Krivoy Rog in the Ukraine (21) and a cluster of new towns in the area; the huge new-town cluster in the Urals (22) and large developments in the Kutznets Basin in western Siberia (1) also relate to iron ore. Copper was important in the Urals, central Kazakhstan, and Noril'sk in the far north (22a). Gold is centered around a cluster of new towns and Susuman (27) shown in Figure 6 and also along the Chinese border in the far east (23). Diamonds are mined in the Yakut Autonomous Republic around Mirnyy (24) to the north. Nickel, copper, and aluminum are centers of a new-town cluster on and near the Kola Peninsula to the north of Leningrad (26).

Agricultural settlements appear to form the basis for settlement in many parts of European Russia and the virgin lands area in north central Kazakhstan (26a).

Functions of New Towns and Their Sizes. The urban functions of the new towns lean toward industry, relying heavily upon the power and raw materials covered above. Table 3 lists 13 urban functions for the third-generation new towns. Overall, the following distribution of primary industrial base for the new towns prevailed for some 634 new towns developed from 1927 to 1960 (excluding new territories): food processing, 115 cities (18.2%); machine building, 87 (13.7%); coal, 86 (13.6%); transportation, 68 (10.7%); lumbering, 56 (8.8%); metallurgy 47 (7.4%); mining, 38 (6%); textile, 26 (1.6%); electrical

energy, 23 (3.6%); chemistry, 23 (3.6%); silicate ceramic, 23 (3.6%); oil, 20 (3.2%); extraction of non-metallic raw materials, 10 (1.6%); resort towns, 8 (1.3%); and scientific research functions, 4 (0.6%).[83]

Nearly 68 percent of all new towns created from 1917 to 1967 were still less than 30,000 population in 1970 when 11 million people lived in these cities. However, 16.4 million lived in new towns ranging from 30,000 to 150,000, which constituted 30.2 percent of all new towns created during that period; 7.1 million lived in 2 percent of the new towns ranging from 150,000 to 800,000 population. Table 5 shows the size and distribution by city size and population.

Figure 6 illustrates even further the large number of very small new towns created. In 1967, 14.5 percent of all people in new towns (about 5 million persons) were in small cities from 10,000 to 20,000; roughly the same number were in cities from 20,000 to 30,000; 10.2 percent (3.5 million) lived in towns from 30,000 to 40,000; 8.2 percent (2.8 million) in towns from 40,000 to 50,000. Approximately 11.3 percent of the people, (3.9 million) lived in new towns ranging from 50,000 to 100,000.

Of the total of 34.6 million living in new towns in 1967, some 13 million were in freestanding new towns (B in Figure 1), many of which were less than 30,000. Eight million were in coal mining regions and 4 million in satellite cities.[84]

The pace of development of new towns is rapid, as is the growth of the major new towns. Table 6 shows over 100 new towns were created in every five-year period from 1951 to 1965. From 1951 to 1955 the average yearly increase in the number of new towns was 20 and from 1961 to 1965 it was 25. This pace continues. Of projects built, 77 percent to 98 percent in each five-year period (by population) were

Table 5 Distribution of New Towns in the Soviet Union Built from 1917 to 1967, by Population Size

Index	Towns with Populations in Thousands					
	10	10–30	30–150	150–300	300–500	500–800
Number of cities	112	547	292	8	9	3
%	11.5	56.3	30.2	0.8	0.9	0.3
Towns with populations in thousands	803	10450	16415	1643	3554	1945
%	2.3	30	47.3	4.7	10.2	5.5

Source: *Novikh Goroda, Planirevochnaya Structura Promishlennova I Nauchno-Pozvodstevenno Profilia.*

Table 6   Construction of New Towns in the Soviet Union for 1951–1967

Years	New Towns		From That Number Built in a New Place	
	Number	Population (in millions)	Number	Population (in millions)
1951–1955	102	3.1	77	2.6
1956–1960	119	2.5	88	2
1961–1965	124	2	98	1.7

NOTE: Those towns are referred to as built in a new place that did not exist as settlements at the time of the population census of 1926. Population is given as of January 1, 1966.
Source: *Novikh Goroda, Planirevochnaya Structura Promishlennova I Nauchno-Pozvodstevenno Profilia.*

freestanding. The others were built around an existing city or town and might be called growth centers. Of special development speed were projects such as Bratsk, Angarsk, Novokuibyshevsk, Tamirtau, and Volzhskiy that did not exist in 1940, but that all grew to over 100,000 by 1967—a period of 20 to 25 years. Equally phenomenal in growth are prewar towns, such as Karaganda and Novokuznetsk, which grew to .5 million during the Soviet hegemony.

The pace of development of average new towns was slower. Of the 134 towns developed from 1926 to 1936, their average size by 1966 was only 20,000. Twenty-four percent (30 towns) grew from 1000 to 3000 a year and were an average size of 75,000 in 1966; 9 percent (nine projects) grew from 3000 to 5000 a year and reached an average size of 155,000 in 1966; only 6 percent of the new towns (seven projects) grew from 5000 to 15,000 a year and reached an average size of 380,000 in 1966.[85] Sixty-one percent (76 towns) grew less than 1000 a year and reached an average size of only 20,000 in 1966.

How was this massive development program accomplished? It was accomplished by central control of the location of industrial development, development of power and raw materials, controls to limit existing city growth, and controls and incentives to entice or require population movement to required locations. The primary tool was the control of location of industry because all industry (except for small farm plots and small entrepreneurs) is in the hands of the state. A primary example of industrial location control is the chain of events that led to the creation of Togliatti. First, a huge hydroelectric plant was built; then some chemical and fertilizer plants were built around the old town of Stravrapol; finally, the decision was made to locate the massive Volga au-

tomobile plant in the new section of Togliatti. This final, single decision caused the town to grow from 20,000 to 450,000 within a period of 20 years.

A supplementary tool was to restrict growth in existing large cities. As early as 1931 the Soviets approved a resolution forbidding the construction of new industrial enterprises in Moscow and Leningrad as of 1932. In 1961 this policy was updated; then in 1966 a party directive specified that new industrial enterprises shall be built mainly in small- and medium-sized towns. In 1971 this was stressed again. In fact, however, this has been difficult to enforce because industries often violate these rules.

According to Matthews, these controls over location of industry are supplemented with control over the movement of people. An internal passport is required of every Soviet citizen, and the local militia must place an approved residence stamp in the passport before residence can be maintained. He points out that if the passport holder wishes to change his place of residence permanently he must get the formal permission of the militia in his chosen area before he moves there. This is only a formality in small towns and less desirable places. However, it may present a problem in republic capitals that have more to offer their inhabitants. At least one eminent American geographer specializing in the Soviet Union indicated that these controls are relatively ineffective because there is large-scale movement from rural to urban areas and from region to region. The movement to find jobs is strong.* Matthews indicates that it is no secret that outsiders are all but excluded from permanent residence in Moscow, for

* Robert Lewis, *Nationality and Population Change in Russia and the USSR* (New York: Praeger, 1976).

example, and some people find that registration there can only be achieved by bribery.[86] In addition, a college senior must go where he is sent for a period of time after completing his state-supported education. Finally, strong monetary incentives are offered. Wages in far east Siberia may be more than one-third higher than in the west.[87]

CONCLUSIONS AND SUMMARY

How successful has this policy been in terms of stated goals? Have regional differences been reduced, large-city size contained, economic efficiency promoted, backward regions advanced, and national security increased? Many of the questions are really unanswerable, given the present state of analysis of Soviet new towns and national growth policy. All that can be done is to cite some opinions and facts tending to throw light on the achievement of these goals.

An unquestionable success has been in bringing up backward areas. From 1922 to 1972, the gross output of industry increased by 601 times in the Kazakh Republic, 532 times in Moldavia, 527 times in Armenia, 513 times in Tadzhikistan, 412 times in Kirgiz, and 343 times in Byelorussia, while the increase in the USSR as a whole was 321 times.

Despite the successes, it should not be inferred that enormous problems do not result from this massive resettlement policy. One expert reported that despite high salaries and other bonuses given to induce Soviet citizens to move to the east, from 1959 to 1970 migration out of Siberia exceeded the number of arrivals. In the Soviet far east only one of every 20 persons who arrived during that 10-year period remained.[88] One Soviet source reported that 924,000 more people left Siberia from 1959 to 1969 than arrived and that the majority of those who left were the able-bodied workers. Shortages of housing and amenities and high prices were given as causes of the reverse movement.[89] One author complains about the unplanned and spontaneous movement to the sunny Caucasus.[90]

One area in which the Soviets have had relatively little success has been in containing city growth. Taubman wrote that in spite of the 1969 prohibition of the construction of new industrial enterprises and expansion of existing ones in 34 cities of the Russian Republic, this rule is flouted on a wide scale. He indicates that plans for economic growth for 91 RSFSR cities show 250 percent growth or over 3 million new

jobs by 1980. Prohibition against industrial construction is no obstacle; in fact the population growth will be proportionally greater in cities where industrial expansion is restricted than in those where it is not.[91] Often industrial and city officials simply circumvent the law, and the professional city planners have no choice but to go along with them.

The failure of controlling growth can be seen by comparing planned and the actual populations. The planned goal for Gor'ky was 840,000, but the actual population in 1969 was 1.1 million; the goal for Tashkent was 800,000, but the 1969 population was 1.3 million. By 1970 Moscow had exceeded its 1981 projections.[92]

Despite early attempts to stop the growth of Moscow, its entire region grew from 4.8 million to 11 million from 1926 to 1959; the area within 50 kilometers including the greenbelt (greater Moscow area) grew from 2.3 to 6.9 million, and the area within the city limits grew from 2.2 million to 6 million.[93] In fact, 1 million persons are in the region of the greenbelt. Included are nine cities and more than 600 tiny populated places within the 10- to 12-kilometer-wide greenbelt. About half of all working population worked in this zone.[94] It could be argued, however, that the metropolitan and large-city growth would have been worse in the absence of a new-town policy.

In 1961 Phillippe Bernard spent several months in the Soviet Union and had extensive interviews with Soviet economic planners and plant managers. He wrote a book on Soviet planning methods in which he addressed the question of whether the geographic distribution of industry is rational and whether at a given moment it is likely to approach what could be regarded as an economic optimum. He concluded:

The answer must on the whole be in the negative. Of all possible distributions for a given production at a given moment, the distribution which one finds in the Soviet Union is assuredly not the one which is the most conducive to minimizing costs, or to take only one element in the latter, to cutting down transportation requirements. The enormous size of the goods traffic involved in the USSR, in relation to an output which is still relatively small, is in itself an indication of this.[95]

He addresses a second question, which is related to long-term development:

Taking the long view, one asks which system is most conducive to economic growth in the various regions, especially those which are the most backward to begin with and, in the end, what system of distribution of industry is most conducive to the growth of the economy as a whole. In this respect, the Soviet experience certainly apears in a much more favorable light than was the case before. . . . Nevertheless, it could not be said that on this count the Soviet system is superior or entirely satisfactory.[96]

Harris treated another aspect of efficiency in terms of transportation costs. He has drawn transportation effort maps that indicate the distance that a perfect transportation system would have to go to all points connected directly by airline distance with all other points. The center of least transportation effort (or within 10 percent of the least effort) is the central industrial district northeast of Moscow, extending east to the Volga oil field in the area of Kazan' and Kuibyshev, south to the Donbas coal center, and west to an area between Khar'kov and Kiev. The urban centers in western Siberia in the Kuznets Basin have 100 percent higher "least effort" transportation cost, and the Baikal region has from 150 percent to 200 percent higher effort.[97] When eastern Europe is taken into account, the point of minimum transportation effort moves west to Poland. Thus the eastern cities pay a high price in transportation to major markets.

Another aspect of efficiency is the relative smallness of the new towns. Harris argues that industry within the center of "least transportation effort," can locate in small- and middle-sized towns because all such settlements in this area are relatively accessible to one another and thus may produce goods efficiently used by other factors.[98] However, for many small new towns (see Figures 6 and 7), industrial location may be less efficient. DiMaio quotes a prominent Soviet specialist, Perevendentsev, as saying that labor productivity is only 90 percent in cities under 50,000; over 138 percent for cities over 1 million. The return of assets is only 82 percent in cities under 50,000 and 211 percent in cities over 1 million. Perevendentsev said:

The restrictive regulation of the growth of cities agrees poorly with the necessity of increasing the efficiency of the national economy. Moreover, a large city, with its possibilities for choice in all respect, offers people far more than medium-sized and small cities do. These economic and social advantages are the main reasons for the ineffectiveness of restrictions on cities which have been unable to prevent the further concentration of the urban population.[99]

The effects of smallness may be partly erased by a good transportation system within a cluster of settlements. In fact, an examination of the second and third generation of new towns in Figure 6 and other new towns and settlements reveals a clustering effect. Harris points out that "other things being equal, most rapid growth has taken place in concentrated clusters of settlements. A negative association with distance to nearest neighbor indicates that the closer a settlement is to other settlements, the faster will be its growth."[100] A detailed review of the regional industrial resource maps of Shabad reveals the same thing.[101]

Other factors bearing on efficiency are climate and wages needed to entice workers to less desirable areas. Kukhanov divided the nation into climatic zones showing relative degree of harshness and other factors including snow, duration of polar night, permafrost, relief, seismicity, swampiness, water supply, remoteness of region and poor transportation, poor power supply, poor social cohesion, and labor shortage. He factored all of these items to show that actual cost increase over construction costs in the central region ranged from 250 percent to 530 percent in the arctic and subarctic zones, depending on the distance east from Europe.[102] Costs in the northern zone, which extended from Sverdlovsk to the north of the Lake Baikal region ran from 160 percent to 230 percent higher; costs in the east, which was bordered by the steppe east of Kazakhstan, was roughly 140 percent higher. Most new towns were not in any of these regions, but some were in the European zone of the northern regions where costs were 160 percent higher or in the eastern region (in western Siberia and Baikal) where costs were 140 percent higher. Only isolated outposts, such as Noril'sk were in the most costly zone.

Most new towns were not in the high-harshness or very-high-harshness zone of climate, which are shown as zones 4 and 3 in Figure 7. Only the Baikal and far east and eastern Urals new towns were in the medium-harshness zone (zone 2). Most were in the zone of low harshness (not shown on Figure 7).[103]

This discussion relates primarily to the question of economic efficiency. What about the quality of life, congestion, and other factors? In all probability, many far eastern locations have diminished the quality of life for those who went there. This explains the high return rate. Harsh climate, housing shortages, and few amenities are found. However, only a small number of new towns are located in the severe climatic regions.

The big issue relates, then, to optimum city size. If the theory of optimum size is correct, many of the new towns would represent an improvement of large city life in that they fall within the optimum range. However, those new towns that are too small (less than 30,000) and not within easy reach of a large urban center would offer many disadvantages compared to life in a large city. These are well documented by accounts in the Soviet press. Taubman finds that neither industry nor higher levels of government are much interested in these smaller cities, and the level of urban amenities and expenditures is very low.[104]

These points are not final judgments, but they raise questions serious enough for Soviet and American scholars to reexamine a policy that places great reliance on a concept of optimum city size. A policy of trying to shape existing growth patterns where it is occurring naturally rather than massive decentralization into small new towns as an end in itself would seem to be supported. This has been the principal philosophy of the current United States new communities program. The advantages of compactness and self-containment of a new town located within a metropolitan area, enjoying the features of both large and small cities, are theoretically possible.

Assessment of achievements at the town level is enormously difficult in light of the relative absence of foreign scholarship in this area and the nature of Soviet publications on the subject. They tend to describe prototypes, not what has actually been achieved or real problems faced. Any overall assessment of new towns and other new development at the town and neighborhood level must remain somewhat mysterious and inconclusive until more serious scholarship is done. However, I offer the following tentative conclusions, based upon three trips to the Soviet Union and the literature reviewed. Most of these conclusions have within them contradictions or inconsistencies.

1. Soviet quantitative achievements in housing and new-town development are massive, particularly in the past 25 years. However, this achievement is dimmed by severe limitations in quality and the small size of housing units and their lack of sophistication. Further, if the Soviets had emphasized housing and community facilities earlier (as opposed to heavy industry), it would not have been necessary for them to hurry so quickly to catch up.
2. There is an enormous contradiction in the pride and talent seen in the Soviet builders, planners, architects, and administrators and the excessive centralization of control and planning standards. Despite the great difference in climate, topography, national tastes, income, and other fac-

tors, virtually all new towns and new housing developments that I viewed on my trips were built to the same general standards (depending upon time of construction), to roughly the same densities, and with the same general neighborhood design.* A pervasive dullness in residential areas makes Soviet new town and new housing developments less diverse, less exciting, and less habitable than they could be. If the diverse creative talents of professionals and aspirations of many Soviet nationalities and groups are to be used, more leeway must be given to republic, regional, and city builders and planners. What can be accomplished is seen in the excellent and attractive monuments, hotels, sports palaces, town centers, and other special structures where more freedom and diversity is permitted.
3. Although there has been an enormous improvement in housing and community facilities compared to the past, a lack of diversity in housing style, density, and space is reducing the freedom of choice even characterized by other sectors of the Socialist economy.
4. The contrast between the beauty, diversity, and human scale of the many old cities viewed with the relative drabness and uniformity of new development, including some new towns, is overwhelming. An outstanding job of historic preservation has preserved much of this historic heritage.
5. Great emphasis is placed on cost savings as the basis for new-town and city planning, particularly in terms of savings in transportation and infrastructure cost; however, many funds are spent on decentralization in harsh climatic zones, which is often aimed at geopolitical goals and, in fact, may be far more expensive than building in existing areas. Some of this building is based upon exploitation of resources existing in harsh climates, and there is little alternative to having some development there; however, other development may not be justified on economic grounds alone. Further, taking into account no cost of land in the Soviet Union, excessive building densities and heights may not be the least-cost solution, even taking into account infrastructure savings.
6. There is little apparent segregation by ethnic group or race in the new towns, at least none obvious to visiting teams. Further, enormous gains

---

* An exception is Akademgorodok. It has lower density, more trees, and a few single-family homes.

in education, health, and physical standards have been made by minority peoples. However, a counterbalancing factor has been that the deepest aspirations and fight for self-determination has been thwarted in efforts to combat nationalism of minority peoples and potential separatist tendencies.

7. The relatively low automobile ownership in new towns and elsewhere in the Soviet Union has saved that country headaches of the automobile: enormous waste of fuel, pollution of air from cars, traffic jams, national plague of auto deaths and injuries, the visual blight of automobile servicing facilities (including parking), and the enormous expense of highway and other facilities. At the same time, low car ownership has denied the benefits known in the West of increased freedom of mobility of shopping, working, and recreation, plus the enjoyment of car ownership.

8. Compared to the West, there is relatively greater equality of homes, wealth, and possessions in new towns and other settlements; however, there is increasing evidence of growing special privileges of the *nachal'stvo* or ruling classes, based upon influence and power, not money.

9. There is an acute shortage of construction labor in every new town and existing city that I visited; yet there is enormous waste of labor power in the inefficient agriculture.

10. There is the provision of low-cost transit, housing, free health care, education, and other services; yet there has been an increase in social control and reduction in freedom of choice due to low disposable incomes. One value must be traded off against the other.

If we are to penetrate the complexity and contradictions of this Soviet housing and community development system, we must be willing to dig far deeper than we have in the past. An occasional quick trip and exchange of a few publications is not enough to reach a mature understanding of this key aspect of Soviet life. If the Soviets are to find transferable ideas from the West, they must undertake the same effort. The hard, tedious work of scholarship and translation and exchange of students and professionals on a long-term basis would supplement this initial formal exchange of information.

The additional effort on both sides should have an even more desirable side effect than the exchange of technical information: it has the potential of laying a good foundation for improved relations. Keeping the peace, reducing tensions, and slowing down the suicidal and wasteful arms race is one of the great challenges of the balance of this century. Destroying stereotypes in many technical fields is one small way to accomplish this goal. The 1000 Soviets and Americans who exchanged visits on technical exchanges last year could certainly help. Differences in approach and philosophy will continue to exist, but these differences need not be made an insurmountable barrier to relations.

Developing countries throughout the world also have a stake in this technical and personal exchange. They are in the process of choosing approaches that appear to be most effective in solving their massive urban problems. Good objective analysis of strengths and weaknesses of different approaches to problem solving in East and West will give them a good basis to evaluate future options. Destructive war, either hot or cold, could bring them to ruin along with the United States and the Soviet Union.

APPENDIX A: PARTIAL LIST OF SOVIET NEW TOWNS TO 1971

A

Abay—K
Abovyan—SC
Ak-Dovurak—WS
Akhangaran—CA
Akhtyskiy—SC
Aksu—K
Alekseyevka—K
Alga—K
Al'met'yevsk—V–U
Amalyk—CA
Angarsk—ES(B)
Apatity—NW
Ararat—SC
Arkalyk—K
Artemoysk—D
Atasu—K

B

Baikal'sk—ES(B)
Baksan—SC
Barda—SC
Belaya Kalitva—SC
Belovo—WS
Belousovka—K
Berezniki—V–U
Berezovskiy—WS
Bestobe—K
Biryusinsk—ES(B)
Bratsk—ES(B)
Bulayevo—K

C

Chaikovskii—V–U
Chardara—K
Charsk—K
Chasniki—SW
Chervonograd—SW
Chervonopartizanski—D
Chebarkul'—V–U
Chiili—K
Chu—K
Chulak-tau—K

D

Denau—CA
Dimitrov—D
Divnogrorsk—WS
Donetsk—SC
Dudinka—NW
Dushanbe—SC
Dzhermuck—SC
Dzherzhinsk—V–U
Dzhusgly—K

E

Ekibastuz—K
Electrostal'—C

G

Gornezavodsk—V–U
Gornyak—D
Gornyatskiy—NW
Gremyanchinsk—V–U
Gribanovskiy—SC
Gubkin—SC
Gulistan—CA

I

Igren'—SW
Inta—NW
Ivdel'—V–U

K

Kachkanar—V–U
Kadzharan—SC
Kaich-na-Donu—SC
Kaltan—WS
Kapchagay—K
Karaganda—K
Karatay—K
Karazhal—K
Kaski—SC
Kayrakkum—CA
Kemerova—WS
Khromtau—K
Kimovsk—C
Kirishi—NW
Kirova Chepatsk—V–U
Kirovskiy—K
Kishniev—SW
Kisilyort—SC
Kohtle Yarve—NW
Komsomol'sk'iy—NW
Korovskiy—D
Kotova—SC
Kovdor—NW
Krasnoarmeysk—K
Krasnogvardeysk—CA
Krovoyrog—SW
Kstovo—V–U
Kubyshevskiy—CA
Kumertau—V–U
Kungrad—K
Kushmurum—K
Kuvandyk—V–U

L

Leninogorsk—V–U
Lipki—C
Lobnia—C
Lusavan—SC

M

Magnitagorsk—V–U
Makinsk—K
Maklakova—ES(B)
Marneuli—SC
Mayli-say—CA
Mezhdurechensk—WS
Mikun'—NW
Mingechaur—SC
Min-kush—CA
Mirnii—FE
Miusinsk—D
Molodogvardeysk—D
Myski—WS

N

Naberezhnye Chelny—V–U
Naftalan—SC
Naueye-Akmiane—NW
Nazarova—WS
Nazyvayusk—K
Neftekamsk—C
Neftekumsk—SC
Nefteyugansk (Siberia)
Nikel'—NW
Nikol'skiy—K
Nizhnekamsk—V–U
Nizhnaya Poyma—ES(B)
Noril'sk—FN
Novayakakhovka—SW
Noviirazdol—SW
Novii Uzen'—K
Novocheboksarsk—V–U
Novodolinskiy—K
Novogrodovka—D
Novokuykbyshevsk—V–U
Novokuznetsk—WS
Novomoskovsk—C
Novopolotsk—SW

Novodruzhesk—D
Novoshakhtinsk—SC
Novovolynsk—SW
Novoulyanovsk—V–U
Nurek—CA

O

Ob'—WS
Oktayabr'skoye—SW
Oktyabr'sk—K
Oktyabr'skiy—V–U
Olaine—NW
Orsk—V–U
Otradnyy—V–U

P

Pechora—NW
Pereval'sk—D
Pevek—FE
Pivdennoe—SW
Polysayevo—WS
Privol'e—D
Promyshelenny—NW
Propop'yesk—WS
Prozhskiy—ES(B)
Pryutova—V–U
Pskent—CA

Pushchino—C
Pushkino—SC

R

Rasdan—SC
Ribnoe—C
Rodinskoye—D
Rudnyy—K
Rustavi—SC

S

Salavat—V–U
Schast'e—D
Schuchinsk—K
Serebryansk—K
Sevan—SC
Severnyy—NW
Severo-zadonsk—C
Svetlovodsk—SW
Shakhtiisk—K
Shelikhov—ES(B)
Shevchenko—K
Shuratovskiy—C
Sokol'niki—C
Soligorsk—SW
Sorsk—WS
Sosnogorsk—NW
Sosnovka—SW
Sovietabad—CA

Stuchka—NW
Sumgait—SC
Surgut (Central Siberia)
Susuman—FE
Svetlogorsk—SW
Syrdar'ya—CA

T

Talas—CA
Taldy-Kurgan—K
Tashtagol—WS
Temirtau—K
Tobol—K
Tol'yiatti—V–U
Tsentral'nyy Kospashskiy—V–U
Tsimlyansk—SC
Tuimazy—V–U

U

Uchaly—V–U
Ukrainsk—D
Uzhur—ES(B)

V

Vale—SC
Valutino—SW
Velikoya Danilovka—SW
Verkhnedovannyy—D
Vidnov—C
Vikhorevka—ES(B)

Vishgorod—SW
Volchansk—V–U
Volgodonsk—SC
Vol'nansk—SW
Vol'nogorsk—SW
Volzhskiy—SC
Vorkuta—NW

Y

Yermak—K
Yermentau—K
Yesl'—K
Yuzhnural'iy—V–U

Z

Zapolarnii—NW
Zaporozh'ye—SW
Zavolzh'ye—VU
Zelenograd—C
Zhanatas—K
Zhdanovka—D
Zheleznogorsk—C
Zheleznogorsk-Ilimskiy—ES(B)
Zherdevka—SC
Zhigulevsk—V–U
Zhodino—SW
Zholymbet—K
Zhovtnevoe—SW
Zimagor'e—D
Zorinsk—D

Letter Designations

C   Central Region, including Moscow, Tula Basin
CA   Central Asia, including Turkemen, Kirghiz, Tadzhik, and Uzbek SSR
D   Donets Basin of the Ukraine
ES   Eastern Siberia (Baikal Region)
FE   Far East
FN   Far North
K   Kazakhstan
NW   Northern European Russia
SC   South Central, including Georgia, Azerbaydzhan, Armenia, and Central Black Earth Region
V–U Volgo-Urals Region
WS   Western Siberia (Novosibirsk area)

APPENDIX B: SOVIET OFFICIALS (1974 TRIP)

1. Moscow

Aleksey Kudryavtsev, chief, State Committee for Civil Construction and Architecture (*Gosgrazhdanstroy*) and head of the Soviet delegation to the United States on the U.S.–USSR Joint Working Group on the Urban Environment.

Mr. Illinsky, deputy to Mr. Kudryavtsev.

Ivan Bordukov, chief specialist, State Committee for Civil Construction and Architecture and an expert in transportation planning.

Anatoliy Romas', an official of the Foreign Relations Administration of *Gosgrazhdanstroy*.

Mr. Sergeev, chief of foreign relations, *Gosgrazhdanstroy*.

The following are officials in the Central Research and Design Institute for Town Planning, Gosgrazhdanstroy, Dmitrovskoye Shosee 9, Moscow:

V. N. Belousov, director.

L. N. Avdot'in, deputy director for research.

E. I. Kutyrev, chief architect.

U. B. Sterengerz, administrative director.

V. A. Vilchenko, secretary of science.

I. M. Smoliar, chief of the New Towns Planning Department.

A. V. Kochetkov, chief of the Department of Economic Problems of Town Planning.

U. A. Stavinchy, chief of the Department of Urban and Interurban Transport.

Vladimir Krogius, head of the Division of Coordination and Foreign Relations.

Edward Tovmasian, senior scientific officer and member of the Presidium of the Moscow Union of Architects.

2. LENINGRAD

Anatoliy Shutov, director of the Leningrad Zonal Research and Design Institute on Town Planning.

Vera Massovkaya, guide and interpreter with Intourist, 3 Rakov Street, Leningrad.

Gennady Buldakov, chief architect of Leningrad, Zodcheva Rossi 1/3, Leningrad.

Marina Palchick, translator, Leningrad Zonal Research and Design Institute of Town Planning, Marata Street 90, Leningrad.

Sergey Ivanovich, Krist'yashin, assistant director for scientific work, "The Institute," Marata Street 90, Leningrad.

Boris Leonodvich Vasel'ev, group director, "The Institute," Chernaya Rechka 18, Leningrad.

3. Sochi

Alexander Dryzhinin, head engineer of the Sochi Special Construction Agency.

Yuriy Petrovich Schliaev, vice chairman, Executive Committee of Sochi, Sochi, 61.

Vera Alexseevna Uliupina, director of the Sanitarium.

4. Minsk

Valadimir Adamovich Korol', director of *Gosstroi* for the Byelorussian Republic.

Leonid Medelevich Levin, chief architect for the Town Center of Minsk, member of the "Minsk Project" Institute, Ulianovskaya Street 31, Minsk.

Yuriy Panteleymonovich Grigoriev, chief architect, city of Minsk.

Mr. Modolinskii, director of "Minsk Project."

NOTES

1. I. M. Smoliar, Ed., *General'nie Plani Novikh Gorodov* (Moscow: Stoyizdat, 1973), p. 3.

2. I. M. Smoliar, *Novikh Goroda: Planerevochnaya Structura Promeshlennova I Nauchno-Pozvodstevenno Profilia* (Moscow: Stoyizdat, 1972), p. 8.

3. William Taubman, *Governing Soviet Cities* (New York: Praeger, 1973), p. 26.

4. This is my personal impression formed during visits to the USSR in 1974 and 1975 plus reports of many other delegations.

5. Taubman, p. 26.

6. See Alfred John DiMaio, Jr., *Soviet Urban Housing: Problems and Policies* (New York: Praeger, 1974).

7. Chauncy D. Harris, *Cities of the Soviet Union: Studies in their Functions, Size, Density, and Growth* (Chicago: Rand McNally, 1970), p. 26.

8. USSR, Tstentral'nye Statitichecheskoe Upravlenie pre Soviet Minstrov SSSR, *SSSR v. Tsefrakh v. 1974 Godu* (USSR, Central Statistical Administration for the Soviet Ministries, *USSR in Figures for 1974*) (Moscow: Statistika, 1975), p. 7.

9. *Ibid.*, p. 239.

10. Fletcher Pope, Jr., et al. "Agriculture in the U.S. and Soviet Union," in *Foreign Agricultural Economic Report No. 92* (Washington, D.C.: U.S. Department of Agriculture, 1973), p. iii.

11. Pope, p. 4.

12. Marvyn Matthews, *Class and Society in Soviet Russia* (New York: Walker, 1970), p. 29.

13. *Ibid.*, p. 189.

14. Harris, p. 237.

15. USSR, Tstentral'nye Statitichecheskoe, p. 7.

16. Harris, p. 240.

17. *Ibid.*, p. 299.

18. *Ibid.*, p. 11.

19. *Gosudarstvenii Pyatilatnii Plan Razvitiya Narodnova Khozyastiva SSSR Na 1971–1975 Gody* (*Five-Year Plan for the Development of the Economy 1971–1975*) (Moscow: Izdatel'stvo Politecheskey Literaturii, 1972), p. 305.

20. DiMaio, p. 21.

21. In 1971 the number of units of urban housing per 1000 population was only 257.9 compared to 353.9 for East Germany (which also suffered enormous wartime destruction); France, 320; Italy, 323, and the United States, 338. Although the housing space standards were greatly improved, the 117 square feet of useful space per person in the Soviet Union was half that of the 224 square feet in 1971 for East Germany, and the 270 per person in the United States. The Soviet Union in 1971 did produce more housing per 1000 population per year (9.2) units than the United States (only 6.7). It also exceeded that of other satellite countries, but it was exceeded by Denmark, West Germany, Greece, The Netherlands, Sweden, and Switzerland. Although it exceeded United States production on a per-unit basis the units were much smaller and less complex. The square feet production per 1000 population was 439 in 1971, compared to 764 for the United States and 947 for Japan. Willard Smith, "Housing in the Soviet Union: Big Plans, Little Action," in *Soviet Economic Prospects of the 70's* (Washington, D.C.: U.S. Government Printing Office, 1973), p. 410. Thus in absolute and relative terms, Soviet production and average space were far behind those of other advanced countries with similar wealth.

22. *Ibid.*, p. 405.

23. Roy A. Grancher, "Housing Industry in the USSR," in *U.S. Delegation Report, Economic Commission for Europe, Third Building Industry Seminar and Russian Study Tour* (Springfield, Va.: National Technical Information Service, 1971), p. 24.

24. DiMaio, p. 73.

25. *Ibid.*, p. 94.

26. *Ibid.*, p. 101.

27. Zev Katz, "Insights from Emigres and Sociological Studies of the Soviet Economy," in *Soviet Economic Prospects in the 70's* (Washington D.C.: U.S. Government Printing Office, 1973), p. 111.

28. *Ibid.*, p. 109.

29. Matthews, p. 94.

30. Hedrick Smith, *The Russians* (New York: Quadrangle/The New York Times Book Co., 1976), Ch. 1, "The Privileged Class: Dachas and Zils," p. 25.

31. Katz, p. 102. Also see Robert G. Kaiser, "A Russian Life Time," Part 7, *The Washington Post*, June 22, 1974.

32. Nelson Foote, "What Can Be Learned from Soviet and American Exchanges Regarding USSR and US New Communities (New York: Hunter College, 1974), (mimeo).

33. Personal observation in 1974.

34. Farley Mowatt, *The Siberians* (Boston: Little, Brown, 1970).

35. Alex Inkeles, "Soviet National Policy in Perspective," in *Russia Under Khrushchev: An Anthology of Problems of Communism*, Abraham Burmberg, Ed. (New York: Praeger, 1962), p. 315.

36. *Ibid.*, p. 301.

37. *Ibid.*, p. 309.

38. *Ibid.*, p. 321.

39. See Edward Allworth, *Central Asia: A Century of Russian Rule* (New York: Columbia University Press, 1967) and Geoffrey Wheeler, *The Peoples of Soviet Central Asia* (London: The Bodley Head, 1966).

40. See USSR, Central Research and Design Institute of Town Planning, *Principles of Town Planning in the Soviet Union, 1966*, trans. Indian National Scientific Documentation Center (New Delhi: Indian National Scientific Documentation Center, 1966), (typescript).

41. V. G. Davidovich, *Town Planning in Industrial Districts*, trans. Israel Program for Scientific Translation (Jerusalem: Israel Program for Scientific Translations, 1968), p. 128.

42. USSR, Central Research and Design Institute, 1966, pp. 231–32.

43. G. M. Lappo, *Tales of Cities* (Moscow: Mysl' Publishing House, 1972), p. 22.

44. Davidovich, *Town Planning in Industrial Districts,* p. 148.

45. Phillippe J. Bernard, *Planning in the Soviet Union* (Oxford: Pergamon, 1966), p. 199.

46. See I. S. Korpeckyj, "Equalization of Regional Development in Soviet Countries: An Empirical Study," *Economic Development and Cultural Change* **21,** No. 1 (1972):68.

47. Bernard, p. 197.

48. Theodore Shabad, "Soviets Support Settlement Near China, Apparently to Affirm Claimes to Lands," *New York Times* (August 5, 1973), p. 18.

49. Foy D. Kohler, "Prepared Statement of Foy D. Kohler," in *Hearings Before the Joint Economic Committee, Soviet Economic Outlook*, 93rd Congress, First Session, 1973, p. 130.

50. Thedore Shabad, *Basic Industrial Resources of the USSR* (New York and London, Columbia University Press, 1969), p. 127.

51. Harris, p. 210.

52. Taubman, p. 22.

53. *Ibid.*, p. 55.

54. See Raymond Burby et al., "New Communities U.S.A.: Results of a National Study," (Chapel Hill: Center for Urban and Regional Studies, University of North Carolina, 1975), (mimeo).

55. DiMaio, p. 55.

56. *Ibid.*, p. 61.

57. Smoliar, 1973, p. 201.

58. Davidovich, *Town Planning in Industrial Districts,* p. 231.

59. Barbara Rosenfeld, "The Soviet Home," prepared for the Soviet and East European Unit, Foreign Information Research Division, Office of Research, United States Information Agency, mimeo. Washington, D.C., 1974. See addendum to the study for reference to poll.

60. See J. F. Skone, "Health and Welfare in High Flats," in *Proceedings of Public Municipal Services Congress* (1962), pp. 225–251; P. Townsend, "Report of Pilot Study of Families Living High in New Blocks of Flats," in *Two to Five in High Flats*, J. Maisel, Ed., (London: The Housing Center, 1961); L. Mackova,

"The Results of Sociological Research Carried Out in Flats and Blocks of Flats and Their Application in Practice," in *The Social Environment and Its Effects on Design of Dwelling and Its Immediate Surroundings* (Stockholm: National Swedish Institute of Building Research, 1968), pp. 39–55.

61. Smoliar, 1973, p. 428.

62. *Ibid.*, p. 249 of the translation by U.S. Department of Housing and Urban Development.

63. USSR, Central Research and Design Institute of Town Planning, "Scientific and Technical Review of Regional Correlation of Public and Individual Transport in Towns of Different Size," trans. 1975 (unpublished), mimeo. p. 5.

64. V. G. Davidovich, "Urban Agglomerations in the USSR," *Soviet Geography* **9** (1964):35.

65. *Ibid.*

66. Herbert E. Meyer, "A Plant that Could Change the Shape of Soviet Industry," *Fortune* (November 1974):230.

67. USSR, Central Research and Design Institute, 1975, p. 7.

68. U.S. Working Group on the Enhancement of the Urban Environment, *Report on the U.S.-USSR Working Group on the Enhancement of the Environment: Second Joint Session* (Washington, D.C.: U.S. Department of Housing and Urban Development, Office of International Affairs, 1973), p. 6.

69. Taubman, p. 91.

70. *Ibid.*, p. 58.

71. See, for example, Grancher, p. 79.

72. See Real Estate Research Corporation, *The Costs of Sprawl: Executive Summary and Detailed Cost Analysis* (Washington, D. C.: U.S. Government Printing Office, 1974).

73. Marshall I. Goldman, "Pollution Comes to the USSR," in *Soviet Economic Prospects for the 70's* (Washington, D.C.: U.S. Government Printing Office, 1973), p. 58.

74. *Ibid.*, p. 67.

75. U.S. Working Group on the Enhancement of the Urban Environment, p. 5.

76. See Smoliar, 1972 and 1973; USSR, Central Research and Design Institute, 1966.

77. U.S. Historic Preservation Team, *A Report of the U.S. Historic Preservation Team of the U.S.-USSR Joint Working Group on the Enhancement of the Urban Environment* (Washington, D.C.: U.S. Department of the Interior, 1975), p. 15.

78. John Reps, *The Making of Urban America: A History of City Planning in the U.S.* (Princeton, N.J., and New York: Princeton University Press, 1967), pp. 420, 428.

79. See Lappo.

80. USSR, Central Research and Design Institute, 1966, p. 61.

81. *Ibid.*, p. 25.

82. I gathered this information from a map, titled "USSR: Major Soviet Petroleum Deposits and Pipeline Systems," that the United States Department of State printed in 1973.

83. B. A. Khorev, "Development of Municipal Agglomerations and the Problem of Satellite Settlements," in *Gorodskiye Poseleniva*, SSR (Moscow: Mysl' Publishing House, 1968), p. 32 of summary translation.

84. Smoliar, 1972, p. 10.

85. Smoliar, 1973, p. 76.

86. Matthews, p. 54.

87. Bernard, pp. 198–199.

88. Shabad, "Soviet Support Settlements Near China," p. 18.

89. R. Ivanova, "On Development of Eastern Regions and Providing Them with Manpower," *Voprosy Ekonomiki* No. 1 (Jan. 1973) reported in *Current Digest of Soviet Press* **25**, No. 12 (1973):8.

90. H. Topilin and E. Gilinkaya, "Regulation of Population Migration in the Eastern Regions of the Russian Republic," *Planovaya Khozyaistva*, No. 1 (January 1973), pp. 121–126; reported in *Current Digest of Soviet Press* **25**, No. 12 (April 18, 1973):6.

91. Taubman, p. 82.

92. DiMaio, p. 47.

93. Khorev, p. 9.

94. *Ibid.*, p. 8.

95. Bernard, p. 216.

96. *Ibid.*, p. 217.

97. Harris, p. 210.

98. *Ibid.*, p. 21.

99. DiMaio, pp. 40–50.

100. Harris, p. 127.

101. Shabad, *Basic Industrial Resources of the USSR*, p. 19.

102. V. F. Bukhanov, "Criteria for Determining an Engineering-Geographic Boundary of the North of USSR," *Soviet Geography* **9**, No. 1 (1970):31.

103. Bukhanov, p. 44.

104. Taubman, p. 73.

BIBLIOGRAPHY

Agranat, G. A. "Research on the Effect of Geographic Conditions on Economic Indicators of Production." *Soviet Geography* **9**, no. 1 (1970), 14.

Allworth, Edward. *Central Asia: A Century of Russian Rule*. New York: Columbia University Press, 1967.

Bernard, Philippe J. *Planning in the Soviet Union*. Oxford: Pergamon, 1966.

Bukhanov, V. F. "Criteria for Determining An Engineering-Geographic Boundary of the North of USSR." *Soviet Geography* **11**, No. 1 (1970), 24.

Bush, Philip D. "Planning and Design Process." In *Report of the U.S. Delegation to the Soviet Union*. Washington, D.C.: U.S. Department of Commerce, National Bureau of Standards, 1969, p. 33.

Burby, Raymond, et al. "New Communities U.S.A.: Results of a National Study." Draft. Chapel Hill: Center for Urban and Regional Studies, University of North Carolina, 1975.

Davidovich, V. G. "On Patterns and Tendencies of Urban Settlement in the USSR." *Soviet Geography* **7**, No. 1 (1966), 3.

———. *Town Planning in Industrial Districts*. Translated and published by the Israel Program for Scientific Translation. Jerusalem, 1968.

———. "Urban Agglomerations in the USSR." *Soviet Geography* **5**, No. 9 (1964); 34.

DiMaio, Alfred John, Jr. *Soviet Urban Housing: Problems and Policies*. New York: Praeger, 1974.

Fitzsimmons, Sharon. "Social Aspects of High Population Density at Cedar-Riverside New Town in Town, Minneapolis. An appendix to the Cedar-Riverside Environmental Impact Statement." Final draft. October 1974, prepared for the New Communities Administration, U.S. Department of Housing and Urban Development. Washington, D.C., unpublished typescript.

Foote, Nelson. "What Can Be Learned from Soviet and American Exchanges Regarding USSR and U.S. New Communities." New York: Hunter College, 1974, 7 pp. Mimeographed.

Forstall, Richard, and Victor Jones. "Selected Demographic, Economic and Governmental Aspects of the Contemporary Metropolis." In *Metropolitan Problems: Internal Perspectives.* Simon Miles, Ed. Toronto, London, and Sydney: Methuen, 1970.

Gallick, Daniel, et al. *Soviet Financial Systems: Structure, Operations and Statistics.* International Population Statistical Reports Series P-90, No. 3. Washington, D.C.: U.S. Department of Commerce, 1968.

Goldman, Marshall I. *Spoils of Progress: Environmental Pollution in the Soviet Union.* Cambridge: M.I.T. Press, 1967.

Gosudarstvenii Pyatiletnii Plan Razvitiya Narodnova Khozyastva SSSR Na 1971–1975 Gody (Five-Year Plan for the Development of the Economy 1971 to 1975). Moscow: Izdatel'stvo Politecheskey Literaturii, Moscow, 1972.

Grancher, Roy A. "Housing Industry in the USSR." In *U.S. Delegation Report, Economic Commission for Europe, Third Building Industry Seminar and Russian Study Tour.* PB 199 418. Springfield, Virginia: National Technical Information Service, 1971.

Harris, Chauncy D. *Cities of the Soviet Union: Studies in Their Functions, Size, Density, and Growth.* Chicago: Rand McNally, 1970.

Inkeles, Alex. "Soviet Nationality Policy in Perspective." In *Russia Under Khrushchev: An Anthology from Problems of Communism.* Abraham Brumberg, Ed. New York: Praeger, 1962.

Ivanova, R. "On Development of Eastern Regions and Providing Them with Manpower" (translation). *Voprosy Ekonomiki,* No. 1 (January 1973); 40–48. Reported in *Current Digest of Soviet Press* **25,** No. 12 (April 1973), 8.

Joint Committee on Tall Buildings. "Character of Life in Residential Tall Buildings." In "Urban Planner Chapter" (draft circulated for comment to committee), 1974 (typescript). Edited by Rai Okomoto, Secretariate of Committee at Lehigh University, Bethlehem, Pennsylvania.

Kaiser, Robert G. "A Russian Life Time." Part I: "The Baby in Russia: Tradition Begins." Part II: "For Russian Babies: Only the Best." Part III: "Creeping Nonconformity." Part IV: "Love, Marriage, Divorce." Part V: "Soviet Life Oriented Toward Family." Part VI: "Growing Old is No Joy." Part VII: "Privileged Soviets." *The Washington Post,* June 16–22, 1974.

Kamenski, V. A. *Leningrad, General'nii Plan Razvitia Goroda* (Leningrad, General Plan for the Development of the City). Leningrad: Lenizdat, 1971.

Khorev, B. A. "Development of Municipal Agglomerations and the Problem of Satellite Settlements." In *Gorodskiye Poseleniya, SSR.* Moscow: Mysl' Publishing House, 1968.

Kistanov, V. "Leninist Nationality Policy and Economic Regionalization in the USSR." *Voposy Ekonomidi* (December 1972), 56–65.

Kohler, Foy D. "Prepared Statement of Foy D. Kohler." In *Hearings Before the Joint Economic Committee, Soviet Economic Outlook.* Joint Economic Committee, 93rd Congress, First Session, 1973.

Korol', V. A. *Minsk: Poslevenny opit Rekonstrukstii i Pazvitiya* (Minsk: Postwar Experience in Reconstruction and Development). Moscow: Izdatel'stvo Literaturii Po Stroitel'stvu, 1966.

Korpeckyj, I. S. "Equalization of Regional Development in Soviet Countries: An Empirical Study." *Economic Development and Cultural Change* **21,** No. 1 (1972), 68–84.

Komashev, K. P. "Application of Quantitative Methods of Settlement to A Lower Level (intra-Oblast) Economic Regionalization." *Soviet Geography* **6,** No. 7 (1970), 545.

Lappo, G. M. *Tales of Cities.* Moscow: Mysl' Publishing House, 1972. (Translation in typescript, July 1973).

Lewis, David F. "Dwelling Unit Satisfaction in New Communities." Chapel Hill: University of North Carolina, December 1974, unpublished draft.

Mackova, L. "The Results of Sociological Research Carried Out in Flats and Blocks of Flats and Their Application in Practice." In *The Social Environment and its Effects on Design of Dwelling and its Immediate Surroundings.* Stockholm: National Swedish Institute of Building Research, 1968, pp. 39–55.

Maisels, J. *Two to Five in High Flats.* London: The Housing Center, 1961.

Matthews, Marvyn. *Class and Society in Soviet Russia.* New York: Walker, 1970.

Movchan, B. S. "Use of Mathematical Methods in Solution of a Location Problem." *Soviet Geography* **11,** No. 8 (1970), 649.

Meyer, Herbert E. "A Plant that Could Change the Shape of Soviet Industry." *Fortune* (November 1974), 152.

Mowatt, Farley. *The Siberians.* Boston: Little, Brown, 1970.

National League of Cities, Department of Urban Studies. "Recreation in the Nation's Cities: Problems and Approaches." Prepared for the Department of Interior, Bureau of Outdoor Recreation. Washington, D.C.: 1968.

Perloff, Harvey, T. Berg, R. Fountain, and D. Vetter. *Modernizing the Central City: New Towns Intown and Beyond.* Cambridge, Mass.: Ballinger, 1975.

Pope, Fletcher, Jr., et al. "Agriculture in the US and Soviet Union." In *Foreign Agricultural Economic Report No. 92.* Washington, D.C.: Economic Research Service, U.S. Department of Agriculture, 1973.

Rapaport, Ames. "Toward Redefinition of Density." *Environment and Behavior* **7,** No. 2 (1974), 133.

Real Estate Research Corporation. *The Costs of Sprawl: Executive Summary and Detailed Cost Analysis.* Washington, D.C.: U.S. Government Printing Office, 1974.

Reps, John. *The Making of Urban America: A History of City Planning in the U.S.* Princeton, N.J. and New York: Princeton University Press, 1967.

Richardson, Harry W. *Economics of Urban Size.* Lexington, Mass.: Saxon House Studies, Lexington Books, 1973.

Rosenfeld, Barbara, "The Soviet Home." Prepared for the United States Information Agency, Washington, D.C., November 1974, mimeographed.

Shabad, Theodore. *Basic Industrial Resources of the USSR.* New York and London: Columbia University Press, 1969.

———. "Soviet Support Settlement Near China, Apparently to Affirm Claim to Lands." *New York Times*, August 5, 1973, p. 18.

Smith, Hedrick. *The Russians.* New York: Quadrangle/The New York Times Book Co., 1976.

Smoliar, I. M., Ed. *General'nie Plani Novikh Gorodov.* Moscow: Stoyizdat, 1973. Trans. U.S. Department of Housing and Urban Development as *General Plans of New Towns,* 1974, typescript.

———. *Novikh Goroda, Planirevochnaya Structura Promishlennova I Nauchno-Pozvodstevenno Profilia.* Moscow: Stoyizdat, 1972. Trans. U.S. Department of Housing and Urban Development, typescript.

Skone, J. F. "Health and Welfare Problems in High Flats." In *Proceedings of Public Municipal Services Congress,* November 1962, pp. 225–251.

Taubman, William. *Governing Soviet Cities.* New York: Praeger, 1973.

Topilin, H., and E. Gilinkaya. "Regulation of Population Migration in the Eastern Regions of the Russian Republic." *Planovaya Khozyaistva,* No. 1 (January 1973), 121–126, reported in *Current Digest of Soviet Press* **25**, No. 12, (April 18, 1973), 6.

Underhill, Jack A. "New Communities Planning Process and National Growth Policy." In *Contemporary New Communities Movement in the United States.* Gideon Golany and Daniel Walden, Eds., Urbana: University of Illinois Press, 1974, pp. 32–67.

———. *Soviet New Towns, Housing and Urban Growth Policy.* Washington, D.C.: U.S. Department of Housing and Urban Development, 1976.

United States Congress. Joint Economic Committee. *Soviet Economic Prospects for the Seventies,* 93rd Congress, First Session, June 27, 1973.

United States Department of Labor. Bureau of Labor Statistics. *Labor Law and Practice in the USSR.* Washington, D.C.: U.S. Government Printing Office, 1964.

United States Historic Preservation Team. *A Report of the U.S. Historic Preservation Team of the US-USSR Joint Working Group on the Enhancement of the Urban Environment, May 25 to June 14, 1974.* Washington, D.C.: U.S. Department of Interior, 1975.

United States Working Group on the Enhancement of the Urban Environment. *Report on the US-USSR Working Group on the Enhancement of the Urban Environment: Second Joint Session.* Washington, D.C.: U.S. Department of Housing and Urban Development, Office of International Affairs, 1973.

USSR. Central Research and Design Institute of Town Planning. "Determination of Criteria for Selecting the Territory for New Towns and Providing a Favorable Environment in New Towns." (in Russian) 1974.

———. *Papers for the International Conference on Improvement of the Environment.* "The New Town of Togliatti;" "General Scheme of Settlement in the Area of the USSR," and "Soviet Town Planning Predictions." Moscow: Central Research and Design Institute for Town Planning, 1973.

———. *Osnovii Sovetskovo Gradostroiitel'strva: Tom 1.* Moscow: Stroyizdat, 1966. Trans. *Principles of Town Planning in the Soviet Union, 1966.* New Delhi: Indian National Scientific Documentation Center, 1970, unpublished typescript.

———. "Scientific and Technical Review on Definition of Regional Correlation of Public and Individual Transport in Towns of Different Size." Translated by Central Research and Design Institute, Moscow, 1975.

USSR, Tstentral'nye Statitichecheskoe Upravlenie pre Soviet Minstrov SSSR *SSSR v. Tsefrakh v. 1974 Godu.* (USSR, Central Statistical Administration for the Soviet Ministries, *USSR in Figures for 1974*). Moscow: Statistika, 1975.

Wheeler, Goeffrey. *The Peoples of Soviet Central Asia.* London: The Bodley Head, 1966.

Wilfred, John A. "Apollo-Soyoz May be Only a Beginning," *New York Times*, Section 4, July 13, 1975, p. 1.

BIBLIOGRAPHIES

Akin, Joy. *Selected Bibliography of Centrally Planned Social Change in the Soviet Union.* Exchange Bibliography No. 149. Monticello, Illinois: Council of Planning Librarians, 1970.

Golany, Gideon. *New Towns Planning and Development: A World-Wide Bibliography.* Section 14: Russia. Washington, D.C.: Urban Land Institute, 1973, pp. 216–221.

Inch, Peter. *Bibliography of Regional Economic Planning in the USSR.* Exchange Bibliography No. 295. Monticello, Illinois: Council of Planning Librarians, 1972.

Zeitlin, Morris. *Guide of the Literature of Cities: Abstract and Bibliography.* Part XI: Socialist Cities. Exchange Bibliography No. 328. Monticello, Illinois: Council of Planning Librarians, 1972.

Figures

Tables

Index

*Tc aid the international readers of this volume, index listings are made in English and, whenever possible, in the language of the country discussed in each chapter. Extensive cross-referencing should be helpful as well. In some cases a subject with descriptive modifiers is listed by those modifiers; e.g., New town, Threshold theory, Urban development. Look for listings by country or by topic. Some listings have the country of origin at the end of the listing; e.g., Act, Community Land, 1975 (Great Britain), *or* CDC, France, *or* Acts, Federal Housing, 1975 (Switzerland). G.G.